la Biennale di Venezia
46. esposizione internazionale d'arte

identity
and alterity

figures of the body 1895 / 1995

la Biennale di Venezia Marsilio

© 1995
Edizioni La Biennale
di Venezia
ISBN 88-208-0390-9

Published by
Marsilio Editori s.p.a.
Venice

First edition
June 1995

Chairman
Gian Luigi Rondi

Secretary-general
Raffaello Martelli

INSTITUTE ACTIVITIES

Managing Director
Dario Ventimiglia

Exhibits Department
Anna Maria Porazzini
Manager
Paolo Scibelli
Roberto Rosolen
Gianpaolo Cimarosti

*Contributions
to the XLVI Esposizione
Internazionale d'Arte
have been made by*
Laurisa Boni
Valentina Castellani
Cristina Cinti
Anna Della Bona
Gaia Donà Dalle Rose
Lia Gardumi
Adriana Scalise
Barbara Tasca

**46. Esposizione
Internazionale d'Arte**

**Director of Visual Arts
Section**
Jean Clair

Visual Arts Committee
Gabriella Belli
Hans Belting
Maurizio Calvesi
Gillo Dorfles
Giulio Macchi

PRESS AND PUBLIC
RELATIONS OFFICE

Managing Director
Adriano Donaggio

Organization
Fiorella Tagliapietra
Manager

**Press, Documentation,
Public Relations,
Communication
Strategy**
Paolo Lughi
*Communication
Manager*
Monica Carrara
Cristina Gatti
Glory Jones
Daria Mariotti
Patrizia Martinelli
Alessandra Pace
Leopoldo Pietragnoli

**Photographic
Documentation**
Barbara Montagner
Pierluigi Varisco

Publicity
Eugenia Fiorin
Manager
Maria Angela
Germanotta

Biennale News
Gian Luigi Rondi
Editor
Adriano Donaggio
Director
Eugenia Fiorin
Paolo Lughi
Leopoldo Pietragnoli
Fiorella Tagliapietra
Veronica Tuzii

Graphic Design
Studio Tapiro

ARCHIVIO STORICO
DELLE ARTI
CONTEMPORANEE

Managing Director
Gabriella Cecchini

Editorial Activities
*Identity and Alterity.
Figures of the Body
1895-1995*
Rosanna Alberti
Massimo Chirivi
Stefano Dal Secco
Maddalena Di Sopra
Maria Barbara
Giacometti
Luisa Sala
Michela Stancescu
*XLVI Esposizione
Internazionale d'Arte*
Alberto Prandi
Coordinator
Stefania Ivanovich
Giovanni Keller
Cristina Menegazzi

**Cataloguing
and Conservation
Department
Photo Archive**
Osvaldo De Nunzio
Pierluigi Varisco

**Laboratories and
Automated Services
Department
Photographic
Laboratory**
Giorgio Zucchiatti

GENERAL AND
INSTITUTIONAL
ACTIVITIES

Managing Director
Gualtiero Seggi

General Affairs
Marina Bertaggia
Maria Cristina Lion
Antonietta Possamai
Andrea Bernardi
Nicola Scolaro
Roberta Savoldello

Hospitality
Roberto Chia
Manager
Susanna Vedova

Personnel
Sandro Vettor
Manager
Carla Mariotto
Graziano Carrer

**General Organization
of Stands and
Transport**
Giuseppa Maugeri
Manager
Aldo Roberto Beltrame
Mauro Momenté
Roberto Fabian

**Transport
and Insurance**
Francesca Semenzato
Alessandra Durand
de La Penne
Carla Ferrari
Michela Renier

Depositary
Donato Mendolia

Stands
Gottardo Bonacini
*Palazzo Grassi,
Museo Correr*
Francesca Mamprin
Padiglione Italia
Manuela Lucà-Dazio
Padiglione Italia

Companies
Official Shippers
Tosetto s.p.a.
Piccin Trasporti d'Arte
Insurance
Assicurazioni Generali,
Venezia
Security
Istituto di Vigilanza
Castellano s.r.l.

Building and Painting
Ditta Coima s.r.l.
Carpeting
Vianello Alessandro
s.a.s.
Electric Work
Bortoli Ettore s.r.l.
Metal Work
Scarpa Officina
Accrochage
Laima s.n.c.
Water Transport
Laguna Trasporti
Manutenzioni
di Tosi Pietro
Cleaning
Cooperativa Mimosa
s.r.l.

ADMINISTRATIVE
AFFAIRS

Managing Director
Angelo Bagnato

Collaboration
Debora Rossi

IDENTITY AND ALTERITY. FIGURES OF THE BODY 1895-1995

Curator
Jean Clair

The Real and Virtual Body 1985-1995

Curators
Jean Clair
and Cathrin Pichler

Imprints of Body and Mind

Curator
Adalgisa Lugli

Assistants to the Director

Pieranna Cavalchini
Dominique Renoux

Advisers to the Director

Marie José
Baudinet-Mondzain
*Iconology
and Oriental Art*
Philippe Comar
*Antropology
and Body Science*
Günter Metken
German Art
Didier Ottinger
Contemporary Art

Catalogue edited by

Manlio Brusatin
and Jean Clair

Installation Design

Gae Aulenti
with
Francesca Fenaroli
and Monica Bonadei

Daniela Ferretti
*Imprints of Body
and Mind*

Lighting Consultant

Piero Castiglioni

PARTICIPATING ITALIAN ARTISTS

Selection Committee

Jean Clair
Gabriella Belli
Hans Belting
Maurizio Calvesi
Gillo Dorfles
Giulio Macchi

Installation Design

Daniela Ferretti

PARTICIPATING COUNTRIES

Argentina

Jorge Glusberg
Commissioner

Australia

Ann Lewis
Commissioner

Austria

Peter Weibel
Commissioner

Belgium

Laurent Busine
Commissioner

Brazil

Edemar Cid Ferreira
Commissioner
Jens Olesen
Assistant Commissioner

Canada

Pierre Granger
Commissioner
Yves Pépin
Assistant Commissioner

Chile

Juan Barattini
Commissioner

Czech Republic

Jiří Ševčik
Commissioner

Denmark

Mette Wivel
Commissioner
Vibeke Dyhrcrone
Assistant Commissioner

Egypt

Magdi Kinawi
Commissioner
Gamal Eldin Bakri
Commissioner

Federal Republic of Yugoslavia

Radislav Trkulja
Commissioner
Vesna Milič
Assistant Commissioner

France

Catherine Millet
Commissioner

Germany

Jean-Christophe
Ammann
Commissioner

Great Britain

Andrea Rose
Commissioner
Brendan Griggs
Assistant Commissioner
Richard Riley
Assistant Commissioner

Greece

Maria Marangou
Commissioner

Hungary

Márta Kovalovszky
Commissioner

Iceland

Bera Nordal
Commissioner

Ireland

Peter Murray
Commissioner

Israel

Gideon Ofrat
Commissioner

Japan

Junji Ito
Commissioner
Masanobu Ito
Assistant Commissioner
Haruhisa Sunami
Assistant Commissioner

Luxemburg

Enrico Lunghi
Commissioner

The Netherlands

Tom van Gestel
Commissioner

Nordic Countries

Timo Valjakka
*Coordinating
Commissioner*

Finland

Timo Keinänen
Commissioner

Norway

Svein Christiansen
Commissioner

Sweden

Svenrobert Lundqvist
Commissioner

Poland

Anda Rottenberg
Commissioner
Hanna Wróblewska
Assistant Commissioner

Portugal

José de Monterroso
Teixeira
Commissioner

Republic of Armenia

Sonia Balassanian
Commissioner

Republic of China on Taiwan

Tsai Ching-fen
Commissioner
Paolo De Grandis
Assistant Commissioner

Republic of Croatia

Igor Zidič
Commissioner

Republic of Korea

Lee Yil
Commissioner

Repubblic of Slovenia

Zdenka Badovinac
Commissioner
Igor Zabel
Assistant Commissioner

Rumania

Dan Hăulică
Commissioner
Coriolan Babeţi
Assistant Commissioner

Russia

Viktor Misiano
Commissioner

Slovak Republic

Katarína Bajcurová
Commissioner

South Africa

Glenn Babb
Commissioner

Spain
Fernando Huici
Commissioner

Switzerland
Pierre André Lienhard
Commissioner
Urs Staub
Commissioner

**United States
of America**
Marilyn A. Zeitlin
Commissioner

Uruguay
Angel Kalenberg
Commissioner

Venezuela
Tahia Rivero
Commissioner
Anunciata Fraino
Assistant Commissioner

**Italo-Latin American
Institute**
Fernando Macotela
Commissioner
Alessandra Bonanni
Assistant Commissioner

**VENICE
AND THE BIENNALE:
JOURNEYS OF TASTE**

In collaboration with
Comune di Venezia
Assessorato alla Cultura

Scientific Committee
Jean Clair
Giandomenico
Romanelli
Commissioner
Diego Arich de Finetti
Gabriella Belli
Maurizio Calvesi
Giuseppina Dal Canton
Fabio Fergonzi
Claudia Gian Ferrari
Mimita Lamberti
Chiara Rabitti
Philiph Rayland
Sileno Salvagnini
Giovanni Sarpellon
*Applied Art and Glass
Curator*
Flavia Scotton
Duccio Trombadori
*Coordinator
and Organizer*

General Coordination
Chiara Alessandri

Installation Design
Umberto Franzoi
Ivano Martino

Press Office
Roberta Lombardo
Gruppo Prospettive

**Great Decorative
Cycles and Applied
Arts
1895-1934**
Curator
Flavia Scotton

**Venetian Glass
1895-1972**

*Project and Historical
Research*
Marina Barovier
Rosa Barovier Mentasti
Attilia Dorigato

Organization
Marina Barovier

**THE SELF AND ITS
DOUBLE. A CENTURY
OF PHOTOGRAPHY
PORTRAITURE IN ITALY
1895-1995
'THE PHOTOGRAPHER'S
STUDIO'**

Scientific Committee
Carlo Bertelli
Jean Clair
Daniela Cammilli
Cesare Colombo
Paolo Costantini
Michele Falzone
del Barbarò
Emanuela Sesti
Susanna Weber
Italo Zannier

**The Self and its
Double**
Curator
Italo Zannier

Editorial Secretary
Giovanna Nardi

Exhibition Organization
Rosa Manno

*Layout and Installation
Design*
Stefano Rovai/Graphiti

Press Office
Silvia Corradini
Michele De Luca

**'The Photographer's
Studio'**
*Coordination
and Realization*
Francesco Barasciutti
Monica Maffioli
Ferruccio Malandrini
Maurizio Rebuzzini
George Tatge

EVENTS

Christian Boltanski
Curator
Martine Aboucaya

Concert & Film
Ensemble Modern

**Ex Machina.
Connected Isolation**
Centre
choréographique
de la Communauté
Française de Belgique,
Compagnie Charleroi/
Danses, Plan κ
and Kunsthochschule
für Medien Köln

**EXHIBITIONS WITH
OFFICIAL PATRONAGE**

**Anni cinquanta,
anni novanta**
Curators
Bruno Passamani
Luigi Serravalli

**Among others/Onder
anderen**
Curators
Bart De Baere
Lex ter Braak

'Aperçus'
Curators
AFAA, Musée National
d'Art Moderne of Paris
ACIF of Venice

**Arte e tecnologia.
Metodi della creatività**
Curator
Enrica Abbate

Artelaguna 1995
Project and Direction
Simonetta Gorreri

Club Berlin
Curator
Klaus Biesenbach

Elytron
Curator
Maria Marangou

L'enigma del campo
Curator
Marakku Valkonen

**General Release:
Young British Artists**
Curator
The British Council,
Visual Arts Department

Histoire de l'infamie
Curator
Jean-Yves Jouannais

**Identità e differenza.
Libri di artiste**
Curators
Francesca Brandes
Vittoria Surian

**L'image dans
la sculpture**
Curator
Catherine Francblin

Mark di Suvero
Curators
Nicolò Asta,
Lowell McKegney,
Enrico Martignoni,
Matteo Martignoni

**Memorie e attesa
1895-1995: il Castello
d'Amore**
Curator
Centro Culturale
'Le Venezie'

Memory
Curator
Vibeke Dyhrcrone

Naduev

**Orizzonti d'arte
in Albania**
Curators
Nicola T. Firmani
Lucia Nadin

**Giulio Paolini
al Palazzo
della Ragione**
Curator
Virginia Baradel

**Sculture e opere
di Richard Hess**
Curator
Francesco Butturini

TransCulture
Curators
Fumio Nanjo,
Dana Friis-Hansen,
Akiko Miki (*assistant*)

**L'uomo, immagine
del cosmo**
Curators
Walter Kugler
Nevia Pizzul Capello

Viva la donna!
Consejo Nacional para
la Cultura y el Arte
de El Salvador,
'Controcultura'

Acknowledgements

La Biennale di Venezia would like to thank museums, art galleries, Italian and foreign art collectors for generously lending their works. A special thank to the exhibiting artists, real protagonists of the XLVI Esposizione. La Biennale also thanks Institutions and State Agencies for their contribution to the demanding realization of this Biennale, particularly Palazzo Grassi for the collaboration given to the 'Identity and Alterity' exhibition. We would like to thank the Mayor of Venice, the Assessore alla Cultura of the Comune di Venezia, the Assessori al Verde Pubblico and Lavori Pubblici. Special thanks to: the President of Palazzo Grassi *Feliciano Benvenuti*, the Vice President *Giuseppe Donegà*, the Director for the cultural activities *Paolo Viti*, the Director for the operative activities *Pasquale Bonagura*, the Comitato Amici di Palazzo Grassi: *Susanna Agnelli* (President), *Marella Agnelli, Umberto Agnelli, Mirella Barracco, Vittore Branca, Cristiana Brandolini D'Adda, Francesco Cingano, Attilio Codognato, Giancarlo Ferro, Gianluigi Gabetti, Knud W. Jensen, Michel Laclotte, Giancarlo Ligabue, Pietro Marzotto, Thomas Messer, Philippe de Montebello, Sabatino Moscati, Giovanni Nuvoletti Perdomini, Richard E. Oldenburg, Giuseppe Panza di Biumo, Alfonso Emilio Pérez Sánchez, Claude Pompidou, Maurice Rheims, Cesare Romiti, Guido Rossi, Francesco Valcanover, Mario Valeri Manera, Bruno Zevi*; the Director of the Civici Musei, *Giandomenico Romanelli*, for organizing the exhibition 'Venice and the Biennale: Journeys of the Taste'; the President of Fratelli Alinari, *Claudio De Polo*, for the exhibition 'The Self and its Double. A Century of Photography Portraiture in Italy, 1895-1995'; the Soprintendenza ai Beni artistici e storici di Venezia and the Soprintendente *Giovanna Nepi Sciré*; the London British Council for the contribution given to the exhibition 'Identity and Alterity'. We also would like to thank State Agencies, Associations and Cultural Institutes which contributed to the organization of the press conferences held in Paris, Association Française d'Action Artistique, Centre Georges Pompidou, and in New York, Museum of Modern Art.

The Director of Visual Arts Section would like to thank the following people for their help, willingness and cooperation: *John Alviti, Gert Ammann, Robert Anderson, Matthew Armstrong, Michael Auracher, Franco Barberis, Ingo Bartsch, Peter Baum, Felix Baumann, Nicolas Bazin, Patrick Bazin, Herbert Beck, Knut Berg, Hans Jacob Brun, E. John Bullard, Klaus Bussmann, Françoise Cachin, Richard Calvocoressi, José Capa Eiriz, Goren Cavalli-Bjorkman, Gabriella Cecchini, Nicolas Cendo, Goran Christenson, Timothy Clifford, Kevin Consey, W.H. Crouwel, Anne d'Harnoncourt, Agnes de Gouvion Saint Cyr, Claudio De Polo, Jacques de Saint Julien, James Demetrion, Wolf Dieter Dube, Jacqueline Dubois, Philippe Durey, Sybille Ebert-Schifferer, Arne Eggum, Dorothea Eimert, Susan C. Faxon, Sabine Fehlemann, Dominique Ferriot, Gerhard Finckh, Kenneth Finkel, Maria Teresa Fiorio, Marianne Fleury, Mark Francis, Helmuth Friedel, Gerbert Frodl, Rudi Fuchs, Anna Luisa Furlan, Silvio Fuso, Oscar Ghez, Vladimir Goussev, Ulrich Grossmann, Carla Guiducci Buonanni, Lorand Hegyi, Cristophe Heilmann, Josef Helfenstein, Margot Heller, Mariusz Hermansdorfer, Wulf Herzogenrath, Lidia Iovleva, Inge Jadi, Paul Jay, Christian Jeambros, Christian Klemm, Heinrich Klotz, Henrik Kondziela, Richard Koshalek, Thomas Krens, William Lang, Steingrim Laursen, Emmanuel Le Roy Ladurie, Helmuth R. Leppien, Veronique Leroux-Hugon, Marion Leuba, William Liebermann, Tomas Llorens, J.L. Locher, Henri Loyrette, Ian Lyle, Monica Maffioli, Fabio Magalhaes, Rosanna Maggio Serra, Rosa Maria Malet Ybern, Eric Mansion,*

Marilyn Martin, Otto Mayr, Helene Mayer, Yves Michaud, Charles S. Moffett, J.R. Molen, Maria Morris Hambourg, Alexandra Noble, I.C. Nolan, Kazimierz Nowacki, Maria Teresa Ocana, Gisèle Ollinger-Zingue, Karin Orchard, Irene Orlova, Frederick S. Osborne Jr., Alfred Pacquement, Suzanne Pagé, Dominique Païni, Mireille Pastoureau, Rosalind Pepall, Eugenia Petrova, Joelle Pijaudier, Anne Pingeot, Bianca Alessandra Pinto, Michel Poivert, Mario Portigliatti, Earl A. Powell III, Jean-Louis Prat, Adrian R. Rance, Urs Raussmuller, Jack Reynolds, Franklin W. Robinson, Thorsten Rodiek, Giandomenico Romanelli, Andrea Rose, Martin Roth, Philip Rylands, Isabelle Sauve-Astruc, Johann-Karl Schmidt, Katharina Schmidt, Carla Schultz-Hoffmann, Peter-Klaus Schuster, Nicholas Serota, Alan Shestack, Lowery S. Sims, Soili Sinisalo, Philippe Sorel, Carol Stanciu, Renata Stradiotti, Ann Temkin, Eugene V. Thaw, Michel Thévoz, Duncan Thomson, Kirk Varnedoe, G. Vilinbankhov, Jacques Villain, John Walsh, Roland Waspe, H. Winter, Beat Wismer, Sylvie Zavatta, Armin Zweite.

Thanks also to: *Martine Aboucaya, Christine von Assche, Sylvie Aznavourian, Cristine Barthe, Elisabeth de Bartillat, Clare Bell, V. Beston, Patti Cadby Birch, Marie-France Bouhours, Maria Brassel, Margrit Brehm, Antonella Brogi, Bernadette Buiret, Pablo Rimenez Burillo, Joseph Casier, Martha Chahroudhi, Tsong-zung Chang, Catherine Chevillot, Roberto Clemente, Pietro Corsi, Jean Coudane, D. Debrot, Fabien Docaigne, Jean-Marie Drot, Carol S. Eliel,*

Beate Ermacora, Paolo Fabbri, Mindy Faber, Martine Ferretti, Ruth Fine, Simonetta Fraquelli, Annamaria Gambuzzi, Marie de Gandry, Claudia Gian Ferrari, Leonardo Giannadda, Elisabeth A. Gibbens, Krystina Gmurzynska, Gregory Hedberg, Françoise Heilbrun, John Hoole, John Ittmann, Victoria Izquierdo, Annie Jacques, Hubert Klocker, Sophie Lam-than, Claude Lamouille, Catherine Lampert, Brigitte Leal, Gaita Leboissetier, Nathalie Leleu, Bernadette Lepeu-Caille, Cassandra Lozano, Laure de Margerie, David Maupin, Brigitte Maury, Denise May, Josette Mazella di Bosco Balsa, Paule Mazouet, Odile Michel, Philippe Migeat, Anne de Mondenar, Augusta Monferini, James Moore, Moniek Nagels, Juliet Nations-Powell, Lars Nittve, Monique Nonne, Jean Nouzareth, Suzanne Petri, Yves Peyre, Suse Pfaffle, Annette Pioud, Colette Piron, Michel Pivert, Andrée Pouderoux, Jean-Marc Prevost, Claudia Reich, Christine Rojouan, Lauren Ross, Christine de Schaetzen, Didier Schulmann, Marie-Paule Serre, Ethel Sheim, Esperanza Sobrino, Béatrice Soule, Monika Spruth, Jeanne-Yvette Sudour, Agnès Takahashi, Lucien Terras, Mme Tissier, Claude Tournay, Dina Vierny, Antonella Vigliani-Bragaglia, Anne Villard, Theodora Vischer, Stephen Vitiello, Georgia Wagner, Ulrich Wilmes, Michèle M. Wong, Gabrielle Wurzel, Margit Zuckriegl.

Thanks also, for the section 'Imprints of Body and Mind', to: *Nino Benati, Jadranka Bentini, Bernard Blistène, Valentina Castellani, Enrica Dorna, Franco Dorna, Liliane Durand-Dessert, Michel Durand-Dessert,*

Riccarda de Eccher, Veronique Legrand, Giancarlo Ligabue, Liliana Martano, Riccardo Passoni, Alessandra Rizzi, Christian Stein.

The Jury
Robert Hughes
United States
of America
Thomas Llorens
Spain
Arturo Carlo
Quintavalle
Italy
Shuji Takashina
Japan
Jacob Wenzel
Germany

Exhibition Locations

Identity and Alterity.
Figures of the Body
1895-1995
Palazzo Grassi, Museo Correr
Imprints of Body and Mind
Giardini di Castello,
Padiglione Italia

Participating
Italian Artists
Giardini di Castello,
Padiglione Italia

Participating Countries
Giardini di Castello,
National Pavilions
Australia
Austria
Belgium
Brazil
Canada
Czech Republic
Denmark
Egypt
Federal Republic
of Yugoslavia
France
Germany
Great Britain
Greece
Hungary
Iceland
Israel
Japan
The Netherlands

NORDIC COUNTRIES
Finland
Norway
Sweden

Poland
Republic of Korea
Rumania
Russia
Slovak Republic
Spain
Switzerland
United States of America
Uruguay
Venezuela

Argentina
Chiesa di San Giovanni Novo,
Castello

Chile
A Venetian Campo

Ireland
Galleria Nuova Icona,
Giudecca

Luxemburg
Provisional space
in the Giardini di Castello

Portugal
Ex Vetrerie,
Procuratie Vecchie,
San Marco

Republic of Armenia
Centro studi
e documentazione
della cultura armena,
Loggia del Temanza,
San Barnaba, Dorsoduro

Republic of China on Taiwan
Palazzo delle Prigioni,
San Marco

Republic of Croatia
Palazzo Barozzi,
Corte Barozzi,
San Moisé

Republic of Slovenia
Ateneo di San Basso,
San Marco

South Africa
Provisional space
in the Giardini di Castello

Italo-Latin American Institute
Chiesa di San Giovanni Novo,
Castello
Colombia
Costa Rica
Cuba
Ecuador
El Salvador
Mexico
Panama
Paraguay
Peru

The Self and its Double
A Century
of Photography
Portraiture in Italy
1895-1995
'The Photographer's
Studio'
Giardini di Castello,
Padiglione Italia,
ala Pastor

Venice and
the Biennale:
Journeys of Taste

Paintings and Sculptures
1895-1972
Palazzo Ducale,
Appartamento del doge

Great Decorative Cycles
and Applied Arts
1895-1934
Venetian Glass
1895-1972
Ca' Pesaro,
Galleria Internazionale
d'Arte Moderna, San Stae

Events

Christian Boltanski
Giardini di Castello,
Padiglione Italia

Concert & Film
Palazzetto dello sport
all'Arsenale, Castello

Ex Machina.
Connected Isolation
Palagalileo,
Lido di Venezia

Exhibitions with
Official Patronage

Anni cinquanta, anni novanta
Galleria d'arte Meeting,
via Mestrina, Mestre

Among others/Onder anderen
Chiostri del convento
di San Francesco della Vigna,
Castello

'Aperçus'
ACIF/Alliance française,
Casino Venier, San Marco

Arte e tecnologia.
Metodi della creatività
Teatro Fondamenta Nuove,
Cannaregio

Artelaguna 1995
Water spaces between
the islands of San Giorgio
Maggiore and San Lazzaro
degli Armeni

Club Berlin
Teatro Malibran,
San Giovanni Grisostomo

Elytron
Istituto ellenico di studi
bizantini e post bizantini,
ponte dei Greci, Castello

L'enigma del campo
Campo Bandiera e Moro
e chiesa di San Giovanni
in Bragora, Castello

General Release:
Young British Artists
Scuola di San Pasquale,
campo San Francesco
della Vigna, Castello

Histoire de l'infamie
Circolo ricreativo
dell'Arsenale, Castello

Identità e differenza.
Libri di artiste
Scuola internazionale
della grafica, Santa Maria
Mater Domini, Santa Croce

L'image dans la sculpture
Florence, Institut Français;
Naples, Institut Français;
Rome, Galerie Française and
Galleria Autori Messa; Turin,
Centre Culturel Français

Mark di Suvero
Riva degli Schiavoni, riva
San Biagio, campo San Vidal,
campo Sant'Agnese, Zattere,
palazzo Cavalli Franchetti
a San Vidal, campo Santa Lucia

Memorie e attesa 1895-1995:
il Castello d'Amore
Stra, Villa Pisani

Memory
Scuola Grande
di San Giovanni Evangelista,
San Tomà

Naduev
To be defined

Orizzonti d'arte in Albania
Tirana, Istituto Italiano
di Cultura

Giulio Paolini al Palazzo
della Ragione
Padua, Palazzo della Ragione

Sculture e opere
di Richard Hess
Vicenza, Teatro Olimpico,
Museo civico di Palazzo
Chiericati, Municipio Palazzo
Trissino

TransCulture
Fondazione Levi, Palazzo
Giustinian Lolin, San Vidal

L'uomo, immagine del cosmo
ACIT, Palazzo Albrizzi,
Cannaregio

Viva la donna!
ACIT, Palazzo Albrizzi,
Cannaregio

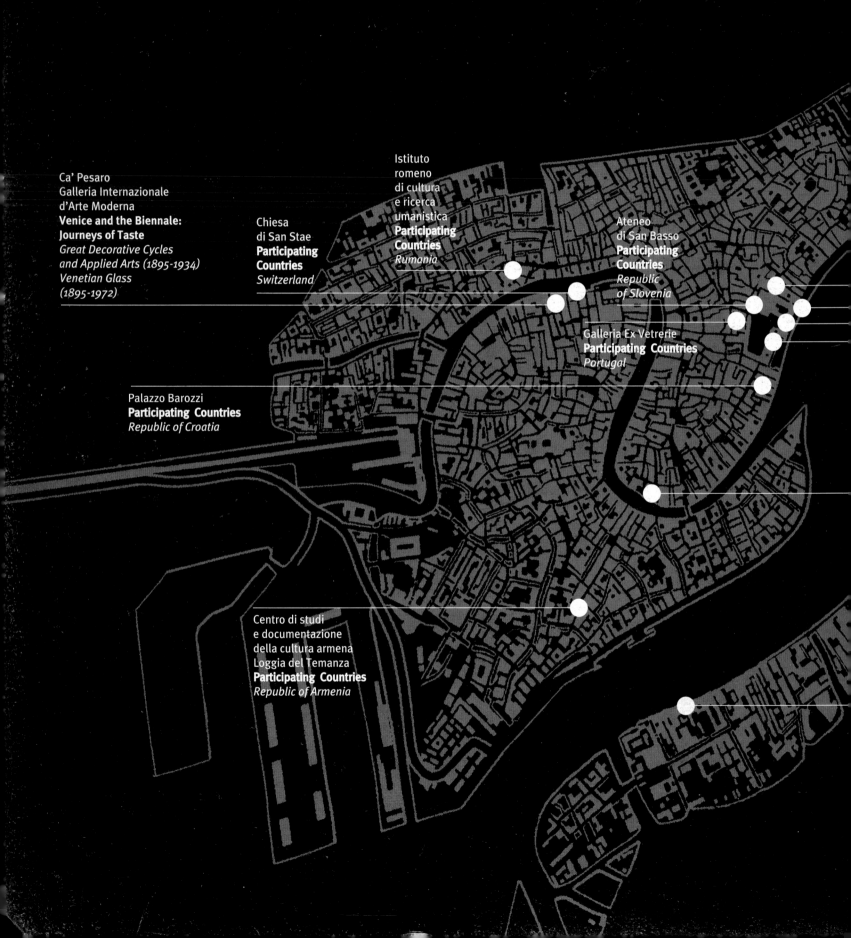

Ca' Pesaro
Galleria Internazionale
d'Arte Moderna
Venice and the Biennale:
Journeys of Taste
Great Decorative Cycles
and Applied Arts (1895-1934)
Venetian Glass
(1895-1972)

Chiesa
di San Stae
Participating
Countries
Switzerland

Istituto
romeno
di cultura
e ricerca
umanistica
Participating
Countries
Rumania

Ateneo
di San Basso
Participating
Countries
Republic
of Slovenia

Galleria Ex Vetrerie
Participating Countries
Portugal

Palazzo Barozzi
Participating Countries
Republic of Croatia

Centro di studi
e documentazione
della cultura armena
Loggia del Temanza
Participating Countries
Republic of Armenia

Exhibition Locations

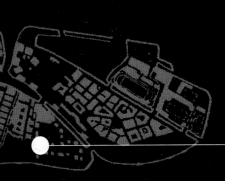

Chiesa
di San Giovanni
Nuovo
**Participating
Countries**
*Argentina,
ITALO-LATIN
AMERICAN
INSTITUTE:
Colombia,
Costa Rica,
Cuba,
Ecuador,
El Salvador,
Mexico,
Panama,
Paraguay,
Peru*

Palazzo
delle Prigioni
Participating Countries
*Republic of China
on Taiwan*

Museo Correr
Identity and Alterity
Figures of the Body
1895-1995

Palazzo Ducale
Appartamento del doge
**Venice and the Biennale:
Journeys of Taste**
*Paintings and Sculptures
1895-1972*

Palazzo Grassi
Identity and Alterity
Figures of the Body
1895-1995

Galleria
Nuova Icona
**Participating
Countries**
Ireland

Giardini di Castello

Padiglione Italia
Identity and Alterity
Imprints of Body and Mind

Padiglione Italia
Participating Italian Artists

National Pavilions
Participating Countries
*Australia; Austria;
Belgium; Brazil; Canada;
Czech Republic; Denmark;
Egypt; Federal Republic
of Yugoslavia; France;
Germany; Great Britain;
Greece; Hungary; Iceland;
Israel; Japan; Luxemburg;
The Netherlands;
NORDIC COUNTRIES:
Finland, Norway, Sweden;
Poland; Republic of Korea;
Rumania; Russia;
Slovak Republic; South Africa;
Spain; Switzerland;
United States of America;
Uruguay; Venezuela*

Padiglione Italia,
ala Pastor
**The Self and its Double
A Century of Photography
Portraiture in Italy
1895-1995**

The Photographer's Studio

The XLVI Esposizione Internazionale d'Arte is heralded as a great
and memorable event, as is to be expected on the historical anniversary
of its extraordinary 100 years of existence.
The Venice Biennale is preparing to celebrate this event with the
commitment and style that have distinguished all its editions and that have
repeatedly captured the attention of the international world of culture.
However, even greater resources have been lavished on the conception
of this edition, which intentionally includes a link with the past, in the sense
of tracing, through an ambitious historical exhibition, an investigation
of Man, his face and his body, as described by prestigious artists from
all over the world, many of whom are indisputable masters in the field
of modern and contemporary art.
The celebration of the Centenary has taken the research of Jean Clair,
curator of the exhibition *Identity and Alterity*, towards artists working
from 1895 to the present. In this context, artists who have made
a considerable contribution to many of the Venice Biennali have, not by
chance, come to the fore and for a scientific and analytical presentation
of this exceptional exhibition (partly housed in Palazzo Grassi, partly in the
Giardini di Castello and partly at the Museo Correr) one needs look no
further than Jean Clair's contribution in the catalogue.
I wish to thank Jean Clair for working to an extremely tight schedule with
great competence and for managing to finish the huge project of *Identity
and Alterity* by the set deadline, contributing with his personal prestige
to obtaining, on loan, delicate and rare works, which have often been
refused on other occasions.
The official Italian contribution, despite the delicate times which
contemporary art is experiencing, is proposed in a stimulating
and prestigious way, open to new experiences such as those of fashion
and scenography.
In keeping with the central theme of the Biennale, *Identity and Alterity*,
the Padiglione Italia will also be hosting a fascinating photographic exhibition
made by from the Fratelli Alinari archives on the theme of a century
of portraiture. To crown the celebratory activities, the Comune di Venezia
and the Biennale have organised an exhibition on 'taste', in the splendid
environment of Palazzo Ducale: a collection of predominantly Italian works,
which have been displayed in past editions of the Biennale and which have
influenced the style and ideas of our century in the field of the visual arts.
Many other exhibitions and events are scattered in locations around
the City that have been specially equipped for the occasion, among which
are those of some foreign countries which have increased the presence
of their artists at the Biennale by exhibiting in these locations other than
at the Giardini. These demonstrate the strong attraction and actuality
of the Biennale Arti Visive, which forms the original nucleus of our Biennale
and makes it a lively and lasting focal point.
Thanks to all those who have taken part for their invaluable contributions
to the realisation of this event, from the Comune di Venezia
to the directors and personnel of our organisation, who have once again
shown their generosity and unselfishness, even in the most difficult of
moments.

GIAN LUIGI RONDI

The invitation to organize the Centenary of such a prestigious event as the Venice Biennale is an honor not unfraught with risks. Quite apart from the fact that the main aim of the Biennale has always tended to be discovery rather than sanctification—and thus the very idea of the usual self-celebration would have been out of keeping—there was also the problem of time: the year which I had at my disposal was far too short for the preparation of a serious retrospective covering the exhibition's 100-year history. Anyway, if such a Biennale of the Biennali was to have had any chance of success I would have had to have teams of researchers, easy access to archives and unlimited recourse to works on loan from public and private collections. Furthermore, I was aware that as a foreigner I would be setting myself a very delicate task in trying to write the history of this important aspect of Italian cultural life when there are so many Italian scholars and historians who, in my place, could so easily have done the job so much better. It was for these reasons that I decided to use the unique opportunity offered by the Centenary to work, along with a team of researchers, on certain questions regarding the actual meaning of these past one hundred years—which, more or less, coincide with the history of so-called 'modern' art. Taking the risk of asking questions seemed to me much more in keeping with the adventurous spirit of the Biennale. The aim was neither to take stock, nor was it to perform some sort of post-mortem. Art is not dead, and the patient, Modernity, is fine. And even less so was it to compile a hit parade. Even supposing such a thing possible, what possible sense could there be to bringing together the one, two... six Hundred Masterpieces of the Biennale, when the very criteria for such value judgements have been undermined? What would be the point in singling out two or three hundred, eight hundred, or a thousand artists, when more than twenty thousand artists have officially participated in the Biennale (and more than double that number have been 'unofficial' participants)—all in all, a group no smaller than the population of Lorenzo il Magnifico's Florence?

If this retrospective was to have a meaning then it should be exploited as an opportunity to assay the validity of the theories that have been propounded during the course of this century. The last decade has seen the collapse of all the ideologies and utopias upon which the last one hundred years have fed. The most obvious defeat is to be seen in the political field, but the same failure can also be seen in Economics (whoever would have thought that Hayek would triumph over Marx?) and in the field of medical research.

In the late-60s people believed in socialism, sexual freedom, the eradication of disease and unlimited technological progress. They had come to look upon themselves as immortal. The young of the 90s have 'recovered' from all that: they are subject to a loathsome economic system, to diseases of previously unknown virulence, to sexuality as a source of stress and to technological progress which has become well-nigh synonymous with the obliteration of humanity. Nationalism, religious fanaticism and ethnic and tribal slaughter have all sprung back from the nineteenth century fully armed. And in saying this, one is not giving voice to nostalgia or 'progressism'. Only the odd provincial would still dare to make an appeal to that 'quaint poetry' which once held such charm.

But whilst all other beliefs crumble, one remains intact —as if no one dare to attack it: the belief in the 'avant-garde' in art. The decade which has formulated a critique of all political, philosophical or technological avant-gardes seems to have steered clear of attacking the *doxa* of the avant-garde itself. The existence of the avant-garde as a veritable touchstone of artistic creativity is a *Credo* no one dares to doubt. By some strange exception, the visual arts seem to enjoy some sort of exemption when it comes to formulating a critique. Kant's *Critique of Judgement* located the visual arts in a domain between knowledge and sensibility—and even today that domain remains one of opinions, diktats and beliefs not of reasoned argument and analyses. Does this fear of thought arise from the particular nature of the image and its power? Ideas are toppled more easily than idols. The image is still protected by a taboo, whilst the written word and books can be more easily contradicted.

This Biennale Centenary, therefore, offered me the opportunity to attempt a critique of the system of avant-gardes and of certain *idées reçues*. What has become of the history of modern art which saw Cézanne as the founding father? What has become of the history of modern art which saw the autonomy the self-referentiality—of the work of art as its ultimate—goal? What has become of the idea of art as shaking off the burden of usefulness that it had been carrying for more than a thousand years? What has become of the Clement Greenberg's ideas, which for more than a quarter of a century were the mainstay of art history—and of the art market? Formalism, the modernist litany of A Cube is a Cube is a Cube, the abrupt tautologies of American Art—did all that and the rest of it really amount to the *nec plus ultra* of artistic creation in the second half of the twentieth century? Pollock as successor to Cézanne and precursor of Robert Morris? A history of triumphs, told in a religious key—with prophets, advents, parousia and rituals? And yet before his death Greenberg himself disowned his own ideas—cruelly, in an article written with lucid despair. Who dares to cite those final words, recall that last pirouette?
And what if there were Meaning where it had always been argued there was only Form? Or if there were the Human where it had always been said there was only Hedonism? And what if Cézanne were no more the origin of Modern Art than was Meissonier, Klinger or De Chirico? Or if the twentieth century had, more than any other, been the century of the Self-Portrait not of Abstraction?... And there are so many other questions to ask.
Posing the problem of the representation of the human body and face seemed, at the end of a century haunted by sex, disease and death, one way to approach such questions. It is the approach we have chosen to follow.

My first thanks go to the Board of Directors of the Biennale, which immediately accepted this Biennale Centenary project when it was proposed in April 1994. I would like to thank President Gian Luigi Rondi for his faith in me and his unqualified support during these long months of work.
My thanks also go to the various teams working within the Biennale, first of all to Dominique Renoux and Pieranna Cavalchini, who with competence, devotion and loyalty have allotted all their time to this project and then in particular to those working in the Visual Arts Section, with a special mention for Raffaello Martelli, Dario Ventimiglia (Section director) and Adriano Donaggio (Director of the Press Office), and for Anna Maria Porazzini, Paolo Scibelli, Roberto Rosolen and Gianpaolo Cimarosti, whose patient help enabled a newcomer to find his way around the intricacies of the Biennale. There was not always time enough to explain the full extent of the project as it should have been explained; yet, with often blind trust, they continued to

work with great dedication and commitment in often difficult conditions. Aware of what a thankless task theirs was, I would like them to know how grateful I am.

Furthermore I'd would like to thank the staff of the Technical Department, Pina Maugeri and Gualtiero Seggi that, considering the Centenary's enormous work, has in cold blood organized the transport of the works.

The manager of the Archivio storico delle arti contemporanee, Gabriella Cecchini, Alberto Prandi and the editorial staff too, who have kindly supplied all the informations I needed have and taken on the load of setting in order the general catalogue.

I would also like to thank the Délégation des Arts Plastiques and its Director Alfred Pacquement, who almost immediately after my appointment put two assistants, Elizabeth de Bartillat and Dominique Renoux, at my disposal to expedite my work, and who also agreed to make a contribution to the financing of Christian Boltanski's project. I am moreso thankful to Xavier North and Brigitte Maury of the Services Culturels de la France who have constantly helped me in Rome and Venice. Equal thanks should also go to my secretary, Odile Michel, who acted as a sort of liaison officer in Paris.

I would also like to express my gratitude to the private patrons who have contributed to the exhibition, and in particular to Patti Cadby Birch and Leonardo Giannadda, whose help made it possible to put certain projects into effect. My thanks also go to all those in Venice who, in spite of inevitable differences of opinion, were willing to work together to ensure the success of this project: the City Mayor, Massimo Cacciari, the Assessore alla Cultura Gianfranco Mossetto , the managers of Palazzo Grassi (and Paolo Viti in particular) and Clarenza Catullo. Special thanks also to my friend and colleague Giandomenico Romanelli. I would also like to express my gratitude to the architects Gae Aulenti and Daniela Ferretti, who in often difficult conditions showed themselves capable of overcoming all obstacles.

I would also like to thank the official and unofficial experts whose advice—and, in some cases, their physical presence—was a great help. First of all, I should mention Gabriella Belli, but also Claudia Gian Ferrari and Giulio Macchi. My gratitude also goes to Prof. Manlio Brusatin, a man of fine erudition who not only saw immediately what I was getting at but has also—with the patient help of his assistant Vittorio Mandelli and the editorial staff—put together a catalogue which is as fine an explication of the ideas behind this exhibition as it was possible to produce in such limited time.

Tribute should also be paid to those Commissioners of national pavilions who have so kindly adapted their individual exhibitions to the theme of the Centenary Biennale. I would also like to take this opportunity to welcome the commissioner of the Korean Pavilion, which opens this year, and extend particular thanks to the Commissioners of the German, Belgian, Spanish, Dutch and Hungarian pavilions, who have had important restoration and renovation work carried out (particularly noteworthy in the case of the Hungarian pavilion, which has regained its former splendor). All of this makes a magnificent contribution to the success of the XLVI Biennale.

Finally I would like to thank my partner, Laura Bossi, whose unfailing affection has sustained me through some difficult moments, and my children Faustine and Johannes Régnier, concrete images of that posterity for which we are working.

JEAN CLAIR

**Preparation
of the catalogue**
Archivio Storico delle
Arti Contemporanee,
Venice

Catalogue edited by
Manlio Brusatin
and Jean Clair

Published by
Marsilio Editori s.p.a.
Venice

Editorial Coordinator
Susanna Biadene

Editor
Isabella Ruol

Editorial Staff
Valeria Bové
Diana Massarotto

Translation
Gus Barker
Marco Bettini
Holly Snapp

Page Layout
Daniela Albanese

Technical Coordinator
Piergiorgio Canale

Contents

Henri Matisse
Académie d'homme
1900-01

Impossible Anatomy 1895–1995

Notes on the iconography of a world of technologies

by Jean Clair

A month before the opening of the first Venice Biennale on March 22 1895, Louis Lumière gave a public demonstration of his new invention, the cinematograph [II. 83]. Legend has it that he came up with the principle of the moving image while watching his mother at work on her sewing-machine. By adapting the presser-foot mechanism to his own purposes he cracked the Zenonian puzzle of how to run still images on a strip of film, thus uniting the continuous with the discontinuous, and movement with immobility. It may come as a surprise that in this way science resuscitates configurations from long before our time. Penelope at her loom, day in day out, weaving images to postpone giving an answer to her suitors: the image leads to the fabled narrative at the origin of all narrative. Speak so as not to die. Reflect so as not to have to pronounce the final word. Unfurl the supple flow of images like skeins of wool, and escape from *rigor mortis*. As long as images are created by the weaving shuttle, as if in another culture, as long as Sheherazade can continue adding one word to another to quell the fury of her sultan, death is deferred. This is the great augural narrative of the genesis of images.

And any stratagem is valid so long as it defers death while the narrative spins its thread, letting the gaze come to rest on its image. Thus every night Penelope unpicks what she has woven during the day. She challenges the very idea that there can be anything new in the production of images—an absolute beginning or a *tabula rasa* of her craft, an empty loom on which to inscribe a sign or glyph no-one had previously imagined. She only ever begins again. She is part of a continuity, herself only a woven link, as she weaves and unweaves through time. She sets to work again, darns, mends. She retraces her craft, returns to her loom. She reminds us of what the French verb *regarder* means: initially a reiteration, a return to the past, a looking back to a previous state; thereafter an act of conservation—as in the German *warten*, and the English 'to ward'. Making images is a remembering and a guarding over. The world exists as long it is held under my gaze, as long as I don't forget to cast my gaze back on it. The *maille* (stitch) in Penelope's cloth is also, in the sense of the old French word, a *méaille*—a medallion or coin (Mail), a precious effigy conserving the memory of those who are no more. This is the coin ('bone') that can never be picked with anyone[1], an effigy that can't be divided because it is good currency, a token of the indivisible identity of being. It is in the name of this *maille*—with its implications of quarrelling, of division, wrangling and death—that all human exchanges take place: contracts, intimate relations and marriages. The fact of drawing a portrait, like drawing a bill of exchange, is a reminder of the deadly stake in the law of retaliation. Stroke for stroke, eye for eye, tooth for tooth, according to Leviticus, which gives some idea of the importance of cutting images. An image is made to retain identity and to respect the rules of exchange. Penelope's suitors discover this to their mortal cost when, one by one, they die stroke for stroke at the hands of Ulysses.

While she is beguiling time, beguiling her suitors and her own long waiting, Penelope is not weaving any random image. The work is connected to her lineage, spun out along the straight line, to which Telemachus' presence bears witness. It is a winding-cloth for Ulysses' father, Laertes. The genealogy of the image—the Odyssey of our culture—closely retraces the narrative of Genesis, the great history of direct human descent, with in the end, the recourse to the Father. All images are rooted in the spectre of carnal begetting. At the end of his interminable travels, Ulysses learns his own story from Demodochus, and he who was Nobody, is finally able to pronounce his own name.

Yet Penelope's patient daily winding-sheet—woven by indefatigable skilful female fingers—is the very opposite of the *icona vera* of the Vernicle, that miraculous, instantaneous 'acheiropoetic' image left by the face of the Son of a God. To take up the terms used by Léon Chestov, the two images are yet further proof of those clear-cut differences between the traditions we have inherited from Athens and Jerusalem.

Having noted the marvellous analogy which led to Louis Lumière's discovery of the principle for his moving picture machine in the small shuttle formerly used by weavers, who could fail to perceive in that history of weft and thread—perpetuating the tradition of images, the descent of men and the mystery of their denomination—the radical difference, the change in the tidemark of images that cinema introduces in our way of seeing the world? It was as if when the hitherto always still body suddenly began flickering on the screen, the quiet of the image was troubled for ever, its repose denied to the gaze. It was as if something—once the paradise of paintings—was slipping away for good. That something was described by Walter Benjamin as *aura*. The unique interior lustre of an individual work is replaced by the flickering and dazzle of an image snatched out of our sight twenty-four times a second. The unfortunate thing about images in our modern culture is not simply that they can be reproduced mechanically (losing substance with each reproduction), but that they have become indefinitely interchangeable, sempiternally fleeting—irremediably labile. We have ceased to trust or find rest in them.

Thus every science has its dark side. In 1895 Lumière's invention pierced the opacity of a darkened room to then place between its own source of light and our eye a screen which lights up and renders the semblances of life. There is an allusion to the enigma of origin itself, to the fact that the images come to us, arise out of darkness, a darkness that is part of them, for without it, they would merely dazzle rather than illuminate.

Forty years after the foundation of the Biennale, when in the 1930s Mussolini set up the Film Festival, he drew conclusions unwittingly reflecting the analyses made by thinkers such as Elie Faure in France and Walter Benjamin in Germany, hardly figures congenial to the *Duce*: cinema was not an industry like any other; nor an art form like any other. It is the Seventh Art, like the Seventh Seal. It accomplishes—and goes beyond—all that the other arts had been trying to do. From this point of view, the history of the Biennale would only be history of the agony of the visual arts enacted in just under a century...

A new regime of images—reproducible, labile, interchangeable images—thus placed itself at the service of new political regimes aspiring to unity, stability and fixity. One People. One Nation. One Leader. While the image was reduced, shifted, eluded, exchanged, revealing its corruptibility, and become a token of nothing, society, stripped of the Palladium which the image represented, formed itself into fixed formidable paintings, aspiring to eternity, or at least to the 'thousand-year kingdom'. The configurations of the latter were delineated in the human architecture of totalitarianisms, in those masses of uniformed men, squared blocks of flesh cancelling out the individual. In those years of the terrible union between the Masses and Power, technological progress led man to transform the union reached with white magic of the still image into a union with the black magic of the moving image. Modernity—as the implementation of technological thought, motion, reproducibility, interchangeability and lability—is thus linked to evil, or rather to what Kant, the first philosopher of modern aesthetics, called *das radikal Böse*—radical Evil[2].

At the end of 1895 the German physicist Röntgen accidentally discovered that non-visible radiation could impress on a photographic plate transparent images of the interior of the living human body. The invention not only opened up the way to the investigation of opaque bodies, it also lent support to a whole current of *Naturphilosophie* which, from Swedenborg to Kerner, postulated the existence of invisible rays able to put us in contact with mysterious universes and—why not?— even make the dead speak.

The advent of radiography suddenly heralded the end of a whole register of European sensibility—what we might call the register of the macabre—which had fuelled the imagination of artists [II. 186; 188-191]. Ancient imagery of skulls and cross was demystified at one fell swoop. But a much more disturbing mystery was about to invite speculation in its place. The range of the colours and forms we are given to perceive is only a tiny window on a vast spectrum of radiations eluding our senses. We are infirm, blind and deaf, immersed in the infinite white noise of the world. We only retain a 'minimum sensation' of it. This humiliation of the artist gave rise to an idea that insidiously permeated the century: the most 'foolish' of all men is the painter who still believes in his pigments, that terebinth and linseed oil will help him to share his 'vision' of the world. Mortified and humiliated, the art of painting would henceforth live off aspects of its own survival, under the obsessive issue of its 'utility'.

From this point of view a clear-cut line was created between those who continued to portray the skull in the traditional way, as if x-rays had never been discovered, and those whose work takes account of the radical semantic and iconographical revolution they implied. The dividing line sometimes cuts unexpectedly, with 'moderns' falling on the side they are not usually placed on. Thus Ensor [II. 30] and Cézanne [II. 17] emerge as traditionalist and outmoded, since they continue to use the *calvarium* as an accessory of Worldly Vanities [II. 37; 186]. Munch and Duchamp, on the other hand, are modern. Looking forward to us, they explore the interiority of the body and its properties. The skeletal arm of the former, the jawbone of the latter, have a new harsh resonance. We are faced with a sort of cold clinical report, whereas Ensor and Cézanne remain hostages to the romantic vignette.

Spiritualistic photos, seance tables and dialogues with the dead—which fascinate not only ordinary people, but also scientists like Crookes and Richet—thus seem to cut out new fields of enquiry just as valid as acceleration, the decomposition of movement or the functional exploration of organisms. All of these démarches of modernity take over the enormous realm of the invisible, which could only be portrayed by *un art non rétinien*—to use Duchamps' phrase—with the artist as *médium* [II. 174-178; 183-184; 186; v. 48]. Albeit in different ways Boccioni, Kupka, Kandinsky and Mondrian were all to share this new credo. But the temptation of angelism is never far away, and we can't be certain that modern art has not had to succumb to it [II. 167-169; 181; 183; IV. 86].

To stay in the realm of the invisible, in 1895 Marconi invented the radio-telephone. And, once again, it seems to be true that scientific and technological advances body forth some of the most ancient dreams inscribed in our mental matrix.

In his *Histories* Herodotus recounts how the Ephesians, when besieged by Croesus, dedicated their city to Artemis and to win over her power they ran a rope from the city walls to the goddess' temple outside[3]. Long before Chappe and Edison, the dream of the telegraph had taken root. In the Sala del Senato of Venice's Café Florian there is a picture of a young woman seated beneath a telegraph pole while the wire crackles with messages: Artemis of Ephesus?

From now on which artist will not be concerned to portray with modern instruments what had once belonged to the iconography of the *Bonus Eventus*? But can the invisible be portrayed? Poles and wires are one thing—Puvis de Chavanne in France and Toorop in Holland were the first to dare depict them, at the height of Symbolism—but how can you depict the wire-*less* telegraph? How can you portray the commandments of the *Mariée* transmitted 'electrically' to the *Célibataires* in the *Grand Verre*? Duchamp was to rack his brains for twelve years over the problem and then in 1923 left his Great Work 'definitively incomplete'.

For centuries, from Dürer to Watteau, the difficulties of painting the nude were tackled following canons inherited from classical geometry; but how could the female anatomy be represented by following the multidimensional geometry arising out of Poincaré's work at the turn of the century? Which Pélerin Viator, which Piero or Uccello would be able to formulate the *regola prospettiva* allowing modern art to take into account the new mathematics?

Again in 1895, with the aid of technical progress in image reproduction the *Iconographie de la Salpêtrière* was illustrated with photographic plates. Up to then it had only been available with original photographs, and therefore had only had a limited distribution for specialists [II. 159-162]. Now it was suddenly attracting a public well outside medical circles. The characteristic posture of *Hysteria major* thus entered the realm of art [II. 140-141]. The arched body of the woman suffering a 'great attack' would become a *topos* of fin-de-siècle modernity, as recognizable as the Mannerist body perfected by Primaticcio and Rosso. Klimt's allegory of *Medicine* and Segantini's *The Bad Mothers* are just two famous examples of that new female body which the medical nosology of the day believed it had isolated: an exasperated, bristling, ecstatic body, twisting and bent under the gaze of her Master, so reminiscent of that of diabolic possessions.

That body was soon removed from the trestles on which

it was exhibited in the hospital, but its artistic career was to last throughout the new century...

In 1935 the Surrealists celebrated the fiftieth anniversary of 'the birth of hysteria' [v. 55]. In the pathetic clinical documents that Bourneville and Régnard had so carefully put together (complete with photographs), the Surrealists wished to see the triumph of Eros. Faces disfigured by suffering were taken to be portraits of sexual ecstasy; wracked bodies, formal prototypes of a 'convulsive beauty'—the only beauty suited to our age. At the end of this century, however, Louise Bourgeois has restored hysteria to its true meaning [II. 128]. Her *Arch of Hysteria* owes more to the models gathered by Charcot in his Musée d'Anatomie-pathologie at the Salpêtrière than to the erotic fantasies of Breton and his disciples.

The history is yet to be written of such museums assembled by various late nineteenth-century doctors, alienists and neurologists and now broken up, lost or destroyed: the Museo Lombroso in Turin, Charcot's museum at the Salpêtrière [II. 130-131; 145], the Trocadero Musée d'Ethnologie founded by Hamy, and the collections of drawings by the mentally-ill put together by Luys, Marie and Réjà (Paul Meunier) and many others [II. 112-118; 149; VII. I]. Models chosen from the crowds of innumerable patients and other poor wretches thronging the mental asylums of the day; the delirious outpourings of the mad, objects, paintings, and other nameless and formless artefacts, all waiting to be described and named, were collected and catalogued. Terrifying wax copies, casts of deformities, infinite series of preserved skulls, insane graffiti were seen as bearing the promise of new canons. This material would be to modern art what the re-opened excavations of Rome had been to the Renaissance: an immense repertory or stock-room in which to find, *a contrario*, new models of the contemporary world. Collected and deciphered, they would become what collections of antique statues and plaster casts had been for the Fine Art Schools of the past: the foundations for a new Science of the Beautiful. And in fact it was the art schools of France and Italy that would gather up what was left of these *mirabilia*. In the vacuum left by the collapse of the classical canons, along with Thomas Eakins in America, Edgar Degas was one of the first artists to see what contribution the nascent discipline of anthropology might make to the artist's gaze [II. 137]. True to his 'scientific realism', Degas was not only interested in Marey's chronophotography but also in Duranty, who since 1867 had been working on a *science physionomique* which drew on Darwin-influenced theories spread by Broca in France and Lombroso in Italy but also by

Bordier and the psychiatrist Morel, author of the very popular *Traité des dégénérescences physiques, intellectuelles et morales de l'espèce humaine*.

When Degas exhibited his *Petite danseuse de quatorze ans* at the sixth Impressionist exhibition, the critics were not taken in. The *facies* of the model corresponded to the descriptions 'science' had made of the 'degenerate' skull type: backward-sloping face, jutting jaw and cheekbones, no forehead—traits which in the popular mind evoked the ignorance and bestiality of the 'dangerous classes'. The *Danseuse* was to be seen as a *petite Nana de quinze ans*, alluding to the recently published Zola novel. In fact, between the preparatory drawings and the maquette, Degas clearly made several changes to his model Marie van Goethem so that she would better exemplify Lombroso's model of the 'born criminal', thus turning this *petit rat d'Opéra*—as the dancers in the corps de ballet were known—into a vicious animal come out of the gutter with the sole purpose of spreading the plague among the bourgeoise.

The glass cage which Degas had thought of using to exhibit the statue was compared to a 'specimen jar', confirming the impression that the *Petite Danseuse* was not so much a work of art as an anatomical waxwork 'made for a museum of zoology, anthropology or physiology'.

At the same exhibition Degas was to have shown two pastels of *Physionomie de criminels* [II. 136], done from sketches taken in the Paris Palais de Justice during the 1879 trial of two young murderers, Abadie and Knobloch. Again there are enough differences between the drawings and the sketches made in the courtroom for it to be clear that in this case Degas was more interested in physiognomical research exemplifying contemporary anthropological classifications than in producing faithful portraits of the accused.

This project for a Science of Beauty was to have been the culmination in the Arts of what Positivism had begun in the Sciences and was to have been to contemporary art what those empirical treatises—from Dürer to Lomazzo—had been to ancient art. But it was doomed to failure. Paul Richer—neurologist, assistant to Charcot at Salpêtrière but also professor of anatomy at the Ecole des Beaux-Arts was a figure in the tradition of William Hunter at the Royal Academy. Richer dreamt of 'offering artists the most recent and incontrovertible scientific acquisitions concerning human proportions'. But all that his *Nouvelle Anatomie artistique du corps humain*, published in 1906, proposed was sterile conventionalism [II. 102; 104]. Only the totalitarian regimes of the 1930s would show any interest in these over-rationalized human bodies, seeing them as *exempla* of the new muscular and healthy humanity they wished to produce.

A much more influential book was Marcel Réjà's *L'Art chez les Fous*, published in 1907, the year of the *Demoiselles d'Avignon*: it was to the abnormal and the 'degenerate' that modern art would turn for themes, if not for models. And although the 'degenerate' might fail to placate modern art's anxiety, at least it would feed its fever.

The year 1895 was also a key date in the career of a man without whom art would not be as we know it today. That year Freud turned his back on neurophysiology and pursued the line of enquiry he would call psychoanalysis.

Significantly, at the beginning of his *I precursori dell'antropologia criminale*, Lombroso cites Aristotle and the treatise on physiology long-attributed to him, in which the appearance of certain criminals is compared to that of the ape. Physiognomy was to be an indispensable part of criminal anthropology as it developed at the end of the nineteenth century. Gall and his followers took up Gianbattista Della Porta's idea of an exact correspondence between facial features and internal dispositions, thus founding the positivist school of metaphysics by postulating that access can be gained to the soul through the body. Inside was to be read from the outside. Lombroso would identify the *stigmata degenerationis* on the body of *Homo delinquens* and claim that they were experimentally verifiable indications of character, visible signs—the body-writing of evil. As in the *Scarlet Letter*, the individual was branded by these signs for all to see. Or rather, they were inscribed upon the body of the crime, just like the tattoos covering the body of the criminals, and Lombroso would become a collector of them.

Although more subtle and scientific than Lombroso's muddled classifications, the theories of cerebral localisations in the positivist neuroanatomy put forward by Broca and Wernicke labour under the same naturalist illusion whereby the various functions of the body and mind—sensations, motor functions, language, etc.— could all be pinpointed to particular sections of the brain [v. 73]. As a pupil of Brücke's, Freud himself was raised in this physicalist school of thought. However, his highly controversial *Project for a Scientific Psychology* was to be abandoned in 1895. A rough draft he would later try to forget, it reduced the whole physiology of the brain to a question of the transmission of electricity in the nervous system. The play of forces within the closed system of the human soul became a simple matter of electrical charge and discharge, with displacements and dissipation of energy, alternating shifts between equilibrium and disequilibrium.

But Freud was not to go far down this reductionist path. In his *Contribution to a Concept of Aphasia* (1892), he had already attacked Meynert's idea that each part of the body could be identified with a particular point in the cortex and that consequently the language apparatus was made up of distinct cortical centres, whose cells contained representations of words. But man is above all a language-using animal and language cannot be reduced to anatomical-physiological processes whose pathways are located in definite zones—this the logic behind Freud's about-turn.

In the year 1895 two parallel approaches would lead him to the re-discovery of the importance of language as something that cannot be pinned down on a map of the brain; first came his study of hysteria with Charcot, then his analyses of dreams, which turned out to be the main route to the unconscious.

In the *Studies on Hysteria*, published the same year, Freud tackled the mystery of the anatomy of the hysteric body which was quite beyond 'location' theories, whose tidy neuronal marking was in a tradition derived from phrenology. This was a problem for the scientist, but also an enigma for the artist, stripped of the rules for his art. What kind of bodily pattern does the hysteric conform to? Hysteria defies the laws of anatomy! It creates a previously unknown body which seems a pure manifestation of language, a pure manifestation of speech, and yet produces physical effects. So, contrary to what the positivists held, the body is not the cause of the soul's troubles, it is the soul which can impose its fantasies on the body, that is—to put it more bluntly—in this case the psyche is the driving force of physical impairment. Abasia and blindness—says Freud—make a mockery of nerves. The body 'speaks'. But this language of the body could not be understood by the neuro-physiological theories of the day. It requires another approach, another way of listening. The organism has an astonishing plasticity, which blissfully transcends localisations, and shatters the fixity of marked-off areas. The continual shifting of its emotions and sensitivity upsets the rigid pattern of localisations and destroys the claim made by Lombroso, Richer and others to have established the rules for a Science of the Beautiful, the Genuine and the Good with its elect and outcasts. Orthopaedics simply does not exist.

And that same year, 1895, the 'doors of dream' opened up to Freud, to use his own words. In 1896 he began writing his *Traumdeutung*, which would be published in 1899. The work of dreams in the sleeping person confirmed what had been hinted at by the work of the hysteric on his or her own body: it is the work of

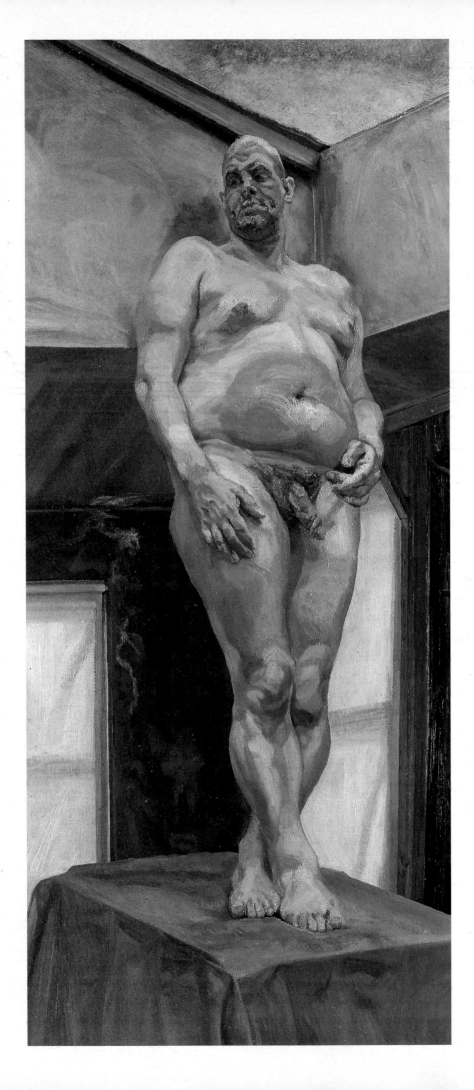

XXX
Jean Clair

Lucian Freud
Leigh under the Skylight
1994

perennially metamorphoses, and Freud set about describing its various figures [v. 70-71; 76-78]. Nothing is fixed, inscribed, labelled or tattooed: everything becomes free, mobile and fleeting. Everything moves, evolves, is transformed. Lapsus, shifts in meaning, deformations, displacements, condensations, approximations and anamorphoses—a whole morphology of aberration was suddenly validated and would hold artists in its sway.

There could be no more topographical adjustments between body and soul. Man is not contained in his body, and he certainly is not 'marked out' in his anatomy by signs revealing his identity and dictating his destiny. The fact that man speaks, and that through language he accedes to the space of interpretations, transcends any 'scientific' definition of his being. In opposition to the body conceived of as *fatum*, as fate marking out the individual with an indelible seal, Freud reinstated the grandeur of a soul. A powerful, dark and perpetually unknowable soul, but, as the source of language, an unlimited potential to manifest human freedom.
What Focillon was to call 'the life of forms' would be inscribed under the sign of that liberating movement.

The anatomies cut up in pieces, fragmented and disarranged of the new photographic techniques; the occulted labile fluctuating bodies of cinematographic phantasmagorias; the filigreed transparent limbs of the new non-invasive exploratory technology; the virtual bodies of multidimensional geometries; the disincarnate bodies of telecommunications, the anarchic or teratological anatomies of hysterics giving birth to limbs or paraesthesia where nothing was expected; and the marvellous, disconcerting anatomies of dreams. Faced with this infinite proliferation of possible bodies obeying no perceptible rules, totalitarianisms would try once more to impose the orthopaedics of a cold tetanic Beauty. Who remembers Breker? He was the last to be honoured by the Biennale in 1942, in the midst of War. Modern art, however, continued on its way. From Rodin to Giacometti, from Martini to Antonio Lopez, from Gerstl to Lucian Freud, perhaps no other century has tried so intensely to restore—against the encroaching deserts—human presence.

[1] *Avoir maille à partir avec quelqu' un* ('to have a bone to pick with someone') means, in a figurative sense, to quarrel with someone, whereas literally, it means to share the 'medal'—the medal being the *sou*, the gold or silver coin on which the monarch's image is stamped as a token of its exchange value.
[2] This critique is usually associated with a certain conservative right, from Spengler to Heidegger and the Jünger brothers. It is often forgotten that it also has a left-wing counterpart in Walter Benjamin, certain philosphers in the Frankfurt School, such as Ernst Bloch, and today Jorge Semprun (see his *Mal et Modernité: le travail de l' Histoire*, Paris, 1995)
[3] Cited by Alberto Savinio, *Divinità per Telegrafo* in *Torre di Guardia* (Palermo, 1977),

Identity
and Alterity

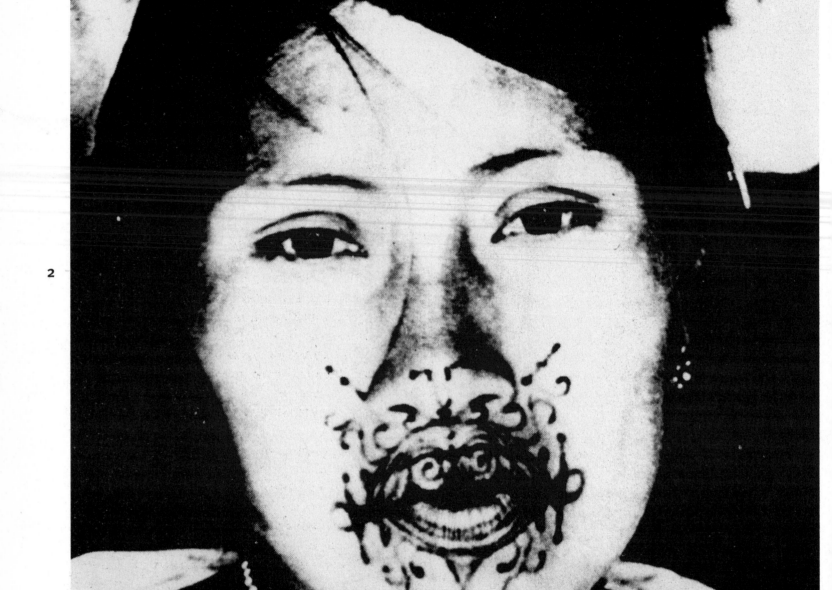

2

Looking at Objects

by Claude Lévi-Strauss

The men of the Indian tribes of the North American Plains painted figurative scenes or abstract decorative patterns on buffalo hides and other skins; but the art of embroidery using porcupine quills was the exclusive preserve of women. They would flatten, soften and dye quills of different lengths and stiffness, then bend, knot, plait and weave them. It was a difficult skill which required years of apprenticeship, and the sharp quills might sometimes wound the embroidress; if they sprang back into the face, they could even take out an eye. Whilst apparently nothing but decoration, these geometric embroideries were rich in significance. The embroidress had meditated for a long time over their shape and content; or she could have received the pattern directly from the double-faced Mother of the Arts in a dream. A pattern thus inspired by the goddess could then be copied by other women and eventually became part of the common repertoire of the tribe. But the woman who first created it retained her special status.

Almost a century ago, an old Indian revealed that 'when a woman has dreamt the Double Lady, then she is without rivals in whatever she does afterwards. But this woman behaves like a complete madwoman. She laughs compulsively, is unpredictable in her behavior. The men who go near her can become possessed. This is why such woman are called double ladies. They will sleep with anyone. But their work surpasses everyone else's. They are great embroiderers of porcupine quills—an art in which they are very skilful. They can also do man's work'.

This astonishing portrait not only outstrips the usual Romantic image of the artist of genius but also surpasses the image of the *poet maudit* which was to develop out of it a century later (complete with pseudo-philosophical meditations on the relationship between genius and madness). Whilst we were being metaphorical, those peoples that had no written culture expressed themselves literally. We have only to transpose what they say for it to be clear that they are not so distant from us, or that we are much closer to them than we thought.

Amongst the Tsimshian Indians, who lived on the Pacific coast of Canada, painters and sculptors formed a distinct, separate group. The very name used to refer to them evokes the mystery that surrounded them. The man, woman or child, who came upon them while they were at work was instantly put to death. There are recorded cases of this happening. In very hierarchical societies the status of artists was generally the preserve of nobles, passed on from father to son, but those whose special gifts had been recognised could also be admitted to the caste. But noble or not, the novice had

3

4
Claude
Lévi-Strauss

Details of paintings
on Tupi Kawahib house-walls

to undergo long and severe trials as part of his initiation. The old artist had to pass on his magic into the body of his successor, who was then carried off to heaven by the protecting spirit of the artist.

In fact, the novice spent a certain length of time hidden in the forest before reappearing in public, invested with all his new powers.

The solid or articulated masks that the artist created had a fearful power. A literate Indian of the beginning of this century has left an account of a supernatural spirit called Boiling-Words who 'had a body like that of a dog. The chief of the tribe never wore his mask over his face or on his head because the mask had its own body and was considered to be an object with terrifying powers. It was very difficult to gets its whistle to work; now no one knows how to. You did not blow with your mouth; you had to place your finger on a certain spot. The only thing that was known about this being was that he lived on a certain rock in the mountains. The mask had a special song; but the mask itself was kept hidden. Only the children of the chief of the tribe—and of the chief of a neighboring tribe—knew the song. But even they were frightened of the voice of Boiling-Words; common people were absolutely terrified of it. Princes and princesses were proud of the fact that they were allowed to touch the mask. The right to exhibit it cost one dear'.

Artists were responsible for decorating the facades of houses and the moving partitions inside, as well as for carving totem poles and creating ritual and ceremonial objects. Most importantly of all they were responsible for designing, making and operating those machines which, among the tribes of this part of America, made important social or religious events into large-scale spectacles.

These 'performances' were held either in the open-air or inside the large single halls which housed several families (and could accommodate a large crowd of guests for the event). A native account dating from last century tells us that during one of these occasions the fire in the centre of the room was suddenly flooded by water surging up from the depths (like something out of *Götterdämmerung*). A life-size whale then appeared, complete with thrashing tail and jets of water. After it had dived beneath the surface again, the water disappeared and, when the earth had dried, the fire was relit.

However, the designers and operators of these machines were not forgiven for mishaps. In 1895 Boas published an account of a ceremony, the 'key moment' of which was the return to his people of a man who was supposed to have been living at the bottom of the sea. The spectators gathered on the seashore saw a large rock appear out of the water and then split open for the man to step forth. The 'stagehands' were hidden in a wood nearby, and operated the whole thing by means of ropes. Everything went well the first two times (the crowd had demanded an encore), but the third time the ropes got tangled and the artificial rock sank back into the sea, taking the man with it. His family appeared unperturbed, saying that the man had decided to stay on the bottom of the ocean, and so the feast continued as planned. But after the guests had left, the dead man's family and those responsible for the mishap tied themselves together and jumped into the sea from the top of a cliff.

It is also recounted that, for the ceremony marking the return of an initiated novice, artists had created a seal-skin model of a whale (again operated by ropes). For the sake of realism, they had red-hot stones inside the model which they plunged into buckets of water to create a convincing water-spout of steam. However, one of the stones fell onto the seal-skins, burnt a hole in them and the whale began to leak. The organizers of the ceremony and the artists who had created the machine all committed suicide, knowing full well that they would have been put to death by the guardians of the mysteries.

These accounts comes from the Tsimshian Indians, who lived along the north coast of British Colombia. The Queen Charlotte Islands directly opposite them were inhabited by the Haida Indians, who had myths of villages of artists situated on the seabed or in the impenetrable heart of forests. The Indians learnt to paint and sculpt as a result of an encounter with one of these artists. So these myths were another way of attributing a supernatural origin to skill in the arts.

However in those ceremonies of which I have quoted some examples, everything was artifice. There was artifice in the solemn moment when the initiator pretended (and just how far did he himself believe in all this?) to be filled with a supernatural spirit which he then drew forth from his body to project it with violence into the novice who was crouched in front of him under a mat (the whole thing being performed to the sound of the whistle, which was taken to be the acoustic 'sign' of this spirit). And the same artifice can be seen in the manufacture of the masks and other automata used to manifest the active presence of the spirit, as well as in the actual 'performances' of which we have a few extant eyewitness accounts.

It was the aesthetic satisfaction provided by a successful 'performance' which, retroactively, justified considering it to be of supernatural origin. This holds true even for

those actually involved in creating or performing the spectacle, who—given that they were obviously aware of the tricks they were using—had at best a hypothetical idea of the link between the performance and the spirit world: 'It must all be true if, in spite of all the difficulties we introduced into the spectacle, everything went off smoothly'. On the contrary, if the gamble on difficulties did not come off and the spectacle went wrong, then there was the risk of shattering the belief that there was no break between the human and supernatural worlds—a conviction that was of paramount importance in a hierarchical society where the power of the nobles, the subordination of common people and the subjection of slaves were all sanctified by the supernatural order on which social order depended. We do not inflict physical death upon those artists who do not have the talent to lift us out of ourselves (financial or social 'death' is another matter, however). Yet, even so, don't we still maintain a link between art and the supernatural? Look, for example, at the etymology of the word 'enthusiasm' which we use to describe our feelings for the work of certain artists. Raphael used to be known as the 'divine' Raphael; and English still has the expression 'out of this world', which can be used to express aesthetic enthusiasm. Here again, we only have to switch from a literal to a figurative key when considering beliefs and practices which seem so disconcertingly alien for us to recognize that they are, in fact, quite familiar.

There is something disturbing, even sinister, about the position of the artist amongst the tribes of this region of North America: enjoying undoubted social status, he was also obliged to fool people (and to commit suicide if he failed to do so). Nevertheless, the myths of this region give a very poetic and fascinating portrait of the artist. The Tlingit Indians of Alaska, who occupy territory immediately bordering upon that of the Tsimshian, have a legend about a young chief from the Queen Charlotte Islands (Haida territory) who was deeply in love with his wife. She feel ill and, in spite of all the care he lavished on her, died. Inconsolable, the young husband sought everywhere for a sculptor who could produce a likeness of his dead wife, but to no avail. Now, in his own village there was a sculptor of some repute who, on meeting the chief one day, said to him: 'You are going from village to village without finding anyone who can make an effigy of your wife, isn't that so? I used to see her often, when the two of you were out walking. But I never studied her face with an eye to one day making an effigy of her for you. Yet if you will allow me, I will try'.

The sculptor took a block of thuja-wood and set to work. When his statue was finished he dressed it in the dead woman's clothes and then called her husband. Overjoyed, the widower seized the statue and asked the sculptor how much he owed him. 'Whatever you want', the artist answers, 'but I acted out of compassion for you, so do not give me too much'. However, the chief pays the sculptor handsomely, in both slaves and other goods.

An artist so famous that even a nobleman does not dare disturb him. An artist who thinks that before undertaking a portrait one should study the physiognomy of the sitter, and who does not allow people to watch him at work. An artist whose works fetch a high price but who, on occasion, can show himself to be sensitive and generous. Aren't they all features of our ideal portrait of a great painter or sculptor (even a contemporary one)? How happy we'd be if all our artists lived up to the same standards. Returning to the myth: the young chieftain treats the statue as a living creature; one day he even has the impression that it moves. His visitors are enthusiastic about the likeness, and in time the statue seems to become identical to a living woman (one can guess what happens then). In fact, shortly after, the statue makes a noise, like that of wood cracking. The chief lifts it up, and there beneath it is the shoot of a young tree. They leave the shoot to grow—and that is why the thuja trees of the Queen Charlotte Islands are so beautiful. When one finds a fine tree, one says 'it is as beautiful as the baby of the chief's wife'. As for the statue, it hardly ever moved and it was never heard to speak. But the chief knew through his dreams that his wife was speaking to him, and he understood what she was saying.

A different version of the story was told among the Tsimshian (whose skill as artists the Tlingit appreciated so much that they often commissioned work from them). In their version it was the widower himself who carved the statue. He then treated it as if it were alive, conversing with it and asking it questions. Two sisters sneak into his hut and see the man embrace and then lie down with the statue. Their laughter betrays them to the chief, who then invites them to eat. The younger sister eats moderately, the elder stuffs her face. Later while she is asleep, she has an attack of colic and 'dirties' herself. The chief and the younger sister decide to get married and make an agreement with each other: they will burn the statue and keep quiet about the elder sister's shame, whilst she herself will not tell anyone 'what he did with the wooden statue'.

The parallel between the (quantitative) abuse of food and the (qualitative) abuse of sexuality is striking because in both cases what we have is an abuse of communication: eating to excess, copulating with a statue as if it were a human being are two distinct registers of behavior which are all the more comparable when one considers that numerous languages often use the same word 'to eat' and 'to copulate' (as does French, at a metaphorical level).

However, the Tlingit and Tsimshian myths treat their common theme in different ways. In the latter there is clear disapproval of treating a wooden statue as if it were a human being. It is true that the statue was the work of an amateur—and I have already mentioned the mystery with which those great professionals, Tsimshian painters and sculptors, surrounded their work. Creating the illusion that art was life was their prerogative and duty; and given that those illusions were intended to emphasise the link between the social and supernatural order, then anyone who used them for his own personal emotional needs would necessarily have been regarded with disapproval. In the eyes of the general public—represented by the two sisters—the widower's behavior would have seemed scandalous or, at the very least, ridiculous.

The Tlingit myth takes a different view of the work of art. The widower's conduct is in no way shocking; people flock to his house to see the effigy. But the statue is the work of a great sculptor and therefore (or, perhaps, nonetheless) occupies a position halfway between life and art. The plant world can only give birth to the plant world, and a woman of wood is brought to bed of a tree. The Tlingit myth views art as an autonomous realm: the work of art lies beyond its creator's intentions. The artist loses his control over it as soon as he has finished a work, which then develops in accordance with its own nature. In other words: the only way a work of art can live is by giving birth to other works of art which, to their contemporaries, will seem more 'alive' than those which have immediately preceded them.

Viewed over thousands of years, humanity seems always to have been moved by the same passions. Time neither adds to nor subtracts from the loves and hates felt by mankind. Man's commitments, struggles and hopes remain unchanged. Yesterday and today. We could omit ten or twenty centuries and the history of mankind would still be substantially the same. The one loss would be the works of art produced during those ten or twenty centuries. Man only distinguishes himself—indeed, he only exists—through his works. Just like the statue of wood which gives birth to a tree, mankind's works are the only evidence we have that over the centuries of human history something has actually happened.

from Claude Lévi-Strauss, Regarder Ècouter Lire, (Paris, 1993), 168–176.

Artists and Group Portraits

by Marc Fumaroli

The self-portrait is undoubtedly the most disturbing genre in European art. The series of self-portraits painted by Rembrandt and van Gogh seem to bear out that modern idea of the solitary, tormented genius, who is as misunderstood as each of us is bound to be. But the Durer's Christ-like self-portrait, Titian's portrait of the artist as an old man, or Poussin's Louvre portrait of the artist as sovereign are all much better defended enigmas. In fact, these are not so much portraits of artists as of Masters. They are the Holy Faces of Painting. The paintings depict mortals and yet they look at us from a world that is not of this world, a world open only to Masters, a world from which the artists look at us and look at themselves.

There is also another genre of painting which defies our insolent interpretative familiarity: the portrait genre which involves a whole group of artists (often shown together with poets) in a sort of *Sacra Conversazione*, with each figure absorbed in his/herself and yet in profound harmony with all the others. The first example of this genre that comes to mind is the *Parnassus* in which Raphael depicts Apollo amidst the Muses and ancient and modern poets, *poëtae ut pictores*.

In fact, the Master's self-portrait already presupposes a similar gathering of chosen disciples. It is painted for such an elect—calls them, points out the path to be followed, holds itself on the threshold to be crossed. Before such a self-portrait we, the non-elect are *de trop*. The *Parnassus*, however, shows us things from a different angle: from below, we look up at the gathering of Master and disciples on one of the slopes or summits of Mount Parnassus. As well as painting a memorable Self-Portrait, Poussin also painted several *Parnassus*, but also two *Sacrement de l'Eucharistie* (Sacrament of the Eucharist)—in one of which (the Chantelous series) he gave the Master among his disciples the features of the Christ of the Holy Shroud.

This was also the period when Le Sueur was painting *La Réunion d'amis* (Gathering of Friends) now in the Louvre: united around the lutist Denys Gautier by friendship and epicurean delight in the spirituality of pleasure, these artists and poets are shown in a realm of 'correspondences' which are no more of this world than are those depicted by the Platonic Raphael and his successor Poussin.

Two centuries later Fantin-Latour painted two admirable group portraits of poets (gathered around Baudelaire) and painters (gathered around Manet). Hung together in the Musée d'Orsay, these works show us the Masters surrounded by their frock-coated disciples in a realm that was misunderstood, feared or despised by the pharisees and bourgeois. These are Pentecost gatherings of French painting.

10
Marc Fumaroli

Max Ernst, Au rendez-vous des amis, 1922:
1 René Crevel, 2 Philippe Soupault, 3 Arp, 4 Max Ernst,
5 Max Morise, 6 Fëdor Dostoevskij, 7 Raffaello Sanzio,
8 Théodore Fraenkel, 9 Paul Eluard, 10 Jean Paulhan,
11 Benjamin Péret, 12 Louis Aragon, 13 André Breton, 14 Baarged,
15 Giorgio De Chirico, 16 Gala Eluard, 17 Robert Desnos

Max Ernst
Au rendez-vous des amis
1922
Detail of the artist's self-portrait

For the Centenary Exhibition of the Venice Biennale Jan Clair has put together a room of 'Gatherings of Artists', including works which show that the genre continued to flourish well into the twentieth century. The most striking of these modern works is Max Ernst's 1922 *Le Rendez-vous des amis*, a work of which there is a fine discussion in Werner Spies *Max Ernst* (Paris, 1991-1992). Raphael's presence amongst these be-suited painters and poets marks both the continuity of an artistic genre, of the tradition of painting itself, and serves to underline the novelty Max Ernst aimed to bring out through this synecdochic allusion to the Vatican *Parnassus*. The disjuncture between this platonic archetype of the Renaissance and its modern *ektype* is a rich source of irony. Allegory, synecdoche and irony— the realm of rhetoric, and it comes as no surprise to see Jean Paulhan himself in the foreground of the group (sitting on Dostoyevsky's knee and resting against Max Ernst himself); at the time, Paulhan was working in his *Fleurs de Tarbes*. But we are also in the realm of poetry, as can be seen from the presence of André Breton (standing), Benjamin Péret (seated) and Eluard, Soupault, Aragon and Desnos. Rhetoric and Poetry set up a magnetic field for the benefit of Painting (here represented by Giorgio De Chirico and Max Ernst himself). The magnetic force is so intense, so unearthly, that the artists seem to move within it like oracular, hieroglyphic marionettes, sketching out what could be dancesteps but might also be mysterious sacramental gestures: their hands appear to communicate in an unknown sign language. At one pole of this magnetic field stands René Crevel, who seems to be leaning over the stage of a toy theatre as over a piano keyboard, whilst children busy themselves about games which are hidden from us by their turned backs. Decorated with a circle and a sun, this is a theatre of Memory, or a theatre of the Infant Unconscious. The other pole is marked by André Breton, a Magus whose arm and hand seem to be held in the concentric circles of an aurora borealis. On the one hand the psychology of human depths, on the other the philosophy of Nietzsche. And while the German philosopher is not directly portrayed there is no doubt that within this Academy of 1922 he has taken Plato's place altogether. Behind the group of artists there is no representation of Parnassus but of the peaks of the Haut-Engadine which were so dear to the author of *Zarathustra*. The black sky behind reminds us that 'God is Dead'; but this is also a place where the spirit can find nourishment—because from that background there already emerge the concentric circles of the Eternal Return. Rhetoric, Poetics, Psycho-analysis, Nietzschean Philosophy, this is the modern Encyclopaedia which lifts this Gathering of Artists out of the vulgar world in a sort of sacred trance. These paintings may be from very different periods, but if we let them speak for themselves we get a powerful impression of an essential feature that is common to both. They create an area of sacred intimidation around themselves. Within the circles there is the order established by Art, its symbolic landmarks, its 'knighthood', its living and its dead. All of which appears in total autonomy, transcending time, place and artistic styles. This objective, vertical order holds the 'art-going public' at a respectful distance from both self-portraits and *Gatherings of Artists*. But it is clear to us that this distance has nothing in common with that idolatry or pose organised in museums around top-ten masterpieces.

These paintings of artists are intended for other artists. They reduce us to the status of the profane, the uninitiated. And yet the most disdainful of all these *Gatherings of Artists* is also the most anti-platonic. In the Banquets of the Platonic Academy, in the Christian or Gnostic Suppers, in Raphael as in Fantin-Latour, the artists were definitely the main guests, but behind them the profane spectator might at least hope to get some share of the leftovers from the feast. To spare us our despair, a formal politeness throws a veil over the enormous distance between the mystery itself and the way it can be received by the uninitiated, between the grace enjoyed by the elect and the stolidity of those who have only just been called. However, while the *Rendez-vous des amis* does not totally ignore this notion of a 'banquet', it presents it simply as a quotation (just as it does with the Platonism of Raphael). A low table at the feet of Dostoyevsky and Max Ernst bears a spare sketch of a 'still life' of cheese and fruit, a few pure signs. The balls on the table indicate that it might also serve for games: but no one is thinking of eating, no one would think of inviting himself to partake of the absent wines and bread. The privilege of modernist culture has replaced the Election to Grace. This modern Rendez-vous is even more impenetrable and exclusive than its disowned ancestors the *Parnassus* and the *Banquet des sages* (Banquet of the Wise), of which it only bears a few traces to jog the memory, to serve as indices of the irony and luxury of culture for the 'happy few'. The Archons of Neo-Nietzscheanism form a sect of intellectuals, poets and artists, cloistered within their esotericism. We are in 1922, at the end point of a tradition which is still capable of renewing itself, but which also runs the risk of snapping the thread. Nevertheless there is still the fact that all these *Gatherings of Artists*, from whatever period they may be, have this common feature of the same impenetrable circle around them holding the 'art-going public' at

a respectful distance. Each one of them bears witness to the transcendence of art. Even the playful aspect of the *Rendez-vous des amis*, its Rimbaudesque *dessus de porte*, cannot hide the gravity, the hieratic concentration, of the players in Ernst's painting. Suspended between two worlds, the *Gatherings of Artists* look towards a beyond that we have no access to without their mediation. Like self-portraits, they are the icons of a religion or of a metaphysics that are peculiar to art.

However after this first frisson we could well recover with a burst of laughter at the idea that what we are really dealing with is something akin to those weeping statues that fool the devout. Only for the naive do these exercises in *trompe-l'oeil* and adulterated holiness transform art into a religion or a metaphysics. The museums where these fake of *acheiropoesis* works are hung are the latter-day heirs of those Christian churches built around relics; they add their own tricks to those the artists have already so skilfully applied to bamboozling the vulgar. The irony of Marcel Duchamp has now freed us from these constructions of illusion, just as Voltaire delivered us from the *Infâme*. We now have clear heads where art is concerned, and those old card tricks no longer fool us. Nowadays there is nothing stopping us from all lining up to approach these images, to have them explained to us without any nonsense, whilst the management busies itself about imposing the laws of the market and of 'democracy' on art. There is even a new species of artist, who are fully tuned in to the general smartness of their public. Produced in great quantity for a well-defined market, their works no longer aim for form but for meaning, for the communication and the consumption of this 'age' of ours, which is so egalitarian and utilitarian.

But let's step back for a moment from this science, this market, of art 'delivered' from all superstition. In both the Self-Portrait and the *Gatherings of Artists* it is the vertical dimension of art, its role as a link between two worlds, which strikes us first. Painting, Music and Poetry—represented by their Masters and disciples—unite to bring us a previously unknown harmony from 'elsewhere' (in Max Ernst's painting this elsewhere could be the mountain peaks beloved of Nietzsche, or the depths of childhood and its secrets, rediscovered by a Crevel who was following the lead given by Freud). This superior harmony descends upon our ordinary world of stolidity and misfortunes. At the same time, this role gives these practicioners of the rite a surprising sociability, which strikes us precisely because it descends from the 'other world'. We view this 'being together' as a grace that is unknown to us in our ordinary social life. From on high, these artists and poets are united by a silent friendship which is all the closer for being tacit. In traditional representations of these Gatherings—Le Sueur's *Réunion d'amis* or in Fantin-Latour's paintings—this friendship is exclusively masculine. But in Raphael's *Parnassus* (which Max Ernst so clearly had in mind in 1922) there is a substantial female presence: not only is the God of Music, Apollo, surrounded by the Muses, but the Greek poetess Sappho is given a prominent place in the foreground of the painting. Along with Homer and Pindar, she represents the Elect of poetry who are gathered around the divinities of Art. In Max Ernst's *Le Rendez-vous des amis*, there is only one woman present: Gala Eluard, the Muse of the entire group. She acts as a synecdoche of all the various Nadjas, Elsas, Nancys and Peggys who will play such a role in the lives of Max's 'Friends'. In the same way, Raphael used the Muses and Sappho in his *Parnassus* to stand for Caterina Cornaro, Vittoria Colonna Elisabetta Gonzaga etc.—all of whom were poetesses themselves and inspired so many of the painters and poets of Italian Neo-Platonism, from Michelangelo to Pietro Bembo.

This participation of superior women in the realm of art, in the friendship that is part of art, does not change anything essential—if it is true that the essential of art is increased by those whom Breton called the 'clairvoyants'. The moral basis of these groups of friends remains fundamentally the same as that described by Cicero in his *De amicitia*: admission to friendship can only be given to those 'who are known to act with rectitude, generosity, honesty and loyalty, those whose firmness of character rules out all avidity, greediness and intemperance; men who have followed nature, the best guide to happiness'. Cicero's definition of this essential virtue fits our Gathering of Artists: 'Friendship is an understanding, in the strict sense of the term, on things human and divine, an understanding nourished by affection'. He then adds: 'I wonder if, apart from wisdom, the gods have given men anything better than friendship. Certain people prefer money, others health, power, honours; many prefer physical pleasure, but they put themselves at the same level as animals. As for the others, the things they desire are fragile and depend less on our will than on capricious chance. Then there are those who see the supreme good as being Virtue. They are undoubtedly right, but virtue is precisely what gives rise to, what nourishes, friendship. Without virtue no friendship is possible'.

The Republic of Arts, like the Republic of Letters, is an exercise of *virtù*. And this *virtù* can become a sacrifice. One did not have to wait for Rousseau to know that. It weaves the strongest, most stable—and rarest—of social bonds: friendship. The artist is a person of *virtù* and not

a mere *virtuoso*, and the 'virtuous' are attracted to each other by natural inclination. The aim of these generous lives is incomprehensible for the vulgar utilitarian (just as he cannot understand the works that express such a life). The phenomenon becomes even more incomprehensible now that vulgar utilitarianism has invented a 'contemporary art' to suit itself and produced the artists to go with it. A misleading nominalism uses the same words for very different things. The artist as Raphael or Max Ernst understood the term had moved beyond the world, he belonged to another order. The artist who pins his hopes on the production line of the 'contemporary' is just acting out a part in the sociology of the art market. Neither friendship nor the other 'divine things' have any meaning or place in such an horizontal scheme of things. The friendship of the ancient world, which was then taken up by Christianity, was able to erase differences in fortune or social rank to establish a society of its own. Amongst artists themselves, or between artists and patrons, it could create a warm, generous atmosphere, without which the vocation of artist or poet is a cold and chilly thing. The sociology of art, the history of art, would be inconceivable without this 'friendship through *virtù*', the means whereby history is graced by an harmony that history can neither understand nor explain. Masters may be rare figures who are solitary by definition yet they should not make us forget the sociability that is part of being an artist (even if their solitude does go beyond such sociability). The Master is, along with Aristotle and Montaigne, the only one who can say: 'O, my friends, there are no friends'.

It is this superior friendship itself which serves as a background to the final contemplative solitude which, in Titian or Poussin's self-portraits, we admire with such trepidation. This very same virtue, worthy of the citizens of Portique, is what is so compelling in Cézanne's self-portraits. It implies a supreme form of voluntary deprivation, which makes the Master the most generous of all the indifferent. The 'unhappiness of being alone', which Cicero referred to when describing the death of friendship, becomes a supreme responsibility for forms within the invisible Republic of the Arts. The humanity of art, the friendship of which it can show itself capable, are sacrificed to an individual and supremely humble Mastership. This was doubtless what André Breton was aiming at—even if it meant breaking up the *Rendez-vous des amis*. But he did not have the humility of the great. This rupture was foreseen by Nietzsche, the Plato invoked with such fervor by Max Ernst in 1922. In *The Gay Science*, he wrote: 'We were friends and we have become strangers to each other. But it is good that it should be like that [...] It was the law *above* us which laid down that we should become strangers to one another: that is the very way in which we have to become more respectable! The way in which the thought of our one-time friendship will become more sacred to us! There is probably an immense, invisible course above, an immense starry way within which our different origins and goals are *inscribed* as trajectories without clear form. Let us raise ourselves up to that thought! But our life is too short, our vision is too feeble for us to be friends other than in the sense of this sublime possibility. And so—should we really want to *believe* in this *astral* friendship, we would have to be asleep here on the earth' (IV, 279).

These constant features, which have survived revolutions, migrations, changes in style, religion and philosophy, we now find, with a sense of remorse, within a Biennale of Modern and Contemporary Art. Max Ernst's Raphael, his small banqueting table, could still co-exist in the twentieth century with the ghost of Nietzsche and the couch of Freud—all within the same painting. The vertical link, the friendly convergence within the same *virtù* meant that, even if rendered with irony, there could still be the same alliance and complicity between Ancient and Moderns, that in 1922 they were both citizens of the same City. The last flashes of modern art are now behind us and have given way to the flat conformism of 'contemporary' art; in such circumstances, the *Gatherings of Artists* painted this century cast a new light on the alibi used to justify the change of regime (or, should one say, to justify the cynical negation of art?)—the alibi, that is, of being 'anti-academic', of being 'avant-garde'.

The great criticism made of the Académie des Beaux-Arts by many twentieth-century artists—both major and minor—is that it corrupts art at the very source with social and commercial considerations which have nothing to do with poetic creation. Academic Art is, in fact, the forerunner of Contemporary Art: it flatters social vanity, it caters to the spiritual and ocular laziness of public and artist alike. It stifles the poetry of art in the cradle. Yet it was possible for artists such as Ingres and Flandrin to be part of the Academy without their art being tainted with academicism. Sincere, poetical art and the emotion that gives rise to it are only possible as the result of an interior quest that has nothing to do with the mondaine passions, self-interest and artifices, which Rousseau was the first 'modern' to criticise. The extraordinary vitality and fertility of French nineteenth- and twentieth-century painting—both within and without the Academy—reveals that among the artists and the public who supported them there were a large number of individuals who were willing to let

themselves be led by the sincere 'sentiment' to which Baudelaire so often referred. For him the term described both the gift and vocation for revealing beauty where it could not be seen and also the virtue of friendship which bound together all those who had such a gift. When that 'sentiment' disappears all that is left is blind sterility and self-interest—hiding behind the cover of Marcel Duchamp.

In the background of the supposed battle between Academicism and the Avant-garde there is really the gradual assimilation by both artists and public of the ideas and sensibility propounded in Rousseau's *Discours sur les sciences et les arts* and his other writings; an assimilation that began at the time of David. The Republic of Arts at the end of the eighteenth century showed itself willing and able of receiving the message of Ciceronian 'virtue' that the *Contrat Social* addressed to a corrupt society. The accusation of Academicism was a Rousseauesque start of disgust; it indicates how mercenary considerations, political interests and an egoistical, artificial culture had compromised the arts, our one inheritance of the unspoilt imagination and sensibility of the natural man. However, nineteenth-century Academicians—whether David's former pupils or not—could often be non-academic in both their works and moral integrity—even if one has to admit that during the Second Empire it was the extra-Academy, the 'fringe' which produced those artists most sensitive to the need for a return to an earlier perception of man and nature. This perception could exercise itself on landscapes far from industrial cities, or it could exercise itself on the industrial cities themselves, viewing them with the unbiased, marvelling, eye of the outsider and thus revealing all their hidden, oppressed poetry (it was in this latter exercise that Baudelaire saw the very beginning of modernity). A painter could take his 'way of seeing' from old and forgotten models that had gone back to their 'savage' state: for the young Manet, for example, the great Spanish artists of the seventeenth century were a revelation (and, indeed, Zurbaran and Velázquez themselves had tried to recapture that profound, innocent eye which they considered to exemplified in early Christian art). One can see the same return to origins, to a fresh, primitive way of seeing, in the Cubists' use of African art.

It is, therefore, difficult to imagine anything more nonsensical than the claim that the Avant-gardes of the nineteenth and twentieth centuries are the ancestors who prove the pedigree of so-called 'contemporary' art, which is nothing but a commodity produced for an amnesic consumerist society that brandishes art like some trusted status symbol. In fact, official 'contemporary' art is entirely devoid of the heroic determination to 'return to the origins' which was so much a part of the creative vitality of the work of Manet and Picasso.

On the other hand there are many deep similarities between the Academies of the Renaissance and of the seventeenth century, and those groups of artists that from the end of the eighteenth century onwards have attempted to create—outside the influence of State, institutions and honours—the 'virtuous' milieu necessary if an artist is to purify his way of seeing (ironically enough, one of these first groups was David's *School*, which was itself later to be accused of academicism). What Rousseau and his socialist ideas were for the rebel artists of the nineteenth and twentieth centuries, Platonism and the various schools of Neo-Platonism had been for artists from the Renaissance to the seventeenth century. A further irony is that the term Academy was coined precisely for those groups in which artists tried to discover the poetry of their art untainted by the institutions and mercenary passions of their day. It was during the nineteenth century—particularly from the Second Empire onwards—that the term became a term of abuse in artists' studios and was confused with the pejorative adjective of 'academicism'. Or is this reversal of meaning anything but an optical illusion? From 1840 onwards Academicism in France became synonymous with the Académie des Beaux-Arts, whilst the 'academy' in the original sense of 'a group of friends' was more flourishing than ever before. In fact, those nineteenth-/ early twentieth-century groups of artists—such as the Barbizon School, the Impressionists, the Nabis etc.— which emerged on the basis of a shared poetics marked a veritable resurgence of Renaissance academies (even if within a very different philosophical and political context). The Renaissance 'academicians' were trying to throw off the suffocating power of the artisan guilds, and the founders of 'movements' in nineteenth-century Paris were trying to break away from the rigidity which had been instilled into the Académie of the Ancien Régime by the new statute introduced during the Napoleonic period. In both cases one sees the stand of poetic invention against social stolidity, of friendship against the machiavellian game of power and self-interest.

I wish I had time to trace a similar parallel in the social history of music, but I will have to limit myself to pointing out that Richard Wagner, the composer who recreated European opera during the time of the Second Empire, was well aware of the parallel between his own desire for a new form of musical academy and the Renaissance academy in which artists worked amongst poets and not among the artisans trained by traditional guilds. In *Die Meistersinger*, the clash between the

Petrarchan musician Walter von Stoltzing and Beckmesser, who had remained faithful to the conventions of the medieval Guild of St. John, is not one of academicism versus the avant-garde, but of poetry against routine, love against endogamy. The only way out from social stolidity is upwards. The desire for a return to origins, to powerful and forgotten ways of seeing was, for the artists and poets of the nineteenth/early twentieth century who had been raised on Rousseau, what the yearning towards Ideas, towards the Divine conjunction of the Good and the Beautiful, had been for the artists of the Renaissance, who had been liberated from the 'mechanical arts' by Plato and Neo-Platonism. The very word 'academy' is Platonic by definition. It had fallen into disuse during the Middle Ages and then been resurrected in the fourteenth century by a poet, Petrarch, for whom it not only referred to a group of friends and disciples gathered around the Master (far from the madding crowd of both populace and court), but also to the country villa or rural retreat in which the group met. The following century Petrarch's *Academia* was followed by Marsilio Ficino's. The very opposite of an institution, this body consisted of a groups of friends drawn together by intellectual affinities and a shared ideal of the contemplative life. This micro-society aimed to free its members from the conventions and stolidities, the blind passions and self-interest of normal social life, from the routine inevitable in the exercise of trade or power. This milieu was one based on creative leisure, on mutual stimulation, cooperation and emulation with a view to something that lay outside the normal goals of human activity: the goal of poetic creation. The Neo-Platonic myth behind this academy (which, at the beginning of the sixteenth century, Sannazzaro named *Arcadia*) was recounted in Petrarch's *Canzoniere*. Laura was the desired object sought after in this poetic quest; the laurels of Daphne, the recompense for achieved poetic form. Like Orpheus ordering the very music of the spheres, Ficino organized poets, literati and artists around him in his villa at Careggi. Among his disciples this Magus and master of Neo-Platonism could count such figures as Lorenzo de' Medici, Alberti, Poliziano, Landino and Pico della Mirandola.

The Roman Academy which 'reinvented' Roman theatre in the late fifteenth century was another group of friends and eager disciples gathered around Pomponio Leto and his spiritual heir Tommaso Inghirami. It was not until 1541, when Cosimo I was doing all he could to get the Pope to recognize him as Grand Duke of Tuscany, that an Academy in Italy received an official statute and became part of a prince's court. However even here, the Florentine Academy pre-existed Cosimo's letters patent, and the friends and literati who made it up hesitated a long time before accepting the Grand Duke's cumbersome offer (which necessarily had political implications).

From the beginning of the fifteenth century onwards painters, sculptors and architects were well-aware of the freedom enjoyed by poets and literati within their academies. Long before there was any actual Academy of artists, the great artists of Florence, Venice, Rome and Naples were already enjoying freedom, inspiration and recognition within these informal academies of literati where they could escape the routine imposed upon them by artisan guilds. Whilst such groups obviously gave the artists a certain recognition, it would be wrong to believe the new members were moved merely by a desire for social glory. Mixing with these poets, literati and musicians gave them poetic stimulation which sustained them in their work. If Raphael lived as a prince and was recognised as such when he walked the streets of Rome surrounded by his pupils, it was because he was aware that he was recognized as a painter-poet by his poet peers; his external behaviour was simply in tune with the inner reality of his work and poetic inspiration. Another reason that he could behave as he did was that he lived in a Rome where the Papal court shared his Christianized Neo-Platonic philosophy—a philosophy which conferred almost priestly dignity on the inspired poet, who in his own way was, like the great preachers, the great cardinals, a mediator between the human and the divine.

It was in Florence that the first Academy of *Disegno* was established (24 May, 1562). The driving force behind the creation of this academy was Giorgio Vasari, painter and historian to the court of Cosimo I, who modelled the new institution on the existing Florence Academy, whose members included the painter-poet Agnolo Bronzino. On 13 January 1563, the painters, sculptors and architects who made up the Academy got duke Cosimo to approve *I Capitoli e Ordini dell'Accademia e Compagnia dell'Arte del Disegno*. One of the passions that bound all these members together was their veritable cult of Michelangelo, who at the time was in voluntary exile in Rome. And, in fact, the first full poetic programme realised by the group was the solemn ceremony planned for the reception into the church of San Lorenzo (on 14 July 1564) of the body of the great artist, architect and poet, which had been practically stolen from Rome. It was the Secretary of the Florentine Academy, Benedetto Varchi, who pronounced the funeral oration. A group of Mannerist artists, the academy would also be a proper school—dominated by the example of the 'divin Buonarroti'—in which young people received not only technical tuition but also a solid cultural grounding in such disciplines as anatomy, perspective and mathematics. In fact, the name of artist, which was gradually being given to the members of the Florentine academy, came from university language (an 'artista' was a student of the Faculty of Arts). The young academicians were working towards becoming a Master; the 'artist' painter or sculptor, had a cultural background which went beyond mere manual craftsmanship; what is more, he was outside the control and rules of the old guilds. Like the poet and literati, he could now invent the 'ideas' for his work himself. So, originally, 'artist' and 'academician' were synonymous terms—used by a certain group to mark a distinction between themselves and artisans and craftsmen. Yet what mattered more than the question of manual skill was the moral nature of the market for which the artist worked: the snares of the guild were totally different from the friendship within the Academy or the relationship established with the patrons and connoisseurs who, in effect, formed an extension of it.

In 1577 Pope Gregory XIII issued a papal bull formally recognizing the Roman Academy of St. Luke which had been founded by Federico Zuccaro. Then came the Accademia degli Incamminati, founded in Bologna by the Carracci in 1584—again a group of poets, literati and artists who had come together to create a stimulating milieu for discussion and artistic invention. This second academy was so linked with the three Carracci—Luigi, Agostino and Annibale—who formed it that it had no official charter and would not survive its three founders. However, the studios of their greatest pupils—Domenichino and Guido Reni in particular—would in their turn become a sort of academy; frequented not just by artists but also by poets and literati, they would offer pupils a complete cultural education rather than just a training in a craft. This was the model Simon Vouet took for the Academy he founded in his Paris studio after his 1627 return from Rome (where Vouet himself had actually been elected Prince of the Academy of St. Luke in 1624).

It would seem that the fertility of an academy of artists is in inverse proportion to its institutionalization. No academy was ever as fertile and productive of great painters as the Carracci Academy, which lasted less than twenty years and owed everything to the personality of its three founders. However, whilst the Rome and Florence Academies did have a legal status that was publicly recognized by Grand Duke or Pope, one cannot deny that they played an important role in stimulating the arts. And from Rome and Florence, the same model made itself felt in Paris. In 1648 a group of like-minded artists decided to break away from the control of the guilds and applied to the king for official recognition of the status of their academy. Their wish was granted; and Colbert later got Louis XIV to renew their official charter. The artists involved were far from seeing this royal stamp of approval as a sign of their enslavement to royal power; on the contrary, it marked a decisive liberation and gave them the chance to practice their art as a free profession. The Royal Academy set no limit as to members (who at times numbered 400); the aim was to involve anyone in Paris who might have artistic talent. However, it was organized hierarchically, with officers, academicians and graduates. The link between art and the monarchy was further exalted by the fact that both the theory behind the Academy and the Monarchy relied heavily on a Platonic-Christian metaphysics. It was during the reigns of Louis XIV and Louis XV that tensions arose between the restraint of royal patronage and the various poetics championed by different painters within the Academy. It was these which gave rise to the, initially unvoiced, feelings of servitude and outraged virtue which would burst to the surface so violently during the Revolution (and David, an attentive reader of Rousseau, would be one of the most fearsome spokesmen of that resentment).

Even though raised and trained within the system of the Royal Academy and of official commissions, David very soon set up his studio—in Paris as in Rome—along the lines of the Carracci Academy, steering clear of the officialdom which had made him such a well-established artist. It was within such an Academy that he was able to create the intense Master-pupil rapport which was to play an important part in the formation of artists of the calibre of Drouais, Wicart, Girodet, Ingres and Granet. The philosophers and literati who frequented David's studio/academy made it into such a stimulating workshop of poetics and ideas that the Royal Academy could not hope to compete with it. The *Vie de David* and Delécluze's *Souvenirs* provide an excellent account of the Socratic method followed by David in teaching his pupils, and also of the transformation of this passionate brotherhood into a veritable School. And like all Schools, this too produced its own doctrinaire theoretician, Quatremère de Quincy. In 1793 the Revolution had become more radical and thus David had the satisfaction of seeing the Royal Academy charged with undermining the integrity of 'genius' and suppressed. Thereafter David became a Jacobin dictator in the arts, and accepted the Directoire's invitation to participate in the setting up a new Académie des Beaux-Arts. And ironically, it was to be this new Academy, limited to just forty members, which during the July Monarchy would be fiercely attacked by the artists trained outside the conservative system of David's

School. The first recorded use of the insult 'academicism' dates from 1840.

From then to the early years of this century there have been numerous groups and movements which have appeared outside the ambit of the Académie des Beaux-Arts, in opposition to its *cursus honorum*, its hierarchy of genres, its rigid fidelity to David. Each one of them, however different the ideas behind it, has been a direct descendant of the Carracci Academy and, ironically enough, of the Academy David created around his studio from 1787 onwards. The seventeenth- and eighteenth-century Academies were much less intransigent than their nineteenth-century counterpart, which concentrated all its teaching on what it considered the highest genre—History Painting (a convenient derivative of which was the official portrait). It was precisely those genres which the Academy condemned as minor (landscape, genre scenes, the domestic scene) and those Old Masters whom it tried to ignore altogether (the Spanish, the Dutch, the Italian Primitives), which were to serve as guiding lines for the energies of those who refused to bow down to the dogma of the *Beaux-Arts* and formed themselves into groups to be able to withstand it.

However, was the official academic discipline of the nineteenth century as sterile as it is now made out to be? It is rather amusing in this age of 'emptiness' to hear people taxing the Académie of the Second Empire or the III Republic with sterility, when we know that the Academicians of the times included artists of the calibre of Michallon, Ingres, Flandrin, Baudry, Forain and Maurice Denis.

The drama of the Académie des Beaux Arts is really the product of the model imposed during the Directoire reorganization of 1796, a model that has since become a dead weight around the Académie's neck. With only forty members there was very little room for renovation and rejuvenation (and it was impossible for the Académie to reflect the variety of the rapidly changing Parisian art scene). This narrowness became even worse after 1816, when as a teaching institution the Académie became the unchallenged master of the teaching geared to the Grand Prix de Rome and, what is more, exercised total control over the work done by the graduates at the Académie de France in Rome. Then, as a means of cultural recognition and glorification, the Académie has had to settle for acting late: it only ever recognizes or rewards artists or movements when they have already become well-established. Nevertheless one has to admit that after the 1839 departure of Quatremère de Quincy, who since 1816 had looked upon himself as some sort of Guardian of Davidian orthodoxy, the Académie has shown itself capable of a certain eclecticism; it may have ignored the artists of Romanticism, but it did eventually elect as members all the leading lights of both Realism and Symbolism. However, unlike the Royal Academy of the Ancien Regime, there was no way the Beaux-Arts could represent all the, happily contradictory, tendencies that are part of the Parisian art scene. After the Revolution, the Academy no longer represented the Republic of the Arts.

The narrowness and sluggishness of the structure inherited from the Napoleonic era proved all the more unfortunate when, during the course of the nineteenth century, it became clear that Paris was turning into a breeding ground for thriving 'academies' in constant and rapid evolution. Cafés, studios and salons continued to spring up all around the Academic fortress—a vast network of small private academies in which musician, actors, writers, painters, sculptors and architects mixed with each other. In its own way, the Goncourt novel *Manette Salomon* gives a fair description of this constant effervescence of young talents. These micro-societies were also veritable art schools—often much more rewarding and stimulating than the official art schools which prepared young people for the Prix de Rome.

However, having said all that, it would be a gross caricature to reduce this cultural wealth to a sort of class warfare between academic committees and gurus of the avant-garde—with academic honours, a place on a museum wall and public commissions all that was at stake. The very number of the Salons in the Paris of the Second Empire or the III Republic disproves this reductive interpretation. Both Baudelaire—whose *Salons* were attentive to all talents (official or otherwise)—and Apollinaire—whose exhibition reviews were so equitable he even had a good word to say for Madeleine Lemaire's flower pictures—prove that such a manichean interpretation of the past is false. The Paris of their day was a new Alexandria, which was proving to be an even more fertile cradle for painting and sculpture than seventeenth-century Rome had ever been. Summary antitheses apply as little to nineteenth-century Paris as they do to a city in which one could find Caravaggio, the Carracci and the last of the Mannerists. Paris had a whole swarm of exceptional talents, and groups of talents—some of them non-academicians. Similarly there was a swarm of mediocre talents—some of them academicians. This vital mix cannot be fixed in a clear-cut scheme. The republican order of art—and the emergence of Masters within that order—takes no account of labels and partisans concepts which do not really understand the nature of that order (or of the role played within it by Grace). Even when being lampooned and attacked, Academic teaching and recognition were

still things on which young talents could 'cut their teeth'. The rebellious sons needed this father-figure against which they could form their own identity. The artistic phratries which arose and disappeared between 1840 and 1940, and which produced such a surprising number of great Masters, would never have been able to maintain their artistic fervour and fellowship at such a high pitch if the frozen model of the official Académie (as quoted in Max Ernst's *Rendez-vous des amis*) had not shown them what they shouldn't do and what they shouldn't be at the very same time as it showed them that they had to 'go on' regardless.

Perhaps our destiny is the desert and an artificial mirage of Las Vegas, but even so we have no right to project that desert back onto our those who have gone before us. Perhaps if we learnt to be honest with their beliefs, if we learnt to feel fellowship for the things they loved, then we might be able to participate through the reverence of memory in those *Gathering of Artists* which occurred amongst them, generation after generation. Perhaps then we will be able to raise our eyes to the self-portraits they have left us without our feeling ashamed.

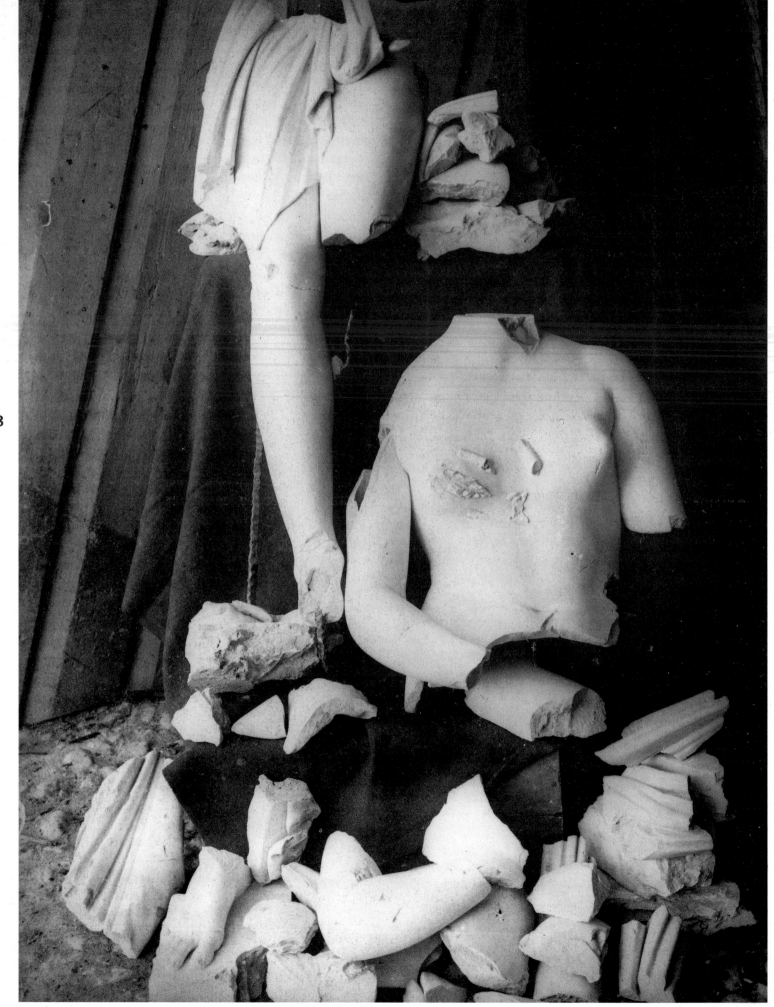

18

Loving Statues

by Maurizio Bettini

Whatever Ovid may have said, Pygmalion was no artist. He may not even have known how to draw. And he certainly didn't have that enviable power that Ovid attributed to him—no divine creation came to life, in the true sense of the word, at the touch of his hands. So what Ovid, and many other poets after him, portrayed as magic power was merely weakness—or mania. It seems that Pygmalion was simply a king of Cyprus, who fell hopelessly in love with a statue of Aphrodite. The famous Christian writer Arnobius wasn't embarrassed to give us a fairly salacious description of him in bed, *demens*, surrendering with vain *libido* to delicious but imaginary embraces. It was only the king's erotic delirium which transformed a sculpted statue into the most perfect of women. Pygmalion's magic was actually sickness, or illusion.

However, whether Pygmalion was a mad king or an artist, he was certainly not the only man to fall in love with a statue. There were actually many stories in circulation on this theme—many of them a good deal racier than Ovid's version of the artist aroused by his own work. It was said, for example, that Praxiteles had sculpted two Aphrodites, one veiled and one nude. And since the Coos preferred the veiled version, the Cnidians got the nude. At the time, many made the trip out to the island just to see Praxiteles' Aphrodite. The temple in which she was housed was left completely open so that the statue could be contemplated from every angle. One night a young man, overcome by a crazed passion for her extraordinary beauty, hid within the temple enclosure, and coupled with the *simulacrum*—leaving a trace of his mad desire on the snowy purity of the marble. Praxiteles had also sculpted an Eros in Parian marble, as beautiful as the Cnidian Aphrodite, and victim to the same offense—for a certain Alcetas of Rhodes fell in love with this superb young masculine specimen, and left a similar mark of profanation upon Praxiteles' innocent marble.

Some Greek authors were actually even more explicit and narrate in vivid detail exactly what occurred within the sacred enclosure of Aphrodite at Cnidus. The young man would go there every morning at dawn, inspired by what seemed great devotion but was instead consuming passion. He would sit in front of the goddess for hours, spellbound, murmuring the incomprehensible words and secret reproaches of lovers. Craving some sort of consolation, he addressed the goddess, but of course Aphrodite never responded. So he then decided to turn to the astrologers. Here his folly conformed to a paradoxically rational model, for it is common knowledge that a god, a silent entity, or at least a being who speaks a language indecipherable to man, often speaks (or is spoken through) by throwing the dice.

19

The young man therefore became a priest, and in the mad language of his passion asked divination to change his lonely soliloquy with the goddess into dialogue. Should the throw be lucky, especially if it should be the throw called the 'stroke of Venus', it would mean that the goddess was willing. If not, the young man would fall into despair and curse all of Cnidus—and of course, he didn't get the right throw on his first try, or on his second.

Unresolved and unrequited, his passion was only further inflamed. And it was during this *crescendo* the walls of the temple were covered with amorous writings, and the bark of all fresh young trees sprouted praises of the beautiful Aphrodite. Praxiteles was as honoured as Zeus, and each precious offering found in the treasure was dedicated to the goddess. As for the end of the story, there's no surprise twist. The kingdom of the dead gave the young man the crazed courage to satisfy his passion with his beloved marble statue. Here, however, the 'popular myth' does add something unexpected, for once the young man leaves the temple, he throws himself off a cliff, or (in other versions) plunges headlong into the sea. It is worth noting that this 'popular myth' reserved these two particular deaths for the unknown statue-worshipper. For it is exactly these types of 'deaths' which were traditionally assigned by ancient cultures to those tainted by the most serious of all types of sexual transgression—incest. Indeed, classical texts frequently mention those guilty of incest undergoing the punishment (or opting for self-punishment) of being flung (or flinging themselves) into the sea or off a cliff. Hence human society has no place for such monsters, and cannot enter into contact with them even for purposes of punishment. Savage nature must instead step in to cast their bodies into the ocean waves or the pit of an abyss. Thus 'popular' myth assigns this lover of Aphrodite and her statue not only intensely dramatic but also culturally significant deaths. We will return to this aspect shortly.

Pygmalion, therefore, was not alone. On the contrary, Ovid's artist who is so pleased by his work—the father in love with his child—has a curious little-known *alter ego* in the letters of Aristhaenetus. In this variation on our theme he is a painter and not a sculptor, a painter who curses his own artistic virtuosity because he has painted a maiden who is too beautiful, so beautiful that he is utterly consumed by his passion. But no goddess of love intervenes with a miracle to save him. He too is described in bed, while attempting a highly unlikely consummation with this image. Now not only the frigid hardness of the stone, but the painter's sensitive canvas also suffers this bizarre 'inconceivable love'. In the nobly

sophisticated intellectual terms of his literary genre, Aristhaenetus consoles his unknown painter with the argument that all Narcissus—another famous protagonist of inconceivable love—had to do was dip his hand in the fountain to see his beloved image fade away. His image, instead, does not vanish if he stretches out his hand to touch it—instead, it remains and smiles at him alluringly. She replies to his offers of love with the classic courtesan's provocative silence, an inferred victory of the painter over the perfection of the mirror and a paradoxical triumph of silence over the word, of the dead image over the life it lacks. By remaining silent, the image seduces. Aristhaenetus' painter seems to say that it is much better that Venus does not grant her life, because otherwise the image would speak, thus destroying its own silent seduction.

Paradoxical loves. But not always tragic—at times they're also amusing. After all, 'Loves Paradoxical and Ridiculous' was the title of a chapter in Helianus' *Varia Storia*, which includes, among other better-known tales, the story of the young Athenian obsessed by a passion for the statue of Agathé Tyche which stood in the city. He used to caress her and kiss her, and in his folly—however impractical—even tried to convince the City Councillors to sell her to him. Up to this point the tale is still fairly ridiculous. The Councillors refuse, so he then swathes the beloved statue with drapery and garlands, and offers her sacrifices. Here things are a bit ambiguous, as is common in this sort of tale. Certainly statues of the gods were offered drapery and garlands, but it was also equally customary that the rejected lover should place garlands of flowers on his beloved's brow—so the young Athenian camouflaged his lover's disappointment behind the cerimony of ritual. As the image is herself the beloved, the two poles of the relationship merge, overlapping and confusing accepted codes of behavior. The end of the tale, however, is unambiguous. Because he has completed his rituals, the lover kills himself before the goddess, just like a true rejected lover.

Inconceivable loves, but if we are to believe Atheneus, the author of *The Banquet of the Sophists*, horrible as well. Cleisophus of Selimbria had himself walled up inside a temple in Samos, victim of a passion for a statue of Parian marble. Unable to satisfy his desire, due to the statue's hard frigidity, he placed a strip of meat between himself and the statue. Here, the love of statues leads to a horror story. Perhaps we should move on to the pilgrim (a more moderate character) who at Delphi also wanted to embrace one of the two male statues erected in the temple. However, on his departure he left an offering of a garland which turned out to be his salvation. When his crime was discovered, the god ordered his absolution, arguing that he 'had paid the price'. It appears that Apollo treated the statues of his temple as if they were prostitutes. It seems more likely, however, that the god at Delphi—he who 'does not hide, does not speak, but signifies'—as Heraclitus defined him, meant something less overt than a prostitute's payment when he spoke of 'paying the price'.

It is easy to see how the intrinsic absurdity of the situation—the love of images—heightened not only the sense of the ridiculous, or drama and horror, but the aspect of the conceptual as well. The rhetoricians didn't let this excellent dissertation theme escape. In his lesson 'On the Painter in Love with His Painted Maiden', Libanius really exercises his rhetorical ingenuity, and claims that the artist has now himself become a subject worthy of portrayal. Any type of amorous subject, says the painter, 'has been the subject of my painting: now I have become a subject for others. Paint, o artists, this my extraordinary love! I have been captured by my own inventions'. But this play of successive embedded images (however strained), this painter in love with an image who as such claims to enter painting in his turn, is not enough to hide the obvious conclusion that 'to couple...and achieve satisfaction is impossible' with this maiden. Despite all conceptualism—the 'silent provocation' of the image, or the 'painted painter' in his turn embracing a painting—the fact remains that the image cannot reciprocate the passion of which it is the object. It is the unrequited pain of the lover that unleashes the cursing and imprecations.
This is why the Sophist Onomarchus could write what seems the best page ever written on the love of images. While the opening lines of his oration *The man who fell in love with a statue* are fairly predictable, he makes up for them in the lover's final curse: 'O living beauty in a body without life, what god formed you? Persuasion? Grace? Or Love himself, the father of beauty? Truly, you have everything: the expression of the face, the flower of rosiness, the sparkling eyes, the enchanting smile, the blush of the cheeks, even the impression that you understand my words. As if you were always just on the point of speech—and speak you will, very soon, that I know—but I will no longer be here because you do not know how to love, you cruel woman, unfaithful to her faithful lover. You have not conceded me a single word. So I will call down upon you the most terrible curse that most makes the Beautiful tremble: you will become old!' An ageing statue is an inconceivable paradox. Cold, dead and immobile, the statue has only one advantage over living beings: it cannot change. Onomarchus is a clever rhetorician, and thus condemns the ungrateful image to the worst possible punishment—a statue

'which becomes old'. Already inferior to living creatures because it is rigid and cold, the statue finally loses its only privilege.

One might be tempted to believe that Roman civilization remained immune to certain paradoxical passions, from certain 'inconceivable loves'. But this would not be entirely true. There does not seem to be anything particularly worrying in Pliny's account of the famous orator Hortensius, who always carried with him a Sphinx he had stolen from Verres, or that the consul Gaius Cestius never allowed himself to be separated, even in battle, from his favorite *signum*. This might be merely an exaggerated form of collecting mania, or a fetishistic affection for an *objet d'art* whose beauty one cannot live without. But we feel a twinge of doubt (partly due to his character and inclinations) when we learn that Nero was never without his Amazon made by Strongylion—and what is more, that he always carried it with him because of its legs (it was actually called 'The Beautiful-Legged'). This love for the 'legs' of a female statue does give rise to the suspicion that Nero may have gone a bit beyond the simple pleasures of collecting. Above all, as we will see when we look at Jensen's *Gradiva*, we know at least one other character who fell in love with the 'step' of an image, the pose of this figure's legs in motion. Here we might note how often the *foot* of an image seems to be a focal point of these 'inconceivable loves'. This is seen in a famous short story by Balzac, *The Unknown Masterpiece*, which tells the tale of the painter Frenhofer, consumed by the passion he harbors for a woman whom he tries to recreate in a painting he keeps jealously concealed. When he finally decides to show his work to two colleagues, Porbus and Poussin, what appears is a *muraille de peinture* from which only the foot of a woman stands out—the only remaining trace of the impossible *chef-d'œuvre*.

To continue with the 'inconceivable loves' of the Romans, if we can possibly absolve Hortensius or Gaius Cestius from the suspicion of having loved statues, and if we are not entirely sure about Nero and his 'beautiful-legged' Amazon, with Caligula there is no doubt. Pliny the Elder recounts that at Ardea there were nude painted statues of Atalanta and Elena. But it so happens that the Emperor, 'inflamed by love' of these images 'tried to take them away from there, and he would have done so had not the nature of the plaster kept him from it'. Then, of course, there is Tiberius. We know for a fact (again, it is Pliny who reminds us) that in front of his own baths Marcus Agrippa had dedicated Lyxippus' famous *apoxyómenos*, a statue which the emperor 'liked very much'. In fact, while 'at the beginning of his reign he was still able to control himself, he was not able to repress his desire and had the statue moved into his bedroom, replacing it with another. But the Roman people reacted so decisively and protested so loudly in the theater, that the *apoxyómenos* be put back in its old place, that the ruler, in spite of his passion, did so'.

The most unusual story, however, we owe to Brutus, Caesar's murderer. It is a fairly harsh tale (as we should expect from a man of his habits) which is precisely why it is so striking. According to Pliny, Strongylion had also sculpted a young boy, 'much loved by Brutus of Philippi, and he had it decorated with his own *cognomen*'. The statue was the recipient of quite a privilege, for the Iunius had borne the *cognomen* of 'Brutus' without interruption from 509 B.C., and it was an integral part of their hereditary aristocratic attitude. Through the link to this name, therefore, Strongylion's boy became 'one of the family'—and what a family. This is a singularly unusual onomastic outcome for this passion for images.

We should now have a sufficent catalogue of 'paradoxical loves' which shows us what an extraordinary number of people have been overcome by mad erotic passion for a statue or a painted image. We could put forth this general observation, though it may seem somewhat obvious—it is common wisdom that *one must never* fall in love with a statue. 'No man of healthy mind' wrote Clement of Alexandria in the chapter on the love of statues 'would couple with a goddess, or have himself buried with a dead person, or fall in love with a demon or a stone...'. He who does so is mad. Clearly something must be done with madmen of this type, someone must make an attempt to intervene. According to the tale by Philostratus, for example, Apollonius of Tiana made a personal appearance to dissuade the lover of the Cnidus Aphrodite from his mad folly. Which was no bad thing—Apollonius was extraordinarily persuasive and a powerful miracle-worker—even if the words he used in this case to convince this lover seem fairly tame. And if, in the modern world, the psychoanalyst were to intervene instead, since we have no Apollo? There is indeed a modern version of Pygmalion which is transformed into a clinical case, no charming myth but rather a long essay which Freud did much to improve: Wilhelm Jensen's *Gradiva*.

The story is well-known. Norbert Hanold, a young German archeologist, falls in love with an ancient female bas-relief which represents a walking girl. What he finds most striking is her step, the way she gracefully arches her foot as she walks. He therefore renames her the 'Gradiva' ('She who walks') and convinces himself that this silent figure cannot possibly come from a metropolis like Rome but a much more remote and serene place—Pompeii.

Tormented by young German married couples flocking to Pompeii as the romantic destination for their honeymoons, Norbert Hanold finally arrives at the scene he has dreamt of so often for his Gradiva. He is astonished when he is approached by a young girl who looks exactly like his marble figure, except that she speaks and moves. She keeps popping up throughout his stay, and it begins to dawn on Hanold that this is no ghost, but something quite different. He discovers that the southern girl is none other than his friend Zoe Bertgang, the daughter of fairly inconsequential naturalist who has been in love with him since childhood. Stolid Teutonic Zoe has taken on the task of curing her friend of his mania—that mania that, in the archeologist's mind, transformed the memory of the face and figure of Zoe into an irresistible marble statue. Of course, the beneficial jolt of this discovery liberates Norbert from his visions of antiquity, and finally allows him to approach the female sex whom before he had only sought in bronze and marble.

Under the incredulous eyes of the lover, the 'Gradiva' slowly undergoes all the stages in the metamorphosis of the Ovidian *simulacrum-bas-relief*, apparition, and finally flesh-and-blood girl. A young, neurotic, very *fin-de-siècle* archeologist has taken Pygmalion's place. The magic of the artist (or the powers of Venus) is replaced by the unconscious, in whose limited and infinite spaces the exhausting game between the archeologist-lover, the Gradiva-portrait and his Germanic all-too-solid 'referent' Zoe Bertgang is played out. In the myth of psychoanalysis the power of Pygmalion is therefore called the 'abandonment of repression': the gift of life to the image, recovery. The only difference is that the metamorphosis does not invest the portrait but the subject-lover instead. Following this line of enquiry, our research would inevitably provide us with a model example of clinical analysis, and we could reduce the myth of Pygmalion to a case of 'delirium' ('hysterical delirium', it would seem)—and frankly, without much damage to Jensen's tale, though it would be a pity for his ancient archetype. As for Pygmalion's mania, we could even give it a psychiatric definition—'fetishistic erotomania'. But since even Freud freed himself, with some irritation, from the exaggerated hyper-psychiatrical flavor of this term, it's better that we stop here. Returning to the path we momentarily abandoned in following the young neurotic archeologist on his Pompeiian wanderings, we should recapitulate so that we can attempt an interpretation.

The statue-lover's passion is founded on a paradoxical and fairly obvious premiss: if the lover seeks perfection in the quest for the love-object, then no living human woman can stand up to comparison with the artificial perfection of a statue. Ovid (that well-known expert on love) put it in exactly these terms. According to the tale in the *Metamorphoses*, Pygmalion was overcome by exasperation towards the female sex, offended by the vices that nature had handed out to women. Thus the artist took refuge in his extraordinary art, and made himself the *simulacrum* of what he could not find anywhere else. Those who fall in love with statues must accept a cruel paradox—that nothing human deserves to be loved, and that nothing human is worthy of their love. So the only thing left is to fall in love with an ideal image constructed by an artist of exceptional virtuosity. It is the paradox of stone, bronze, ivory, that they are as cold and perfect as real human beings are warm but flawed. A statue cannot partake of love, certainly, but as we know from Onomarchus' curse, it can neither age nor lose its beauty.

Perhaps we can now better understand the paradox that is the characteristic aberration of the 'statue-lover'. But how can we imagine and categorize this aberration? Loving images certainly constitutes sexual transgression—but it is so unusual (so 'paradoxical') that it is worth trying to understand how it was perceived and represented in cultural imagination.
The ending of a story has to be the best way of understanding it, for actions make sense because of their consequences. We can therefore expect to find our explanation at the *finale* of these inconceivable loves. We saw how the young lover of the Cnidus Aphrodite ended up by throwing himself off a cliff or into the sea, as do those guilty of incest—the fate assigned him by this 'popular myth'. His behavior greatly resembles that of those who, by loving a forbidden woman such as the mother or sister, trangress the elementary law that governs amorous behavior. The statue-lover commits such a serious transgression that he merits the same punishment as those guilty of incest—this is what the story tells us.
The fact that the lover of images is considered to have committed a sexual crime as extreme and monstruous as incest seems confirmed by other clues. First of all there is the fact that Pygmalion—the true Pygmalion—was a 'king'. Then tales of erotic passions for an image were also told about Tiberius, Caligula and Nero, emperors and tyrants. Now we know that it is always kings and tyrants who are the protagonists of tales involving monstruous sexual transgression, and they don't step back from incestuous loves—on the contrary, they seem

On page 18
Stefano and **Siro Serafin**
Venere Italica
di Antonio Canova
December 1917

Stefano and **Siro Serafin**
Perseo e l'Italia piangente
di Antonio Canova
December 1917

to have a real weakness for them. There is of course a reason for this. For the tyrant, the opportunity to commit incest follows from the license guaranteed him by the absolute power he wields, but it is also true that incest constitutes both the basis and the explicit declaration. Beyond and above the laws that govern the behavior of all men, the tyrant selects incest to affirm once and for all his privileged status. When Caracalla hesitated over entering into an incestuous marriage with his own stepmother, he was asked 'Don't you know that you are the emperor, that you lay down the laws, not receive them?' Returning to tyrant lovers of images, Nero was reputed to have loved his own mother, and Caligula was said to have loved his sister. These depraved and incestuous tyrants also share a singular weakness for images.

Narcissus clearly comes in here, for he too loved an image—the image of himself. In love with a *simulacrum*, but this time of himself, Narcissus too was just as much the protagonist of an inconceivable love, and can be placed in the paradoxical category of 'lovers of images'. Only that even this sad and wistful character shows up (somewhat unexpectedly) as an example of incestuous love, for other versions of the myth actually portray him as the lover of his twin sister. This time, however, it is a sister who dies—so that Narcissus is leaning over the notorious mirror of the fountain to contemplate not his own reflection, but that of his dead sister, so very like his own. Narcissus' link with incest remains strong even if we stick to the best-known variant of his myth. The vice that struck him, love of his own reflected image, links Narcissus to one of the most lascivious of animals, the horse. The classical world considered the horse the incestuous animal *par excellence*—and also prone to a passion for its own reflected image. Image-lovers are therefore placed outside culture's realm, and must fearfully set out for the world of lawless nature, just as those who love animals, a love which is severely and strictly prohibited. Like lawless tyrants, or lovers flung from cliffs, like those who commit incest, those who love their sisters, or are overcome by bestiality, the lover of images is a kind of sophisticated and artistic Oedipus whom society thrusts away like a *pharmakòs*. The sense of exile and separation communicated by the paradoxical lover in his tales and myths corresponds to any negative paradigm. His tale of inconceivable love is an authentic myth of prohibition.

The tales linked to the love of images therefore constitute a discourse (as we will soon see, a discourse strictly limited 'to men') related to a supremely important issue in cultural organization. These stories help to establish the rules governing behavior with these 'substitute' beauties who are even more beautiful than real beings, with their seductive marble bodies and subtle illusionistic colored forms that are more and more common in the landscape of culture. There is the risk that man may want to forge unacceptable links with the image, which is exposed to a power it cannot defend itself from. Images are creatures entrusted to men, placed under their *fides* or protection, and this trust must not be broken by exploiting the weakness of the image which completely depends on those who create them and surround them.

But here another question emerges: what 'temptation' is concealed in this forbidden creature, the image? If there are reasons 'to forbid it', it follows that there must be equally strong motives 'for desiring it'. It is easy to see the sexual attraction aroused by anything that is forbidden. But beyond this we should also perceive that the image possesses a peculiar feature which radically differentiates it from live beings—its immobility, its silent and 'passive willingness'. Its utter inability to reciprocate love certainly corresponds to a consequent absolute passivity.

This feature could explain why the image-lover is always 'male'—which may not at first be readily apparent. Of course, all the 'inconceivable lovers' we have examined are masculine. In a culture in which the 'practice of pleasure' is conceived 'based on the stereotype of penetration, and a polarity setting the active against the passive' (as Foucault expressed it) the image may represent the prototype of sexual passivity itself, thus heightening, in the paradox of inconceivable loves, the unique 'intrinsically important role exploited to its fullest extent, the essential definition of the active being—domination'.

Along with the beauty of the work and its perfection, this could quite possibly create a strong stimulus of desire—for the cultural imagination as well—to create 'myths' that revolve around the 'love of images'. Myths in which the frustrated desire of passivity (perfectly represented by the image) clashes yet merges with the sexual prohibition which strikes all who are too submissive and vulnerable to violent masculine possession.

But perhaps we're being a bit too hard on poor Pygmalion. Perhaps it was not just disgust with a woman—his woman—or terror of living beings, which led him to replace reality with something as perfect as it was docile and passive. Perhaps we could also be more generous with all the other lovers of the inconceivable. It may not be so much an evil disregard for life, as the fact that each of them had glimpsed, in those sculpted or painted images, an extraordinary gesture, an 'obsessive apparition' which they are driven to seek eternally in real beings. But this glimpse is sadly absent or wiped out by the reality of life. Thus, once they are inside the temple, these lovers finally see before their very eyes the true (if not living) image of what they seek. Or even better, if less noble, they manage, as artists, to set that apparition permanently in a work of art, where the 'stereotypes of art' (Klossowsky) sustain rather than suppress the original gesture. Goethe's Werther speaks of the moment in which 'the stairs climbed and the threshold crossed' he sees, for the first time, 'the most enchanting sight in the world'— Carlotta, the girl he will fall in love with, cutting brown bread for the children. This astonishing shock of love takes place in a scene which, framed by the pantry door, will dominate his life and death, and his love is fixed into one single image. Commenting on this episode in his famous *Frammenti di un discorso amoroso* (Fragments of an amorous discourse), Roland Barthes claims that 'first *we love a painting*'. He continues: '...among all the combinations of objects, what we seem to see best for the first time is the painting: the curtain suddenly goes up, and what was never before seen is completely unveiled, and from that moment devoured by the eyes...'. Norbert Hanold is fixated on a gesture, the step of the *Gradiva*. And what was the pose of the Agathé Tyche which cost that young Athenian his life? What spirit did she conceal?

In a famous passage from the *Ars poetica*, Horace reminds us that 'Poets and painters have the license to dare whatever they desire'. Yet this is not just a banal authorization to flout the conventions of verisimilitude—it is as if the image possessed an inherent capacity to portray even the 'impossible', all that the creatures, objects and situations inhabiting the living world could never accept. The kingdom of the image not only reproduces the real but enlarges it, finding room not only for what exists, or could exist, but also for everything that would never have any chance to exist in the real world. The myth expert Antonino Liberale tells us that once on the plane of Thebes, the dog of Cephalus (a hound from which no prey escaped) and the fox Teumexia (an animal able to escape any pursuer) faced each other. But how is this perfect *mise-en-scène* of a logical paradox solved? Following the scene to its inevitable yet infinitely repetitive conclusion, it is obvious that neither the dog nor the fox can win. When Zeus, however, saw the two animals overwhelmed by the paradox, he changed them to stone. In the figurative language of the mythical tale, the statue explicitly gives shape and place to the 'impossible'. What the real world can never accept (even from a logical point of view) finds refuge in the world of images.

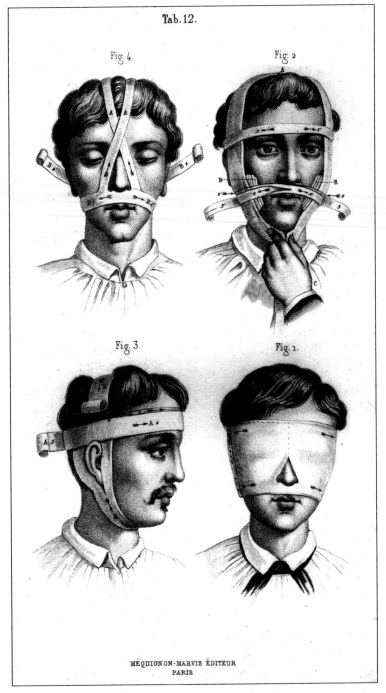

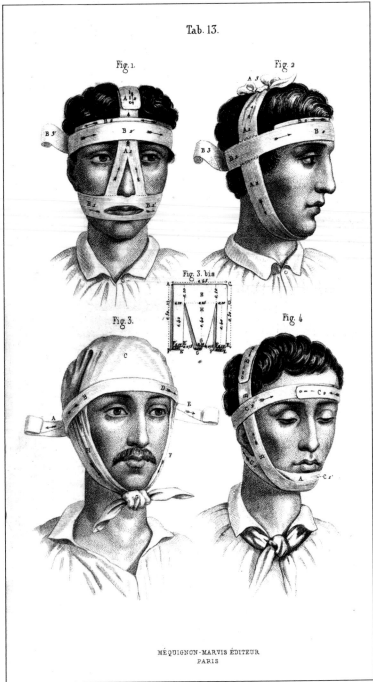

Cornuel and **Davesne**
*Examples of bandaging
in Goffres,* Sommario
iconografico di fasciature,
medicature ed apparecchi,
Naples 1858

Deformities of the Face

by Paolo Fabbri

Visual Signs: a Plumper Minerva

The human face has long been an object of study for both the arts and the sciences. But whilst art is once more concerning itself with the delineation of facial features and characteristics, the received conceptual wisdom on the subject is that such things are illegible. The excesses of the Physiognomists and Phrenologists of the nineteenth century have left indelible marks. Ever since Lichtemberg, the reading of the physiognomical paradigm, the pathognomic deciphering of physical stereotypes has been considered 'a coagulated prejudice, a foolhardy application of the theory of meaning'. Whilst admitting that the face could well bear the traces of past experience, no one would now support the theories current in early twentieth-century criminology which claimed there was a grammar to the face, the application of which enabled us to identify the genius or the criminal. Given that any such hermeneutics is out of the question, that any genealogy of expression, any attempt at facial typology is a mere extortion of signs, then such 'sciences' are condemned to insignificance, to being 'collections of symptoms of a (rather singular) grammar of the unconscious'.

Eppur si muove. Just as there are arts of sensual pleasure that do not fall within the scope of the science of sexology, the art of practical living has continual resort to knowledge of the human face. The respected 'commonplace' is the face science puts on for the world at large; but the results of science—like all results—are only a small part of experience.

Anyway, the view of Cubism as simply 'covering the face of man with headstones' is as untenable as the view of science as a metalanguage obeying pre-established norms (rather than as the set of rules by which modern epistemology chooses to play the game). And as for grammar—it is the thing which 'guarantees language the necessary degree of freedom'.

What we need therefore is 'a plumper Minerva', who is willing to do without a priori typologies. Those sorts of typologies 'which take the human nose and deduce that it can be divided into base, bridge and tip, then described as long or short, hooked, straight or average, thin or fleshy, etc.—and thence come up with 81 categories of nose, all of which reflect different virtues or vices. These methods can also come up with 58 types of forehead, 43 types of eye, 50 chins and 18 mouths!' (Giraud)[1]. What does need to be traced in, however, is a genealogy of human expression which (i) illustrates the way contemporary morphology is a break *within* the history of physiognomy and (ii) the connection between artistic practice and the way we think about the 'visual' sign. Painting and writing have always thought of expression as both forming and giving color to human affections and emotions, and the great physiognomist/morphologists such as Piderit or Bell have used the arts as a source of observational material. The former wrote a penetrating outline of the 'veiled look' (as a sort of visual *faux pas*), and the latter made interesting comments on Michelangelo and classical sculpture (the *Dying Gaul* and the *Laocoon*) [2].

But the 'semiotics of affections' (K. Bühler, *Theory of Expression*) has changed as well. The 'visual' sign is no longer seen as constructed of a fixed correlation between expression (*significant*) and inner feelings (*signifié*), but as the provisional outcome of a number of processes that involve both facial muscles and inner feelings. From Wundt's psycho-physics of human expression up to recent studies of deaf-and-dumb sign language, icastic studies of the human face (that is, the investigation of the face's role as an expressive whole—*Gestaltungskraft*) argue that a facial expression is to be considered as having meaning within a veritable mimic language, as an abstraction of action, 'Expression, one might say, is only to be understood within a mimic *Mienenspiel*' (L. Wittgenstein, *Observations on the Philosophy of Psychology*). These facial signs are the body representing itself; the body actually experiences them—and so they can be either active or passive (think of the difference between the movement of the eyes or the facial gestures which accompany tasting something). However, they let us know if they are transitive or reflexive: as Wittgenstein observed, they obey the grammar of exclamations.

Facial 'signs' are not entirely arbitrary. They begin as underdetermined facial movements, and might be considered as the grammatical 'roots' or *etyma* of feeling in affective processes. The 'motivational' link is between signs and motions—not states—of mind. The facial signs are like corporeal *shifters* (in the grammatical sense): that is, they start out undefined and are gradually made precise and individual [3]. Their meaning relates to the iconic meaning of the whole face in the same way as the meaning of a metaphor relates to the literal meaning of the words used. In this sense 'it is precisely the meaning that I *see*'. Or rather, 'in general, I do not impute fear to someone, I *see* it in him'. The question changes then. The 'epigonal' facial sign as it appeared in old Aristotelian or Thomistic studies of physiognomy was something that required us to progress from knowledge of a facial trait or gesture to the emotion it 'portrayed'. Whilst Bühler, following Husserl and Marty, argues that the meaning of an expression is an existential one which involves empathy (and therefore the connection of *signifié* and *significant* cannot be totally arbitrary).

The results of science's morphological studies of the expressions of the human face would thus seem to bear out the ideas of Wittgenstein, who was an untiring researcher into the ways whereby the human face might have 'meaning' (he was much more attentive than Carnap and James to the language games of physiognomy, and to our general blindness as to the form and meaning of those games). Learning to read a face does not mean learning to decipher it. What it means is discovering how different forms—for example, a face seen full frontal or in profile—can be seen as variants of a single whole and integrated as part of a history of feelings seen and depicted with forms and colors. For Wittgenstein, artistic representation is literal. 'Imagine a face shown full frontal and in profile at the same time, like in some modern paintings. A representation which encloses movement, change, the shifting of sight. Doesn't a picture like this depict what one *really* sees?'.

Better still, Wittgenstein argued that the understanding of feelings through physiognomy is not another application of linguistic semantics. It is words that have a physiognomy, a face and emotions. 'Each word can have a different character in different contexts, but it always has a character, a face. It looks at us always. One might imagine that each word is a small face, the written sign could be a face. And one could also say that an entire sentence is a group portrait, in which glances meet and produce a relation between the faces which leads to the emergence of a group with meaning'. The gaps in our knowledge shift—as do our certainties—but I think that key to the secret of the human face and passions is to start from this point of clarity. There is always time for making an explanation into an enigma, whilst it is likely that by searching for clarity over things that have been declared incomprehensible one might come across a few good ideas.

The Linguistic Physiognomies of Appearance
The words that refer to the human face have their own features—family similarities and differences. *Faciem*, *vultum* and *visum* are not the same thing. Their variations can not be reduced to differences of register. The words have different physiognomies. *Visum* is the animation of the *faciem*, and *vultum* is orientated in relation to others. The face is closest to behavior; it is a surface of features open to the sight of others. The *faciem* sees and lays itself open, but the *visum*—and, even more so, the *vultum*—are more 'aligned', they are turned outwards, towards the Other, in varying degrees of synergy or allergy.

This is not the place to go into the semantic prototypes of appearance that occur in our metaphors (a study similar to those which certain linguists have carried out into the extension of the idea of *choler*), but it is undoubtedly true that these metaphors reflect and hide more than our mirrors and our masks (how could one not recognise, *prima facie*, the connection between *vultus* and *vulva?*).

One point, however, on lineaments and character. The face, a concentration of sense organs, stands out on the 'head'. The 'lineaments'—a chorus of active and passive actors—are a collection of its distinctive 'traits', but also its outline. The character, on the other hand, exhibits the properties that are attributed to it. Old physiognomists—from Alberti and Della Porta to Klages—always read the face in terms of character (Alberti and Della Porta were, in this field, the equivalent of cryptographers). But as often happens in science, a metaphor may have had its day at a heuristic level but that does not mean it is totally played out (think, for example, of the planetary metaphor of the atom). Wittgenstein compares the written sign to a face showing emotion: writing could be seen as the locus of the tension and distension, of the fast and loose, of the syncopation and duration, which are the *etyma* of our emotional life.

In any case, the writing in question has all the features of textual ambiguity. The face is the place of identification and distinction. The moral guarantor of our persistence in being, of our subjective identity, the face can also suffer from the loss of all modesty and reserve. Appearance is also an artifice, the ceremonial locus for recognition and transfiguration. Appearance can be just that—and so become fiction and dissimulation, a reversal of the truth. Cosmetics are truly cosmic—make-up, plastic surgery and hair-dos can vary the contours of the face, change the relation between body and head. The rhythm of eyebrows, lips and eyelids (the black or white magic of the eyes can only shine in that face, made-up in that way, said Wittgenstein; whilst Canetti said: 'What would eyes be without their far-sightedness, without their eyelids?'). A Poetics of the face which is also a contribution to knowledge. The technique used in measuring the shadows cast on different planets in order to calculate the exact height of their mountains is derived from our knowledge of pictorial depth and of *maquillage*.

Grimaces, Disfigurements and Metamorphoses
The face is not a heraldic device which assigns to an individual a livery and a lineage. Physiognomy is disparity, a relation between differences which resemble each other, nuances of which we only become aware when they change. An expression is caught (or one is caught in it) only through the act of alteration. And nothing amorphous can change. Simmel is right to see the face as a principle of order, a collimator in which the least shift in the features (that is, the least malformation) is rich is meaning. Caricatures prove the 'felicity' of these procedure of change which do not so much reveal meanings and feelings as create new ones. Playing with the correlation between forms and meanings, Nabokov inverted the medieval hieroglyph which saw the face as represented by a 𝄞, the name of man, and replaced it with oȷo—so that the disappearance of the eyebrows and the extension of the nose turns the face of man into his genitals.

The grimace is a twist in the form, a de-formity (which may initially have been limited to the mouth) which leads to the 'disfigured' reading of the face and feelings. An example that is set in Venice. In *Death in Venice*, a grimace is enough to change the indescribable beauty of the Polish Tadzio when he sees a family of despised Russians.

'A storm of anger clouded his face. His expression dulled, his mouth contracted, turning upwards, and his lips tensed in a grimace of irritation which deformed his cheeks; his frown was such that his eyebrows overhung his eyes, which, dark and evil, sank back muttering the language of hate'.

Disfigurements which lead to a change in color, temperature and consistency. This is how, in *La Coscienza di Zeno*, Svevo describes his hero's perception of the *facies* of his former beloved, who is just recovering from a long illness. 'Ada's face was ill-constructed because the cheeks were back, but in the wrong place; as if the flesh had forgotten where it should go—so that, upon returning, it had settled too low down. They looked more like swellings than cheeks. Her eyes were back in their sockets, but no one had been able to repair the damage they had done by leaving in the first place. They had shifted or destroyed precise and important lines [...] In the blinding winter sunshine I could see that there was none of the colouring of the face I had loved so much. She was pale and the fleshy parts of her face where marked with red blemishes. Good health did not look as if it belonged to that face; she looked as if she had faked it'. Thus the face of the loved one changes—and we will never know if it is really the face or our love that has changed.

A face can also be a prey to tics, compulsive grimaces created by 'the unceasing struggle between a feature of the face which tries to escape from the overall organization of the face, and the face itself which tries to seize hold of this feature, block its escape, force it to accept organization'[4]. Here the face is seen as a virtual diagram, a 'voltage machine', which can impress itself on anything, starting from the head of man. The fate of man is to escape from the inhumanity of the face with all its possible grimaces. Art and science, madness and dreams are always throwing down challenges to the norms imposed by the face, smudging distinctions, switching faces and features, multiplying and fracturing ('freckles which flit at the horizon, hair streaming in the wind, eyes passed through rather than seen [...]'), condensing and dilating the face within animal or landscape metamorphoses. 'There is no face that does not contain an unknown or unexplored landscape, there is no landscape that does not take on a face which is loved or dreamed about, that does not call up a face for the future or from the past. What face has not suggested the landscape that goes with it (be it sea or mountain landscape), what landscape has not evoked the face that would have completed it, that would have given it its unexpected complement in facial features and lineaments?'.

I am thinking of Bacon's faces, whose mouths are as wide open as the dawn, of De Chirico's metaphysical faces—which are sometimes absorbed within the head, sometimes present as Still Lifes (unquiet depths which are peopled with secrets)—of the *Natura Morta* of the faces which appear in Serrano's *The Morgue* series of photographs.

To portray is to distort ('to deliberately change something', says the dictionary, 'to alter something in exhibiting or interpreting it', to 'alter reality'). And this applies both to portraits of a human face (to be read upside down, in an experiment that was dear to the Gestaltists) and to those of the earth itself (geological maps are provisional visualizations, which have to be continually updated to take account of shifts in constantly changing relations).

But such alteration can also be a disfiguring, a scarring of the face—the infliction of a permanent tic on constantly changing appearance. There is a character in Verga who caresses the face of an adulteress with a sharpened coin between his fingers: 'you have shown the sign of nature to others beside me', he says. 'Now everyone will be able to see the sign of it'.

The disfigurement of the face—the very opposite of 'transfiguration', in which things dissolve together. That very circle which appeared in thee / Conceived as but reflection of a light / When I had gazed on awhile, now seemed / To bear the image of a human face / Within itself, of its own colouring– / Wherefore my sight was wholly fixed in it (Dante, *Paradiso*, XXXIII, 127–132).

The Monster and the Mug

'Names in language are only the basis in which concrete elements are rooted. But the abstract elements in language are rooted in our judgement' (Benjamin). The monstrous face is not an error of genetic or visual syntax. Its task is neither to de-monstrate nor to represent. Monster comes from the Latin word 'mostra' which, in its turn comes from the verb 'moneo'—to advise and warn. The concern here is not with description or reference but with moral qualities. This was the case with the bestial face, the anthropomorphic 'mug'—the monstrous paradigm of otherness that is to be found in totems and fairytales. It is here that we find the remnant of myth and allegory within the concept of metamorphosis.

But science has exorcised the indecipherability of the alien 'mug' (Darwin followed the opposite procedure to that adopted by Della Porta and superimposed the human physiognomy on the animal). We can now see such mugs on the glossy pages of ecology magazines. An attempt is being made to overcome their mutism: the signs of the mug are under observation (and the hope is that we will be able to transplant our language onto it). Experimental killing (vivisection) marks a definite break with the intimacy of the sacrifice, which linked us with the animal world whilst preserving its otherness. If the 'mug' has no ethical value, one can no longer think about animals in the same way as one thinks about concepts.

Modern media abound in terrible faces and have exorcised the ambivalent message of the bestial 'mug', which could be twisted an infinity of ways and become the source of all sorts of deep-seated terrors. Since King Kong passed from the jungle to the music hall, it is only camera distortions which generate monsters: the monster is now machine-made.

Nature was poor in monsters, whilst imagination was rich in them; but now monsters are—and will be— produced in large quantities by the awakening of scientific reason. Yet genetic manipulation offers us ill-advised monsters, without any moral standards—like those same-faced settlers which Wittgenstein feared: 'With beings different from ourselves could things be different? If, for example, these beings all had the same face and the same features, many things would still be different'.

The monstrous face is a rhetorical tactic—a visual correction—in the exercise of our cognitive faculties. Now it is no ethical allegory, the monstrous face can be part of mass culture without tormenting it. Is art all that is left to us of a moral response to, of a sense of responsibility when dealing with, the human face? Incisions, transplants and ablations: van Gogh's self-mutilations, Giacometti's growing nose?

That face is new to me

Our face is not a code for connecting the heraldry
of expressions to the zodiac of emotions.
But what is left for us, once it has been declared that
we cannot know the face? A neutral mask animated by
a mechanical etiquette of mannered passions. A *carte du
tendre* on offer to plastic surgeons? The iconic paradigm
for the face ends up being the funeral mask, bereft
of that language which is part of the face.
We need new concepts and a new sense of proportion
in both contemporary science and art, which should not
limit themselves to representing and describing but to
bringing out properties that can be made the most of.
The white faces of screen stars are the only myth of
seduction we have. This encounter of mass culture and
reproducible images has produced those cold creatures of
artifice who are at the same time archetypes of seduction
which figure in our initiation rites (Baudrillard would
call them our very own Easter Island statues).
Are there other places where our affective capacities can
be drawn and drawn up? Where can we find an
embodied model which would provide us with another
point of view from which to read the feelings within the
face, these 'icons of values' (Nozick)? A *Semio-gnomics*
which responds to the interplay of the parts and sees
feeling immediately, without any interference from logic.
A Poetics of the Face, which can draw upon an open
and varied body of meaning: a secret, a-subjective and
metaphoric face such as that to be seen in Arcimboldo's
'curious' paintings. An indirect, free text, written on
one's own face by the face of the 'other' to which it lays
itself open. A narration of varying rhythm and intensity,
in which the facial features are actors. A narration which
presents, demonstrates and responds to passions that
have yet to be spoken.
Not everyone can lend an ear to this vision.
One possibility remains. Instead of trying to understand
how the eye is smiling in that face, one can respond
with a smile. 'If you now say that that face is smiling,
what is easier: describing the position and form of the
various parts of the face, or smiling back?'
(Wittgenstein).
Wittgenstein adds: 'Now I know how to continue'.

[1] P. Fabbri, *Le passioni del volto*, in *Effetto Arcimboldo*, catalogue of the Palazzo Grassi exhibition, Venice (Milan, 1987), 259–272.
[2] Ch. Bell, *The Anatomy and the Philosophy of Expression as Connected with the Fine Arts* (London, 1806).
[3] Fabbri, *Op. cit.*
[4] G. Deleuze, F. Guattari, *Mille Plateaux* (Paris, 1980).

Louis Corinth
26 Februar 1910

Behind the Mirror
Notes from the Portrait in the Twentieth Century

by Günter Metken

Let's start with a paradox. One might imagine the history of twentieth-century art as a series of self-portraits. And this very centenary of the Biennale invites comparison with a series of portraits. The one hundred years of this exhibition practically coincide with that period over which the individual has become a unit in mass planning, to the point where individuality has dissolved itself in the collectivization of war, consumerism and, most recently, electronic entertainment. And yet, this same period—which is so problematic where subjective consciousness is concerned—has also been the one where the art of portraiture has flourished as almost never before.

Up to now the history of modern art has dwelt on abstractionism (assuming it to be a progressive tendency) and deliberately ignored portraits (assumed to be reactionary). Such a view is mistaken because the portrait in this century has rarely been understood as a study of human temperament and character (though there are notable examples of this type of portraiture in the 1920s); more often than not, the genre has functioned as a workshop in which to make daring experiments.

Since time immemorial, facial lineaments have been taken as revealing the inner state of an individual. In the eighteenth century, under the stimulus of the work of Johann Caspar Lavater, the scientific study of physiognomy tried to create a system for reading these traits. Modernism, however, has posed a totally different problem: the face is less an expression of the sitter than of art itself. The system of pictorial representation that has come down to us is built on a classical system of coordinates: point and line, curved and straight lines, flat or rounded forms all make a complex whole that is both resonant and 'essential'. From the iconic reductions of Alexej von Jawlensky to the contoured physiognomical landscapes of Stanley Spencer, Francis Bacon and Lucian Freud there is a whole range of possibilities, that have been even further extended by the shifts in the direction of delirium and schizophrenia which can be seen in the works of Ernst Josephson, Franz Pohl, Karl Brendel (Prinzhorn has, in fact, called the work of the last two 'the art of the mentally-ill'). The human face was the terrain on which the abolition of limits was tried out for the first time. It is also the terrain which, thanks to the mirror, can be checked on and assessed like no other. The mirror gives the artist the experience of that apparently familiar thing there in front of him being taken away from him. 'J'est un autre'—as Rimbaud saw so clearly. Ernst Mach, a physicist and psychologist who studied vision, pointed out that continuous observation breaks down what is observed into a network of fragments. And if one's own reflect is something that one cannot grasp, then the image of another person must be well beyond our reach!

'My facial expression is too changeable'

The drama of the individual 'turned out' of his own reflection is clear in the work of Vincent van Gogh (and, in a profoundly similar way, in that of Antonin Artaud). Van Gogh's self-portraits are a veritable Via Crucis: to fight against the imminent menace of a split in his consciousness, this heir of protestant psychoanalysis felt he had to be continually checking up on his expression. The hysteria and disturbance that can be seen in the lineaments he portrays are the clear demonstration of how vain his attempts were. European culture at the turn of the century seems to have been obsessed with penetrating to the spiritual core of the 'I'; a quest due in no small part to the influence of Theosophy and the works of Rudolf Steiner. Rembrandt, the artist who had measured and recorded all the heights and depths of existence, every joy and sorrow, every happiness and misery, was more than just appreciated—he was practically venerated. Book after book was written to discuss the changes from one Rembrandt self-portrait to another (the greatest being the discussion in George Simmel's essay); whereas nowadays we would surely see that these self-portraits are also efficient and well-designed exercises in 'image-making', performed by an artist who was a very good manager of his own talents. The turn-of-the-century aphasia yearned towards expression, and thus viewed this game of images as something that had a sort of animistic power—just as the pulverization or regeneration of Monet's sun- or rain-soaked Rouen Cathedral seemed to make the building into a sort of living being. 'My facial expression is too changeable' Richard Wagner said when he saw photographs of himself, and thus scrupulously controlled which ones were released in order to create a solid, reliable portrait of himself. The sculptors Rodin, Medardo Rosso and the late Giacometti were all fascinated by this shifting, changeable quality of facial lineaments, by how one expression could turn into another; the futurists Boccioni and Balla also studied this changeability, interested as they were in movement and mobility. Something similar can be found in the sketches and drawing produced by Ferdinand Hodler in the years 1914–15 to record with clinical ruthlessness the illness and death of his lover Valentine Godé-Darel. He broke up the previously static portrait into phases, creating an almost filmic sequence showing the gradual dissolution of his lover's face, the approaching blankness in the eyes of a woman he had initially portrayed in a frontal symmetrical pose (like something in Fayoum's Coptic portraits).

Psycoanalysis and X-Rays

Inevitably psychoanalysis opened up new dimensions for portraiture. From the 1900 *Interpretation of Dreams* onwards, Freud was constantly arguing the stratified nature of man's inner being, with each layer either repressed or trying to push its way to the surface. Something of the same thrust to the surface can be seen in the portraits which Oskar Kokoschka painted in the years before the First World War, following on the lead set by Anton Romako. However, those paintings also call to mind the contemporary fascination with x-rays, which at the time were seen as sounding out the depths of the human body. Skin became parchment, whilst beneath it one could glimpse what used to be only intuited: suspended particles, translucid structures and layers. The spiritual as concrete. Alice's look through the looking-glass had here become reality: one could see front and back at the same time. From now on the portrait-painter will not stop at the skin, and the Belgian artist Léon Spilliaert would turn the portrait into a vision of spectres, thus widening the concept of the individual to a disturbing extent. Inside and outside, the facade and the continent which lies behind it—they all emerge at the same time and mix together without any regard for rhythm or composition. This is particularly clear in those works by Lovis Corinth, in which paint offers high-intensity condensations of the betrayal felt because of a ruthless mirror and an obsession with old age (veritable *memento mori* in the Rembrandt sense). There is a clear, link here with Georg Baselitz's early portraits of 1960s.

One can see the same thing in music, with the written text offering composers the same opportunity for freedom as that the human face offered the painters of the time. Lieder and the setting of words to music account for a large part of the work of the young Arthur Schönberg. The composer used literary texts to obtain greater freedom from traditional schema, and then from polytonality he moved on to the arrangement of sound in total atonal freedom. During this phase, he was helped and sustained by the structure and message of contemporary poetry, which was used to organize and hold together his constructions of sound.

In painting—and not least of all in that of Schönberg himself—the face was taken as a reference point (which served in place of the text). Whatever deformations it is subject to, the face is still a recognizable sign. Almost no one has gone as far as Richard Gerstl in mixing and dissolving the material of the facial lineaments, and yet even here the form is used to hold together the centrifugal forces which, like madness, would otherwise tear the 'I' apart. This was also the case with his pupil, Arnold Schoenberg, whose face during his 1909–10 crisis decomposes into some sort of hallucinatory optical game which reminds one of neurotically obsessive behaviour. One could follow this sequence of Viennese portraits of anxiety all the way to the 'touched-up', intersecting faces painted by Arnolf Rainer.

A Masked Ball

The Man in the Crowd is the title of an Edgar Allan Poe story set in London which recounts how, on a particularly busy thoroughfare, an individual continually appears and disappears within the crowd. From the innumerable anonymous faces there eventually arises a crowd physiognomy—and that is what we see in Edward Munch's *Spring Evening in the Karl-Johann-Gade in Oslo* (1892). These groups are entirely without will-power and react in unforeseeable ways. At about the same period, James Ensor used the image of the mask for such a crowd. The metaphor would have been known to him thanks to the Ostend Carnival and the various shops of ethnic rubbish that abounded in the port town; he applied it to any city crowd, making them into processions of masked figures—like that surrounding Jesus Christ on his entry to Brussels. The mask has numerous connotations in modern culture. It can symbolize the demoniac aspect of man (who under cover of the crowd explodes in momentary hysteria), but it can also symbolize homogeneity and uniformity. In the art of totalitarian regimes, for example, the human face is as rigid and fixed as a mask, with a square-jawed virility and a determined, sharp-edged beauty which are a harsh, stiff parody of classical canons. This is why all the portraits of the leaders of Communist China began to look the same (especially during the Cultural Revolution)—that is, they began to look more 'western': they were adapting to a standard which, irony or ironies, Roy Lichtenstein was in those very years raising to be one of the icons of Pop Art. By isolating the genetically-pure facial features of strip-cartoon heroes from their context, he transformed them into enormous outlines.

But for the artists of the early avant-gardes, a mask represented a formal synthesis within painting. Working on *Les Demoiselles d'Avignon* (1907), Picasso gradually reduced the clients and prostitutes of a Barcellona brothel into figures in a provocative frieze; taking African masks as his model, he totally broke with the expectations of Mimesis and depersonalized the faces of all the figures.

The same sort of thing was happening in the work of Matisse, Derain and the artists of the Dresden Brücke (as well as in the paintings of Emil Nolde, whose work was so close to theirs). The series could be continued to include Brancusi's masks and the masks later produced by Giacometti (up to *Naso*/Nose, a symbol of sexuality and a parody of Pinocchio). In the First World War, gas masks made soldiers even more like automata. The mask then served to underline the absurdity of a humanity which had become cannon fodder. Here one should mention Max Beckmann and his scenes from the Frankfurt Carnival, represented as some sort of Theatre of Cruelty. Beckmann was just one of the many twentieth-century artists (from Rouault and the Picasso of the Pink Period) who have portrayed themselves as clowns. The eternal 'stand-in', the artist takes upon himself all the flaws of his day and unmasks Huxley's Brave New World as a world-turned-upside-down. It is as if the larva were the true face of the twentieth century—a face that has been geometrically reconstructed by artists such as Giorgio De Chirico, Carlo Carrà, Mario Sironi and their followers amongst the Dadaists and the Magical Realists (Raoul Hausmanun, Max Ernst, Anton Räderscheidt and Felix Nussbaum, the man with the Star of David). Hunted by the Nazi, Nussbaum took refuge in Brussels but was eventually denounced by his neighbours. His self-portraits from 'underground' reflect the turmoil of a 'degenerate'. Often there is no face at all behind the mask, only emptiness. Rudolf Schlichter has defined these faceless persons as 'the new type', embodied in either fascists or technocrats. His *Blinde Macht* is dedicated to the German Resistance against the Nazis and shows one such automaton of terror, whose face and armour are clearly derived from the mannequins of Metaphysical painting.

The Reticence and Eloquence of Faces

On this point one should mention Walter Benjamin's description of the sight of masses of silent troops returning from the First World War. They had been exposed to a technological hell for which they had no preparation, and thus had no means of grasping or communicating what they had actually experienced. Their faces were the only means they had for communicating their experiences at the Front—and artists and physiognomists fell upon those faces with eagerness. This why Walter Benjamin's account, in *Experience and Poverty* (published in 1933), is a comment on portraiture in the twentieth century. He observes: 'No, this at least is clear: the 'stock' of experience has fallen—in a generation that, between 1914–18, had one of the most terrifying experiences in the history of the world. But perhaps this is not as surprising as it seems. Everyone must have noticed it— that people returning from the battlefield were silent, poorer not richer in communicable experience. All the material that ten years later found its way into the flood of books on the war was anything but the experience of the war as recounted by word of mouth. No, it was no surprise. Never had personal experience been more totally denied than it was by trench warfare, by economic inflation, by hunger as the means of knowing one's body, by the interests of the Great Powers presented as identical with morality. A generation that went to school by horse-drawn tram suddenly founded itself in an open landscape where the clouds were the only thing that had not changed; the poor frail human body was there, in the middle of it all, within range of destructive assaults and explosions.

A whole new type of misery descend on the men caught up in that terrifying unfurling of technological resources. And the other side of the coin was the descent on people generally of a suffocating wealth of ideas generated by the revitalization of astrology and yoga, of Christian Science and Chiromancy, of Vegetarianism and Gnostic Philosophy, of Scholastic Philosophy and Spiritism. Because this was not real revitalization but a sort of galvanization. One need only think of the large-scale paintings by Ensor: a wicked spell has filled the streets of large cities with petty bourgeois in carnival masks; crowned with glitter, distraught figures in make-up wander aimlessly along the streets. These pictures are perhaps nothing but the effigy of the chaotic, horrifying renaissance on which so many had put all their hopes. But here something becomes strikingly clear: our poverty of experience is only a part of that larger poverty which has once more acquired a face—and this time the face has all the sharpness and cunning of a medieval beggar'.

The Theatre of Physiognomy
One can speak of a veritable theatre of physiognomy. The early 1920s resurgence of figurative art inclining towards realism was welcomed, above all in France, as a return to order and, in part, to Neo-classicism. At the same time, Italy had its Novecento movement, and the USA its Regionalism. The USSR was Constructivist by decree, but the Supremacist Kasimir Malevich was gradually returning to a figurative tradition. In that paradise for Workers and Peasants, based on the ambiguous motto *mens sana in corpore sano*, Alexandr Deineke created an eurhythmics of bodies which both at work and play moved as if part of a dance. They could be compared with Malevich's 'atheletes' and with the mannequins that the Bauhaus Dakar Schlemmer was producing, all of them with identical faces. The aim was to redeem the individual who had been isolated within industrialised society by placing him within a social harmony. Hans Bellmer responds to the voyeur with a doll of articulated limbs, which denies human instincts altogether. It would be too easy to see this return to

figurative art as a step backwards. In fact, the avant-garde had never broken away from the nineteenth century and its iconography as radically as the manifestoes would have one believe.

The renewed attention paid to the real world was particularly apparent after 1916–17; and actually benefited from those movements that had tried to undermine it. The effects were not only to be seen in painting and sculpture (think of Otto Gutfreund and Arturo Martini, of Adolfo Wildt and Wilhelm Lehmbruck) but also, and especially, in photography (with various famous series of pictures investigating the human face and its significance). August Sender wanted to establish a table of identifiable social types, whilst others were more interested in ethnography, social hierarchies, professional 'types' or studying the social outcast. And at the very moment that people began to have a first full understanding of the human physiognomy, they also became aware that the differences between individuals were about to be flattened.

Alongside this sort of photography, which was concerned with the variations between individuals, there was also the propaganda photography of totalitarian regimes, concerned simply to impose unification and a *Volksgemeinschaft* which would not tolerate deviations or contradiction. Whilst in democratic countries photographers revealed an insatiable appetite for the human face. The face was all the rage; and illustrated magazines showed more, and more types, of human images than ever before. Quite apart from whatever exotic interest it might have, the human image served both to entertain and instruct.

The same fascination with the human face can be seen in the painting produced between the wars. Otto Dix, New Objectivity and the Italian Novecento all showed an interest in the social portrait: the doctor, the architect, the engineer, the modern woman, the factory worker and the writer were all portrayed with the emblems of their trade.

At the same time there was an almost irrational explosion of interest in the 'science' of physiology, which made it possible to read facial features (this, little-studied, phenomenon was particularly evident in Weimar Germany).

In response to the compartmentalization imposed by experimental science, there was a desire for a psychology of the human expression which would 'reveal all'. People were already beginning to distrust language, and facial features seemed much more likely to provide reliable information on one's fellow man.

The exaggerations of still photograph and the staggering close-ups used in silent cinema taught the public how to decode facial features—the faces of Asta Nielsen, Pola Negri, Falconetti and Greta Garbo are still part of the collective imagination. Faces were an argument presented visually. Racial theories necessarily fell back on differences in facial features, and the human face was studied throughout the 20s and early 30s by German psychologists and critics as different as Oswald Spengler, Georg Simmel, Max Picard, Ernst Kretschmer, Rudolf Kassner, Ludwig Klages and Ernst Jünger. As contemporary photographs reveal, people were fascinated by external appearance as something that could be used to evaluate character, intelligence, sensibility and talent. Along with the facial features went the hand—in particular, the index finger—in a gestuality without words. The creases on the forehead provided clues as to personal future and character which it was as well to know rightaway.

All of this prepared the way for the violent, hyper-gestual portraits painted under the Weimar Republic, for the works of Georg Grosz (the artist with the cruel eye), Max Beckmann, Rudolf Schlichter, Christian Schad and even Ludwig Meidner (in whose pictures the eruption of punished lineaments turns into the forced articulation of a silent scream).

Photo and 'Image'

After the Second World War photography made further contributions in the field of portraiture. Impressionistic, abstract and subjective photography had obviously existed before, but what happened after the war was that 'objective' photography also became an art form. Photographers such as Bernd and Hille Becher took photographs of abandoned factories in a neutral, even light, as if they were historical monuments or works of sculpture. This technique was then applied to portrait photography by some of their students at the Dusseldorf Academy; the animated human face assumed the rigidity of a monument, became a work of sculpture. The face became a neutral building captured once and for all within its natural tendency to change. Photography had initially robbed painting of the realm of realist reproduction of appearance; now it achieved its dream and became a tangible, long-lasting monument in its own right.

The forms of contemporary portraits often owe a lot to these changes. Like when Cindy Sherman insinuates herself into the agitated dreams of American woman, or has herself photographed within the agitated 'dreams' of history and the history of art. Think of the products turned out in Andy Warhol's Factory. These are not mimetic reproductions but clichés, as Hans Belting says, passed on by the mass media which reduce not the person but his 'image' into a visual slogan.

Another American painter, Chuck Close, has reconstructed on canvas the photos of friends and family, starting with a photo of himself, enormously enlarged within a grid of lines and points. The result is not a reproduction but an icon. This is even more the case when, as recently, the artist works to compose his puzzle with luminous particles of color. The sparkle of mosaics, the aura thus created, evoke not only the works of Gustav Klimt but also those of his very sources: the mosaics of Venice and Ravenna (and even further back, the pre-Christian paintings of Fayoum, Egypt). The large female faces of Dominique, Doris and Natascha produced by the Swiss artist Franz Gertsch are totally different. Gertsch too started out trying for radical photographic realism in painting, then in the 80s he began to produce these enormous pieces out of colored wood. More than two meters high, these pale figures have a narcotic effectiveness, with the apparition of the face mysteriously hovering between presence and absence.

Ghosts

The embarrassment can only increase when the visitor is faced with the contemporary works of video art. Having turned on the video we find ourselves encountering faces that come towards us, behave with deceptive appropriateness. Being and Appearing enter into contact with each other within a world of shadows. But, as with ghosts, there is always that 'almost', that non-contact, in the zone of the transitional.

Often, and this is the case with Bruce Nauman, the artist shows himself, in a situation of extreme narcissism. Bill Viola, on the other hand, uses mirrors to draw the spectator into a happening; the dark space creates theatrical suspense, as if one were participating in an existential drama. Aud yet there is no real interlocutor. Within the subjectivity of the spectator, the work splits up into images that follow on from one another; words here are reproduced words. These ephemeral, deceptive *mise-en-scène* require the experience of the spectator to give them an identity, to make them into something like portraits.

Gary Hill has radically deconstructed this situation. He works with fragments of the human body which are connected with the passage of the spectator, to represent a presentiment of life, an allusion to a person and a face. The various fragments are never present all at the same time: portrait and person are no longer analogous, the images have become immaterial.

Lovis Corinth
Selbstbildnis umgesen
von Ausdrucksstudien
26 February 1910

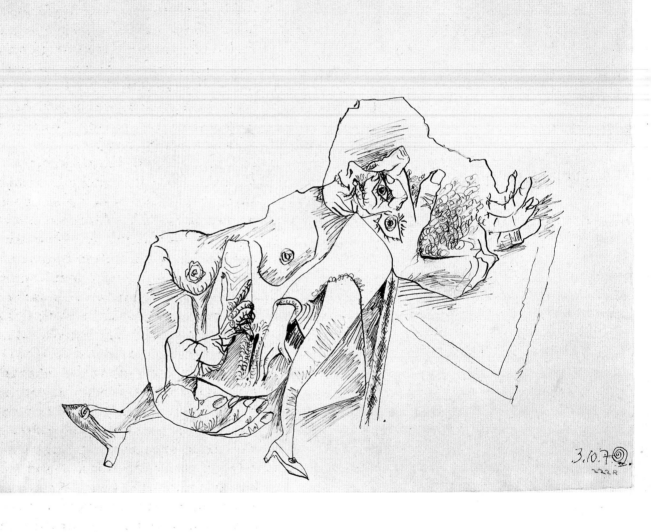

Pablo Picasso
Nu dans un fauteuil
3 October 1972

From the day it was decided to submit the body to the requirements
of the fourth dimension, the body suffered the most serious disorders.
...Certain organs found themselves shifted outside the body and, under
the natural thrust of the muscles, they grouped themselves
in an indescribable heap, disobeying all known rules.
GASTON DE PAWLOWSKI, *Voyage au Pays de la Quatrième Dimension*

In the portraits I have drawn... I have often put objects, trees or
animals alongside the human heads because I am still not sure about
where to fix the limit at which the body of my human self stops.
ANTONIN ARTAUD

The Body Beside Itself

by Philippe Comar

The invention of photography caught man on the hop;
then radiography overcame his opacity and now even
the most secret functions of his body can be made
visible by fibre optics. Each new means of investigation
offers a new purchase on the object being studied. As
Paul Valéry said half a century ago, we are on a slope
where it is impossible to stop and form, for a particular
hour and a particular day, a precise idea of the human
body. We have never had so much knowledge about the
body, and yet the body has never seemed so difficult to
delimit 'at a single blow'.

In Descartes' day the mechanical model of levers, cogs,
pumps and tubes was applied to anatomy and
physiology, thus justifying the metaphor of the body as
'automaton', a stable collection of moving pieces, a fixed
and measurable system. Apart from the problems of
reproduction and of the exact nature of the force
animating the living being (which was considered a
question for metaphysics), there was no *a priori* reason
why the body could not be known exhaustively. A
complete description of the organs which made it up
would be enough to delimit all aspects of the body.
Then, at the beginning of the industrial era, came
the notion of 'Energy', which meant metaphysical
considerations no longer played a central role in
discussions of the source of movement in a living body.
The human machine, which had been almost completely
delimited, suddenly found itself wide open again and
became a place when things were transformed, burnt up,
exhausted; the physiologist began to borrow his tools
from the chemist and physicist rather than the
locksmith and the plumber. A collection of new factors
were taken into consideration which meant that the
body had to be seen as part of a larger whole. Around
the 1860s, Claude Bernard was introducing the notion
of 'milieu' into biology, then came Ernst Haeckel with
the notion of 'ecology'. For his part, Etienne-Jules Marey
showed that any analysis of movement had to include
the notions of 'time' and 'space'. The visible mechanism
of the dead body were abandoned in favour of the
invisible mechanism of the living body; the
encyclopaedic statue of the flayed body started running.
The study of locomotion by then involved the study of

39

air resistance, of surface reaction and friction, of inertia and gravity. And on those questions, the anatomist was not likely to be enlightened by looking under the skin of a corpse. The dissection of a leg tells us nothing about the laws of gravity, without which it is impossible to offer an accurate description of running.

Since the second half of the nineteenth century we have learnt more about the human body from mastering the physical laws of the universe within which it moves than from studying its own secret cogs and wheels. This new approach 'exteriorises' the human machine, undermines the very notion of a body. How can a body be envisaged when its limits are less and less certain? How have artists reacted to this change? The body was once represented with great care as a 'finite' object to be given 'finish', but now it no longer appears to be strapped into itself. What becomes of the notion of identity when the contours of the body are more and more difficult to delimit?

In this essay I will limit myself to discussing various stages in this transformation, from Manet to the present day. First of all I will discuss the gradual disappearance of skin as the natural boundary of the human body, then the emergence of a whole fabric of relations and constraints which envelope the body and make it impossible to individualise it any more.

At the end of 1863 a French ministerial decree concerning the reform of art-teaching caused a violent controversy. In response to criticism from the Académie (where the rule of the ageing Ingres was still unchallenged), Viollet-le-Duc supported the government and launched a bitter attack on the methods used in teaching drawing at the École des Beaux-Arts. He had great fun mocking this academic discipline, the very backbone of art-school training, which he described as involving a student copying 'a naked man, always lit by the same daylight in the same room, and forced into a pose which would generally pass for some sort of torture paid for by the hour'[1]. Against this moribund, closeted activity, Viollet-le-Duc championed the teaching of drawing in the fresh air, from life. His faith in the observation of the body in motion and of the role of intelligent memory lent support to the then-fashionable theories of Lecoq, who in his *Éducation de la mémoire pittoresque* of a few years earlier had given enthusiastic accounts of certain 'pleasure parties', with teachers and students settled by the side of a pond in some clearing under luxuriant trees. The models 'had to walk, sit, run—in short, give themselves over to spontaneous movement... We poor mercenaries of the pose were liberated by this splendid vivifying milieu, we seemed truly transfigured'[2]. The studio was abandoned in favour

of the open air, the conventional pose gave way to living movement. It is, of course, almost impossible to read Lecoq's description of his 'pleasure party' with thinking of Manet's *Déjeuner sur l'herbe*, painted in the same year (1863) and taken by art historians as marking the very beginning of all modern art. In less than a decade, the Impressionists would have gradually blurred the outlines of the human figures to blend it into the whole field of the picture, to make everything shift and move. Figurative painting gave up the pose and the fixed form in favour of the 'movement' and 'memory' (which Marey would champion a few years later). This meant that the artist could free himself entirely of the presence of his model, liberate himself from objective limits. Manet (whom some consider to be a painter of 'appearance') was well aware of this inward 'step back' from the world, and in a letter to Georges Jeanniot wrote: 'Cultivate your memory, because nature will never provide you with anything but information'[3]. The body would no longer be enclosed within its appearance. Movement, the shaky and blurred line—together with the no-doubt accidental discovery of out-of-focus photography—all opened up the contours of the human body; on one side, the mechanically organized structure disappeared; on the other, turbulence and blood made their getaway.

Among the various traces to be found of this etiolation of the human form one might mention how important the relation body-water becomes in the work of certain painters (most notably Degas and Bonnard). The significance of the theme goes well beyond the classical connotations evoked by a scene in which a figure is getting washed. Tubs and baignoires re-immerse the body in a milieu that is both tepid and impinging. Flesh and water are elements of the same density, and between them the skin acts as a very slight dividing membrane. The mass of the body seems to be breaking out of its own space to extend itself into the water. The liquid also has another effect of decisive plastic importance within the painting: the troubled surface of the water contorts the contours of the human form; sometimes the alterations are so violent that the refracted image seems to be an outburst of soluble flesh. The flaccidity of the corporeal envelope was taken to paroxysmal lengths by the Surrealists. The list of the examples of stretched skin and soft, spongy excrescences in the works of Dalì, Masson and Miro, as well as in the distorted photographs produced by André Kertész would be endless. In the works of Tanguy the human form is bathed in the atmosphere of a weightless, glaucous universe and floats like some old cast-off—thus prefiguring the destiny of that other skin, the canvas of the painting itself (the last convulsion of the *peau de chagrin*). Trust or mistrust of the corporeal envelope is, according to the rather categorical judgement laid down by André Breton, the supreme criterion for distinguishing between conformists and those who have freed themselves from visual platitudes: 'I know two sorts of painters: those who believe and those who don't believe in the skin'[4].

Alongside this pictorial dermatology one should of course mention all the inflammatory troubles and tissue necroses which afflicted the Expressionists—whose works illustrate the critical point of a integument about to give. One might also look at the obsessional repetition of lines in Alberto Giacometti's portraits, with the artist emphasizing the impossibility of giving a figure a sharp defined outline, suggesting the permeability of human contours.

The Cubists do not emphasize the *non finito* of outlines in the same way, but they too end up pushing the body to its very limits. Edges and lines of force are everywhere. Supple, elastic skin is stretched over its framework, ready to snap. In fact, where skin is concerned, *Les Demoiselles d'Avignon* marks a true passage to the limit. In the years that followed, from 1907–12, Picasso confirmed this rupture: the entire body exploded, and participated in the diapason of the universe around it. The opposition between inside and outside was abolished, and in the *Portrait de Kahnweiler*, the crushed face seems to be entirely submerged in a mosaic of forms. The painting is left to the interpretative skills of the spectator, to his ability to appreciate a visual whole; it reminds one of those tests which were being perfected at the time by *Gestalt* psychologists, in which the spectator was required to make out a figure amongst a mess of lines and marks.

By opening up the limits of the human body, and bricking up the body inside the picture with which it forms a whole, the Cubists and their heirs followed on from the Symbolists and developed a whole series of relations and 'correspondences' between the inner and outer world. The loss of the corporeal envelope reveals not only what lies in the depths of the organism but also reveals how the outside world plays a part in the body's inner workings. Surrounded by stimuli and influences of all types and intensity, but responding to them all, the body becomes a cog in a vast universal machine (a myth which culminates in the role of Artist-Machine to which Andy Warhol aspired).

In the 1930s Raoul Hausmann, Francis Picabia and Georges Grosz—along with comic illustrators such as Rube Golberg (whose machines were always turning against those who used them)—all painted a picture of the body subordinate to its physical and social

environment. The question was no longer one of recreating a facsimile of the body on the basis of knowledge of its interior structure, but rather of tracking the course of its evolution and then enclosing it within a sort of 'virtual' cage, or experimental enclosure. Giacometti's 1932 *Main prise* (Held Hand) is certainly the most perfect example of this *exo-automaton*, with the levers, cogs and straps enclosing the hand they operate upon as in a sort of reliquary. The mechanism of movement used to be hidden beneath the skin, now its constrains the body from outside. Hoffmann's machine which dreamt of acting freely under the impulse of its own cogs and springs has now been turned back on itself and becomes a formidable mechanism for holding the body in traction. The hand that holds is held. The other aspect of this approach to the body, this undoing of the human form, arises less from the mechanical causes of movement than from the consequences of movement. These consequences are not only the intentional goal of an action but also those secondary side-effects that inevitably, parasitically, accompany any action. In this case, the artist follows the body-in-motion so as to be able to make out the disturbances it produces. Sharp contours, the certainty that the body had clearly-defined limits are really nothing but the effect of incomplete, interrupted observation—that is to say, they are a consequence of that illusion of the 'instant', which was so dear to the age of the Enlightenment.

Umberto Boccioni dared to fix his attention on a living man for a whole second. Without using what he knew to correct what he saw, he showed the whole thing in a single block. *Forme uniche di continuità nello spazio* (Single Form of Continuity in Space), which was influenced by Matson's aerodynamic theories, is the most successful example of this man/trajectory. Taken in full movement, the human form dissolves into the flow and eddies of the fluid milieu through which it progresses; the body is no more distinct from the milieu than a whirlpool from the water. Man only holds together through action.

Whilst the Futurists were championing this energetic waste, Marcel Duchamp was—without much effort, it's true—applying himself to the study of 'small wasted energies' in such things as the fall of tears, the growth of hair and excessive pressure applied to a light switch[5]. This interest in waste, in entropy, is a prelude to the aesthetics—of consumption which underlies Performance Art and Happenings.

Between these two extremes—of Giacometti's *Main prise*, which externalises the mechanism of human man movement, and Boccioni's *Forme uniche di continuità nello spazio*, which extends the corporeal envelope well beyond the skin—our Museum of Bodies with Uncertain Contours, will have to include a whole series of *Machines Célibataires*, which show the human form as indistinguishable from the tissue of relations within which it is caught. This new generation of machines take the relation between body and external world one step further. Whilst Giacometti and Boccioni represent the Realist and Impressionist aspects of the mechanistic world, the Celibate Machine represents its 'mythical' aspect.

There is no doubt that, with a few exceptions, the gradual disappearance of the limits of the human body which can be noticed in period between Manet and Duchamp is, to varying degrees, the result of artists' encounter with the real or imagined mechanism of the human body. This primacy of function over form leads, from the 1950s onwards, to artists seeing their own bodies as the 'raw material' on which they should question themselves—and thence, of course, as the raw material of their work itself.

Whilst it is easy to reduce someone else's body to appearance, make it a pure form or statue, our perception of our own body is necessarily linked to a perception of it at work. For ourselves we can never be a mere form. When we consider our bodies, function is more important than appearance.

Bruce Naumann's facial contortions, Mona Hatoum's endoscopies, the pitfall-ridden Via Crucis Gary Hill takes with his video camera on his shoulder, the bloody entrails of Gina Pane, the refundable excrement and spilt bile and humours of a number of other artists (not to mention physical performance art) are all intended 'to make the body present' and to make a symbolic reference its physical function. A corollary of the trials to which the body is submitted is that the integrity of the corporeal envelope is both undermined and made into a sort of disguise (and thus denied as a limit). Skin is not where the body ends.

The art of the past century has presented an increasingly chaotic, derisory image of man. This crushed, deliberately subjective, image may conflict with the image which science (but not only science) presents of a well-scrubbed mankind, of measured creatures subject to the tyranny of scientific exactitude, but it also follows the lead given by science on two basic points.

The first point is that of the very status of skin. In the Age of Enlightenment, skin was a simple enclosure protecting the body from outside aggression, but as a result of the nineteenth-century developments in histology and dermatology skin is now a veritable 'organ'[6]—just like the heart or the liver. As well as being a protective and sensorial membrane, it performs a number of metabolic functions which regulate the exchanges between the body and the outside world. A very significant change in itself, this shift in status only scratches the surface with regard to the much vaster contemporary change in the way life itself was considered, which resulted in the human body no longer being envisaged as a closed system. It is now only one piece in the entire puzzle of the world of living organisms. What is more, the study of the body now involves chemistry and physics, which were once thought to have nothing to do with 'life sciences'. At whatever level man is now considered, he can no longer be studied without taking his milieu into account. Most of the artists of the last one hundred years seem to have grasped the extent of this change. They have abandoned the veil of appearances, through which there shone a hidden reality which has since become dim, and are now trying to show us the invisible interplay of relations between the body and universe within which it evolves. In short, the aim is now to delimit the 'inappearance' of man; that inappearance which so appealed to Apollinaire when he dreamt of a statue which would take the form of a mould set up underground, and thus negate all the usual norms of human figuration. Classical art believed that form came from inside—hence the need to study anatomy. Modern art is built on the opposite idea: form is the result of the pressures exerted by milieu. In their own immediate way Body Art and Performance Art use many scientific techniques—from live experimentation to ethology—in investigating exaltation, fear and protest (consider also, for example, Beuys defense of ecology).

The second point at which art and science—two different ways of 'remaking' the world—converge is undoubtedly the result of the vast field of interests covered by a study of the body. Nowadays there is so much data of so many kinds that the idea of forming an ordered sum of our knowledge (the old goal of science) is not only daunting but senseless. The further science advances on all fronts, the more the individual man has to settle for fragmentary knowledge. The validity of encyclopaedic knowledge has been undermined, and now there are only scraps of knowledge and white-coated specialists.

When one looks at the representation of the human body from Cubism to Body Art there can be no doubt that we are more tormented than ever by the dismemberment of the body, by the loss of unity. No envelope seems adequate enough to hold such a multi-faceted entity as man. The 'individual', in the sense of an 'individual body', almost seems to be a notion that has had its day. The individual's status is crumbling as his statue might. Isn't it true that we no longer feel the body to be a unique mechanism governed by a reassuring and maternal 'I' but rather an ensemble of mechanisms, most of which do not respond directly to our will? And in trying to coordinate the different roles and appearances these mechanisms impose upon us we find ourselves the victims of the Earthworm Syndrome: split into a legal, social, moral, physical and emotional person, one may not feel exactly that one has been cut up into bits but one certainly feels the need to cast one's skin.

The *disiecta membra* which art puts before us are clearly the result of the explosion of scientific knowledge of the body. Nowadays it is almost impossible for man to have a clear representation himself, for him to buckle on an image. Certainly there is no shortage of images; nor is it their abundance which makes it difficult to get them to agree with one another. The problem is that so many of these images are mutually incompatible but nonetheless fertile—a sure sign of a deep disturbance (which is also revealed by the growing number of contradictions within all of us). The idea of an overall approach, of a contemplation of a final organization of the facts, is no longer tenable; and in its demise, it takes with it the Ideal of Beauty, the canons of perfect proportions. Broken up, pulverized, the body can only take root in the vast nebula of possibilities. The only limit to this dispersion, to this glittering meta-body, is language itself, the exhaustion of language.

But perhaps the unity of the body was only ever a chimera, an illusion of the self, to which centuries of art have given a definite form—a form which now finds that the ground has disappeared from under its feet.

One last piece of news: the fingerprint has disappeared from our identity cards, and the photograph has given way to DNA. What has become of that opaque membrane which, smooth or wrinkled, was for the mankind of yesterday the very seal of identity? It seems to have had its hide saved. Cleaned, tanned and made-up, it is now, thanks to computer technology, selling well in clone form. Reduced to a electronic rag behind a screen, a virtual image, our skin can now be played upon by others, can now be transposed into situations that bear no relation to lived experience.

[1] Viollet-le-Duc, *À propos de l'enseignement des arts et du dessin*, (Paris, 1984), 94.
[2] Lecoq de Boisbaudran, *L'Éducation de la mémoire pittoresque et la formation de l'artiste*, (Paris, 1848, reprinted 1913), 43.
[3] Edouard Manet, letter to Georges Jeanniot, 1882, in *L'œuvre peint de Manet*, (Paris, 1970), 14.
[4] A. Breton, *Le Surréalisme et la peinture*, (Paris, 1928, reprinted 1965), 23.
[5] M. Duchamp, *Duchamp du signe*, ed. by M. Sancuillet, (Paris, 1975), 272.
[6] Long considered a mere covering for the body, the skin became an organ during the 19th century. Certain stages of the change include: Antoine Lavoisier's description of perspiration (1791); Xavier Bichat's presentation of tissue as the basic structure of bodily organs (1801); Jean Alibert's study of illnesses specific to the skin (1814); the coining of the word 'dermatology' (1836); Etienne-Jules Marey's calculation of heat exchange (1863); the development of histological pathology during the second half of the 19th century, mainly through the work of Paul G. Unna. The skin—dermis, epidermis and subcutaneous tissue—is the heaviest organ of the human body: about 7 kgs.

> To live is to be blind to one's own dimensions.
> CIORAN

One characteristic of the second half of this century is the 'boom' of anthropology—that is 'of a monographical natural history of mankind, written as a zoologist might write a study of an animal' (De Quatrefages). Man has become an object of study for himself and expects to be able to put together a body of knowledge centred round himself. Just like the form and functions of his body, his moral standards are approached from a 'scientific' point of view, in full accordance with a methodology based on careful observation and experimentation. These 'Lessons on Mankind' move in two interconnected but contradictory directions. On the one hand, they try to find the deep identity that is shared by a particular group, to produce the single figure of a 'type'; on the other, they emphasize the inexhaustible differences between subjects, and thus emphasis the single as against the whole and try to describe the identity of an 'individual'.

A Made-to-measure Identity

by Philippe Comar

The Measure of the Individual

The only plates in Diderot and d'Alembert's *Encyclopédie* which give tables of figures and measurements are those with images of the human body that are used to illustrated the entry 'Drawing'. The figure given exemplifies the proportions established by Classical canons of beauty—rules that are the last vestiges of a science of the beautiful, of a belief that one could measure beauty. One century later anthropology was imposing a new approach to the human body; ideal proportions had been replaced by the measurement of individual variations. Hundreds of thousands of individuals had been exhaustively measured then compared and classified. In 1876 Paul Topinard wrote: 'anthropometry is one of the most promising areas of anthropological research'. In attempting to reduce the multiple variations between individuals to a few physical measurements, anthropologists were in fact attempting to establish some sort of correlation between the measurement of the corporeal and of the mental. A number of theories, which have now been abandoned, tried to establish such things as the correlation between skull size and intelligence, or between the inclination of facial bones and the degree of evolution. The measurement of the human form was, therefore, not aimed simply at establishing a physical morphology but also at describing intellectual, moral and cultural identity.

Judicial Identity

Over the period 1880–90, Alphonse Bertillon reformed the system used by the judiciary in establishing identity.

45

Up to then police descriptions had used a few vague morphological features but had had no reliable criteria for the certain identification of an individual—because it was easy for suspects to lie about their background or previous convictions. To resolve this shortcoming with regard to those who already had a criminal record, Bertillon decided to index all prisoners on the basis of the most durable feature of the human body—the length of its bones. He perfected a system of anthropometric classifications which made it possible to establish the identity of one individual out of the hundreds of thousands who had been registered, simply on the basis of seven measurements. This system, he wrote, 'made it possible to identify a person previously measured, whatever physical changes may have occurred to them during the period since measurement'. The anthropometric information was backed up by fingerprints, a note on the colour of the eyes and by full-face and profile photographs (complete with an indication of scale reduction). When Bertillon published his *La Photographie judiciaire* in 1890, the reform of the criminal identification system was practically complete—and the success of 'Bertillonnage' led to it being adopted in most Western countries. Gradually, photographic identification, which had initially been reserved for those members of society who were considered dangerous, was extended to cover the entire population. In 1990, a century after the creation of the police identification records, the whole system was computerised.

Human Catalogues

On the eve of the twentieth century the compilation of inventories of individuals spread from the more restricted fields of scientific study and law enforcement to all domains in which the body played a part— fashion, health and fitness, beauty care, art, eroticism. Photographic albums such as those put together by Calavas inventoried thousands of bodies (of men, women and children), which were offered for perusal by the curious, or by amateur and professional artists looking for possible models. In the United States, Muybridge tried to compile a catalogue of all the possible poses of the human body in motion, and created the monumental encyclopaedia which became an ABC for painters and sculptors. In France Charcot's assistant at Salpêtrière, Richer (who later became professor of anatomy at the École des Beaux-Arts) photographed hundreds of men and women, measured them exhaustively and completed his morphological identification files with a few more general notes on each model: 'Playful character. Heart on his sleeve. Loves life, the pleasures of the flesh. Solid appetite, Straight sternum. Pelvis very sloping. Depression at the

top of the Sacrum. The top of the division between the buttocks not very deep'. At about the same time Pierre Louÿs was compiling another sort of inventory with rather different files. Over a period of almost thirty years the writer kept a scrupulous account of all his female acquaintances and supplemented his clinical observations with photographs, which are numbered and classified by organ, form, position, size. Thus the body became something that could be compiled, like a table of figures.

From the Average Man to Typology

At the turn of the century, whilst anthropology was revealing the extent of the physical variations between individuals, it was also making a contribution to the emergence of typology—the classification of racial, morphological and psychosomatic types. The aim was to lump together a group of individuals in one image that reflected their shared characteristics. The use of scientific measurement revolutionized the approach to the study of human types, which in itself dates back to Antiquity. Applying statistical methods to the study of the human and social body, the Belgian mathematician, Adolphe Quételet, proposed a theory of The Average Man. This ideal, which stripped men of all individuality, was the first concrete example of an attempt to portray Mr Man-in-the-Street.
The search for the unchanging physical traits within a given human group led anthropologists to stress the existence of different human types, which could be identified by the predominance of a specific morphological characteristic. But whilst the analysis of types makes it possible to base arguments on certain simple models, it has the disadvantage of relying on arbitrary criteria that are often open to criticism. Which body meets the norm? Which is discarded because it fails to meet it? As Paul Broca was already commenting last century: 'the definition of a group precedes precise knowledge of all the elements of which it is made up'. Categories are not safe from the influence of prejudices—and in Italy Lombroso tried to compile the portrait of Criminal Man, Prostitute Woman and Man of Genius; whilst in England Francis Galton, a cousin of Darwin's, suggested superimposing the photographs of various criminals one on top of the other so as to create a 'general portrait' in which all the shared stigmata of the criminal would be apparent. In France, Sigaud and Mac Auliffe directed research towards the discovery of types based on bodily constitution. On the eve of the First World War the French Ministry of War actually set up a Morphology Laboratory which would screen soldiers physiologically: according to whether the recruits were of the 'muscular', 'respiratory', 'digestive' or

'cerebral' type, they would be employed as infantrymen, cavalrymen, gunners or clerks. In 1930s Germany typology was even introduced in psychiatry, with Kretschmer trying to establish a link between physical formation and mental condition (both normal and abnormal).

The Model of the 'Healthy' Man
At the turn of the century, the inventoried images of the human body led to the emergence of artistic canons which were based solely on statistics derived from data. The ancient notion of harmony—which saw beauty as depending on proportion between parts and whole—was replaced by the notion of the average. All pathological or 'deviant' forms were excluded, and the authors of these new canons aimed to promote the image of the 'healthy man' as an artistic model. 'We have replaced the aesthetic notion of the beautiful with the scientific notion of the perfect', wrote Richer in 1902. The treatises on artistic anatomy published in the first quarter of this century took the body of the athlete as their ideal—as a result partly of the recent discoveries on the physiology of bodies in motion, but also as a result of the theories put forward by those social reformers who advocated the development and improvement of the human species. In 1902 Marey's assistant, Georges Demeny wrote: 'We submit our animals to selection, breeding and training, in order to benefit from them more. However, we do not have the energy to apply the same procedures to ourselves—even if we are sure the results of such an application would excede our expectations'. Demeny was also sure of 'the influence of physical exercise on beauty'. Just as Europe was about to experience the explosion of Cubist and Abstractionism, this praise of the athletic body did not only set new aesthetic norms it also opened the way to Eugenics, to the quest for a superior type of humankind—something which would be central to the Nazi ideology.
Perhaps the 1937 Munich exhibition designed to show the enormous gap between New German Art and Degenerate Art was the most pathetic demonstration there could have been of the split between an official art which was characterized by a return to order and measure, and a 'non-official' art which refused to submit to established norms and aimed to give the human body a new appearance. The art which claimed it was creating a new human body on scientific criteria could do no better than Arno Breker's stiff and academic nudes. Whilst the art which, in the name of those same biometric criteria, was being set up for public ridicule included powerful and innovative works by the likes of Otto Dix, Emil Nolde and Max Beckmann.

At the beginning of this century, therefore, anthropometry set itself the task of enclosing identity within an unvarying construction of measurements. In 1913, Marcel Proust opens the first volume of *La Recherche* with a discussion of the fluidity of the features of the human face, which makes all portraiture relative. He describes the mixture of joy and fear he felt as a child when he projected the magic lantern image of Golo onto the walls of his bedroom and the body of the knight adapted itself to the mouldings of the cornice, the folds of the curtains: 'The body of Golo himself, as supernatural in essence as that of his horse, adapted itself to every material obstacle, every hindrance he encountered, by absorbing it and making it part of the body itself. Just as his pale face immediately adapted itself to the doorknob'. The superficial identity of the face is here doubled by an alterity behind the surface. No fixed measure holds the depth in place, and thus there opens up another dimension to being.

Judicial signalling lesson in Paris, early XX cent.

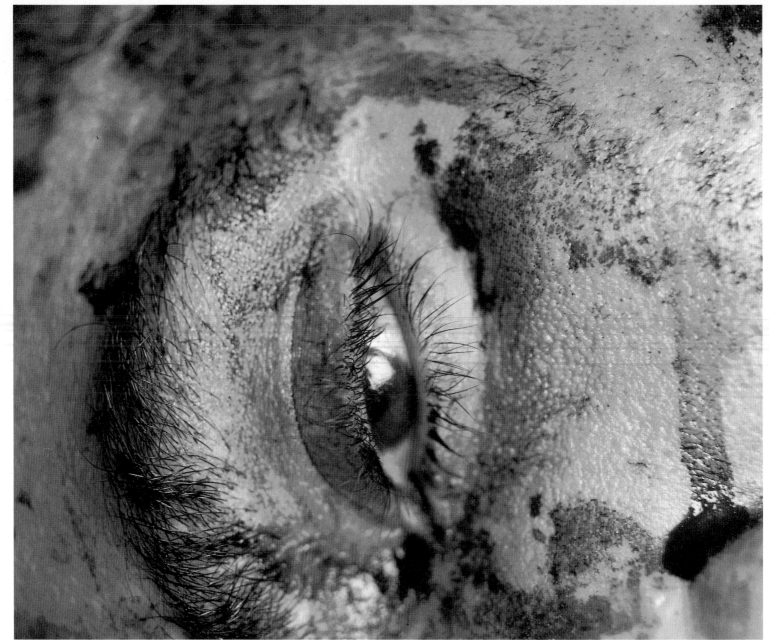

Andres Serrano
Hacked to Death II
1992

Ars moriendi: Andres Serrano

by Marcel Brisebois

Montreal. Seven o'clock in the evening, the time for the TV news on both channels—one from Paris, the other from New York. Time to relax after work. Time to eat. The television has pictures of the fighting in Grozny, the bodies of Russian and Chechen civilians who have been shot and left to rot in the streets. Yesterday there were the same sort of pictures from Bosnia and then from Ruanda. Pictures of violence and disasters. Pictures of the horrors of war, the same horrors that were portrayed by Jacques Callot, Francisco Goya or Leon Golub. No one is scandalized, no one protests. The journalists are only doing their job: providing information. The media are only doing theirs too: continually outbidding each other with offers of news. Any news is fit to be reported or shown. As for the viewers; they either want to be informed or else are willing to settle for an entertainment which allows some escape from the suffocating daily routine. And journalists, media and viewers are all equally concerned by the need for objectivity. In submitting to these almost apocalyptic images, one confesses oneself both irresponsible and helpless. At best one will join one of those humanitarian organizations which try to help the victims. At the same time, on another channel, the presenter of a talkshow is protesting about the presence in a state-run museum of a series of photographs by Andres Serrano entitled *The Morgue*. Public indignation will subsequently become such that the Minister of Culture himself will consider it opportune to appear in a later programme to explain his own position on the matter.

Let's admit it, these large colour photographs (125.7×152.5 cm) are so shocking that one's first reaction is one of repulsion, even disgust. But what exactly is at stake here? How are these pictures using the ambiguous ways in which western societies both expose and hide the bodies of the dead? What do they add to the ways in which art represents death?

The Morgue is a corpus of some twenty photographs which present fragments of bodies that have suffered accidental death (*Death by Fire, Burnt Victim*), violent death (*Hacked to Death II*, on exhibition here, *Knifed to Death*) or death from natural causes (*Fatal meningitis, Infections Pneumonia*). The pictures were taken in an American morgue, but the actual setting of the bodies is never shown; the reference to the morgue is, therefore, a metonymic one. What is more, no body is shown in its entirety—so that in many cases if we were not forewarned we would think we were looking at a photograph of a new-born baby, or perhaps of someone sick or asleep.

In this work *The Morgue* was Andres Serrano trying to break a taboo? Was he not perhaps trying to oppose

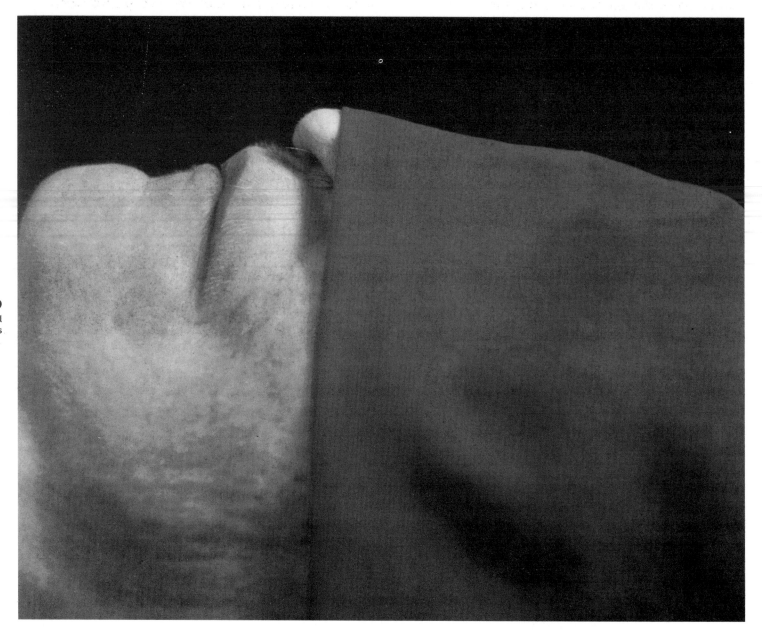

Andres Serrano
Infections Pneumonia
1992

that bourgeois vision of death as something strictly private, the source of feelings that are too intimate to be shared? Was he looking back to a world of past feelings or forward to the emergence of a new image of death? The conventions governing the representation of death in Western art have often changed. There was the representation of the anonymous dead, the representation of a dead body which could be identified by its attributes, and the dead man recognisable by his facial features. There is the allegorical representation of Death at work: the blind Fate cutting the thread, the old man with a scythe harvesting his victims, vanities which remind one of the passage of time and the inevitable end of all human beings. Other representations chose to show the glorious, immortal body of a saint or hero. And each one of these works reflected western man's changing sensibility with regard to death. Sometimes they emphasized the ineluctability of death, of the fate which gives gravity and weight to the 'unbearable lightness of being'. *Memento mori*, in effect. On other occasions, the works emphasized the regenerative role of death in the evolution of the species. Like sex, death was seen as a force of nature, an irresistible violence which could be mastered by rituals, tamed by being transformed into spectacle. But whilst it is the common lot of mankind, the final act of justice—that is, deliverance from a miserable existence—death is also the last action of my life, the last action which makes sense of all the rest, which enables me to achieve my true identity, to express my essential self. 'Would you die if you were forbidden to write?' But repugnant, absurd, distressing death does not make sense of anything. And even that end is not the end: life does not come to a stop, it changes and transforms itself—and once started, the dialogue continues in the commemorations which keep the memory of the dead alive. Grünewald, Holbein, Zurbaran, Titian, Poussin and Delacroix are only a few who have dealt with these themes, putting them together as the leitmotifs of a very personal music.

And Serrano? You will already have understood that this work is in no way a piece of reportage on the working and personnel of a modern morgue; even if the way the works are hung cannot but remind one of the refrigerated drawers used in such establishments. However, if the purpose of the medical/legal institution of the morgue is to identify the dead body and establish the cause of death, then these pictures are of very little practical worth. Serrano's subjects have no social identity apart from that which we afford them; their biography is limited to the terse description the artist gives of their death. These corpses are not whole: we only see fragments of them. Was this to spare us images that would be even more harassing, or was it because only what is shown to us was worthy of interest? Where does one draw the line between censure and attention to strictly significant details, between the incapacity to describe continuity and the expression of a reality that cannot be grasped any other way? 'Fragments' wrote Pontalis, 'overwhelm one at first'.

Serrano achieves the desired effect, even more so because he presents this nightmarish reality in such a refined way: picture-format, neutral background, careful attention to details, an eye for colour—these all mean that images of the unbearable are presented as works of art. In spite of his Latin-American origins, Serrano cannot be situated in the baroque tradition. There is no emphatic gesture here, but rather a neo-classical purity which rejects all appeal to sentiment. Voyeurism is equally absent from these works. What is left is that one eye in the middle of a close-up on part of a human face. The haunted stare of an sightless eye which, without love or animosity, seems fixed on those fateful events which deprived it of life. 'Both the world and life are, in truth, too fragmentary', said Heine. Beauty and abjection, illness, hate, death and art themselves are all equally fragmentary. They reveal their rent nature when they do not emphasize the fracture.

Jean Hélion
La jeune fille et le mort
1957

Portrait, Mask, Hood
Otto Dix, Jean Hélion, Philip Guston

by Didier Ottinger

The face and the human body have always opposed stubborn resistance to any sort of formalist manipulation. Logically enough it was Futurism, the first of the great avant-garde movements, which made the banishment of the Nude part of its official 1911 manifesto: 'We demand the total suppression of nudes in paintings for the next ten years!'[1]. Cubism then neglected the nude and more or less ignored the portrait, developing instead through a study of landscape to then fully express itself in the Still Life. If Fernand Léger's stove-pipe robots or the automata of Malevitch and Gromaire prefigure modern man, then one has to admit that History did actual bring this Modernist future to pass: artists had only just conceived the man-robot when the chaos of the First World War made him a reality. Modernist man fitted in nicely with his destiny: anonymous, functional, interchangeable. In post-war Germany, Otto Dix's work first expressed caustic disappointment with progress then very soon became a fully-fledged accusation against the pure spirit, the irrelevance, of the avant-garde. Dix had been amongst the first to express his faith in technological progress. In fact, he gave the impression of being positively inebriated by the future it seemed to herald and, like the Italian Futurists, he sang the praises of the machine and became an apologist for speed and movement. Like the Futurists, he believed that the war and violence unleashed by technology would have a regenerating effect upon mankind. Enraptured by the contemplation of the Futurist god, Mars[2], Dix euphorically envisaged the birth of a new order and a new type of mankind. Avant-garde painting had caught a glimpse of what this New Man would be like, then along came the war and, in the trenches of Flanders, reality had the bad taste to take over from Utopia. Before turning the landscape into linear abstractions, the gunshells in the sky traced dynamic lines which could have come from a painting by Carra or Severini. In St. Petersburg one year before war broke out, Malevitch and the co-signatories of a 'futurist' manifesto put on a theatrical piece entitled *The Victory over the Sun*. 'The bodies were sliced into pieces by light beams. Turn and turn about, they lost arms, legs, head, because for Malevitch they were only geometrical bodies subject not only to division into constituent parts but also to complete disintegration within the space of the picture'[3]. The future by then was close at hand: the explosions and battlefield surgery of Verdun would make the survivors into strange Cubist-futurist figures. And Otto Dix had a front row seat for the entire show. First of all, he painted the portrait of the 'smashed faces' of the survivors, but then he quickly moved on from recording reality to denouncing it. His *Card Players* of 1920 is full

53

of references to Cubism. The cane-chairs, the newspapers, the playing-cards, however, are even less 'cubist' than the actual faces of the players: the chin turned up into the cheek, the metal jaw, the feet that can grip cards as hands might do—the anatomical inventivity would be masterful, almost insanely daring, if it weren't that the picture simply records reality itself. Dix is burying his illusions, deliberately mixing up the formalism of the avant-garde with the work of History. He adopts the realism of New Objectivity so as to better denounce the flightiness, the incurable naiveté of the formalist avant-gardes of his day. Georges Grosz gives voice to the same sort of disillusionment: 'It is an error to think that because an individual paints circles, cubes or the profound troubles of the human soul he is therefore a revolutionary'[4]. Schad, a leading figure in Zurich Dadaism, moved to Bavaria in 1920, and he too expresses the same sort of feelings: 'Once I'd got to Munich, in a Germany that had been abandoned to its destiny, I initially wanted to go on with the typewritten images; but the context had changed, and the whole thing seemed to have suddenly become derisory'[5]. War had made Utopia impossible.

In his 1923 *Self-portrait with model* Otto Dix answers the smooth surfaces and ideal forms of Gromaire's humbug, the robotic forms of Léger and Sclemmer, with a depiction of his own wrinkle-lined face and the streaked skin of his model. The realism of Dix, Schad and Grosz also contradicts another type of New Man— the utopian figures that were beginning to emerge from the official Academies of Stalin, Hitler and Mussolini— all those stereotypes of some sort of racial utopia, which in their attempts to accumulate all the characteristics of Aryan or Soviet Man in fact produce nothing but synthetic figures that nowadays remind us of computer graphics. In their attempt to incarnate all the virtues of motherhood and fertility, Saliger's *Grâces* (The Graces) look like inflatable women—proving, once more, that 'functional' art always ends up performing its task by the creation of laughable, pitiable organs. Otto Dix's *The Graces* are very different: the models alongside whom he portrays himself in 1923 and 1924, are such vital individuals that they almost verge on caricature. Real blood is coursing beneath their loose skin; their body hair is unashamedly luxuriant.

Dix's realism, his headstrong attachment to the *principium individuationis* are his answer to the abstractions which would reduce the image of man to the simple application of an equation. At the beginning of the 1930s, Jean Hélion saw radical abstraction as the militant, committed alternative to the figurative art being churned out by the totalitarian regimes in Europe. Like Mondrian (whose Neo-

plasticism he was to adopt himself), like the Russian Constructivists or the painters of the Bauhaus (whose definition of Concrete Art he made his own), Hélion saw objectivity, rationality and 'constructed art' as expressing values which were part of a much vaster cultural and social project. In 1930, together with van Doesburg, Carlsund,and Tutundjan, he formed the first French avant-garde movement to champion non-figurative art. 'One cannot deny that these paintings have a social power', he wrote in the first issue of the review *Abstraction-Création*[6]. To prove that abstract painting was truly the standard, the emblem of a new humanism, he gave his mid-1930s compositions all the hieratic pose, the proud majesty of Philippe de Champaigne's ceremonial paintings. The message was clear: a new type of mankind, a regenerate classicism, could emerge from the values of measure and clarity that lay at the very heart of Abstract Art. This enthusiasm culminated in the large compositions painted at the end of the 1930s; but it did not withstand the upheavals brought about by History.

In the very year that the Second World War broke out, Jan Hélion painted a *Composition dramatique* (Dramatic Composition) and a *Figure tombée* (Fallen Figure) which are very clear on this point. Here we see the cones, cylinders and spheres that had made up the *Figures* of the previous years thrown to the ground in disorder— and their downfall marks the crumbling of Hélion's own ideals, of his faith in the irresistible progress of culture and reason. The Nazi tanks unleashed on Europe, the cowardice of international politics had rased his utopia to the ground, smashed the monuments he had raised to it.

Hélion enlisted but was taken prisoner in June 1940 and interned in a camp in Pomerania, from which he escaped to the U.S.A. It was there he published an account of his imprisonment and escape which was also an act of defiance against his former jailers—*They shall not have me*. In it he says 'I have travelled the length of Europe, as far as the Soviet Union, and I have come back laden with human problems. The more I threw myself into abstraction, the more concerned I was with human problems—which is a bloody contradiction because I have always thought that art should express everything the man has inside. Other people can separate things—their ideas to one side, their art on the other'[7].

In the U.S.A, he took up his paintbrush again and produced several *Saluers* (Saluters) and some *Allumeurs* (Igniters), which it is tempting to see as self-portraits. These figures have the insolence of those who are braving the enemy. Shortly before going back to Europe, in 1939, Hélion painted some rigid formalist heads which are still inspired by an abstract geometrical logic. But after the war—after his own war—Hélion's style changed radically. The *Salueurs* are supple; their sinuous lines are a clear announcement that the painter now sides with the moving, organic forms of the real world. 'Avoid straight lines in human beings', he notes in his 1946 *Carnets*[8]. Like Dix, Hélion was converted to realism by the tragic events of war. The proud, casually elegant figure of the *Allumeur* is reacting to the humiliations, the greyness of war.

However, in 1945 the number of victims far exceeded the number of those who had escaped or managed to resist. First American soldiers, then the entire American nation, discovered the full extent of Nazi barbarity, and the numerous 'melancholic' nudes which Hélion drew and painted after 1945 represented his own state of mind. The *Figures gothiques* (Gothic Figures) are the answer to the abstract *Figures* of the 1930s—with abstraction now a question of mutilation and crutches. Between the two groups of paintings came the war, after which the intolerable sight of the concentration camps had dealt a hard blow to the very image mankind might have of itself. Fautrier painted 'hostages' who have been rendered into shapeless matter by the cruelty and contempt of their torturers. Bacon and Giacometti dedicated themselves to depicting a mankind that had been stripped of all identity by the barbarity of recent history. Four years before his death, in 1984, Jean Hélion looked back at this period: 'I think that all the important things in this world are connected; they echo each other, explain each other. The total exclusion of natural images from painting—in part, the result of the development of painting itself—coincided, accidently one might say, with the exclusion from humanity of millions of human beings. I am not saying that this caused that; but that these things happened at the same time reveals disturbances of equal profundity'[9]. Modernism in painting has always judged the portrait as an obsolete genre. Whilst Hegel could still claim that 'progress in painting, from its first imperfect attempts, has always been in the direction of perfect portraiture'[10], Modern Art seems to see the evolution of art in terms of the gradually effacement of the portrait.

After the Second World War the re-awakening of belief in an avant-garde utopia stimulated new controversies in America about the validity of figurative art. Clement Greenberg, the champion of the New Formalism, repeated André Breton's anathemas against portraits painted from nature. Recalling no doubt how Breton had fallen out with Giacometti the day the painter had told him how much he wanted to go back to painting 'from life', Greenberg declared that portraiture was impossible for modernist painters.

Otto Dix
Selbstbildnis
mit nacktem Modell
1923

At the end of the 1940s Guston became such a modern painter, abandoning the figurative painting he had previously practiced (though he did go on producing caricatures, which were intended for himself alone). The adaptation to Action Painting was not without its difficulties, but after the deaths of Jackson Pollock and Franz Kline in 1956 and 1962 respectively, Guston was one of the few survivors of the historic generation of Abstract Expressionists left in New York. Thus one can imagine the scandal when he decided to paint his self-portrait in 1969. In a style which was soon being compared to that of contemporary underground comic-strips, Guston showed himself at work in his studio, his face hidden by a Klu Klux Klan hood. 'A Mandarin making fools of idiots,' wrote the critic Hilton Kramer in the *New York Times*[11].

But the scandal was due less to the fact of Guston's volte-face than to the fact that his painting had the appearance of an act of accusation. No one missed the point—the hooded figure was that of the modernist painter in general, the type of painter Guston himself had been, the type of painter who would denounce this figurative development in his art. At the bottom of the work Guston put Greenberg's anathema against portraits—thus making his painting into a 'portrait' of formalist bigotry and intolerance.

A few years later another modernist painter made his self-portrait into an act of accusation. For his Spring 1974 exhibition at the Leo Castelli Gallery in New York, Robert Morris produced a poster which shows him stripped to the waist, with a chain round his neck and a Nazi helmet on his head. Morris's work had continually tried to undermine the conscious and unconscious structures of power, so he had already taken a critical stance with regard to the ideological forms of modernism; but now he was denouncing its puritanism and authoritarianism.

In 1977, when he read the English translation of Michel Foucault's *Discipline and Punish*, his intuitions became certitudes. He took grids and other minimalist schema and, on the basis of Foucault's work, reinterpreted them as panopticon prisons. The 1974 self-portrait had already revealed the shady, the unconscious side of the link between a modernist artist and his public. Just as Guston had done in 1969, Morris offers an image of himself (this time, a sado-masochist one) which serves as an emblem; the image is the paradoxical mask which reveals the real face.

After that first 1969 self-portrait, Guston returned to the genre several times (producing works in which his face was clearly recognisable, however). He portrays himself as a tubercle with an hypertrophied eye; he shows himself as a slave to tobacco or drink, or both

at the same time. In other paintings he is whipping himself—and soon the whip becomes like another brush for the figurative painter, the painter of self-portraits. After his irremediable return to figurative painting, Guston increasingly used symbols which identified his art with vice, with evil in the widest possible sense. Ironic and provocative, Guston played with the historic and moral heresy which made him paint the way he did: artistic 'purity', avant-garde 'idealism' were associated with culpable indifference to the world. '...The world, what happened in America, the brutality of the world. What sort of a man am I, sitting in my house, reading magazines, getting angry over nothing—and then going to my studio to put some red together with some blue. I told myself that there must be another way of acting. I knew that a road was opening up before me—the beginning of a road that still wasn't clear. I wanted to be whole again, like when I was a kid... when thought and feeling went together'[12]. When he paints himself giving in to vice in the pampered solitude of his studio, Guston is attacking the indifference and egoism of the formalist artist.

In this century has the self-portrait ever been anything other than an act of resistance, defiance? How can one help thinking so when one looks at Malevitch's 1933 self-portrait, in which the artist has adopted the costume and pose of a fifteenth-century merchant? Or again, when one looks at the whole range of historical costumes that De Chirico chose for his self-portraits, finally ending up in 1959 depicted with all the derisive grandeur of a seventeenth-century gentleman. And what about Beckmann—whose self-portraits mix together proud insolence and the costumes of clown or acrobat? More recently there has been Lucian Freud, who chose to portray himself as some sort of Apelles in carpet slippers, short-circuiting gravitas and provocation[13].

In the present century, self-portraiture is no anodyne exercise. Modernism repressed it because it knew that a self-portrait is uncontrollable, that one cannot neatly circumscribe its meaning or form. A self-portrait overflows, spreading doubt and confusion in an aesthetic universe which aspires to be one of norms and measure. Meaning trickles through a self-portrait. For a long time the genre was considered synonymous with introspection. In the distant light of Romanticism, a self-portrait opened the door to the fever and torture racking the creative soul. From van Gogh to Schönberg, a self-portrait was the most eloquent image of genius. From Antonin Artaud to Franz Pohl it reveals the upheavals, the convulsions of the soul. A self-portrait was considered the most direct means of access to the mystery of inspiration. Modernism was only too willing to abandon the grimy smithies of feverish genius, preferring to be with the erudite, the experimenters who operate by the light of day. For modernism, self-portraiture is too heavily tainted with unfathomable interiority. However, even in its relation with the external world the self-portrait refuses to be mastered. More than other paintings it imposes itself as a 'presence'. It is the subject par excellence. It stares back at us.

Modernism has always been against works which establish a dialogue with the spectator. Michael Fried sees this exchange as belonging to the world of 'theatre'. In a famous essay [14] in which he attacks the aesthetics of Minimalist Art, the critic cites the theatricality of the works of Judd and Morris. He reproaches them for being anthropomorphic, for being obstinately 'objective' and thus imposing a 'presence', setting up moments of dialogue with their spectator. This theatricality, which invites spectator and actor to switch roles, is, according to Michael Fried, the very negation of painting. 'There is a war between theater and modernist paintings, between theater and the pictorial' [15].

If Minimalism does contravene the Modernist orthodoxy that Fried defends it is because it inverts that Cartesian order which guarantees the spectator, the observer, an unshakeable grasp on the world. (In this sense, modernist aesthetics are heir to that paradigm of classic vision which Michel Foucault traced so well in the structure of Velázquez's *Las Meninas*). Fried casts light on this aesthetic 'inversion' by analysing the sculptor Tony Smith's account of his immersion in a landscape. This experience is interpreted as 'coming from outside', as being the 'source of an exchange which turns the subject into object' [16]. Like Tony Smith's landscape, Minimalist works usurp the place traditionally occupied by the spectator because they are autonomous *qua* objects. Fried describes Smith's sculptures as 'defying' the spectator. Philip Guston, who was well-aware of the full power of self-portraits, offers an explicit illustration of this stance in a series of works consisting of eyes painted on bare canvas.

This exchange, this dialogue, this 'theatricality' all undermine the chronometry of the aesthetic experience. In fact, formalism requires that such experience be instantaneous. Fried says that 'if we were infinitely perspicacious then only one, infinitely brief, instant would be enough to see and experience the work in all its depth and plenitude...' [17].

The atavistic links between the self-portrait and the revelation of Romantic genius necessarily mean that paintings of this genre are subject to a careful scrutiny which attempts to decipher the imprint of a soul within the work. Such paintings, therefore, reject the idea of a uni-directional, 'instant' aesthetic experience. Self-portraits are, for modernist orthodoxy, the most heretical of works.

In painting portraits and self-portraits, artists are implicitly attacking the idealism behind modernism; they are rejecting its authoritarianism, its belief in 'the progress of art', its obsessive manipulation of feelings and faculties. The self-portrait does not set up one order to combat another; its world is one of uncertainty, of a goal that is never reached (which explains why the genre can become an obsession with some artists). A self-portrait is an open question. And nowadays those are more important than all the certainties in the world.

[1] Conclusion to *Manifeste technique des peintres futuristes*, 11 April 1910, in the catalogue to the exhibition *Le Futurisme*, Paris, Musée national d'Art moderne, 19 September–19 November 1973, 57–60.
[2] Cf. *Autoportrait en Mars* (Self-portrait as Mars), 1915.
[3] J.–H. Martin, *Casimir Malévitch. Fonder une ère nouvelle*, in the catalogue to the exhibition *Malevitch*, Paris, Musée national d'Art Moderne, 14 March–15 May 1978, 11.
[4] George Grosz and Wieland Herzfelde, 1925, quoted by Berthold Hinz, *La peinture durant le IIIe Reich et l'antagonisme de ses origines*, in the catalogue to the exhibition *Les réalismes 1919–1939*, Paris, Musée national d'Art moderne, 17 December 1980–20 April 1981, 120.
[5] Quoted by I. Lebeer, *Entretien avec Christian Schad, Cahiers du musée national d'Art moderne*, 79, 1, July–September 1979, 75.
[6] Quoted by D. Abadie, *Hélion ou a force des choses*, (Brussels, 1975), 77.
[7] Op. cit., 16–17
[8] J. Hélion, *Journal d'un peintre. Carnets 1929–1962*, (Paris, 1992), 93.
[9] J. Hélion, *Mémoires de la chambre jaune*, (Paris, 1994), 201.
[10] G.W.F. Hegel, *Aesthetics*.
[11] *A mandarin pretending to be a stumblebum, New York Times*, 25/10/1970.
[12] *In the Realm of the Carceral*, 1978.
[13] *Travail du peintre, réflexion*, 1993.
[14] *Art and objecthood, Artforum*, New York, June 1967.
[15] Op. cit., 27.
[16] Op. cit., 20.
[17] Op. cit., 27.

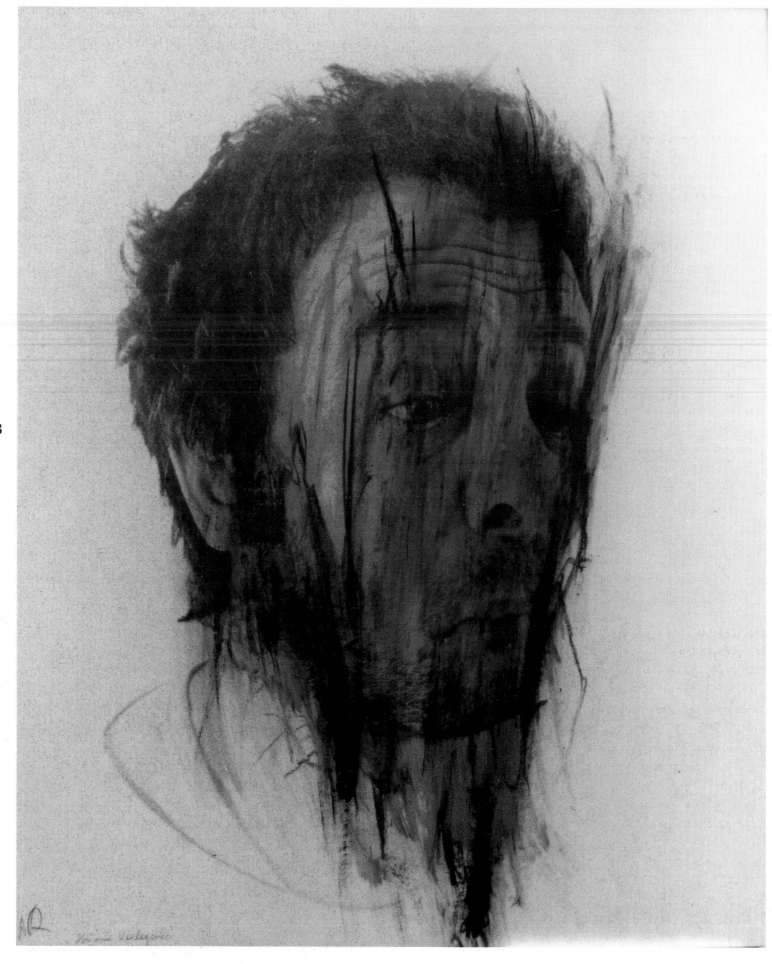

Arnulf Rainer
Stumm Verlegenes
1970

Sacrifice

Arnulf Rainer, Rudolf Schwarzkogler and Günter Brus: works on the human body

by Cathrin Pichler

What I am / is not written / is not represented in man / Man is simply an opaque block / moved by what is repressed / rejected / what is not revealed / in which each gesture is spontaneous revelation.
ANTONIN ARTAUD

'I spit on you. I spit on your shirts'.
Thus Arnulf Rainer to those present at a vernissage in Vienna in the 1950s. A provocative way of presenting oneself to the public, which was taken even further by the Viennese 'Actionists' of a few years later (Otto Mühl, Hermann Nitsch, Günter Brus and Rudolf Schwarzkogler) and culminated in the 1968 'Art and Revolution' (involving Günter Brus, Otto Mühl, Peter Weibl, Oswald Weiner, Franz Kaltenbäck and others)—an exhibition which marked the end of Viennese Actionism (with some of the artists being legally prosecuted and others actually expelled from Austria).
Rainer's confrontational approach and the Actions of the 1960s can all be seen as a reaction against the atmosphere of 'restoration' in Austrian art and society during the post-war years. Rainer had in fact been a member of the *Hundsgruppe*, whose Galerie St. Stephan was where contemporary art movements made their first appearance in 1950s Vienna.
There was a clear parallel between Austria's hidebound political life and the country's artistic isolation: the art world looked to the past and seemed to exclude any sort of discussion of what was happening internationally.
'A sort of moderate, well-mannered Modernism was tolerated; but the subversive revolutionary forces that are an integral part of art were ignored altogether—as was the reciprocal influence of art on our ways of seeing and thinking and vice versa (even though such influence was clear to everyone). Modern art irritated the "homely" way of seeing things which happened to be dominant at the time'[1].
Arnulf Rainer was thus the first artist to search out new approaches, to open up new paths for the spiritual in art (this was why he was to play such an important part in subsequent artistic movements which set themselves the same goals). Already in 1948, he had exhibited a painting entitled *Entry wound in the abdominal area caused by a 7 mm pistol fired at close range.*
From 'automatic painting' he moved on to Informal art—and in 1951 he exhibited a series of *Blind Drawings* and held an exhibition of empty frames (*Nadamalerei*). Action Painting then seemed to offer Rainer a way of revitalizing *Tachisme*. 'Painting to move beyond painting', was his programme. In the period up to 1965 he produced a number of action paintings and monochromes. This is how Werner Hofmann interpreted the idea behind his Action Painting: 'What does he put in place of what he rubs out? The maniacal act of

painting itself, which is constantly renewed and uninterruptedly paints and repaints picture after picture. Behind these icons of plenitude-vacuum there lies the desire for a meta-painting, something which embraces all painting within itself'[2]. Rainer would later see Action Painting as the pedagogical antithesis of his work using the language of the human body, which he began in 1972. The series of photographs he took of himself in various poses or pulling various faces, were explained as attempts at experiencing his own body: 'To make progress in my research into myself, I try to reproduce myself in concentrated form'. The products of this 'work with one's own body in front of a camera', were often modified and 'scratched' by Rainer, in an attempt to add to the intensity of expression and to emphasize individual features. Werner Hofmann has spoken of the 'paradox' of the fact that these formal modifications make the expressiveness of the work more intense—that the more the photograph is attacked, the fuller of life and energy it seems. And yet the wounds inflicted on the photograph are merely a continuation of the ill-treatment Rainer subjected himself to when he was in front of the camera, grimacing and pretending to strangle or torture himself'[3]. The act of painting becomes rooted on the surface of the photograph, and is then projected onto the human body through an elementary act of the body itself. Rainer describes the artistic intention behind these works by saying that art must be able 'develop new corporeal categories, new ways of expressing the body'.

Painting whilst under the influence of drugs was one of the ways Rainer had experimented with personal identity; and a similar concern can be seen behind his interest in the paintings of the mentally-ill (*l'art brut*). Reinhard Priessnitz has argued that the origin of this fascination is to be found in the resurgent slander of art as a mental disease: artists reacted against this commonplace and thence discovered 'forms of creative expression... [whose] intentions they feel not so very different from their own, given they deal with aspects of the problem of identity, which is fundamental to their own work'[4]. One can see a close link between Rainer's first series of grimaces (1969) and photographs that document the expressions of the mentally-ill. The later *Face Farces* were similarly reworked—as were the other figurative objects Rainer used (the representations of movement, the death masks, etc.). 'Through re-painting I emphasize corporeal expression, I analyze the movements and gestures of my own body'. The result is 'independent works of art whose aesthetic effectiveness is based on the tension between two processes of representation, and on the dialectical relation between identity and re-identity'[5].

Madness—the 'other side'—is seen as an unexplored region of new artistic experiences and opportunities. In his essay *Beauty and Madness*, Rainer says. 'while there: is enough oxygen left, one should plunge into the abyss where even madness is at home. Endless riches, convulsive beauty, incredible beings, kings, woods, gardens, princesses, buildings, precious stones, cherubs... I have seen them all there—and all of them more splendid than they appear in our culture'.

Rainer's gaze into the abyss seems to evoke all the myths that lay at the root of modernity: the breaking through the crust of reality, the discovery of identity beyond conventions and traditions, the use of self-experience in its most radical forms—all of these features, which can be found in Rimbaud and Artaud, are present in various forms in the artistic innovation and research that were integral to Viennese Actionism.

One of the first aims of the movement was to move beyond painting, to rupture the surface of the painting itself. This soon became a desire to move beyond the limits of art, to create a new link between art and life. This involved both a new metaphysical understanding of reality beyond the reality of being, and a practical programme of 'actions' which would introduce a salutary rupture into art and society. In all its forms, Actionism was a rebellion against the 'making-do' that was so much a part of post-war Austrian society. This 'making-do' had to be overcome by means of art: at the base of all the Actionists' programs and projects was an attempt to found identity—be it through self-therapeutic models, through experiences that were at the very limit of the self, or through asceticism, purification and mystical-religious experiences.

The first joint Actions took place shortly after 1960. In 1962 the manifesto *Die Blutorgel* (The Blood Organ) was published and Otto Mühl and Hermann Nitsch undertook a three-day Action entitled *Einmauerrungsaktion* (Closure of spaces through the construction of walls). Otto Mühl's first Concrete Action came in 1961, with his destruction of a painting. 'This is what Concrete Action is: action with materials and bodies in space. Painting has extended from the surface of the canvas into space itself'.

'Concrete Action is a representation of painting. It is self-therapy made visible through food products'[6]. Hermann Nitsch's idea for an *O.M. Theater* (Theater of Orgies and Mysteries) dated from 1957, and had already laid the foundations of Actionist Painting.

'My Actionist theater developed out of Informal Art and *Tachisme*. Painting itself—the production of a painting—becomes a visible process; and this led Action Painting to become the exhibition of the act of painting'[7].

Günter Brus's Actions started in 1963 and were centred

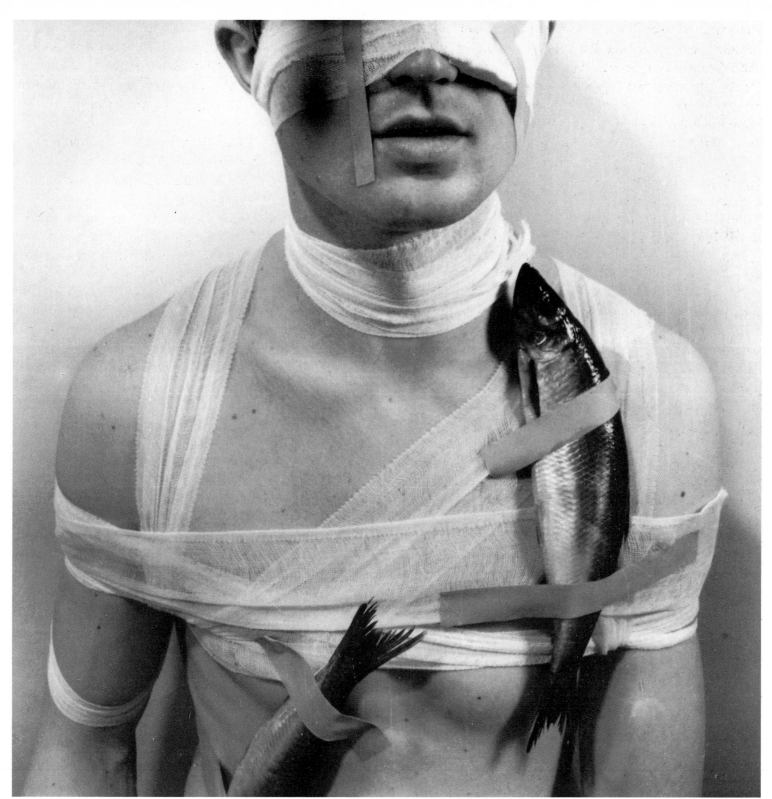

Rudolf Schwarzkogler
Action
Summer 1965

on the human body.

'Self-painting is a development in painting. Canvas is no longer the only possible surface for paint. Painting has moved back to its origins—to the wall, the living being, the human body. Self-painting is a controlled form of self-mutilation. Self-painting is suicide that can be savoured forever'[8].

At the beginning of his career as an actionist, Rudolf Schwarzkogler worked in collaboration with Otto Mühl and Hermann Nitsch. In 1965 he produced a number of Actions together with the latter.

In his manifesto *Panorama*, he says: 'Instead of constructing a painting one constructs the conditions for the act of painting—that is, one determines its range of action (the space around the painter, the real objects that are to be around him). The act of painting itself is released from the need to leave "remains", given that there are now machines that can reproduce images, that have taken over responsibility for passing on information. The timespan of the act of painting coincides with the time of exhibition. With the objects and elements of PANORAMA, moved within space and modified [...] it becomes possible to extend the act of painting into a complete action that can be experience through all five senses. As a spatial and temporal construct, the work becomes a plastic image that is open to multiple comprehension, through all the different apparatus of sense'[9].

The Actions of the 60s were concerned with radical renovation; they were also an occasion to confront and provoke the public. The artists imposed a radical challenge upon themselves, put themselves on the line be breaking taboos—something which often met with a hostile reception. Thus an attempt to renew art became part of a social and political critique. Events both within and without Actionism seem to have borne out what Otto Mühl said: 'It is all a reaching after the new, and the even newer—until, in the end, everything explodes'. Quite apart from their individual characteristics, all the works of Actionism can be broadly divided into two main categories—the Dionysiac and the Apollonian. The former would include the opulent, dramatic Concrete Actions of Otto Mühl along with the sensual Abreactions and ecstatic experiences exploited by Hermann Nitsch, whilst the latter would include Günter Brus's more hermeneutic works, in which reflection goes beyond the confines of the human body. A fundamental aim of Viennese Actionism was the conjunction of Art and Life—almost an identification of the two. And the means for achieving this identification was provided by the bodily senses. Experience and inner experience both play a central role in Actionism. Whilst Concrete Actions (Mühl) and the *O.M. Theater* (Nitsch) use the senses to mediate between experience and experience of the self, the works of Brus and Schwarzkogler operate at a more analytical or self-analytical level. But those analyses and the representative forms used in Actionism all serve to cast light on Being as exposed and surrendered to constrictions and commands from outside—and thus to precariousness and 'making-do'. 'Brus and Schwarzkogler [...] deal with the task of representing the destiny of man and his inability to adapt to it in a more complex and subtle way. Whilst Nitsch preferred planned, choral ritual, they—like Sartrean man—prefer to be alone, naked on the stage of the world. No hand is stretched forth to save them; everyone must work by himself to rid himself of his feelings of guilt—the straitjacket in *Ana* (Brus, 1964)— or accept the challenge of social indifference—*A walk in Vienna*, (Brus, 1965)'[10].

Schwarzkogler's Actions came after those of Mühl and Nitsch, and were all concentrated in the brief period from the beginning of 1965 to the spring of 1966—all in all, six fully-documented Actions along with numerous sketches and outlines. In line with Schwarzkogler's artistic manifesto as an Actionist, these works were not intended for the public but were photographed for circles of friends. Most of them were so-called 'table-top actions', with various material and objects arranged on a table in relation with the circumambient space and a human body.

Whilst the first Action, *Wedding*, makes clear references to the works of Nitsch and Mühl, the Actions that followed showed Schwarzkogler developing his own concrete, expressive language. He makes repeated use of white—white space, a white ball, white gauze—along with a black square of glass, fish, electric wires and surgical material. The organization of these materials in 'still lifes' highlights their connotations of coldness, menace and death. The quartering of the fish, the bandaging of head and penis, the conjunction of fish-head and penis—all symbolise wounding and castration. In his last Action, the artist covered his entire body in bandages, transforming it into an object amongst objects. These paintings-in-theater reduce and condense the language of figuration whilst giving expression to a chill, aggressive aesthetics. They symbolize existential menace, fear and vulnerability.

Schwarzkogler described art as a 'purgatory of the senses'. He spoke of a 'regeneration of our capacity for inner experience', with art helping us to 'kick the habit'. The central concern of both his art and life was our experience of self. Looking back, after his suicide in 1968, we can see just how radical his experiment with art really was. Bernd Matthaeus spoke of Schwarzkogler as of a *corps aliené*: 'he tore down the barriers of identity. His style was exhaustive without regard for limits. His indifference to suffering was a provocation to all of those who [...] consider suffering as something negative, and consider the loss of identity, the conscious transformation of identity, as the equivalent of death, negativity and closure'[11].

One might also describe Günter Brus's Actions as acts of aggression, as stepping-over the boundary of experience of the self. Naturally enough, this once more meant the extrovert 'exposure' of oneself to the public. After the 1964 Action *Painting in a space transformed into a labyrinth*, Günter Brus began work on *Ana*, a series of Actions using his own body: *Self-Painting/Self-Mutilation, Self-Mutilation, A Walk in Vienna, Tetanus* and *Transfusion* (all dating from 1965). In 1966 came two Total Actions (in collaboration with Otto Mühl), and a number of other Actions centred on his own body (*Action in a Circle, Destruction of the Head*). Günter Brus was the first Actionist to use his own body as a surface for paint and then as part of the Action itself. The artist painted his entire body white than decorated it with black signs, creating a 'corporeal object' that was then placed in relation to an axe painted black (*Painted Head*, 1964). *A Walk in Vienna* brought the self-painting out before the public. The stroll by the white-painted artist ended with the arrival of the police.

In his 1965 *Extract from a Self-Mutilation*, Günter Brus wrote: 'I am lying, white on white, in a white bedroom / I am sitting, white on white, on a white toilet / I am sitting, white on white, in a white police station / amongst white policemen / White on white, in a white meeting hall in Parliament amongst / white M.P.s / I am making a white speech. /

I am preaching in a white church, white on white / I take off my left hand. Somewhere there is a foot. A suture at the metacarpus. I stick a drawing-pin in my spine. I nail the thumb and index finger. On a white plate there is pubic hair and head from my head and armpits. I use a (Smart) razor blade to cut along the length of the aorta. I drive a steel point into my ear. I split my head in two lengthways...'[12].

The special characteristic of Actionism was its use of the human body as a surface for paint, as a substitute *tout court* for the material of art. A way of integrating the 'subject' within the artistic process. The body was the centre of the scene and of the action; through the use of its appearance, movement, and spatial relations with other objects, the body was made to represent the message directly. The medium and message were united in the 'original' material of the body, which appears in Rainer's 'body language' works and in the Actions of Brus and Schwarzkogler with a radical significance—as a gesture, a scream, a grimace. The theatrical search for identity in the body and on the body brings out the profound analogy between the work of art and the human body. Merleau-Ponty described works of art as 'beings in which expression and the thing expressed cannot be distinguished; the sense of which is only accessible through direct contact; beings which radiate their meaning without shifting from their spatio-temporal coordinates. From this point of view, one might compare the work of art and our own bodies'.

[1] R. Priessnitz, *Malerei, Plastik etc. Aufsätze*, (Linz-Wien, 1988), 75.
[2] W. Hofmann, *Fragmentarisches über Rainer*, in *Raineriana*, (Wien-Köln, 1989), 15.
[3] W. Hofmann, *Jenseits des Schönheitlichen*, in Op. cit., 45.
[4] Preissnitz, *Malerei*, Op. cit., 74.
[5] Op. cit., 79.
[6] Weibel/Export (ed.), *Wien - Bildkompendium Wienner Aktionismus und Film*, (Frankfurt, 1970), 248.
[7] Op. cit., 248.
[8] Op. cit., 246.
[9] E. Badura-Triska, H. Klocker, *Rudolf Schwarzkogler. Leben und Werk*, (Klagenfurt, 1992), 245.
[10] B. Mattheus, *Jede wahre Sprache ist unverständlich*, (München, 1977), 112.
[11] Op. cit., 117.
[12] Weibel/Export, *Wien*, 305.

Giuseppe Sammartino
Cristo Velato
1753

Imprints of Mind and Body
The Continuity and Change of the Ancient in the Modern

by Adalgisa Lugli

To be in the body and to see it from outside, as if the air were an uninterrupted mirror around you. This is what centuries of the visual arts—painting, sculpture and drawing—have given us; a gift that has been further supplemented by the advent of photography. The most striking thing in all this is that while we observe ourselves—that is, while we observe the representation, the study of the human body with which artists have provided us—we are ourselves within a body. We can sink our feet into the sand, search out the point where the ground is softest, leave an imprint of the front part of our foot, spreading our toes so that each of them is clear.

In fact, the artist's perception of the human body is never made up of visual representation alone. The artist has continual resort to the sense of touch, to his own personal experience, for information that confirms his representation of reality, widens the range of mimesis—and thus leads to the affirmation of a new experience of art. This subterranean work of complete mimesis, of resort to the whole body, has never been totally abandoned by artists—and it is this that transports the creator of the work inside his creation. The person looking at the final result of such creation will experience another aspect of mimesis: that representation is always the work of someone working 'inside a body'. Using a wide range of experimental approaches, the artists of the twentieth century have made us fully aware of great opportunities open to art which goes beyond representation. The material and material existence of the work of art have been essential concerns for artists whose methods of working and creating have often either bordered upon or imitated the magical.

Since the 1950s this theme has been a central concern of all the great avant-garde movements; as we shall see below, they have used a range of artistic languages to achieve surprising results—all of them characterised by the gestuality and ritual of poesis. The body is seen from the inside. Marcel Duchamp's 1959 *With My Tongue In My Cheek* is emblematic of this new 'point of view', whilst the late 50s also saw Klein and Manzoni actually impressing the human body on canvas or exhibiting it as living sculpture. For the artist the body is more than a three-dimensional reality to be depicted; it can be carried over into an illusionary form of life within the work itself. Its whole mass can leave a mark, or perhaps a part of the body might become imprinted on the work (parts of the body became particularly frequent when the avant-garde took the liberty of—or felt forced into—expressing itself in fragments). Everything changes and new avenues open up. Other experiments provide equally surprising signs of a close, continuing, link with the art of antiquity.

65

Imprint

Leaving an imprint is so potent a gesture that in black magic one of the ways to cast a fatal spell on someone is to wipe out an imprint left by a part of his body. Such imprints are an immediate, unmediated sign of existence, a powerful link with the earth.

The imprint left by the body is an object of wonder, curiosity and emotion. At one and the same time it is the mark of a living being, of a form and of an inanimate object; it constitutes a more or less indecipherable sign.

The earth has borne countless examples of imprints and 'bodywriting'. It itself leaves its imprint on space, casting a shadow on other heavenly bodies. This elementary, unmediated dialogue between distant bodies is created by the passage of light and shadow, and culminates in a perfectly synchronized geometrical embrace. The trace of man's passage on the surface of the moon is not the print left by a machine but a simple footprint. Something which the soft surface of the moon might preserve and fossilize, just as the earth has preserved the traces of small swamp amphibians which existed 230–250 million years ago, or of the massive dinosaurs of some 300 million ago.

Imprints, representations, visions

Bodies cast shadows, leave imprints. And in various ways these imprints and shadows have been a constant source of fascination to artists. Prehistoric Man left prints of his paint-covered hand on the walls of a cave. An elemental, magic gesture that one cannot easily break away from, especially when—after the masterly command of mimesis which artists acquired over the period stretching from the Renaissance to Impressionism—more efficacious, abbreviated, artistic approaches have been opened up.

In the centuries from the Renaissance to the present day, painting and sculpture have aimed to provide a 'double', a perfect imitation of the real world. The techniques used in this mimesis have accumulated layer upon layer. Ghiberti, in the mid-fifteenth century, was the first to give what he considered an exhaustive list of the disciplines that should be mastered in the pursuit of this skill. His list gives the measure of the change in status of the *artes mechanicae*, with painters and sculptors being expected to be proficient in writing and geometry, know the works of the Ancients, History, Philosophy, Medicine and Astrology—as well as be expert in Perspective and the science of optics. All of these skills went into creating the basis for the figurative conventions used in the depiction of the real world up to this century. Romanticism might look inwards and shift its attention to the world of imagination and

dreams, but its ghosts were still represented realistically. Or else, using the same tactic of splitting and doubling reality, artists tried to point out escape routes, abstractions, distant paradises, closed, immutable gardens. The hand was guided by the mind and eye. It obeyed conventions, neglecting part of its gifts to be guided by the painter's intelligence, his cultural background, his ability to reason and to acquire both knowledge and know-how. The hand was at the service of a mind nourished not only by all the expertise listed by Ghiberti, but also as by myth, poetry, religious wisdom, dreams, visions and symbolism.

To understand the stages by which this 'hand' became attracted by the perfect mimesis of a real world which in itself has no perspective, no geometric grids or visual conventions, one has to move back to the experimentalism of the Renaissance, to the re-reading of the techniques used by the Ancients. And in doing so one is struck by the parallels between that period and the twentieth century, in which there has been a resurgence of experimentalism within the visual arts. The use of plaster casts of face or body play a central role here. In fact, no matter how much it was supplemented by increasing knowledge of anatomy, the use of perspective and proportion to portray the human body would not have been enough. Every now and again, someone had to feel the need to move back to the very beginning of figurative art, to the moment when the caveman left a print on a cave wall of his paint-stained hand (that very hand which would become the artist's main tool). The cavemen was expressing his own identity, speaking the elemental language of life: I am here, I have a body. I can exert pressure. I express myself from within a body and I represent the first thing that I see before me: my hand.

It is important to recover that hand and the logic behind its use. And, above all nowadays, it is important to dwell on those moments when the artist feels the need to make the elemental, disruptive, primitive gesture described above. A peak in technical, scientific or cultural achievements has often been accompanied by a felt need to go back to basics. It is as if the work of art had, every now and again, to recover all those emotions that do not depend on vision and give them a place within an artistic language which, in its turn, is enriched by the addition.

Natural Imprints

Polybius' account of Roman funeral ceremonies lays great stress on the need for the effigies of the dead to be as accurate as possible (*Historiae*, 167–151 B.C.). In his *Naturalis Historia* Pliny reveals the secret of this close adherence to the 'real' and describes the procedures used

> If a picture could be expressed in words, there would be no point in painting it.
> EDWARD HOPPER

Il Supremo Convegno: Body and Soul

by Manlio Brusatin

From 22 to 24 August 1895 even Sigmund Freud was in Venice (with his brother Alexander, he was almost certainly staying at the Casa Kirsch, where he would later become a regular guest). It was a very special summer, when dreams began to talk and to become more real than reality: 'a dream of the other night confirmed in the most amusing way that dreams are wish-fulfilment'. The secret of dreams was revealed in the Bellevue house on the night of 15 July to a Freud who was more interested in cultivating his hobbies of 'chess, art history and pre-history' and whose main desire was for a place where 'science does not exist'[1]. Psycho-analysis without dreams would be like art history without colors. Freud's presence at the 1895 Venice International Art Exhibition is undoubtedly a fact; but a fact which explains nothing.

The first Biennale of Art should have opened on 22 April 1895, but was, as usual, late and opened only on the 30th of the month. The delay, however, was due to the scandal caused by the painting *Il Supremo Convegno* (The Supreme Encounter)—the first of many publicity scandals at the Biennale. Riccardo di Sambuy, the President of the Turin Accademia Albertina, had declared that the painting by Giacomo Grosso, painter, photographer and teacher of drawing at the Accademia di Belle Arti since 1889, was an 'impudent, fanciful composition'. In fact, the 'Grosso Affair', as some would call it, had actually exploded when the large wooden casing of the painting had been removed in the presence of council workmen and the Secretary to the Biennale, the art connoisseur Antonio Fradeletto (like every Biennale since, the first involved this hybrid critical ritual performed before a collection of workmen and 'initiates' to the mysteries of art). *Il Supremo Convegno* immediately became a 'case'—perhaps because of its very lack of substance as a work of art and because it was caught in the crossfire of judgments from 'above' and 'below'. The painting was inconsequentially 'immediate', and thus 'obscene'. And its obscenity did more than create indignation, it impinged upon the 'common sense of decency', involving everyone but probably not really scandalizing anyone.

It is difficult to 'see' the obscenity of a picture after the fact; especially when we would now be more inclined to describe the work as ugly rather then obscene. However, it is not difficult to recreate the network of interpretations which were behind this 'publicity event', which led to the painting becoming a 'visual event' for the public. The case of *Il Supremo Convegno* is not one of the public execrating a work of art which it does not understand because it has never seen the like of it before. What we have here is one of those cases of the public expressing its solidarity with the artist, and successfully insisting that its 'rulers' show more respect for its ability to appreciate and judge a work of art (these sort of things happen every now and again in regimes based upon ' freedom of opinion'). The case shows a clear awareness, on the part of the public, that their own powers of judgement were being undervalued—with the result that they insisted on their right to decide for themselves. Every now and again even a democratic public fails to respond to an appeal from its rulers; in fact, though, these small-scale public triumphs (in which the public enjoys the feeling of being ahead of its time) are almost always bound within rigid conditions and turn out to be a mere display of supposed freedom. 'The people' became 'the public' and preferred to regard itself as ignorant rather than useless when faced with a stream of opinions which were beginning to express new powers—powers which included a renewed, and much firmer, assertion of one's right to one's own opinion and one's own personal freedom. This meant that everyone wanted to have their say on such an important issue as Morality in Art, which involved a painting that everyone could see. Judging the obscenities of a picture that one understands is much less frustrating than admitting one's ignorance when faced with a painting one does not like because one cannot understand it. Giacomo Grosso's painting therefore stands (and perhaps represents) the encounter of tendencies that would become historic. But what one is really doing in discussing his work is evaluating a certain level of reaction to the obscene as a test of 'reserved libido'.

The painting is a markedly theatrical composition in which the space immediately sets before us a dangerous mix of sacred and profane. The dark decorated halls of the licentiously opulent palazzo which invites one to decadence and ruin might be taken for the large room of a sacristy. The most ambiguous feature is the 'catafalque-bed' on which lies the still-warm body of the deceased. The dead man's lady friends are probably the cause of his premature end but they are there to re-evoke the life of the past—perhaps their presence was explicitly requested by the dead man, who was the one spectator of this final encounter. *Convegno* could also be 'congress' as in 'sexual congress', which may be 'supreme' when Death is the severe judgmental spectator—that is, within our last habitation, the coffin. A coffin which here is sufficiently sober and simple for an aesthete who still believes much more in Life than in Death (given that he has set up this floral spectacle to challenge the power of the latter).

It is curious that the author of a diary who describes himself as *Un imbecille all'esposizione...* [2] should express amazement that this painting is 'unanimously judged to be immoral', when really it is simply 'the last meeting of Don Juan's lovers around the body of their seducer.' The ironic visitor gives a clear, swaggering verdict on the picture: 'if those ladies had been behaving indecorously then they would have been confused with what are commonly referred to as Meretrices; but while the substance may be the same, appearances distinguish between them and the said Meretrices... Around the coffin of their great seducer are gathered his victims, who have no decency, no modesty, and no charms—all treasures that he used up during his life. The dead man has before him the eternity in which we are promised eternal beauty; but for the moment he is surrounded by these living corpses. How much philosophy there is in Grosso's picture!' And, in fact, that is about the long and the short of it.

We have no way of knowing what Freud thought of this painting, which he must certainly have seen; but perhaps we should recall that when he returned to Vienna he recommended his friend Wilhelm Fliess to study the rather curious subject of *The Nose and Female Sexuality* (which Fliess would later publish as *Die Beziehungen zwischen Nase...*, Vienna, 1897) [3]. Anyway, the public in front of Grosso's painting can be divided into two groups: those who were looking at the painting, and those who were looking at those who were looking at the painting.

Given that a painting of this kind is a window thrown open too wide, there should be some protection provided for 'the simple folk' who 'in looking at the mere surface would have a very bad impression of it'. This was how the Patriarch of the Venetian Church, Giuseppe Sarto, phrased his invitation to Mayor Riccardo Selvatico and other public authorities to ban the exhibition of the picture. Selvatico, a laic politician and a gifted dialect playwright, was not about to be intimidated by the man who, in later years, would be the pope that was the most hale-and-hearty but also the most stubborn in his relations with the 'moderns'. Thus there arose the problem of the moral authority of the Church. The Church may not exactly have posed itself as standing between artistic freedom and artistic morality, but the Cardinal clearly expected obedience from the Mayor over a question on which the Church could not only state its opinion but also mobilize the opinion and actions of the faithful.

The Cardinal forbid all Catholics to go and see the painting; a reaction which may seem extreme and bigoted but certainly marks a change from the political detachment inherent in the position of *non expedit* the

Vatican had been taking ever since Italian unification. The episode marks the first example of the general mobilization of Catholic opinion. And while the public did not follow the Cardinal's diktat to the letter (being unwilling to forego the opportunity to judge the picture for themselves), they would later follow him on much more serious issues. At the end of the nineteenth century the problem of morality in art involved such things as funereal statues or photographs of prostitutes, and while the Venice 'case' shows just how lacking in substance the question is, it also sparked off a far more substantial reaction: in July of that same year Riccardo Selvatico was defeated as Mayor and replaced by Filippo Grimani, supported by both liberals and catholics (described by the Cardinal as being 'all practising catholics' who, more importantly, were also 'obedient'[4]). Patriarch Sarto's anathema against the ungodly *Supremo Convegno* turned out to be the rallying-call for the Veneto crusade that would 'bend' post-Unification liberalism/free masonry and modernist idealism to a respect for catholic morality. Subsequently it led to the establishment of the parish civilization—built of small rural savings banks and 'homes of Christian doctrine'—that would form the 'kingdom' to which the body of Pope Sarto would return in 1954 (after his canonization).

1895 marked the entry of Catholics into modern political life; and Pope Sarto's subsequent Gentiloni Pact can now be seen as consummating the Catholic union with the powers-that-be in Italian politics. That same political life which is now characterised by the spread of a new type of populist religiosity (which offers us an insight into both the past and future), a religiosity that features Madonnas who no longer simply appear but also weep tears of blood and make appeals for a new maternity for the church, for politics, for women themselves...

One possible obscenity: Grosso's pictures proposes the aesthetic redemption of those women who are 'slaves to love' whilst at the same time immorally depicting an anti-maternal type of femininity. The ideal of 'maternity' was a new ethical and aesthetic image, which was being reconstructed with religious fervour under the auspices of a religion that presents itself as a Mother: not only was the pastoral action of the priest making itself felt through the spread of Azione Cattolica, but a new moral appreciation of motherhood was emerging. The priest 'Father' became a Mother himself, and motherhood was the be-all and end-all of femininity. Art, therefore, had to depict the eternal, sublime task of motherhood in opposition to the idleness of the mistress. Gaetano Previati's *La maternità* (1890–1891) extends as far as Umberto Boccioni's 'material' and

'explosive' portrait of his aged mother (1909–1912). Grosso's work therefore showed an insulting lack of maternity in women (whilst many works in that Biennale were singing the praises of just such maternal feelings); and Grosso went even further in a large-scale work of the same year, *La Femme*, which now hangs in the Museo Civico, Asti (1895). Here again, our *Imbecille* comments, that the imperious attitude which says 'Look at Me', reveals a not too distant past when the invitation was 'Take Me' (which may or may not have involved payment): all the regal splendor of the woman is based on the capital gained through the exercise of a 'certain' profession. Presented at the same time as *Il Supremo Convegno*, this painting offers an eloquently unappealing image of a Venus past her prime—a women whose lack of appeal is reflected in her excessively fulsome garments, in the heavy room hangings and the flowery gown that falls in folds at her feet, in the overdone decoration of the bodice enclosing an unattractive bust surmounted by a far from pleasant face. The whole figure seems to express a destiny in which Will has become Power; and judging from the firm way she is gripping her fan it seems likely that the Power can only go on increasing.

This picture explains a lot of the latent immorality in the *Supremo Convegno*, which in many parts is even technically 'decadent'; this unusual sloppiness in Grosso's work was perhaps due to hurry to finish the picture for the Biennale.

The 1895 exhibition also included more stringent portrayals of the condition of Woman the Slave. This was particularly the case with the work of the Divisionisti, and Angelo Morbelli's *Per 80 Centesimi (in risaia)* (For 80 cents; in the ricefield) (now in the Museo Civico Borgogna, Vercelli) takes a diametrically opposite approach to that taken by Grosso's *Supremo Convegno*: even Catholics could feel solidarity for these poor rice-pickers tramping their way up a long steep road in the middle of an interminable ricefield—could, that is, if the painter had avoided that unfortunately 'socialist' title. Our *Imbecille* was moved to comment that a day in the rice fields (pay: 80 cents) would not be enough to buy an entry ticket for the Biennale (cost: one lira). However, this 'photographic' chronicle in painting offers the visitor nothing but *riso amaro*: the technical elaborateness of a divisionist painting only complicates things for untrained eyes and thus squanders the expressive value of the picture (which tended to get forgotten amidst all the hullabaloo over the *Supremo Convegno*). Similarly Giuseppe Pellizza da Volpedo's *Processione* (1892–1895) was a rather tentative narrative; the public tended to miss the oblique message conveyed by its swarms of girls in white dresses following the

Giovanni Biadene
Caricature
of Giacomo Grosso and
the patriarch Giuseppe Sarto
1895

Crucifix in an eternal journey towards the adventure of life. The Patriarch's intransigent ban on the *Supremo Convegno*, also prevented Catholics from seeing the speech in favour of country workers—for fear of the disorderly procession of the *Fiumana* (Human River) (sketch of 1895) and of *Il Quarto Stato* (The Fourth Estate) (1898–1900) which cries out so silently. Giovanni Segantini's *Ritorno al paese* (Homecoming) (now in Berlin, Nationalgalerie) was also on display at the Biennale: it centres on that embarrassing object, the coffin, borne on a cart and wept over by a woman (mother). The picture tells of the sad return to the church among the mountains—the place to which one returns whether one wants to or not—and is very fragile if one compares it to the final scene of the triptych *La vita, la natura, la morte* (Life, Nature, Death) (1898) (Winterthur, Stiftung für Kunst, Kultur und Geschichte). There the white snow is positively filigreed with multi-colored threads which make it into a desirable burial place even for the aesthetically-demanding (for the likes of D'Annunzio, for example, who would be inconsolably attached to the heroic end of a painter such as Segantini in a scene set on a vast glacier). But Segantini's novel-in-pictures starts with *Due Madri* (Two Mothers) (1889) to conclude with the castigation of the 'bad mothers' who have not overcome their sensuality through motherhood. *Il Castigo delle Lussuriose* (Punishment of Licentious Women) (1895) (Washington, Private Collection) and a single drawing (shown in Florence in 1896) are the forerunners of all those various paintings in which women seem to float in a bed of air above a violet sheet of snow. Through abortion they have sinned against their role as mothers, and thus they will wander, inconsolable, above the snow until their hair catches in some tree and, through penance, they are brought back to the solid soil they have abandoned. Their halo is 'within' a tree, as we can see in that stark image *Angelo della Vita* (Angel of Life) (1896) (St. Moritz, Museo Segantini). This was the necessary legend of women who are necessarily mothers which Segantini weaves out of the silent nature of 'true loves': without Segantini's mothers we would all feel more like orphans.

This was the powerful nucleus of good painting of good sentiments, of a common sense of decency which can arise from painting itself. Alongside such works the one really 'deviant' painting on show at the 1895 Biennale was Francesco Paolo Michetti's *La Figlia di Jorio* (Jorio's Daughter) (now in Pescara, Municipio), which shows the girl who 'sinned through love' courageously standing up for a 'new morality' in the midst of mocking peasants and shepherds who are barbarian outsiders to sentiment. Gabriele D'Annunzio dedicated to Michetti his *Trionfo della morte* (finished in 1894); perhaps the gesture was more one of friendship than anything else, and a tribute to the untamed calm of Michetti's life—so far from the intense struggles that racked the novel's hero, Giorgio Aurispa, who has the strength finally to eliminate both himself and his lover Ippolita Sanzio through a dream of metamorphosis. D'Annunzio's tastes in painting were well represented at the first Biennale; there were Mario de Maria, Laurens Alma-Tadema, Aristide Sartorio, Segantini, the last Pre-Raphaelites, John Everett Millais, William Holman Hunt and Edward Burne-Jones[5]. But it was to Francesco Paolo Michetti that D'Annunzio seems to dedicate 'the images of the joy and sorrow of our people beneath an heaven prayed to with such savage faith, on a earth that has been worked with immemorial patience'. This was the tenor of regretted realism which D'Annunzio will play out the following year (1895) when he gives the closing speech of the Biennale—which from April to November had grown in a way no one could possibly have foreseen. D'Annunzio was in Venice to be with Eleonora Duse, and his presence there would lead to the one modern novel 'about art' *Il Fuoco* (1898–1900). According to Stelio Effrena, that novel takes up the ideas expounded in the closing speech to the Biennale—The *Glosa all'Allegoria dell'Autunno* became an aesthetic project 'for living a more intense life, or dying a more noble death' in the 'city of water and stone' which had never known an autumn so full of colour and sublime inquietude. And part of that inquietude was due to the First International Exhibition of Art, and to the events to which I will now return.

The special embarrassing nature of Giacomo Grosso's painting can in no way be traced back to 'D'Annunzianism', given that it falls so far below the *pittura, poesia muta* as propounded by the writer. *Il Supremo Convegno* has an indiscreet, novelettish vulgarity which makes the link with *art pompier* inevitable. The funereal setting has nothing imposing, mythical or symbolic about it; the realism is merely banally, wilfully ambiguous.

Upon the suggestion of Antonio Fradeletto, Riccardo Selvatico met the Patriarch's call to ban the painting by setting up (one week before the official opening) a jury of cultural 'experts' who would make a final decision on the matter. This committee consisted of Enrico Panzacchi, Giuseppe Giacosa, Enrico Castelnuovo and Antonio Fogazzaro—the latter, a practicing Catholic who had just published *Piccolo mondo antico*, was appointed as Chairman.

The verdict given was unanimous: 'the painting does not offend public morals', indeed it illustrates an unmistakable moral prohibition because, says Fogazzaro's letter clearing Grosso, 'it shows violent, terrifying and close links between licentiousness and death'—a horror made all the clearer, it is explained, by the nudity of sin. This judgement only partially reassured the Patriarch—who expressed his respect for the verdict given by people 'to whom no one could take exception', but reiterated his claim that the picture would make a 'bad impression' on the general public 'who only look superficially' (17 April, 1895).

The unconditional appreciation voiced by Antonio Fogazzaro carried the public with it; they were not about to shirk the task of judging for themselves and finally absolved the painting altogether by awarding it the Public Prize (awarded on the basis of visitors' votes): a victory of public 'taste' won in the face of a risk of being disturbed. The prize was proposed by the President of the Biennale itself; another provocation for which the Mayor would pay dearly at the ballot box. Giacomo Grosso's painting got the popular vote (549 altogether)[6]; and this popular sanctification was actually 'made real' at the award ceremony, when the picture was accidentally referred to as 'Il Sacro Convegno'. The runner-up, Michetti's *Figlia di Jorio* (185 votes) had the consolation of knowing that it had appealed to a more literary public with interests in the visual arts. The ultrapopular *Sotto la pioggia* (In the Rain) by Vizzotto Alberti only came third with 144 votes; later bought by King Umberto and Queen Margherita, the work depicts key scenes from the novels of Carolina Invernizio and the dialect comedies of Giacinto Gallina and the Mayor Riccardo Selvatico himself. Henry Davis's *Frutteto in Picardia* (Orchard in Picardy) (136 votes) is a very 'aesthetic', pre-raphaelite rendering of nature in sharp contrast to the De Amicis style socialism of Oreste Da Molin's *Diurnisti a Due Lire* (Two-lire daylaborers) (103 votes), which is a fair-day's-pay-for-a-fair-day's-work picture in an almost Macchiettisti style (in comparison to which Morbelli's *Per 80 centesimi* is positively seditious). The *Diurnisti* seem to be too hungry to gnaw on a bone, and—our *Imbecille* points out—'too well-dressed'.

Silvio Rotta was the portrait-painter for the House of Savoia and for Cesare Lombroso; his *Morocomio* (Mental Asylum) shows the 'desperate' courtyard of a lombrosian madhouse; for very different reasons, his picture appealed to the same sort of public taste that made Grosso's painting such a triumph.

The same public, both 'high and low', was also the reader of Antonio Fogazzaro. The Vicenza writer had already ready marked his divorce from a certain type of local, diocesan Catholicism by judging *Il Supremo Convegno* as he had; that same Catholicism would get its own back when Patriarch Sarto, by then elected Pope, would put Fogazzaro's novel *Il Santo* on the Index; Sarto, in fact, said he had actually read the book himself, and up to his dying day he refused to grant the author a papal audience.

In a public conference held in Turin (11 April, 1900), Fogazzaro gave a forceful illustration of his own 'aesthetic programme' in a lesson which seems inspired by *Il Supremo Convegno*. The work was published a year later in Milan with the title *Dolore nell'arte*[7]. It seems to circumscribe and then develop that marble beauty to be found in Leonardo Bistolfi's *La Bellezza della morte* (The Beauty of Death) (also shown at the first Biennale), a work which decants the spirit of Fogazzaro's ideas with a more D'Annunzian idea of pleasure. But perhaps this is an illusion, because the Pain-Love described by Fogazzaro is undoubtedly exemplified in the fate which meets the *Santo* (aka Piero Maironi), who drags his beloved Jeanne Dessalle, a woman philosopher, to conversion after a fierce struggle between mondanity and sanctity (her end being the same as that as of Livia, the heroine of *Senso*, 1883 and 1895). It is the final, and most unfortunate, expression of a sort of Catholic Romanticism which would get short shrift from the dialect stubbornness of good old Pope Pius. 'The hidden beauty of suffering,' according to Fogazzaro, 'should explode or recharge itself from the springs of the sunken shadows (sic) of conscience where there lie the obscured treasures of memory and there are glimmering traces of marvellous faculties which depend on neither sense nor rationality.' Obscure presentiments and artistic inspiration lie at the bottom of a large pond which we might almost call the unconscious 'where hilarity and melancholy go together.' And it is this that Fogazzaro identifies as an inexhaustible source of aesthetic sensibility: 'an arcane beauty of sorrow' which arises from 'shadows of the subconscious', a sorrow-love which exists in a simple, original culture as some sort of archetype (and Jung would have agreed about this). Fogazzaro thought the tormented female souls, the 'sweet creatures sacred to sorrow' around the body of Grosso's mustachioed corpse (was the model Nietzsche, who died in Turin in 1889?) had the faces of the Madonnas painted by Giovanni Bellini and Sassoferrato. The origin of the artistic view of sorrow was profoundly Christian, and this is why the naively sacred art promoted by Pius x (which would include, for example, the primitivism of Tullio Garbari) could not hope to deal with the condensation of powerful intellectual and spirtual issues that it had to face.

Fogazzaro sprinkles his *Dolore nell'Arte* with Dantesque quotes, and sees Grosso's work as portraying the 'wretchedness' of 'amorous ghosts'. Certainly that 'simple' sorrow which is caused by social-moralistically conditioned reflexes cannot move one as much as the sorrow which 'arises from the ineluctable, the fated conditions of life on earth—from death, love, from the problems of the human condition, from the shadows of the afterlife.' As a picture which seems to throw itself onto death but then be held back so that it can speak to the 'heart', Fogazzaro sees *Il Supremo Convegno* as a perfect, sublime work; so the mistake made in the award ceremony is justified and the painting really becomes a 'Sacro Convegno'. 'Think of the numerous representations in modern art of death, which are all the more powerfully felt by us when the reality of death—a reality that is abhorred by nature—is shown in all its horror, when it contradicts all our notions of what is just and reasonable, when it strikes innocence, beauty, grace, love and young hopes.' And perhaps this is where the picture redeems itself. *Il Supremo Convegno* shows a mocking, disturbing disorder of slumped women, and in the joyous exultation of the woman who has 'mounted' the coffin seems to shift the bacchanal of recent death back into the realm of life. But at the same time it slips in another figure, on which a virtuous interpretation could be based: that adolescent girl who has been dragged unknowingly into this house of pleasure, to this party with its tragic sense of disappointed expectations. She is kneeling by an overturned, guttering candle which marks the snuffing out of pleasures even before they arise: it is in this figure that one sees the seed of an *ethos* that will cause *eros* to wilt. Fogazzaro could suggest that in that isolated figure it is not suffering which art makes voluptuous but the idea of a type of suffering which carries the spectator of the painting towards a state of aesthetic pietas. It's a miracle just what Fogazzaro manages to get out of that picture. By almost unthinkable chance, I have come across a study Grosso made for that adolescent girl's face (now in a private collection)—the face which, together with Fogazzaro's commentary leads one towards the 'moral' reading of the picture. This key-fragment is called *L'Adolescente* (1895) and is an intense portrait of 'sorrow in art' showing the terrible disillusionment of an adolescent forced into a premature death of the spirit whilst around her lies the life which should be hers, a life with all the beauty and fragility of a flower. Flowers unfortunately are all over the place in *Il Supremo Convegno*. 'Trop de fleurs!', commented the Empress Elizabeth of Austria[8], unaware that her own tragic death was not far away (1898). A youth betrayed by the tragic spectacle of love and death: this is the note Fogazzaro uses when shouting that the picture redeems itself through the beauty/truth of the sorrow which emerges unvoiced from the face of a little girl who has been made to grow up too fast. But the note is both too high and too forced.

Fogazzaro argues for his modernist, catholic aestheticism in opposition to that 'moralist' and 'socialist' art which dwells 'on the sorrow which results from social inequality, sorrow that cries out for justice to be done (just as civic art dwells on the sorrow that results from disorder within the Patria, the sorrow that stirs one to fulfill one's civic duty); but I cannot forget that the sorrow in a work of art appears to be more attractive for being inexplicable, for being represented without some ulterior aim that lies outside the realm of Art.' Aesthetic balance and detachment from the promises and hopes raised by both socialism and the social Catholicism (introduced in the Veneto by the future Pope Pius); but also indifference towards a patriotism which, with the Great War and the death of the Pope, will prove itself to be something very different. Fogazzaro's argument needs both the guilt and absolution of a death which cannot, however, be compared to that in *Canto della bellezza che va verso la Morte*[9], the last chapter of Maurice Barrès's *Mort de Venise* (1903), in which the most pathetic and inviting sight is that of man who decomposes just thinking of death whilst standing in front of 'the four dancing women who float in the incense of a closed room… proud and sad beauties who satisfy the dreams of death of which I can never have enough. Perhaps they are chimeras of my own heart, a pure metaphysical idea'. Perhaps this is also another possible interpretation of this picture seen from the point of view of the dead man, of someone who gets a short sentence or proverb from each woman in turn: 'desire everything', 'despise everything', ' I was outraged' and lastly 'Grow old'. How much could be said by the women of the *Supremo Convegno*, who are orchestrated parts of the eternal motif of death through an excess of life. It is a banal but simple explanation put forward by Barrès, after the fervent contortions of Fogazzaro, whose aim was to emphasize the evanescent ethical nature of the sorrow linked to art (a type of ethical sorrow that was no longer available even to the Church) and thus redeem a picture which subsequently became interesting again precisely because of the way it disappeared—into the diabolical element itself.

The Patriarch who detested excessively difficult interpretations of the world and of the *Supremo Convegno* was elected Pope on 1903. He was born and raised in the Veneto, which he had transformed into a sort of modern Vandée, a happy land of popes and wet-nurses, and one should perhaps end with an illustration which gives an idea of the new regality of the 'peasant pope'. An image taken from Hugo von Hofmannsthal's *Viaggio d'estate* of the very year of that papal election,

1903; in which the writer recalls how the Veneto, proud of its new pope, was beginning to think it might also have a new king (something made 'technically' impossible by the advent of the Great War). This was still the land of Fogazzaro and of the 'battling' monsignors appointed by Pius X, the last religious Arcadia to exist before the battles of Monte Grappa and the Piave changed everything. Hofmannsthal walked this landscape from Cadore to Vicenza: 'just as the faun plays his happiness on his pipes, so nature exalts in her triumph in this place through the dream of Palladio. Now she has laid the pipes aside, and leaves them to rot by a pond, and has instead gently seized the Rotunda from the circle of human creations and included it in the shifting, umbrous web of her own realm. What crowns the hill in Vicenza is neither a temple not a house, it is more than either. An immortal dream, the goal of marvellous form towards which the distant mountains seem to long, towards which the moving waters seem to long. It achieves that goal; surrounding its circle, holding its four flights of steps to itself, the frame redeemed by a symbol'.

The accursed painting of *Il Supremo Convegno* was bought by the Venice Art & Co, for an international tour and seems to have gone up in flames on the first day of its exhibition in the United States, in Chicago).

[1] S. Freud, *Le origini della Psicoanalisi. Lettere a W. Fliess, abbozzi e appunti 1887–1902*, (Turin, 1961), letter of 16 August 1895, 105–106; letter of 23 September 1895, 105–106; letter of 12 June 1900, 176–177.
[2] G. Ottolenghi, *Un imbecille all'esposizione internazionale con un catalogo umoristico delle 516 opere esposte*, (Venice, 1895), ch. I, 3–25, also for the following quotes.
[3] Freud, Op. cit., letter of 8 October 1895, 107–108.
[4] P. Fernessole, *Pie X*, 2 vols. (Paris, 1953), Vol. I, 187–192.
[5] B. Tamassia Mazzarotto, *Le arti figurative nell'arte di Gabriele D'Annunzio*, (Milan, 1949), 495–515.
[6] *Prima Esposizione Internazionale d'Arte della città di Venezia. Catalogo illustrato*, ed. by A. Fradeletto, (Venice, 1895), *passim*. For the cultural background of the Secretary Antonio Fradeletto: *Conferenze. Malattie d'Arte. La Volontà come forza sociale. La letteratura e la vita. La idealità della scienza. La psicologia della letteratura italiana*, (Milan, 1911). Cf. the first conference dated 1895–1903.
[7] A. Fogazzaro, *Il Dolore nell'Arte*, (Milan, 1901), 29–75, also for following quotations.
[8] Bladinius (Giovanni Biadene), *Il primo Convegno degli artisti italiani ed esteri alla Esposizione di Venezia*, (Milan, 1895), 12, but also the entire work for its interesting vignettes.
[9] M. Barrès, *Il canto della bellezza*, in *Amori et Dolori Sacrum. La Mort de Venise*, (Paris, 1921).
[10] H. von Hofmannsthal, *L'Ignoto che appare. Scritti 1891–1914*, (Milan, 1991), 168–169.

Il Supremo
Convegno

82

Il Supremo Convegno

I found that the old question of morality in art was raging away in Venice because of a painting by Grosso showing the 'supreme encounter' between Don Juan's mistresses, all gathered around the corpse of their seducer. The public version of the facts is as follows.

The painting by the powerful artist was unanimously judged to be immoral by all of those whose mighty intellect had raised them to a position from which they could judge. Riccardo Selvatico, who has often shown himself more than willing to get hold of the wrong end of the stick, decided to be of the opposite opinion and so three arbitrators were sought out to settle the question.

All good Venetians would have preferred a jury of four: the Patriarch, the Armenian bishop, the Rabbi and the Turkish Consul. But the Law of Odd Numbers required there to be only three. Three educated gentlemen who, like Selvatico, got hold of the wrong end of the stick and thus Don Juan (plus courtesans) was admitted.

Will the public settle for a verdict when they don't know the reasons for it? [...]

What greater restraint on immorality than, artfully, putting a stop to the terror that can thunder from pen and paintbrush? And is there anyone of so august an intellect that, under this sweltering sun, he will stop before the imposing scene of the death of Don Juan to ask himself if those ladies who make up the rest of the company are really *comme il faut*? If there is then I suggest no more art exhibitions be held, ever. You can always find something obscene in a painting—like the Mother Superior who objected to a picture of the Virgin and Child because the poor baby happened to be facing her. The artist re-did it; but she was no happier with the rear view. So in the end, he painted the poor Virgin looking with maternal affection at a Cross, underneath which was written: 'The Christ Child will come back enlarged so as not to scandalize the Mother Superior'.

And if Grosso had painted this Last Encounter with a dead Don Juan seeing four or five fine matrons in one of those fine, secluded houses where modern Don Juans meet their wealthy mistresses—whose chastity is simply a question of wardrobe—would the painting have been moral? It is not easy to come up with an answer. If the ladies in question had had the modest, well-mannered air of classical *preficae*, the painting might have been considered a pamphlet. But from the *La Boetie* pamphlet on *servitude volontaire* onwards—through the work of all the most famous pamphleteers—such works have always had a high moral content (the Romans raised the pamphlet to an instrument of law, branding criminals with the initial of their crime). Such branding had a moral purpose; and this picture of the modern *preficae* might well have served as a warning to those of the future (to avoid becoming the subject of art). Nono's *Berlina* (Ridicule), on exhibition in Venice, is a pamphlet.

And if the painter had shown the women to be graceful muses, he would have implied that Don Juan was a poet of the soul rather than a mere hack of the senses; misrepresenting the character of the protagonist, the corpse could have been seen as that of Frate dell'Allighieri surrounded by Bianca, Pia, Sophia and Beatrice.

Nothing true, nothing repugnant, nothing moral—except for the artist's technique (which is something—even if it does belong to the art of thirty centuries ago).

If those ladies had been behaving indecorously they would have been confused with what are commonly known as Meretrices; but while, in substance they may be so, appearances distinguish between them and the said Meretrices.

But the public honor and venerate according to appearances and so would not have believed the painter—and, with credibility gone, the picture would have been immoral all the same.

84

However the former victims around the coffin of the great seducer have neither shame nor grace (gifts which he himself used up during his lifetime): as he faces that very eternity wherein we are all promised Eternal Beauty, this corpse is surrounded by living cadavers. How much philosophy there is in Grasso's [sic] painting!

But this is not all. I am still wondering if Grosso— whose fame as an artist extends to the very borders of Italy— wasn't perhaps trying to get himself banned from this temple of art for immorality.

Giacomo Grosso

L'adolescente, *1895*
Study for Il Supremo
Convegno
Oil on canvas
30×28 cm
Turin, Private collection

from G. Ottolenghi, *Un imbecille all' esposizione internazionale con un catalogo umoristico delle 516 opere esposte*, Venezia 1895, 20–24.

Giacomo Grosso
L'adolescente
1895

I
**Group
Portraits**

88

Maurice Denis
Hommage à Cézanne [I. **3**]
1900

Group Portraits

The Seven Years' War marked an irreparable break between the old and the new; the etiquette of the old society centred around the court was no longer enough—and a reform of manners entailed a new type of education, a knowledge of the laws of political economy (not the usual mercantile skills but an acquired ability to 'balance the books'). Such was the programme of reforms proposed by the *Società dei Pugni* founded by Verri after his return from the war—a body whose press organ was the newspaper *Il Caffè* (published from 1764 to 1766).

The group which met at Caffè Demetrio had little in common with the *Accademia dei Trasformati*, with arcadian dreamers or with the *Accademia di Vigilianti* and the *Società Palatina*. The themes of discussion had changed. Instead of poetical compositions, elogies, clever riddles and caricatures, there was criticism of the pedantry of the Academicians and a debate which ranged over various aspects of agriculture and commerce. But the main concern was the promotion of public morality through a new form of education and reformed social manners.

Verri's *Caffè* was neither a real café nor a mere institution; for the champions of the new ideas, it served the same functions as the *salon* in eighteenth-century France or the coffee-house in early-eighteenth-century England.

Italy had, in fact, never had a salon society—partly because there was no aristocracy independent of the Court, partly because the clerical/military nature of society had prevented the emergence of the type of woman who might host a salon, and, above all, because respectable *literati* were already members of the *accademie*.

Whilst Verri's Caffè was no *Accademia*, it was perhaps less than a salon (even if it did have something of the spirit of its French counterpart). There's no doubt, however, that it was much more than a coffee-house (which had been a public place, open to both sexes of all social stations).

The Café makes its appearance in literature at the end of the seventeenth century, in French theater. First there is J.B. Rousseau's comedy *Le Café*, followed in 1750 by Goldoni's *La Bottega del caffè* and ten years later by Voltaire's *L' Ecossaise ou le café*.

In the café truth lies elsewhere. In the debate over vices and virtues, over human passions and interests, personal qualities and defects, it is no longer the *maitre* who counts but the *esclave*; the literati and scholar count for less than the gazetteer and the libertine. The old world of the mondaine has been replaced by a much wider awareness of the world; the *verité de l' espèce* distinguished between the old use values of honesty and good manners and the new use values of education, training and information. The café is the stage for the switch from courtly to educational values of apprenticeship, morality and utility. There is a shift from the values dear to Castiglione's courtier to those values inculcated by wretched teachers. The basis for all accepted values becomes utility and self (public) interest (as is well-known, private vices are destined to become public virtues).

But the café was more than a simple stage set, it was also a cultural *topos* that functioned on three levels: as a 'factory of wit and spirit', as a veritable 'encyclopaedia' (on all sorts of subjects), and finally as a transmitter of discourse (open to both input and feedback).

from A. Fontana, J.-L. Fournel, *Piazza, Corte, Salotto, Caffè*, in *Letteratura italiana*, vol. V: *Le questioni*, Turin 1986, 672–678.

Tullio Garbari
Gli intellettuali alla «Rotonde» [I. 5]
1916

From the Academy to the Café

Michael Andrews

I **1**
The Colony Room, *1962*
Oil on canvas
121×182.8 cm
London, Private collection

Amerigo Bartoli

I **2**
Amici al caffè, *1929*
Oil on canvas
120×200 cm
Rome, Galleria Nazionale
d'Arte Moderna
e Contemporanea

Maurice Denis

I **3**
Hommage à Cézanne,
1900
Oil on canvas
180×240 cm
Paris, Musée d'Orsay

Otto Dix

I **4**
Gruppenbildnis
Günther Francke,
Paul Ferdinand Schmidt
und Carl Nierendorf,
1923
Oil on canvas
40×74 cm
Berlin, Staatliche Museen
zu Berlin, Nationalgalerie

Tullio Garbari

I **5**
Gli intellettuali
alla «Rotonde», *1916*
Oil on canvas
101×101 cm
Geneve,
Musée du Petit Palais

Renato Guttuso

I **6**
Caffè Greco,
1976
Acrylic on cardboard
pasted on canvas
193.4×250.7 cm
Madrid,
Fundación Colección
Thyssen-Bornemisza

Jörg Immendorff

I **7**
Eigenlob stinkt nicht,
1983
Oil on canvas
150×200 cm
Cologne,
Galerie Michael Werner

Oskar Kokoschka

I **8**
Die Freunde,
1917–18
Oil on canvas
102×151 cm
Linz,
Neue Galerie der Stadt

**Boris Michajlovič
Kustodiev**

I **9**
Gruppovoj portret
chudožnikov obščestva
'Mir Iskusstva',
1920
Oil on canvas
52×89 cm
St. Petersburg,
Gosudarstvennyj Russkyj
Musej

William Roberts

I **10**
The Vorticists at the
Restaurant de la Tour
Eiffel: Spring 1915,
1916
Oil on canvas
182.9×213.4 cm
London, Tate Gallery

Oskar Kokoschka
Die Freunde [I. **8**]
1917-18

**Boris Michajlovič
Kustodiev**
Gruppovoj portret
chudožnikov obščestva
«Mir Iskusstva» [I. **9**]
1920

Otto Dix
Gruppenbildnis
Günther Francke,
Paul Ferdinand Schmidt
und Carl Nierendorf [I. **4**]
1923

Amerigo Bartoli
Amici al caffè [I. **2**]
1929

William Roberts
The Vorticists
at the Restaurant de la Tour
Eiffel: Spring 1915 [I. **10**]
1962

Michael Andrews
The Colony Room [I. **1**]
1962

Renato Guttuso
Caffè Greco, [I. **6**]
1976

Jörg Immendorff
Eigenlob stinkt nicht [I. **7**]
1983

II
**The Age
of Positivism**
1895-1905

The Age of Positivism

1895-1905

A Science of Beauty that turns into an Unhappy Science; a shift from the Academy's drawing lessons to criminal anthropology.

An individual's body and habits are studied experimentally to draw up a 'typology' and establish individual 'identity' (Bertillon). It's well-known that the differences between individual countries change in a situation where the environment is a question of urgency and conflict, the preserve of 'technicians' who practise organization and dominion. To define, delineate, count, regroup and subdivide is to understand. This is no logical grammar but a morphology and a topology. The social space (be it of a people, crowd, tribe or gang) becomes the locus and implement of mind and individuality. No order has been given; but practical action is taken against those who resist.

Cesare Lombroso's *Criminal Anthropology* (1905) will try to name and classify the unnameable and unclassifiable, outline the normal breaker of norms (the rebel, the criminal, the madman).

This new 'science' aims to be humanitarian, to protect the majority against the minority, to protect the majority from itself, through the application of preventive norms (there lies the task of society). Darwin (1859) emphasised the necessity of change; the Theory of Evolution is a hymn to the power and pleasure of movement. Lumière's Cinematograph does not yet fool the eye completely; the image has a 'vis comica' but has none of the soul and rhythm of dance to be found in the strict and joyful education of a *corps de ballet* trained like a small army (Degas). Post-Impressionism and Divisionism—as well as Rodin's sculpture of 'matter and memory'—are created against the background of photography, the dissimulation of animal and human 'souplesse' (Eakins). Callimetry now concerns itself with 'before' and 'after', with the evaluation and delineation of movements rather than the application of static canons (the Academy and its plaster-cast statues).

These 'new impressions' of life and psyche tend to remark more upon degeneration than generation: the new style casts a clinical eye on the genius of madness; like the *Museo Lombroso*, it puts together a maniacal collection that 'looks forward to' art brut, dadaism, surrealism, body art and viennese actionism. Lombroso had his own head conserved in formaldehyde to show he simply did unto others what he was willing to have done unto him.

But when the 'contact' between the criminal body and genius began to throw off sparks, the residual body— the 'poor soul'—began to twist and twitch, to speak in strange tongues, to sigh its life away in hysteria and neuroses. Charcot and Richer put on a new 'theater' for pathology and forensic medicine; the stage was that embarrassing object, the bed. Sleep and Waking began to overlap, to get confused (like those new miracles that science cannot explain). The spirits were no longer frightening, merely eager to communicate. Even the Sacred could be photographed (what would the Holy Shroud be if a photographic negative had not visibly restored it to its place as a 'sublime icon'?) . New lives and shadows lie within us; we can hear their whispering and their screams. Doctor Freud is already listening (1895) and will take up the ancient art of oneiromancy—*The Interpretation of Dreams* (1899).

Luigi Russolo
Autoritratto [II. **105**]
1909

From Callimetry
to Metric
Anthropology

II **1**
Craniometro, *about 1890*
Cast iron
60×50×40 cm
Turin, Museo
di Istituto di Scienze
Medico-forensi
dell'Università di Torino

II **2**
10 moulages ethnologiques
de types raciaux (visages),
about 1880
Plaster moulds
15×7 cm each
Paris, Ecole Nationale
Supérieure des Beaux-Arts,
Département
de Morphologie

II **3**
Photographie signalétique
d'une prisonnière juive
du camp d'Auschwitz
(vue de face)
Photograph (recent print)
18×24 cm
Paris, Ministère de la
Défense, Secrétariat d'Etat
chargé des Anciens
Combattants et Victimes de
Guerre, Délégation à la
Mémoire et à l'Information
Historique

II **4**
Photographie signalétique
d'une prisonnière juive
du camp d'Auschwitz
(vue de face)
Photograph (recent print)
18×24 cm
Paris, Ministère de la
Défense, Secrétariat d'Etat
chargé des Anciens
Combattants et Victimes de
Guerre, Délégation à la
Mémoire et à l'Information
Historique

II **5**
Photographie signalétique
d'une prisonnière juive
du camp d'Auschwitz
(vue de face)
Photograph (recent print)
18×24 cm
Paris, Ministère de la
Défense, Secrétariat d'Etat
chargé des Anciens
Combattants et Victimes de
Guerre, Délégation à la
Mémoire et à l'Information
Historique

II **6**
Photographie signalétique
d'un prisonnier juif
du camp d'Auschwitz
(vu de face)
Photograph (recent print)
18×24 cm
Paris, Ministère de la
Défense, Secrétariat d'Etat
chargé des Anciens
Combattants et Victimes de
Guerre, Délégation à la
Mémoire et à l'Information
Historique

II **7**
Photographie signalétique
d'un prisonnier juif
du camp d'Auschwitz
(vu de face)
Photograph (recent print)
18×24 cm
Paris, Ministère de la
Défense, Secrétariat d'Etat
chargé des Anciens
Combattants et Victimes de
Guerre, Délégation à la
Mémoire et à l'Information
Historique

II **8**
Photographie signalétique
d'un prisonnier juif
du camp d'Auschwitz
(vu de face)
Photograph (recent print)
18×24 cm
Paris, Ministère de la
Défense, Secrétariat d'Etat
chargé des Anciens
Combattants et Victimes de
Guerre, Délégation à la
Mémoire et à l'Information
Historique

Anonymus

II **9**
Anatomic photograph,
late 19th century
Celloidin print
35×26 cm
Venice, Civici Musei,
Palazzo Fortuny

Alphonse Bertillon

II **10**
Mallette Bertillon servant
à l'anthropométrie et au
relevé des empreintes
digitales
Wood, other media
6.5×72×26 cm
Paris, Musée des Collections
Historiques de la Préfecture
de Police

II **11**
Vitrine photographique
d'einseignement du
signalement descriptif,
1890
Wood, photographs
on glass plates
217×310×31 cm
Lyon, Ecole Nationale
Supérieure de la Police

II **12**
Séance de mensurations:
mensuration du crâne,
face et plongée,
1890
Photograph pasted on
cardboard, albumin print
28.5×22 cm
Paris, Musée des Collections
Historiques de la Préfecture
de Police

II **13**
Portrait parlé:
famille Bertillon,
face et profil (Françoise),
1895 (13 December)
Photograph pasted on
cardboard, albumin print
13.5×14.5 cm
Paris, Musée des Collections
Historiques de la Préfecture
de Police

II **14**
Portrait parlé: François
Bertillon enfant,
face et profil,
1902 (14 December)
Photograph pasted on
cardboard, albumin print
13.5×14.5 cm
Paris, Musée des Collections
Historiques de la Préfecture
de Police

II **15**
Portrait parlé: Alphonse
Bertillon, face et profil,
1912 (7 August)
Photograph pasted on
cardboard, albumin print
13.5×14.5 cm
Paris, Musée des Collections
Historiques de la Préfecture
de Police

Umberto Boccioni

II **16**
Io-Noi-Boccioni,
1907–10
Photomontage
9×13.5 cm
Milan, Angelo and Silvia
Calmarini collection

Paul Cézanne

II **17**
Nature morte au crâne
et chandelier, *1900*
Oil on canvas
61×50 cm
Stuttgart, Staatsgalerie

Marcel Duchamp

II **18**
Stoppages étalons,
1913–14
Assembling
28×129×23 cm
Paris, Musée National
d'Art Moderne,
Centre Georges Pompidou

II **19**
Marcel Duchamp
autour d'une table, *1917*
Photomontage
10.4×17 cm
Private collection

II **20**
Ready made rectifié:
Wanted / $2.000 Reward,
1923–63
Print (1/20)
87.5×69 cm
Antwerpen,
Ronny Van de Velde

Marcel Duchamp
and **Man Ray**

II **21**
'La Tonsure'(1) et 'La
Tonsure' (2), points de
vue différents, *1924–25*
Photograph, old silverprint
11.5×9 cm each
Paris, Lucien Treillard
collection

II **22**
Rrose Sélavie, Belle
Haleine, 'Eau de Voilette',
1924–25
Photographs: old silverprint,
recent print, old silverprint
11.5×8.3 cm each
Paris, Lucien Treillard
collection

Paul Cézanne
Nature morte au crâne
et chandelier [II. **17**]
1900

105
The Age
of Positivism

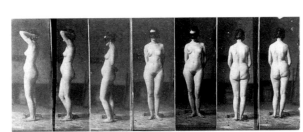

Thomas Eakins
«Brooklyn N° 1»
Masked Girl [II. **29**]
1883-84

Thomas Eakins
Anatomical Cast:
Left Arm [II. **25**]
about 1877-80

Thomas Eakins

II **23**
Anatomical Cast: Torso,
about 1877–80
Bronze
36×24×12 cm
Philadelphia, Philadelphia
Museum of Art
(lent by R. Sturgis Ingersoll)

II **24**
Anatomical Cast:
Right Leg, *about 1877–80*
Bronze
42×12×12 cm
Philadelphia, Philadelphia
Museum of Art (donation
of R. Sturgis Ingersoll)

II **25**
Anatomical Cast:
Left Arm, *about 1877–80*
Bronze
36×14×6 cm
Philadelphia, Philadelphia
Museum of Art
(lent by R. Sturgis Ingersoll)

II **26**
Nine Studies of Figure
after Photographs of Nude
Models, *about 1883*
Ink and pencil on paper
9.8×24.7 cm
Washington, Hirshhorn
Museum and Sculpture
Garden, Smithsonian
Institution (donation
of Joseph H. Hirshhorn)

II **27**
Masked Female Student
or Model in Pennsylvania
Academy Studio, *1883–84*
Photographs, albumin prints
8.3×19 cm
Philadelphia, Philadelphia
Museum of Art, Smithkline
Beecham Corp. Fund for
the Ars Medica Collection

II **28**
Unknown Female Student
or Model in Pennsylvania
Academy Studio, *1883–84*
Photographs, albumin prints
7.6×19.4 cm
Philadelphia, Philadelphia
Museum of Art, Smithkline
Beecham Corp. Fund for
the Ars Medica Collection

II **29**
'Brooklyn N° 1'
Masked Girl, *1883–84*
Photographs, albumin prints
7.8×20.5 cm
Philadelphia, Philadelphia
Museum of Art, Smithkline
Beecham Corp. Fund for
the Ars Medica Collection

James Ensor

II **30**
Les masques et la mort,
1897
Oil on canvas
99×100 cm
Liege, Musée d'Art Moderne

**Francesco Paolo
Michetti**

II **31**
Donna nuda (4 foto),
about 1890
Celloidin print
8.9×15 cm
Florence, Museo di Storia
della Fotografia Fratelli
Alinari, Palazzoli collection

II **32**
Donna nuda seduta
(4 foto), *about 1890*
Celloidin print
8.9×15 cm
Florence, Museo di Storia
della Fotografia Fratelli
Alinari, Palazzoli collection

II **33**
Studio per il dipinto
'La figlia di Jorio': pastori,
about 1890
21 photographs,
Celloidin print
8.4×12 cm
Florence, Museo di Storia
della Fotografia Fratelli
Alinari, Palazzoli collection

II **34**
Donna con abito
(36 foto), *about 1890*
Celloidin print
9×12 cm
Florence, Museo di Storia
della Fotografia Fratelli
Alinari, Palazzoli collection

Paul Richer

II **35**
L'écorché vivant:
mannequin en plâtre
demi-écorché,
about 1903
Plaster
62×27×14 cm
Paris, Galerie Alain Brieux

II **36**
Album de modèles
féminins,
1911 (June)
Album
2 tomes, 55 tables,
photographs from silver
bromide emulsion glass
plates, drawings
Paris, Ecole Nationale
Supérieure des Beaux-Arts,
Département
de Morphologie

II **37**
Buste de Descartes
avec montage incorporé
de son crâne, *1913*
Plaster
44×40×28 cm
Paris, Ecole Nationale
Supérieure des Beaux-Arts,
Département de Morphologie

Auguste Rodin

II **38**
12 têtes (3 bourgeois
de Calais, 2 femmes Slaves,
1 femme au chignon,
1 amour, 1 squelette, 1
tête d'expression, 3 divers),
about 1900
Plaster and coated plaster
Various dimensions
Paris, Musée Rodin

II **39**
8 bras (en extensions,
pliés, squelette),
about 1900
Plaster and terracotta
Various dimensions
Paris, Musée Rodin

II **40**
3 jambes, *about 1900*
Plaster and terracotta
Various dimensions
Paris, Musée Rodin

II **41**
5 pieds (en extensions,
contractés, squelette),
about 1900
Plaster, coated plaster
and terracotta
Various dimensions
Paris, Musée Rodin

II **42**
14 mains (en extensions,
pliées, contractées,
main tenant un pied),
about 1900
Plaster, coated plaster
and terracotta
Various dimensions
Paris, Musée Rodin

II **43**
Balzac: étude
de nu en athlète, *1892-97*
Plaster
93.3×42×34.5 cm
Paris, Musée Rodin

II **44**
Balzac: petite étude
de nu en athlète, *1892-97*
Coated plaster
40.6×23.9×17.3 cm
Paris, Musée Rodin

II **45**
Assemblages: têtes
et mains de bourgeois
de Calais en réduction,
surmontées d'une figure
ailée, *about 1900*
Plaster
24×28×23.5 cm
Paris, Musée Rodin

Willy Selke

II **46**
Stufenrelief der Königin
Luise, *1893–94*
Plaster bas-relief
for photosculpture
Munich, Deutsches Museum
von Meisterwerken
der Naturwissenschaft
und Technik

II **47**
Gipsbüste der Königin
Luise, *1893–94*
Clay with the trace
of photosculpture
16.6×10.7 cm
Munich, Deutsches Museum
von Meisterwerken
der Naturwissenschaft
und Technik

Andy Warhol

II **48**
Most Wanted Man
N° 12: Franck B.,
1964
Diptych, synthetic
and serigraph on canvas
121.9×99.1 cm each
Pittsburgh, The Andy
Warhol Museum, Founding
Collection, Contribution
The Andy Warhol
Foundation for the Visual
Arts

James Ensor
Les masques
et la mort [II. **30**]
1897

Willy Selke
Stufenrelief der Königin Luise
[II. **46**]
1893-94

Gipsbüste der Königin Luise
[II. **47**]
1893-94

 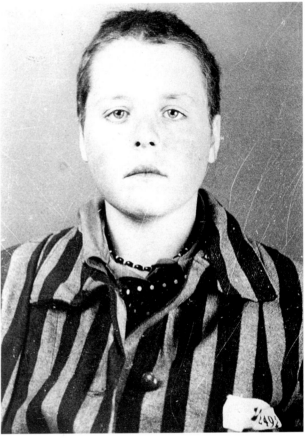

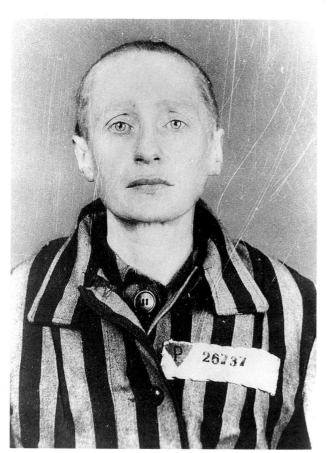 

Photographies signalétiques
de prisonniers juifs
du camp d'Auschwitz [II. **3-6**]

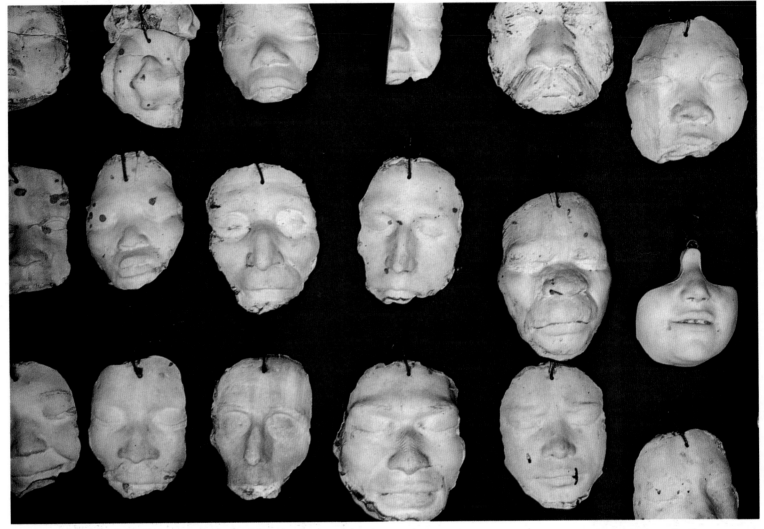

10 moulages ethnologiques
de types raciaux (visages) [II. **2**]
c. 1880

Craniometro [II. **1**]
c. 1890

Anonymous
Anatomic photograph [II. **9**]
late 19th century

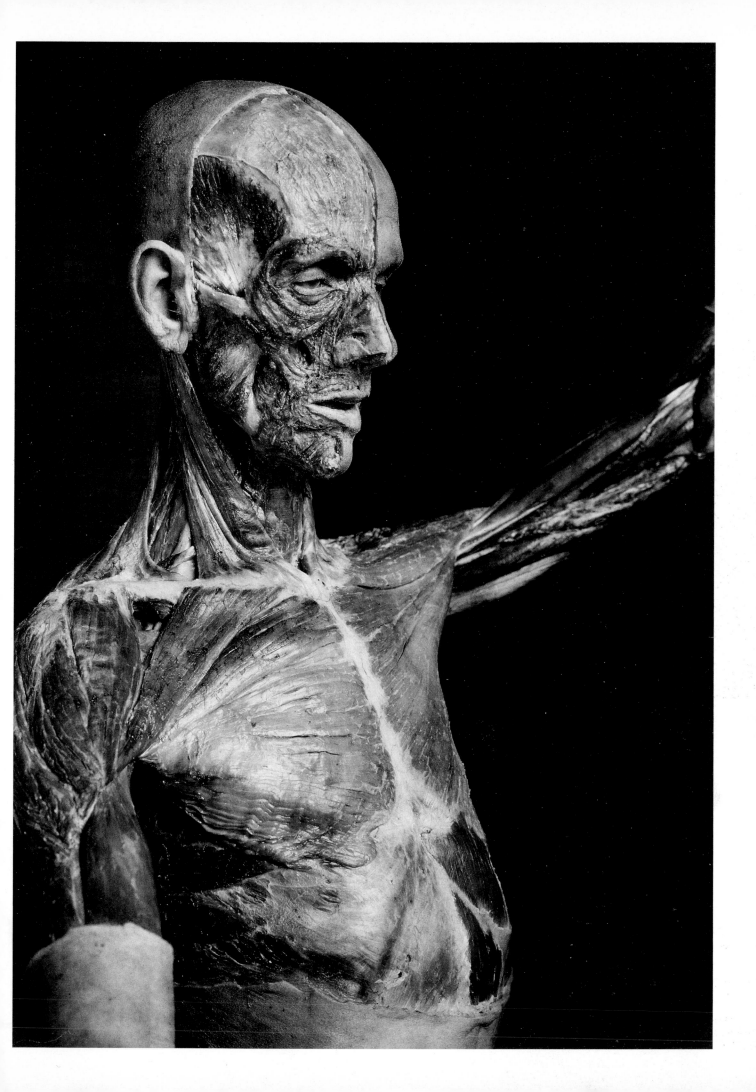

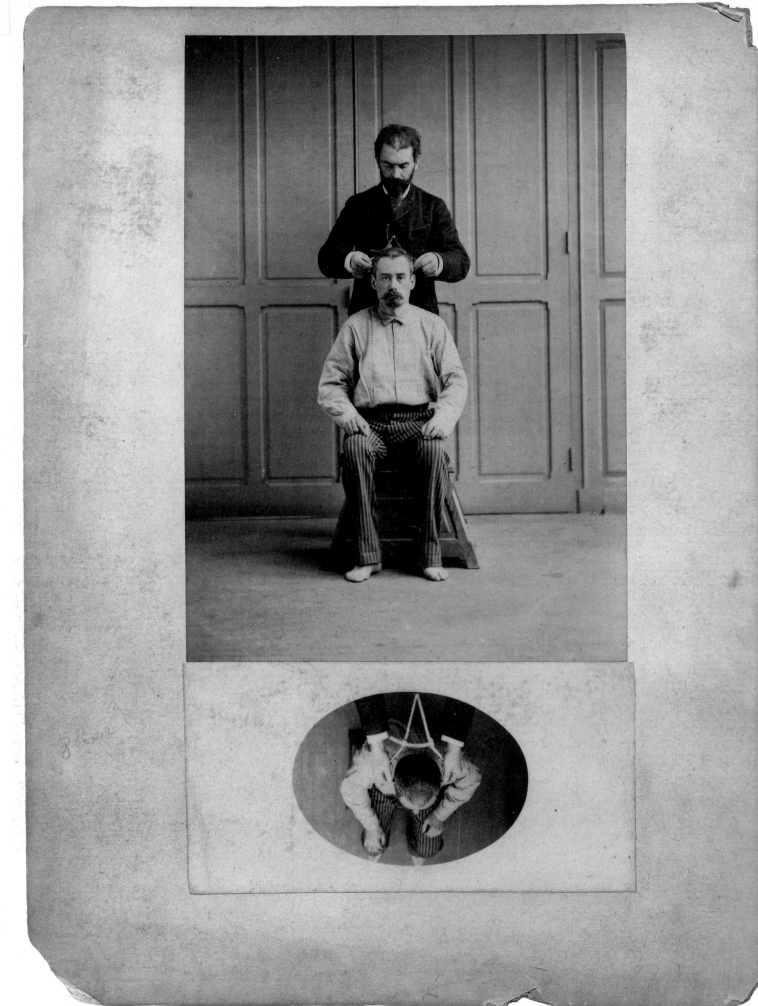

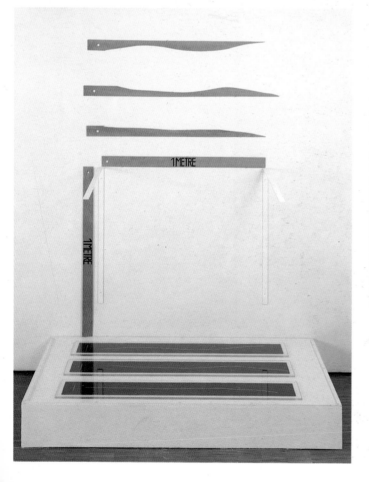

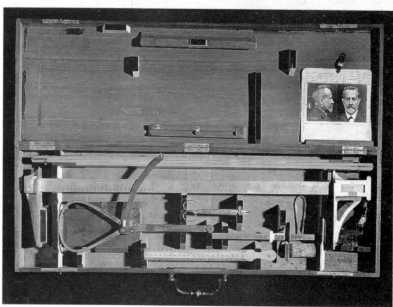

Alphonse Bertillon
Séance de mensurations: mensuration du crâne, face et plongée [II. **12**], *1890*
Vitrine photographique d'einseignement du signalement descriptif [II. **11**], *1890*

Marcel Duchamp
Stoppages étalons [II. **18**], *1913-14*

Alphonse Bertillon
Mallette Bertillon servant à l'anthropométrie et au relevé des empreintes digitales [II. **10**]

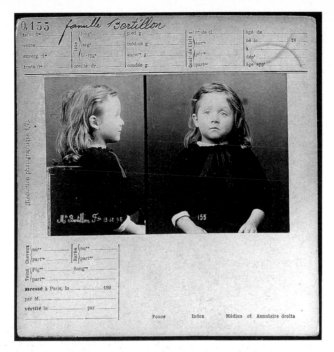

Alphonse Bertillon
Portrait parlé: famille Bertillon,
face et profil (Françoise) [II. **13**]
1895

Portrait parlé: François
Bertillon enfant, face et profil [II. **14**]
1902

Portrait parlé: Alphonse
Bertillon, face et profil [II. **15**]
1912

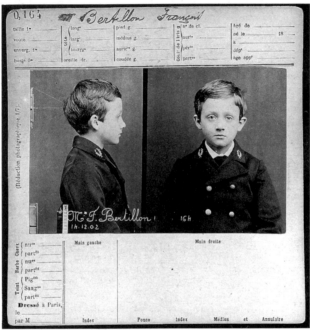

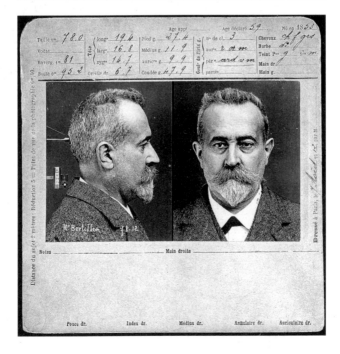

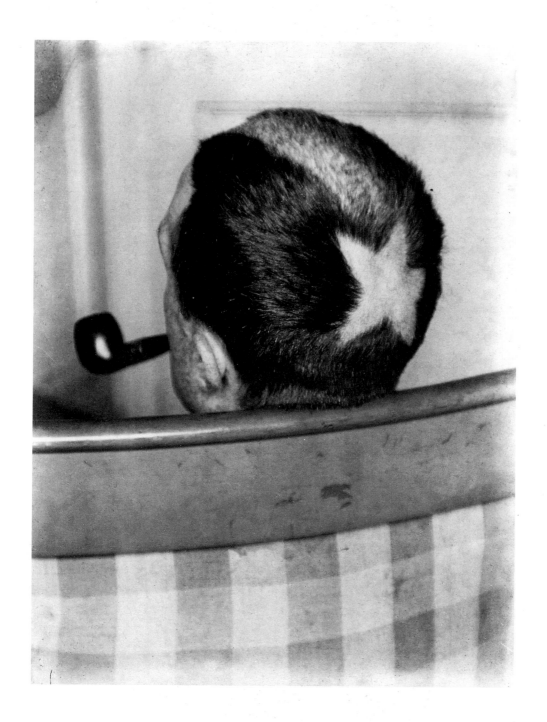

Marcel Duchamp
e **Man Ray**
«La Tonsure» [II. **21**]
1924-25

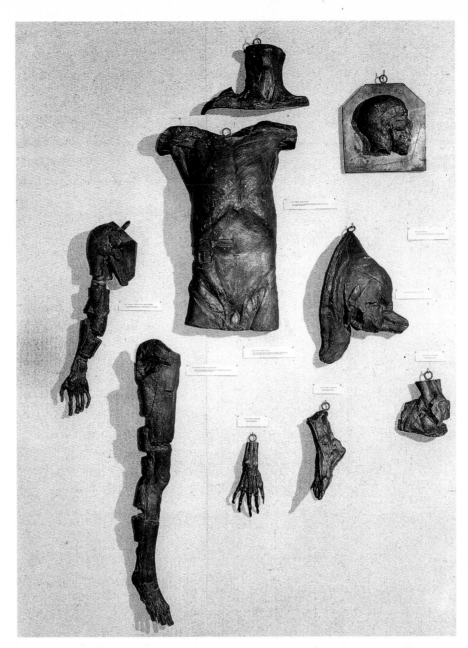

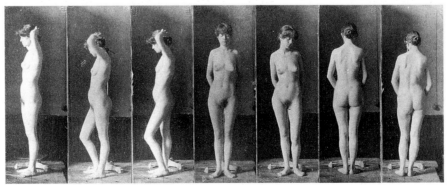

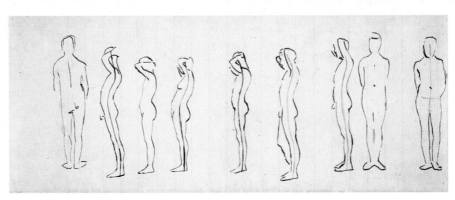

Francesco Paolo Michetti
Studio per il dipinto
«La figlia di Jorio»:
pastori [II. **33**]
c. 1890

Donna nuda [II. **31**]
c. 1890

Donna nuda seduta [II. **32**]
c. 1890

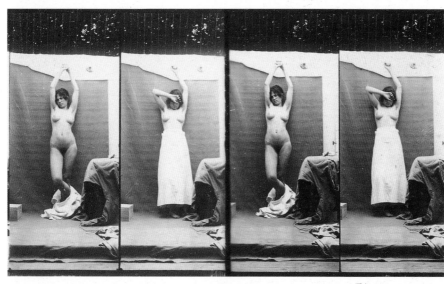

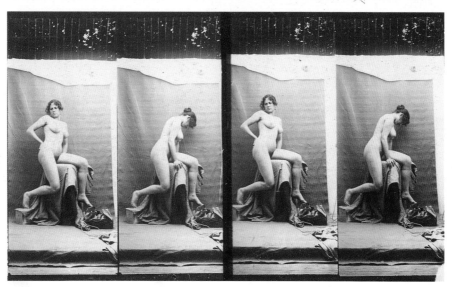

Paul Richer
Buste de Descartes
avec montage incorporé
de son crâne [II. **37**]
1913

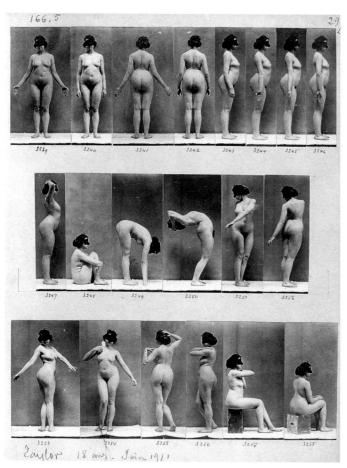

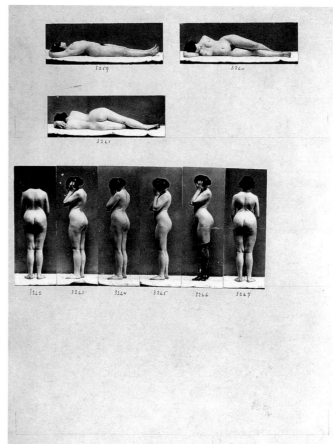

Paul Richer
Album de modèles féminins [II. **36**]
1911

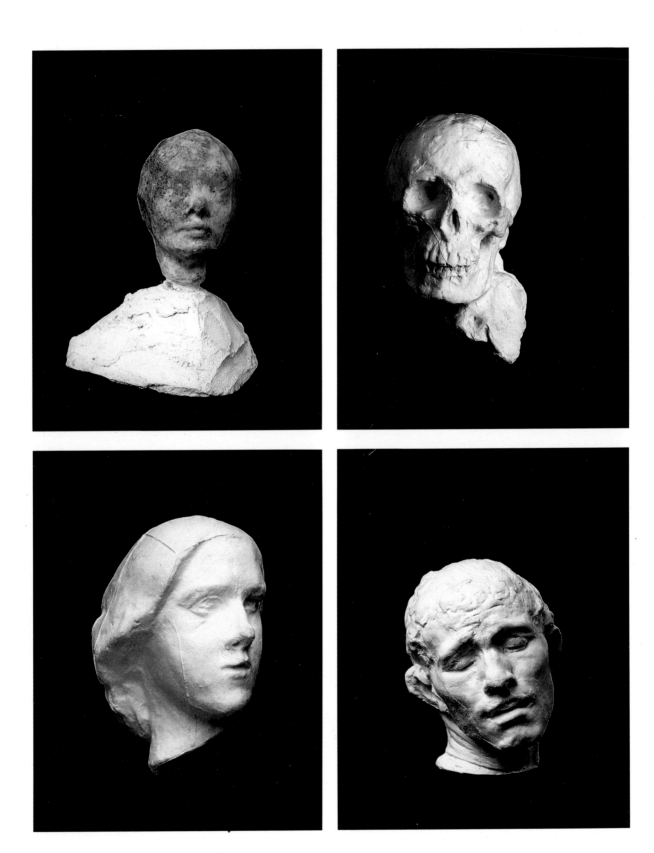

On this page and the following:
Auguste Rodin
Têtes, bras, jambes, pieds, mains [II. **38-42**]
c. 1900

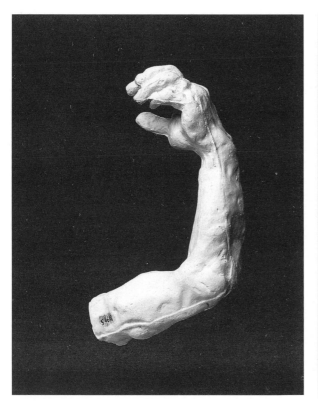

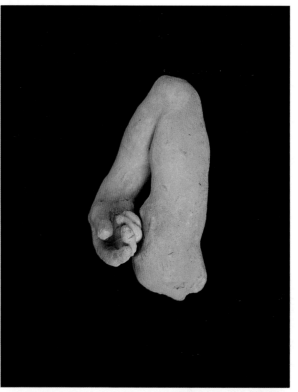

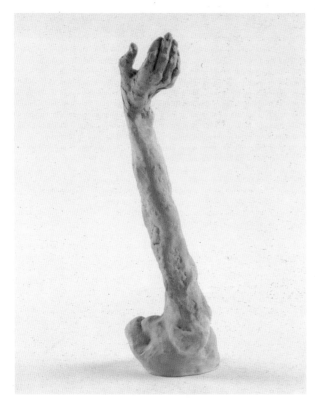

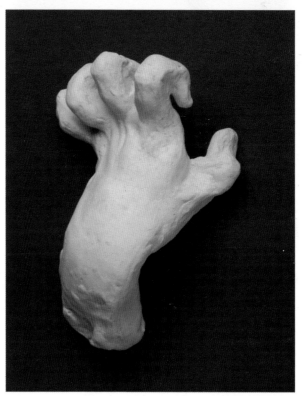

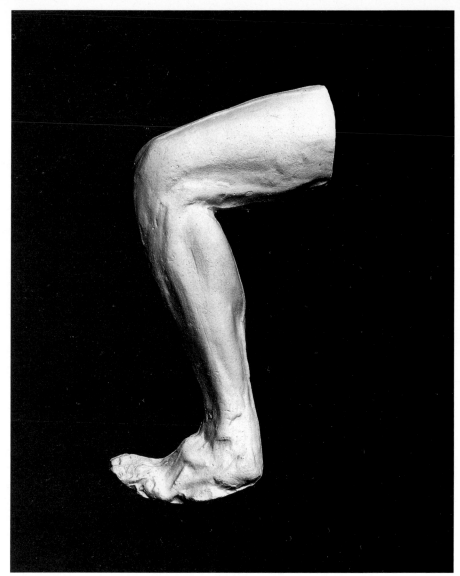

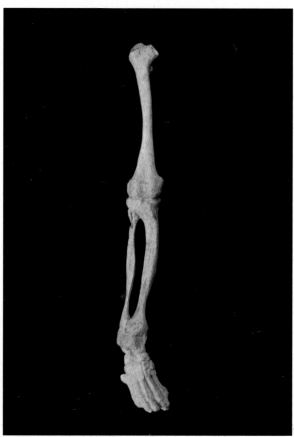

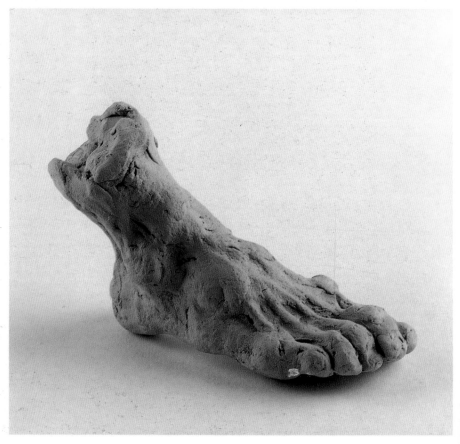

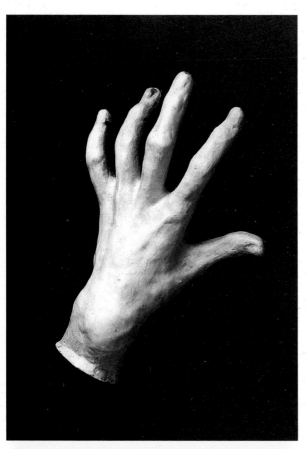

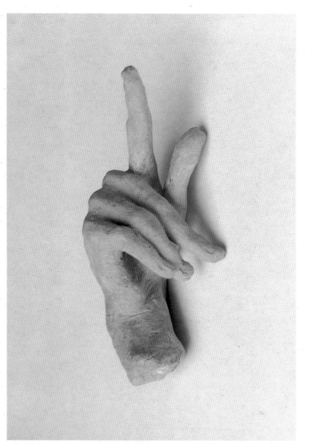

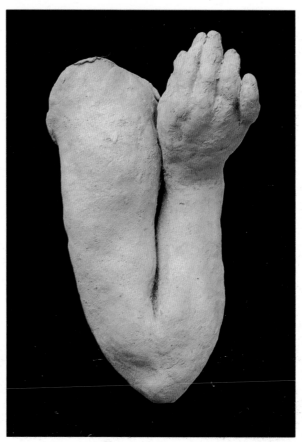

Auguste Rodin
Assemblages: têtes
et mains de bourgeois
de Calais en réduction,
surmontées d'une figure ailée [II. **45**]
c. 1900

Balzac: petite étude de nu
en athlète [II. **44**]
1892-97

Balzac: étude de nu
en athlète [II. **43**]
1892-97

Umberto Boccioni
Io-Noi-Boccioni [II. **16**]
1907-10

Marcel Duchamp
Marcel Duchamp
autour d'une table [II. **19**]
1917

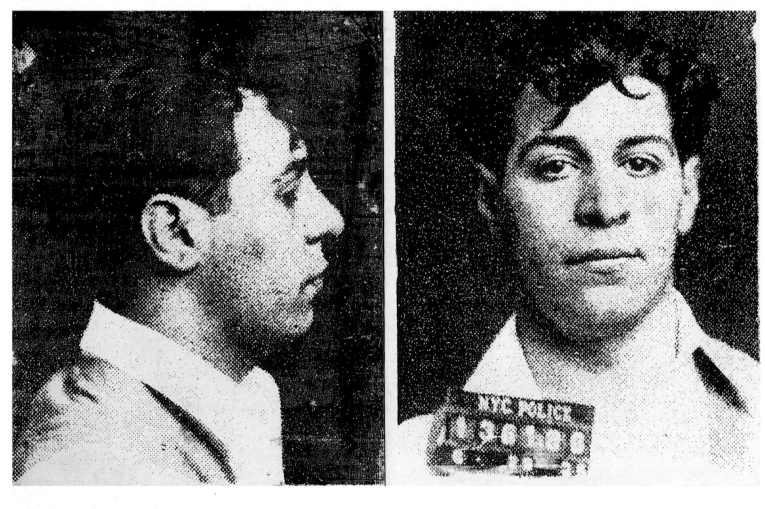

Andy Warhol
Most Wanted Man N° 12:
Franck B. [II. **48**]
1964

Marcel Duchamp
Ready made rectifié:
Wanted / $2.000 Reward [II. **20**]
1923-63

at the

Pasadena Art Museum

46 north los robles avenue
pasadena, california

WANTED

$2,000 REWARD

For information leading to the arrest of George
W. Welch, alias Bull, alias Pickens, etcetry,
etcetry. Operated Bucket Shop in New York under
name HOOKE, LYON and CINQUER Height about
5 feet 9 inches. Weight about 180 pounds. Com-
plexion medium, eyes same. Known also under name RROSE SÉLAVY

a retrospective exhibition

by or of

Marcel Duchamp

or

Rrose Sélavy

october 8 to november 3, 1963

II 49
Fusil
chronophotographique
de Marey, *1882*
Metal, wood, leather
39×12×86 cm
*Paris, Musée National
des Techniques du C.N.A.M.*

II 50
L'humanité féminine,
Paris 1907
*Weekly magazine,
4 issues of 7 pp.*
*Paris, Ecole Nationale
Supérieure des Beaux-Arts,
Département
de Morphologie*

II 51
Etudes académiques,
Paris 1909
*Fornightly magazine,
270 pp.*
*Paris, Ecole Nationale
Supérieure des Beaux-Arts,
Département
de Morphologie*

II 52
La Renaissance physique,
Paris 1912 (November)
*Monthly magazine, n. 7,
22 pp.*
*Paris, Ecole Nationale
Supérieure des Beaux-Arts,
Département
de Morphologie*

II 53
La Renaissance physique,
Paris 1912 (December)
*Monthly magazine, n. 8,
22 pp.*
*Paris, Ecole Nationale
Supérieure des Beaux-Arts,
Département
de Morphologie*

Giacomo Balla

II 54
La mano del violinista,
1912
Oil on canvas
52×75 cm
*London, Eric and Salome
Estorick Foundation*

Umberto Boccioni

II 55
Autoritratto,
1905
Oil on canvas
51.4×68.6 cm
*New York, The
Metropolitan Museum
of Art (bequest of Lydia
Winston Malbin)*

II 56
Idolo moderno,
1911
Oil on board
59.7×58.4 cm
*London, Eric and Salome
Estorick Foundation*

II 57
Forme uniche nella
continuità dello spazio,
1913
Bronze
112×40×90 cm
*Milan, Civico Museo
d'Arte Contemporanea*

Anton Giulio Bragaglia

II 58
Fotodinamica pubblicata
in 'Fotodinamismo
futurista', *Rome 1912*
Volume

Anton Giulio
and **Arturo Bragaglia**

II 59
Un gesto del capo,
fotodinamica, *1911*
Photograph
57×41 cm
*Rome, Centro Studi Anton
Giulio Bragaglia, Antonella
Vigliani Bragaglia collection*

Carlo Brogi

II 60
Il Ritratto in Fotografia,
Florence 1896
*Volume, 182 pp., 4 tables
with original photographs
Florence, Museo di Storia
della Fotografia Fratelli
Alinari*

Edgar Degas

II 61
Après le bain,
1895
Oil on canvas
46.3×65.4 cm
*Philadelphia, Philadelphia
Museum of Art (donation
of Orville H. Bullitt)*

II 62
Après le bain, femme
s'essuyant le dos,
1896
*Modern print from the
original bromide plate
Malibu, California,
The J. Paul Getty Museum*

II 63
Danseuse de corps
de ballet ajustant son
épaulette droite,
1895
*Recent print from a glass
plate coated with collodion
13×18 cm
Paris,
Bibliothèque Nationale,
Cabinet des Estampes*

II 64
Danseuse de corps
de ballet, *about 1896*
*Recent print from a glass
plate coated with collodion
18×24 cm
Paris,
Bibliothèque Nationale,
Cabinet des Estampes*

II 65
Danseuse, position de
quatrième devant sur la
jambe gauche, première
étude, *1896–1911*
Bronze
41×25×26 cm
Paris, Musée d'Orsay

II 66
Danseuse, position de
quatrième devant sur la
jambe gauche, deuxième
étude, *1882–95*
Bronze
60.3×36×37 cm
Paris, Musée d'Orsay

II 67
Danseuse, position de
quatrième devant sur la
jambe gauche, troisième
étude, *1882–95*
Bronze
57.5×33.3×38.5 cm
Paris, Musée d'Orsay

Georges Demenÿ

II 68
Chronophotographie
de la parole. Demenÿ
prononçant la phrase
'Je vous aime', planche:
'Je vous...', *about 1890*
*Chronophotography
on film cut and pasted
on cardboard
22.5×28 cm
Beaune, Musée Marey*

II 69
Chronophotographie
de la parole. Demenÿ
prononçant la phrase
'Je vous aime', planche:'
...ai...me...', *about 1890*
*Chronophotography
on film cut and pasted
on cardboard
22.5×28 cm
Beaune, Musée Marey*

II 70
Les bases scientifiques
de l'éducation physique,
Paris 1902
Volume, 328 pp.
*Gentilly, Philippe Comar
collection*

Thomas Eakins

II 71
Four Horses (Studies for
Painting 'Fairman Rogers
Four-in-Hand'), *1879*
*Bronze, marble pedestal
24×30×7 cm
Philadelphia, Philadelphia
Museum of Art (bequest
of Lisa Norris Elkins)*

II 72
Marey-Wheel Photograph
of Georges Reynolds,
1884
*Albumin print
5.9×9.9 cm
Washington, Hirshhorn
Museum and Sculpture
Garden, Smithsonian
Institution*

II 73
Marey-Wheel Photograph
of Jesse Godley, *1884*
*Cyanotype on paper
5.7×8.4 cm
Washington, Hirshhorn
Museum and Sculpture
Garden, Smithsonian
Institution*

II 74
Marey-Wheel Photograph
of Unidentified Model,
1884
*Celloidin print
17.3×22.6 cm
Washington, Hirshhorn
Museum and Sculpture
Garden, Smithsonian
Institution*

II 75
A Man Walking Full-Face.
Marey-Wheel Photograph
by Eakins, *1884*
*Photograph, recent print
from the original glass plate
25.4×25.4 cm
Philadelphia, The Franklin
Institute Science Museum,
Thomas Eakins Collection*

II **76**
History of a Jump. Marey-
Wheel Photograph by
Eakins, with his
Notations, *1884–85*
Photograph, albumin print
25.4×27.9 cm
Philadelphia, The Library
Company of Philadelphia

II **77**
Wrestlers,
1899
Oil on canvas
101.6×127 cm
Philadelphia, Philadelphia
Museum of Art (bequest of
Fiske and Marie Kimball)

II **78**
The Wrestlers,
1899
Oil on canvas
122.9×60 cm
Columbus,
Columbus Museum of Art,
Derby Found

II **79**
Wrestlers in Eakins's
Studio, *about 1899*
Photograph, platinum print
9×15.2 cm
Washington, Hirshhorn
Museum and Sculpture
Garden, Smithsonian
Institution

Otto von Geyer

II **80**
Der Mensch, *Stuttgart,*
Leipzig, Berlin 1902
Volume, 136 pp.
Paris, Ecole Nationale
Supérieure des Beaux-Arts,
Département
de Morphologie

Paul Godin

II **81**
Les proportions du corps
pendant la croissance,
Paris 1910
Volume, 27 pp.
Paris, Ecole Nationale
Supérieure des Beaux-Arts,
Département
de Morphologie

Julius Kollmann

II **82**
Plastische Anatomie
des Menschlichen Körpers
für Künstler und Freunde
der Kunst, *Leipzig 1910*
Volume, 624 pp.
Paris, Ecole Nationale
Supérieure des Beaux-Arts,
Département
de Morphologie

Louis and Auguste Lumière and Jules Carpentier

II **83**
Cinématographe Lumière,
35 mm, *1895*
172×96×56 cm
Paris, Musée National des
Techniques du C.N.A.M.

René Marage

II **84**
Appareil du docteur
Marage pour l'étude de
la parole et la mesure de
l'acuité auditive, moulage
de la bouche prononçant
les voyelles, *about 1908*
Metal, glass, plaster
35×30×45 cm
Paris, Musée National des
Techniques du C.N.A.M.

Etienne-Jules Marey

II **85**
La méthode graphique
dans les sciences
expérimentales, *Paris 1885*
Volume, 560 pp.
Paris, Ecole Nationale
Supérieure des Beaux-Arts,
Département
de Morphologie

II **86**
Développement
de la méthode graphique
par l'emploi de la
photographie, *Paris 1885*
Volume, 52 pp.
Paris, Ecole Nationale
Supérieure des Beaux-Arts,
Département
de Morphologie

II **87**
'L'Etude des mouvements
au moyen de la
chronophotographie',
in 'Revue Générale
Internationale', Paris,
about 1895
Abstract, vol. 18,
pp. 200–218 1 table
Paris, Ecole Nationale
Supérieure des Beaux-Arts,
Département
de Morphologie

II **88**
2 Chronophotographies:
'Analyse
chronophotographique
de la course, station
physiologique', 'Image
réduite d'un marcheur,
coté droit'
Photographs, modern prints
18×24 cm each
Paris, Gérard Régnier
collection

II **89**
2 Chronophotographies:
'Trajectoire parabolique
d'une boule lancée à la
main', 'Variations d'une
verge élastique'
Photographs, modern prints
18×24 cm each
Paris, Gérard Régnier
collection

II **90**
2 Chronophotographies:
'Homme vêtu de noir
avec des points blancs
et des bandes blanches
pour l'analyse
chronophotographique
de la locomotion',
'Homme vêtu de noir
avec des points blancs
et des bandes blanches
pour l'analyse
chronophotographique
de la locomotion,
station physiologique'
Photographs, modern prints
18×24 cm (each)
Paris, Gérard Régnier
collection

Eadweard Muybridge

II **91**
Animal Locomotion,
tav. 607, 1887
Phototypy
48×60 cm
Philadelphia, Courtesy Free
Library of Philadelphia,
Print and Picture
Collection

Bruce Nauman

II **92**
Mouths, *1967*
Pencil on paper
48.3×69.2 cm
New York, Joseph Helman
collection, Courtesy
Blum Helman Gallery

II **93**
Studies for Holograms:
Pulled Lips, *1970*
Photograph
on polaroid paper
66×66 cm
Humleback, Louisiana
Museum of Modern Art

II **94**
Studies for Holograms:
Pulled Neck, *1970*
Photograph
on polaroid paper
66×66 cm
Humleback, Louisiana
Museum of Modern Art

II **95**
Studies for Holograms:
Pinched Cheeks, *1970*
Photograph
on polaroid paper
66×66 cm
Humleback, Louisiana
Museum of Modern Art

II **96**
Studies for Holograms:
Pulled Lower Lips, *1970*
Photograph
on polaroid paper
66×66 cm
Humleback, Louisiana
Museum of Modern Art

II **97**
Studies for Holograms:
Pinched Lips, *1970*
Photograph
on polaroid paper
66×66 cm
Humleback, Louisiana
Museum of Modern Art

Ludwig Pfeiffer

II **98**
Handbuch der
Angewandten Anatomie,
Leipzig 1899
Volume, 502 pp.
Paris, Ecole Nationale
Supérieure des Beaux-Arts,
Département
de Morphologie

Francesco Leopoldo Pullè

II **99**
Italia Genti e Favelle
(disegno antropologico-
linguistico), Atlante,
Turin 1927
Volume, n.p.n.,
60 illustrated tables
Florence, Museo di Storia
della Fotografia Fratelli
Alinari, Biblioteca
Malandrini

Paul Richer

II **100**
La course, commencement
et fin de phase d'appui,
phase de suspension
Plaster
h 49 cm
Paris, Musée de l'Assistance
Publique, Hôpitaux de Paris

II **101**
Le coureur,
Phénakistiscope
Polychromatic plaster
and wood
70×45×40 cm
Paris, Ecole Nationale
Supérieure des Beaux-Arts,
Département
de Morphologie

II **102**
Canon de proportions
du corps humain,
Paris 1893
Volume, 95 pp.
Paris, Ecole Nationale
Supérieure des Beaux-Arts,
Département
de Morphologie

II **103**
Introduction à l'étude
de la forme humaine,
Paris 1902
Volume, 190 pp.
Paris, Ecole Nationale
Supérieure des Beaux-Arts,
Département
de Morphologie

II **104**
Nouvelle anatomie
artistique, vol. II:
Morphologie. La Femme,
Paris 1915
Volume, 287 pp.
Paris, Ecole Nationale
Supérieure des Beaux-Arts,
Département
de Morphologie

Luigi Russolo

II **105**
Autoritratto, *1909*
Oil on canvas
67×50 cm
Milan, Civico Museo
d'Arte Contemporanea

Carl Heinrich Stratz

II **106**
Über ... Frauen auf Java,
Braunschweig 1898
Volume, 10 pp.
and 6 photographic tables
Paris, Ecole Nationale
Supérieure des Beaux-Arts,
Département
de Morphologie

II **107**
Die Schönheit
des weiblichen Körpers,
Stuttgart 1899
Volume, 236 pp.
Paris, Ecole Nationale
Supérieure des Beaux-Arts,
Département
de Morphologie

Paul Topinard

II **108**
L'Anthropologie,
Paris 1876
Volume, 560 pp.
Gentilly, Philippe Comar
collection

II **109**
L'Homme dans la nature,
Paris 1891
Volume, 352 pp.
Paris, Ecole Nationale
Supérieure des Beaux-Arts,
Département
de Morphologie

Francesco Trombadori

II **110**
Autoritratto, *Photodynamic*
realized in collaboration
with Arturo Bragaglia,
about 1919

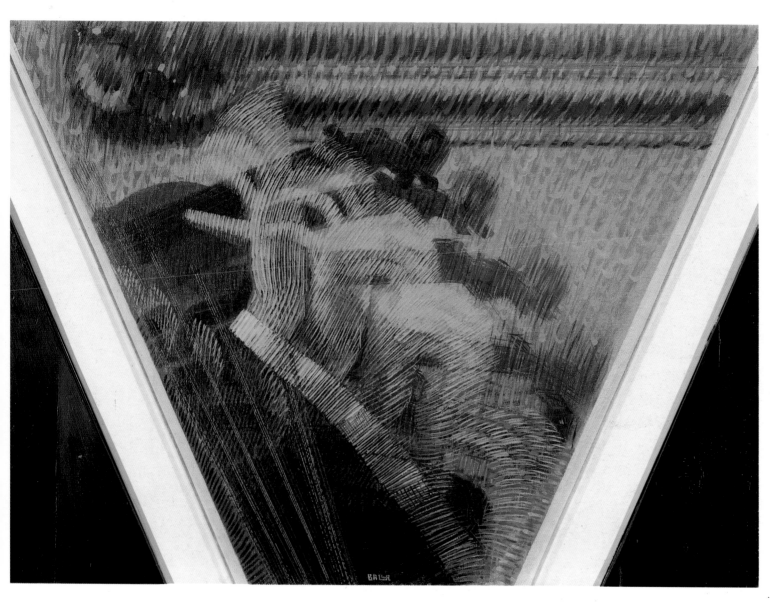

Giacomo Balla
La mano del violinista [II. **54**]
1912

Fusil chronophotographique
de Marey [II. **49**]
1882

Louis and **Auguste Lumière**
and **Jules Carpentier**
Cinématographe Lumière,
35 mm [II. **83**]
1895

Thomas Eakins
History of a Jump.
Marey-Wheel Photograph
by Eakins, with his Notations [II. **76**]
1884-85

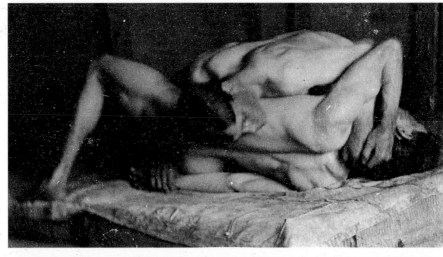

Thomas Eakins
Wrestlers
in Eakins's Studio [II. **79**]
c. 1899

Wrestlers [II. **77**]
1899

The Wrestlers [II. **78**]
1899

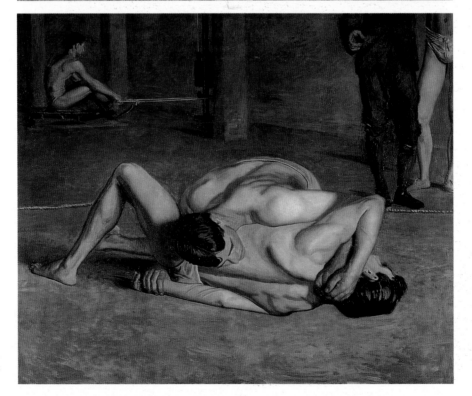

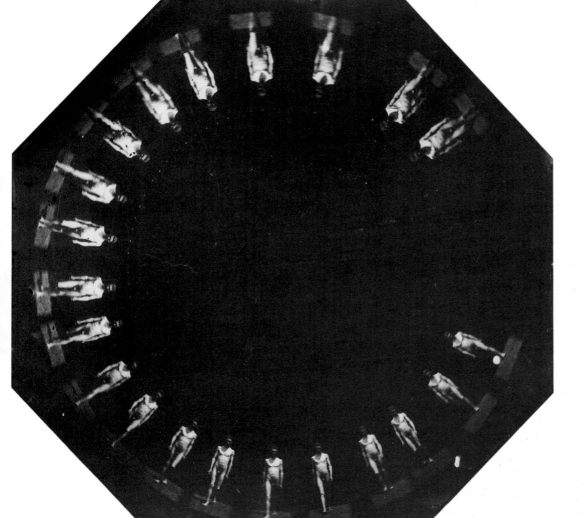

Eadweard Muybridge
Animal Locomotion,
tav. 607 [II. **91**]
1887

Thomas Eakins
A Man Walking Full-Face.
Marey-Wheel Photograph
by Eakins [II. **75**]
1884

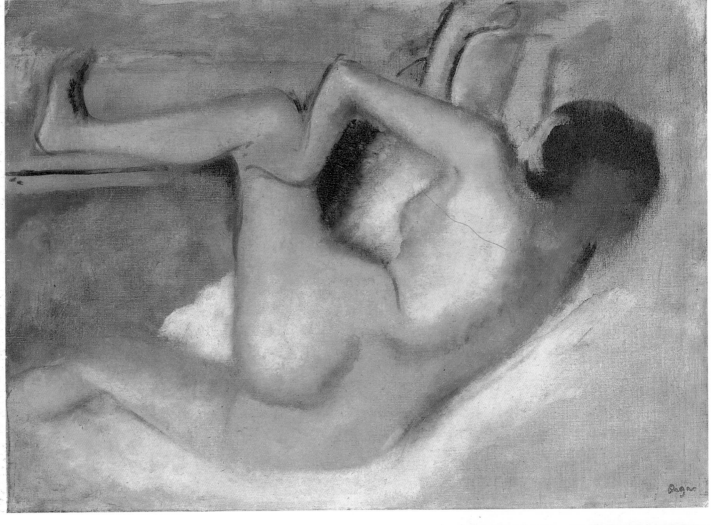

Edgar Degas
Après le bain [II. **61**]
1895

Après le bain,
femme s'essuyant le dos [II. **62**]
1896

Danseuse de corps de ballet
ajustant son épaulette [II. **63**]
1895

Danseuse de corps de ballet [II. **64**]
c. 1896

Danseuse, position de quatrième
devant sur la jambe gauche,
deuxième étude [II. **66**]
1882-95

Danseuse, position de quatrième
devant sur la jambe gauche,
première étude [II. **65**]
1896-1911

Danseuse, position de quatrième
devant sur la jambe gauche,
troisième étude [II. **67**]
1882-95

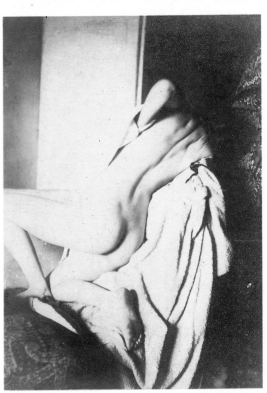

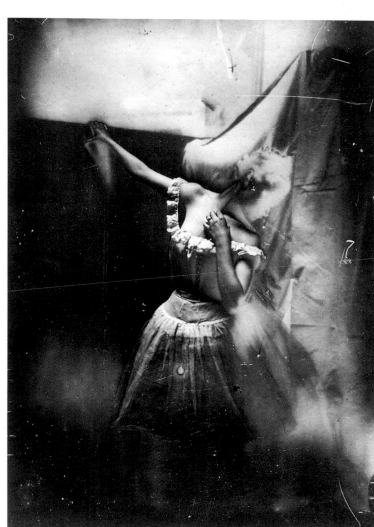

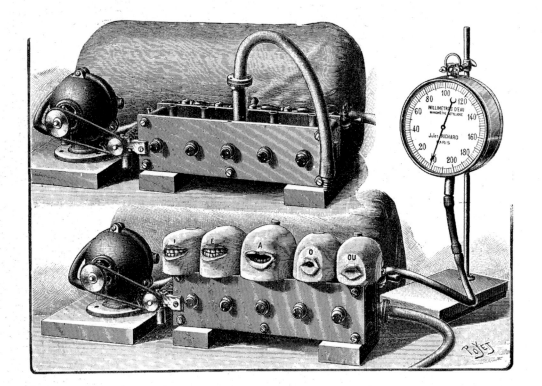

René Marage
Appareil du docteur Marage pour l'étude
de la parole et la mesure de l'acuité auditive,
moulage de la bouche prononçant les voyelles [II. **84**]
c. 1908

Georges Demenÿ
Chronophotographie de la parole.
Demenÿ prononçant la phrase
«Je vous aime», planche: «Je vous...» [II. **68**]
c. 1890

Chronophotographie de la parole.
Demenÿ prononçant la phrase
«Je vous aime», planche: «...ai...me...» [II. **69**]
c. 1890

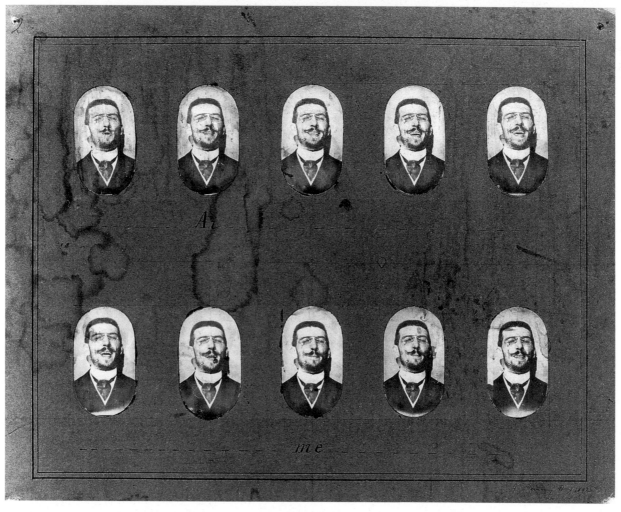

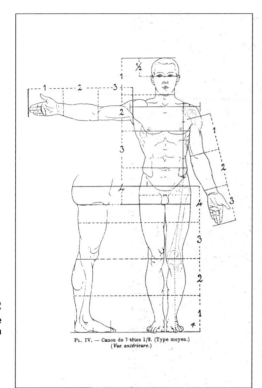

Pl. IV. — Canon de 7 têtes 1/2. (Type moyen.)
(*Vue antérieure.*)

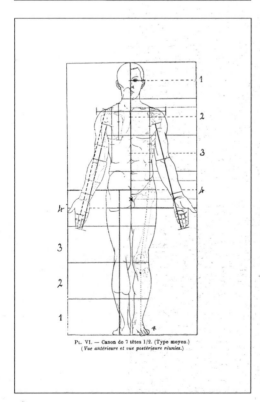

Pl. VI. — Canon de 7 têtes 1/2. (Type moyen.)
(*Vue antérieure et vue postérieure réunies.*)

Paul Richer
Canon de proportions
du corps humain [II. **102**]
Paris 1893

Le coureur,
Phénakistiscope [II. **101**]

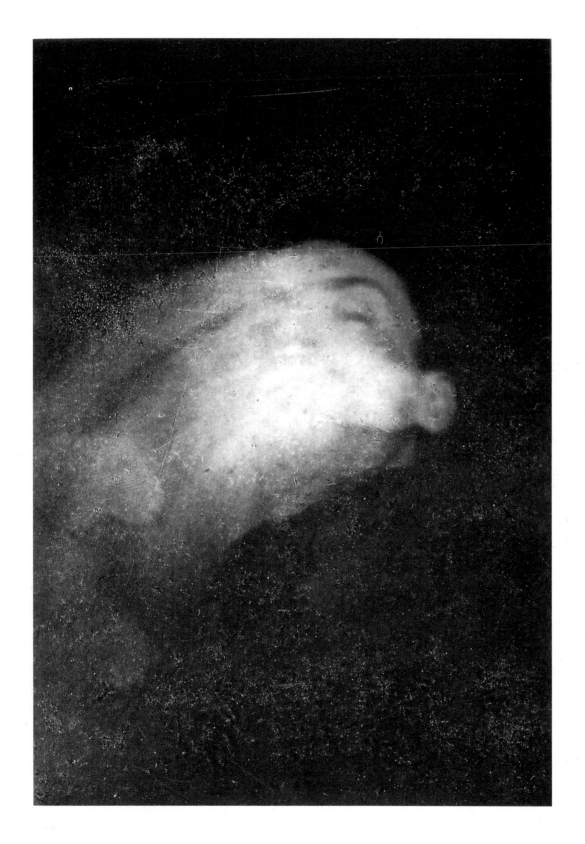

Anton Giulio
and **Arturo Bragaglia**
Un gesto del capo,
fotodinamica [II. **59**]
1911

Umberto Boccioni
Autoritratto [II. **55**]
1905

Forme uniche
nella continuità
dello spazio [II. **57**]
1913

Umberto Boccioni
Idolo moderno [II. **56**]
1911

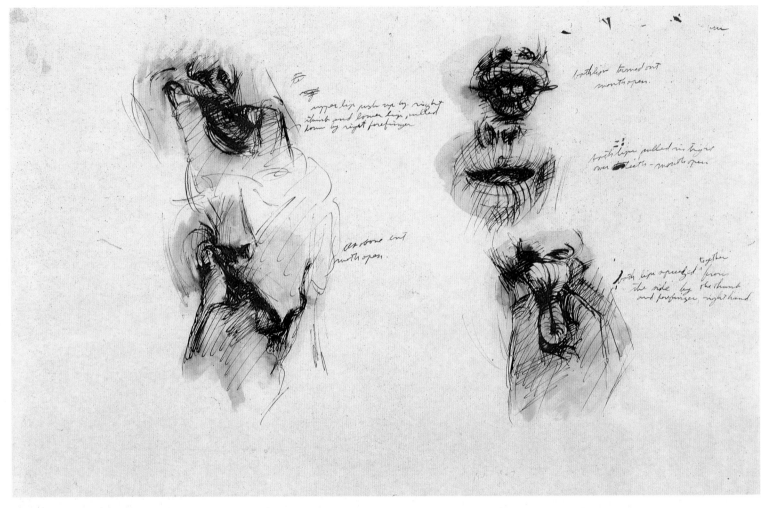

Bruce Nauman
Mouths [II. **92**]
1967

Studies for Holograms:
Pinched Cheeks [II. **95**]
Pulled Lower Lips [II. **96**]
Pinched Lips [II. **97**]
Pulled Lips [II. **93**]
1970

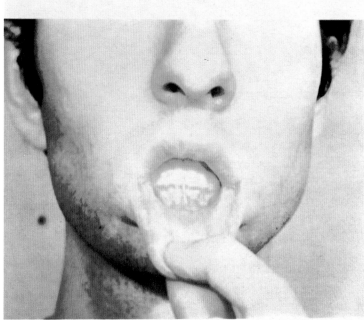

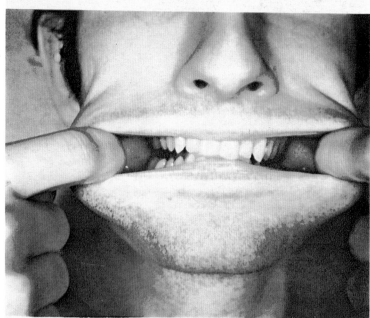

II **111**
Degenti degli anni 1873
e seguenti
*2 original case sheets
with identity photographs
of patients
38×25.5 cm
Venice, Archivio della
Fondazione S. Servolo
I.R.S.E.S.C and Archivio
dell'Ospedale Psichiatrico
di S. Clemente*

II **112**
Fotografie di identità
di degenti, *1874*
*25 original photographs
in 2 albums
59×39 cm
Venice, Archivio della
Fondazione S. Servolo
I.R.S.E.S.C and Archivio
dell'Ospedale Psichiatrico
di S. Clemente*

II **113**
Tipologie psichiatriche:
'epilessia', *about 1890*
*Photograph
12×9 cm
Turin, Istituto di Scienze
Medico-forensi
dell'Università di Torino*

II **114**
Tipologie psichiatriche:
'schizofrenia', *about 1890*
*Photograph
12×9 cm
Turin, Istituto di Scienze
Medico-forensi
dell'Università di Torino*

II **115**
Tipologie psichiatriche:
'mania', *about 1890*
*Photograph
12×9 cm
Turin, Istituto di Scienze
Medico-forensi
dell'Università di Torino*

II **116**
Tipologie psichiatriche:
'imbecillità', *about 1890*
*Photograph
12×9 cm
Turin, Istituto di Scienze
Medico-forensi
dell'Università di Torino*

II **117**
Tipologie psichiatriche:
'melancolia', *about 1890*
*Photograph
8×7 cm
Turin, Istituto di Scienze
Medico-forensi
dell'Università di Torino*

II **118**
Esempi della classificazione
lombrosiana dei deliquenti:
camorristi, *about 1890*
*Photograph
25×19 cm
Turin, Istituto di Scienze
Medico-forensi
dell'Università di Torino*

II **119**
Boîte contenant des iris
*Glass and wood
5×20×10 cm
Paris, Gérard Régnier
collection*

Alphonse Bertillon

II **120**
La Photographie judiciaire,
*Paris 1890
Volume, 115 pp.
Paris, Ecole Nationale
Supérieure des Beaux-Arts,
Département de
Morphologie*

II **121**
Assassinat de Mme
Debeinche-8 mai 1903,
*1903
Photograph
17×23 cm
Paris, Musée des Collections
Historiques de la Préfecture
de Police*

II **122**
Affaire de la plaine Saint-
Denis: assassinat de Mme
Pouillaude-4 janvier 1906,
*1906
Stereometrical photographs
35.5×26.5 cm
Paris, Musée des Collections
Historiques de la Préfecture
de Police*

II **123**
Affaire de l'impasse
Ronsin-31 mai 1908,
*1908
Metric photograph
20.9×27.2 cm
Paris, Musée des Collections
Historiques de la Préfecture
de Police*

II **124**
Affaire de Colombes-
2 janvier 1909, *1909
Planimetrical sketch from
photographic views
28×35 cm
Paris, Musée des Collections
Historiques de la Préfecture
de Police*

II **125**
Affaire de Colombes-
2 janvier 1909: assassinat
des époux Mathieu-Vue de
la salle à manger, *1909
Metric photograph
36×26.8 cm
Paris, Musée des Collections
Historiques de la Préfecture
de Police*

II **126**
Affaire de Colombes-
2 janvier 1909)-
Vue du bureau, *1909
Photograph
36×26.8 cm
Paris, Musée des Collections
Historiques de la Préfecture
de Police*

Alphonse Bertillon
and **Arthur Chervin**

II **127**
Anthropologie métrique,
*Paris 1909
Volume, 228 pp.
Paris, Ecole Nationale
Supérieure des Beaux-Arts,
Département
de morphologie*

Louise Bourgeois

II **128**
In and Out, *1995
Installation
243.8×243.8×243.8 cm
New York, Artist collection
(courtesy Robert Miller
Gallery)*

Paul Broca

II **129**
Nuancier des couleurs
de la peau et du système
pileux *in* Instructions
anthropologiques
générales, *Paris 1879
Volume, 290 pp.
Gentilly, Philippe Comar
collection*

Franz Karl Bühler
(Franz Pohl)

II **130**
Ohne Titel
(Selbstportrait),
*about 1909
Crayon on drawing paper
41.5×30.9 cm
Heidelberg, Prinzhorn-
Sammlung, Psychiatrische
Universitätsklinik,
Ruprecht-Karls-Universität
Heidelberg*

II **131**
Ohne Titel, *1909–16*
Crayon on watercolour
paper
41.5×31 cm
Heidelberg, Prinzhorn-
Sammlung, Psychiatrische
Universitätsklinik,
Ruprecht-Karls-Universität
Heidelberg

II **132**
Ohne Titel
(Selbstportrait),
1918 (September)
Pencil on drawing paper
27.7×18.9 cm
Heidelberg, Prinzhorn-
Sammlung, Psychiatrische
Universitätsklinik,
Ruprecht-Karls-Universität
Heidelberg

II **133**
Das Selbst,
1919 (26–27 March)
Pencil on drawing paper
17.4×12.9 cm
Heidelberg, Prinzhorn-
Sammlung, Psychiatrische
Universitätsklinik,
Ruprecht-Karls-Universität
Heidelberg

F. Holland Day

II **134**
The Seven Last Words,
1898
7 platinum prints
in sequence
14×41.5 cm
New York, The Metropolitan
Museum of Art

Edgar Degas

II **135**
Physionomie de criminel,
1880
Pastel on paper
45.5×59.5 cm
Belgrade, Narodni Muzej
(Nationalmuseum)

II **136**
Physionomies de criminels
(à gauche Emile Abadie, à
droite Michel Knobloch),
1880–81
Pastel
48×63 cm
Private collection

II **137**
Petite danseuse de
quatorze ans, *about 1921*
Partially coloured bronze,
cotton skirt, silk bow,
wooden pedestal
h 99 cm
(base: 7.9×49×50 cm)
São Paulo, Museu de Arte
de São Paulo

II **138**
Etude de nu pour
la 'Danseuse' habillée,
about 1921
Bronze
72×33.6×25.2 cm
São Paulo, Museu de Arte
de São Paulo

Robert Demachy

II **139**
Femme mimant une
expression sous hypnose
(l'effroi), *about 1900*
Recent print from the
original positive plate
24×18 cm
Paris, Société Française
de Photographie

II **140**
Femme mimant une
expression sous hypnose
(la joie), *about 1900*
Recent print from the
original positive plate
24×18 cm
Paris, Société Française
de Photographie

Johan Karl Genzel
(Karl Brendel)

II **141**
Doppelfigur:
Frau mit Maßstab
und Mann mit Hobel
und Kehlkopfkanüle
Wood
30×8×7 cm
Heidelberg, Prinzhorn-
Sammlung, Psychiatrische
Universitätsklinik,
Ruprecht-Karls-Universität
Heidelberg

Richard Gerstl

II **142**
Selbstbildnis vor
blaugrünem Hintergrund,
1906–07
Oil on cardboard
100×72 cm
Innsbruck, Tiroler
Landesmuseum
Ferdinandeum

II **143**
Lachender Mann
(Selbstbildnis), *1908*
Oil on canvas
39×30.4 cm
Vienna,
Österreichische Galerie

Carl Fredrik Hill

II **144**
August Strindberg
Charcoal and pencil
on paper
41.5×34 cm
Malmö, Konstmuseet

II **145**
Untitled
Bronze, gold
and silver paper
30.5×36.5 cm
Malmö, Konstmuseet

Ernst Josephson

II **146**
Extatiska huvuden,
1851–1906
(Ecstatic Heads)
Oil on wood
41×31 cm
Stockholm, Nationalmuseum

II **147**
Adam skapelse, *1893*
(The Creation of Adam)
Indian ink drawing
37.5×22.8 cm
Stockholm, Nationalmuseum

Emile Laurent

II **148**
Les habitués des prisons
de Paris, *Paris 1890*
Volume, 616 pp.
Paris, Ecole Nationale
Supérieure des Beaux-Arts,
Département
de Morphologie

Cesare Lombroso

II **149**
Il direttore del manicomio
Wood
125×45×41 cm
Turin, Istituto di Scienze
Medico-forensi
dell'Università di Torino

II **150**
L'uomo delinquente in
rapporto all'antropologia,
giurisprudenza
e alle discipline carcerarie,
Milan 1876
Volume, 256 pp.
Turin, Istituto di Scienze
Medico-forensi
dell'Università di Torino

II **151**
La perizia psichiatrico-
legale coi metodi per
eseguirla e la casistica
penale classificata
antropologicamente,
Turin 1905
Volume, 643 pp.
Florence, Biblioteca
Nazionale Centrale

II **152**
La femme criminelle
et la prostituée,
Paris 1896
Volume, 679 pp.
Turin, Istituto di Scienze
Medico-forensi
dell'Università di Torino

II **153**
L'uomo delinquente,
Turin 1878²
Volume, 746 pp.,
8 tables
Private collection

Pierre Louÿs

II **154**
Quatre photographies
de nus féminins,
1897
Black and white
photographs
24.5×18.5 cm each
Private collection

II **155**
Cinq pages manuscrites,
(Five handwritten pages),
late 19th century
24.5×18.5 cm each
Paris, Alain Kahn-Sribert
collection

Lucien Mayet

II **156**
Les stigmates anatomiques
et physiologiques
de la dégénérescence,
Paris, Lyon 1902
Volume, 164 pp.
Paris, Ecole Nationale
Supérieure des Beaux-Arts,
Département
de Morphologie

Ludwig Meidner

II **157**
Selbstbildnis,
1912
Oil on canvas
79.5×60 cm
Darmstadt, Hessisches
Landesmuseum Darmstadt

Charles Perrier

II **158**
La grande envergure et ses
rapports avec la taille chez
les criminels, *Lyon 1909*
Volume, 71 pp.
Paris, Ecole Nationale
Supérieure des Beaux-Arts,
Département
de Morphologie

Paul Richer

II **159**
Grande attaque hystérique,
3ème période, attitude
passionnelle: 'Ernest, viens'
Pencil on paper
11.2×17.1 cm
Paris, Collection Richer-
Coutela Alain Sourdille

II **160**
Grande attaque hystérique,
3ème période, attitude
passionnelle: 'Viens'
Pencil on paper
21.8×16.1 cm
Paris, Collection Richer-
Coutela Alain Sourdille

II **161**
Grande attaque hystérique,
période de clownisme:
période des contorsions
Pencil on paper
24.5×15 cm
Paris, Collection Richer-
Coutela Alain Sourdille

II **162**
Variété de la grande
attaque hystérique:
attaque démoniaque
Pencil on paper
28.5×20 cm
Paris, Collection Richer-
Coutela Alain Sourdille

Jules Seglas

II **163**
De l'examen
morphologique chez les
aliénés et les idiots, *in*
Nouvelle Iconographie de
la Salpêtrière, *Paris 1889*
Abstract, 37 pp.
Paris, Ecole Nationale
Supérieure des Beaux-Arts,
Département
de Morphologie

Otto Stuß

II **164**
Luftzeichnung, *about 1909*
Pencil on paper
32×20 cm
Heidelberg, Prinzhorn-
Sammlung, Psychiatrische
Universitätsklinik,
Ruprecht-Karls-Universität
Heidelberg

Louis Umgelter

II **165**
Religiöser Wahnsinn, *1906*
Pencil and pastel
on cardboard
39×50.6 cm
Heidelberg, Prinzhorn-
Sammlung, Psychiatrische
Universitätsklinik,
Ruprecht-Karls-Universität
Heidelberg

II **166**
Allkohollismus, *1906*
Pencil and pastel
on cardboard
39×50.6 cm
Heidelberg, Prinzhorn-
Sammlung, Psychiatrische
Universitätsklinik,
Ruprecht-Karls-Universität
Heidelberg

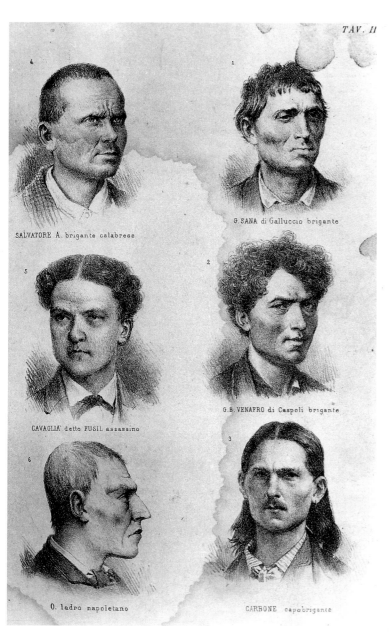

Cesare Lombroso
L'uomo delinquente [II. **153**]
*Turin 1878*²

Edgar Degas
Physionomie de criminels
(à gauche Emile Abadie,
à droite
Michel Knobloch) [II. **136**]
1880-81

Petite danseuse
de quatorze ans [II. **137**]
c. 1921

Etude de nu pour
la «Danseuse» habillée [II. **138**]
c. 1921

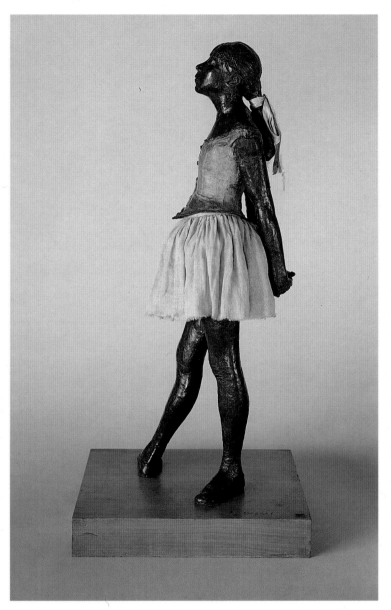

Franz Karl Bühler (Franz Pohl)
Ohne Titel
(Selbstportrait) [II. **130**]
c. 1909

Ohne Titel [II. **131**]
1909-16

Das Selbst [II. **133**]
1919

Ohne Titel
(Selbstportrait) [II. **132**]
1918

Richard Gerstl
Selbstbildnis vor blaugrünem
Hintergrund [II. **142**]
1906-07

Lachender Mann
(Selbstbildnis) [II. **143**]
1908

Richard Gerstl
Selbstbildnis vor blaugrünem
Hintergrund [II. **143**]

Ludwig Meidner
Selbstbildnis [II. **157**]
1912

Ernst Josephson
Extatiska huvuden [II. **146**]
1851-1906

Adam skapelse [II. **147**]
1893

Carl Fredrik Hill
Senza titolo [II. **145**]

Otto Stuß
Luftzeichnung [II. **164**]
c. 1909

Carl Fredrik Hill
August Strindberg [II. **144**]

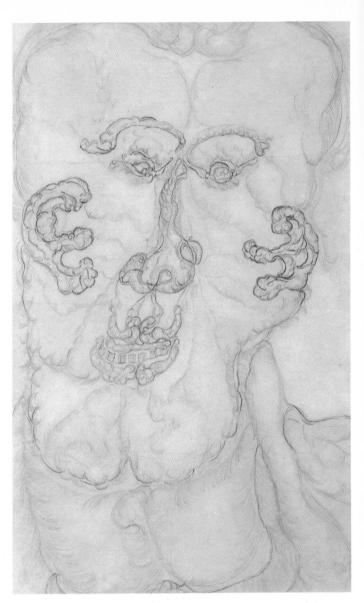

Johan Karl Genzel
(Karl Brendel)
Doppelfigur: Frau mit Maßstab
und Mann mit Hobel
und Kehlkopfkanüle [II. **141**]

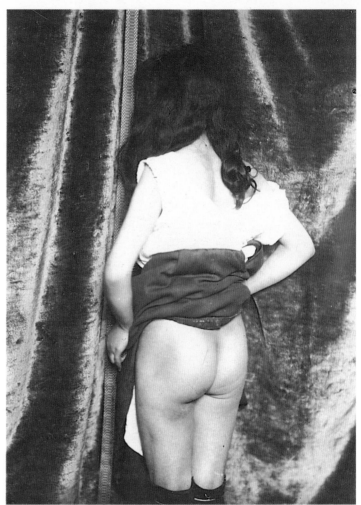

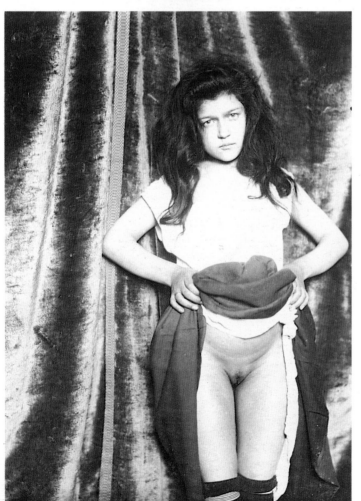

Pierre Louÿs
Quatre photographies
de nus féminins [II. **154**]
1897

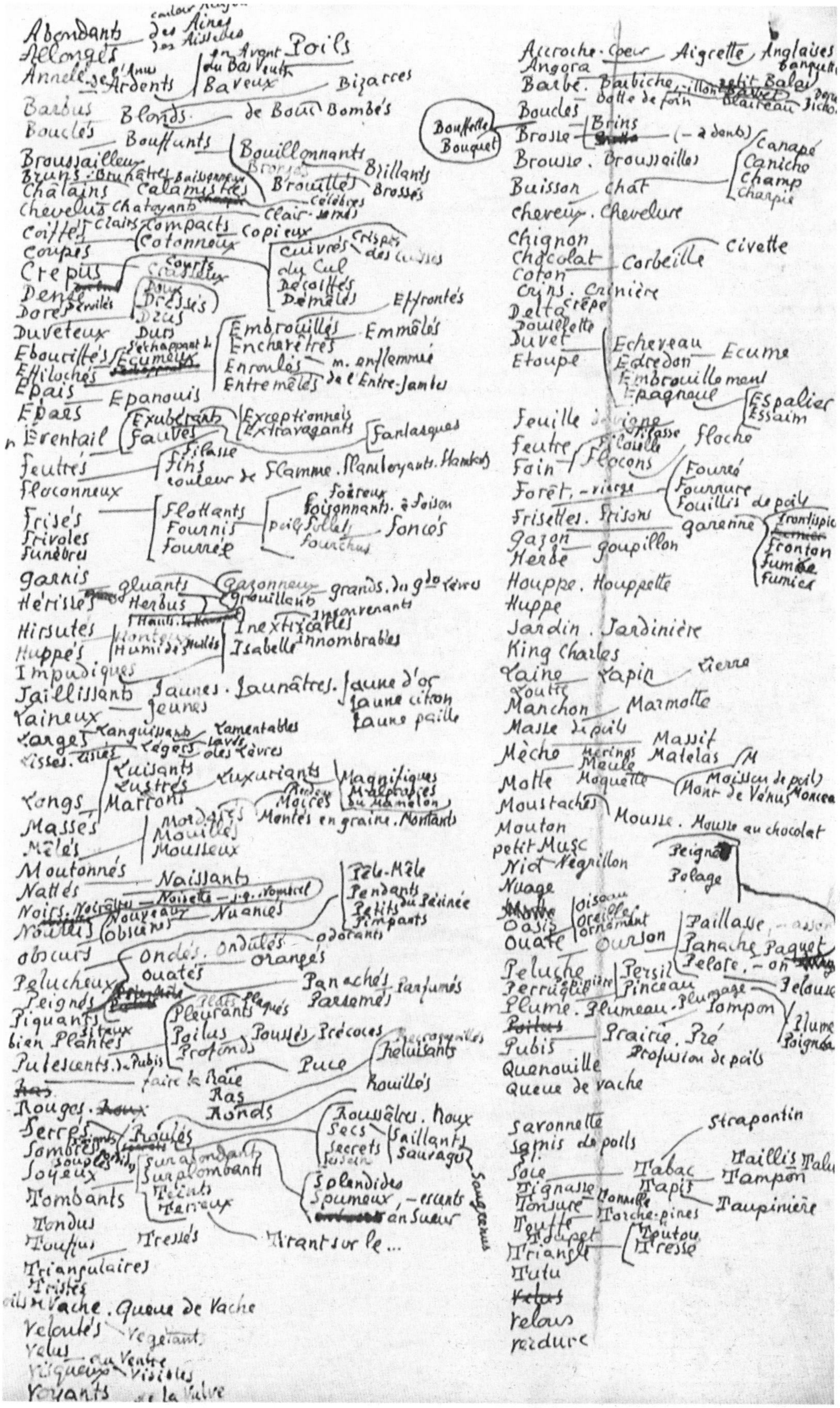

Page manuscrite [II. **155**]
late 19th century

Louis Umgelter
Religiöser Wahnsinn [II. **165**]
1906

Allkohollismus [II. **166**]
1906

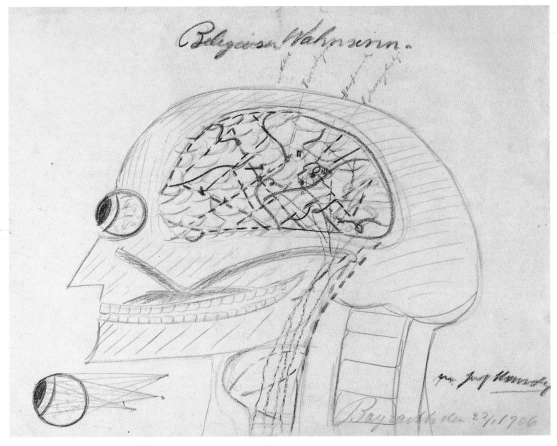

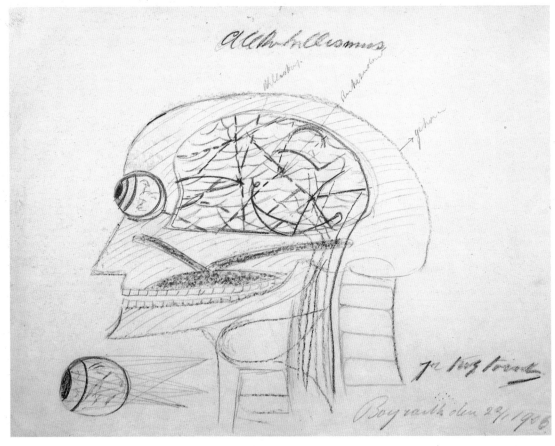

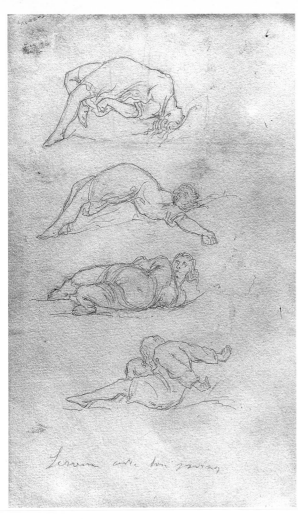

Paul Richer
Grande attaque hystérique, période de clownisme:
période des contorsions [II. **161**]

Grande attaque hystérique,
3ème période, attitude passionnelle: «Viens» [II. **160**]

Grande attaque hystérique, 3ème période,
attitude passionnelle: «Ernest, viens» [II. **159**]

Variété de la grande attaque hystérique:
attaque démoniaque [II. **162**]

F. Holland Day
The Seven Last Words [II. **134**]
1898

Robert Demachy
Femme mimant une expression
sous hypnose (la joie) [II. **140**]
c. 1900

Femme mimant une expression
sous hypnose (l'effroi) [II. **139**]
c. 1900

Louise Bourgeois
In and Out (Cell) [II. **128**]
1995

Umberto Boccioni
Stati d'animo:
quelli che vanno [II. **167**]
1911

**The Discovery
for the Invisible**

Umberto Boccioni

II **167**
Stati d'animo:
quelli che vanno, *1911*
Oil on canvas
71×95.5 cm
Milan, Civico Museo
d'Arte Contemporanea

II **168**
Stati d'animo: quelli che
restano, *1911*
Oil on canvas
71×96 cm
Milan, Civico Museo
d'Arte Contemporanea

II **169**
Stati d'animo: gli addii,
1911
Oil on canvas
71×96 cm
Milan, Civico Museo
d'Arte Contemporanea

Umberto Boccioni
Stati d'animo:
quelli che restano [II. **168**]
1911

Stati d'animo: gli addii [II. **169**]
1911

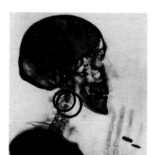

Meret Oppenheim
Röntgenaufnahme
des Schädels
Meret Oppenheim [II. **189**]
1964

II **170**
Eusapia Paladino, *in*
'L'illustrazione italiana',
1902 (23 February)
Magazine
Florence, Biblioteca
Nazionale Centrale

Anonymous

II **171**
Untitled
*Photograph: stereoscopic
view on cardboard
9×18 cm
Châlon-sur-Saône,
Musée Nicéphore Nièpce*

II **172**
Untitled
*Photograph: stereoscopic
view on cardboard,
late 19th century
9×18 cm
Châlon-sur-Saône,
Musée Nicéphore Nièpce*

Hippolyte Baraduc

II **173**
L'âme humaine, ses
mouvements, ses lumières
et l'iconographie
de l'invisible fluidique,
*Paris 1896
Volume, 299 pp.,
70 separate photographic
reproductions
Paris, Bibliothèque
de l'Institut de France*

II **174**
Méthode de radiographie
humaine..., La force
courbe..., photographies
des vibrations de l'éther,
*Paris 1897
Volume, 51 pp.
18×24 cm
Paris, Bibliothèque de
l'Institut de France*

Edouard-Isidore Buguet

II **175**
Photographie 'spirite':
le spectre de Balzac
*Albumin print
10.5×6.8 cm
Paris, Angel-Sirot Collection*

II **176**
Photographie 'spirite':
Jeanne Leymarie
(l'esprit de Mlle Finet),
*about 1870–80
Albumin print
10.5×6.8 cm
Paris, Angel-Sirot Collection*

II **177**
Photographie 'spirite':
Miss Bluwald évoquant
Napoléon III,
*about 1870
Albumin print
10.5×6.8 cm
Paris, Angel-Sirot Collection*

II **178**
Photographie 'spirite':
Mr Destanon reconnaissant
le spectre de sa femme
*Albumin print
10.5×6.8 cm
Paris, Angel-Sirot Collection*

Miss Houghton

II **179**
Chronicles of Spirit
Photography,
*London 1882
Volume, 273 pp.,
photomechanical
reproduced illustrations
Florence, Museo di Storia
della Fotografia Fratelli
Alinari*

Enrico Imoda

II **180**
Fotografie di Fantasmi,
*Turin 1912
Volume, 254 pp., 48
original photographic tables
Florence, Museo di Storia
della Fotografia Fratelli
Alinari, Biblioteca
Malandrini*

Wassily Kandinsky

II **181**
Dame in Moskau, *1912*
*Oil on canvas
108.8×108.8 cm
Munich, Städtisches Galerie
im Lenbachhaus*

II **182**
Succession, *1935*
*Oil on canvas
81×100 cm
Washington,
The Phillips Collection*

František Kupka

II **183**
Duše lotosu, *1898*
*(Lotus' soul)
Watercolour and gouache
on paper
38.6×57.8 cm
Prague, Národni Galerie
v Praze*

**Littleton Views
Company Publishers**

II **184**
The Haunted Lovers,
*1893
'Spiritic' stereoscopic
photograph
8.6×18 cm
Paris, Angel-Sirot Collection*

Cesare Lombroso

II **185**
Ricerche sui fenomeni
ipnotici e spiritici,
*Turin 1909
Volume, 319 pp.
Florence, Biblioteca
Nazionale Centrale*

A. Mori

II **186**
Fotografia di un piede
alla luce Crookes,
*1896 (February)
Fototypy
11.1×15.5 cm
Venice, Italo Zannier
collection*

Enrico Morselli

II **187**
Psicologia e spiritismo,
*Turin 1908
Tome I, 464 pp., 7 tables;
Tome II, 586 pp.
Florence, Biblioteca
Nazionale Centrale*

Edvard Munch

II **188**
Selvportrett med
knokkelarm, *1895*
*(Self-portrait with
Armbone)
Litograph
45.5×31.5 cm
Oslo, Munch Museet*

Meret Oppenheim

II **189**
Röntgenaufnahme
des Schädels Meret
Oppenheim, *1964
X-ray
25.3×20.5 cm
Hamburg, Thomas Levy
collection*

Robert Rauschenberg

II **190**
Booster (*from* Booster
and Seven Studies), *1967*
*Colour litograph
and screenprint
183×89 cm (framed)
New York, Marlborough
Gallery Inc., Richard Kahn
collection*

Edouard-Isidore Buguet
Photographie «spirite»:
Jeanne Leymarie
(l'esprit de Mlle Finet)
[II. **176**]
c. 1870-80

Photographie «spirite»:
Mr Destanon reconnaissant
le spectre de sa femme
[II. **178**]

Thiébault
Photographie «spirite»:
Spectres Robin - n° 2 -
(photomontage publicitaire
pour le prestidigitateur
Dunkel, dit Robin) [II. **195**]

Remy
and **Contremoulins**

II **191**
Radiographie grandeur
nature d'un homme, *1896*
X-ray mounted on
cardboard
97.5×58.6 cm
Paris, Bibliothèque
de l'Institut de France

Saint-Edme

II **192**
Photographie 'spirite':
homme et apparition
(enfant), *about 1860*
Albumin print
10.5×6.8 cm
Paris, Angel-Sirot Collection

Giovanni Segantini

II **193**
L'eroe morto, *1879*
Oil on canvas
161×90 cm
St. Gallen, Kunstmuseum

Thiébault

II **194**
Photographie 'spirite':
Spectres Robin–n° 1–
couché (photomontage
publicitaire pour le
prestidigitateur Dunkel,
dit Robin)
Albumin print
10.5×6.8 cm
Paris, Angel-Sirot Collection

II **195**
Photographie 'spirite':
Spectres Robin–n° 2–
(photomontage publicitaire
pour le prestidigitateur
Dunkel, dit Robin)
Albumin print
10.5×6.8 cm
Paris, Angel-Sirot Collection

II **196**
Photographie 'spirite':
Spectres Robin–n° 3–
(photomontage publicitaire
pour le prestidigitateur
Dunkel, dit Robin)
Albumin print
10.5×6.8 cm
Paris, Angel-Sirot Collection

II **197**
Photographie 'spirite':
Spectres Robin–n° 4–
(photomontage publicitaire
pour le prestidigitateur
Dunkel, dit Robin)
Albumin print
10.5×6.8 cm
Paris, Angel-Sirot Collection

Remy and **Contremoulins**
Radiographie grandeur nature
d'un homme [II. **191**]
1896

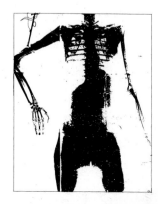

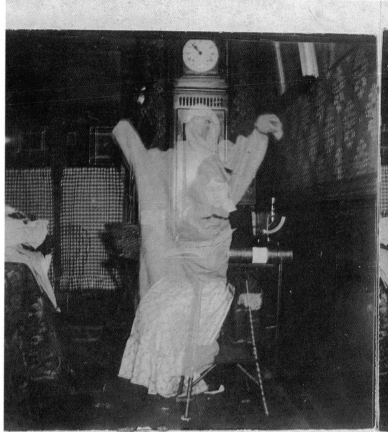

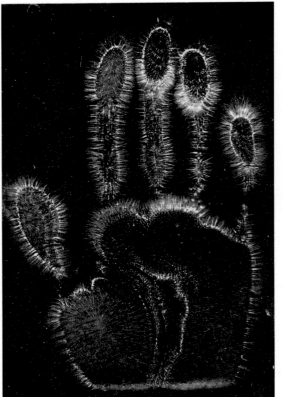 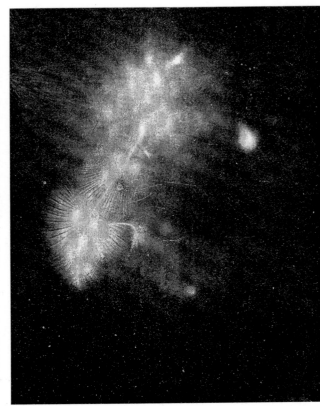

Hippolyte Baraduc
L'âme humaine,
ses mouvements, ses lumières
et l'iconographie
de l'invisible fluidique [II. **173**]
Paris 1896

Edouard-Isidore Buguet
Photographie «spirite»:
le spectre de Balzac [II. **175**]

Photographie «spirite»:
Miss Bluwald évoquant
Napoléon III [II. **177**]
c. 1870

Thiébault
Photographie «spirite»:
Spectres Robin - n° 1 -
couché (photomontage
publicitaire pour le
prestidigitateur Dunkel,
dit Robin) [II. **194**]

Photographie «spirite»:
Spectres Robin - n° 4 -
(photomontage publicitaire
pour le prestidigitateur
Dunkel, dit Robin) [II. **197**]

Miss Houghton
Chronicles of Spirit
Photography [II. **179**]
London 1882

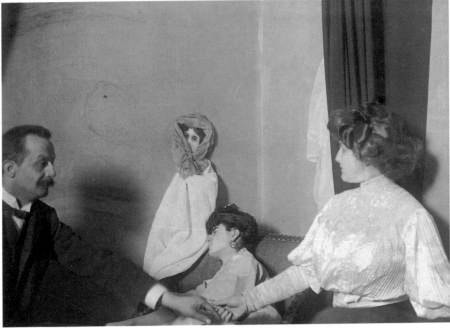

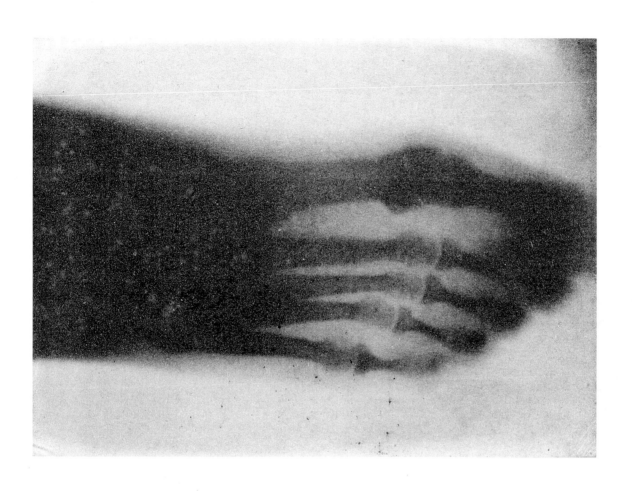

Saint-Edme
Photographie «spirite»:
homme et apparition (enfant) [II. **192**]
c. 1860

Enrico Imoda
Fotografie di Fantasmi [II. **180**]
Turin 1912

Littleton Views Company Publishers
The Haunted Lovers [II. **184**]
1893

A. Mori
Fotografia di un piede
alla luce Crookes [II. **186**]
1896

František Kupka
Duše lotosu [II. **183**]
1898

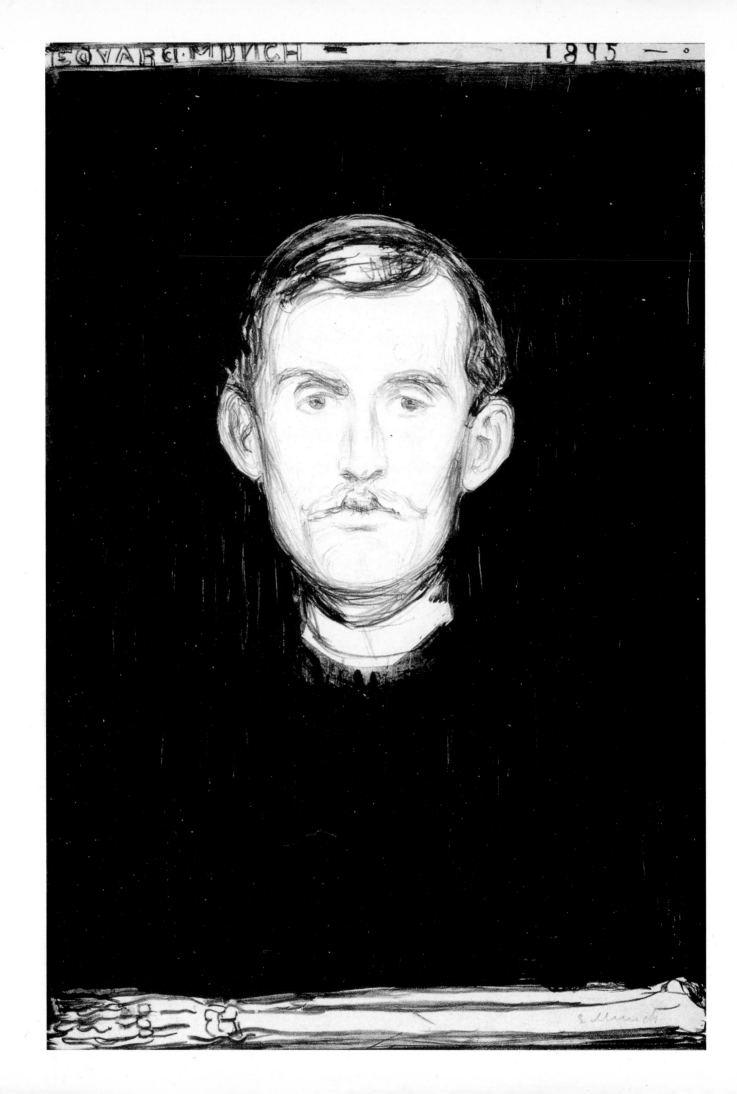

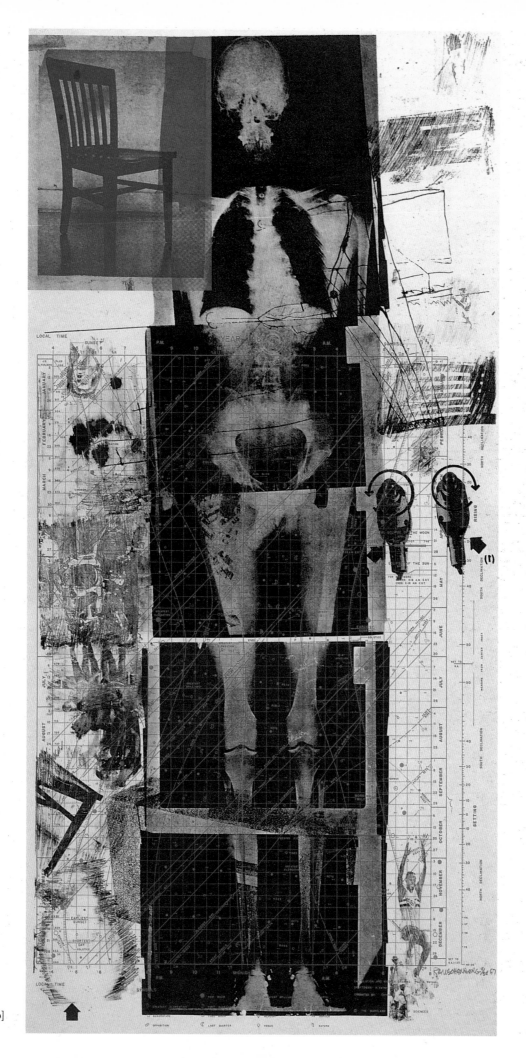

Edvard Munch
Selvportrett
med knokkelarm [II. **188**]
1895

Robert Rauschenberg
Booster (*from* «Booster
and Seven Studies») [II. **190**]
1967

Giuseppe Enrie

II **198**
Ostensione
della S. Sindone
a ricordo delle fauste nozze,
delle LL. AA. RR. i Principi
di Piemonte, *1868*
Photograph
10.5×39.2 cm
*Florence, Museo di Storia
della Fotografia Fratelli
Alinari, Zannier collection*

II **199**
Positivo fotografico
della S. Sindone
in grandezza 1/1,
1931
*Colour print from the
original black and white
plate of the exclusive official
photographs taken by
Giuseppe Enrie in 1931*
110×436 cm
*Turin, Centro
Internazionale
di Sindonologia*

II **200**
Positivo della fotografia
ufficiale della Sindone,
1931
*Silver bromide emulsion
positive picture*
10×40 cm
*Turin, Centro
Internazionale
di Sindonologia*

II **201**
Negativo fotografico
del S. Volto
(fotografia ufficiale
della Sindone), *1931*
*Silver bromide emulsion
negative print*
40×30 cm
*Turin, Centro
Internazionale
di Sindonologia*

II **202**
Negativo della fotografia
ufficiale della Sindone,
1931
*Silver bromide emulsion
negative print*
10×30 cm
*Turin, Centro
Internazionale
di Sindonologia*

Giovanni Tamburelli and Nello Balossino

II **203**
Immagine in tre
dimensioni del volto
dell'uomo del S. Sudario
di Torino
Photograph
20×30 cm
*Turin, Centro
Internazionale
di Sindonologia*

Giovanni Tamburelli
and **Nello Balossino**
Immagine in tre dimensioni
del volto dell'uomo
del S. Sudario di Torino [II. **203**]

Giuseppe Enrie
Ostensione della S. Sindone
a ricordo delle fauste nozze
delle LL.AA.RR. i Principi
di Piemonte [II. **198**]

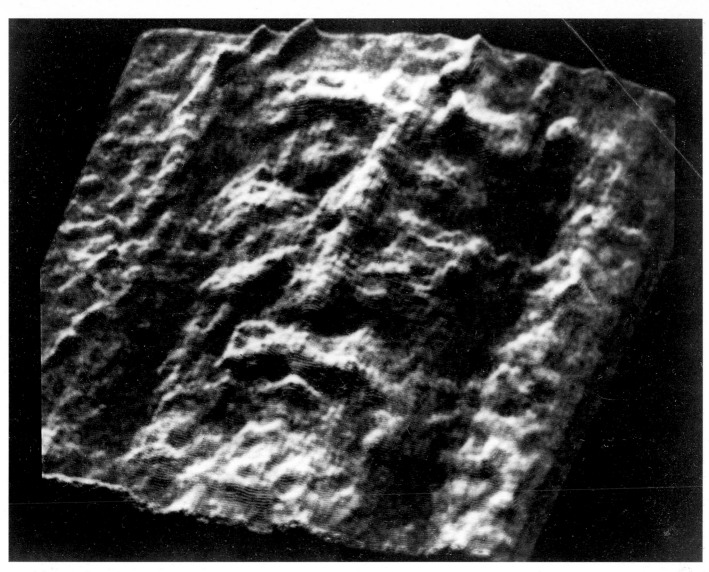

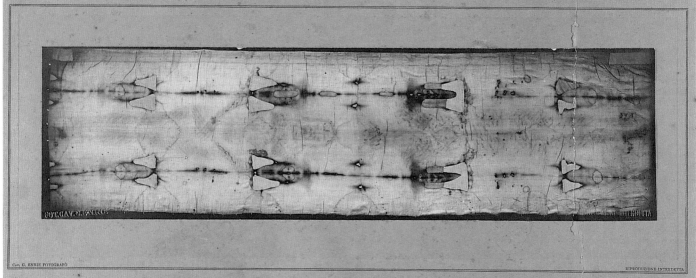

OSTENSIONE DELLA S. SINDONE

A RICORDO DELLE FAUSTE NOZZE DELLE LL. AA. RR. I PRINCIPI DI PIEMONTE

CAV. G. ENRIE FOTOGRAFÒ

RIPRODUZIONE INTERDETTA

Tuam Sindonem veneramur, Domine, et Tuam recolimus Passionem

IL PRESIDENTE DELLA COMMISSIONE ESECUTIVA

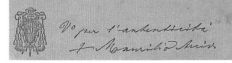

III
The
Incoherence
of the
Avant-garde
1905-1915

The Incoherence
of the Avant-garde
1905-1915

The eruption which usually 'sweeps' artistic avant-gardes from their explosive utopias and scatters them to the four winds is here recounted as a Remains of the Avant-Garde. The two opposite poles around which the original 'Rule' can be constructed are to be found in Ethnology and 'Multidimensional representation': thus the re-discovered idol is not immobile but dynamic (Brancusi).
Picasso's *Les Demoiselles d' Avignon* (1907) is not graceful with those ambiguous 'young ladies': the creative energies which are so extraordinarily present are themselves The New Graces.
Even when concerned with new anatomies (Matisse) or new studies of physiognomy (Corinth), portraits are concerned with 'expressions', with images that are decidedly 'turned in on themselves' (a sort of reaction to the 'artist' portrait). Expression and Depression (Munch) felicitously catch those artists in whom one can see a sublime confusion of face and life (Picasso). Artists are Old Young Men—see Gauguin's last portrait (1903). The portrait of male artists can, however, be read backwards, to discover a younger nature within appearance; whilst if we look at the series of portraits of Schjerfbeck, we see a biological process that it is not easy to reverse (the female face is read from youth to age, but not vice versa). Male senescence can lead to youth through a final act of wisdom (Bonnard).
The dilated expressions in Jawlesky's 'chroma' tend towards the creation of an insinuating mask, a modern 'mask' to withstand the world. Malevich is understandably attentive to popular tradition and offers his public the original geometry of color and form.

A New Norm
beyond Norms

193

Umberto Boccioni

III **1**
Antigrazioso, *1913*
Bronze
58.4×52.1×50.8 cm
New York, The Metropolitan
Museum of Art
(bequest of Lydia Winston
Malbin)

Constantin Brancusi

III **2**
Muse endormie, *1910*
Glazed bronze
16.5×26×18 cm
Paris, Musée National d'Art
Moderne, Centre Georges
Pompidou

Robert Gie

III **3**
Distribution d'effluves
avec machine centrale
et tableau métrique, *1916*
Black and blue pencil
on tracing-paper
48×69 cm
Lausanne,
Collection de l'Art Brut

Otto Gutfreund

III **4**
Kubistické poprsí,
1913–14
(Cubist Bust)
Bronze
h 60 cm
Prague, Národni Galerie
v. Praze

Katharina

III **5**
Corps humain, *1965*
Pencil and crayons on paper
126×90 cm
Lausanne,
Collection de l'Art Brut

Henri Matisse

III **6**
Académie d'homme,
1900–01
Oil on canvas
82×29 cm
Marseille, Musée Cantini

III **7**
Tête blanche et rose, *1914*
Oil on canvas
75×47 cm
Paris, Musée National
d'Art Moderne,
Centre Georges Pompidou

Pablo Picasso

III **8**
Buste de femme, *1907*
Oil on canvas
65×50 cm
Prague, Národni Galerie v
Praze

III **9**
Etude pour 'Les
Demoiselles d'Avignon':
nu de face aux bras levés,
1907 (Spring)
Oil, pencil and charcoal
on paper pasted on canvas
134×81.5 cm
Paris, Musée Picasso

III **10**
Etude pour 'Les
Demoiselles d'Avignon':
nu debout, *1907*
Pen and China
on tracing-paper
31×12.6 cm
Paris, Musée Picasso

III **11**
Etude pour 'Les
Demoiselles d'Avignon':
nu debout, *1907*
Pen and China
on tracing-paper
22.7×12.2 cm
Paris, Musée Picasso

III **12**
Etude pour 'Les
Demoiselles d'Avignon':
nu debout, *1907*
Pen and China
on tracing-paper
25.5×12 cm
Paris, Musée Picasso

III **13**
Etude pour 'Les
Demoiselles d'Avignon',
1907
Charcoal
47.6×63.5 cm
Basel, Öffentliche
Kunstsammlung
Kupferstichkabinett

III **14**
Etude de nu au visage
hiératique, les bras croisés
au-dessus de la tête,
1908 (Summer)
Lead-point on tracing-paper
31×21 cm
Paris, Musée Picasso

III **15**
Trois Etudes: femme de
dos au chignon, les bras
levés, *1908 (Summer)*
Lead-point and China
on tracing-paper
48.2×67.2 cm
Paris, Musée Picasso

III **16**
Tête de femme
(Fernande),
1909 (Autumn)
Bronze
40.5×23×26 cm
Paris, Musée Picasso

Medardo Rosso

III **17**
Madame x, *1896*
Wax
30×19×24 cm
Venice, Galleria
Internazionale d'Arte
Moderna Ca' Pesaro

Ardengo Soffici

III **18**
Donne che si lavano,
1911
Oil on canvas
137×112 cm
St. Eraclio in Foligno,
Primo De Donno collection

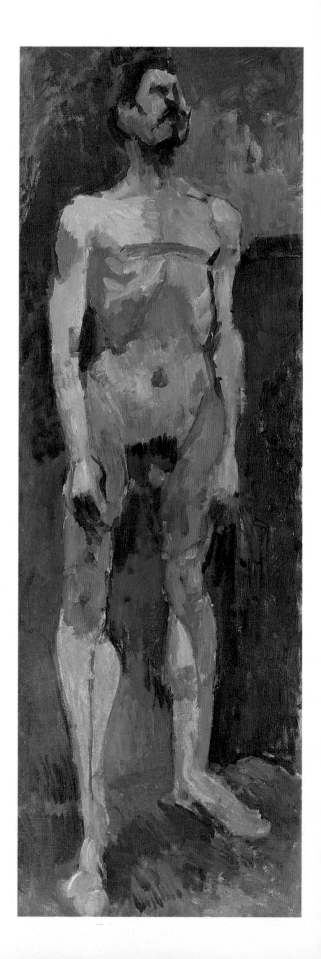

Henri Matisse
Académie d'homme [III. **6**]
1900-01

Tête blanche et rose [III. **7**]
1914

On page 192
Pablo Picasso
Buste de femme [III. **8**]
1907

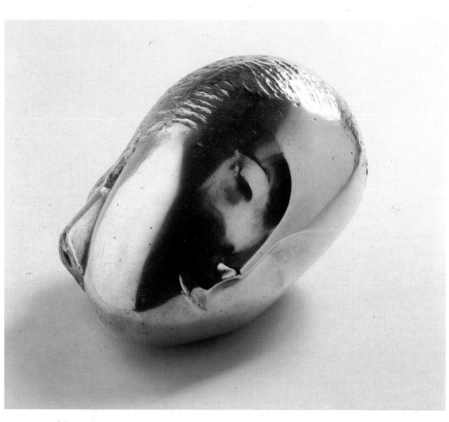

Constantin Brancusi
Muse endormie [III. **2**]
1910

Pablo Picasso
Tête de femme (Fernande)
1909
[III. **16**]

Medardo Rosso
Madame x [III. **17**]
1896

Otto Gutfreund
Kubistické poprsí [III. **4**]
1913-14

Umberto Boccioni
Antigrazioso [III. **1**]
1913

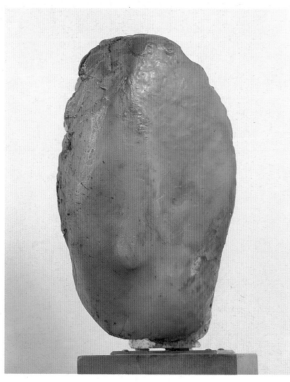

Pablo Picasso
Etude pour «Les Demoiselles
d'Avignon»: nu de face
aux bras levés [III. **9**]
1907

Etude pour «Les Demoiselles
d'Avignon»: nu debout [III. **10**]
1907

Trois Etudes: femme de dos
au chignon,
les bras levés [III. **15**]
1908

Etude de nu au visage
hiératique, les bras croisés
au-dessus de la tête [III. **14**]
1908

Katharina
Corps humain [III. **5**]
1965

Robert Gie
Distribution d'effluves
avec machine centrale
et tableau métrique [III. **3**]
1916

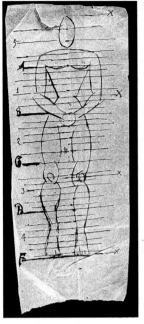 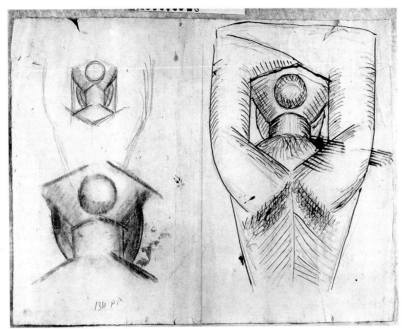 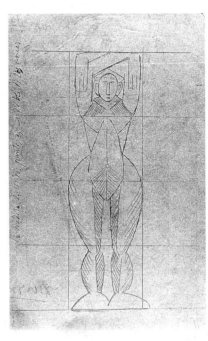

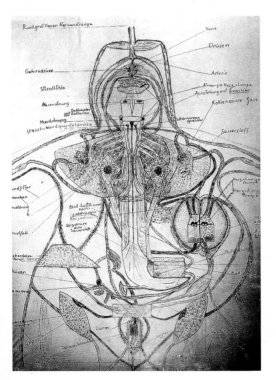 

Pablo Picasso
Etude pour «Les Demoiselles
d'Avignon» [III. **13**]
1907

Ardengo Soffici
Donne che si lavano [III. **18**]
1911

**The Demands
of Expressionism
Self-portraits**

Paul Gauguin

III **19**
Autoportrait, *1903*
Oil on canvas
42×25 cm
*Basel, Öffentliche
Kunstsammlung
Kustmuseum*

Edvard Munch

III **20**
Selvportrett, *1886*
Oil on canvas
33×24.5 cm
Oslo, Nasjonalgalleriet

III **21**
Morderen, *1910*
Oil on canvas
94×154 cm
Oslo, Munch Museet

III **22**
Selvportrett ved vindvet,
1940
Oil on canvas
84×108 cm
Oslo, Munch Museet

Helene Schjerfbeck

III **23**
Omakuva, *1895*
Oil on canvas
38×31 cm
*Tammisaari, Tammisaaren
Museo*

III **24**
Omakuva, *1912*
Oil on canvas
43×42 cm
Helsinki, Private collection

III **25**
Omakuva, musta tausta,
1915
Oil on canvas
45×36 cm
Helsinki, Ateneum

III **26**
Punatäpläinen omakuva,
1944
Oil on canvas
45×37 cm
Helsinki, Ateneum

III **27**
Omakuva, *1945*
Oil on canvas
35×23 cm
Helsinki, Private collection

Jacek Malczewski

III **28**
Autoportret z hiacyntem,
1902
Oil on canvas
78×59 cm
Poznan, Muzeum Narodowe

III **29**
Autoportret w Jakuckiej
czapce, *1907*
*(Self-portrait with the
Iacutian Hat)*
Oil on cardboard
40.5×32.5 cm
Poznan, Muzeum Narodowe

III **30**
Tobiasz i Parki, *1912*
(Tobias and the Parcae)
Oil on canvas
96×125 cm
*Poznan, Muzeum
Narodowe*

III **31**
Przekazanie palety
(Autoportret Mieczysław
Gąsechim), *1922*
*(Handing the Palette.
Self-portrait with
Mieczyslaw Gasecki)*
Oil on cardboard
74.5×102 cm
Krakow, Muzeum Narodowe

Pablo Picasso

III **32**
Autorretrato con peluca,
1897
Oil on canvas
55.8×46 cm
Barcelona, Museu Picasso

III **33**
Vieil homme assis,
*26 September 1970–14
November 1971*
Oil on canvas
145.5×114 cm
Paris, Musée Picasso

III **34**
Tête (Autoportrait),
1972 (2nd July)
Pencil on paper
65.5×50.5 cm
*Saint-Moritz,
Gilbert de Botton*

Pierre Bonnard

III **35**
Portrait de l'artiste, *1889*
Oil on cardboard
21.5×15.8 cm

III **36**
Autoportrait, *1930*
*Gouache, watercolour
and pencil on paper*
60×55 cm
Private collection

III **37**
Le boxeur (Autoportrait),
1931
Oil on canvas
54×74 cm
Paris, Private collection

III **38**
Autoportrait dans la glace,
1938
Oil on canvas
56×68.5 cm
Private collection

Lovis Corinth

III **39**
Selbstbildnis mit Modell,
1903
Oil on canvas
121×89 cm
Zurich, Kunsthaus

III **40**
Selbstporträt mit Glas,
1907
Oil on canvas
120×100 cm
Prague, Národni Galerie

III **41**
Selbstbildnis umgeben
von Ausdrucksstudien,
1910 (26 February)
Pencil
51.5×34 cm
Bremen, Kunsthalle

III **42**
Selbstbildnis mit Palette,
1924
Oil on canvas
100×80.3 cm
New York, Museum
of Modern Art
(donation of Curt Valentin)

III **43**
Selbstporträt, *1924*
Oil on canvas
55.5×41.3 cm
Stuttgart, Staatsgalerie

Arnold Schönberg

III **44**
Blick, *1910 (March)*
Oil on canvas
28×20 cm
The Schönberg Estate

III **45**
Der rote Blick,
1910 (26 March)
Oil on cardboard
28×22 cm
The Schönberg Estate

III **46**
Vision (Augen),
1910 (April)
Oil on cardboard
25×31 cm
The Schönberg Estate

III **47**
Grünes Selbstportrait,
1910 (23 October)
Oil on board
33×24 cm
The Schönberg Estate

III **48**
Hände, *1910*
Oil on canvas
22×33 cm
Munich, Städtische Galerie
im Lenbachhaus

III **49**
Selbstportrait, *1910*
Oil on board
31×22 cm
The Schönberg Estate

III **50**
Blick, *about 1910*
Oil on cardboard
31.5×28 cm
The Schönberg Estate

III **51**
Christus-Vision (Kopf),
about 1910
Oil on cardboard
50×37 cm
The Schönberg Estate

III **52**
Selbstportrait,
about 1910
Gouache on paper
23×19 cm
The Schönberg Estate

III **53**
Selbstportrait,
about 1910
Oil on canvas
38×28 cm
Private collection (courtesy
Galerie St. Etienne, New
York)

III **54**
Selbstportrait, *about 1910*
Oil on cardboard
40×30 cm
The Schönberg Estate

III **55**
Tränen, *about 1910*
Oil on canvas
29×23 cm
The Schönberg Estate

Jean Fautrier

III **56**
Autoportrait, *1916–17*
Oil on canvas
61×41 cm
Paris, Private collection

Jacek Malczewski
Autoportret
w Jakuckiej czapce [III. **29**]
1907

Paul Gauguin
Autoportrait [III. **19**]
1903

Edvard Munch
Selvportrett [III. **20**]
1886

Edvard Munch
Selvportrett
ved vindvet [III. **22**]
1940

Morderen [III. **21**]
1910

Helene Schjerfbeck
Omakuva
musta tausta [III. **25**]
1915

Punatäpläinen
omakuva [III. **26**]
1944

Omakuva [III. **27**]
1945

Jacek Malczewski
Przekazanie palety
(autoportret Mieczysław
Gaseckim) [III. **31**]
1922

Tobiasz i Parki [III. **30**]
1912

Autoportret z hiacyntem [III. **28**]
1902

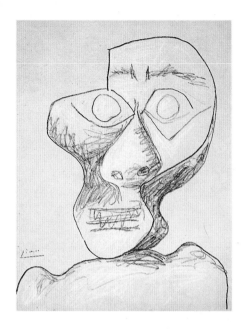

Pablo Picasso
Autorretrato con peluca [III. **32**]
1897

Tête (Autoportrait) [III. **34**]
1972

Vieil homme assis [III. **33**]
1970-71

Pierre Bonnard
Portrait de l'artiste [III. **35**]
1889

Autoportrait [III. **36**]
1930

Bonnard 1930

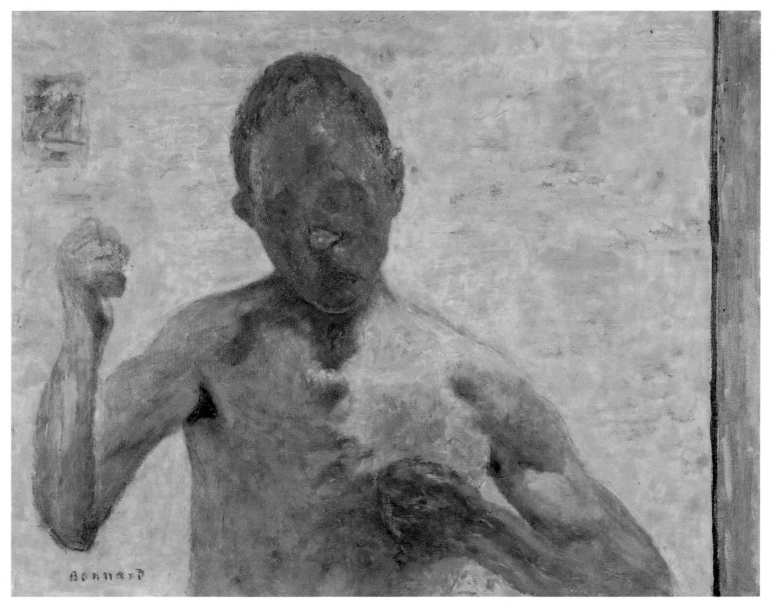

Pierre Bonnard
Le boxeur
(Autoportrait) [III. **37**]
1931

Autoportrait
dans la glace [III. **38**]
1938

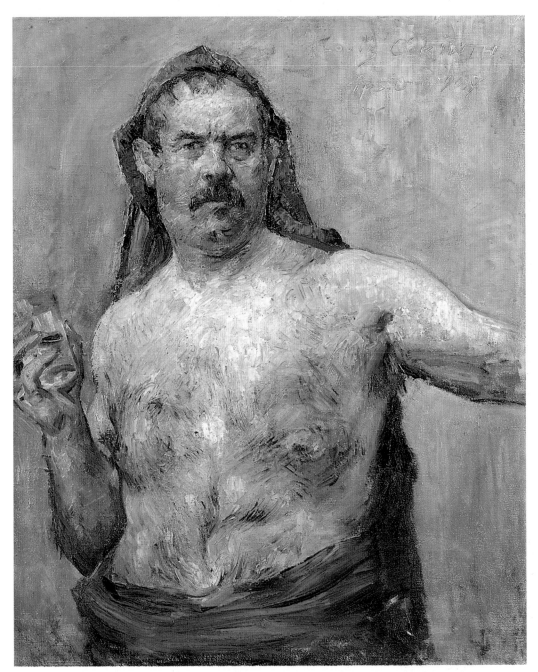

Lovis Corinth
Selbstbildnis mit Palette [III. **42**]
1924

Selbstporträt mit Glas [III. **40**]
1907

Selbstbildnis mit Modell [III. **39**]
1903

Arnold Schönberg
Der rote Blick [III. **45**]
1910

Christus-Vision (Kopf) [III. **51**]
c. 1910

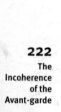

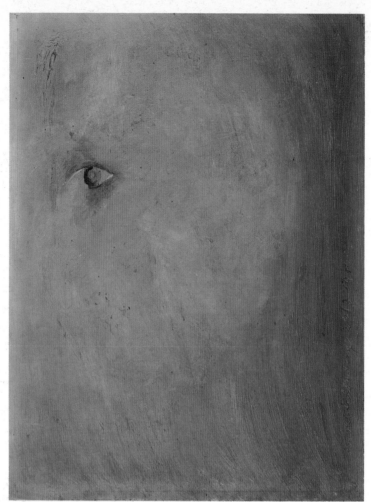

 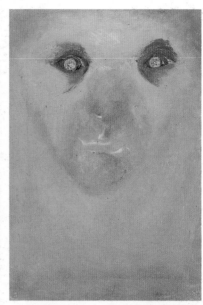 

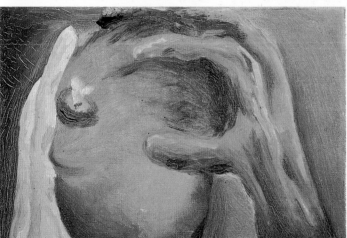  

Arnold Schönberg
Selbstportrait [III. **49**]
1910

Vision (Augen) [III. **46**]
1910

Blick [III. **44**]
1910

Hände [III. **48**]
1910

Blick [III. **50**]
c. 1910

Tränen [III. **55**]
c. 1910

Arnold Schönberg
Selbstportrait [III. **53**]
c. 1910

Grünes Selbstporträt [III. **47**]
1910

Selbstportrait [III. **52**]
c. 1910

Selbstportrait [III. **54**]
c. 1910

From the Espressionist Image to the Abstract Icon

Alexej von Jawlensky
Meduse [III. 58]
1923

Alexej von Jawlensky

III **57**
Jünglingskopf Herakles,
1912
Oil on cardboard
59×53.5 cm
Dortmund,
Museum am Ostwall

III **58**
Meduse, 1923
(Medusa)
Oil on canvas
42×31 cm
Lyon, Musée des Beaux-Arts

III **59**
Sonne-Farbe-Leben,
1926
Oil on cardboard
52.8×46.4 cm
Frankfurt,
Deutsche Bank AG.

III **60**
Kopf, 1931
Oil on cardboard
23.1×23.4 cm
Dortmund,
Museum am Ostwall

III **61**
Frauenkopf
(Abstrakter Kopf), 1932
Oil on cardboard
34×26 cm
Berlin, Staatliche Museen
zu Berlin, Nationalgalerie

III **62**
Homer, 1933
Oil on cardboard
42.7×33 cm
Emden, Kunsthalle,
(donation of Henri
Nannen)

III **63**
Meditation, 1935
Oil on cardboard
17.7×12.6 cm
Dortmund,
Museum am Ostwall

III **64**
Meditation IX/35 w1,
1935
Oil on cardboard
18.5×13.4 cm
Dortmund,
Museum am Ostwall

III **65**
Meditation, 1936
Oil on cardboard
25×18.5 cm
Dortmund,
Museum am Ostwall

Kazimir Malevič

III **66**
Golova krest'janki, 1912
(Countrywoman's Head)
Oil on canvas
80×95 cm
Amsterdam,
Stedelijk Museum

III **67**
Ženskij tors, 1920
(Feminine Bust)
Oil on board
73×52.5 cm
St. Petersburg,
Gosudarstvennyj Russkyj
Musej

III **68**
Suprematizm, 1920–27
Oil on canvas
72.5×51 cm
Amsterdam,
Stedelijk Museum

III **69**
Černyj krest, 1925–30
(Black Cross)
Oil on canvas
106×106 cm
St. Petersburg,
Gosudarstvennyi Russkyj
Musej

III **70**
Dačnik, 1928–32
(The holidayer)
Oil on canvas
106×69.5 cm
St. Petersburg,
Gosudarstvennyj Russkyj
Musej

III **71**
Dve mužskie figury,
1928–32
(Two male figures)
Oil on canvas
99×74 cm
St. Petersburg,
Gosudarstvennyj Russkyj
Musej

III **72**
Golova, 1928–32
(Head)
Oil on canvas
61×41 cm
St. Petersburg,
Gosudarstvennyj Russkyj
Musej

III **73**
Krest'janin v pole,
1928–32
(Farmer on the field)
Oil on canvas
71×44 cm
St. Petersburg,
Gosudarstvennyj Russkyj
Musej

III **74**
Portret ženy Natalija
A. Mančenko, 1933
(Portrait of the wife
Natalija A. Mancenko)
Oil on canvas
67.5×56 cm
St. Petersburg,
Gosudarstvennyj Russkyj
Musej

III **75**
Mužskoj portret
(Nikolaj Nikolaevič
Punin),
1933
(Portrait of Nikolaj
Nikolaevič Punin)
Oil on canvas
70×57.5 cm
St. Petersburg,
Gosudarstvennyj Russkyj
Musej

III **76**
Portret dočeri
Una Kazimirovna
Uriman-Malevič, 1934
(Portrait of the Daughter,
Una Kazimirovna Uriman-
Malevič)
Oil on canvas
85×61.8 cm
St. Petersburg,
Gosudarstvennyj Russkyj
Musej

Alexej von Jawlensky
Jünglingskopf Herakles [III. **57**]
1912

Alexej von Jawlensky
Sonne-Farbe-Leben [III. **59**]
1926

Kopf [III. **60**]
1931

Frauenkopf
(Abstrakter Kopf) [III. **61**]
1932

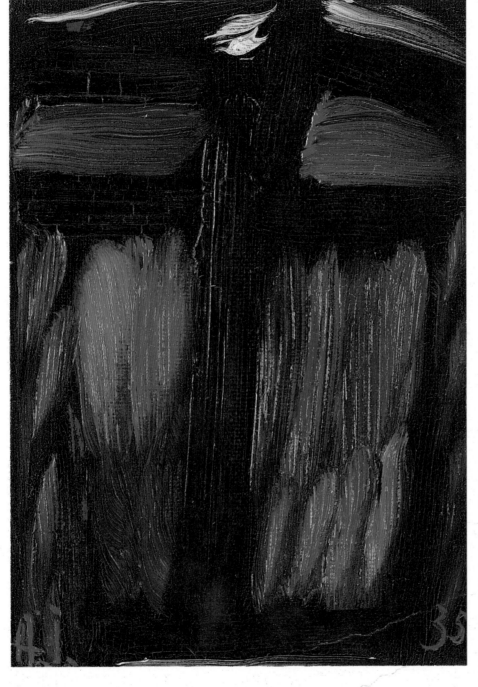

Alexej von Jawlensky
Meditation [III. **63**]
1935

Homer [III. **62**]
1933

Meditation IX/35 w1 [III. **64**]
1935

Meditation [III. **65**]
1936

Kazimir Malevič
Čërnyj krest [III. **69**]
1925-30

Suprematizm [III. **68**]
1920-27

Kazimir Malevič
Golova krest'janki [III. **66**]
1912

Ženskij tors [III. **67**]
1920

Dačnik [III. **70**]
1928-32

Dve mužskie figury [III. **71**]
1928-32

Kazimir Malevič
Portret dočeri
Una Kazimirovna
Uriman-Malevič [III. **76**]
1934

Portret ženy Natalija
A. Mančenko [III. **74**]
1933

Mužskoj portret Nikolaj
Nikolaevič Punin [III. **75**]
1933

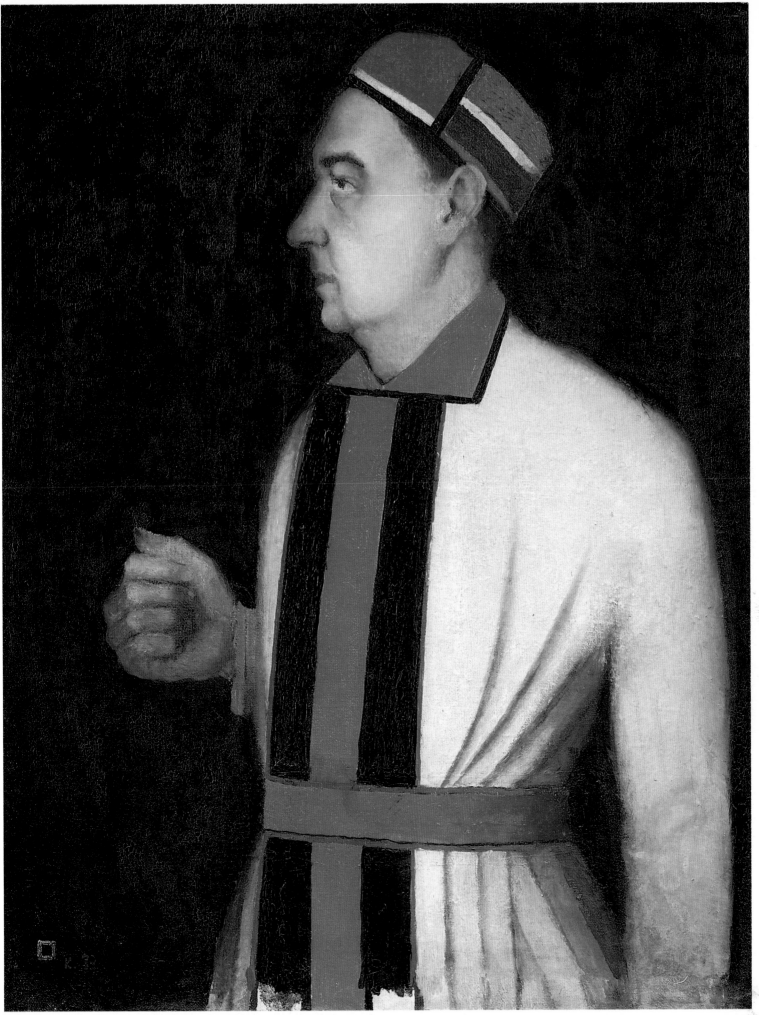

Kazimir Malevič
Krest'janin v pole [III. **73**]
1928-32

Golova [III. **72**]
1928-32

IV
**Towards
a New Man?**
1915-1930

242

Towards a New Man?

1915-1930

Beauty in cars is acceleration and the consumption of space and time. Archaic time never ended, modern time is shifted forward; it is seen in relation to space and therefore to speed. Alongside this Futurist beauty, there is also a beauty that can be contemplated—the geometry of a machine that evokes some Modern Prometheus, some Metaphysical mannequin (*Il Trovatore*), which manages to harness together Frankenstein's excess of untamed energy and the shortfall in humanity to be found in the Golem created out of the residue of human creativity.

The New Man is a son who returns to his father in a sort of classic parable (De Chirico). The Metaphysical mannequins can be related to Dedalo's mechanical dolls, or to marionettes constructed for children (Depero) or adults (Schlemmer).

Certain mechanical rigidities and 'plaster casts' remind one of the grim puppets of war, of the tragi–comedy of a retreat of invalids or a parade of veterans. The last war of the old world was the first of the modern world, and Otto Dix portrayed the misery and misfortunes of a 'modernity' which simply made it easier to kill people in larger numbers. Along with traditional weapons—of enormous size—there were new chemical weapons; gases became the modern equivalent of plague and epidemic (propagated by the precious element of air, which is only noticed when it is missing). The first anti–gas masks were the monstrous face of the fear which could save your life. Thereafter poison gas was one of the 'benefits' of progress—the air pollution that forms a hallow around our cities.

But the sufferings of 'cannon fodder' did not always end with gassing and a mass grave in a trench; there were those who brought their stigmata home, bearing a disfigured face which was nevertheless human. Henry Tonks' disfigured faces are, in a sense, the response to the abstract science of military camouflage as perfected by the Englishman

Wilkinson. Disfigurement is an irreversible disguise. It is not the transformation of a face by the 'human' means of laughter, speech or other expressions of feeling. The disfigured are identified with a 'lost' face, which does not even have the dignity of a skull. Seventeenth–century preachers had taught an *Ars moriendi* based on preparation to meet one's Maker, and a similar art of 'recomposition' was now sought for. The violent death of the suicide contrasts with the slow agony in which death makes an immobile statue of a body which loses its form (Ferdinand Hodler's *Valentine* sequence). Andreas Serrano offers us peaceful details of the stigmata of Eternal Rest. And the next order? A magic—or very unmagic—realism which fixes the form of a new genealogy (van den Berghe) in a mundane tramcar of desire (Guidi), in the logo of a boasted artistic aristocracy (De Chirico) or in a colorful popular dignity (Gutfreund). Is it a call to order—or a return to order? The magic work of a *camera obscura* fixes on light–sensitive paper the new faces of those who hold to appearance in our everyday world (Wulz).

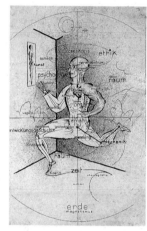

243

Oskar Schlemmer
Der Mensch
im Ideenkreis [IV. **17**]
1928

The Beauty
of the Machine

Rudolf Belling

IV **1**
Dreiklang, *1919*
Bronze
90×68×72 cm
Nuremberg, Germanisches
Nationalmuseum

Giorgio De Chirico

IV **2**
Il Trovatore, *1917*
Oil on canvas
80×55 cm
Milan, Private collection

IV **3**
Il figlio prodigo, *1926*
Oil on canvas
100×80 cm
Verona,
Galleria dello Scudo

IV **4**
Il figliol prodigo, *1929*
Oil on canvas
81×65 cm
Milan, Renato Cardazzo
collection

Aleksandr Dejneka

IV **5**
Parvekkella, *1931*
(At the Balcony)
Oil on canvas
100×105 cm
Moscow, Tret'jakovskaja
Galereja

IV **6**
Aamuvoimistelu,
1932
(Morning Exercise)
Oil on canvas
91×118 cm
Moscow, Tret'jakovskaja
Galereja

Fortunato Depero

IV **7**
Clavel nella funicolare,
1918
Oil on canvas
59×59 cm
Lugano, Private collection

Jacob Epstein

IV **8**
Torso in Metal from 'The
Rock Drill', *1913–14*
Bronze
h 70.5 cm
London, Tate Gallery

Henri Gaudier-Brzeska

IV **9**
Tête hiératique
de Ezra Pound, *1914*
Marble
95×50×50 cm
Venice,
Fondazione Giorgio Cini

Marcel Gromaire

IV **10**
La guerre, *1925*
Oil on canvas
130×96.5 cm
Paris, Musée d'Art Moderne
de la Ville de Paris

Raoul Hausmann

IV **11**
Kutschenbauch dichtet,
1920
Watercolor and China ink
on paper 42.5×31.9 cm
Saint-Etienne,
Musée d'Art Moderne

Heinrich Hoerle

IV **12**
Drei Invaliden, *1930*
Oil on board
100×50 cm
Zurich, Private collection

Oskar Kokoschka

IV **13**
Mann mit Puppe, *1922*
Oil on canvas
80×120 cm
Berlin, Staatliche Museen
zu Berlin, Nationalgalerie

Fernand Léger

IV **14**
Femme au bouquet, *1924*
Oil on canvas
65×50 cm
Villeneuve-d'Asq,
Musée d'Art Moderne
de la Communauté
urbaine de Lille
(donation of Geneviève
and Jean Masurel)

Markus Lüpertz

IV **15**
Zyklop-dithyrambisch,
1973
Gouache and glued paper
on canvas
240×190 cm
Cologne,
Galerie Michael Werner

Oskar Schlemmer

IV **16**
Der Kopftypus, *1928*
Ink and pencil on paper
30×21 cm
Oggebbio, Como, C. Raman
Schlemmer collection

IV **17**
Der Mensch
im Ideenkreis, *1928*
Pencil, spray ink
and crayon on gray paper
74.5×48.9 cm
Oggebbio, Como, C. Raman
Schlemmer collection

IV **18**
Einfachste
Kopfkonstruktion
von vorn, *1928*
Pencil, crayon
and ink on paper
30×21 cm
Oggebbio, Como, C. Raman
Schlemmer collection

IV **19**
Einfachste
Kopfkonstruktion
(Profil), *1928*
Pencil on paper
30×21 cm
Oggebbio, Como, C. Raman
Schlemmer collection

IV **20**
Gruppe am Geländer I,
1931
Oil on canvas
91.5×60.5
Düsseldorf, Kunstsammlung
Nordrhein-Westfalen

**Walter
Schulze-Mittendorf**

IV **21**
Copie du robot du film
'Metropolis' de Fritz Lang,
1926 (original),
re-make (1970)
Copy in layered polyester
resin (1995)
190×60×45 cm
Paris, Cinémathèque
Française collection, Ateliers
de Moulage du Louvre

Fortunato Depero
Clavel nella funicolare [IV. **7**]
1918

Rudolf Belling
Dreiklang [IV. **1**]
1919

Henri Gaudier-Brzeska
Tête hiératique
de Ezra Pound [IV. **9**]
1914

Jacob Epstein
Torso in Metal
from «The Rock Drill» [IV. **8**]
1913-14

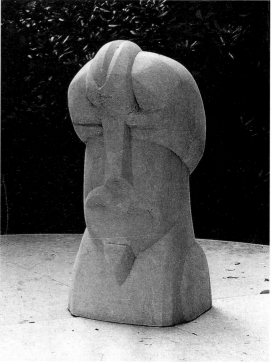

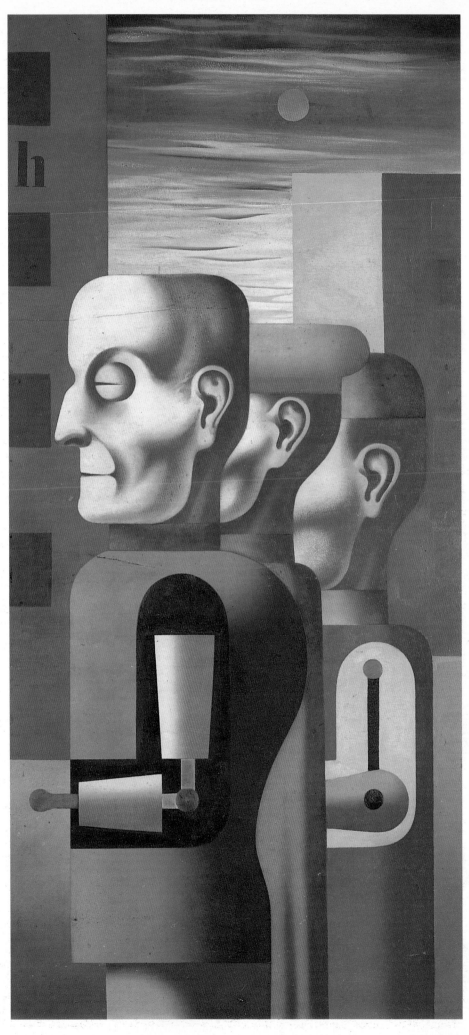

Marcel Gromaire
La guerre [IV. **10**]
1925

Heinrich Hoerle
Drei Invaliden [IV. **12**]
1930

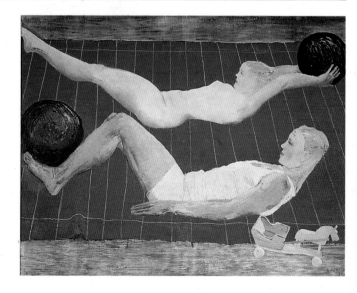

Aleksandr Dejneka
Parvekkella [IV. **5**]
1931

Aamuvoimistelu [IV. **6**]
1932

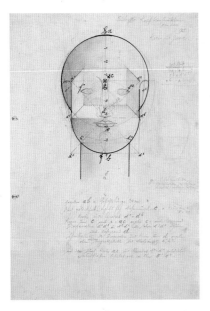

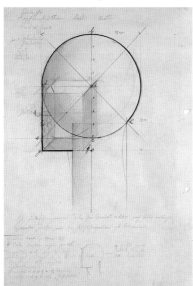

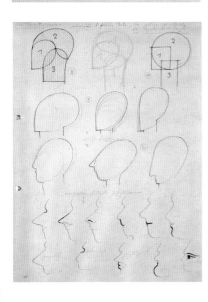

Oskar Schlemmer
Einfachste Kopfkonstruktion von vorn [IV. **18**]
1928
Einfachste Kopfkonstruktion (Profil) [IV. **19**]
1928
Der Kopftypus [IV. **16**]
1928
Gruppe am Geländer I [IV. **20**]
1931

Giorgio De Chirico
Il figliol prodigo [IV. **3**]
1926

Il figliol prodigo [IV. **4**]
1929

252
Towards
a New Man?

Markus Lüpertz
Zyklop-dithyrambisch [IV. **15**]
1973

Oskar Kokoschka
Mann mit Puppe [IV. **13**]
1922

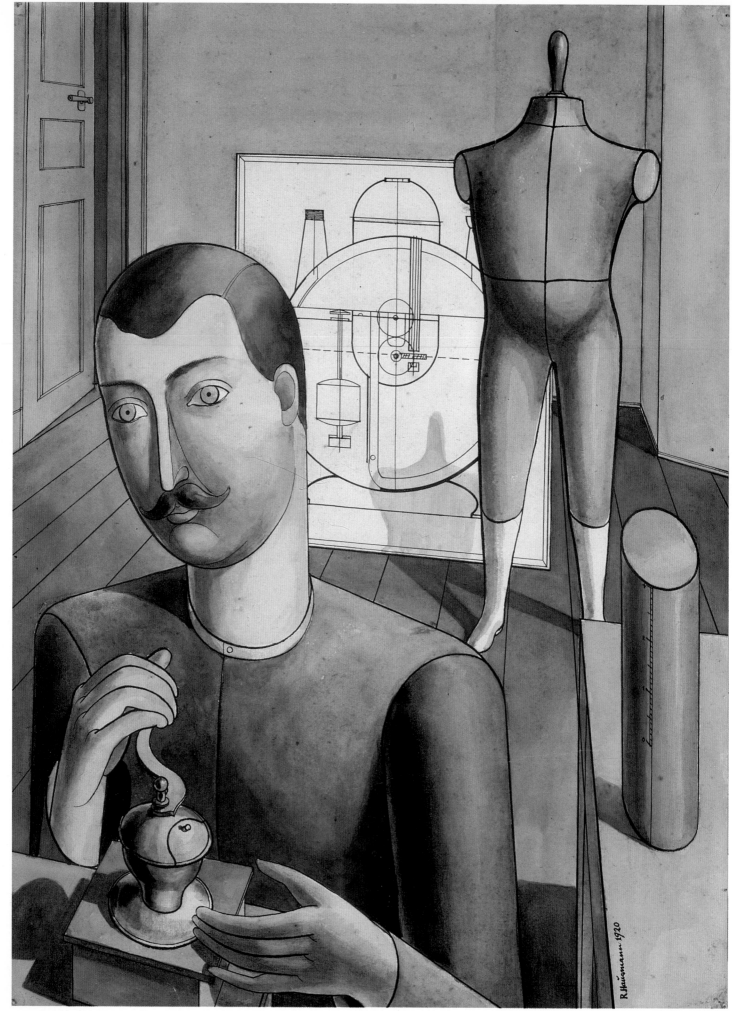

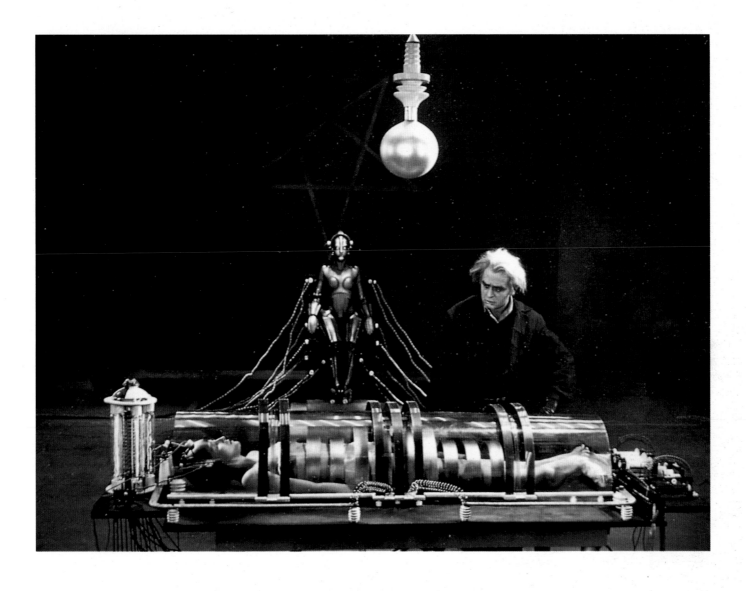

Raoul Hausmann
Kutschenbauch dichtet [IV. **11**]
1920

Frame from Fritz Lang's movie
Metropolis
1926

'Tempests of Steel': The Great War

Anonymous

IV **22**
Masques en cire d'un
blessé de guerre (Double
bec de lièvre traumatique
et fracture des os du nez.
Aspect du blessé après
opération. Pose de la
prothèse nasale. Pose
d'une prothèse nasale de
travail), *1917*
Wax mould
30×100 cm
Paris, Musée du Service
de Santé des Armées
au Val-de-Grâce

IV **23**
Tampon servant
de masque à gaz (Tampon
avec lunettes cousues.
Cette combinaison marque
un premier essai de
masque complet qui sera
réalisé peu après les
masques LTN et THN. Le
masque est présenté sur
un moulage en plâtre
polychrome), *1915*
Wax, fabric, plaster
28×17×17 cm
Paris, Musée du Service
de Santé des Armées
au Val-de-Grâce

IV **24**
Tampon servant de
masque à gaz (Tampon P2
à 3 compresses. Lunettes
caoutchoutées. Le masque
est présenté
sur un moulage en plâtre
polychrome), *1915*
Wax, fabric, plaster
27×17×16 cm
Paris, Musée du Service
de Santé des Armées
au Val-de-Grâce

IV **25**
Tampon servant
de masque à gaz (Deux
tampons de tissue éponge
cousus à la face interne
du baillon assurent une
application plus étanche
de chaque côté du nez.
Les cordons peuvent
s'attacher sous le menton.
Le masque est présenté
sur un moulage en plâtre
polychrome), *1915*
Wax, fabric, plaster
15×25×16 cm
Paris, Musée du Service
de Santé des Armées
au Val-de-Grâce

IV **26**
Tampon servant
de masque à gaz (Tampon
de toile avec lunettes
de caoutchouc. L'appareil
possède 3 compresses.
Le masque est présenté
sur un moulage en plâtre
polychrome), *1915*
Wax, fabric, plaster
27×20×18 cm
Paris, Musée du Service
de Santé des Armées
au Val-de-Grâce

Max Beckmann

IV **27**
Das Leichenhaus, *1915*
Dry-point and etching
25.6×36 cm
Frankfurt, Städtische
Galerie im Städelsches
Kunstinstitut

Otto Dix

IV **28**
Toter Soldat, *1922*
Watercolor and tempera
48×37 cm
Stuttgart, Galerie der Stadt

IV **29**
Dirne und Kriegsverletzter,
1923
Pencil
47×37 cm
Munster, Westfalisches
Landesmuseum für Kunst
und Kulturgeschichte

IV **30**
Die Irrsinnige
von St. Marie-à-Py, Bl. 5,
Mappe IV der Folge
'Der Krieg', *1924*
Etching
28.8×19.8 cm
London,
The British Museum

IV **31**
Gesehen am Steilhang von
Cléry-sur-Somme, Bl. 8,
Mappe III der Folge
'Der Krieg', *1924*
Etching and aquatint
26×19.6 cm
London,
The British Museum

IV **32**
Mahlzeit in der Sappe
(Lorettohöhe), Bl. 3,
Mappe II der Folge
'Der Krieg', *1924*
Etching and aquatint
19.6×29 cm
London,
The British Museum

IV **33**
Schädel, Bl. 1, Mappe IV
der Folge 'Der Krieg',
1924
Etching
27.5×19.5 cm
London,
The British Museum

IV **34**
Sterbender Soldat, Bl. 6,
Mappe III der Folge
'Der Krieg', *1924*
Etching and aquatint
19.8×14.8 cm
London,
The British Museum

IV **35**
Tote bei der Stellung vor
Tahure, Bl. 10, Mappe V
der Folge 'Der Krieg',
1924
Etching and aquatint
19.5×25.8 cm
London,
The British Museum

René Leriche
Statuette d'un homme
atteint d'hémiplégie
post-commotionnelle [IV. **38**]
1918

On page 258
Otto Dix
Toter Soldat [IV. **28**]
1922

IV **36**
Transplantation, Bl. 10,
Mappe IV der Folge
'Der Krieg', *1924*
*Etching, dry-point and
aquatint*
19.9×14.9 cm
*London, The British
Museum*

René Leriche

IV **37**
Statuette d'un homme
atteint de contracture
de la masse sacro-lombaire
des obliques et des
muscles de la hanche,
1914-18
Plaster mould
35×16×11 cm
*Paris, Musée du Service
de Santé des Armées
au Val-de-Grâce*

IV **38**
Statuette d'un homme
atteint d'hémiplégie
post-commotionnelle,
1918
Plaster mould
29×15×15 cm
*Paris, Musée du Service
de Santé des Armées
au Val-de-Grâce*

**Société du Petit
Parisien, Dupuy et Cie**

IV **39**
Le soldat Brunier,
avant sa guérison, *1916*
(21 June and 7 October)
*Two prints in silver
chloride bromide emulsion,
one of which retouched
in tempera*
11.5×8.7 cm
*Florence, Museo di Storia
della Fotografia Fratelli
Alinari*

Henry Tonks

IV **40**
Study of Facial Wounds,
n° 57, *1916*
Pastel on paper
24.8×18 cm
*London, The Royal College
of Surgeons of England*

IV **41**
Study of Facial Wounds,
n° 58, *1916*
Pastel on paper
24.8×18 cm
*London, The Royal College
of Surgeons of England*

IV **42**
Study of Facial Wounds,
n° 59, *1916*
Pastel on paper
24.8×18 cm
*London, The Royal College
of Surgeons of England*

IV **43**
Study of Facial Wounds,
n° 60, *1916*
Pastel on paper
24.8×18 cm
*London, The Royal College
of Surgeons of England*

IV **44**
Study of Facial Wounds,
n° 61, *1916*
Pastel on paper
24.8×18 cm
*London, The Royal College
of Surgeons of England*

IV **45**
Study of Facial Wounds,
n° 62, *1916*
Pastel on paper
24.8×18 cm
*London, The Royal College
of Surgeons of England*

IV **46**
Study of Facial Wounds,
n° 63, *1916*
Pastel on paper
24.8×18 cm
*London, The Royal College
of Surgeons of England*

IV **47**
Study of Facial Wounds,
n° 64, *1916*
Pastel on paper
24.8×18 cm
*London, The Royal College
of Surgeons of England*

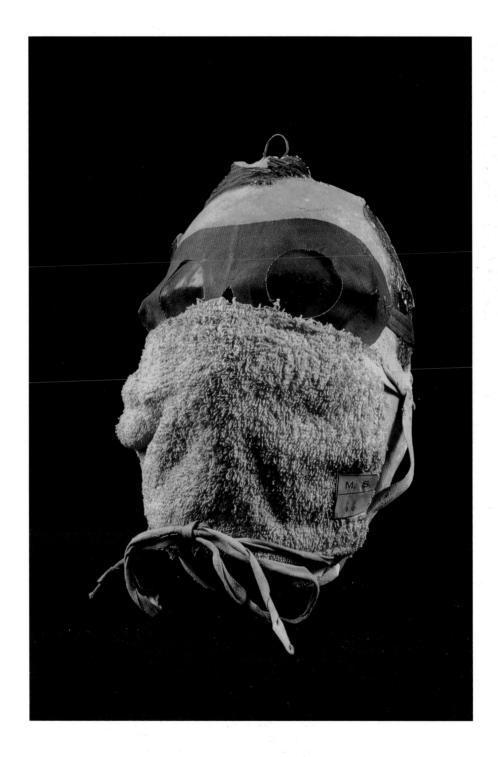

Anonymous
Tampon servant
de masque à gaz [IV. **25**]
1915

Max Beckmann
Das Leichenhaus [IV. **27**]
1915

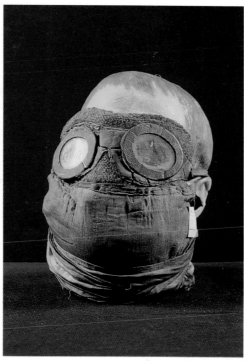
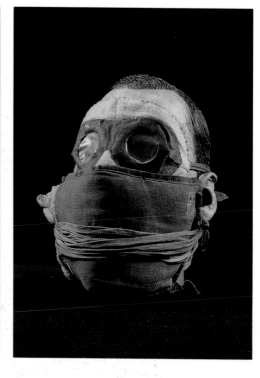

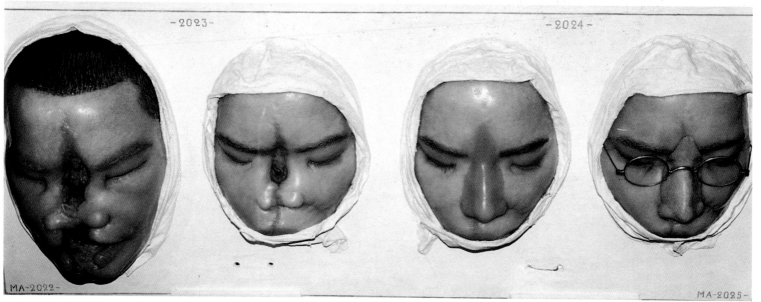

Anonymous
Tampons servant de masque
à gaz [IV. **23-24-26**]

Masques en cire d'un blessé
de guerre [IV. **22**]
1917

Otto Dix
Mahlzeit in der Sappe
(Lorettohöhe), Bl. 3,
Mappe II der Folge
«Der Krieg» [IV. **32**]
1924

Sterbender Soldat,
Bl. 6, Mappe III der Folge
«Der Krieg» [IV. **34**]
1924

Gesehen am Steilhang
von Cléry-sur-Somme,
Bl. 8, Mappe III der Folge
«Der Krieg» [IV. **31**]
1924

Schädel, Bl. 1, Mappe IV
der Folge «Der Krieg» [IV. **33**]
1924

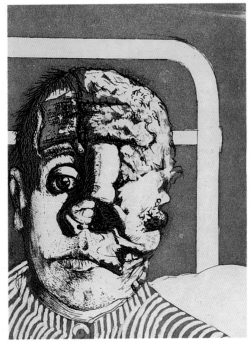

Otto Dix
Die Irrsinnige
von St. Marie-à-Py,
Bl. 5, Mappe IV der Folge
«Der Krieg» [IV. **30**]
1924

Transplantation,
Bl. 10, Mappe IV der Folge
«Der Krieg» [IV. **36**]
1924

Dirne und Kriegsverletzter [IV. **29**]
1923

Tote bei der Stellung
vor Tahure, Bl. 10, Mappe V
der Folge «Der Krieg» [IV. **35**]
1924

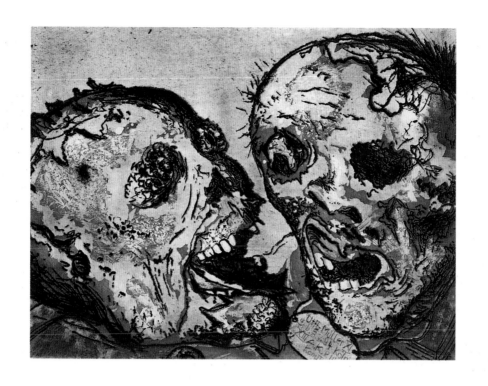

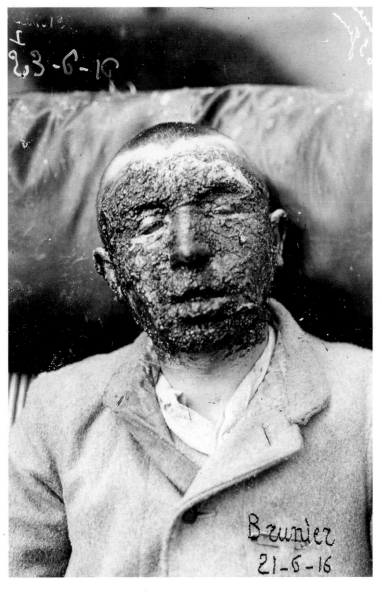
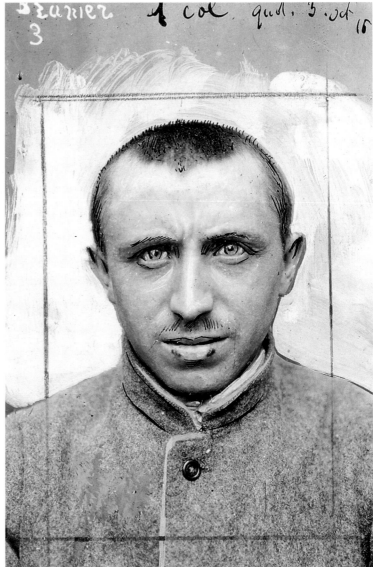

Société du Petit Parisien, Dupuy et Cie
Le soldat Brunier
avant sa guérison [IV. **39**]
1916

Henry Tonks
Study of Facial Wounds,
n° 57; n° 58; n° 64;
n° 59 [IV. **40-41-47-42**]
1916

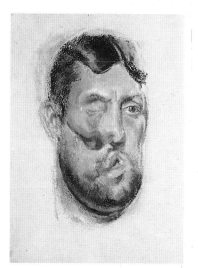 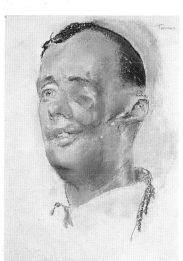  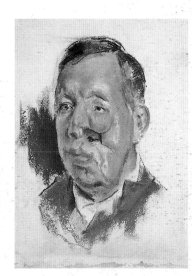

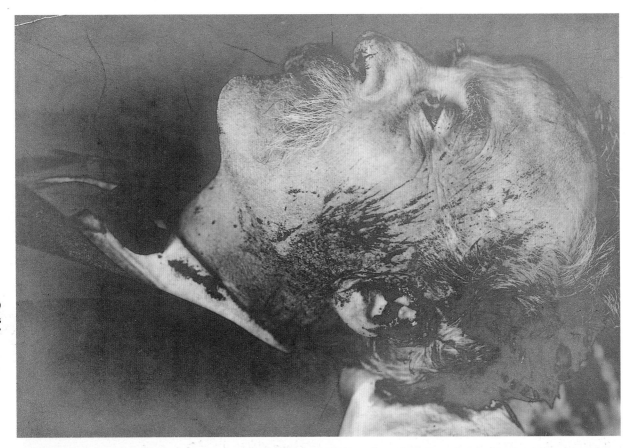

Anonymous
Suicida per arma
da fuoco [IV. **48**]
c. 1905

Jeffrey Silverthorne
Morgue Work:
Old Man [IV. **63**]
1986

'Ars moriendi'

Anonymous

IV **48**
Suicida per arma da
fuoco, *about 1905*
*Photograph, print on silver
bromide paper*
17.3×11.7 cm
*Venice, Italo Zannier
collection*

Camille Claudel

IV **49**
Torse de Clotho,
about 1893
Plaster
44.5×25×14 cm
Paris, Musée d'Orsay

Ferdinand Hodler

IV **50**
Die kranke
Valentine Godé-Darel,
1914
Lead pencil on white paper
62.5×46.8 cm
*Zurich, Kunsthaus,
Graphische Sammlung*

IV **51**
Die tote Valentine
Godé-Darel, Halbfigur,
Rechtsprofil, *1915*
*Lead pencil, gouache
and oil on beige paper*
45.8×64 cm
*Zurich, Kunsthaus,
Graphische Sammlung*

IV **52**
Kopf der Sterbenden
Valentine Godé-Darel
in Kissen gebettet, *1915*
Lead pencil on white paper
47×31 cm
*Zurich, Kunsthaus,
Graphische Sammlung*

IV **53**
Die sterbende
Valentine Godé-Darel,
1915 (4 January)
*Lead pencil
on Fabriano paper*
40×52 cm
*Zurich, Kunsthaus,
Graphische Sammlung*

IV **54**
Die Sterbende Valentine
Godé-Darel, Linksprofil,
1915 (24 January)
*Lead pencil and gouache on
beige paper*
34.5×45.5 cm
*Zurich, Kunsthaus,
Graphische Sammlung*

IV **55**
Die Tote
(Valentine Godé-Darel),
1915 (26 January)
*Lead pencil and oil on
paper 39.5×64 cm*
*Basel, Öffentliche
Kunstsammlung,
Kunstmuseum*

Gustav Klimt

IV **56**
Die drei Lebensalter, *1905*
Oil on canvas
180×180 cm
*Rome, Galleria Nazionale
d'Arte Moderna
e Contemporanea*

Pablo Picasso

IV **57**
Nu dans un fauteuil,
1972 (3 October)
Pen and China ink
59×75.5 cm
Paris, Musée Picasso

Paul Richer

IV **58**
Cire d'une vieille femme
morte des suites d'un
rhumatisme, déformant
(Richer/Londe)
Polychromatic wax
18×160×53 cm
*Paris, Musée
de l'Assistance Publique,
Hôpitaux de Paris*

IV **59**
Femme atteinte de la
maladie de Parkinson,
1895
Bronze 47×16×16 cm
*Paris, Bibliothèque Charcot,
Hôpital de la Salpêtrière*

Andres Serrano

IV **60**
The Morgue (AIDS Related
Death), *1992*
Cibachrome 1/3
125.7×152.4 cm
*Paris,
Galerie Yvon Lambert*

IV **61**
The Morgue (Hacked
to Death II), *1992*
Cibachrome 1/3
125.7×152.5 cm
*Montreal, Musée d'Art
Contemporain*

IV **62**
The Morgue (Rat Poison
Suicide II), *1992*
Cibachrome 1/3
125.7×152.4 cm
*Paris, Fonds National d'Art
Contemporain (F.N.A.C.)*

Jeffrey Silverthorne

IV **63**
Morgue Work: Old Man,
1986
Color photograph
40×50 cm
*Stuttgart, Courtesy of the
Galerie A. Vera Amor*

IV **64**
Morgue Work:
Beating Victim, *1972*
Black and white photograph
50×40 cm
*Stuttgart, Courtesy of the
Galerie A. Vera Amor*

Paolo Vallorz

IV **65**
Nudo di Violette Leduc,
1964
Oil on canvas
150×75 cm
*Milan,
Alain Toubas collection,
Compagnia del Disegno*

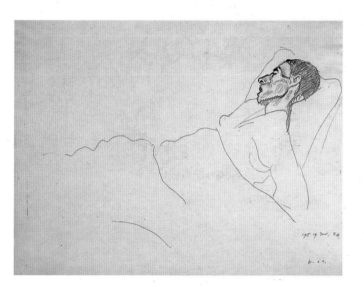

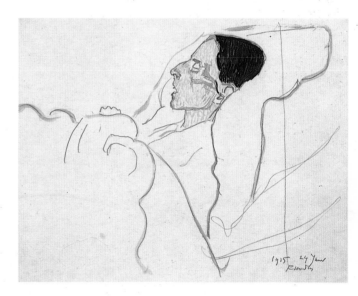

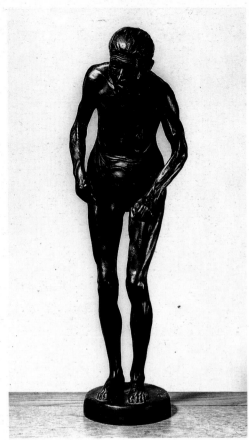

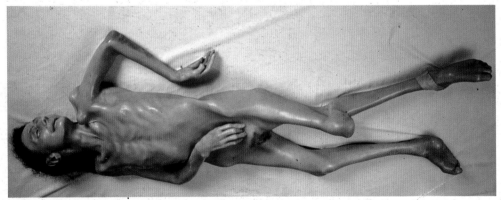

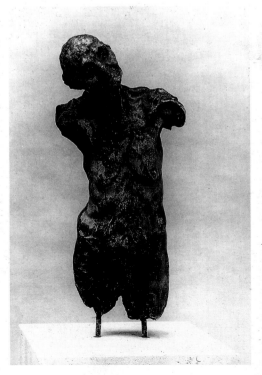

Paul Richer
Femme atteinte de la maladie
de Parkinson [IV. **59**]
1895

Cire d'une vieille femme
morte des suites
d'un rhumatisme déformant
(Richer/Londe) [IV. **58**]

Camille Claudel
Torse de Clotho [IV. **49**]
c. 1893

Gustav Klimt
Die drei Lebensalter [IV. **56**]
1905

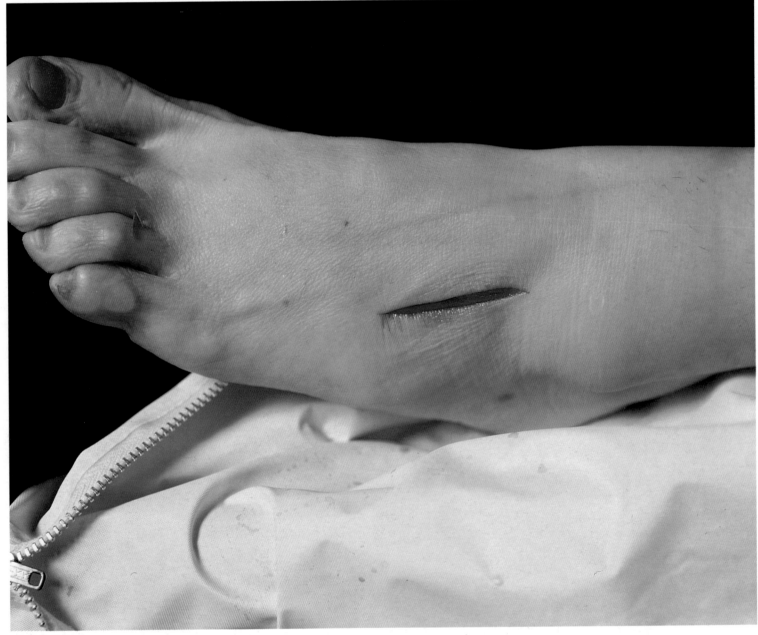

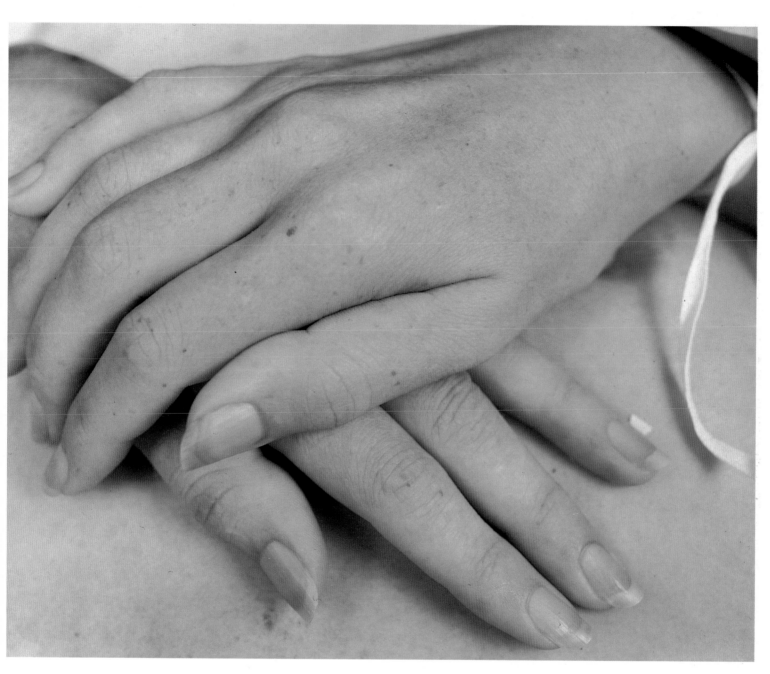

Andres Serrano
The Morgue
(Rat Poison Suicide II) [IV. **62**]
1992

The Morgue
(AIDS Related Death) [IV. **60**]
1992

An Impossible Call to Order

Frits van den Berghe

IV **66**
Genealogie, *1929*
Oil on canvas
146×114 cm
Basel, Kunstmuseum
(bequest of Emanuel
Hoffmann Stiftung)

Massimo Campigli

IV **67**
Le cucitrici, *1925*
Oil on canvas
161×96.5 cm
St. Petersburg,
Ermitage Museum

Felice Casorati

IV **68**
Silvana Cenni, *1922*
Tempera on canvas
205×105 cm
Turin, Francesco Casorati
collection

IV **69**
Doppio ritratto, *1924*
Tempera on board
122×91 cm
Milan, Private collection

IV **70**
Conversazione platonica,
1925
Oil on canvas
78.5×100.3 cm
Rome, Private collection

Giorgio De Chirico

IV **71**
Autoritratto, *1911*
Oil on canvas
82.5×68.5 cm
New York, Metropolitan
Museum of Art (donation
in memory of Carl Van
Vechten and Fania
Marinoff)

IV **72**
Autoritratto, *1920*
Oil on canvas
32×41.5 cm
Milan, Renato Cardazzo
collection

IV **73**
Autoritratto in veste
di Odisseo, *1922*
Tempera on canvas
90×70 cm
Milan, Private collection

IV **74**
Autoritratto con busto
d'Euripide,
1922–23
Tempera on canvas
59.5×49.5 cm
Private collection (courtesy
of the Galleria dello Scudo,
Verona)

IV **75**
Autoritratto con la rosa,
1923
Oil on canvas
75×60 cm
Piacenza, Private collection

IV **76**
Autoritratto,
1925
Oil on canvas
75×62 cm
Venice, Giovanni Deana
collection

Otto Dix

IV **77**
Liegende auf
Leopardenfell:
Vera Simailova, *1927*
Oil on wood
70×99 cm
Ithaca (New York), Herbert
F. Johnson Museum of Art
Cornell University
(donation of
Samuel A. Berger)

G. Givaudan

IV **78**
Profil d'Emile Givaudan
('Méthode de la troncature
apparente par tranches
lumineuses'),
about 1920 (original)
36 contact prints 6×6
(recent prints)
52.4×99.6 cm
Chalon-sur-Saône,
Musée Nicéphore Nièpce

Virgilio Guidi

IV **79**
In Tram, *1923*
Oil on canvas
160×190.5 cm
Rome, Galleria Nazionale
d'Arte Moderna
e Contemporanea

Otto Gutfreund

IV **80**
Vlastní portrét, *1919*
(Self-portrait)
Polychromatic terracotta
h 45 cm
Prague, Národni Galerie v
Praze

IV **81**
Podobizna umělcovy zěny,
1923
(Portrait
of the Artist's Wife)
Polychromatic terracotta
h 33 cm
Prague, Národni Galerie v
Praze

**Nikolaj Aleksandrovič
Ionin**

IV **82**
Portret F.N. Ioninoj,
about 1925
(Portrait of F.N. Ionina)
Oil on board
36×31 cm
St. Petersburg,
Gosudarstvenuyj Russkyj
Musej

Aristide Maillol

IV **83**
Torse de Vénus, *1921*
Bronze
114×47×30 cm
Paris, Dina Vierny
collection

Arturo Martini

IV **84**
La Nena, *1928*
Terracotta
51×33×33 cm
Varese, Private collection
(courtesy of the Galleria
GianFerrari)

IV **85**
La Pisana, *1928*
Kaolin and sand
55×135×50 cm
Milan, Private collection

Piet Mondrian

IV **86**
Zelfportret, *1918*
Oil on canvas
88×71 cm
The Hague, Haags
Gemeentemuseum

Ubaldo Oppi

IV **87**
Le amiche, *1924*
Oil on canvas
120.5×101 cm
Private collection (courtesy
of the Galleria dello Scudo,
Verona)

**Kuz'ma Sergeevič
Petrov-Vodkin**

IV **88**
Rabočie, *1926*
(Workers)
Oil on canvas
'97×106.5 cm
St. Petersburg,
Gosudarstvenuyj Russkyj
Musej

Christian Schad

IV **89**
Dr. Haustein, *1928*
Oil on canvas
80.5×55 cm
Madrid,
Fundación Colección
Thyssen-Bornemisza

Gino Severini

IV **90**
Portrait de la famille
Severini, *1936*
Oil on canvas
175×122 cm
Lyon, Musée des Beaux-Arts

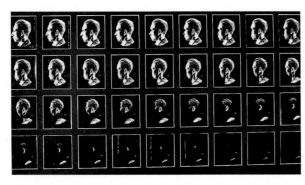

Giorgio De Chirico
Autoritratto [IV. **72**]
1920

G. Givaudan
Profil d'Emile Givaudan
(«Méthode de la troncature
apparente par tranches
lumineuses») [IV. **78**]
c. 1920

On page 278:
Frits van den Berghe
Genealogie [IV. **66**]
1929

IV **91**
Projections conjuguées
de la tête, *about 1920*
China ink on paper
55×61 cm
Rome, Gina Severini
Franchina collection

Mario Sironi

IV **92**
L'architetto, *1922*
Oil on canvas
70×60 cm
Milan, Private collection

IV **93**
Nudo con lo specchio,
1923–24
Oil on canvas
97×73 cm
Bergamo, Private collection

IV **94**
L'allieva, *1924*
Oil on canvas
97×75 cm
Private collection (courtesy
of the Galleria dello Scudo,
Verona)

Carlo Wulz

IV **95**
L'attrice triestina Ducaton,
about 1910
Print on silver bromide
emulsion
18.2×16.6 cm
Florence, Museo di Storia
della Fotografia Fratelli
Alinari, Wulz Archive

IV **96**
Ritratto di donna,
about 1910
Print on silver bromide
emulsion
24.2×12.3 cm
Florence, Museo di Storia
della Fotografia Fratelli
Alinari, Wulz Archive

IV **97**
Sphinx, *about 1915*
Print on silver bromide
emulsion
41×24.5 cm
Florence, Museo di Storia
della Fotografia Fratelli
Alinari, Wulz Archive

IV **98**
Nudo femminile,
1920-25
Print on silver chloride
bromide emulsion
27×22 cm
Florence, Museo di Storia
della Fotografia Fratelli
Alinari, Wulz Archive

IV **99**
Marion e Wanda, con
Bianca Baldussi, *1920–25*
Enlargement on silver
chloride bromide emulsion
28.2×21.1 cm
Florence, Museo di Storia
della Fotografia Fratelli
Alinari, Wulz Archive

IV **100**
Mia figlia Marion,
about 1922
Print on silver bromide
emulsion 24.5×22.8 cm
Florence, Museo di Storia
della Fotografia Fratelli
Alinari, Wulz Archive

Wanda Wulz

IV **101**
Ritratto di donna,
1925–30
Print on silver bromide
emulsion 29.2×21.3 cm
Florence, Museo di Storia
della Fotografia Fratelli
Alinari, Wulz Archive

IV **102**
Ritratto di donna,
about 1928
Print on silver chloride
bromide emulsion
29.5×23.3 cm
Florence, Museo di Storia
della Fotografia Fratelli
Alinari, Wulz Archive

Felice Casorati
Silvana Cenni [IV. **68**]
1922

Felice Casorati
Doppio ritratto [IV. **69**]
1924

Conversazione platonica [IV. **70**]
1925

Giorgio De Chirico
Autoritratto [IV. **71**]
1911

Autoritratto
in veste di Odisseo [IV. **73**]
1922

Giorgio De Chirico
Autoritratto
con busto d'Euripide [IV. **74**]
1922-23

Autoritratto [IV. **76**]
1925

Autoritratto
con la rosa [IV. **75**]
1923

Otto Dix
Liegende auf Leopardenfell:
Vera Simailova [IV. **77**]
1927

Christian Schad
Dr. Haustein [IV. **89**]
1928

Piet Mondrian
Zelfportret [IV. **86**]
1918

Mario Sironi
L'architetto [IV. **92**]
1922

Mario Sironi
L'allieva [IV. **94**]
1924

Nudo con lo specchio [IV. **93**]
1923-24

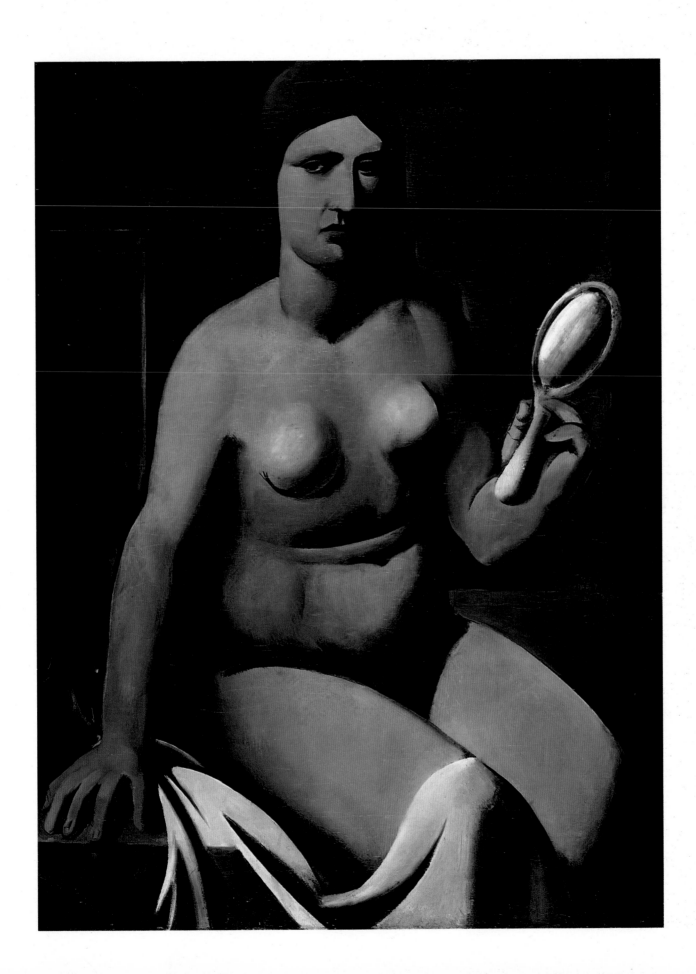

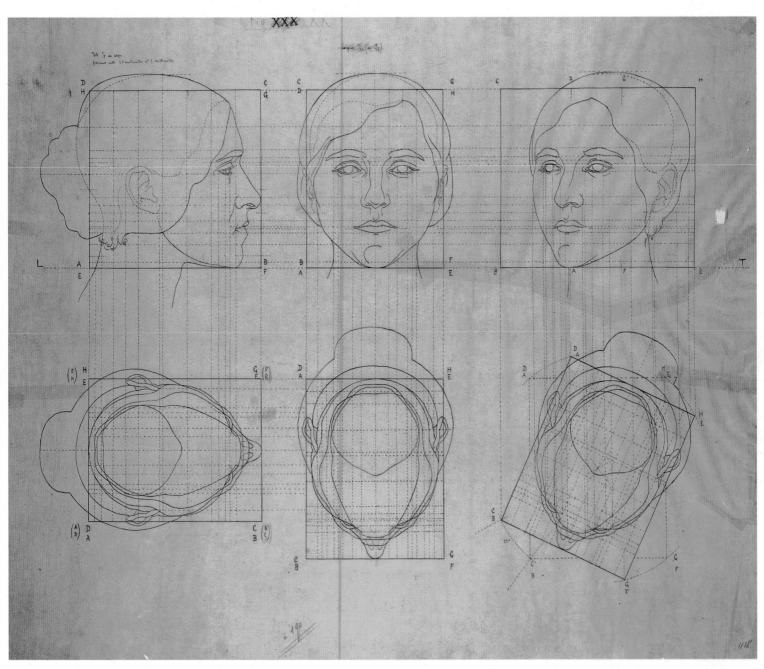

Gino Severini
Portrait de la famille
Severini [IV. **90**]
1936

Projections conjuguées
de la tête [IV. **91**]
c. 1920

Otto Gutfreund
Podobizna umělcovy
zěny [IV. **81**]
1923

Vlastní portrét [IV. **80**]
1919

Nikolaj Aleksandrovič Ionin
Portret F.N. Ioninoj [IV. **82**]
c. 1925

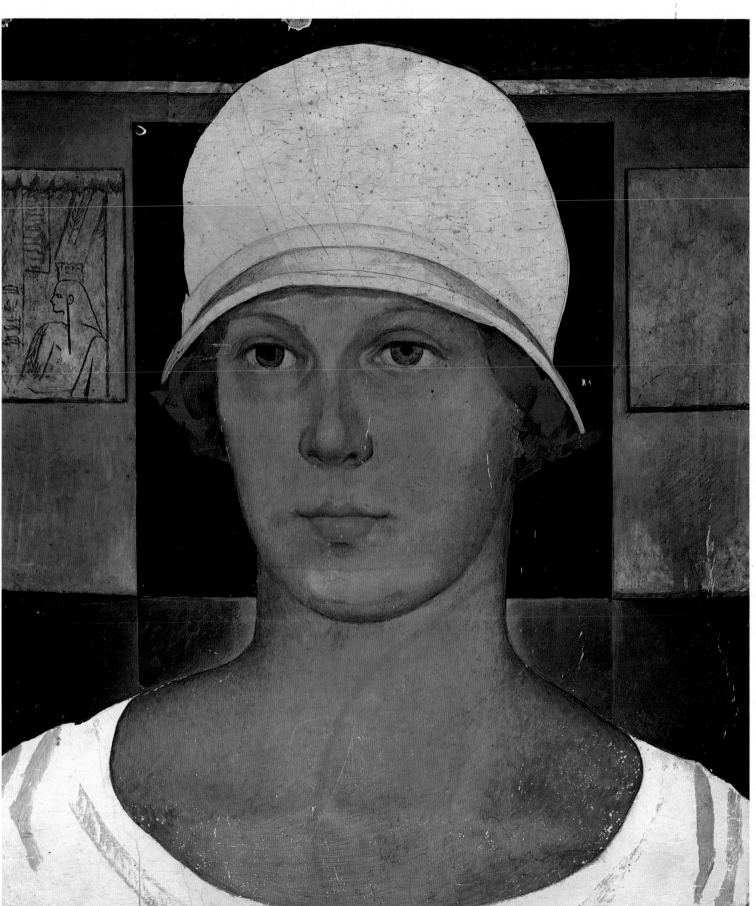

Arturo Martini
La Nena [IV. **84**]
1928

La Pisana [IV. **85**]
1928

Aristide Maillol
Torse de Vénus [IV. **83**]
1921

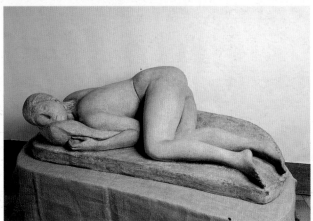

Ubaldo Oppi
Le amiche [IV. **87**]
1924

Virgilio Guidi
In tram [IV. **79**]
1923

Carlo Wulz
Marion e Wanda,
con Bianca Baldussi [IV. **99**]
1920-25

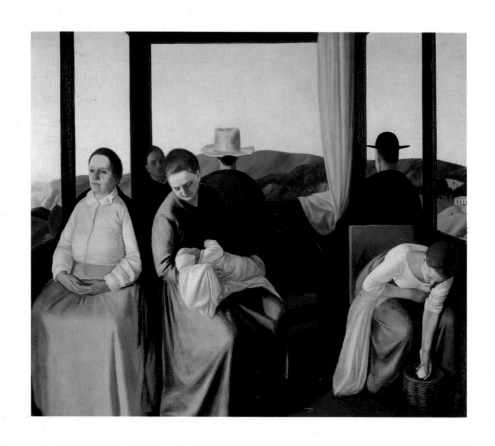

Wanda Wulz
Ritratto di donna [IV. **102**]
c. 1928

Carlo Wulz
Ritratto di donna [IV. **96**]
c. 1910

L'attrice triestina Ducaton [IV. **95**]
c. 1910

Wanda Wulz
Ritratto di donna [IV. **101**]
1925-30

Carlo Wulz
Mia figlia Marion [IV. **100**]
c. 1922

Sphinx [IV. **97**]
c. 1915

Nudo femminile [IV. **98**]
1920-25

V
**Totalitarian Arts
and
Degenerate Art**
1930-1945

Enrico Prampolini
Mussolini - sintesi plastica [V. **14**]
1924

Totalitarian Arts and Degenerate Art
1930-1945

The image of the Leader is a head above a bust, a head toppling from a bust. This beloved bust is raised from being a wee thing—like everyone else—to being enormous—like no one at all. The wonder of the Leader's body and face is that it grows to giant size in the midst of shattered fragments. This sterile 'chill beauty' feds on the terrible will of the small folk who fear defeatism like the plague, who look upon the degeneration of their peers as a threat to the Leader and the nation. The last in line, the degenerate are 'the others'—up to that revolutionary rallying–cry *We are not the Last* (Music), which makes it clear that we could all be the last in line.

This public, 'civic' history is played out against a strictly private novel which incorporates the fantasy of bodies desired and abandoned. Eros as autonomous desire becomes an intellectual prison, an intricate dislocation ('liberation' has its price). Love produces heteronomies (newspaper tragedies) or disquiet homophilies. Beyond narcissism lie the censure and constrictions of the 'other world', that of intolerant normality.

Surrealism's use of an existential concentrate of realism starts from those deformations that were produced 'technically' (by cameras or pantographs). Anamorphoses, new 'caricatures' projected onto a wall (Ducos du Hauron and Gimpel) become a source of entertainment for a gathering of friends.

Surrealism enjoyed drawing forth the compelling beauty of imagination like some little monster that pops out of the mouth (or a spirit that might possess one by the corresponding orifice). Metabolic and biomorphous flux rub against the spirit 'in the body'. Kertész's distorsions are 'internal' and external corporeal flux. In the same way, Miró constructs a 'sinuous corporeality' to contain and perhaps to capture using the pleasant tricks of nature. Slow and snapping vegetable forms—like so many carnivorous plants—accompany the flux of desire in Brauner; the very contrary of the broken, agitated disharmony of

Art Brut—whose bodies are dried out by a sort of interior nausea, an irony which functions as a sort of balsamic poison.

In their portraits, artists can be forced into public or military uniforms (Beckmann and Dix); or, when off-duty, they flash a cigarette which could be a knife (or might be a pen). Witkiewicz answers this masculine intellectual portrait with its female counterpart—a new 'parity' which goes together with the freedom of the writer and artist 'out on parole' (and so zealously watched over by Communism).

Penfield's *Homunculus* becomes a post–modern hero—a three–dimensional caricature in which growth is no longer a harmonious arrangement but a sort of paradoxical gymnastics imposed on the body by the parts (by the eyes, the hands, the sexual organs)—and perhaps by the brain itself (which turns out to count less than the thumb and index finger). A 'degenerative' disease develops—dilating and drying out the parts according to deceptively constructive rules. The rules, that is, of metastasis.

Matisse's tranquil description of the artist is both a caricature and a self–portrait—the wise mania of Cézanne's domesticated rusticity, far from the madding crowd. If the work of the artist is not necessary to others, it is at least recognised as a job 'like any other'.

Renato Bertelli
Profilo continuo
(Testa di Mussolini) [V. **1**]
1933

Images
of the Leader.
A Chill Beauty

Renato Bertelli

v **1**
Profilo continuo
(Testa di Mussolini),
1933
Painted terracotta
29 cm
Milan, Paolo Curti
collection

Isaak Brodskij

v **2**
Portret S.M. Kirov,
about 1930
Oil on canvas
117×125 cm
Moscow, Muzej Revoljucii

Pavel Nikolaevič Filonov

v **3**
Živaja golova, *1926*
(Head)
Oil on paper
pasted on canvas
105×72.5 cm
St. Petersburg,
Gosudarstvenyj Russkyj
Musej

v **4**
Poste nalëta, *about 1930*
(After the incursion)
Oil on paper
pasted on canvas
82×69 cm
St. Petersburg,
Gosudarstvenyj Russkyj
Musej

J. Jacquin-Chatellier

v **5**
L'Homme, les hommes
(Etudes morphologiques),
Paris 1932
Volume, 142 pp.
Gentilly, Philippe Comar
collection

Oskar Kokoschka

v **6**
Bildnis eines 'Entarteten
Künstlers',
1937
Oil on canvas
110×85 cm
Edinburgh, Private
collection (courtesy
of Scottish National Gallery
of Modern Art)

Léon Mac Auliffe

v **7**
Développement et
croissance,
Paris 1923
Volume, 226 pp.
Paris, Ecole Nationale
Supérieure des Beaux-Arts,
Departement
de Morphologie

v **8**
Les mécanismes intimes
de la vie,
Paris 1925
Volume, 100 pp.
Paris, Ecole Nationale
Supérieure des Beaux-Arts,
Departement
de Morphologie

Eugen Matthias

v **9**
Der Männliche Körper,
Zurich-Leipzig 1931
Volume, 58 pp.
Paris, Ecole Nationale
Supérieure des Beaux-Arts,
Departement
de Morphologie

Zoran Music

v **10**
Non siamo gli ultimi,
1974
Oil on canvas
114.5×146 cm
Venice, Archivio Storico
delle Arti Contemporanee
de La Biennale di Venezia

Félix Nussbaum

v **11**
Selbstbidnis mit Judenpaß,
1943
Oil on canvas
56×59 cm
Osnabrück,
Kulturgeschichtliches
Museum

**Kuz'ma Sergeevič
Petrov-Vodkin**

v **12**
Trevoga, *1934*
(Restlessness)
Oil on canvas
169×139 cm
St. Petersburg,
Gosudarstvenyj Russkyj
Musej

Enrico Prampolini

v **13**
Autoritratto, *1914*
Oil on canvas
100.6×100.6 cm
New York, Solomon
R. Guggenheim Museum

v **14**
Mussolini-sintesi plastica,
1924
Oil on plywood
75×75 cm
Milan, Matteo Lorenzelli
collection, Lorenzelli Arte

Ivan Šadr

v **15**
Junoša so zvezdoj
i znamenem, *1937*
(Boy with Star and Flag)
Bronze
h 117 cm
Moscow, Tret'iakovskaja
Galereja

Ivo Saliger

v **16**
Urteil der Paris, *1939*
Oil on canvas
160×200 cm
Munich,
Oberfinanzdirektion
München

Aleksandr Nikolaevič Samochvalov

v **17**
Osoaviachimovka, *1932*
(Feminine figure
of the voluntary Association
for Support and Defence
of Aviation
and Chemical Industry
Sectors-Osoaviachim)
Oil on canvas
120×116 cm
St. Petersburg,
Gosudarstvenyj Russkyj
Musej

v **18**
Deruška s jadrom, *1933*
(Girl with a load)
Oil on canvas
124.5×65.8 cm
Moscow, Tret'jakovskaja
Galereja

Franz Tschackert

v **19**
Der Gläserne Mensch,
1962
Cellon, synthetic material,
copper wire, lead,
aluminium, electric
material
206×100 cm
Dresden, Deutsches
Hygiene-Museum

Adolfo Wildt

v **20**
Ritratto ideale
di Benito Mussolini,
about 1925
Marble
89×137×61 cm
Brescia, Civici Musei d'Arte
e Storia

Adolf Wissel

v **21**
Kalenberger Bauernfamilie,
1939
Oil on canvas
150×200 cm
Munich,
Oberfinanzdirektion
München

Enrico Prampolini
Autoritratto [v. **13**]
1914

Oskar Kokoschka
Bildnis eines «Entarteten
Künstlers» [v. **6**]
1937

Adolfo Wildt
Ritratto ideale
di Benito Mussolini [v. **20**]
c. 1925

Aleksandr Nikolaevič Samochvalov
Osoaviachimovka [v. **17**]
1932

Devuška s iadrom [v. **18**]
1933

Isaak Brodskij
Portret S.M. Kirow [v. **2**]
c. 1530

Ivan Šadr
Junoša so zvezdoj i znamenem [v. **15**]
1937

Kuz'ma Sergeevič Petrov-Vodkin
Trevoga [v. **12**]
1934

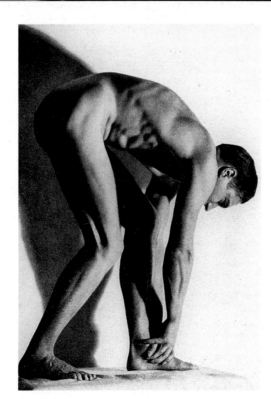

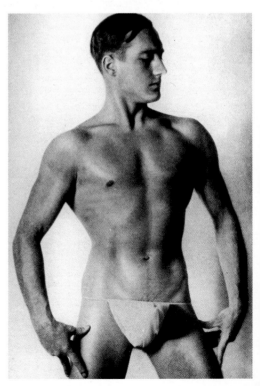

Ivo Saliger
Urteil der Paris [v. **16**]
1939

Eugen Matthias
Der Männliche Körper [v. **9**]
Zurich-Leipzig, 1931

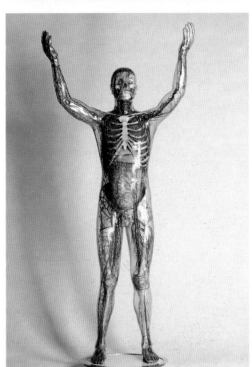

Adolf Wissel
Kalenberger Bauernfamilie [v. **21**]
1939

Franz Tschackert
Der Gläserne Mensch [v. **19**]
1962 (original 1932)

Félix Nussbaum
Selbstbildnis mit Judenpaß [V. **11**]
1943

Zoran Music
Non siamo gli ultimi [V. **10**]
1974

**Eros and
the Body in parts**

Paul Delvaux

v **22**
Le bois sacré (Le temple),
1946
Oil on canvas
160×180 cm
Milan, Renato Cardazzo
collection

Gaston Lachaise

v **23**
Bust of a Woman,
about 1924
Pencil on paper
25.4×19.7 cm
New York,
The Metropolitan Museum
of Art (ambassador
Scofield Thayer)

v **24**
Figure of a Woman,
about 1924
Pencil on paper
25.4×16.5 cm
New York,
The Metropolitan Museum
of Art (ambassador
Scofield Thayer)

v **25**
Standing Nude,
about 1925
Pencil on paper
24.8×16.8 cm
New York, The
Metropolitan Museum
of Art (donation of
The Lachaise Foundation)

v **26**
Abstract Figure,
about 1930–32
Bronze
13.9×33×14.6 cm
New York, The Lachaise
Foundation (courtesy
Salander O'Reilly Galleries)

v **27**
Dynamo Mother, *1933*
Bronze
28.3×45×18.4 cm
New York, The Lachaise
Foundation (courtesy
Salander O'Reilly Galleries)

v **28**
Walking Figure, *1934*
Brush, ink and pencil
on paper
59.7×47 cm
New York, The
Metropolitan Museum
of Art (donation of The
Lachaise Foundation)

v **29**
Abstract Figure,
about 1935
Bronze
41.9×25.4×28.6 cm
New York, The Lachaise
Foundation (courtesy
Salander O'Reilly Galleries)

Alberto Savinio

v **30**
I costruttori del Paradiso,
1929
Oil on canvas
73×91 cm
Private collection (courtesy
of Galleria dello Scudo,
Verona)

Stanley Spencer

v **31**
Portrait of Patricia Preece,
1933
Oil on canvas
83×73.7 cm
Southampton, Southampton
City Art Gallery

v **32**
Nude (Patricia Preece),
1935
Oil on canvas
50.8×76.2 cm
London, Ivor Braka
Limited

Gaston Lachaise
Abstract Figure [v. **29**]
c. 1935

Gaston Lachaise
Abstract Figure [v. **26**]
c. 1930-32

Dynamo Mother [v. **27**]
1933

Figure of a Woman [v. **24**]
c. 1924

Walking Figure [v. **28**]
1934

Standing Nude [v. **25**]
c. 1925

Bust of a Woman [v. **23**]
c. 1924

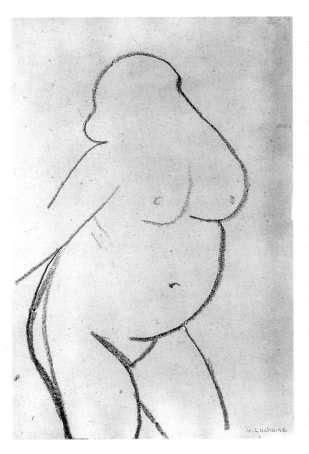

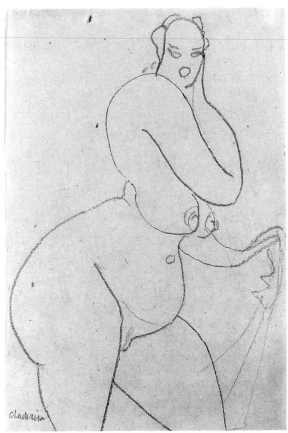

Alberto Savinio
I costruttori
del Paradiso [v. **30**]
1929

Paul Delvaux
Le bois sacré
(Le temple) [v. **22**]
1946

Stanley Spencer
Portrait of Patricia Preece [V. **31**]
1933

Nude (Patricia Preece) [V. **32**]
1935

Man Ray
A l'heure de l'Observatoire -
Pour *Les Amoureux* [v. **67**]
1932

Surrealism and 'Convulsive' Beauty

Hans Bellmer

v **33**
Die Puppe, *1932-45*
Painted wood and various materials (hear, socks and shoes)
61×170×51 cm
Paris, Musée National d'Art Moderne, Centre Georges Pompidou (donation of the artist to the State)

v **34**
Unica, *1958 and 1983*
Recent print from the original negative
24×18 cm
Paris, Galerie André-François Petit

v **35**
Unica, *1958 and 1983*
Recent print from the original negative
24×24 cm
Paris, Galerie André-François Petit

Jacques André Boiffard

v **36**
Le pouce, *1929*
Silverprint
29.1×22.1 cm
Paris, Musée National d'Art Moderne, Centre Georges Pompidou (donation of Mme Boiffard)

v **37**
Sans titre, *1930*
Silverprint
28.8×21.8 cm
Paris, Musée National d'Art Moderne, Centre Georges Pompidou

v **38**
Sans titre (pieds), *1930*
Silverprint
18.5×22.8 cm
Paris, Musée National d'Art Moderne, Centre Georges Pompidou (donation of Lucien Treillard)

v **39**
Sans titre (nu), *1930*
Silverprint
28.2×21.2 cm
Paris, Musée National d'Art Moderne, Centre Georges Pompidou (donation of Lucien Treillard)

v **40**
Sans titre, *1930*
Silverprint
29×21.7 cm
Paris, Musée National d'Art Moderne, Centre Georges Pompidou (donation of Mme Boiffard)

v **41**
Sans titre (visage masqué par un bas), *1930*
Silverprint
22.7×16.9 cm
Paris, Musée National d'Art Moderne, Centre Georges Pompidou

v **42**
Sans titre ('Les yeux levés'), *about 1930*
Recent contact copy
13×9 cm
Paris, Lucien Treillard collection

v **43**
Sous le masque-Pierre Prévert, *1930*
Silverprint
22.4×16.8 cm
Paris, Musée National d'Art Moderne, Centre Georges Pompidou

v **44**
Sans titre, *1932–33*
Silverprint
16.1×20 cm
Paris, Musée National d'Art Moderne, Centre Georges Pompidou

Victor Brauner

v **45**
Petite morphologie, *1934*
Oil on canvas
53×63.5 cm
Paris, François Petit collection

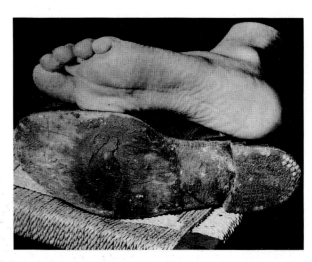

Jacques André Boiffard
Sans titre (pieds) [v. **38**]
1930

Jacques André Boiffard
Le pouce [v. **36**]
1929

Sans titre (nu) [v. **39**]
1930

Sans titre (visage masqué
par un bas) [v. **41**]
1930

Sous le masque-Pierre
Prévert [v. **43**]
1930

v **46**
L'étrange cas
de Monsieur K., *1934*
Oil on canvas
81×100 cm
Private collection

v **47**
Projet pour Anatomie
du désir, *1935*
China on paper
26.9×20.6 cm
Paris, Musée National d'Art
Moderne, Centre Georges
Pompidou (donation
of Mme Brauner)

v **48**
Anatomie du désir,
1936
China and colored inks
drawing on paper
65×50 cm
Paris, Musée National d'Art
Moderne, Centre Georges
Pompidou (donation
of Mme Brauner)

Louis Ducos du Hauron

v **49**
Autoportrait
anamorphique, *1889*
Recent print from the
original negative plate
18×24 cm
Paris, Société Française
de Photographie

v **50**
Autoportrait
anamorphique, *1889*
Recent print from the
original negative plate
24×18 cm
Paris, Société Française
de Photographie

Max Ernst

v **51**
Un jeune homme chargé
d'un fagot fleurissant,
1921
Collage and tempera
on paper
15.5×11 cm
Turin, Private collection

v **52**
Castor et Pollution, *1923*
Oil on canvas
73×100 cm
Geneva, Private collection

Léon Gimpel

v **53**
Autoportrait
anamorphique, *1905–10*
Recent print from the
original negative plate
18×24 cm
Paris, Société Française
de Photographie

v **54**
Autoportrait
anamorphique, *1905–10*
24×18 cm
Paris, Société Française
de Photographie

Robert Heine

v **55**
Le phénomène de l'extase,
about 1928
Photomontage
15×11.4 cm
Milan, Arturo Schwarz
collection

André Kertész

v **56**
Distorsion n° 4,
1933 and 1976
Silverprint
16×22 cm
Lyon, Bibliothèque
Municipale de Lyon

v **57**
Distorsion n° 9,
1933 and 1976
Silverprint
22×16.5 cm
Lyon, Bibliothèque
Municipale de Lyon

v **58**
Distorsion n° 49,
1933 and 1976
Silverprint
22.5×17.5 cm
Lyon, Bibliothèque
Municipale de Lyon

v **59**
Distorsion n° 51,
1933 and 1976
Silverprint
17×22.5 cm
Lyon, Bibliothèque
Municipale de Lyon

v **60**
Distorsion n° 93,
1933 and 1976
Silverprint
16.5×22 cm
Lyon, Bibliothèque
Municipale de Lyon

v **61**
Distorsion n° 128,
1933 and 1976
Silverprint
16.5×22.5 cm
Lyon, Bibliothèque
Municipale de Lyon

v **62**
Distorsion n° 132,
1933 and 1976
Silverprint
22×13.5 cm
Lyon, Bibliothèque
Municipale de Lyon

v **63**
Distorsion n° 134,
1933 and 1976
Silverprint
22.5×17.5 cm
Lyon, Bibliothèque
Municipale de Lyon

v **64**
Distorsion n° 137,
1933 and 1976
Silverprint
18.5×24 cm
Lyon, Bibliothèque
Municipale de Lyon

v **65**
Distorsion n° 138,
1933 and 1976
Silverprint
22×13 cm
Lyon, Bibliothèque
Municipale de Lyon

v **66**
Distorsion n° 140,
1933 and 1976
Silverprint
22.5×17.5 cm
Lyon, Bibliothèque
Municipale de Lyon

Man Ray

v **67**
A l'heure
de l'observatoire-Pour
Les amoureux, *1932*
Original photograph
9×21.5 cm
Milan, Arturo Schwarz
collection

Joan Miró

v **68**
Autoportrait, *1919*
Oil on canvas
73×60 cm
Paris, Musée Picasso

v **69**
La statue, *1925*
Oil on canvas
80×55 cm
New York, Private collection

v **70**
La statue, *1926*
Conté pencil on paper
62.3×47.6 cm
New York, The Museum
of Modern Art

v **71**
Personnages devant une
métamorphose,
1936 (January)
Egg tempera on masonite
50.2×57.5 cm
New Orleans, New Orleans
Museum of Art

v **72**
Autoportrait,
1937/38–60
Oil and pencil on canvas
146.5×97 cm
Barcelona, Fondació Joan
Miró (deposit of Maria
Dolors Miró)

Wilder Graves Penfield

v **73**
The Cerebral Cortex
of Man: Human Sensory
Homunculus, *1952*
Plaster
95×46×52 cm
Paris, Private collection

Pablo Picasso

v **74**
Métamorphose I, *1928*
Bronze (only copy extant)
22.8×18.3×11 cm
Paris, Musée Picasso

v **75**
Femme assise dans un
fauteuil rouge, *1932*
Oil on canvas
130×97.5 cm
Paris, Musée Picasso

v **76**
Une anatomie:
trois femmes, II,
1933 (Paris, 25 February)
Lead-point
20×27 cm
Paris, Musée Picasso

v **77**
Une anatomie:
trois femmes, VI,
1933 (Paris, 27 February)
Lead-point
20×27.1 cm
Paris, Musée Picasso

v **78**
Une anatomie:
trois femmes, X,
1933 (Paris, 1st March)
Lead-point
19.7×27.1 cm
Paris, Musée Picasso

Wilder Graves Penfield
The Cerebral Cortex of Man:
Human Sensory Homunculus [v. **73**]
1952

Louis Ducos du Hauron
Autoportrait
anamorphique [v. **50**]
1889

Léon Gimpel
Autoportrait
anamorphique [v. **53**]
1905-10

Autoportrait
anamorphique [v. **54**]
1905-10

Louis Ducos du Hauron
Autoportrait
anamorphique [v. **49**]
1889

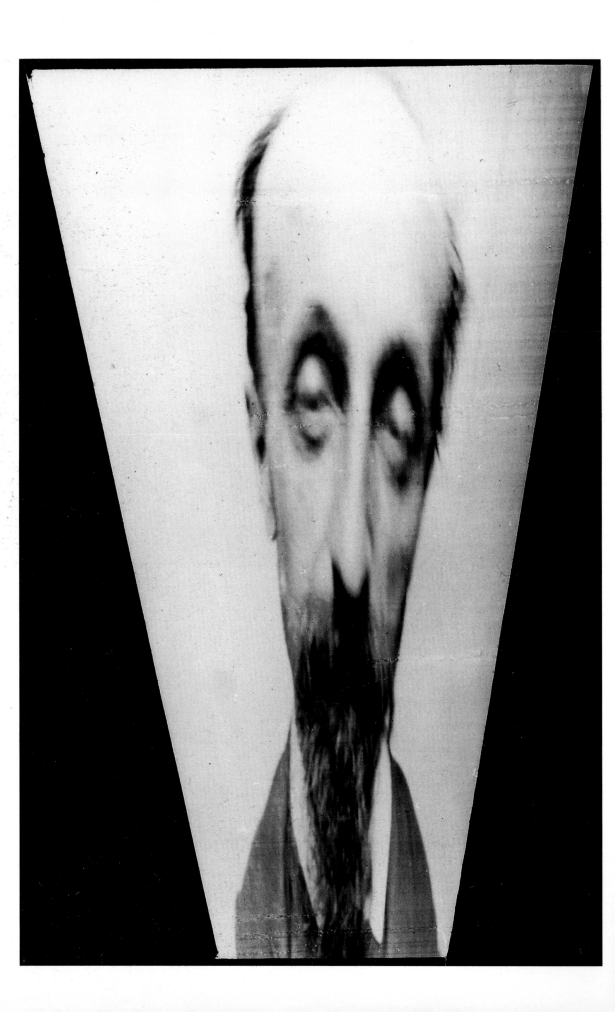

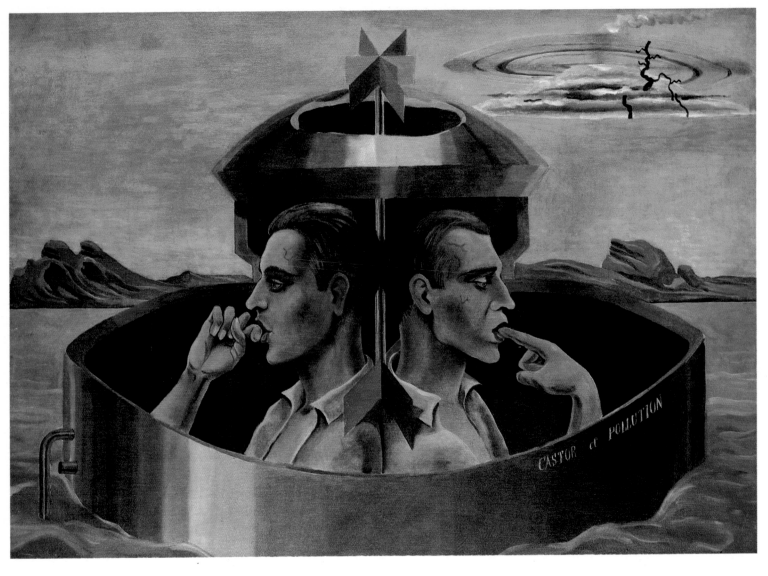

Max Ernst
Castor et Pollution [v. **52**]
1923

Un jeune homme chargé
d'un fagot fleurissant [v. **51**]
1921

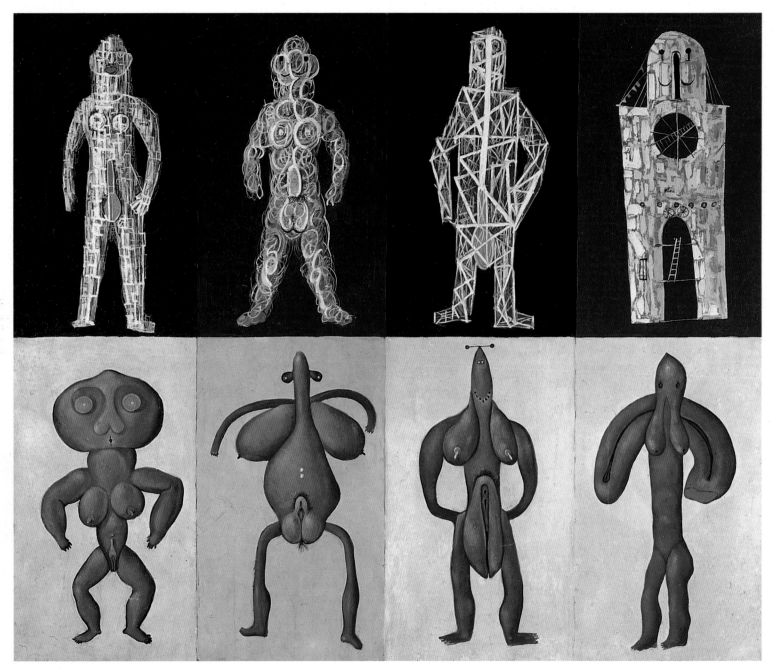

Victor Brauner
Petite morphologie [V. **45**]
1934

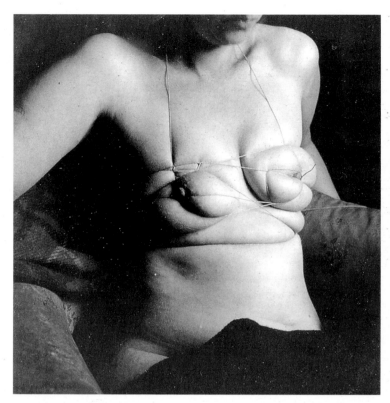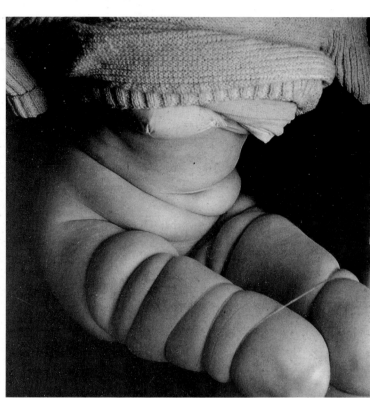

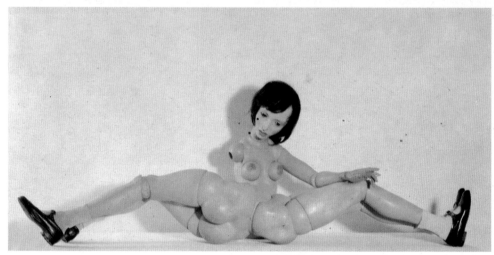

Hans Bellmer
Unica [v. **34**]
1958 and 1983

Unica [v. **35**]
1958 and 1983

Die Puppe [v. **33**]
1932-45

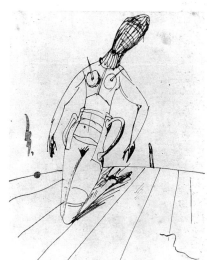

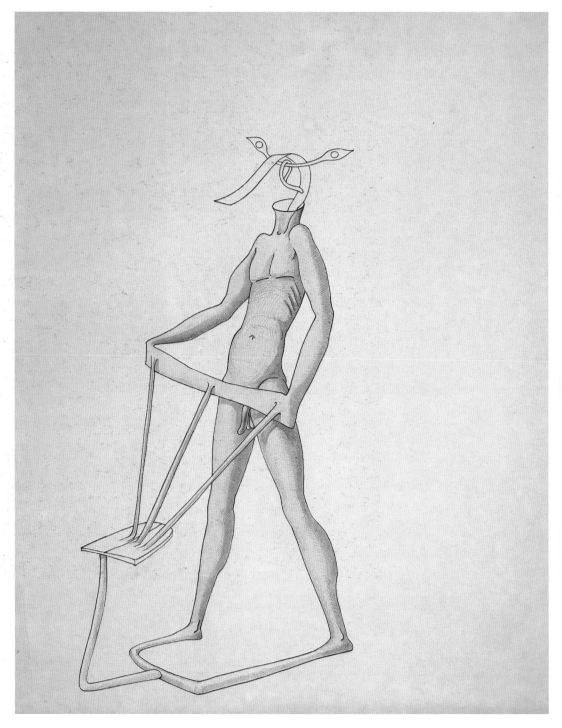

Victor Brauner
Projet pour Anatomie
du désir [v. **47**]
1935

Anatomie du désir [v. **48**]
1936

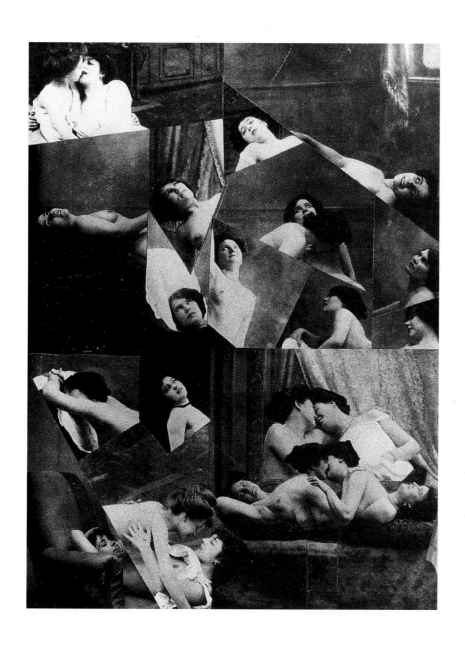

Robert Heine
Le phénomène de l'extase [v. **55**]
c. 1928

Joan Miró
La statue [V. **69**]
1925

Personnages devant
une métamorphose [V. **71**]
1936

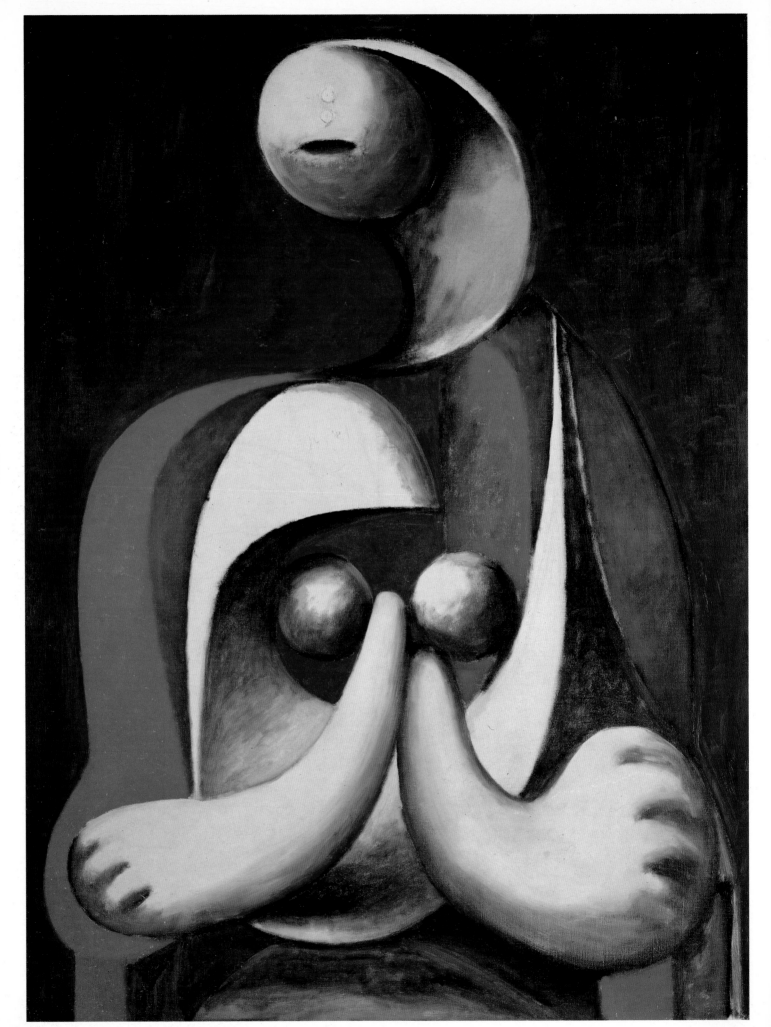

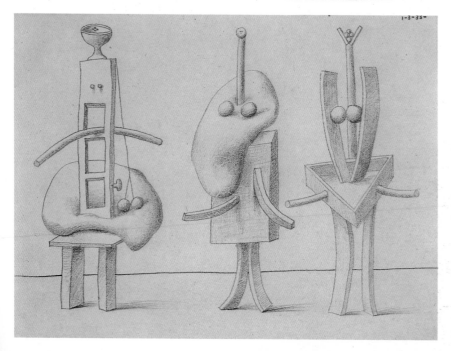

349
Totalitarian
Arts and
Degenerate
Art

Pablo Picasso
Femme assise dans
un fauteuil rouge [v. **75**]
1932

Une anatomie:
trois femmes, II [v. **76**]
1933

Une anatomie:
trois femmes, VI [v. **77**]
1933

Une anatomie:
trois femmes, X [v. **78**]
1933

Métamorphose I [v. **74**]
1928

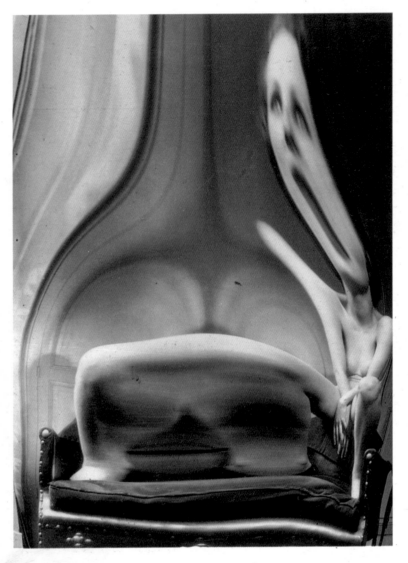

André Kertész
Distorsion n° 4; n° 51; n° 93;
n° 137 [v. **56-59-60-64**]
1933 and 1976

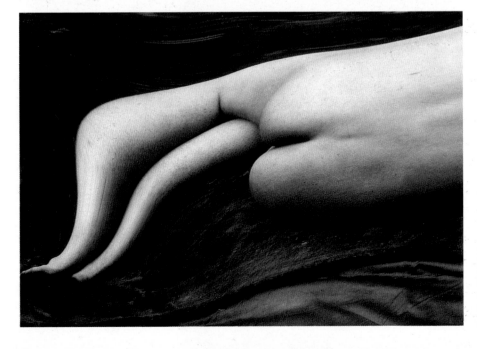

André Kertész
Distorsion n° 140; n° 132;
n° 49; n° 138; n° 134;
n° 9 [v. **66-62-58-65-63-57**]
1933 and 1976

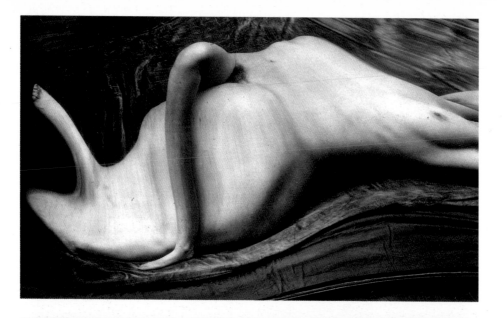

Self-portraits
in the 1930s

Max Beckmann

v **79**
Selbstbildnis in Florenz,
1907
Oil on canvas
98×90 cm
Hamburg, Private collection

v **80**
Selbstbildnis
(Unvollendet), *1908*
Oil on canvas
55×45 cm
Madrid,
Fondación Colección
Thyssen-Bornemisza

v **81**
Selbstportrait als
Krankenpfleger, *1919*
Oil on canvas
55.5×38.5 cm
Wuppertal,
Von der Heyt Museum

v **82**
Selbstbildnis auf gelbem
Grund mit Zigarette,
1923
Oil on canvas
60.2×40.5 cm
New York, The Museum
of Modern Art

v **83**
Selbstbildnis mit Zigarette,
1947
Oil on canvas
63.5×45.5 cm
Dortmund,
Museum am Ostwall

Otto Dix

v **84**
Selbstbildnis als Soldat,
1914
Oil on paper
68×53.5 cm
Stuttgart, Galerie der Stadt

v **85**
Selbstbildnis mit Staffelei,
1926
Oil on wood
98.1×73 cm
Düren,
Leopold-Hoesch-Museum

Henri Matisse

v **86**
Autoportrait sans barbe,
1927
Graphite on paper
22.7×17.4 cm
Paris, Musée National
d'Art Moderne,
Centre Georges Pompidou

v **87**
Autoportrait, *1937*
Charcoal on paper
25.4×20.3 cm
Paris, Musée National
d'Art Moderne,
Centre Georges Pompidou

v **88**
Autoportrait au chapeau
de paille (chapeau
Panama), *1945*
Black ink on paper
40.1×26 cm
Paris, Musée National
d'Art Moderne,
Centre Georges Pompidou

Stanislaw Ignacy
Witkiewicz

v **89**
Portret Neny Stachursskiej,
1929
(Portrait of Nena
Stachurska)
Pastel on paper
65.5×50 cm
Poznan, Muzeum
Narodowe w Poznaniu

v **90**
Portret Heleny
Bialynickiej-Biruli, *1930*
(Portrait of Helena
Bialynicka-Birula)
Pastel on paper
64×48 cm
Poznan, Muzeum
Narodowe w Poznaniu

v **91**
Portret Erwardy
Szmuglarowskiej, *1930*
(Portrait of Erwarda
Szmuglarowska)
Pastel on paper
70×50 cm
Poznan, Muzeum
Narodowe w Poznaniu

v **92**
Portret Heleny
Bialynickiej-Biruli, *1934*
(Portrait of Helena
Bialynicka-Birula)
Pastel on paper
65×49.5 cm
Poznan, Muzeum
Narodowe w Poznaniu

Henri Matisse
Autoportrait au chapeau
de paille
(chapeau Panama) [v. **88**]
1945

Autoportrait [v. **87**]
1937

Autoportrait sans barbe [v. **86**]
1927

Otto Dix
Selbstbildnis als Soldat [v. **84**]
1914

Selbstbildnis
mit Staffelei [v. **85**]
1926

Max Beckmann
Selbstbildnis in Florenz [v. **79**]
1907

Selbstbildnis
mit Zigarette [v. **83**]
1947

Selbstbildnis
(Unvollendet) [v. **80**]
1908

On pages 360-361:
Max Beckmann
Selbstportrait als
Krankenpfleger [v. **81**]
1919

Selbstbildnis auf gelbem
Grund mit Zigarette [v. **82**]
1923

Stanislaw Ignacy Witkiewicz
Portret Neny
Stachursskiej [v. **89**]
1929

Portret Heleny
Bialynickiej-Biruli [v. **90**]
1930

Portret Erwardy
Szmuglarowskiej [v. **91**]
1930

Portret Heleny
Bialynickiej-Biruli [v. **92**]
1934

VI
**The Post-war
Period**
1945-1962

366

The Post-war Period
1945–1962

The face is no longer recognizable. The wall on which the face is sketched hides a thousand possibilities. After the war the face remains 'its own hostage' (Fautrier); it can be a simple fracture above an inanimate object, or a 'lunar' outline in search of its double (Artaud). At a certain point in our lives we are all responsible for our own faces. Identity is the adventure of loss, of what cannot be had. A loss of meaning and a sense of alienation with regard to one's own body and its products—which can become crushed and crumpled threads (Dubuffet), or 'significant' refuse (Piero Manzoni).

Pollock's portraits look like the completion of a portrait scratched on a photographic plate with a pin. Here one might discover a black pond or some starry depths; there is the informal form of 'drips' which become the trace of a face that attracts our eye because it emerges from chance elements. The drops of paint which rain down on the white vacuum create a picture which faces us—even if every trace seems to be rubbed out by a voluntary action or an involuntary happening (Rauschenberg).

Their 'refractory and resistant' character makes those who don't get out of the way quickly enough into survivors. Freaks reappear to make a plea for a new pity to be shown towards deviance, deformity, visual punishment. We are all handicapped.

When 'otherness' is not visible, then the image of humanity is impoverished in its search for 'poor liberty'. Arbus' portraits show the deformities of the healthy and the profound sanity and resistance of the deformed, plucky heroes in a room of nightmares.

Bacon's portraits—which reflect that butchery which fills the stomach of modern cities—might be 'explained' as new anamorphoses. Giacometti's non–virtual ghosts walk in solitude, in high inaccessible places, set apart by their corporeal lightness and their lucid spirit of expectation.

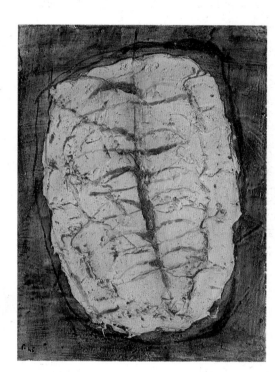

Jean Fautrier
Tête d'otage n° 14 [VI. **10**]
1945

Jackson Pollock
Number 7 [VI. **27**]
1952

Piero Manzoni
Achrome [VI. **23**]
1958

The Eclipse
of the Face

Aloïse (Aloïse Corbaz)

VI **1**
Mickens,
about 1950
Wax-pastel and collage
on paper
100×146 cm
Lausanne,
Collection de l'Art Brut

Antonin Artaud

VI **2**
Portrait de Yves Thévenin,
1947 (21 June)
Pencil and color crayons
on paper
64×48 cm
Paris, Musée National
d'Art Moderne,
Centre Georges Pompidou

VI **3**
Portrait de Colette
Thomas, *1947 (August)*
Pencil on paper
59×45 cm
Paris, Musée National
d'Art Moderne,
Centre Georges Pompidou

VI **4**
Portrait de Jacques Marie
Prevel, *1947*
Soft pencil shading
on paper
57.4×45.6 cm
Paris, Musée National
d'Art Moderne,
Centre Georges Pompidou

Jean Dubuffet

VI **5**
Gymnosophie, *1950*
Oil on canvas
97×146 cm
Paris, Musée National
d'Art Moderne,
Centre Georges Pompidou

Jean Fautrier

VI **6**
Le torse nu d'otage,
1943
Oil on canvas
45.5×37.5 cm
Rome, Fabio Sargentini
collection

VI **7**
Nu, *1943*
Oil on paper glued
on canvas
55×38 cm
Los Angeles, The Museum
of Contemporary Art,
Panza di Biumo collection

VI **8**
Otage, *1944*
Mixed media on canvas
34×26 cm
Paris, Philippe and Denyse
Durand-Ruel collection

VI **9**
Tête d'otage n° 1,
1944
Oil on paper glued
on canvas
35×27 cm
Los Angeles, The Museum
of Contemporary Art,
Panza di Biumo collection

VI **10**
Tête d'otage n° 14,
1945
Oil on paper glued
on canvas
35×27 cm
Los Angeles, The Museum
of Contemporary Art,
Panza di Biumo collection

VI **11**
Otage, *1945*
Mixed media on canvas
27×23 cm
Paris, Philippe and Denyse
Durand-Ruel collection

VI **12**
Tête d'otage n° 11,
1945
Oil on paper glued
on canvas
35.5×26.5 cm
Paris, Galerie Di Meo

Jean Hélion
Charles [VI. **14**]
1939

Francis Gruber

VI **13**
Job, *1944*
Oil on canvas
162×130 cm
London, Tate Gallery

Jean Hélion

VI **14**
Charles, *1939*
Oil on board
39×28 cm
Paris,
Galerie Pascal Lansberg

VI **15**
Edouard, *1939*
Oil on board
33×26 cm
Paris, Jacqueline Hélion
collection

VI **16**
'Edouard 1939', *1939*
Oil on board
39×30 cm
Paris, Private collection

VI **17**
'Emile II 1939', *1939*
Oil on board
38×28 cm
Paris, Private collection

VI **18**
Homme à la joue rouge,
1943
Oil on canvas
65×49.5 cm
Paris, Private collection

VI **19**
Homme au chapeau,
1943
Oil on canvas
57×49 cm
Fontenay-sous-Bois,
Private collection

VI **20**
A rebours, *1947*
Oil on canvas
113.5×146 cm
Paris, Musée National
d'Art Moderne,
Centre Georges Pompidou

VI **21**
La Jeune fille et le mort,
1957
Oil on canvas
114×146.5 cm
Paris, Jacqueline Hélion
collection

René Magritte

VI **22**
Les voies et les moyens,
1948
Oil on canvas
55×46 cm
Antwerp, Ronny Van de
Velde

Piero Manzoni

VI **23**
Achrome, *1958*
Kaolin on creasy canvas
130×162.5 cm
Turin, Galleria Civica
d'Arte Moderna
e Contemporanea

Raymond Mason

VI **24**
Le départ des fruits et
légumes du coeur de Paris,
le 28 février 1969,
1969–71
Epoxy resin and acrylic
310×315×135 cm
Paris, Raymond Mason
collection

Jackson Pollock

VI **25**
Self-Portrait,
about 1930–33
Oil on plaster and clay on
canvas 18.4×13.3 cm
New York (courtesy
of Jason McCoy Inc.)

VI **26**
Eyes in the Heat, *1946*
Oil on canvas
137.2×109.2 cm
Venice, Peggy Guggenheim
collection

VI **27**
Number 7, *1952*
Paint and oil on canvas
134.8×101.6 cm
New York,
The Metropolitan Museum
of Art (donation of Emilio
Azcarraga in honour
to William S. Lieberman,
1987)

Robert Rauschenberg

VI **28**
Untitled, *about 1951*
Oil on canvas
182.8×91.4 each
New York, Property
of the artist

VI **29**
Erased de Kooning
drawing, *1953*
Ink and pencil on paper
64.1×55.2 cm
New York, Property
of the artist

Jean Fautrier
Otage [VI. **11**]
1945

Francis Gruber
Job [VI. **13**]
1944

Aloïse (Aloïse Corbaz)
Mickens [VI. **1**]
c. 1950

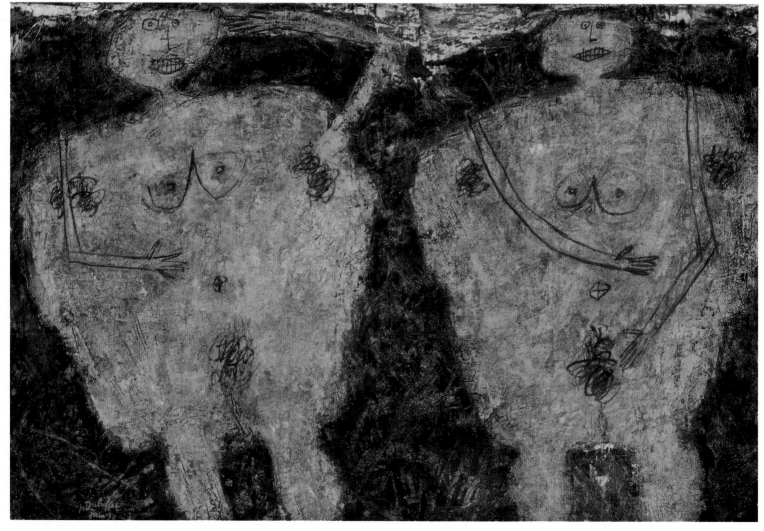

Jean Dubuffet
Gymnosophie [VI. **5**]
1950

Antonin Artaud
Portrait de Jacques
Marie Prevel [VI. **4**]
1947

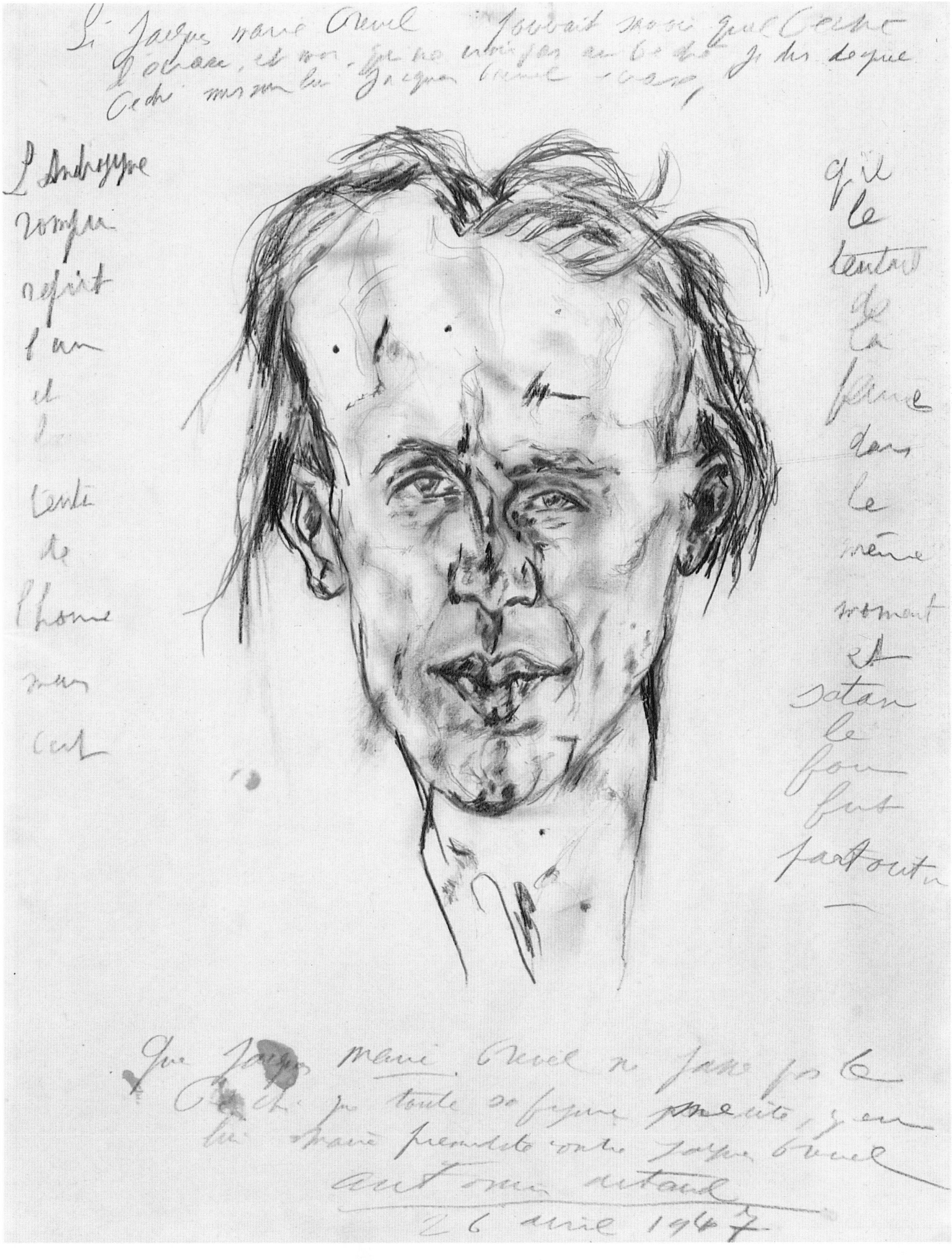

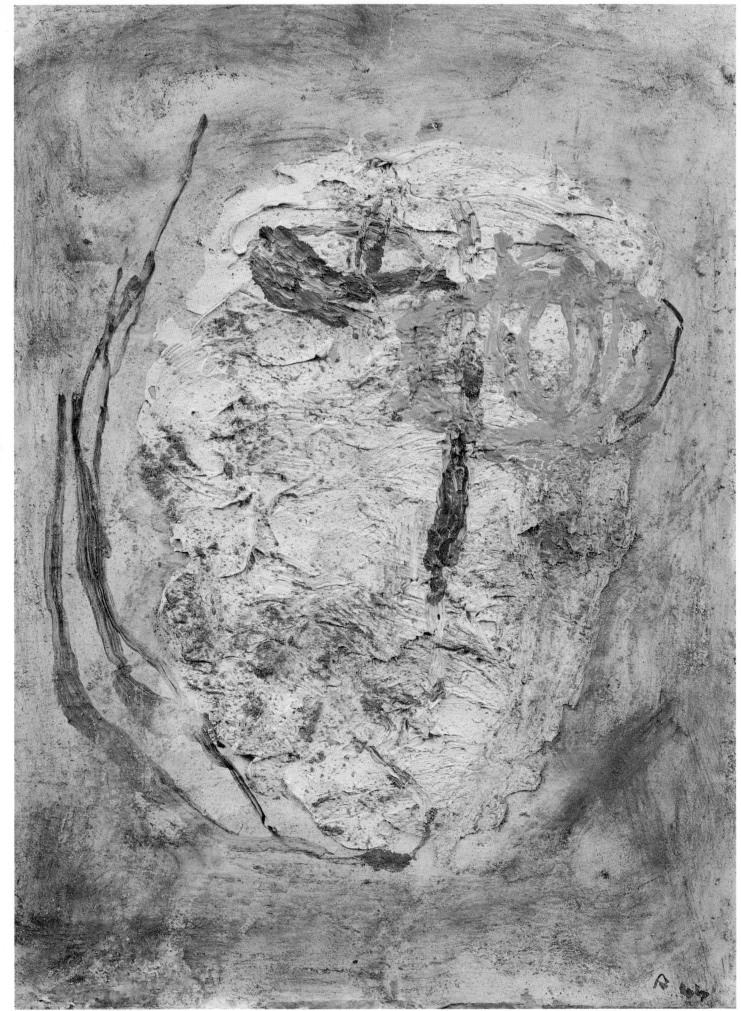

  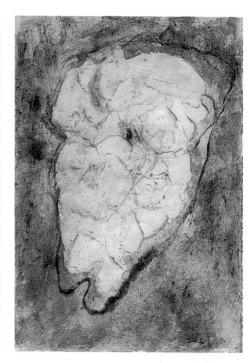

Jean Fautrier
Otage [VI. **8**]
1944

Tête d'otage n° 1 [VI. **9**]
1944

Tête d'otage n° 11 [VI. **12**]
1945

Nu [VI. **7**]
1943

Jean Hélion
«Edouard 1939» [VI. **16**]
1939

Edouard [VI. **15**]
1939

A rebours [VI. **20**]
1947

Homme au chapeau [VI. **19**]
1943

René Magritte
Les voies et les moyens [VI. **22**]
1948

Raymond Mason
Le départ des fruits
et légumes du coeur de Paris,
le 28 février 1969 [VI. **24**]
1969-71

On pages 382-383:
Jackson Pollock
Self-Portrait [VI. **25**]
c. 1930-33

Eyes in the Heat [VI. **26**]
1946

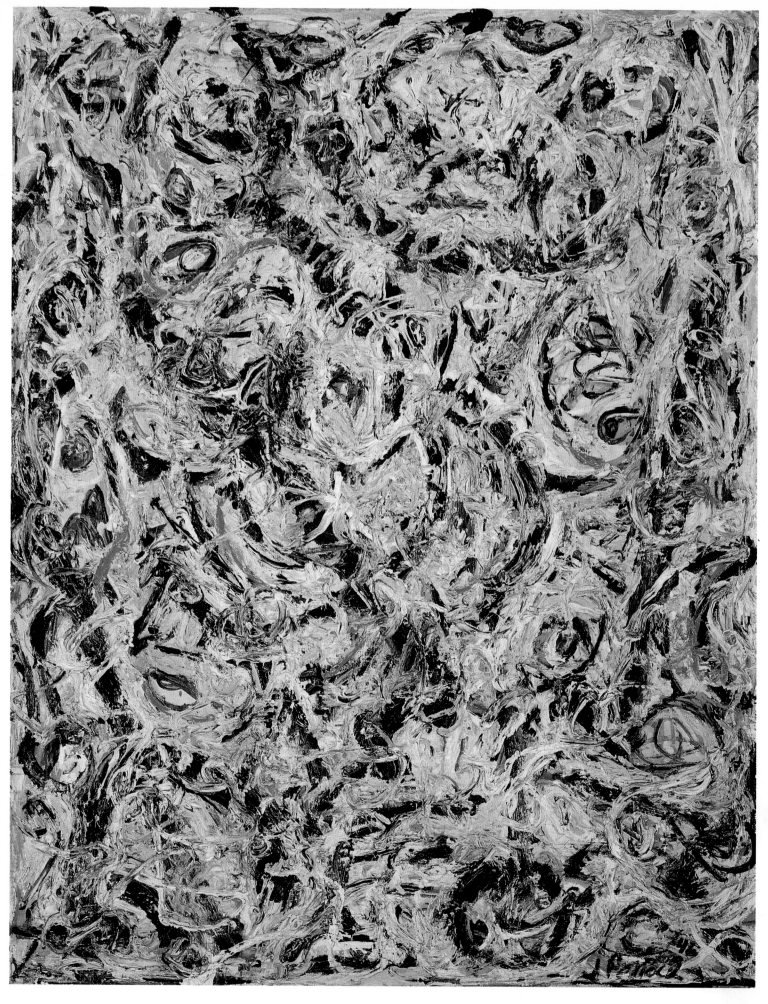

Robert Rauschenberg
Untitled [VI. **28**]
c. 1951

Erased de Kooning
drawing [VI. **29**]
1953

ERASED de KOONING DRAWING
ROBERT RAUSCHENBERG
1953

Diane Arbus

VI **30**
Exasperated Boy with
a Toy Hand Grenade,
New York, 1963
Photograph
32.5×32.5 cm
Paris, Bibliothèque
Nationale,
Cabinet des Estampes

VI **31**
Man and Wife
in a Nudist Camp,
early Evening, *1963*
Silver bromide print test
36.5×35.5 cm
Paris, Bibliothèque
Nationale,
Cabinet des Estampes

VI **32**
Man and Wife with their
Shoes on in a Cabin
at Nudist Camp, *1963*
Silver bromide print test
36×36 cm
Paris, Bibliothèque
Nationale,
Cabinet des Estampes

VI **33**
Retired Man and his Wife
at Home in a Nudist
Camp One Morning,
New Jersey, *1963*
Photograph
36×34.5 cm
Paris, Bibliothèque
Nationale,
Cabinet des Estampes

VI **34**
Nudist Lady with Swan
Sunglasses (reminiscent
of Myrna Loy and Betty
Grable), *1965*
Silverprint test
38×37.4 cm
Paris, Musée National d'Art
Moderne,
Centre Georges Pompidou

VI **35**
Man in Curless Dressing
for a Drug Ball, *1966*
Silver bromide print test
40×37.5 cm
Paris, Bibliothèque
Nationale,
Cabinet des Estampes

On the Sidelines: the Unmanageable, the Resistant

Francis Bacon
Sphinx [VI. **41**]
1954

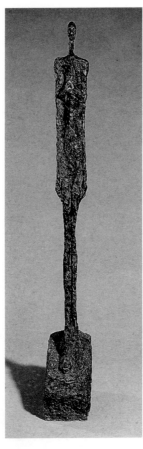

Alberto Giacometti
Femme de Venise I [VI. **46**]
1956

VI **36**
Male Travestite Wearing
a Torn Stocking, *1966*
Silver bromide print test
38.5×38.5 cm
Paris, Bibliothèque
Nationale,
Cabinet des Estampes

VI **37**
Boy in Pro-war Parade,
with Button and Flag,
New York, *1967*
Silver bromide print test
37×37 cm
Paris, Bibliothèque
Nationale,
Cabinet des Estampes

VI **38**
Identical Twins (Cathleen
and Coleen) Roselle,
1967
Silver bromide print test
36.5×36.5 cm
Paris, Bibliothèque
Nationale,
Cabinet des Estampes

VI **39**
Woman with Accessories,
1967
Silver bromide print test
36.5×36 cm
Paris, Bibliothèque
Nationale,
Cabinet des Estampes

Francis Bacon

VI **40**
Head II, *1949*
Oil on canvas
84.5×100.7 cm
Belfast, Ulster Museum

VI **41**
Sphinx, *1954*
Oil on canvas
151×116 cm
Private collection
(courtesy of Galleria
dello Scudo, Verona)

VI **42**
Self-portrait, *1973*
Oil on canvas
198×147 cm
Private collection

VI **43**
Study of the Human
Body, *1981–82*
Oil and pastel on canvas
198×147.5 cm
Paris, Musée National
d'Art Moderne,
Centre Georges Pompidou

Balthus

VI **44**
La partie des cartes,
1948–50
Oil on canvas
140×194 cm
Madrid,
Fundación Colección
Thyssen-Bornemisza

VI **45**
Grande composition
au corbeau, *1983–86*
Oil on canvas
200×150 cm
New York, Private collection

Alberto Giacometti

VI **46**
Femme de Venise I,
1956
Bronze
106×13.5×29.5 cm
St. Paul-de-Vence,
Fondation Maeght

VI **47**
Femme de Venise II,
1956
Bronze
121.5×15.5×33 cm
St. Paul-de-Vence,
Fondation Maeght

VI **48**
Femme de Venise III,
1956
Bronze
119×17×33.5 cm
St. Paul-de-Vence,
Fondation Maeght

VI **49**
Femme de Venise IV,
1956
Bronze
116×15.5×33.5 cm
St. Paul-de-Vence,
Fondation Maeght

Alberto Giacometti
Femme de Venise III [VI. **48**]
1956

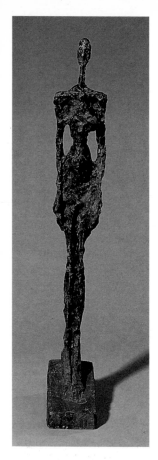

Alberto Giacometti
Femme de Venise II [VI. **47**]
1956

VI **50**
Femme de Venise V, *1956*
Bronze
111×13.5×31 cm
St. Paul-de-Vence,
Fondation Maeght

VI **51**
Femme de Venise VI, *1956*
Bronze
133×15.5×33 cm
St. Paul-de-Vence,
Fondation Maeght

VI **52**
Femme de Venise VII,
1956
Bronze
117×16.5×36.5 cm
St. Paul-de-Vence,
Fondation Maeght

VI **53**
Femme de Venise VIII,
1956
Bronze
120.5×14.5×33 cm
St. Paul-de-Vence,
Fondation Maeght

VI **54**
Femme de Venise IX,
1956
Bronze
115×16.5×34.5 cm
St. Paul-de-Vence,
Fondation Maeght

William de Kooning

VI **55**
Woman II, *1952*
Oil on canvas
149.9×109.3 cm
New York, The Museum
of Modern Art (donation
of John D. Rockfeller III)

Léon Kossof

VI **56**
Two Seated Figures,
1962
Oil on board
182.9×152.4 cm
Private collection (courtesy
Louver Gallery)

VI **57**
Nude on Red Bed, *1972*
Oil on board
121.9×182.9 cm
Los Angeles,
Private collection

Eugène Leroy

VI **58**
Autoportrait, *1960*
Oil on canvas
92×74 cm
Private collection (courtesy
of Galerie de France, Paris)

VI **59**
Autoportrait, *1962*
Oil on canvas
82.5×60.5 cm
Private collection

VI **60**
Autoportrait, *1962*
Oil on canvas
117×81.5 cm
Private collection

VI **61**
Autoportrait en Flandre,
1962
Oil on canvas
54×73 cm
Paris, Eugène Jean Leroy
collection (courtesy
of Galerie de France, Paris)

Eugène Leroy
Autoportrait [VI. **58**]
1960

Diane Arbus
Nudist Lady with Swan
Sunglasses (reminiscent
of Myrna Loy and
Betty Grable) [VI. **34**]
1965

Woman with Accessories [VI. **39**]
1967

Boy in Pro-War Parade,
with Button and Flag,
New York [VI. **37**]
1967

Male Travestite Wearing
a Torn Stocking [VI. **36**]
1966

Man in Curless Dressing
for a Drug Ball [VI. **35**]
1966

Exasperated Boy with
a Toy Hand Grenade,
New York [VI. **30**]
1963

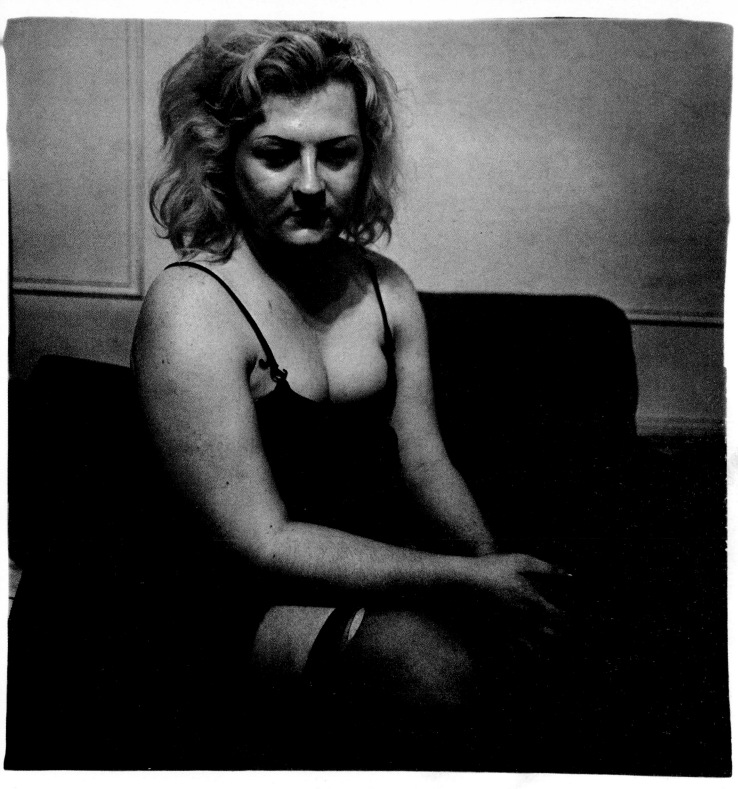

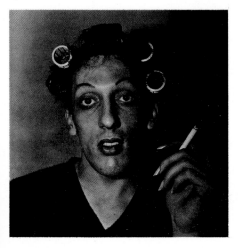

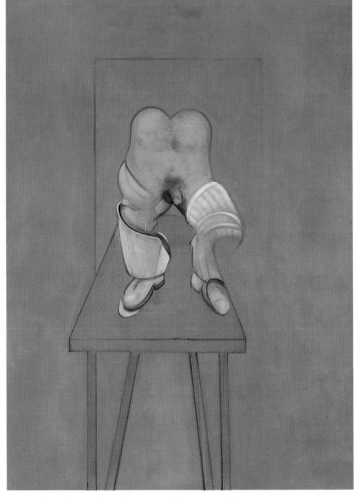

Francis Bacon
Head II [VI. **40**]
1949

Study of the Human
Body [VI. **43**]
1981-82

Self-portrait [VI. **42**]
1973

Balthus
La partie des cartes [VI. **44**]
1948-50

Grande composition
au corbeau [VI. **45**]
1983-86

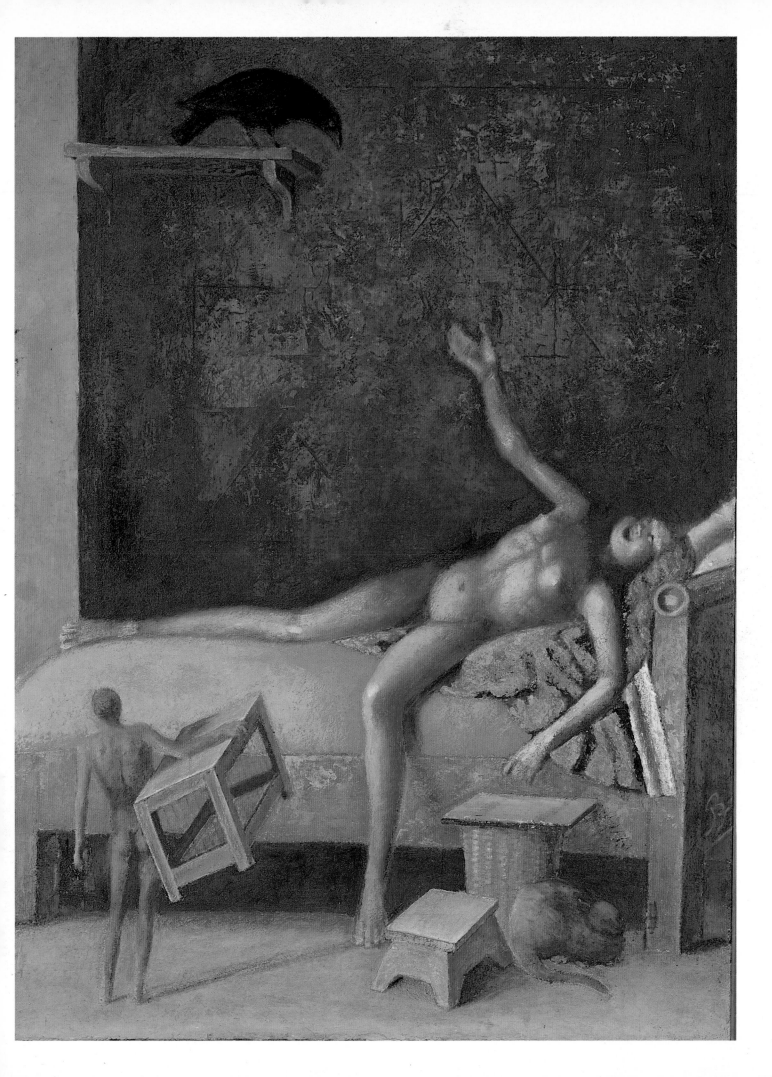

Alberto Giacometti
Femme de Venise IV [VI. **49**]
1956

Femme de Venise V [VI. **50**]
1956

Femme de Venise VI [VI. **51**]
1956

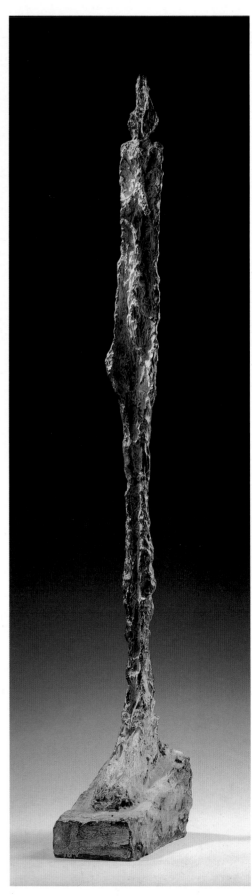

Alberto Giacometti
Femme de Venise VII [VI. **52**]
1956

Femme de Venise VIII [VI. **53**]
1956

Femme de Venise IX [VI. **54**]
1956

William de Kooning
Woman II [VI. **55**]
1952

Léon Kossof
Two Seated Figures [VI. **56**]
1962

Nude on Red Bed [VI. **57**]
1972

On pages 400-401:
Eugène Leroy
Autoportrait [VI. **60**]
1962

Autoportrait [VI. **59**]
1962

VII
**The Return
of the Body**
1962-1985

404

Georg Baselitz
Porträt Franz Dahlem [VII. **4**]
1969

The Return of the Body
1962-1985

Attitude, behavior, personality and opinions are the marks of modern character. The image is being reversed by infantile 'revolutionary' games, the rules laid down by a power subject to the imagination. Baselitz turns his portraits upside down, making them the formal opposite of any official gallery. There is a sense of optimism with regard to the 'body' — freedom of sexuality and decision now seem to be possible. Youthful enthusiasm compounds itself within the 'commune' — in a lifestyle that rejects all consumerism. The opium trail leads to eastern religions, which replace ideologies that have collapsed, disciplines which have revealed themselves to be punitive. The ideal body of a new orientalism (Kitaj) can — like the Shaman — destroy itself to return into life and obtain a full recomposition (which up to then had been 'unpresentable'). Moving 'on the tip of his pencil', Hockney gathers up the repeated gestures of a walk around his own room, whilst time is 'kept' silently by a digital clock. Lopez and Freud use traditional instruments to make the drawing of the human body into an exercise unto itself, whilst Close patiently puts together the stereotype brilliance of pixels. The dilation of desire (O'Keeffe) soon encounters the limits set by the degenerative diseases which besiege the human body. The Ars Amandi, therefore, becomes a contemplative virtue, a reserved and 'technically' simple 'masturbatory freedom' (Nauman).

There is both iconoclasm and iconolatry in the images of the human body. The face (and the body) veils and 'unveils' itself, conforms to, deforms itself within, the new exotic–plastic aestheticism (de Clérambault and Newton). Perhaps the mystery of fundamentalism is to be understood as opposition to the victory of a war fought through images.

The Turning-point
1962-1973

Georg Baselitz
Porträt Elke I [VII. **3**]
1969

Georg Baselitz

VII **1**
Der werktätige Dresdener-Porträt M.G.B., *1969*
Synthetic resin on canvas
162×130 cm
Private collection

VII **2**
Fünfziger Jahre Porträt-M. W., *1969 (September)*
Synthetic resin on canvas
162×130 cm
Private collection

VII **3**
Porträt Elke I, *1969*
Synthetic resin on canvas
162×130 cm
Private collection

VII **4**
Porträt Franz Dahlem, *1969 (October)*
Synthetic resin on canvas
162×130 cm
Private collection

VII **5**
Porträt H.M. Werner, *1969*
Synthetic resin on canvas
162×130 cm
Private collection

VII **6**
Porträt K.L. Rinn, *1969*
Synthetic resin on canvas
162×130 cm
Private collection

VII **7**
Kaspar König, *1970–71*
Oil on canvas
162×130 cm
Private collection

Philip Guston

VII **8**
The Studio, *1969*
Oil on canvas
122×107 cm
New York, Private collection
(courtesy McKee Gallery)

VII **9**
Painting, Smoking, Eating, *1973*
Oil on canvas
197×263 cm
Amsterdam, Stedelijk Museum (purchased with the assistance of Vereniging Rembrandt)

VII **10**
East Coker T.S.E., *1979*
Oil on canvas
106.7×122 cm
New York, Museum of Modern Art

VII **11**
Ravine, *1979*
Oil on canvas
173×203 cm
New York, Property of the artist (courtesy McKee Gallery)

Georg Baselitz
Fünfziger Jahre Porträt
- M.W. [VII. **2**]
1969

Der werktätige Dresdener
- Porträt M.G.B. [VII. **1**]
1969

Porträt H.M. Werner [VII. **5**]
1969

Kaspar König [VII. **7**]
1970-71

Porträt K.L. Rinn [VII. **6**]
1969

Philip Guston
Painting, Smoking, Eating [VII. **9**]
1973

The Studio [VII. **8**]
1969

Ravine [VII. **11**]
1979

East Coker T.S.E. [VII. **10**]
1979

David Hockney
Paul Hockney
& Grandson Timothy,
March 7th 1994 [VII. **37**]
1994

Gregory Evans,
June 27th 1994 [VII. **31**]
1994

'Human Clay'
1973–1985

Avigdor Arikha

VII **12**
Marie-Catherine,
1982 (3 January)
Oil on canvas
60.9×65 cm
Paris, Musée National
d'Art Moderne,
Centre Georges Pompidou

VII **13**
Nu à l'écharpe noire,
1985 (29 March)
Oil on canvas
195×130 cm
Djion,
Musée des Beaux-Arts

VII **14**
Autoportrait nu de dos,
1986 (30 July)
Oil on canvas
65×45.5 cm
Paris, Property of the artist

VII **15**
Lord Home (Alexander
Frederick Douglas),
1988 (16 March)
Oil on canvas
91.5×71.3 cm
Edinburgh, Scottish
National Portrait Gallery

Chuck Close

VII **16**
Fanny (Fingerpainting),
1985
Oil on canvas
259×213 cm
Washington, National
Gallery of Art (donation
of Lila Acheson Wallace)

VII **17**
Alex, *1991*
Oil on canvas
254×213 cm
Los Angeles, Collection
Lannan Foundation

Lucian Freud

VII **18**
Naked Portrait,
1980–81
Oil on canvas
90×65 cm
London, Private collection

VII **19**
Evening in the Studio,
1993
Oil on canvas
200×169 cm
New York, Private collection
(courtesy British Council)

VII **20**
Painter Working,
Reflection,
1993
Oil on canvas
101.1×81.7 cm
Private collection
(courtesy British Council)

VII **21**
Benefits Supervisor
Resting,
1994
Oil on canvas
297.2×120.6 cm
New York, Acquavella
Contemporary Art

VII **22**
Leigh under the Skylight,
1994
Oil on canvas
227×121 cm
New York, Acquavella
Contemporary Art

David Hockney

VII **23**
Henry and Eugene,
1977
Acrylic on canvas
183.2×183.2 cm
Private collection

VII **24**
Model with Unfinished
Self Portrait,
1977
Oil on canvas
152×152 cm
Private collection

VII **25**
Jonathan Silver,
Dec. 30th 1993, *1993*
Pencil on paper
76.8×57.1 cm
Private collection

VII **26**
Mum, Dec. 20th 1993,
1993
Pencil on paper
76.8×57.1 cm
Private collection

VII **27**
Mum, Dec. 28th 1993,
1993
Pencil on paper
76.8×57.1 cm
Los Angeles,
David Hockney Studio

VII **28**
Celia Birtwell,
May 30th 1994, *1994*
Pencil on paper
76.8×57.1 cm
Los Angeles,
David Hockney Studio

VII **29**
Dr. Wilbur Schwartz,
Feb. 15th 1994, *1994*
Pencil on paper
76.8×57.1 cm
Los Angeles,
David Hockney Studio

VII **30**
Frank Watanabe,
May 25th 1994, *1994*
Pencil on paper
76.8×57.1 cm
Los Angeles,
David Hockney Studio

VII **31**
Gregory Evans,
June 27th 1994, *1994*
Pencil on paper
76.8×57.1 cm
Los Angeles,
David Hockney Studio

VII **32**
Henry Geldzahler,
May 1st 1994, *1994*
Pencil on paper
76.8×57.1 cm
Los Angeles,
David Hockney Studio

R.B. Kitaj
A Visit to London
(Robert Creeley and
Robert Duncan) [VII. **42**]
1977

Ivan Theimer
Ercole [VII. **52**]
1987-88

VII **33**
Jonathan Brown,
Jan. 2nd 1994, *1994*
Pencil on paper
76.8×57.1 cm
Los Angeles,
David Hockney Studio

VII **34**
Mum sleeping I,
March 9th 1994, *1994*
Pencil on paper
76.8×57.1 cm
Los Angeles,
David Hockney Studio

VII **35**
Nicholas Hockney,
March 5th 1994, *1994*
Pencil on paper
76.8×57.1 cm
Los Angeles,
David Hockney Studio

VII **36**
Paul Bartel,
April 10th 1994, *1994*
Pencil on paper
76.8×57.1 cm
Private collection

VII **37**
Paul Hockney
& Grandson Timothy,
March 7th 1994, *1994*
Pencil on paper
76.8×57.1 cm
Private collection

VII **38**
Rebecca Ryan,
March 7th 1994, *1994*
Pencil on paper
76.8×57.1 cm
Los Angeles,
David Hockney Studio

VII **39**
Shirley Goldfarb
& George Masurovsky,
1994
Acrylic on canvas
76.2×106.7 cm
Los Angeles,
David Hockney Studio

R.B. Kitaj

VII **40**
The Arabiste (Moresque),
1976–77
Oil on canvas
243.8×76.2 cm
Rotterdam, Museum
Boymans-van Beuningen

VII **41**
The Orientalist, *1976–77*
Oil on canvas
244×76.8 cm
London, Tate Gallery

VII **42**
A Visit to London
(Robert Creeley and
Robert Duncan), *1977*
Oil on canvas
182.9×61 cm
Madrid,
Fundación Colección
Thyssen-Bornemisza

VII **43**
The Hispanist
(Nissa Torrents), *1977*
Oil on canvas
244×76.2 cm
Oslo, Astrup Fearnley
Collection

VII **44**
Selfportrait as a woman,
1984
Oil on canvas
246×77.2 cm
Oslo, Astrup Fearnley
Collection

Antonio Lopez

VII **45**
Hombre y mujer, *1968–90*
Painted wood
man: 195×59×46 cm
woman: 169×42.5×38 cm
Madrid,
Property of the artist

VII **46**
Emilio, *1985*
Pencil on paper
204×101 cm
Madrid,
Galeria Marlborough,
Property of the artist

VII **47**
Manuel, *1985*
Pencil on paper
186×92 cm
Madrid,
Galeria Marlborough,
Property of the artist

VII **48**
J. Enrique, *1986*
Pencil on paper
205×100 cm
Madrid,
Galeria Marlborough,
Property of the artist

VII **49**
L. Fernando, *1986*
Pencil on paper
199×92 cm
Madrid,
Galeria Marlborough,
Property of the artist

VII **50**
Croquis con medidas 1,
1986–92
Pencil on paper
184×140 cm
Madrid,
Galeria Marlborough,
Property of the artist

VII **51**
Croquis con medidas 2,
1986–92
Pencil on paper
190×91.5 cm
Madrid,
Galeria Marlborough,
Property of the artist

Ivan Theimer

VII **52**
Ercole, *1987–88*
Wax and plaster model
182×66×63 cm
Paris, Private collection

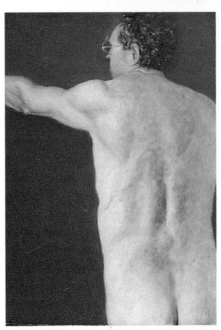

Avigdor Arikha
Nu à l'écharpe noire [VII. **13**]
1985

Marie-Catherine [VII. **12**]
1982

Autoportrait nu de dos [VII. **14**]
1986

Lord Home (Alexander
Frederick Douglas) [VII. **15**]
1988

Chuck Close
Fanny (Fingerpainting) [VII. **16**]
1985

Alex [VII. **17**]
1991

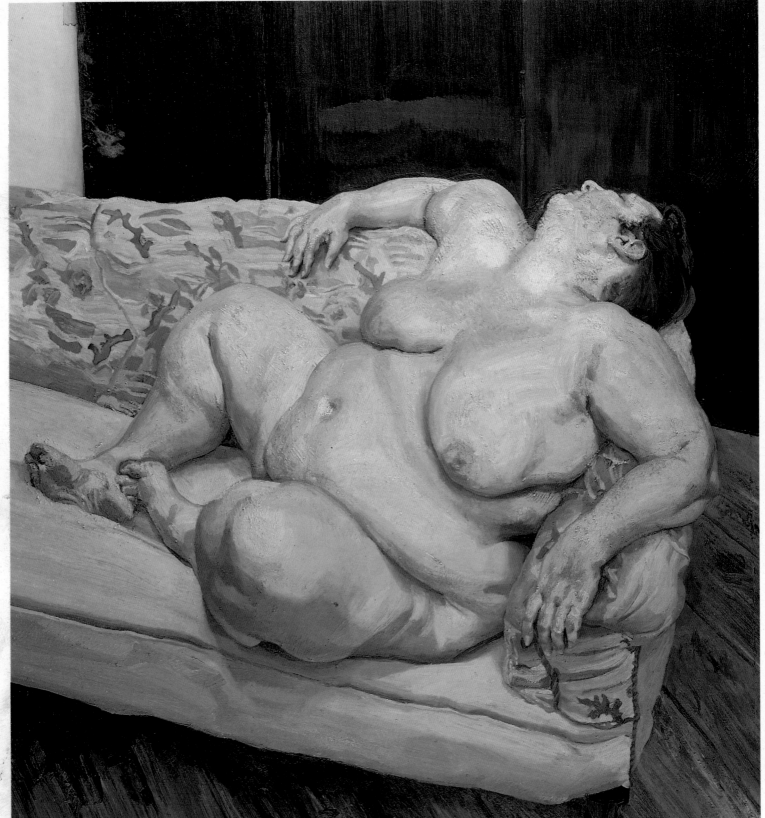

Lucian Freud
Benefits Supervisor Resting [VII. **21**]
1994

Leigh under the Skylight [VII. **22**]
1994

Painter Working, Reflection [VII. **20**]
1993

Evening in the Studio [VII. **19**]
1993

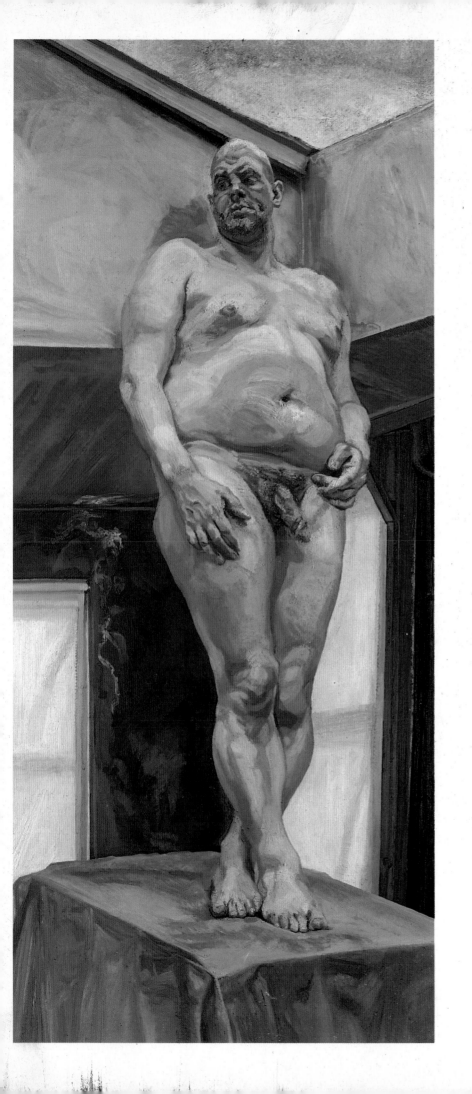

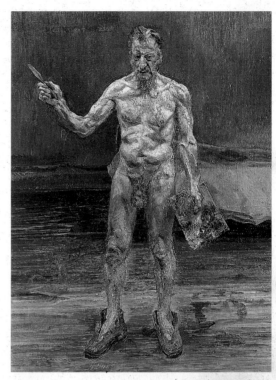

 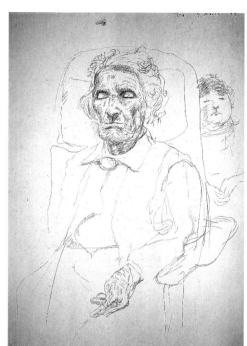 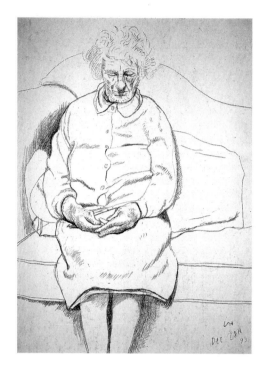

**The Return
of the Body**

David Hockney
Jonathan Silver,
Dec. 30th 1993 [VII. **25**]
1993

Celia Birtwell,
May 30th 1994 [VII. **28**]
1994

Jonathan Brown,
Jan. 2nd 1994 [VII. **33**]
1994

Mum, Dec. 20th 1993 [VII. **26**]
1993

Mum sleeping I,
March 9th 1994 [VII. **34**]
1994

Mum, Dec. 28th 1993 [VII. **27**]
1993

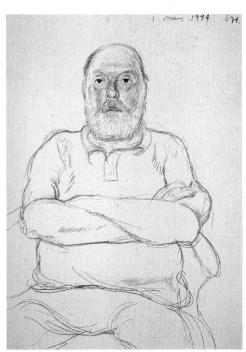
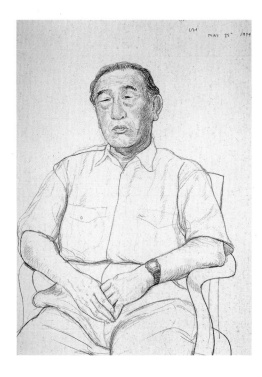

David Hockney
Dr. Wilbur Schwartz,
Feb. 15th 1994 [VII. **29**]
1994

Nicholas Hockney,
March 5th 1994 [VII. **35**]
1994

Rebecca Ryan,
March 7th 1994 [VII. **38**]
1994

Paul Bartel, April 10th 1994 [VII. **36**]
1994

Henry Geldzahler,
May 1st 1994 [VII. **32**]
1994

Frank Watanabe,
May 25th 1994 [VII. **30**]
1994

David Hockney
Model with Unfinished
Self Portrait [VII. **24**]
1977

Henry and Eugene [VII. **23**]
1977

R.B. Kitaj
The Arabiste (Moresque)
[VII. **40**]
1976-77

The Hispanist
(Nissa Torrents) [VII. **43**]
1977

The Orientalist [VII. **41**]
1976-77

Selfportrait as a woman
[VII. **44**]
1984

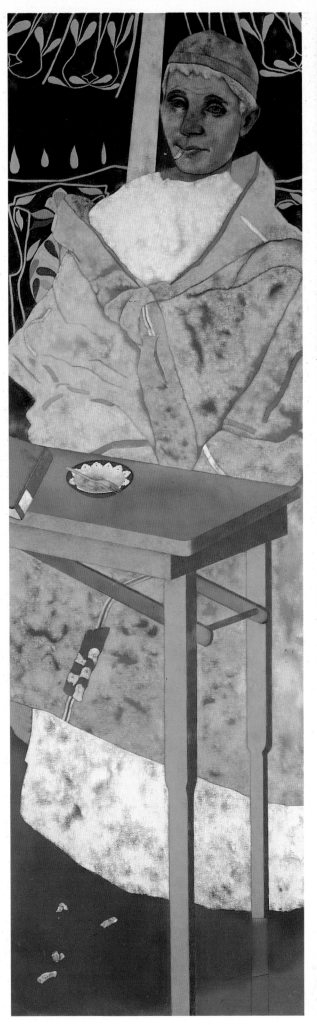

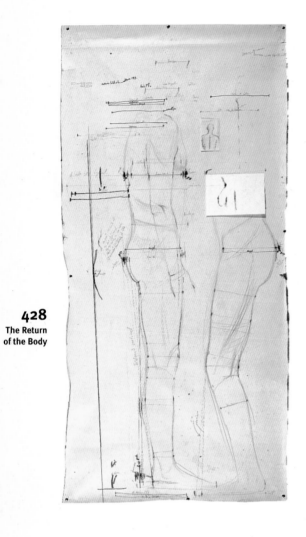

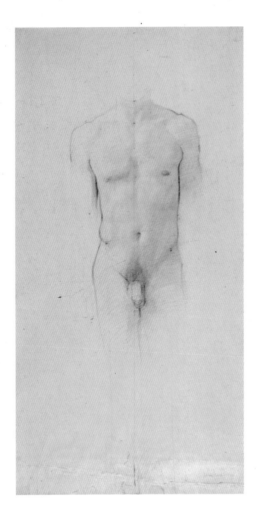

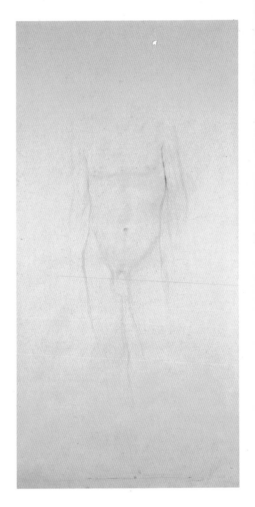

Antonio Lopez
Croquis con medidas 2 [VII. **51**]
1986-92

Manuel [VII. **47**]
1985

Emilio [VII. **46**]
1985

J. Enrique [VII. **48**]
1986

L. Fernando [VII. **49**]
1986

Croquis con medidas 1 [VII. **50**]
1986-92

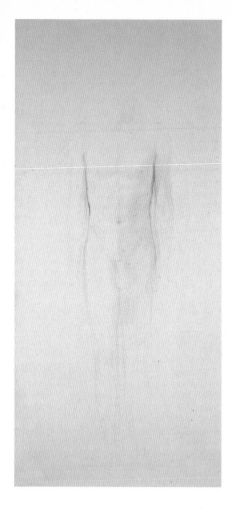

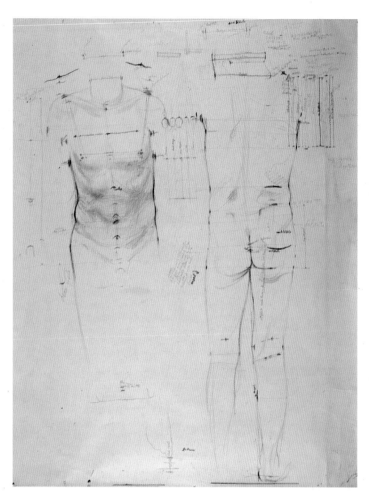

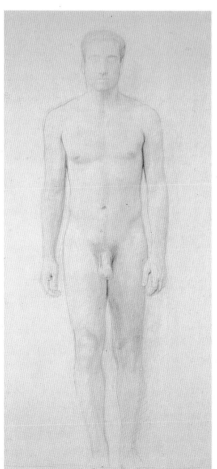

Antonio Lopez
Hombre y mujer [VII. **45**]
1968-90

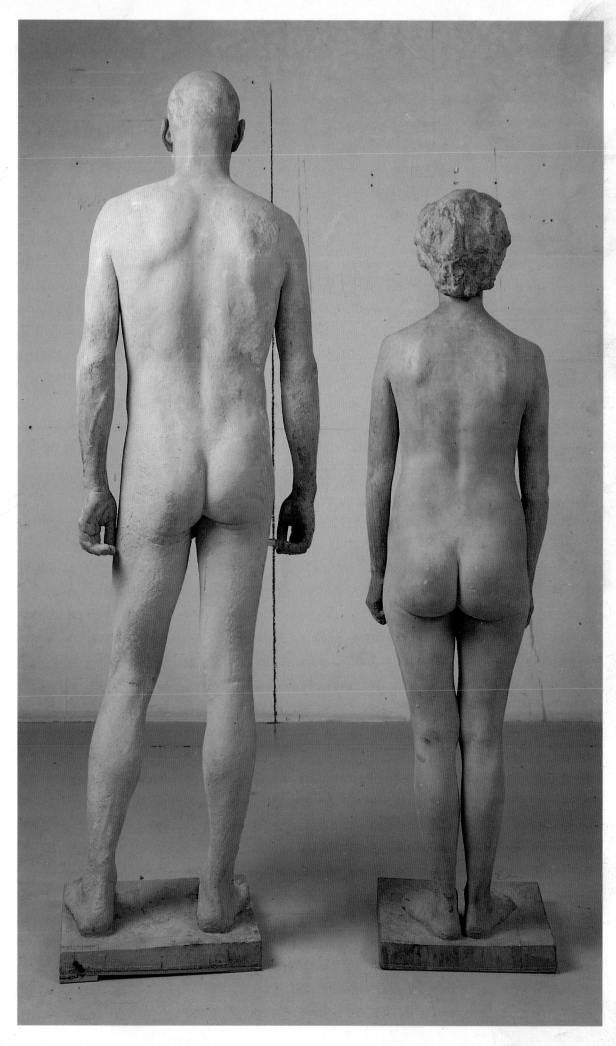

Pablo Picasso
Nu couché sur fond jaune
[VII. **65**]
1967

'Ars amandi'

Andrea Cascella

VII **53**
La nascita di Venere,
1962
Marble
70×40×70 cm
*Florence, Beatrice Monti
Rezzori collection*

Marcel Duchamp

VII **54**
Feuille de vigne femelle,
1950–51
Galvanized plaster
9×14×12.5 cm
*Milan, Arturo Schwarz
collection*

VII **55**
Objet-Dard,
1951–63
Bronze
6×7.5×20.1 cm
*Milan, Arturo Schwarz
collection*

VII **56**
Coin de chasteté,
1954–63
Bronze and dental plastic
5.6×4.2×8.5 cm
*Milan, Arturo Schwarz
collection*

Lucio Fontana

VII **57**
Venezia era tutta d'oro,
1961
Acrylic on canvas
149×149 cm
*Madrid,
Fundación Colección
Thyssen-Bornemisza*

Robert Morris

VII **58**
House of the Vetti,
1983
*Gray and pink felt,
metal studs*
240×244×92 cm
*Madrid,
Fundación Juan March*

Bruce Nauman

VII **59**
Untitled, *1965*
*Fibreglass and
polyester resin*
101.6×12.7×21.6 cm
*Buffalo, Albright-Knox
Art Gallery*

VII **60**
Storage Capsule for
the Right Rear Quarter
of My Body, *1966*
Galvanized metal sheet
182.9×24.1×15.2 cm
*Basel, Öffentliche
Kunstsammlung, Museum
für Gegenwartskunst*

VII **61**
Female Masturbation,
1985
*Pencil and watercolor
on paper*
127×96.5 cm
*Paris, Yvon Lambert
collection*

VII **62**
Male Masturbation, *1985*
*Pencil and watercolor
on paper*
127×96.5 cm
*Paris, Yvon Lambert
collection*

Georgia O'Keeffe

VII **63**
Grey Line with Lavender
and Yellow, *1923*
Oil on canvas
121.9×76.2 cm
*New York,
The Metropolitan
Museum of Art*

VII **64**
White Iris n° 7,
1957
Oil on canvas
76.2×102 cm
*Madrid,
Fundación Colección
Thyssen-Bornemisza*

Pablo Picasso

VII **65**
Nu couché
sur fond jaune,
1967 (9 October)
Oil on canvas
114×146 cm
*Paris, Bernard Ruiz-Picasso
collection*

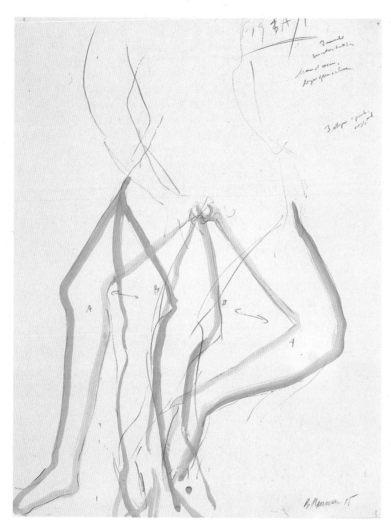 

Bruce Nauman
Female Masturbation [VII. **61**]
1985

Male Masturbation [VII. **62**]
1985

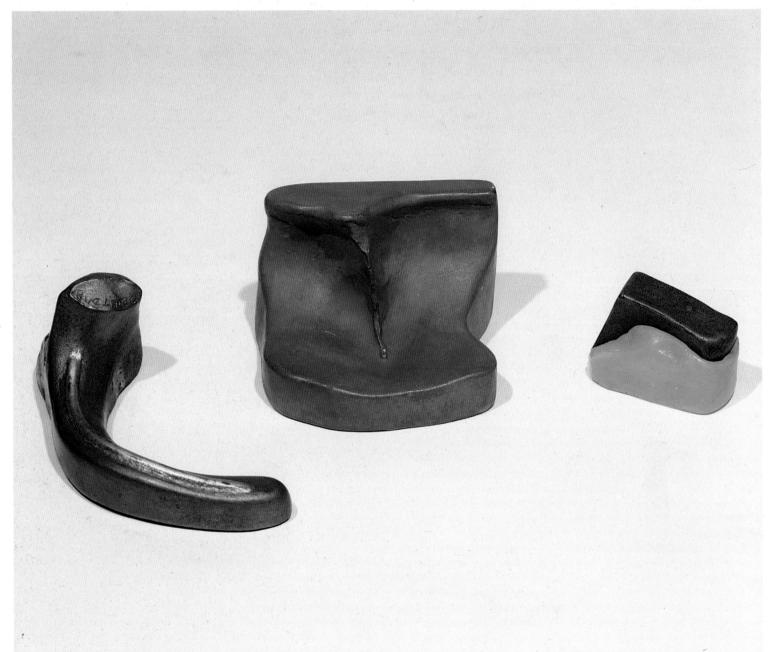

Marcel Duchamp
Objet-Dard [VII. **55**]
1951-63

Feuille de vigne femelle [VII. **54**]
1950-51

Coin de chasteté [VII. **56**]
1954-63

Lucio Fontana
Venezia era tutta d'oro [VII. **57**]
1961

Robert Morris
House of the Vetti [VII. **58**]
1983

Bruce Nauman
Storage Capsule for
the Right Rear Quarter
of My Body [VII. **60**]
1966

436
**The Return
of the Body**

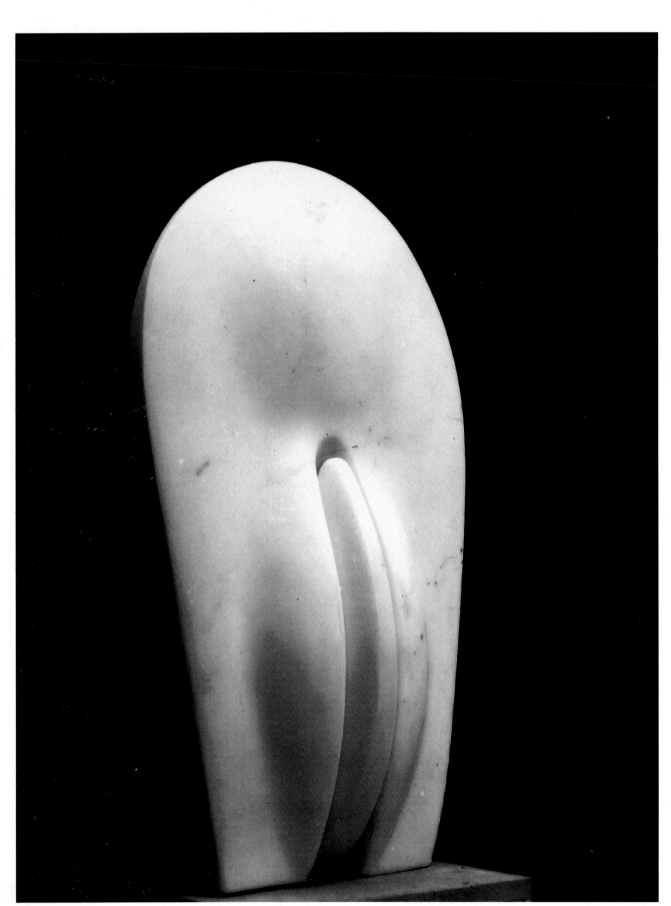

Georgia O'Keeffe
Grey Line with Lavender
and Yellow [VII. **63**]
1923

White Iris n° 7 [VII. **64**]
1957

439
**The Return
of the Body**

Marc Garanger
Femme algérienne [VII. **66**]
1960

A Veiled and Unveiled Face

Marc Garanger

VII **66**
Femme algérienne,
1960
Photograph
26.8×27.4 cm
Paris, Property of the artist

VII **67**
Femme algérienne,
1960
Photograph
26.8×27.4 cm
Paris, Property of the artist

VII **68**
Femme algérienne,
1960
Photograph
26.8×27.4 cm
Paris, Property of the artist

VII **69**
Femme algérienne,
1960
Photograph
26.8×27.4 cm
Paris, Property of the artist

VII **70**
Femme algérienne,
1960
Photograph
26.8×27.4 cm
Paris, Property of the artist

VII **71**
Femme algérienne,
1960
Photograph
26.8×27.4 cm
Paris, Property of the artist

**Gaëtan Gatian
de Clérambault**

VII **72**
Etudes d'étoffes, 1918–34
5 prints on silver bromide
emulsion mounted
on cardboard
28×51 cm
Paris, Bibliothèque
du Musée de l'Homme

VII **73**
Etudes d'étoffes, 1918–34
5 prints on silver bromide
emulsion mounted
on cardboard
28×51 cm
Paris, Bibliothèque
du Musée de l'Homme

VII **74**
Etudes d'étoffes, 1918–34
4 prints on silver bromide
emulsion mounted
on cardboard
30×70 cm
Paris, Bibliothèque
du Musée de l'Homme

VII **75**
Etudes d'étoffes, 1918–34
3 prints on silver bromide
emulsion mounted
on cardboard
28×51 cm
Paris, Bibliothèque
du Musée de l'Homme

VII **76**
Etudes d'étoffes, 1918–34
4 prints on silver bromide
emulsion mounted
on cardboard
28×51 cm
Paris, Bibliothèque
du Musée de l'Homme

VII **77**
Etudes d'étoffes, 1918–34
4 prints on silver bromide
emulsion mounted
on cardboard
30×70 cm
Paris, Bibliothèque
du Musée de l'Homme

VII **78**
Etude d'étoffes, 1918–34
Print on silver bromide
emulsion mounted
on cardboard
54.5×37 cm
Paris, Bibliothèque
du Musée de l'Homme

VII **79**
Etude d'étoffes, 1918–34
Print on silver bromide
emulsion mounted
on cardboard
54.5×37 cm
Paris, Bibliothèque
du Musée de l'Homme

VII **80**
Etude d'étoffes, 1918–34
Print on silver bromide
emulsion mounted
on cardboard
54.5×37 cm
Paris, Bibliothèque
du Musée de l'Homme

VII **81**
Etude d'étoffes, 1918–34
Print on silver bromide
emulsion mounted
on cardboard
54.5×37 cm
Paris, Bibliothèque
du Musée de l'Homme

Helmut Newton

VII **82**
'Sie Kommen' dressed,
1981
Black and white photograph
200×115 cm
Cologne, Leon Gustantiner
collection (courtesy Galerie
Rudolf Kicken)

VII **83**
'Sie Kommen' naked,
1981
Black and white photograph
200×115 cm
Cologne, Leon Gustantiner
collection (courtesy Galerie
Rudolf Kicken)

Marc Garanger
Femmes algériennes [VII. **67-71**]
1960

**Gaëtan Gatian
de Clérambault**
Etudes d'étoffes [VII. **72**]
1918-34

Helmut Newton
«Sie Kommen» dressed [VII. **82**]
1981

«Sie Kommen» naked [VII. **83**]
1981

VIII
**The Real
and Virtual
Body**
1985-1995

450

The Real and Virtual Body
1985-1995

The body of humanity opens in two, between the real and the virtual, showing exactly what art can and cannot do. 'We cannot bear the whole and the perfect' (Bernhard, *Alte Meister*, 1985). Or else we want them beyond ourselves. Arnulf Rainer's comedy of Viennese grimaces is a prologue of great immediacy—followed by the incomplete tragedy of the dispersal of his images and his 'ugly signs'. We are still left wondering how the spectator–less, body–less Minimal Art, could be 'paired off' with a Body Art in which the single spectator strips himself of the bandages of 'victimism' and becomes a curious man–ghost (Nitsch and Brus), who likes silent landscapes and the black vacuum.

'Protect me from what I want' is one of the truisms and proverbs that form the 'neo–classical' inscriptions Jenny Holtzer has engraved on the edifice of Post–Modernism. Cindy Sherman and Kiki Smith offer an archaeological reconstruction of the emblem of Painting and Sculpture after the fragmentation of semiology and aesthetics—the last word belongs to 'retrospective contemporaneity', which is necessarily more contemporary. Nancy Burson and Gerhard Lang create ultra–human and subhuman images that draw on the fear of extinction of a species caught between hostile philosophy and animal–mania. These are not the coy animals you see on the cover of a glossy magazine; they can also represent the animal within us that has to be tamed (Wulz and Ousmane Sow). Graffiti and wind–writing never come to an end, and we must try to understand the infinite stories told in the hieroglyphics. Clemente's ideogrammed *Meditations* are exchange tokens between old and new currencies: 'City of shadow and City of the Sun'. Such an alphabet arises out of the slow transformations in the sign messages of the body, which can be compared to those slight modifications in faces which are both the same and different, those instinctive reactions (Wicki) which lead towards the recomposition of a 'larger family portrait' (Zhang) —

in which we can see all the peculiarities and constant features of the physiognomical imprinting of East and West.

The black and white photographs taken in the 1930s by the musician Wols form a catalog of succulent alimentary cruelty. Beans, cheese, fruit, meat, the head of a rabbit, a bird, kidneys—all are becoming someone else's body and flesh; and all that is left of the life of the bodies is a market–scene. Nutrition is a vast silent production of life, which extends throughout a diffuse body. Bulimia or anorexia are the excessive acceptance or negation of the body. The virtual aspiration is always the same: the possession of a clone of oneself to act out one's orders and thus 'double' a body which mourns for its soul.

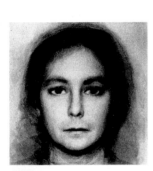

Nancy Burson
Androgyny [VIII. **10**]
1982

The Real and Virtual Body
1985-1995

VIII **18**
Untitled 89–22, *1989*
Polaroid Polacolor ER Land
film Print pasted on
cardboard
74×65.5 cm
Paris, Fonds Régional
d'Art Contemporain
de Basse-Normandie

VIII **19**
Untitled 90–2, *1990*
Polaroid Polacolor ER Land
film Print
73×68 cm
Paris, Alain Burger
collection

VIII **20**
Untitled 90–1 (Pinhead
Man), *1990*
Polaroid Polacolor ER Land
film Print
78.6×66.8 cm
Courtesy of Jayne H. Baum
Gallery, New York
and Galerie Michèle
Chomette, Paris

VIII **21**
Untitled 90–10 (Nathaniel
on Bed), *1990*
Silverprint,
reproduction 2/8
53.3×53.3 cm
New York, courtesy of Jayne
H. Baum Gallery and
Galerie Michèle Chomette,
Paris

VIII **22**
Untitled 91–10 (Danny),
1991
Silverprint,
reproduction 1/8
53.3×53.3 cm
Courtesy of Jayne H. Baum
Gallery, New York
and Galerie Michèle
Chomette, Paris

VIII **23**
Untitled 91–04
(Jessica & Mom),
1991
Silverprint,
reproduction 1/8
53.3×53.3 cm
Courtesy of Jayne H. Baum
Gallery, New York
and Galerie Michèle
Chomette, Paris

VIII **24**
Untitled 91–09
(The Twins), *1991*
Silverprint,
reproduction 1/8
53.3×53.3 cm
Courtesy of Jayne H. Baum
Gallery, New York
and Galerie Michèle
Chomette, Paris

VIII **25**
Untitled 92–04, *1992*
Silverprint,
reproduction 1/8
53.3×53.3 cm
Courtesy of Jayne H. Baum
Gallery, New York
and Galerie Michèle
Chomette, Paris

VIII **26**
Untitled 92–05, *1992*
Silverprint,
reproduction 2/8
53.3×53.3 cm
Courtesy of Jayne H. Baum
Gallery, New York
and Galerie Michèle
Chomette, Paris

VIII **27**
Untitled 92–06, *1992*
Silverprint,
reproduction 1/8
53.3×53.3 cm
Courtesy of Jayne H. Baum
Gallery, New York
and Galerie Michèle
Chomette, Paris

VIII **28**
Untitled 92–07, *1992*
Silverprint,
reproduction 1/8
53.3×53.3 cm
Courtesy of Jayne H. Baum
Gallery, New York
and Galerie Michèle
Chomette, Paris

VIII **29**
Untitled 93–01, *1993*
Silverprint,
reproduction 2/8
53.3×53.3 cm
Courtesy of Jayne H. Baum
Gallery, New York
and Galerie Michèle
Chomette, Paris

VIII **30**
Untitled 93–02, *1993*
Silverprint,
reproduction 2/8
53.3×53.3 cm
Courtesy of Jayne H. Baum
Gallery, New York
and Galerie Michèle
Chomette, Paris

Nancy Burson
David Kramlich

VIII **31**
Anomaly Machine
and Age Machine 1990–92,
1994
Interactive installation
162.5×61×122 cm and
162.5×61×38 cm
Courtesy of Jayne H. Baum
Gallery, New York
and Galerie Michèle
Chomette, Paris

E.A. Cabanis,
M.T. Iba-Zizen,
R. Cavezian, Ph. Trocme,
T.H. Nguyen, D. Payet,
N. Mottier, Ph. Comar

VIII **32**
Anatomie médicale:
du réel au virtuel, *1995*
Videotape, 5'
Paris, Emmanuel Cabanis
collection

Mary Carlson

VIII **33**
Toile Figures, *1990*
Sewn nylon fabric
17×90×200 cm
New York, Pamela
Jo Rosenau collection

VIII **34**
Rice Paper, *1992*
Glued paper
8×115×150 cm
New York,
Property of the artist

Helen Chadwick

VIII **35**
Enfleshings I, *1989*
Cibachrome, glass, steel,
electronic equipment
106.7×91.4×15.2 cm
London, Jim Moyes and
Joanna Price collection

VIII **36**
Eroticism, *1990*
Photograph electronic
equipment
76×122 cm
London, Saatchi Collection

Clegg & Guttmann

VIII **37**
Vérité, *1994*
Installation
500×800 cm
Cologne,
Galerie Christian Nagel

Francesco Clemente

VIII **38**
Méditation: Helvétius
and Tracy, *1992–94*
Mixed media on canvas
186×197 cm
Zurich,
Galerie Bruno Bischofberger

VIII **39**
Meditation: Fioriture,
1992–94
Mixed media on canvas
186×197 cm
Zurich,
Galerie Bruno Bischofberger

VIII **40**
Meditation: Journal
des deux ponts, *1992–94*
Mixed media on canvas
186×197 cm
Zurich,
Galerie Bruno Bischofberger

VIII **41**
Meditation: Hampden,
1992–94
Mixed media on canvas
186×197 cm
Zurich,
Galerie Bruno Bischofberger

VIII **42**
Meditation: Effet
nécessaire, *1992–94*
Mixed media on canvas
186×197 cm
Zurich,
Galerie Bruno Bischofberger

VIII **43**
Meditation; Le Docteur
Edwards, *1992–94*
Mixed media on canvas
186×197 cm
Zurich,
Galerie Bruno Bischofberger

VIII **44**
Meditation: Trigonometrie,
1992–94
Mixed media on canvas
186×197 cm
Zurich,
Galerie Bruno Bischofberger

VIII **45**
Meditation: Improbus,
1992–94
Mixed media on canvas
186×197 cm
Zurich,
Galerie Bruno Bischofberger

Vincent Corpet

VIII **46**
'2606 P 15, 20, 21, 27 IX;
14, 21, 26 X; 1, 4, 10 XI
94 H/T 191×64', *1994*
Oil on canvas
191×64 cm
Paris, Property of the artist

VIII **47**
'2608 P 31 X; 1, 2, 8, 11,
15 XI; 5 XII 94 H/T
60×171', *1994*
Oil on canvas
171×60 cm
Paris,
Property of the artist

VIII **48**
'2610 P 21, 23, 24 XI; 2,
7, XII; 26, 28, I 95 H/T
60×179,5', *1994–95*
Oil on canvas
179.5×60 cm
Paris, Property of the artist

VIII **49**
'2612 P 10, 19, 31 I; 3,
10 II; 1, 9 III 95 H/T
58×176,5', *1995*
Oil on canvas
176.5×58 cm
Paris, Property of the artist

VIII **50**
'2614 P 25 I 95 ... H/T
71×195', *1995*
Oil on canvas
195×71 cm
Paris, Property of the artist

Hans Danuser

VIII **51**
In Vivo: Medizin I
(1984), Chemie II (1989),
1984–89
Photograph
40×50 cm and 50×40 cm
Aarau,
Aargauer Kunsthaus,
Aargauische Stiftung für
Fotografie, Film und Video

Marlene Dumas

VIII **52**
Snowhite and the Next
Generation, *1988*
Oil on canvas
140×200 cm
Utrecht, Centraal Museum

VIII **53**
Belly, *1993*
Oil on canvas
30×24 cm
Milan, Pasquale Leccese
collection

VIII **54**
Bondage, *1993*
Oil on canvas
30×24 cm
Milan, Alessandro Grassi
collection

VIII **55**
Young boys, *1993*
Oil on canvas
100×300 cm
New York, Lois & Richard
Plehn collection

Jeanne Dunning

VIII **56**
Sample 4, *1990*
Cibachrome on plexiglas
45×38 cm
Turbigo, Milan,
Private collection

VIII **57**
Crack 3, *1991*
Photograph
122×11 cm
Geneva, Galerie
Analix-B & L Polla

VIII **58**
Untitled Hole, *1991–93*
Cibachrome on plexiglas
64.3×64.3 cm
Paris, Courtesy of Galerie
Samia Saouma

VIII **59**
Untitled Hole, *1991–93*
Cibachrome on plexiglas
64.3×64.3 cm
Paris, Lewis Kaplan
collection (courtesy of
Galerie Samia Saouma)

VIII **60**
Detail 16, *1992*
Cibachrome on plexiglas
65×83 cm
Milan, Private collection

VIII **61**
Detail 17, *1993*
Cibachrome
54.2×42.8 cm
Bruxelles, Andrée Levy
collection (courtesy of
Galerie Samia Saouma)

VIII **62**
Detail 18, *1993*
Cibachrome
54.2×42.8 cm
Bruxelles, Andrée Levy
collection (courtesy of
Galerie Samia Saouma,
Paris)

VIII **63**
Untitled Part, *1993*
Cibachrome on plexiglas
83.2×59.2 cm
Paris, Courtesy of Galerie
Samia Saouma

Eric Fischl

VIII **64**
Questionable pleasure
n° 3, *1994*
Oil on canvas
178×114 cm
Paris,
Galerie Daniel Templon

Judy Fox

VIII **65**
Saint Theresa, *1993*
Hydrostone, casein paint
95×80 cm
Vienna, Courtesy
of Christine König Galerie

VIII **66**
The Virgin Mary, *1993*
Hydrostone, casein paint
h 95 cm
Innsbruck, Private collection
(courtesy of Christine König
Galerie, Vienna)

Betty Goodwin

VIII **67**
La mémoire du corps,
n° XVII, *1991–92*
Pastel and graphite
on photostat and steel
185.5×206 cm
Montreal, Stéphanie Dudek
collection

VIII **68**
Untitled Nerves, n° 1,
1993
Oil pastel, oil crayons,
wax and chromoflex print
on Mylar
193×134.5 cm
Toronto, Alan and Alison
Schwartz collection

Michel Haas

VIII **69**
Les Etreintes, *1994*
Mixed media
163×70 cm
Geneva, Krugier-Ditesheim
Art Contemporain

VIII **70**
Figure, *1994*
Mixed media
176×65 cm
Paris,
Property of the artist

VIII **71**
Assis, *1994*
Mixed media
105×65 cm
Geneva, Krugier-Ditesheim
Art Contemporain

Mona Hatoum

VIII **72**
Corps étranger, *1994*
Installation with video-
projectors and wooden
framework
350×305×305 cm
Paris, Musée National
d'Art Moderne,
Centre Georges Pompidou

Gary Hill

VIII **73**
Untitled, *1995*
Video installation
Seattle,
Property of the artist

Stephan von Huene

VIII **74**
14 Zeichnungen, *1988–93*
Drawings
170×115 cm each
Karlsruhe,
Zemtrum für Kunst
und Medientechnologie

VIII **75**
Tisch-Tänzer: sculpture
with one forward and
back movement, *1988–93*
Various materials,
electronic components
200×80×50 cm
Karlsruhe,
Zemtrum für Kunst
und Medientechnologie

VIII **76**
Tisch-Tänzer: sculpture-
object with one side to
side movement, *1988–93*
Various materials, electronic
components
200×80×50 cm
Karlsruhe, Zemtrum für
Kunst und
Medientechnologie

VIII **77**
Tisch-Tänzer: sculpture-
object with one diagonal
movement, *1988–93*
Various materials,
electronic components
200×80×50 cm
Karlsruhe,
Zemtrum für Kunst
und Medientechnologie

VIII **78**
Tisch-Tänzer: object tall
with no trousers and
Baroque, *1988–93*
Various materials, electronic
components, air compressor
275×70×40 cm
Karlsruhe,
Zemtrum für Kunst
und Medientechnologie

Mike Kelley
and **Paul McCarthy**

VIII **79**
'Fresh Acconci', *1995*
Video installation
Los Angeles,
Rosamund Felsen Gallery

Peter Kogler

VIII **80**
Ohne Titel, *1994*
Video installation
with 2 monitors
Vienna, Property of the artist

Inez van Lamsweerde

VIII **81**
Thank you Thigmaster,
Pam 1993, *1993*
Duraflex print, perspex
and aluminium
187×120 cm
Amsterdam, Courtesy
of Torch Gallery

VIII **82**
Final Fantasy: Wendy
1993, *1993*
Duraflex print and perspex
100×150 cm
Amsterdam, Courtesy
of Torch Gallery

VIII **83**
The Forest: Marcel 1995,
1995
Colour print, perspex
and aluminium
135×180 cm
Amsterdam, Courtesy
of Torch Gallery

Gerhard Lang

VIII **84**
Palaeanthropische
Physiognomie: Unbekannt,
1991
Photograph
230×120 cm
London, Private collection

VIII **85**
Palaeanthropische
Physiognomie: Unbekannt,
1991
Photograph
230×120 cm
London, Private collection

VIII **86**
Palaeanthropische
Physiognomie: Fridmana
Christ, *1992*
Photograph
230×120 cm
London, Private collection

VIII **87**
Palaeanthropische
Physiognomie: Unbekannt,
1992
Photograph
230×120 cm
London, Private collection

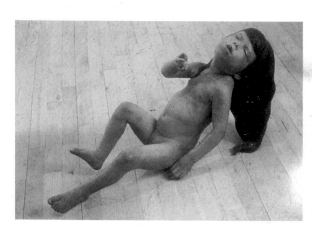

Judy Fox
Saint Theresa [VIII. **65**]
1993

VIII **88**
Palaeanthropische
Physiognomie: Unbekannt,
1992
Photograph
230×120 cm
London, Private collection

VIII **89**
Palaeanthropische
Physiognomie: Strigiedel
Homisbeth, *1992*
Photograph
230×120 cm
London, Private collection

Greer Lankton

VIII **90**
Untitled (Torso
with Red Edge), *1982*
Fabric, wire, color
60×25×8 cm
Cologne, Courtesy
of Galerie Tanja Grunert

Maria Lassnig

VIII **91**
Last des Fleisches, *1973*
Oil on canvas
185×251 cm
Vienna, Austria Center

VIII **92**
Rast der Kriegerin, *1978*
Oil on canvas
142×177.5 cm
Vienna, Austria Center

VIII **93**
Sensenmann, *1991*
Oil on canvas
200×145 cm
Vienna, Property of the artist

VIII **94**
Der Verstopfte, *1991*
Oil on canvas
200×145 cm
Vienna, Property of the artist

Wei Liu

VIII **95**
'You Like Pork?', *1995*
Oil on canvas
200×150 cm
Hong Kong, Property of the
artist (courtesy of Hanart
TZ Gallery)

Bruce Nauman

VIII **96**
Falls, Pratfalls and Sleights
of Hands, *1993*
Video installation with
5 monitors
12×12 m
Düsseldorf, Konrad Fischer

Yan Pei-Ming

VIII **97**
Tête, *1992*
Oil on canvas
207×155 cm
Paris, Courtesy of Galerie
Liliane & Michel Durand
Dessert

VIII **98**
Tête, *1992*
Oil on canvas
207×155 cm
Paris, Courtesy of Galerie
Liliane & Michel Durand
Dessert

VIII **99**
Tête, *1992*
Oil on canvas
207×155 cm
Paris, Courtesy of Galerie
Liliane & Michel Durand
Dessert

Arnulf Rainer

VIII **100**
Jalousie, *1969–70*
Ink, oil crayons
on photograph
60×47.7 cm
Vienna, Galerie Ulysses

VIII **101**
Stumm Verlegenes, *1970*
Ink, oil crayons
on photograph
60.8×50.8 cm
Vienna, Galerie Ulysses

VIII **102**
Tragkranz, *1971*
Ink, oil crayons
on photograph
60.5×50.1 cm
Vienna, Galerie Ulysses

VIII **103**
Augenschlag, *1972*
Graphite, oil crayons
on photograph
50.3×59.6 cm
Vienna, Galerie Ulysses

VIII **104**
Schnecke, *1972*
Graphite, oil crayons
on photograph
47.5×59.7 cm
Vienna, Galerie Ulysses

VIII **105**
ss, *1972*
Graphite, oil crayons
on photograph
60.5×50.3 cm
Vienna, Galerie Ulysses

VIII **106**
Was dann?, *1972–73*
Graphite on photograph
60.7×47.8 cm
Vienna, Galerie Ulysses

VIII **107**
Stand am Rand, *1972–73*
Graphite on photograph
60.9×48.2 cm
Vienna, Galerie Ulysses

VIII **108**
Stand und Hand,
1972–73
Graphite, oil crayons on
photograph
60.9×47.6 cm
Vienna, Galerie Ulysses

VIII **109**
Ohne Titel, *1972–73*
Graphite, oil crayons
on photograph
60.8×48.3 cm
Vienna, Galerie Ulysses

VIII **110**
Auch eine Daseinshöhung,
1972–73
Graphite, oil crayons
on photograph
60.8×40.2 cm
Vienna, Galerie Ulysses

VIII **111**
... (Titel unleserlich),
1972–73
Graphite on photograph
60.8×48 cm
Vienna, Galerie Ulysses

VIII **112**
Rätseln, *1973*
Graphite, oil crayons
on photograph
47.3×60 cm
Vienna, Galerie Ulysses

VIII **113**
Pause (Weder noch I),
1973
Oil crayons on photograph
47.4×59.7 cm
Vienna, Galerie Ulysses

VIII **114**
Ohne Titel, *1973*
Soft ink, oil crayons
on photograph
59.6×47.2 cm
Vienna, Galerie Ulysses

VIII **115**
Abend, *1973*
Oil crayons on photograph
48.6×60.7 cm
Vienna, Galerie Ulysses

VIII **116**
Kniefall, *1973–74*
Graphite, oil crayons
on photograph
47.2×60 cm
Vienna, Galerie Ulysses

VIII **117**
Ohne Titel, *1979*
Pastel, oil crayons
on photograph
50.7×61 cm
Vienna, Galerie Ulysses

VIII **118**
Ohne Titel, *1979*
Pastel, oil crayons
on photograph
50.7×61 cm
Vienna, Galerie Ulysses

VIII **119**
Ohne Titel, *1979*
Pastel, oil crayons
on photograph
50.7×61 cm
Vienna, Galerie Ulysses

VIII **120**
Ohne Titel, *1979*
Pastel, oil crayons
on photograph
50.7×61 cm
Vienna, Galerie Ulysses

Alberto Savinio

VIII **121**
La fidèle épouse, *1930–31*
Oil on canvas
81×65 cm
Private collection (courtesy
of Galleria dello Scudo,
Verona)

Carolee Schneeman

VIII **122**
Up and Including
Her Limits, *1976*
2 photographs
100×127; 95×120 cm
Vienna,
Collection Hubert Klocker

Rudolf Schwarzkogler

VIII **123**
3. Aktion, *1965*
30 photographs
30 cm
Vienna, Museum Moderner
Kunst Stiftung Ludwig

VIII **124**
6. Aktion, *1965*
34 photographs
30 cm
Vienna, Museum Moderner
Kunst Stiftung Ludwig

Cindy Sherman

VIII **125**
Untitled n° 209, *1989*
Color photograph (1/6)
75×61 cm
New York, Courtesy of
Metro Pictures and the
artist Cindy Sherman

VIII **126**
Untitled n° 214, *1989*
Color photograph
75×61 cm
New York, Courtesy of
Metro Pictures and the
artist Cindy Sherman

VIII **127**
Untitled n° 223, *1989*
Color photograph (5/6)
75×61 cm
Switzerland, L.A.C.
collection

VIII **128**
Untitled n° 225, *1990*
Color photograph
122×84 cm
New York, Courtesy of
Metro Pictures and the
artist Cindy Sherman

VIII **129**
Untitled n° 226, *1990*
Colour photograph (2/6)
122×76.2 cm
New York, Courtesy of
Metro Pictures and the
artist Cindy Sherman

Kiki Smith

VIII **130**
Scaffold Body, *1995*
White bronze and steel
259×239×91 cm
New York,
The Pace Gallery

Ousmane Sow

VIII **131**
Nouba: Lutteur debout,
1984
Mixed media
185×110×100 cm
Dakar, Property of the
artist (courtesy Béatrice
Soulé)

VIII **132**
Nouba: Lutteur assis,
1984
Mixed media
115×130×85 cm
Dakar, Property of the
artist (courtesy Béatrice
Soulé)

Nigel Van Wieck

VIII **133**
Face to Face
Oil pastels
56.5×75.5 cm
New York, Hazel
S. Kandall collection

VIII **134**
Black Tie, *1987*
Oil pastels on paper
77×56 cm
Riverside, Wendy
E. Ormond collection

VIII **135**
Sleep Tight, *about 1987*
Pastel on paper
56×75 cm
Madrid, Penn Sicre
collection

VIII **136**
Late Night Call, *1988–89*
Oil pastels on paper
34.3×43.2 cm
New York, Spencer
Harper III collection

VIII **137**
Two Manhattans, *1989*
Oil pastels on paper
56×89 cm
New York, Private collection

VIII **138**
American Landscape, *1989*
Pastel on paper
58×77 cm
Madrid, Penn Sicre
collection

Chantal Wicki

VIII **139**
Phantombilder-Gaby 1–
30, *1993–95*
Oil on canvas
20×20 cm each
Zurich,
Property of the artist

Wols (Alfred Otto Wolfgang Schulze)

VIII **140**
Sans Titre (Champignons)
Photograph
24×18 cm
Freiburg, Private collection

VIII **141**
Sans Titre (Haricots)
Photograph
24×18 cm
Freiburg, Private collection

VIII **142**
Sans Titre (Fromage)
Photograph
24×18 cm
Freiburg, Private collection

VIII **143**
Sans Titre (Fruit)
Photograph
24×18 cm
Freiburg, Private collection

VIII **144**
Sans Titre (Viande)
Photograph
24×18 cm
Freiburg, Private collection

VIII **145**
Sans Titre
(Branche et viande)
Photograph
24×18 cm
Freiburg, Private collection

VIII **146**
Sans Titre (Tête de lapin)
Photograph
24×18 cm
Freiburg, Private collection

VIII **147**
Sans Titre (Lapin avec
peigne et harmonica)
Photograph
24×18 cm
Freiburg, Private collection

VIII **148**
Sans Titre (Oiseau)
Photograph
18×24 cm
Freiburg, Private collection

VIII **149**
Sans Titre (Rognons)
Photograph
24×18 cm
Freiburg, Private collection

Wanda Wulz

VIII **150**
'Io + Gatto', *1932*
Silver chloride emulsion
print
29.5×23.5 cm
Florence, Museo di Storia
della Fotografia Fratelli
Alinari, Wulz Archive

Xiaogang Zhang

VIII **151**
Comrades, *1995*
Oil on canvas
130×100 cm (4 paintings)
Hong Kong, Property of the
artist (courtesy of Hanart
TZ Gallery)

VIII **152**
Bloodline: The Big Family,
n° 1, *1995*
Oil on canvas
180×230 cm
Hong Kong, Property of the
artist (courtesy of Hanart
TZ Gallery)

VIII **153**
Bloodline: The Big Family,
n° 2, *1995*
Oil on canvas
180×230 cm
Hong Kong, Property of the
artist (courtesy of Hanart
TZ Gallery)

VIII **154**
Bloodline: The Big Family,
n° 3, *1995*
Oil on canvas
180×230 cm
Hong Kong, Property of the
artist (courtesy of Hanart
TZ Gallery)

VIII **155**
Bloodline: The Big Family,
n° 4, *1995*
Oil on canvas
180×230 cm
Hong Kong, Property of the
artist (courtesy of Hanart
TZ Gallery)

Wanda Wulz
«Io + Gatto» [VIII. **150**]
1932

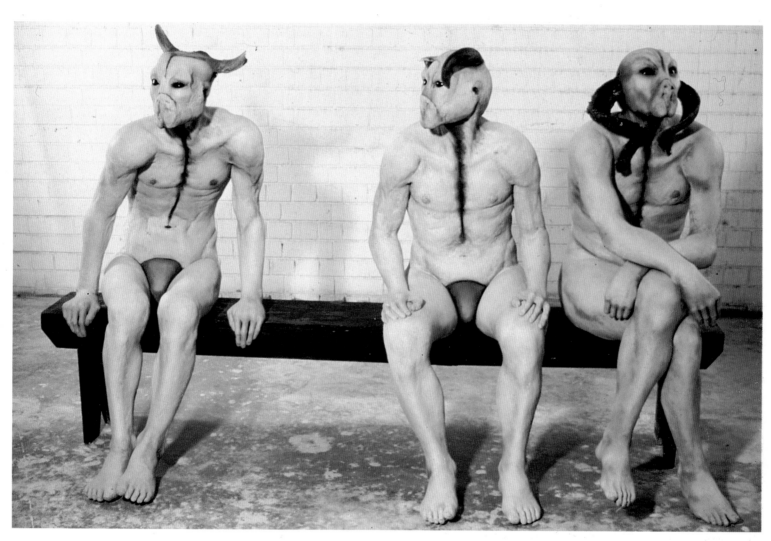

Jane Alexander
Butcher Boys [VIII. **2**]
1985-86

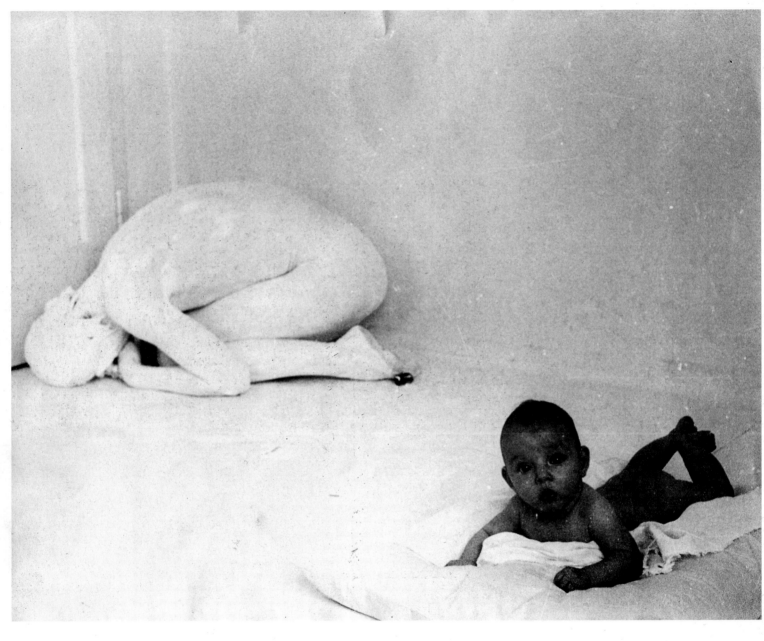

Günter Brus
Aktion mit Diana
1967

Wiener Spaziergang
1965

Malerei, Selbstbemalung,
Selbstverstümmelung
Galerei Junge Generation
1965

Selbstverstümmelung
1965

 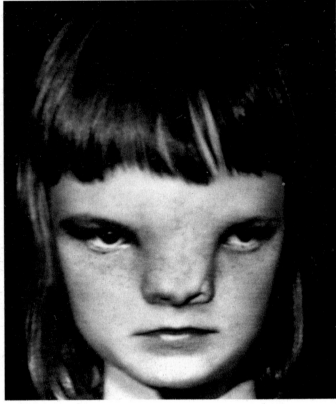

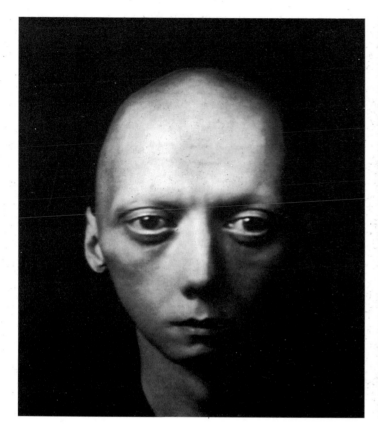 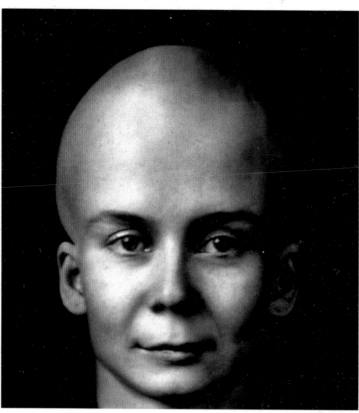

Nancy Burson
Evolution II [VIII. **12**]
1984

Untitled 89-8 [VIII. **15**]
1988

Untitled 89-22 [VIII. **18**]
1989

Untitled 90-2 [VIII. **19**]
1990

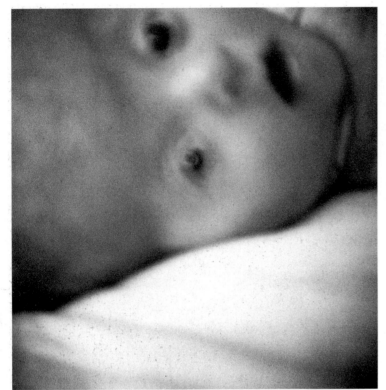
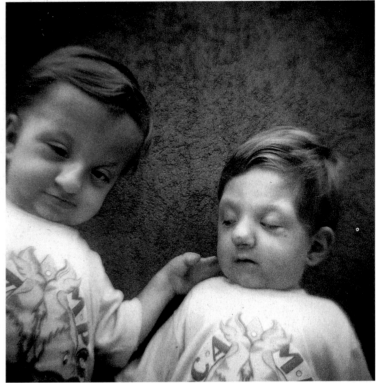

Nancy Burson
Untitled 90-10
(Nathaniel on Bed) [VIII. **21**]
1990

Untitled 91-09 (The Twins) [VIII. **24**]
1991

Untitled 92-07 [VIII. **28**]
1992

Untitled 93-02 [VIII. **30**]
1993

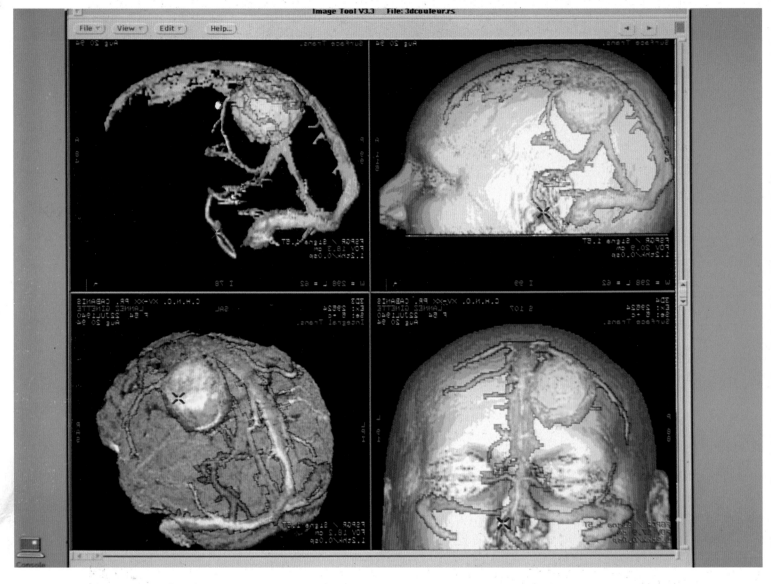

**E.A. Cabanis, M.T. Iba-Zizen,
R. Cavezian, Ph. Trocme,
T.H. Nguyen, D. Payet,
N. Mottier, Ph. Comar**
Anatomie médicale:
du réel au virtuel [VIII. **32**]
1995

Mary Carlson
Toile Figures [VIII. **33**]
1990

Rice Paper [VIII. **34**]
1992

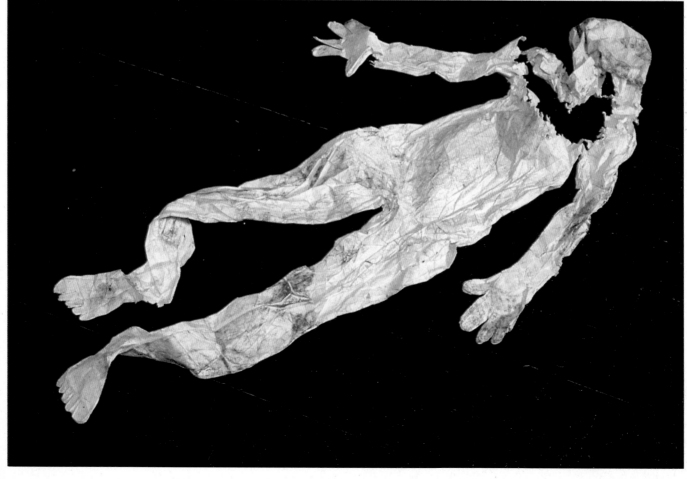

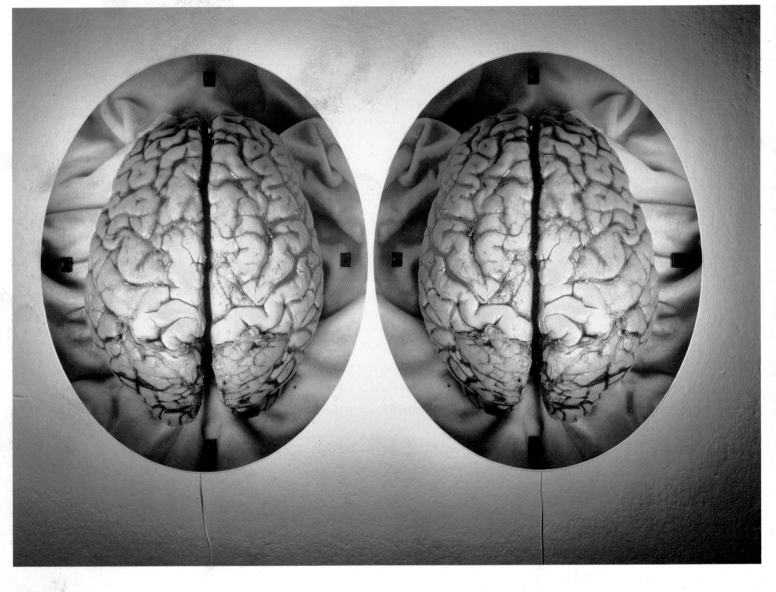

Helen Chadwick
Eroticism [VIII. **36**]
1990

Clegg & Guttmann
Vérité [VIII. **37**]
1994

Francesco Clemente
Méditation: Helvétius
and Tracy [VIII. **38**]
1992-94

Méditation: Fioriture [VIII. **39**]
1992-94

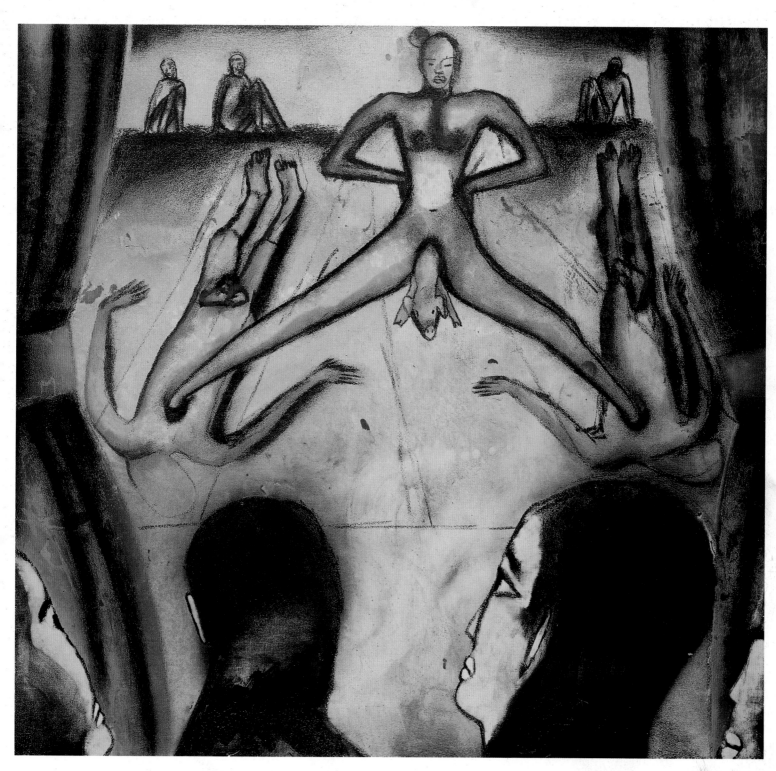

Francesco Clemente
Méditation: Journal
des deux ponts [VIII. **40**]
1992-94

Méditation: Improbus [VIII. **45**]
1992-94

Vincent Corpet
«2608 p 31 x; 1, 2, 8, 11, 15 xi;
5 xii 94 н/т 60×171» [viii. **47**] *1994*

«2612 p 10, 19, 31 i; 3, 10 ii; 1, 9 iii 95 н/т
58×176,5» [viii. **49**] *1995*

Eric Fischl
Questionable pleasure n° 3 [viii. **64**] *1994*

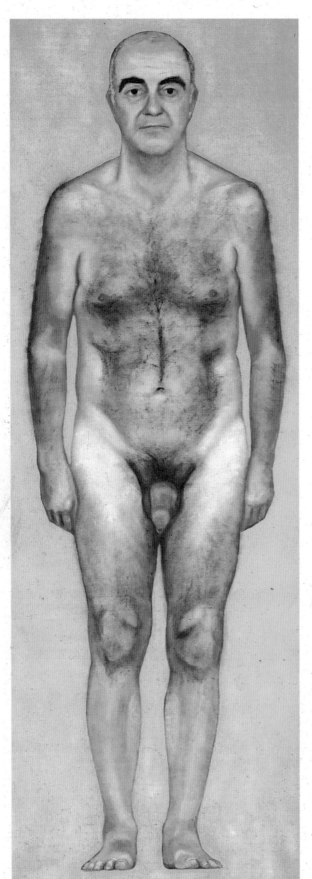

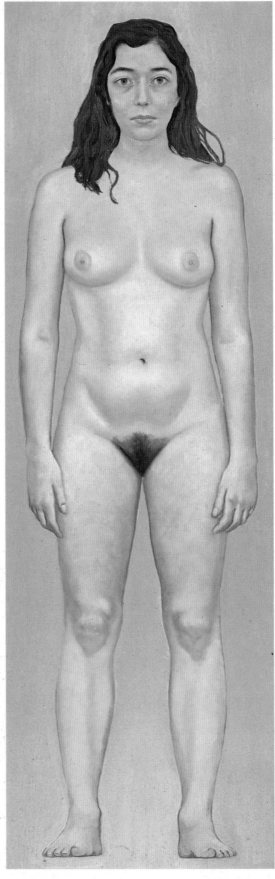

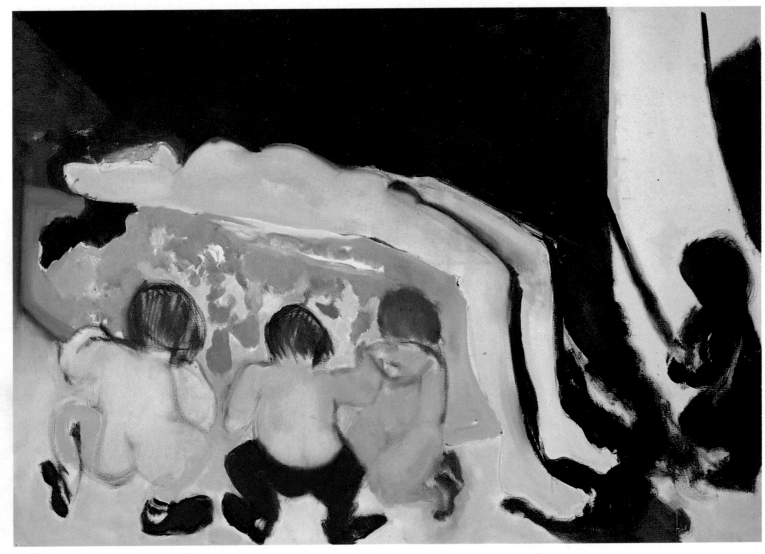

Marlene Dumas
Snowhite and the Next
Generation [VIII. **52**]
1988

Belly [VIII. **53**]
1993

Bondage [VIII. **54**]
1993

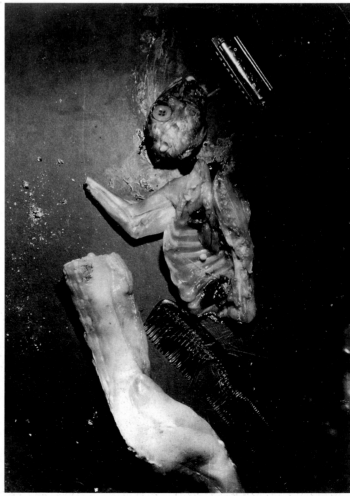

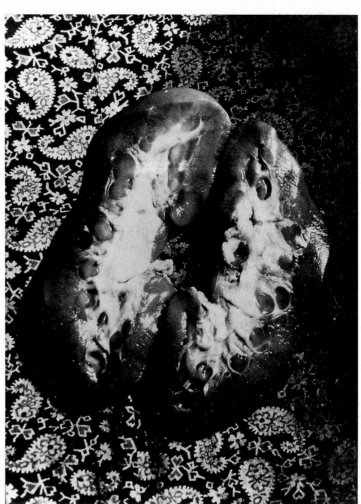

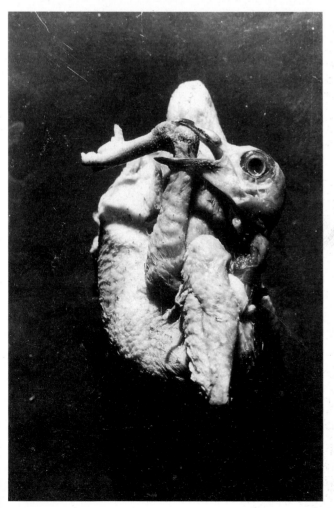

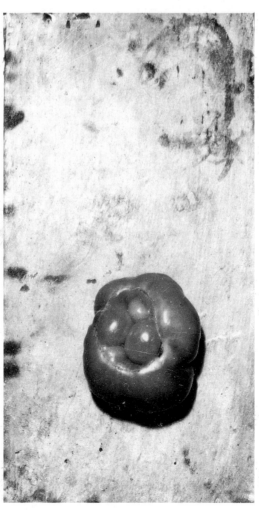

Wols
(Alfred Otto Wolfgang Schulze)
Sans Titre
(Champignons) [VIII. **140**]

Sans Titre (Haricots) [VIII. **141**]

Sans Titre (Branche et viande)
[VIII. **145**]

Sans Titre (Lapin avec peigne
et harmonica) [VIII. **147**]

Sans Titre (Viande) [VIII. **144**]

Sans Titre (Rognons) [VIII. **149**]

Sans Titre (Oiseau) [VIII. **148**]

Sans Titre (Fruit) [VIII. **143**]

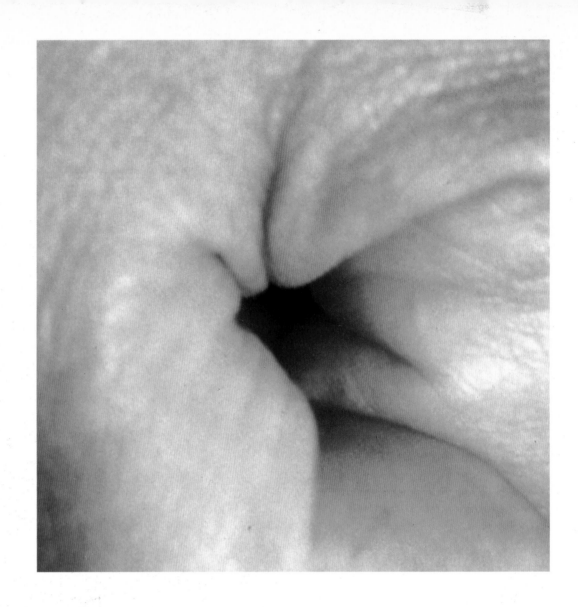

Jeanne Dunning
Untitled Hole [VIII. **58**]
1991-93

Detail 16 [VIII. **60**]
1992

Crack 3 [VIII. **57**]
1991

Untitled Part [VIII. **63**]
1993

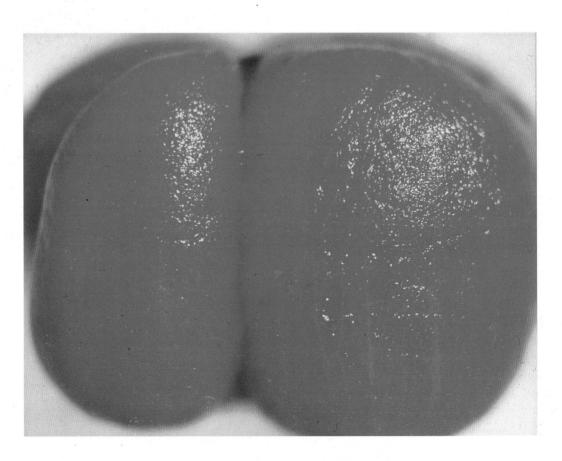

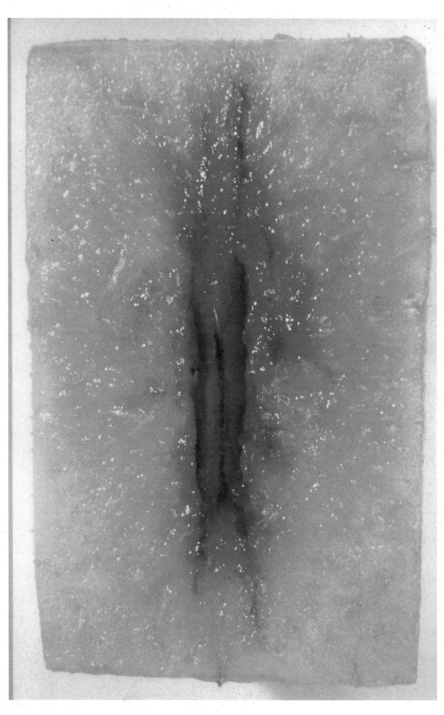

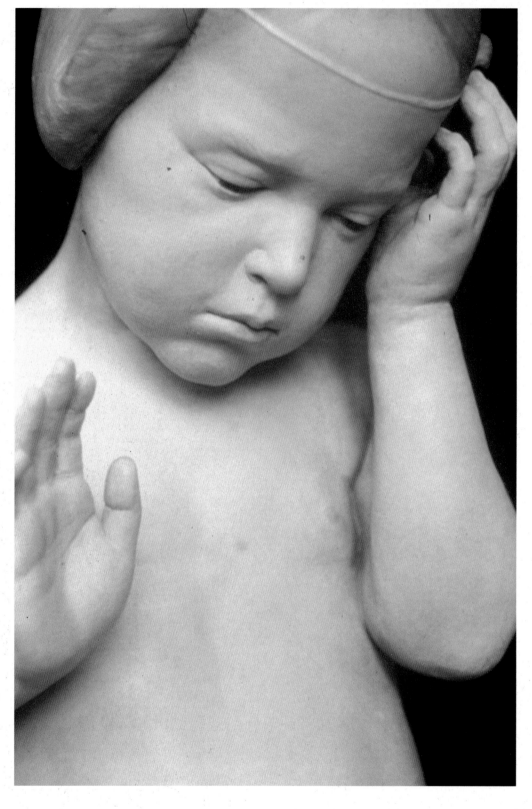

Judy Fox
The Virgin Mary [VIII. **66**]
1993

Michel Haas
Figure [VIII. **70**]
1994

Les Etreintes [VIII. **69**]
1994

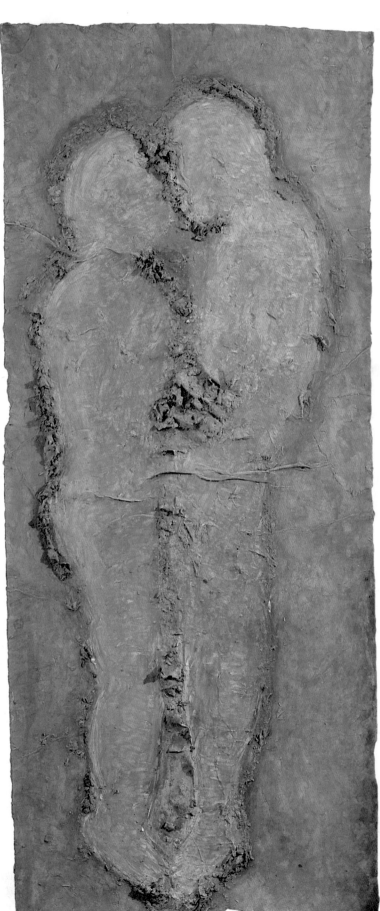

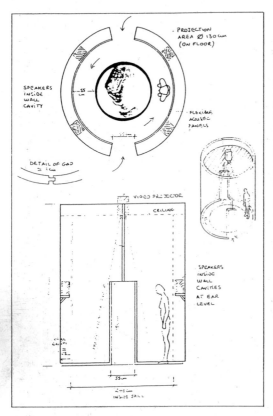

Mona Hatoum
Corps étranger [VIII. **72**]
1994

Stephan von Huene
Tisch-Tänzer: sculptures [VIII. **75-78**]
1988-93

14 Zeichnungen [VIII. **74**]
1988-93

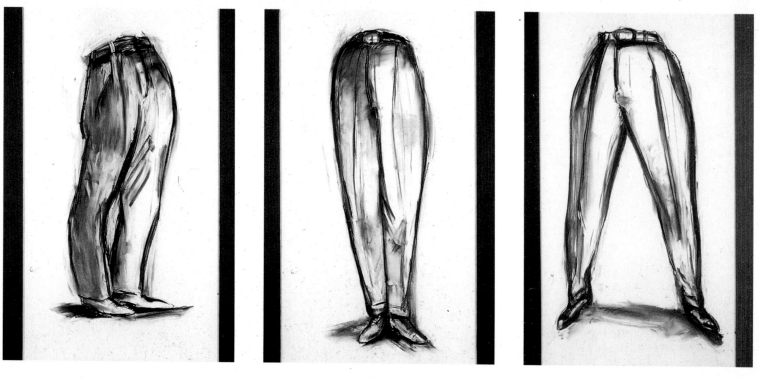

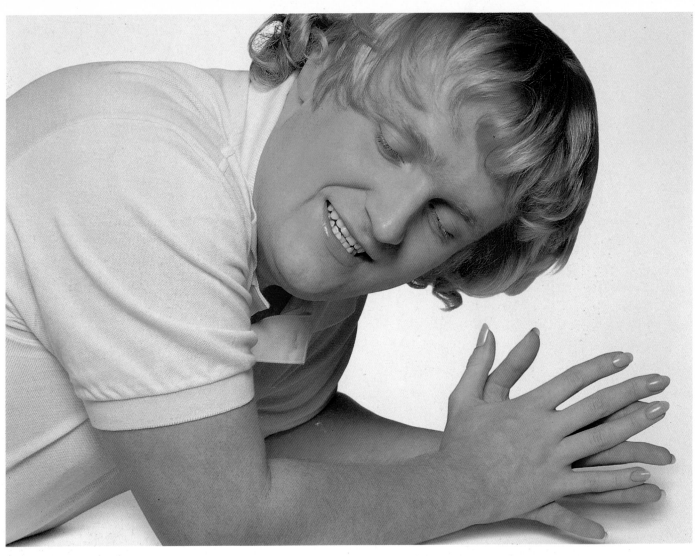

Inez van Lamsweerde
The Forest: Marcel 1995 [VIII. **83**]
1995

Thank you Thigmaster,
Pam 1993 [VIII. **81**]
1993

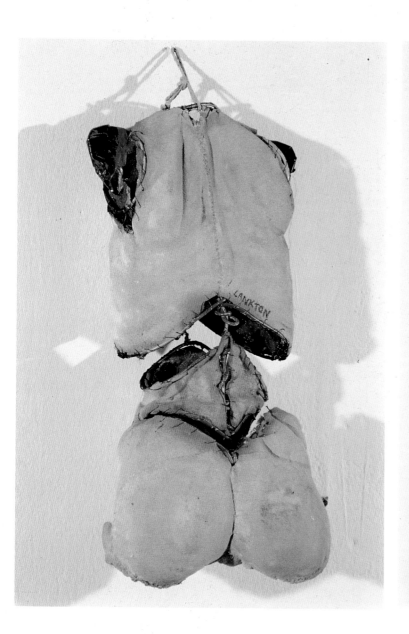

Greer Lankton
Untitled (Torso
with Red Edge) [VIII. **90**]
1982

Alberto Savinio
La fidèle épouse [VIII. **121**]
1930-31

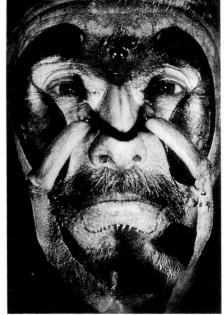

Gerhard Lang
Palaeanthropische
Physiognomie: Unbekannt
[VIII. **85**]
1991

Palaeanthropische
Physiognomie: Fridmana
Christ [VIII. **86**]
1992

Palaeanthropische
Physiognomie: Unbekannt
[VIII. **84**]
1991

Palaeanthropische
Physiognomie: Unbekannt
[VIII. **88**]
1992

Palaeanthropische
Physiognomie: Unbekannt
[VIII. **87**]
1992

Palaeanthropische
Physiognomie: Strigiedel
Homisbeth [VIII. **89**]
1992

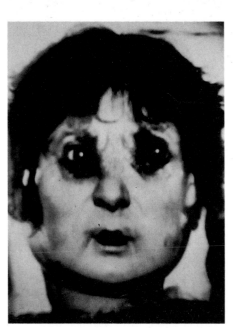

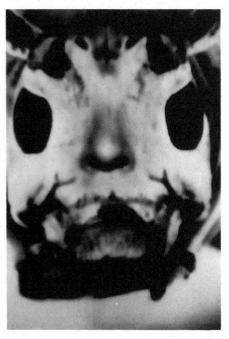

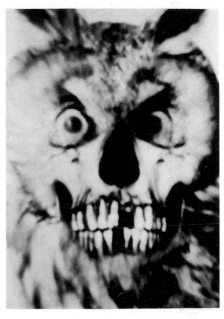

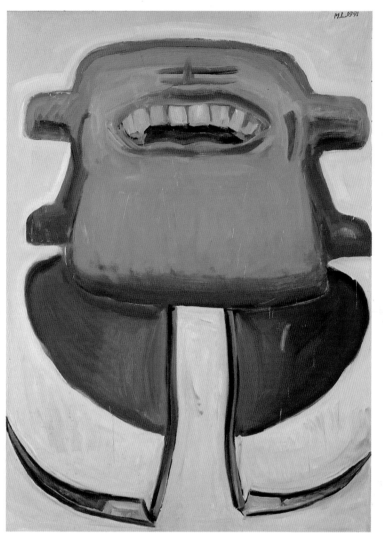

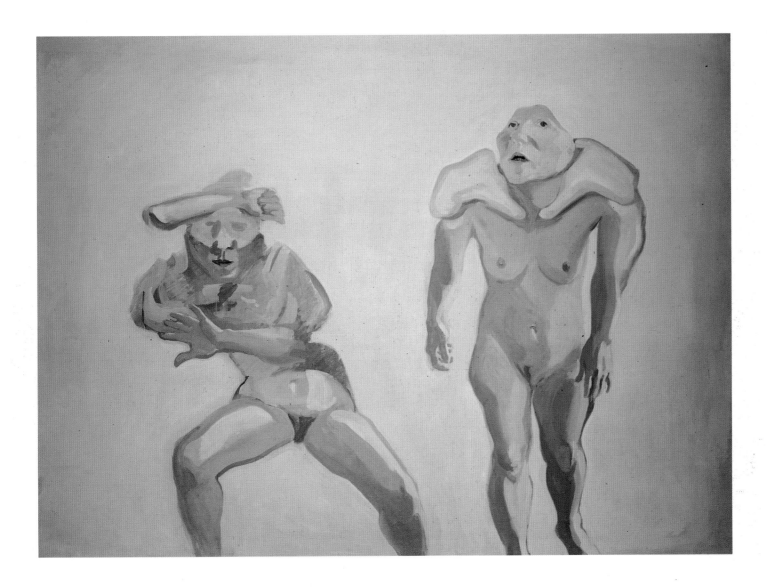

Maria Lassnig
Sensenmann [VIII. **93**]
1991

Der Verstopfte [VIII. **94**]
1991

Last des Fleisches [VIII. **91**]
1973

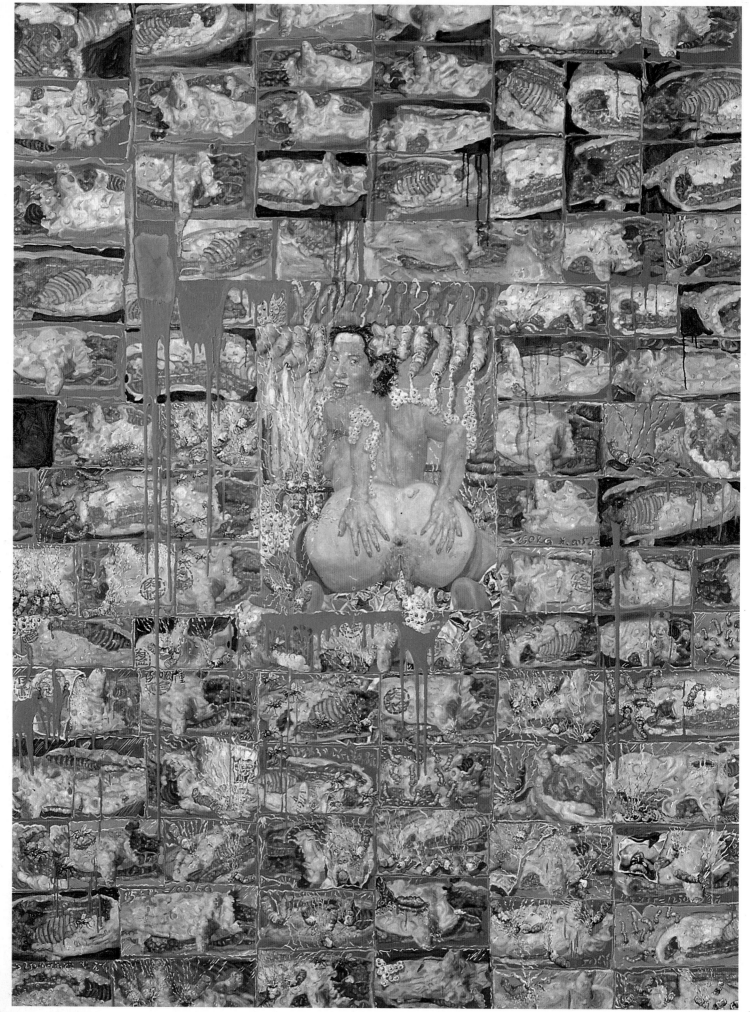

Wei Liu
«You Like Pork?»
[VIII. **95**]
1995

Yan Pei-Ming
Tête [VIII. **97**]
1992

493
The Real
and Virtual
Body

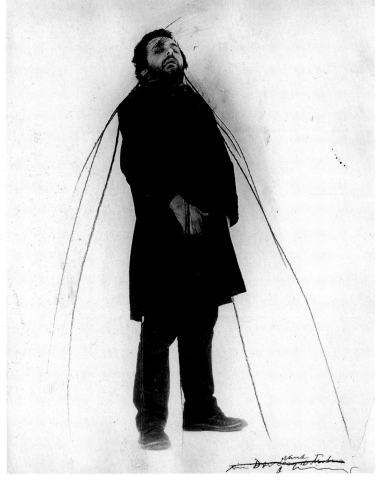

Arnulf Rainer
Auch eine Daseinshöhung
[VIII. **110**]
1972-73

Stand am Rand [VIII. **107**]
1972-73

Kniefall [VIII. **116**]
1973-74

Rätseln [VIII. **112**]
1973

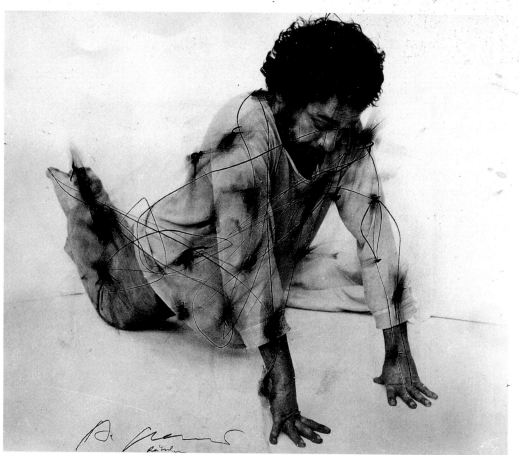

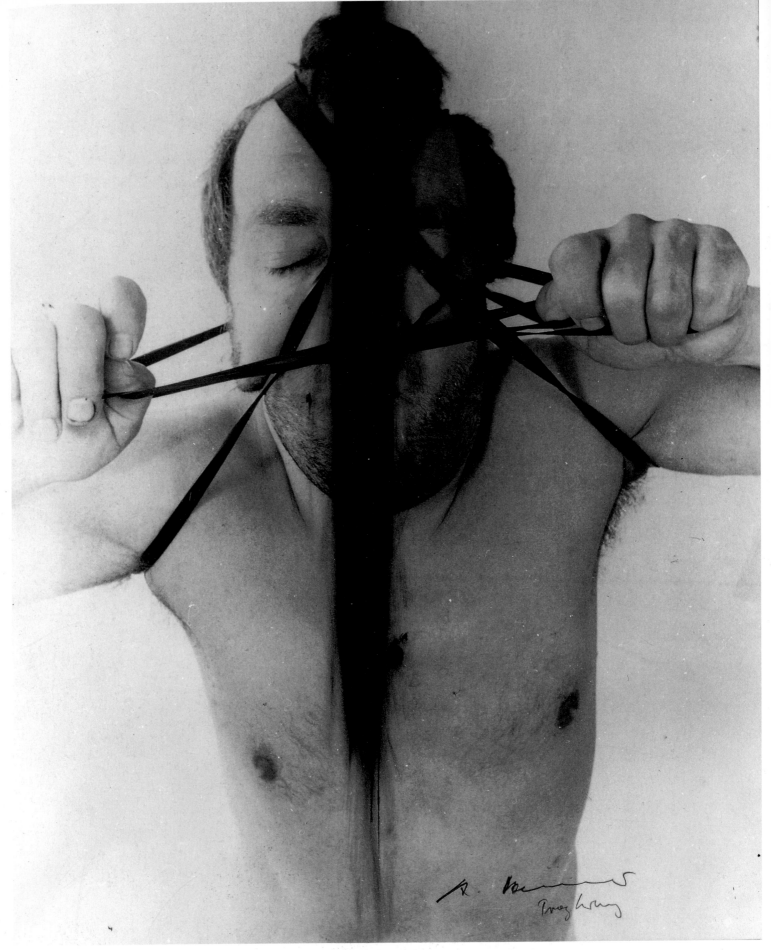

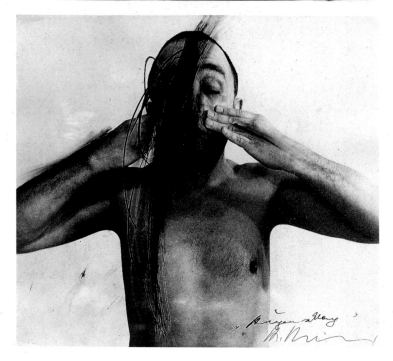

Arnulf Rainer
Tragkranz [VIII. **102**]
1971

Pause (Weder noch I) [VIII. **113**]
1973

Abend [VIII. **115**]
1973

Augenschlag [VIII. **103**]
1972

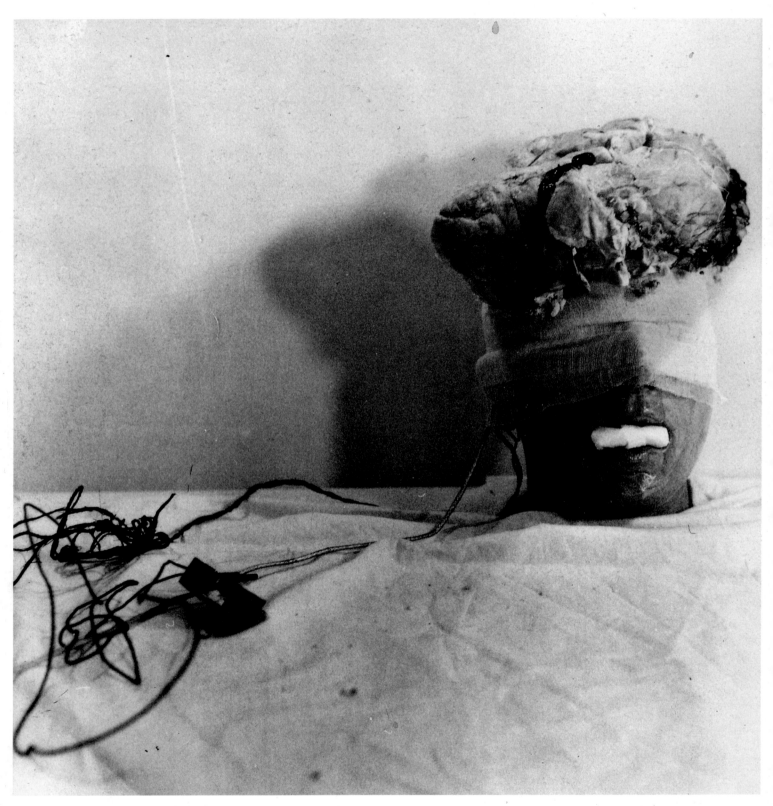

Rudolf Schwarzkogler
3. Aktion [VIII. **123**]
1965

Ousmane Sow
Nouba: Lutteur assis [VIII. **132**]
1984

Nouba: Lutteur debout [VIII. **131**]
1984

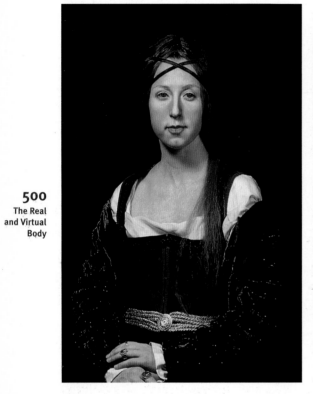 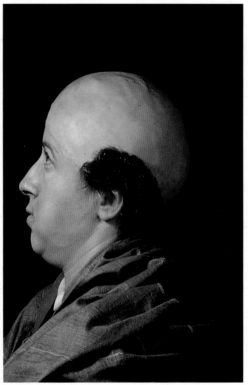 

Cindy Sherman
Untitled n° 209 [VIII. **125**]
1989

Untitled n° 214 [VIII. **126**]
1989

Untitled n° 223 [VIII. **127**]
1989

Untitled n° 225 [VIII. **128**]
1990

Chantal Wicki
Phantombilder - Gaby 1-30 [VIII. **139**]
1993-95

Xiaogang Zhang
Bloodline:
The Big Family, n° 1 [VIII. **152**]
1995

Bloodline:
The Big Family, n° 2 [VIII. **153**]
1995

Bloodline:
The Big Family, n° 3 [VIII. **154**]
1995

IX
**Imprints of Body
and Mind**
curator:
Adalgisa Lugli

Claudio Parmiggiani
La notte [IX. **41**]
1964

Imprints of Body and Mind

An imprint is the mark left by passing through, by being there. It is an immediate form of identification — an elementary gesture, similar to the impression of a prehistoric hand on a cave wall. From this point of view there is a dual polarity in art — making and representing. In the latter case, the artist reconstructs dream or reality, represents the natural world or the products of his imagination. Whilst in the former case, the artist is himself present in his work — either his body itself or some trace of it.
It is this aspect in the work of artists from the 50s up to the present day that we look at here. The artist rediscovers his 'hand' and abandons a merely formal, stylistic presence in his work. The visitor is invited to pause before those moments when an artist felt the clear need to return to an elemental, disruptive gesture, to bring his hand or body into the work of art (directly, not through figuration).
These are not new techniques. Artists have always known how to reproduce the body directly — techniques such as body prints and plaster casts have existed since classical antiquity. The cast, in fact, was described by Pliny — and has been present in artists' studios since the Middle Ages.
It is surprising to note the frequency with which these techniques are used by avant-garde artists (from Duchamp and Man Ray to Klein and Manzoni). Obviously there are changes in artistic language and in the materials used, but an unbroken link with the concerns of the past can still be traced.
The work on imprints was at its height in the 60s and 70s — particularly in Italy, where younger artists took up the lessons to be learnt from Klein, Manzoni, Fontana and Burri (the most 'materialist' of Informal artists). Different materials were used. There was experimentation with photography and performance art; outlines and imprints became a more common feature in the work of art.
The plaster cast played a central role in a certain type of art. Not only as a way of directly reproducing the body but also as constituting a 'trace' of previous works of sculpture. The cast could be an *objet trouvé*, to be used in a shifting game of reference and meaning.

AL

Outline of an object imprinted
on a wall in Hiroshima,
6 August 1945 [IX. 1]

Imprints of Body and Mind

Anonymous

IX **1**
Gigantografia delle vittime
di Hiroshima stampate
come ombre sui muri
dalla deflagrazione
nucleare
*(Enlarged photograph of the
human figures imprinted
on the walls of Hiroshima
by the nuclear explosion)*

IX **2**
Maschera del defunto
*Turin, Soprintendenza
Archeologica del Piemonte*

IX **3**
Moulage du visage
de André Breton, *1929*
Plaster sculpture
30×18×16 cm
Paris, Private collection

IX **4**
Ritratto romano
*Turin, Soprintendenza
Archeologica del Piemonte*

IX **5**
Calco dell'impronta
della zampa posteriore
di un sauropode
proveniente dal Niger,
dintorni di Agadesh, *(Cast
of the rear foot print of a
plesiosaur, from Agadesh,
Niger) about 1980*
Plaster mould 60×50 cm
*Venice, Giancarlo Ligabue
collection*

Vincenzo Agnetti

IX **6**
Libro dimenticato
a memoria, *1969*
*Volume, fabric
and book-mark*
71×51 cm
*Milan, Germana Agnetti
collection*

Franco Angeli

IX **7**
Autoritratto, *1985*
Mixed media 140×100 cm
*Bologna, Livio Collina
collection*

Alighiero Boetti

IX **8**
Io che prendo il sole
a Torino il 19 gennaio
1969, *1969*
*Quick-setting cement
and yellow butterfly*
h 177 cm
*Turin, Massimo Sandretto
collection*

André Breton

IX **9**
Moulage du visage
de Paul Eluard
Plaster mould
Private collection

Alberto Burri

IX **10**
Rosso plastica 5, *1962*
*Red plastic and combustion
on canvas*
65×100 cm
Rome, Private collection

Mario Ceroli

IX **11**
Corradino di Svevia, *1965*
Wood
200×80×60 cm
*Rome, Nicola Maria
De Angelis collection*

César

IX **12**
Le pouce, *1965*
Iron
252×143×102 cm
*Marseilles, Musées
de Marseille (donation
of César)*

Tony Cragg

IX **13**
Hunters,
1989
Plaster, wax, black elastic
155×185×70 cm
Marseilles, Fonds Regional
d'Art Contemporain
Provence-Alpes-Côte d'Azur

Jean-Pierre Dantan

IX **14**
Buste de Rossini,
1836
Plaster
h 19.2 cm
Paris, Musée Carnavalet

IX **15**
Masque de Rossini
Plaster
h 36 cm
Paris, Musée Carnavalet

Marcel Duchamp

IX **16**
Elevage de poussière,
1920–64
Photograph
24×30.5 cm
Milan, Arturo Schwarz
collection

IX **17**
With my Tongue
in my Cheek,
1959
Plaster, pencil on paper
mounted on board
25×15×5.1 cm
Paris, Musée National
d'Art Moderne,
Centre Georges Pompidou

Barry Flanagan

IX **18**
Ring n° 1966,
1966
Sand
300×120×120 cm
Ibiza, Private collection

IX **19**
Sand Muslin 2, *1966*
Muslin and sand
10×40×40 cm
Paris, Liliane & Michel
Durand Dessert collection

Lucio Fontana

IX **20**
Figure nere, *1931*
Painted terracotta
41×30×12.5 cm
Milan, Fontana Collection

IX **21**
Concetto spaziale,
Natura A, *1959–60*
Bronze
42×54 cm
Milan, Fontana Collection

IX **22**
Concetto spaziale,
Natura B, *1959–1960*
Bronze
40×48 cm
Milan, Fontana Collection

Pietro Gallina

IX **23**
Bambino/spazio, *1967*
Oil and enamel on plywood
180×43×43 cm
Turin, Property of the artist

IX **24**
Ombra di ragazza seduta,
1967
Shaped plywood
163×38×34 cm
Turin, Galleria Civica
d'Arte Moderna
e Contemporanea

Andy Goldsworthy

IX **25**
A Stone Laid On
Previously For Several
Hours..., *1994*
Cibachrome
(only copy extant)
100×80 cm
London, Property of the
artist (courtesy Michael
Hue-Williams)

Enrico Job

IX **26**
Metamorphosis, *1972*
Bread mould
of a male body thrown
to wild beasts and men
180×90×40 cm
Bolognano (Pescara),
Lucrezia Durini de
Domizio collection

Yves Klein

IX **27**
Anthropométrie sans titre,
1961
Pure blue pigment and
synthetic resin on paper
mounted on canvas
156×108 cm
Marseilles, Musée Cantini

IX **28**
Portrait-relief Arman,
1962
Blue bronze from mould
plaster on golden plywood
175×95×26 cm
Paris, Musée National
d'Art Moderne,
Centre Georges Pompidou

Tony Cragg
Hunters [IX. **13**]
1989

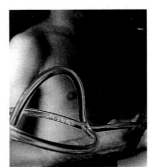

Gilberto Zorio
Odio [IX. **57**]
1974

Jean Jacques Lebel

IX **29**
Empreintes digitales des
spectateurs du happening
120 minutes dédiés
au Divin Marquis,
4 April 1966
Mixed media; play-bill
90×75 and 46×36 cm
Paris, Private collection

Man Ray

IX **30**
Autoportrait, *1933*
Plaster painted
with silver-dust
31×17×10,5 cm
Milan, Giorgio Marconi
collection

Piero Manzoni

IX **31**
Fiato d'artista, *1960*
Rubber, lead, wood
18×18 cm
Milan, Courtesy Galleria
Blu

IX **32**
Uovo, esemplare 43,
1960
Egg, ink and wood
5.6×8.2×6.8 cm
Milan, Courtesy Galleria
Blu

Eliseo Mattiacci

IX **33**
Riflessi del cielo, *1989*
Installation (aluminum
and antimony casting)
angle 500×500 cm
Turin, Galleria Martano

Guido Mazzoni

IX **34**
Testa di vecchio,
1475
Polychromatic terracotta
44×19×23 cm
Modena, Galleria Estense

Fausto Melotti

IX **35**
Il sapiente,
1936
Plaster
229.5×55×35 cm
Milan, Private collection

Meret Oppenheim

IX **36**
Tisch mit Vogelfüßen,
1938
Golden engraving on wood,
leaden legs
65×70×50 cm
Basel, Private collection

Giulio Paolini

IX **37**
Astrolabe, *1967*
World map,
silhouette on plexiglas
4.5×4.5×9 cm
Turin, Property of the artist

IX **38**
Proteo I, *1971*
Pencil on paper, plexiglas,
plaster
195×50×50 cm
Milan, Private collection

IX **39**
Proteo II, *1971*
Pencil on paper, plexiglas,
plaster
195×50×50 cm
Milan, Private collection

IX **40**
Proteo III, *1971*
Pencil on paper, plexiglas,
plaster
195×50×50 cm
Milan, Private collection

Claudio Parmiggiani

IX **41**
La notte, *1964*
Painted plaster mould,
fabric, wood, glass
36×36×29.5 cm
Modena,
Mattia Parmiggiani
collection artist

IX **42**
Delocazione, *1970*
Smut and dust marks
on canvas
106×130 cm
Turin,
Galleria Christian Stein

IX **43**
Autoritratto, *1979*
Photograph on canvas
65×48 cm
Paris, Remo Guidieri
collection

Giuseppe Penone

IX **44**
La mia altezza,
la lunghezza delle mie
braccia, il mio spessore
in un ruscello, *1968*
3 black and white
photographs
60×50 cm
San Raffaele Cimena
(Turin), Private collection

IX **45**
Soffio di creta,
1978
Clay
160×80×80 cm
San Raffaele Cimena
(Turin), Private collection

IX **46**
Soffio di foglie,
1979
Box-leaves
30×250×250 cm
San Raffaelle Cimena
(Turin), Private collection

IX **47**
Gesto vegetale con foglia,
1981
Bronze casting
150×60 cm
Turin,
Galleria Christian Stein

IX **48**
Contour Lines, *1989*
Cast-iron and glass, 7 pieces
10×250×120 cm
San Raffaelle Cimena
(Turin), Private collection

Vettor Pisani

IX **49**
Venere di cioccolato, *1970*
Mixed media (chocolate
coating)
Rome, Property of the artist

IX **50**
L'androgino (carne umana
e oro), *1971*
Mixed media (gilded
Bronze)
120×50×50 cm
Rome, Property of the artist

Giuseppe Spagnulo

IX **51**
Archeologia, *1978*
Cardboard, terracotta
(2 pieces)
126×126×6 cm
Gaggiano (Milan),
Property of the artist

N.H. (Tony) Stubbing

IX **52**
Spring Ceremonial,
1959
Oil on canvas
168×196 cm
London, England & Co.
Gallery

Giuseppe Uncini

IX **53**
Cemento armato n° 12,
1961
Concrete
92×154 cm
Turin,
Galleria Christian Stein

Ben Vautier

IX **54**
Zen For Head,
1967
Documentary pictures of the
performance at the Museo
Sperimentale di Torino
Nizza, Property of the artist

Gilberto Zorio

IX **55**
Fluidità radicale, *1969*
Tin object and photographs
Turin, Michelangelo
Pistoletto collection

IX **56**
Pugno fosforescente, *1971*
Installation: phosphorescent
wax, two Wood lamps
170×180×50 cm
Paris, Musée National
d'Art Moderne, Centre
Georges Pompidou

IX **57**
Odio, *1974*
Turin, Property of the artist

Yves Klein
Portrait-relief Arman [IX. **28**]
1962

Calco dell'impronta della zampa posteriore
di un sauropode proveniente dal Niger,
dintorni di Agadesh [IX. **5**]
c. 1980

Lucio Fontana
Concetto spaziale, Natura A -
Natura B [IX. **21-22**]
1959-60

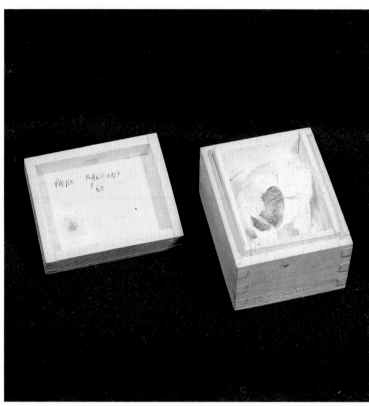

Piero Manzoni
Fiato d'artista [IX. **31**]
1960

Uovo, esemplare 43 [IX. **32**]
1960

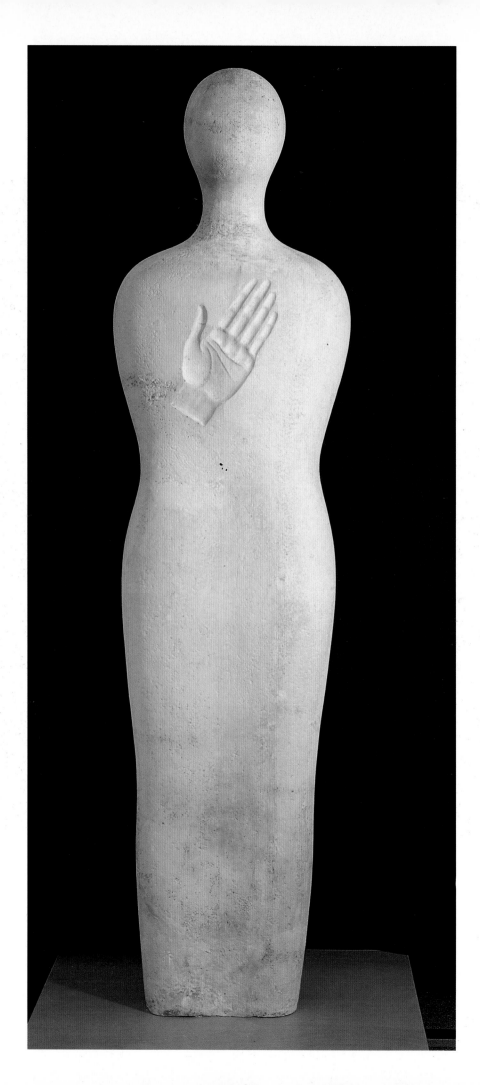

Meret Oppenheim
Tisch mit Vogelfüßen [IX. **36**]
1938

Alberto Burri
Rosso plastica 5 [IX. **10**]
1962

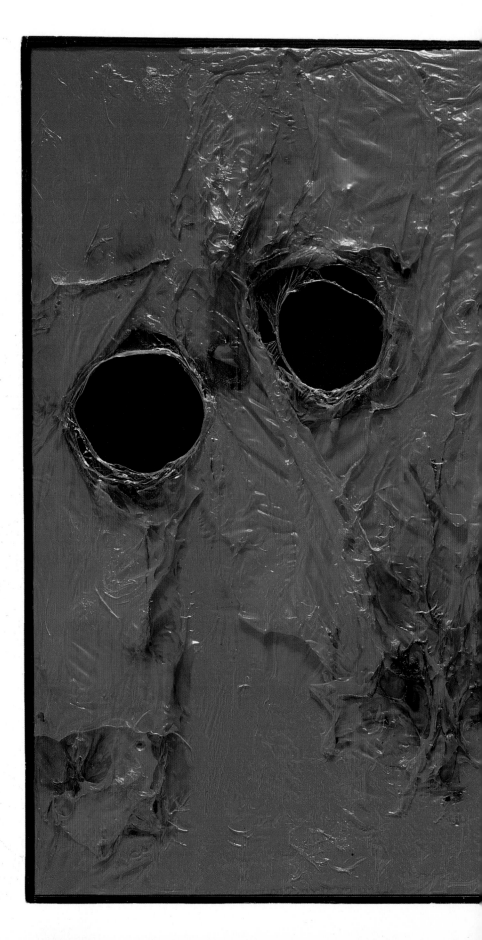

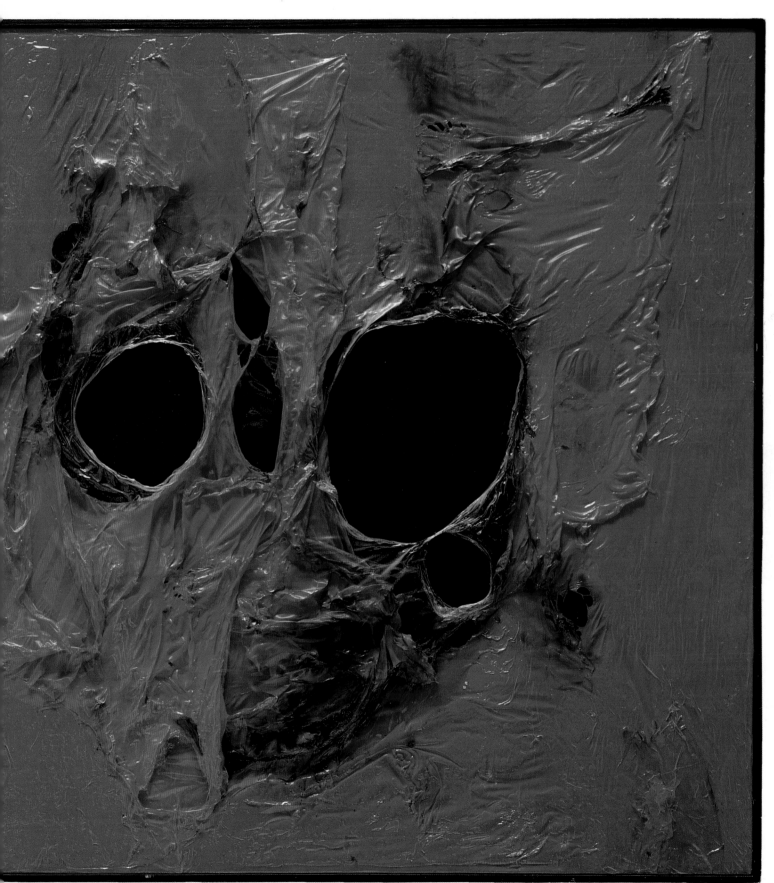

Ben Vautier
Zen For Head, *1967* [IX. **54**]

Claudio Parmiggiani
Delocazione [IX. **42**]
1970

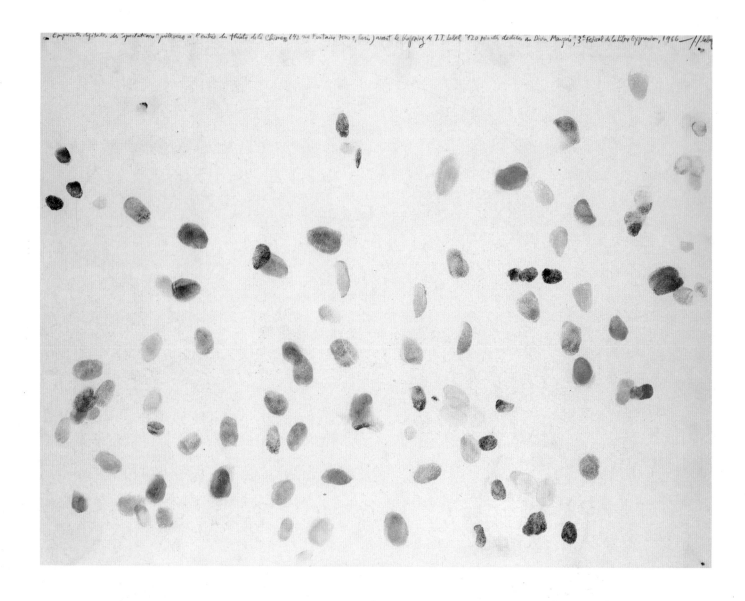

Jean-Jacques Lebel
Empreintes digitales
des spectateurs du happening
120 minutes dédiés
au Divin Marquis [IX. **29**]
1966

Franco Angeli
Autoritratto [IX. **7**]
1985

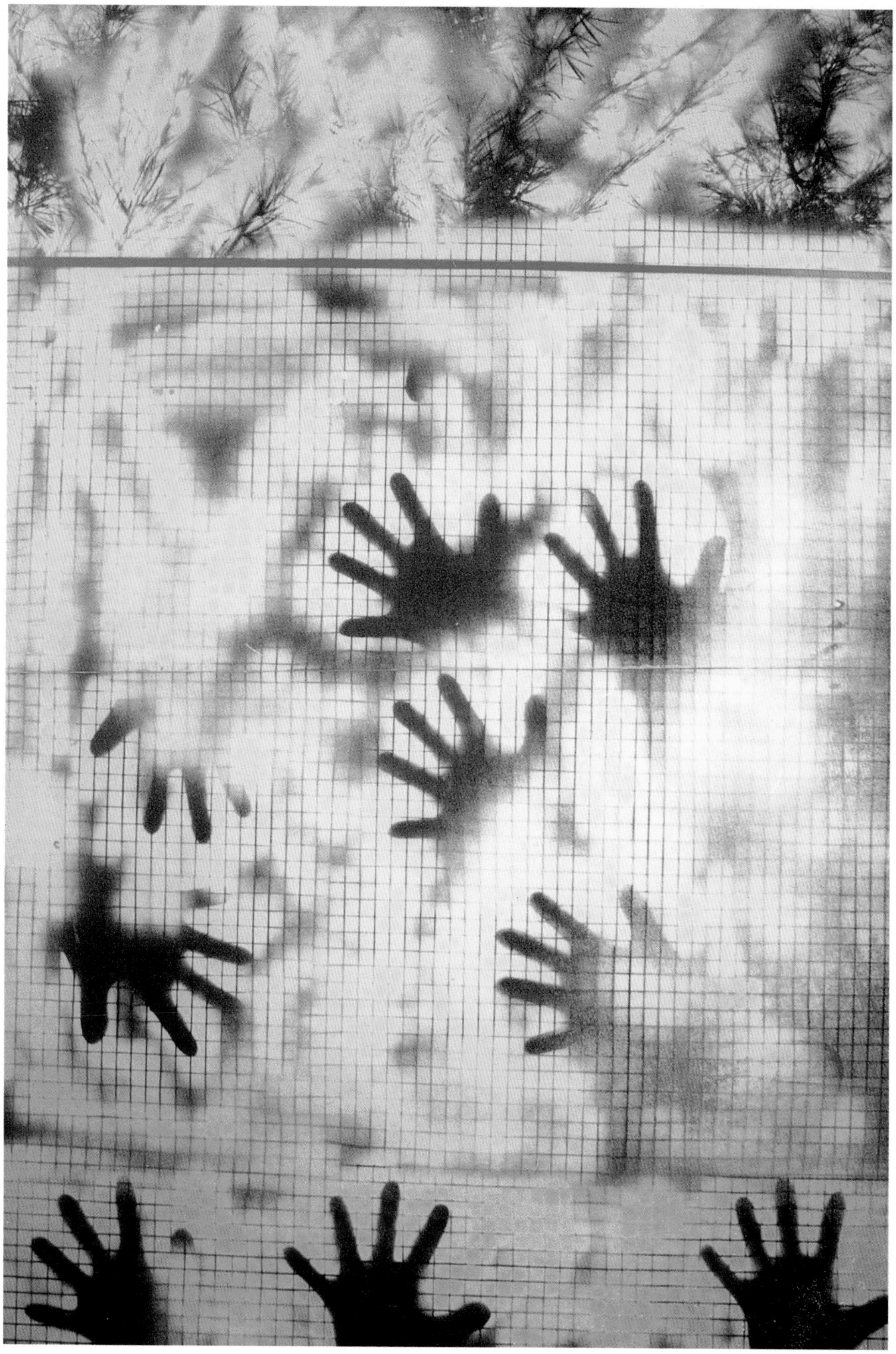

Giuseppe Penone
Soffio di foglie [IX. **46**]
1979

Soffio di creta [IX. **45**]
1978

Giuseppe Penone
Contour Lines [IX. **48**]
1989

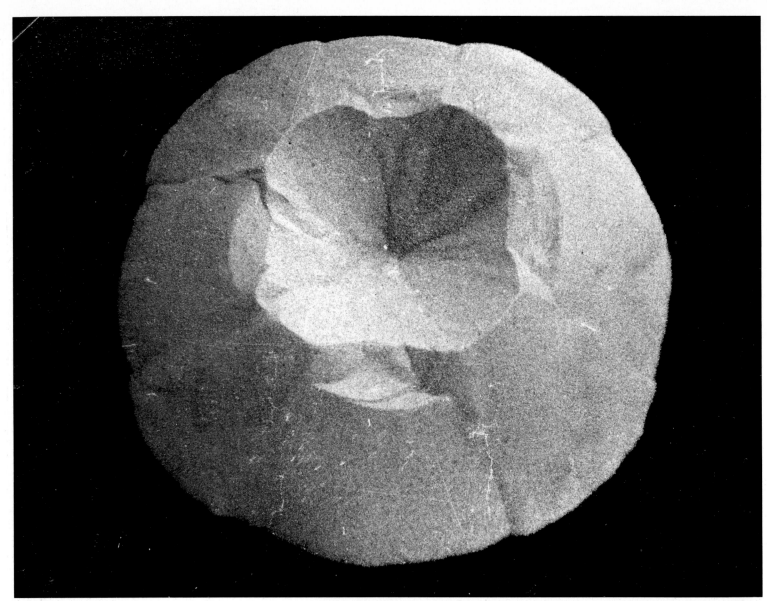

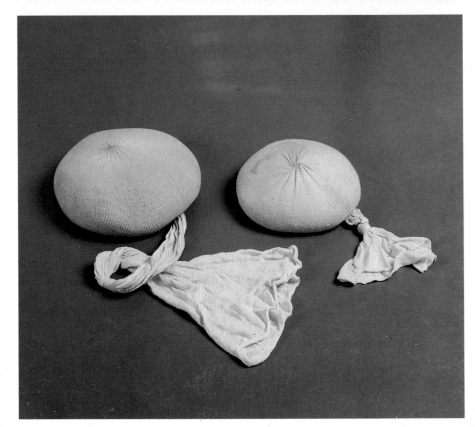

Barry Flanagan
Ring n° 1966 [IX. **18**]
1966

Sand Muslin 2 [IX. **19**]
1966

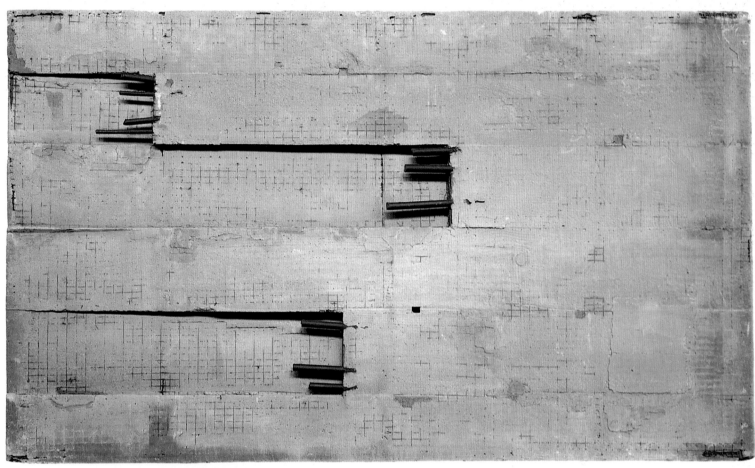

Giuseppe Uncini
Cemento armato n° 12 [IX. **53**]
1961

Giuseppe Spagnulo
Archeologia [IX. **51**]
1978

Guido Mazzoni
Testa di vecchio [IX. 34]
1475

Jean-Pierre Dantan
Masque de Rossini [IX. 15]

Buste de Rossini [IX. 14]
1836

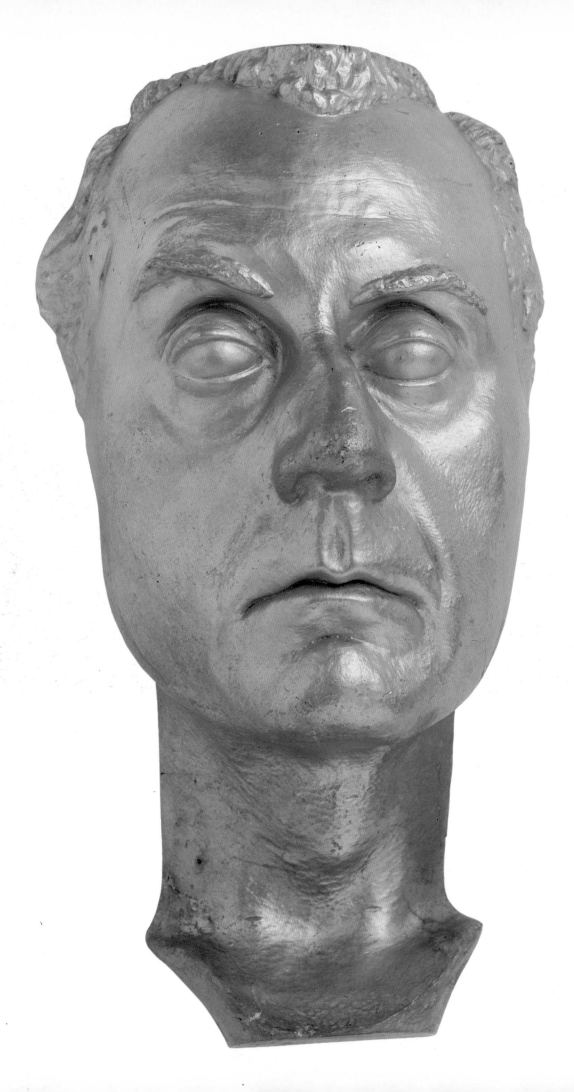

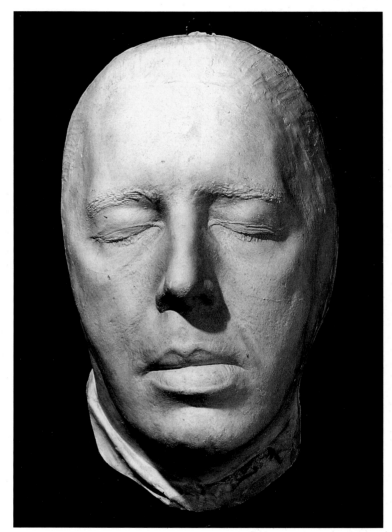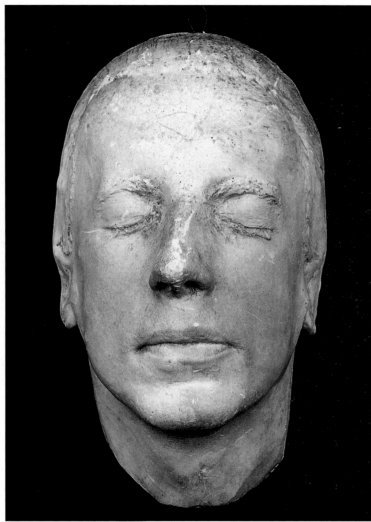

Man Ray
Autoportrait [IX. **30**]
1933

Paul Eluard
Moulage du visage
de André Breton [IX. **3**]
1929

André Breton
Moulage du visage
de Paul Eluard [IX. **9**]

Marcel Duchamp
With my Tongue
in my Cheek [IX. **17**]
1959

Yves Klein
Anthropométrie sans titre [IX. **27**]
1961

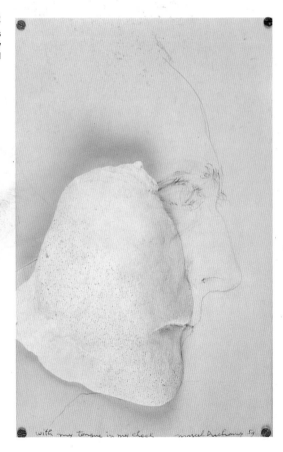

 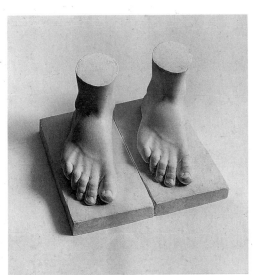 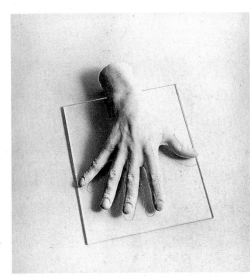

Giulio Paolini
Proteo I; Proteo II; Proteo III [IX. **38-40**]
1971

Vettor Pisani
Calco della Venere di Milo
(cioccolato) [IX. **49**]
1970

Androgino (carne umana
e oro) [IX. **50**]
1971

Gilberto Zorio
Pugno fosforescente [IX. 56]
1971

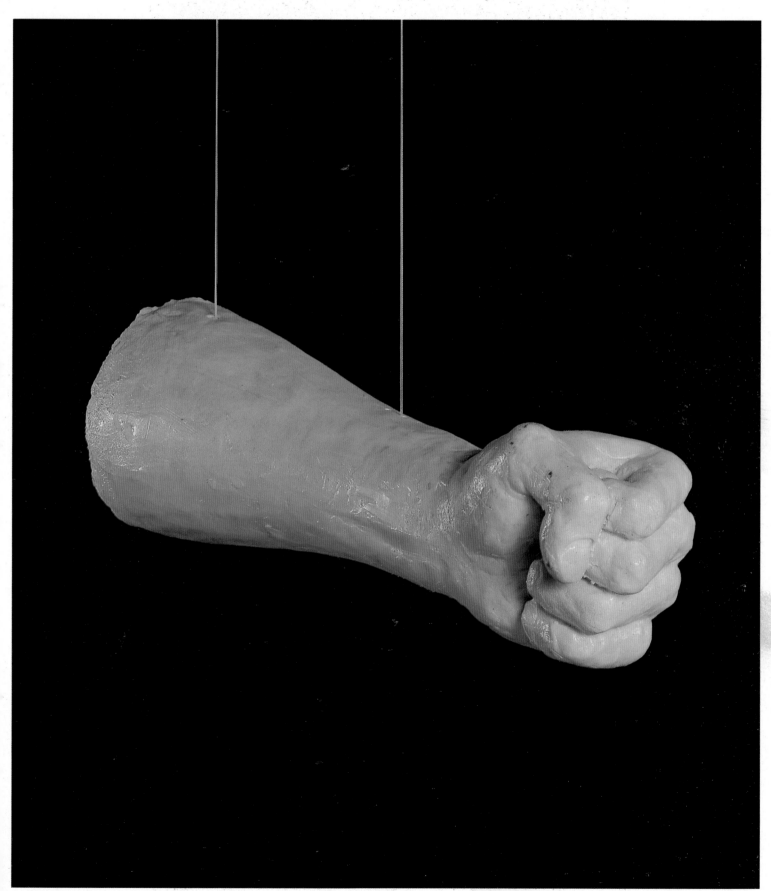

Alighiero Boetti
Io che prendo il sole
a Torino il 19 gennaio 1969
[IX. **8**] *1969*

Enrico Job
Metamorphosis [IX. **26**]
1972

Giuseppe Penone
Gesto vegetale con foglia
[IX. **47**] *1981*

Marcel Duchamp
Elevage de poussière [IX. **16**]
1920-64

Lucio Fontana
Figure nere [IX. **20**]
1931

Claudio Parmiggiani
Autoritratto [IX. **43**]
1979

Giuseppe Penone
La mia altezza, la lunghezza
delle mie braccia,
il mio spessore in un ruscello [IX. **44**]
1968

Pietro Gallina
Ombra di ragazza seduta [IX. **24**]
1967

Mario Ceroli
Corradino di Svevia [IX. **11**]
1965

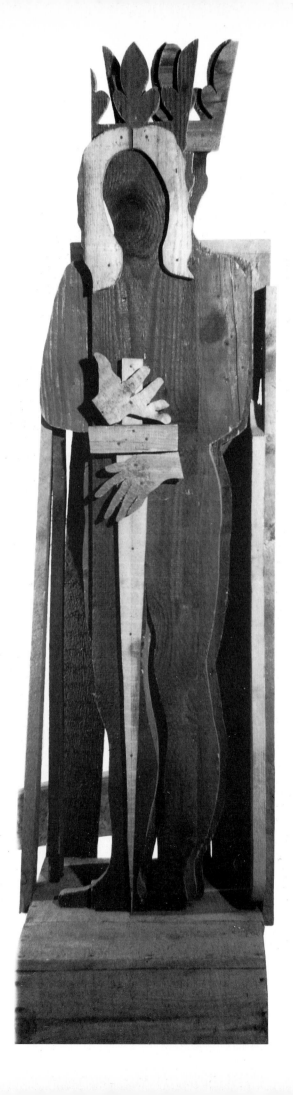

Eliseo Mattiacci
Riflessi del cielo [IX. **33**]
1989

Andy Goldsworthy
A Stone Laid On Previously
For Several Hours... [IX. **25**]
1994

**Critical
and
Biographical
Index**

550 Rosanna Alberti RA
Nathalie Boulouch NB
Valentina Castellani VC
Massimo Chirivi MC
Philippe Comar PC
Stefano Dal Secco SDS
Maria Barbara Giacometti
MBG
Vittorio Mandelli VM
Susanne Richter SR
Luisa Sala LS

Agnetti Vincenzo
Milan, 1926–1981
Conceptual painter, essayist, writer and critic, he received his diploma at the Brera *liceo artistico*, and made his debut in the Informal in the late 1950s. In 1960 he abandoned painting to explore the border areas between physical objects, and their ideas and mental images, employing numbers, words, photography and audio and visual tapes. With Enrico Castellani and Piero Manzoni he founded the review *Azimuth*, and later worked with Sottsass at *Domus*. He published *Un Quadro nero non può essere un quadro dipinto di nero*, and *Libro dimenticato a memoria* in 1969, in which 'the pages have lost the space that is usually occupied by words'. *Pagine dimenticate a memoria* came out in 1972. His many writings include the experimental novel *Obsoleto* (1963-64), *Ciclostile. Elenco progetti e idee per una mostra di sole Idee* (1969), and *Machiavelli 30* (1978). After his first one-man show at the Palazzo dei Diamanti in Ferrara, he took part in many shows in Italy and abroad. One of the most original figures in Italian conceptual art, in 1972 he exhibited at the Kassel Documenta 5. In 1973 he was invited to the São Paulo Biennale and the Rome Contemporanea, and in 1974 and 1978 he participated in the Venice Biennale.

BIBLIOGRAPHY
Vincenzo Angetti, *Spazio perduto e spazio costruito*, (Macerata, 1972); Vincenzo Agnetti, *Tradotto, Azzerato, Presentato*, (Milan, 1974); Vincenzo Agnetti, *I Dicitori*, (New York, 1979); *Vincenzo Agnetti*, catalogue, Milan Padiglione d'Arte Contemporanea 1981.
VC

Alexander Jane
Johannesburg, 1959
In 1982 she won the first prize at the National Fine Arts Students Exhibition with a sculpture made of mixed materials, also characteristic of her later works. She uses both natural objects (bone, wood) and industrial (plastic, synthetic clay, and other substances). She also works in black and white photomontage. In the work she has exhibited in both one-man (Market Gallery, Johannesburg 1986) and group shows (*State of the Art*, Everard Read Contemporary Gallery, Johannesburg 1994) she aproaches the real by manipulating it to emphasize unusual and disturbing fragments of everyday life, expressing 'the awareness that the atrocities committed by men become an integral part of their bodies, their shapes'.

BIBLIOGRAPHY
Un art contemporain d'Afrique du sud, catalogue (n.p., 1994), ed. Jean-Yves Jouannais, preface Marilyn Martin (Barcelona, 1994), 22.
VM

Aloïse (Aloïse Corbaz) *see* **Art Brut**

Andrews Michael
Norwich, 1928
He studied at the Slade School of Fine Arts (1949), and taught at the Norwich School of Art (1959), and the Chelsea School of Art (1960). He is one of the major figures in the 'School of London' (name coined in 1976 by Kitaj), together with Francis Bacon, Lucian Freud, Leon Kossoff, Franck Auerbach and R.B. Kitaj. The movement began in 1945 with the exhibition of Bacon's triptych *Three studies of figures at the base of the crucifixion* (London, Tate Gallery) at the Lefèvre Gallery; Andrews joined it in 1952 when he showed his work at the Beaux–Arts Gallery in London. The characteristic features of the movement, shared by Andrews, are the focus on the figurative and the interest in the understanding and practice of painting, an attitude that leads to isolation in an all–consuming dedication to painting. The painting *The Colony Room* is considered the School's icon; it portrays a well–known Soho bar, 'The Colony', frequented by some of these 'hermit' artists in the Sixties. Bacon and Freud were some of its better–known patrons. In 1977 Andrews abandoned the London artistic haunts of Camden and Chelsea, and moved to Norfolk.

BIBLIOGRAPHY
Max Rabino, 'I sei eremiti della Scuola di Londra', *Arte*, 208 (June 1990), 68–75.
RA

Angeli Franco
Rome, 1935–1988
His début at the La Salita gallery in Rome (with Festa and Uncini in 1958) marked him as one of the generation that Cesare Vivaldi called the 'Giovane Scuola di Roma'. His work at that time was representative of the New Dada, a mixture of Informal influences including sign-symbols such as swastikas, eagles, stars, and the wolf of Rome. His one-man show was held at the Tartaruga gallery in Rome in 1963, where he exhibited works like *Cimitero partigiano* (a hammer and sickle arranged around a five-pointed star) which reveals the political and social content that would be accentuated during the years of student revolt. He took part in the 1964 Biennale, which intro-duced Italy to Pop Art, whose influence can be felt in *Frammenti* (1964–65), enlarged symbols and slogans of Rome, and in the dollar-inspired series (*Half Dollar*, 1966), the emblem of American capital-ism. In 1964 he exhibited in the group show at the Galleria Odyssia in Rome with Festa, Schifano, Del Pezzo, and Baruchello, who were defined as the 'Scuola di Piazza del Popolo'. In 1972 he exhibited in the Rome Quadriennale. In the Eighties he joined the Neo-Metaphysical movement, marking a partial return to the figurative.

BIBLIOGRAPHY
Angeli, catalogue, Rome Galleria la Tartaruga, M. Calvesi (1968); *Franco Angeli. Opere 1958–1972*, catalogue, San Casciano Val di Pesa Antica Fattoria Machiavel-li, ed. G. Battistini (1988); *Franco Angeli. Il canto del cigno*, catalogue, Aosta Toru Fromage April–July 1989, ed. F. Gallo (1989).
VC

Arbus Diane
New York, 1923–1971
After studying photography with Lisette Model in New York (1955–57) she worked for fashion magazines and as an assistant to her husband, the photographer Allan Arbus. In the early Sixties she began to do individual and group portraits in photographs that reflect a profound sense of detachment between sub-stance and appearance. The nudist camps where she found some of her subjects show that '... the human body is not as beautiful as it's said to be, and when it's looked at closely, all its mystery vanishes ...' . Her photographs are crowded with marginal characters, 'ordinary' people, socially and physically different individuals, whose inimitable tragic existences are highlighted by the objectivity of the mechanics involved: '... I don't mean that all the photographs are malicious. Sometimes they demonstrate something better than you expected, or something curiously different. The point is that facts can't be avoided, you can't escape reality as it really is ...' (Diane Arbus, quoted in Doon Arbus, 2). In 1967 she exhibited some photographs at the New York Museum of Modern Art, which marked the beginning of her many exhibitions in American and European collections. She committed suicide in New York in 1971. Her photographs were exhibited in the United States Pavilion in the Venice Biennale XXXVI (1972).

BIBLIOGRAPHY
XXXVI Esposizione Biennale Internazionale d' Arte (Venice, 1972), 142; Doon Arbus and Marvin Israel (eds.), *Diane Arbus* (New York, 1972); Nigel Wartburton, 'Diane Arbus and Erving Goffmann: the Presen-tation of Self', *History of Photography* (Winter 1992), 401–4.
MBG

Arikha Avigdor
Bukovina, 1929
A survivor of the Holocaust concentration camps, he studied at the Bezalel school in Jerusalem and the Ecole des Beaux-Arts in Paris (1949) where he moved permanently. He alternated between the figurative and the abstract until the late Sixties when his 'hungry eye' pushed him from abstraction and led him to paint 'from truth'. He then began to study the plastic relationships of very simple objects in compositions permeated with such drama and tension that they evolve into forms of spiritual conceptualization (Channin). The portraits, drawn or painted, play a special role in his œuvre: his subjects, always people he knows or loves, are placed right in front of the spectator, who feels empathy when confronted by this immediate physical presence. In his more recent work the portrait transcends detail to take on aspects of universal humanity (*Marie-Catherine*, 1982) or transmit the restlessness born of the encounter between the artist and his subject (*Alexander Frederick Douglas–Home*, 1988). Arikha exhibited at the Venice Biennale in 1962 and 1982.

BIBLIOGRAPHY
Richard Channin, André Fermingier, Robert Hughes, Jane Livingstone, Barbara Rose and Samuel Beckett, *Arikha* (Paris, 1985); Duncan Thomson, *Arikha* (London, 1994); *Avigdor Arickha. Works 1992–93*, catalogue, London Marlborough Fine Art 6 May–4 June (London, 1994).
MBG

Art Brut
Although the genre of expressive, spontaneous and immediate manifestation, stripped of all cultural mediation, was first introduced to the general public by the painter Jean Dubuffet (Le Havre, 1901–Paris, 1985), at the end of the nineteenth century scholars such as Hans Prinzhorn (Hemer, Germany, 1876–Munich 1933), and later W. Morgenthaler, had already distributed a massive amount of material to doctors and artists (Litch, 36). It was, however, Dubuffet '... who recognized its true significance and directed all his energies towards spreading the questions and possibilities that his speculation on the theme of *Art Brut* opened up in art and artists in the Fifties and Sixties ...' (Litch, 36). Thus from the very first show onwards (Galerie René Drouin, 1948), the work of alienated or schizophrenic artists like Adolf Wölfli, Aloïse (Aloïse Corbaz, Lausanne, 1886–1964), Katharina, and Robert Gie received attention. They were generally called by just their Christian name following the custom of psychiatric hospi-tals. Due to the *Publications de la Compagnie de l' Art Brut*, the periodical edited by Dubuffet himself, Michel Thévoz and other specialists, the conviction gained credence that there cannot be an '... art of the mad, separate from, say, the art of someone with an injured knee ...' (Dubuffet, quoted in Litch, 33).

BIBLIOGRAPHY
L' art brut préféré aux arts culturels, catalogue, Paris Galerie René Drouin October 1949 (Paris, 1949), n. 74; Jacqueline Porret-Ferel (ed.), 'Aloïse', *Publications de la Compagnie de l' Art Brut*, 7 (Paris, 1966); Michel Thévoz, *L' Art Brut* (Lausanne, 1975); Fred Litch, *Oltre i confini della critica?*, in *Jean Dubuffet & Art Brut*, catalogue, Venice Peggy Guggenheim Collection Winter 1986–1987 (n.p., [1986]), 33, 36.
VM

Artaud Antonin
Marseille, 1896–Paris, 1948
Suffering from serious nervous disorders and bouts of depression from 1915 on, he was forced to travel frequently in search of a cure. In 1920 he went to Paris where he acted in film and theater with

Charles Dullin. He began to publish in several journals, including the *Nouvelle Revue Française*. He joined the Surrealism movement, although he had disagreements with the leaders of the movement. He founded the Théâtre Alfred Jarry (1927) where he staged works by Claudel, Strindberg and Vitrac. He published *L' ombilic des limbes* (1927), *Le Pèse-nerf* (1925), and *A la grande nuit ou Le Bluff surréaliste* (1929). He began *Le Théâtre et son double* published in 1938. He traveled in Mexico (1936) and Ireland (1937), and returned after yet another severe depression. He began a long period of confinement in the Rodez psychiatric hospital (1943–46) where he underwent electro-shock therapy, wrote, drew, and painted the *Cahiers de Rodez* published in 1946. On his return to Paris he contacted the editor Gallimard for the publication of his complete works. He was close friends until his death with Adamove, Colette and Henri Thomas, Dubuffet, Paulhan, Jacques Prevel, and Paul Thévenin. His drawing is closely connected to his literature, both together expressing the world of the conscious, deformed in time and space, experienced through the body. His furrowed wrinkled portraits reveal his years of living, marked by the undeniable signs of the inexorable passage of time.

BIBLIOGRAPHY
Monique Borie, *Antonin Artaud. Il teatro e il ritorno alle origini. Un approccio antropologico* (Bologna, 1994); Nicoletta Scalabrin, '"Dessins ecrits" di Artaud', *Terzocchio*, 63 (June 1992), 28–30.
RA

552
Critical and Biographical Index

Bacon Francis
Dublin, 1909–Madrid, 1992
Because of poor health in his youth (he suffered from chronic asthma) and his family's peripatetic existence, Bacon never received a regular education. In his mid-twenties he left his parents and lived in London, Paris and Berlin making enough to live on by doing odd jobs. In Paris in 1927 he was profoundly impressed by Picasso's recent work: 'Only Bacon, among all the painters of his generation, realized that [...] vast unexplored sinister territory was opening up in the representation of the human body' (*Gowing* in *Francis Bacon*, 1989, 12). Bacon's reputation began to grow in the mid-Forties and has never waned,

so that he is now one of the 'sacred monsters' of this century. In 1954 he exhibited at the Venice Biennale, in 1959 at the Documenta II and the Biennale of São Paulo, and in 1962 the Tate Gallery put on his first major retrospective. Bacon always declared a deep-seated hostility to any form of abstraction, which he considered mere decoration; instead, he felt that art must not be afraid to engage in life and 'get its hands dirty': 'Bacon reached the conviction that for him the subject of painting must be human, detailed, real [...] he remained firm in his belief that art is an obssession with life' and 'after all, from the moment we become human beings, our greatest obsession is with ourselves' (*Gowing* in *Francis Bacon*, 1989, 18).

BIBLIOGRAPHY
La Biennale di Venezia (Venice, 1954), 317-19; *Francis Bacon*, catalogue, Washington D.C. Hirshhorn Museum and Sculpture Garden Smithsonian Institute 11 February–29 April 1990, ed. James Demetrion (New York–London, 1989); *Francis Bacon*, catalogue, Lugano Museo d'Arte Moderna Villa Malpensata 7 March–30 May 1993, ed. R. Chiappini (Milan, 1993); *Figurabile. Omaggio a Francis Bacon*, catalogue, Venice Museo Correr La Biennale di Venezia 13 June–10 October, ed. Achille Bonito Oliva (Milan, 1993).
SDS

Balla Giacomo
Turin, 1871–Rome, 1958
Studied violin at an early age and later began to draw and paint. He made his debut as a landscape painter in Turin in 1891. He acquired his intellectual training on his own, based on the teachings of Lombroso and the scientific positivism of the time. This cultural model, within which all his creative choices would be made, gave birth to an artistic career focused on the quest for an experimental language to express concrete evidence in objective and scientific terms. This quest is combined with an interest in a photographic vision of reality, which he absorbed from his father and matured through his acquaintance with various photographers. Moving to Rome, he came into contact with Gino Severini and Umberto Boccioni (1895). He signed the Futurist manifestoes (1910 and 1915), and joined the movement in 1912 with three works (*Guinzaglio in moto*; *La mano del violinista*; *Bambina che corre*

sul balcone) which achieved the analytical breakdown of motion, taking movements from Marey's chronophotographs and Bragaglia's photodynamics. Anton Giulio Bragaglia and Balla influenced each other, sharing an interest in motion that, compared to other Futurists (Boccioni), tends to include the temporal dimension within the problem of dynamism. Among the three mentioned, *La mano del violinista* (painted in Düsseldorf, 1912) is the work closest to Bragaglia's photodynamics which portray musicians playing instruments. After this painting Balla continued his process of movement analysis, including an increasing quantity of data and abstract applications of chronophotographic multiplication. His works were exhibited at the Venice Biennale from 1926 to 1968.

BIBLIOGRAPHY
Maurizio Calvesi, *Quattro maestri del primo futurismo italiano*, in *XXXIV Esposizione Biennale Internazionale d' Arte* (Venice, 1968), XLI–XLVIII; Giorgio De Marchis, *Giacomo Balla. L' aura futurista* (Turin, 1977); Giovanni Lista, *Balla* (Modena, 1982) (with catalogue of works and bibliography).
MBG

Balossino Nello *see*
Shroud of Turin

Balthus
Paris, 1908
His father an art critic, his mother a painter, Balthazar Klossowski de Rola, known as Balthus, was raised in an artistic environment where he made contact early on with painters such as Pierre Bonnard, André Derain, and Pierre Jean Jouve, and literary figures such as Rainer Maria Rilke who first made him reproduce his drawings (1921). He had his first one-man show in Paris (Galerie Pierre, April 1934), where he became friends both with Surrealists (André Breton, Paul Eluard, Alberto Giacometti) and the 'Forces Nouvelles' (1935). A great admirer of Piero della Francesca, Masaccio and Paolo Uccello, whom he studied in Florence in 1926, he also looks to Cézanne and contemporary German Realists (Otto Dix, George Grosz, Max Beckmann), completing the foundation of his refined but complex and personal style. He was Director of the Académie de France in the Villa Medici in Rome from 1961

to 1976. He was invited to the Venice Biennale XXXIX (1980) and had a one-man show in the Scuola di San Giovanni Evangelista (*Balthus*, 114-7).

BIBLIOGRAPHY
Stanislas Klossowsky de Rola, *Balthus* (Paris, 1983), 97, nn. 40–41, figs. 40–41; Jean Clair, *Metamorphosen des Eros. Essay über Balthus* (Munich, 1984); *Balthus, Zeichnungen*, catalogue, Berne Kunstmuseum 18 June–4 September 1994, eds. Jean Leymarie and Josef Helfenstein (Basle, 1994), 114-7.
VM

Baraduc Hippolyte Ferdinand
Hyères, 1850–Paris, 1909
The son of Hippolyte André Ponthion (1814–1881), he was a doctor and scientist like his father, and assistant to Jean Martin Charcot (Paris, 1825–Nièure, 1893) at the Salpêtrière clinic in Paris. Baraduc was among the very first to use photography within the world of psychiatry. His work attempted to document an iconography of the invisibile by '... recording on plates, developed traditionally, the marks formed by streaking and swirling, which sometimes resemble badly-developed shadowy negatives, where [Baraduc] searches for the *signature* of the human soul, the center of luminous power maintaining its existence by means of a double movement of attraction and repulsion of special forces achieved in the invisible cosmos ...' (Bovien, 164–5). He was interested in spiritualist photography and wrote a number of classic if by now obsolete texts in this field, including *L' âme humaine, ses mouvements, ses lumières* (Paris, 1896).

BIBLIOGRAPHY
Hippolyte F. Baraduc, *La Force vitale, notre corps vital fluidique, sa formule biométrique, par le D'r H. Baraduc* (Paris, 1893); Hippolyte F. Baraduc, *Démonstration photographique des tourbillons et anses ellipsoïdales de la force vitale cosmique du zoéther* (Vichy, 1896); Hippolyte F. Baraduc, *L' âme humaine, ses mouvements, ses lumières* (Paris, 1896); Hippolyte F. Baraduc, *Méthode de radiographie humaine de Hippolyte Baraduc,... La force courbe cosmique, photographies des vibrations de l' éther* (Paris, 1897); J. Bovien, 2. Baraduc, in *Dictionnaire de Biographie Française*, vol. v (Paris, 1951), 164–5.
VM

Bartoli Amerigo
Terni, 1890–Rome, 1971
He studied at the Rome Istituto di Belle Arti where he graduated in 1912, and later attended advanced courses given by Aristide Sartorio. He traveled to Florence, Turin and Paris on a scholarship. In 1915 he exhibited at the *Secessione romana III*, in 1921 at the Rome *Biennale I*, and in 1926 at the *I Mostra del Novecento Italiano* together with De Chirico, with whom he shared his studio around 1920. A painter as well as a satirical cartoonist, caricaturist, and writer, he pursued his painting along with his graphic work for journals and books, and was an active contributor to *La Ronda* and *Valori Plastici*. He exhibited in the I Mostra del Sindacato fascista (First show of the fascist union), at several Venice Biennales (1930, 1932, and 1950), and at the Rome Quadriennale (1931-59, 1965). The lively Roman cultural setting focused around the Caffè Aragno is reflected in his painting *Gli amici al caffè* (1930), a portrait of this gathering place for many *La Ronda* artists and intellectuals. In this group portrait, his painting takes on the stylistic accents of Courbet and Fantin-Latour, but also demonstrates his great skill as a painter, in the transformation of the implicitly extravagant intellectual tone into witty caricature. From 1938 to 1960 he held the chair in painting at the Accademia di Belle Arti in Rome.

BIBLIOGRAPHY
Catalogo della XVII Esposizione Internazionale d' Arte La Biennale di Venezia (Venice, 1930), 108; *Amerigo Bartoli*, catalogue, Acquasparta Palazzo Cesi 19 June–19 September 1982 (n.p., 1982).
RA

Baselitz Georg
Deutschbaselitz, 1938
Hans Georg Kern studied at the Hochschule für Bildende und Agenwandte Kunst in East Berlin. In 1958 he moved to the Hochschule für Künste in West Berlin, where he was to teach until 1988. It was there that he began to develop an interest in anamorphosis and the work of alienated mental patients from the Prinzhorn collection (1960). In 1961 he adopted the pseudonym Georg Baselitz, the name he exhibited under at his first one-man show in Berlin (1 *Pandämonium*). The cycles *Idol* (1964), *Helden* (1965) and *Fraktur* (1966) followed, along with experiments in woodcut and sculpture. In 1969 he

produced his first upside-down painting, a conceptual solution he explains with provocative simplicity: '... you paint for years, in a state of intoxication, without any great goal in sight. You're oppressed by health problems, financial problems, social problems, and suddenly you realize that the bases for your previous work have shifted. I had to paint new images, so I turned them upside down ...' (Baselitz, quoted in *Georg Baselitz*, 28). He was a guest of the Venice Biennale XXXIX (1980) and is invited to all major international art exhibitions.

BIBLIOGRAPHY
Fred Jahn, *Baselitz, peintre-graveur*, 2 vols. (Berlin, 1983 and 1987); *Georg Baselitz*, ed. Franz Dahlem, (Berlin, 1990), 18; *Georg Baselitz-Retrospektive 1964–1991*, catalogue, Munich Kunsthalle der Hypo-Kulturstiftung 20 March–17 May 1992, ed. Siegfried Gohr (Munich, 1992).
VM

Beckmann Max
Leipzig, 1884–New York, 1950
He studied at the Weimar Grandducal School of Art (1900–03) and in 1907 he moved to Berlin and joined the Berlin Sezession. He traveled to Paris and Florence. Like other German artists, he volunteered for service in 1914, and his drawings (inspiration for his graphic work, 1909–29), realistic portrayals of the atrocities of the war, stand as eloquent testimony to this period. In 1937 he was exiled in Amsterdam where he remained until 1947, when he set off for the United States. He lived and taught first in St. Louis and later in New York (1949). The German Pavilion dedicated a retrospective to him at the Venice Biennale XXV in 1950, where he won the Gran Premio in painting. In his portraiture Beckmann brings out his subject's individuality, the unique psychology and spirituality of the person represented. In his self-portraits he maintains a profound sense of detachment, thus modifying his own personality and letting us intuit his intimate understanding of himself. His approach to gesture is revealing, and the hands and their movements play a fundamental role in the portrayal of the subject.

BIBLIOGRAPHY
Catalogo della XXV Biennale di Venezia (Venice, 1950), 319–20; *Max Beckmann*.

Gemalde 1905–1950, catalogue, Leipzig Museum der Bildende Kunste 21 July–23 September 1990, ed. Klaus Gallwitz (Stuttgart, 1990); *Max Beckmann. Gravures (1911–1946)*, catalogue, Les Sables d'Olonne Musée de l'Abbay Sainte-Croix 12 March–5 June 1994 (Les Sables d'Olonne, 1994).
RA

Belling Rudolph
Berlin, 1866–Krailing, 1972
He began his apprenticeship as a specialist in small-scale three-dimensional decoration, while studying drawing and sculpture. He worked with Max Reinhardt on several theater pieces, and in 1912 he studied with the sculptor Peter Breuer at the Kunstakademie in Berlin. He became a member of the 'Novembergruppe' and the 'Arbeistrat für Kunst'. In the Twenties he held several important exhibitions in Germany. In 1931 he joined the Prussian Akademie der Künste and exhibited in New York and Zurich. Assisted by the architect Hans Poelzig, he emigrated to Turkey in 1937; he taught at the Academy of Fine Arts and at the Technical University of Istanbul until 1956. Many of his works were destroyed by bombs in Berlin, while others were confiscated by the authorities who considered Belling a degenerate artist. In 1966 he returned to Germany where he moved to Munich; his former reputation restored, a major retrospective was dedicated to him in 1967.

BIBLIOGRAPHY
J.A. Schmoll Gen. Eisenwerth, *Rudolf Belling* (Erker, 1971); '*Degenerate Art'. The Fate of the Avant-Garde in Nazi Germany*, catalogue, Los Angeles, Los Angeles County Museum of Art 17 February–12 May 1991 (Los Angeles, 1991).
RA

Bellmer Hans
Katowice, 1902–Paris, 1975
He studied perspective and technical drawing at the Technische Hochschule of Berlin (1923–24), and later became close friends with George Grosz and Otto Dix. In 1933, disgusted by the climate of suspicion generated by the Nazi rise to power, he decided to 'abandon any work useful to the state' and devoted himself to the creation of a life-size articulated doll, *Die Puppe*. The images related to the doll's construction were printed at Bellmer's expense (1934). 'The limbs [of this

doll], joined by forces external to them, know that the principle of their life... could be cut off at any moment... The tragic interior suggested by the face fights a possibility that Bellmer leaves open, which is an essential component of sadism—the reduction of a living body to the exhaustive external aspect of an algebraic equation'. He was discovered by the Surrealists in Paris, where he moved in 1938. At the outbreak of World War II he was interned with Max Ernst in the prison camp at Mille, in the south of France, an experience which inspired a series of designs. In 1945–46 he illustrated Bataille's *Histoire de l'œil*. He met the writer Unica Zürn who posed, nude and bound, for a violent series of photographs (*Unica*). Zurn, who suffered from schizophrenia and had spent much time in psychiatric clinics, committed suicide in 1970.

BIBLIOGRAPHY
Hans Bellmer, catalogue, Paris Centre National d'Art Contemporain 1971 (Paris, 1971); *Obliques*, monograph dedicated to Hans Bellmer (1975); *Hans Bellmer Photographien*, catalogue, Hanover Kestner-Gesselschaft 1984 (Hanover, 1984); *Formas del abismo. El cuerpo y su representación extrema en Francia 1930–1960*, catalogue, Gipuzkoa Sala de Exposiciones Koldo Mitxelena, 21 October 1994–15 January 1995 (Gipuzkoa, 1994).
LS

van den Berghe Frits
Gand, 1883–1939
After his study at the Académie and the Ecole des Arts e Métiers in Gand, he spent the summers from 1904 to 1913 in Laethem–Saint Martin, where he formed, with Albert Servaes, Léon and Gust De Smet, and Constant Permeke the so-called 'Second Group of Laethem'. After six months in the United States, he spent the war years in Holland, where he remained until 1922. There he became acquainted with the Futurism and Expressionism of Jan Sluyters, as well as the constructivist fauvist work of Henri Le Fauconnier, artists who would influence his work until the post-war period. In Holland, 1930, he and Gust De Smet began to create the 'constructive version of Flemish Expressionism' (Leen, 240). In 1926 fantastical images started appearing in his work, confirmation of his visionary talent, which reveals references to the formal and structural experimentation of

Max Ernst's surrealism. In 1931 he began to work as an illustrator for the Socialist periodical *Vooroit*.

BIBLIOGRAPHY
Robert Hoozee, Monique Tahon-Vanrose and Sabine Bown-Taevernier, *Frits van den Berghe* (Brussels, 1983); Frederick Leen, ad vocem *Frits van den Berghe*, in *L'avant-garde en Belgique. 1917–1929*, catalogue, Brussels Musée d'Art Moderne, 18 September–13 December 1992 (Brussels, 1992).
LS

Bertelli Renato
Lastra a Signa, Florence, 1900–1974
A student of Domenico Trentacoste (Palermo, 1859–Florence, 1933), a Sicilian sculptor influenced by Auguste Rodin (1840–1917), he came to public attention in 1922 with a *Ballerina* selected for the Esposizione Primaverile of Florence. Later he worked with poor materials (terracotta, majolica), favoring simple themes linked to everyday life. In the Thirties he began to explore Futurist concerns and the theories of Filippo Tommaso Marinetti which he expressed in the innovative lines of the 1933 bronze *Profilo continuo (testa di Mussolini)*. He was influenced by the work of Ernesto Michaelles Thayaht (Bietoletti, 50). He participated in the Venice Biennale XVI (1928).

BIBLIOGRAPHY
S. Bietoletti, *Bertelli, Renato*, in *Saur-Allgemeines Künstler-Lexicon-Die Bildenden Künstler aller Zeiten und Völker*, vol. 10 (Munich and Leipzig, 1995), 50.
VM

Bertillon Alphonse
Paris, 1853–Münsterlingen, 1914
From 1880 the director of a method for criminal identification created for the Paris police, he invented the recognition system based on a photographic portrait (frontal and profile) completed by a card recording descriptions, distinctive characteristics, and detailed measurements of the parts of the body (*Nascita*, 47). Known as *bertillonnage*, this method was adopted by police throughout the world between 1888 and 1905, and was later replaced by the fingerprint system. It was based on constant parameters guaranteed by a device made of a camera and a graduated measuring rod. Inspired by

Quételet's work in anthropology and statistics, Bertillon's theory, vigorously opposed by Cesare Lombroso and his school, is described in his book *La photographie judiciaire*.

BIBLIOGRAPHY
Alphonse Bertillon, *La photographie judiciaire avec un appendice sur la classification et l'identification anthropologique* (Paris, 1890); Alphonse Bertillon, *Identification anthropologique. Instructions signalétiques* (Melun, 1893); Alphonse Bertillon, *Anthropologie métrique. Conseils pratiques aux missionnaires scientifiques sur la manière de mesurer, de photographier des sujets vivants et des pièces anatomiques. Anthropologie, photographie métrique, portraits descriptifs, crâniométrie* (Paris, 1909); *Nascita della fotografia psichiatrica*, catalogue, Venice Ca' Corner della Regina 31 January–8 March 1981, eds. Franco Cagnetta and Jacqueline Sonolet (Venice, 1981), 45 ff.
VM

Beuys Joseph
Krefeld, 1921–Düsseldorf, 1986
In 1941 he was mobilized as an officer pilot. He was shot down during a raid in the Crimea (1943) and was rescued by the Tartars (Kuspit, 83). Shortly after the war he attended the Düsseldorf Kunstakademie where he studied with Joséph Enseling and Ewald Mataré. Just after his first one-man show (Krannenburg, 1953) in which he exhibited in bronze and wood recovering the primary sense of these materials, he opened an atelier in Düsseldorf and began teaching at the Kunstakademie (1961–72) where he had students such as Jörg Immendorff (1964). In the Sixties he began to employ waste or perishable material in his work, and he began to participate in 'Fluxus' group events (1963). He was very active in happenings and installations both in Europe and in the United States. He took part in the Venice Biennale XXXVII (1976) with his *Tram Stop I* installation, and also participated in the Biennale XXXIX (1980) with the piece *Das Kapital Raum 1970–1977*. At the same time he was standing as a Green party candidate for the EEC elections.

BIBLIOGRAPHY
Donald Kuspit, 'Joseph Beuys: The Body of the Artist', *Artforum*, vol. XXXIX, 10 (Summer 1991), 83; *Joseph

and used for teaching human anatomy. In 1903 he went to Munich and later moved to Paris (1904) where he attended the Ecole Nationale des Beaux–Arts and worked in Antonin Mercié's studio. He refused to become an apprentice in Rodin's atelier to free himself from his influence. He then moved towards a stylization of pure primordial forms, beginning with the variations of the *Muse endormie* (1909–10). His taste for abstraction and exploration of the 'shape–type' intensified after World War I. He was the subject of an *Omaggio a Brancusi* organized by Dan Haulica at the Venice Biennale XL (1982).

BIBLIOGRAPHY
Sidney Geist, *Brancusi–A Study of the Sculpture* (New York, 1968); Pontus Hulten, Natalia Dumitresco, Alexander Istrati, *Brancusi* (Paris, 1986); Anne C. Chave, *Constantin Brancusi: Shifting the Bases of Art* (New Haven–London, 1994).
MC

Brauner Victor
Piatra-Neamt, 1903–Paris, 1966
Influenced by his father who interested him in spiritualism, he attended the Budapest School of Fine Arts (1924) where he was especially influenced by Cézanne (Semin, 275). In 1930 he moved to Paris where he met his compatriot Constantin Brancusi, and at the same time Yves Tanguy, André Breton and other members of the Surrealist movement (1934). After the failure of his first one-man show (Galerie Pierre, Paris, 1934) he began a series of paintings representing distorted human figures with mutilated eyes. At the outbreak of World War I, he took refuge in the Pyrenees, Marseilles and finally Switzerland where he studied the tarot and ancient mytholo-gy (Egyptian, Colombian and Mexican), and developed a personal graffito encaustic technique. He resumed his work immediately after the war with a Surrealist show at the Galerie Maeght (Paris, 1947), when he finally achieved international fame, confirmed by his participation at the Venice Biennales of 1954 and 1966 (Semin, 280).

BIBLIOGRAPHY
Didier Semin, *Victor Brauner* (Paris, 1990); *Victor Brauner*, catalogue, Saint Etienne Musée d'Art Moderne 1992, eds. Martine Dancer and Sylvie Lecoq-Ramond (Paris, 1992).
VM

Broca Paul
1824–1880
French surgeon and anthropo-logist. He is best–known for his research on the localization of the cerebral nerve centers of the word. He founded the *Société*, the *Revue* and the *Ecole d' Anthropologie* in Paris, and is considered the father of modern physical anthropology.

BIBLIOGRAPHY
Instructions générales pour les recherches anthropologiques à faire sur le vivant (1864); *Mémoires d' anthropologie* (1871–75); *Instructions craniologiques et cranio-métriques* (1875).
PC

Brodskij Isaak Izraejlevič
Sofievka, 1884–Saint Peters-burg, 1939
After early studies in Odessa he moved to Saint Petersburg where he was a student of Ilya Ephimovič Repin (1844–1930). He went through a Symbolist phase in which he produced traditional landscapes and portraits, and was a member of various groups ('Mir Iskusstva'; 'The Painter's Union'). Later he dedicated himself to Realism. After the 1917 Revolution his work centered primarily on historical events, with particular focus on Stalin. In the Thirties he was first professor (1932) and later director (1934) of the Academy of Fine Arts in Leningrad.

BIBLIOGRAPHY
Arte Russa e Sovietica 1870–1930, catalogue, Turin Lingotto 1989, ed. Giovanni Carandente (Milan, 1989), 455–6.
VM

Brogi Carlo
Firenze, 1850 c.–1925
Following in the footsteps of his father Giacomo, he did excellent work on the photographic portrait in his family's studio in Florence. He would later write an essay on this subject (*Il ritratto in fotografia*, 1895). On his father's death (1881) he took over the management of the family firm. In 1895 he also wrote another interesting treatise, *Dell' Arte del ritratto fotografico*, which compares the psychological relationship between the photograph and the photographed subject. He became friends with Paolo Mantegazza with whom he would work on the *Atlante delle espressioni del dolore*. He was associate, then member of the board of directors, and finally vice–president of the Società Fotografica Italiana. He defended the legal rights of photographers and supported a bill for the protection of author's rights in photo-graphic-editorial projects. Some of his major exhibitions were those in Vienna (1873), Milan (1881) and the Florence Esposizione Universale (1889).

BIBLIOGRAPHY
Piero Bechetti, *Fotografi e fotografie in Italia. 1839–1880* (Rome, 1978); *Fotografia italiana dell' Ottocento*, catalogue, Florence Palazzo Pitti October–December 1979 and Venice Ala Napoleonica-January–March 1980 (Venice, 1979).
MC

Brus Günter
Ardning, 1938
He began to attend the School of Arts and Crafts in Graz in 1953, and from 1957 on he studied at the Vienna Academy of Applied Arts. He finished his training in 1960, when he traveled throughout Spain and visited the Venice Biennale. The same year he met the artist Otto Mühl, whose studio was the scene for his first auto-painting action (*Selbstbe-malung*) entitled *Aktion Ana*, which was filmed by Kurt Kren and photographed by Siegfried Klein. He was to perform another forty actions in the years up to 1970. His first one-man show was held at the *Galerie Junge Generation* in Vienna, which was also part of action 10 *Starrkampf* (tetania) In Mühl's studio he also performed action 17 *Aktion in einem Kreis* (action in a circle). During his exhibition action 33 he sang the Austrian National Anthem, and performed acts of sado-masochism and self-mutilation. He fled from prosecution and moved to Berlin in 1969. In 1971 he took up drawing and graphics, and created the genre of the *Bild-Dichtung* (image-poem). In later years he has exhibited throughout Europe, and he returned to Austria in 1976 where he is developing the *Bild-dichtung* which still remains his preferred genre.

BIBLIOGRAPHY
Peter Weibel and Valie Export, *Wien-Bildkompendium Weiner Aktionismus und Film* (Frankfurt, 1971); *Aktions-malerei-Aktionismus 1960-1965*, catalogue, Kassel Winterthur, Edinburgh Vienna 1988-89 (Klagenfurt, 1988); *Günter Brus–Limite du visible*, catalogue, Paris Centre Georges Pompidou 1993, ed. Caterine Grenier (Paris, 1993).
SR

Bühler Franz Karl (Franz Pohl)
see **Prinzhorn-Sammlung**

Burri Alberto
Città di Castello, 1915–Nice, 1994
After graduating with a degree in medicine (1940), he was taken prisoner in World War II and sent to Hereford, Texas (1943).
He began to paint there, and once he returned to Italy took up painting professionally. He made his debut in the galleria Santa Margherita (Rome, 1947). In 1951, along with Balocco, Colla and Capogrossi, he signed the manifesto of the *Origine* group which encouraged new informal trends. At the same time he began his *Sacchi* cycle which brought him to international notice. He took part in the Venice Biennale XXVI (1952) and several later ones. His *Combustioni* period, followed by the *Ferri* and *Legni*, actually anticipate the series of *Plastiche* which confirmed his acclaim, as it pre–dates the work of Jasper Johns and Robert Rauschen-berg (*Grande Rosso Plastica*, 1962). In the Seventies he continued his work in materials.
These were works such as the *Cretti*, synthetic and polyvinyl acetate structures, which he followed with thematic series such as *Sestante*, eighteen pieces for the Giudecca shipyards in Venice (1983).
In 1981 the Museo Burri opened in Città di Castello, which houses a representative selection of his work.

BIBLIOGRAPHY
Burri. *Contributi al catalogo sistematico*, ed. Fondazione Palazzo Albrizzini (Città di Castello, 1990), 174 n. 734, 175 (extended bibliography).
VM

Burson Nancy
Saint Louis, 1948
She studied at Colorado Women's College in Denver, and then moved to New York City where she now lives and works.
Her first one-man show was at the Bertha Urdan Gallery (New York, 1974).
Her photography is based on her interest in the analysis of the portrait and its limits, and she has alternated between multi-media work, installations and videos in which the images are worked out with the use of a computer and *video-disk* to explore its boundaries (*Composite portraits*, 1986). *Faces* (1993), one of her more recent works, consists of a series of black and white photographs of children affected by illnesses that lead to cranial deforma-tion. Fired with passion and altered perspectives, they lead the observer, through analysis of concepts such as alternative physical beauty, to recreate the experience of children.

BIBLIOGRAPHY
Christine van Assche, *Vidéo et après–Le collection vidéo du Musée national d' art moderne* (Paris, 1992), 86; Nancy Burson, *Faces* (Santa Fe, 1993).
VM

Cabanis Emmanuel A.
1943
Head of Neuro-Imagerie and Radiologie at the Centre Hospitalier National d'Ophtalmologie des Quinze-Vingt in Paris, he is a professor of radiology at the faculty of medicine Pitié-Salpétrière (Université Pierre et Marie Curie, Paris VI), and a national legal expert.
He has written many medical texts on *neuro-imagerie* (*Imagerie par Résonance Magnétique*; *L' Anatomie numérique et l' informatique*; *Anatomie historique*), and he prepared the 1996 report of the Société Française d'Ophtalmologie (*L' Imagerie en Ophtalmologie*) and the catalogue of the Musei Delmas-Orfila-Rouvières.
RA

Campigli Massimo
Max Ihlenfeld
Berlin, 1985–Saint Tropez, 1971
He first encountered Futurism in Milan in 1909. In 1919 he moved to Paris, where he worked both as a painter and a journalist. He began to explore Cubism which inspired his taste for rigid geometry of figures. His painting united allusions to Egyptian art with the influence of contemporary painters such as Léger, Ozenfant, Carrà and Picasso. He frequented *Novecento* circles and the 'Italiens de Paris' group. On his return to Rome in 1928 he discoverd Etruscan art, and, renouncing his earlier styles, he achieved his accomplished final style, populated with pre-Hellenic female images, which he would remain faithful to for the rest of his life. *Le cucitrici* recall Léger, Giotto and Chaldean art. There are further references to the corsetted women of Seurat, in which a female sensuality of form is contrasted with the geometry of composition, and the

reiteration of the two paired figures typical of Picasso's work in the Twenties. The painting is part of a series portraying female figures involved in various domestic chores. The intimacy of the scenes contrasts with the balanced symmetry of composition. In the Thirties he worked a great deal in fresco (the Geneva Palace of Nations, the Milan Palazzo di Giustizia, the Italian Pavilion of the Venice Biennale 1937, and the Atrio del Liviano, in the Faculty of Lettere in Padua).

BIBLIOGRAPHY
Campigli, catalogue, Padua Palazzo della Ragione 1994.
LS

Carlson Mary
Steven's Point, 1951
She studied at the School of Visual Art in New York (1973). Her first one-man show was in 1986 at the Curt Marcus Gallery of New York, and in 1988 she received the sculpture prize from the National Endowment for Arts. In 1993 she received a John Simon Guggenheim Fellowship. She creates swollen bodies, which are actually suits carefully completed by hands and feet in different types of found material, like flayed skin, which are placed on the ground or hung in a corner, sewn together with other bodies. The latex versions are clean and clinical. They reflect a pathological obssession with the private, and evoke the fear of the prophylactic wrapping of the vulnerable body. Some bodies are in paper (*Rice paper*, 1992), and are placed outside, subject to the stress of city traffic and exposed to denting and buckling. Others, in sponge, dirtied by the absorption of body stains, seem a metaphor for depression, hung as they are in a corner, as if ashamed. A fabric body (*Toile figures*, 1990) hung on a wall, like a kind of lining of the soul, serves both as a container for prophylactics (a recurrent motif in the AIDS era) and bodily by-products.

BIBLIOGRAPHY
Amie Wallach, *Dialogue Among Curators Is a Mind Game with Art*, in 'New York Newsday', 30 December 1994; Holland Cotter, 'Art in Review', *The New York Times*, 10 April 1992.
RA

Carpentier Jules
Paris, 1851–Joigny, 1921
After studying engineering at the Polytechnic, he worked as a fitter to complete his practical training. Specializing in mechanical constructions, he invented a portable photographic instrument around 1892, known as the *photo–jumelle*, which was considered one of the best on the market. This helped spread the popularity of small format photography in France (which was then 6.5 x 9). On 15 March 1895 he patented the *cinégraphe*, which used two connected lens. In the same year he volunteered to help the Lumière brothers for the industrial construction of the *cinématographe*. By mid–October he had finished the first prototype of a series which was an improvement over Charles Moisson's version, both in terms of construction and aesthetics. After the first public projection of the *Cinématographe* at the *Grand–Café* on the *Boulevard des Capucines* on 28 December 1895, the Lumière brothers ordered from Carpentier 200 models of this device which was soon in great demand all over the world. He later became the owner of Ruhm-korff electrical works which he greatly improved and developed.

BIBLIOGRAPHY
Georges Sadoul, *Il cinematografo dei fratelli Lumière*, in *Storia generale del cinema–Le origini e i pionieri (1832–1909)* (Turin, 1965), 147–66; Bernard Chardère, Guy and Marjorie Borgé, *Les Lumière* (Lausanne, 1985).
MC

Cascella Andrea
Pescara, 1920–Milan, 1990
Raised in an artistic environment, he studied under Domenico Rambelli. He had his first one–man show in Rome (1949) after the war, when he had been active in the Resistance in Piedmont. He later moved to Rome where he and his brother Pietro worked for many years in ceramics and stone sculpture applied to architecture. He was one of the winners of the competition for the Auschwitz memorial (1958) and he worked with many Milanese architects including Zanuso, Gardella, and Gregotti. Eight of his works were exhibited in a room dedicated to him at the Venice Biennale XXXII (1964), including *La Nascita di Venere* (1962), and he won the Gran Premio for sculpture. His work is based on the embedded combination of simple abstract and geometrical forms, permeated, however, by a symbolic and mythical dimension, '... as if the imagination of the sculptor, because of subtle ambiguity and attraction, could never completely abandon the shapes of the human figure ...' (*XXXII Esposizione Biennale*, 76–7).

BIBLIOGRAPHY
XXXII Esposizione Biennale Internazionale d' Arte Venezia (Venice, 1964), 76–7; *Andrea Cascella. Il corpo della scultura: proposte e ipotesi*, catalogue, Milan Studio Reggiani 31 May 1990, ed. Luciano Caramel (n.p., [1990]); *Scultura a Milano 1945–1990*, catalogue, Milan Palazzo della Permanente 1 June–22 July 1990 (Milan, 1990).
MC

Casorati Felice
Novara, 1883–Turin, 1963
He first achieved critical recognition in the Venice Biennale of 1907. Klimt's one-man show in Venice (1911) influenced his work, and inspired his brilliant colors and decorative styles. He joined the group of artists at Ca' Pesaro, where he was given a room (1913) and returned there to exhibit in later years. However, he always maintained his relationship with the Biennale, where he exhibited often (1909, 1910, 1912, 1914). Over the years his work was taken up as the emblem of the 'return to order' in Italian painting. *Silvana Cenni* is considered one of his characteristic paintings because of its 'immediate recognizability of cultured sources (Piero della Francesca and fifteenth-century inlay), the apparent harshness of perspective... the optical ambiguity of a construction completely defined by orthocentric planes and axes, by subtly falsified symmetries: an assertion of severity and serenity placed... in a context of breaks, pauses, and deliberate incompletions, noticeable primarily in the foreground of the still-lifes and in the wing of the wall to the left' (Lamberti, 87). *Conversazione platonica* was exhibited at the first show of the Italian Novecento: 'although the sensual echo of the nature study is so vivid, the eroticism of the painting lies, in harmony with the title,... frozen, unexpressed except in purely mental terms; and not because... the characters are not touching each other, but because of the control of the drawing, which encloses the flesh of the woman in an intangible veil, in an aura of absolute perfection' (Lamberti, 107).

BIBLIOGRAPHY
Felice Casorati 1883–1963, catalogue, Turin Accademia Albertina di Belle Arti 19 February–31 March 1985, eds. Maria Mimita Lamberti and Paolo Fossati (Milan, 1985); *Felice Casorati a Milano*, ed. Maria Mimita Lamberti (Milan, 1990).
LS

Cavezian R.
see **Cabanis Emmanuel A.**

Ceroli Mario
Castelfranco, Chieti, 1938
After having attended the Istituto d'Arte in Rome, he began to produce Informal ceramics under the guide of Leoncillo, which he exhibited at his first one-man show at the Galleria San Sebastianello in 1968. In the Sixties he started using wood panels and plywood packing crates to create repeated model figures (*L' Addio, L' ultima cena*) and objects (*Lettere, Telefono, Orologio Si-No*), which he exhibited in a group show at La Tartaruga gallery in Rome in 1964. At the same time he was conducting a re-assess-ment of great painters of the past (*L' uomo di Leonardo*, 1964; *Le Veneri botticelliane*, 1965; the *Mobili nella valle di De Chirico*). He was in the United States between 1966 and 1967. On his return he began to work extensively in stage design, and did the sets for *Richard III* at the Teatro Stabile in Turin in 1968. Though he took part in the first group show of the Arte Povera movement, he continued to work independ-ently. His one-man shows include those at the Palazzo Ducale of Pesaro in 1972, the Forte Belvedere in Florence in 1983, and the Galleria Cleto Polcina in Rome in 1990.

BIBLIOGRAPHY
Mario Ceroli, catalogue, Florence 1983, ed. Maurizio Calvesi (Florence, 1983); *Roma anni '60. Al di là della pittura*, catalogue, Rome 1990, ed. M. Calvesi and R. Siligaro (Rome, 1990).
VC

César
Marseilles, 1921
His early production, which denies both the abstract constructivist as well as the neo-constructivist, then predominant in the Paris of the Forties and Fifties, is an exploration of the relationship with nature and the sugges-tion of materials that led to his *assemblages* of reject scrap from foundries. He took his conception of symbolist objects from Surrealism, and in 1960 he joined Nouveau Réalisme. He then began to produce prismatic blocks, obtained by crushing old cars into cubes. His first one-man show was at the Galerie Lucien Durand in Paris. In the Sixties and Seventies he was creating large blown-up objects (*Le pouce di César*, 1966) and later explored the idea of liquefying objects. Among his many shows were those at the Palais de Beaux-Arts in Brussels in 1971, and at the Musée Picasso in Antibes in 1978.

BIBLIOGRAPHY
César. Les Expansions, catalogue (Paris, 1979); L. Vinca Masini, *L' arte contemporanea*, vol. II (Florence, 1993).

Cézanne Paul
Aix-en-Provence, 1839-1906
Cézanne's work represents the great watershed in the history of the composition of space, and his influence can be found behind all modern painting: Cubism, Expressionism, the Abstract' (Guerney, in *Cézanne. The Late Work*, p. 73). His early interest in painting was a reaction to his provincial life working as a clerk in his father's bank, longing to experience the artistic life of Paris. Cézanne witnessed early on the conflict between official art and the revolutionary realism of Corbet and Manet. Later he would experience every phase in the develop-ment of Impressionism, without coming to the fore until the early 1890s. His final period established him as an extraordinary painter. He painted a remarkable series of works (from *Sainte-Victoire* to the still-lifes, to his *Bathing nudes*) which challenge the earlier 'ephemeralism' of Impressionism. There are two sets of reflections to be made about his *Still life with skull and candelabra* (1900-04), which are true of all his late work. First of all, the two objects are both traditional subject matter of the *memento mori*: this preoccupation with approaching death runs throughout all his late production. Another feature from this period were large unworked spaces, deliberately creating 'a different effect from the "not-finished"' (Reff, in *Cézanne. The Late Work*, 36).

BIBLIOGRAPHY
Cézanne. The Late Work, catalogue, New York Museum of Modern Art, 1977 (New

York, 1977); Kathleen Adler, 'Cézanne's Bodies', *Art in America*, 78, March 1990, 234-237, 277.
SDS

Chadwick Helen
Croydon, 1953
She studied at the Brighton Polytechnic (1973–76) and at the Chelsea School of Art (1976–77). She lives and works in London. Involved in a number of different fields, she held her first one-man show in 1978 in London. She won the Greater London Arts Association prize in 1981 and the Artist in Schools prize in 1983. In 1984 she exhibited at the Venice Biennale *Aperto '84*. She focuses on female identity in the attempt to eliminate historical imbalance, but her final goal is to understand the universal human condition. Seeing is a complex process that requires the manipulation of signs and symbols. Chadwick questions the significance of the body; if it is a specimen, a machine, an archetype, light or colour—if it is even possible to know it. She asks herself if two bodies, two spirits, two brains (*Eroticism*, 1990) can ever understand each other intimately, if eroticism is their reciprocal exchange or a narcissistic projection towards an 'invisible other'. To understand the social body, man must know his own flesh.

BIBLIOGRAPHY
The British Art Show, catalogue, Birmingham City of Birmingham Museum and Art Gallery and Ikon Gallery, 2 November–22 December (London, 1984), 117, 137; William A. Ewing, *Le corps. Oeuvres photographiques sur la Forme Humaine* (1994), 335.
RA

Chervin Arthur
French doctor and anthropologist. A craniology specialist, he worked with Alphonse Bertillon on the development of metric photography and anthropometry. He took part in several ethnological expeditions in South America, especially Bolivia.

BIBLIOGRAPHY
Essai de géographie médicale en France, 1880; *Anthropologie métrique*, 1909.
PC

Claudel Camille
Fère–en–Tardenois, 1864–Montdevergues, 1943.
In 1882 she moved with her family to Paris where she was educated at the Académie Colarossi and studied with the sculptor Alfred Boucher. In 1885 she began to work with Auguste Rodin, marking the beginning of a long and tormented relationship. Between 1885 and 1888 she exhibited regularly at the Société des Artistes Français, and assisted Rodin with several works (*Les Portes de l'Enfer*, 1888). The *Torse de Clotho* (1893) is a poignant illustration of the suffering she experienced after her tragic separation from Rodin (1892). In this, Claudel took representation to its extreme, transferring her own pain to the debased torso topped by a completely bald head. For a brief period she continued to sculpt, especially small figures (*La Vague*, 1900). Although she exhibited at the Société Nationale des Beaux–Arts, the Salon d'Automne and received public commissions, she abandoned herself to solitude and despair, and destroyed some of her own work. In 1913 her family took the decision to commit her to a psychiatric hospital, first in Ville–Evrard, then at Mondevergues, where she categorically refused to sculpt until her death.

BIBLIOGRAPHY
Camille Claudel, catalogue, Paris Musée Rodin n.d. (Paris, 1984); Reine–Marie Paris, Arnaud de La Chapelle, *L'œuvre de Camille Claudel, Catalogue raisonné* (Paris, 1991); Enzo Fabiani, 'Camille Claudel, sequestrata e morta in manicomio', *Arte*, 230 (June 1992), 76–81.
RA

Clegg & Guttmann
Michael Clegg (*Dublin, 1957*) and Martin Guttmann (*Jerusalem, 1957*) live and work in New York and San Francisco. Their work must be classified as Postmodern, a movement that has opted for the critical function of art in its confrontation with the cultural industry. Photography furnishes critical reflections of reality, in recording the mise-en-scène of a declared fiction. They deal primarily with landscape and the portrait, especially the group portrait, both inspired by seventeenth-century Dutch and Flemish painting. The character, however, has no individual identity, but is introduced as an actor placed against a previously photographed backdrop, clearly revealing its scenic construction. At the same time, the landscape is not identifiable, and reproduces the environment of industrialized culture—open spaces plowed through by highways, dotted with advertising billboards and lampposts, in a recognition of lives dictated by consumerism.

BIBLIOGRAPHY
Clegg & Guttmann. *Portraits de groupes de 1980 à 1989*, catalogue, Bordeaux Musée d'Art Contemporain 10 March–23 April 1989 [Paris, 1989]; *Sguardo di Medusa*, catalogue, Castello di Rivoli Museo d'Arte Contemporanea 5 July–27 September 1991, ed. Ida Gianelli, Milan 1991.
RA

Clegg Michael *see* Clegg & Guttmann

Clemente Francesco
Naples, 1952
Clemente made his debut in Rome in 1970, with early work in conceptual photography, and he began painting in the late Seventies. His extensive travel in India has been an important source of inspiration in his work. Along with Chia, Cucchi, De Maria and Paladino he arrived at international fame in the early Eighties as an exponent of the Italian *Transavanguardia*. In his figurative work from the Eighties he recorded 'the visibility in the sea of objectivity' (Gallo in *Transavanguardia*, 1992, 92). Clemente uses an iconography developed in painting cycles linked to the human figure, to eroticism and especially to the self-portrait. Clemente is extremely multi-faceted in his expressive matter, and not only uses drawing, painting, and watercolour, but also mosaic, miniature and fresco with a classical and Eastern flavor. 'To Clemente art is always the production of opulence, even when he seems to use severe and minor topics in drawing, in fresco, in murals [...] This is a light-bearing language which puts the spotlight on the excess that is the image' (Bonito Oliva in *Transavanguardia: Italia/America*, 7).

BIBLIOGRAPHY
Transavanguardia: Italia/America, catalogue, Modena Galleria Civica del Comune 21 March–2 May 1982, ed. Achille Bonito Oliva (Modena, 1982); *Transavanguardia*, catalogue, Milan Galleria GianFerrari Arte Contemporanea, 25 November 1992–23 January 1993, ed. Francesco Gallo (Milan, 1992).
SDS

Close Chuck
Monroe, 1940
He studied at the University of Washington (1958–62), the Yale Summer School of Music and Art in Norfolk (1961), and at the Yale University School of Art and Architecture in New Haven (1962–64). In 1967 he moved to New York, where he lives and workds today. He taught at the University of Massachusetts (1965–67), the School of Visual Arts of New York (1967–71), the University of Washington (1970), and New York University (1970–73). In 1965 he began to experiment with photography, and adopted different artistic techniques in painting, creating a mosaic effect in oil by using three–color processes, streaking, and fingerpainting. Through his intimate relationship with the sitter, Close seeks to highlight the essential character of the subject, creating a new realism and a new intensity. In the delicate texture of the skin created by fingerprints, *Fanny* (1985) expresses, in black and white, both the technical effect and the artist's affection for the older woman he portrays. In spite of the size of the canvas, *Alex* (1991), the subject of many paintings, reveals a man internally anguished and externally vulnerable.

BIBLIOGRAPHY
Chuck Close, catalogue, Baden Baden Staatliche Kunsthalle 10 April–22 June 1994, eds. Jochen Poetter and Helmut Friedel (Ostfildern, 1994).
RA

Comar Philippe
see Cabanis Emmanuel A.

Contremoulins *see* x–Rays or Röntgen

Corinth Lovis
Tapiau, 1858–Zandvoort, 1925
After studying in Paris under Bouguereau, where he admired the naturalistic painting of Wilhelm Leibl, Corinth followed Böcklin to Munich in 1891, where he was one of the founding members of the 'München Sezession' (1892). He later moved to Berlin where, with Max Liebermann and Walter Leistikow, he created the 'Berliner Sezession' (1900). In the first decade of the 20th century his palette became lighter and his painting revealed a freer brushstroke, typical of the German Impressionism of which he was the principal representative, along with Liebermann and Slevogt. A serious illness (1911–12) from which he never completely recovered hastened the development of his artistic vision, so that the monumental aspect of his last paintings is associated with a certain dissolving of formal structure. The extreme mellowness of colour of *Ecce Homo* (1925) seems to display traces of Modernism. He died during a trip to Holland, where he had gone to study Rembrandt and Frans Hals. The Venice Biennale XVI (1928) dedicated a retrospective to him. His last works were condemned by the Nazis, removed from museums, and exhibited in the show on Degenerate Art (*Entartete Kunst*, 1937).

BIBLIOGRAPHY
Lovis Corinth: die Bilder vom Walchensee, catalogue, Regensburg Ostdentsche Galerie 27 April–15 June 1986, eds. Werner Timm and Hans Jürgen Imiela (Regensburg, 1986); *Lovis Corinth 1858–1925*, catalogue, Essen Museum Folkwang 10 November 1985–12 January 1986, eds. Zdenek Felix, Gerhard Gerkens, Friedrich Gross, Joachim Hensinger von Waldegg (Cologne, 1985).
LS

Corpet Vincent
1958
He held his first one-man show at the gallery *Mesdames-Messieurs* in Montpellier in 1982, and has exhibited in many group shows in France and abroad. An intransigent realism pervades his series of nudes, male and female figures realistically represented with a cruel and objective, almost photographic approach. The realism of these images seems to oscillate between violent demystification and objective neutral observation of a body subject to anthropometry.

BIBLIOGRAPHY
Bataille. Georges Bataille: une autre histoire de l'oeil, catalogue, Las Sables d'Olonne Musée de l'Abbaye Sainte-Croix March–June 1991 (Les Sables d'Olonne, 1991), 59–60, 67; Jean Clair, 'Two or Three Things about Vincent Corpet's Paintings', *Art Press*, 194 September 1994, 51–53.
RA

Cragg Tony
Liverpool, 1949
After having worked as a technician at the laboratories at the Natural Rubber

Producers Research Association (1966–68), he attended (1968 to 1977) Gloucester College of Art and Design in Cheltenham, the Wimbledon School of Art and finally the Royal College of Art in London where he took his degree. His work immediately stands out from that of other new English sculptors, although he shares with them an underlying relationship with reality. He starts from fragments, rejects, and discards which are arranged so as to form 'other' figures, in which the original figure can be deduced. He uses, for example, pieces of bottles with which he constructs larger bottles on the walls, a work in which the object becomes a sign, to demonstrate that it itself is only a fragment of the mass production process. Among Cragg's many exhibitions are his one-man shows in 1986 at the La Jolla Museum of Contemporary Art in California, the Hayward Gallery in London (1987), and the Tate Gallery in London (1989). In 1987 he took part in the Chicago exhibition dedicated to British sculpture, and in 1988 in the Venice Biennale.

BIBLIOGRAPHY
Tony Cragg, *Ecrits, Writings, Geschriften* (Brussels, 1992); *Tony Cragg, Early Forms* (Basle, 1994); *Tony Cragg*, catalogue (Trento, 1994).
VC

Dantan Jean-Pierre
Paris, 1800–Bade, 1869
Also known as Dantan le jeune (his father, Antoine-Laurent, was also a sculptor), Dantan began to work as an apprentice to his father when still very young. He became a ornamental sculptor when he about twenty, and among other projects worked on the restoration of the cathedral of Saint Denis (1819) and the Bourse in Paris. In 1823 he began to attend the Ecole des Beaux-Arts. He exhibited various busts at the 1827 Salon and the next year he left for Italy. Continued in Italy, his career as a satirical and caricature portraitist (begun in 1826) exploded on his return to Paris in 1831. His plaster busts (of Paganini, Rossini, Hugo, Balzac) came to form a true gallery of the grotesque. His great success as a satirical sculptor overshadowed the fact that Dantan was actually an artist of great talent: his serious production included a statue of Philibert Delorme at the Louvre and others at the church of the Madeleine, as well as a remarkable series of marble busts (*Portrait de*

Rossini, 1836).

BIBLIOGRAPHY
Dictionnaire de Biographie Française, vol. x (Paris, 1965), 138; Lami, *Dictionnaire des sculptures du XIX siècle*, vol. II (Paris, 1916), 24–26.
SDS

Danuser Hans
Chur, 1953
A photographer who splits his work between Switzerland, Great Britain and the United States. Between 1979 and 1989 he worked on the cycle *In Vivo*, 'in which he confronts the themes of life and the human being in their widest significance—even in the moment of their absence as definition and negative presence' (Stahel, 54). These studies are extremely contemporary, both in terms of contents as well as photographic technique, and explore the most problematic areas of our culture and civilization such as the economy, science, research and technology. His work is placed right in the middle of the consequent crisis of man. 'The triptych combination formula-experiment-formula becomes symbol of the system of knowledge to acquire: the power over the body allows a physiological and organic knowledge: through this knowledge, the body becomes language and with this we investigate substance again' (Stahel, 56).

BIBLIOGRAPHY
Hans Danuser, *In Vivo: 93 Photographien* (Baden, 1989); Urs Stahel, 'In Vivo: The Photo-Essays of Hans Danuser', *Arts Magazine*, vol. 66, December 1991, 54-57; Roto Hänny, *Helldunkl–Ein Bilderbuch* (Frankfurt, 1994).
MC

Day F. Holland
1864–1933
From childhood he showed great interest in literature and painting, and was already collecting books and decorative objets d'art. At the age of sixteen he enrolled in Chauncy Hall in Boston where he received highest marks in English literature, acting and stage design in 1884. The independence and economic freedom granted him by his parents allowed him to develop his creative interests and become an active participant in the intellectual life of bohemian Boston, whose passion he shared for the Middle Ages. His aesthetic, exotic and sometimes erotic use of the camera is typically

late Victorian. During a visit to Great Britain in 1893 he met Oscar Wilde, and later shocked Boston by publishing his *Salomé*. In 1898 he had already created some photographic tableaux inspired by the Crucifixion which were considered outrageous. 'In *The Seven Words* Day completely focuses his interest on the agony expressed on the face of Christ, with a series of foregrounds that suggest the convulsed movement and the visceral suffering associated with the agony of Christ. The sequence of Day's poses intensifies the vulnerability and the stages of suffering' (James Crump in 'History of Photography', 325).

BIBLIOGRAPHY
Estelle Jussim, *Slave to Beauty: The Eccentric Life and Controverisal Career of F. Holland Day, Photographer, Publisher, Aesthete* (Boston, 981); Verna Posever Curtis (ed), 'F. Holland Day', *History of Photography*, vol. 18, 4, Winter 1994.
MC

De Chirico Giorgio
Volos, 1888–Rome, 1978
His birthplace, Greece, became part of the painter's personal mythology, doubly fascinating because of its childhood associations and its cultural heritage. De Chirico spent the years from 1911 to 1915 in Paris, after his work in Florence and his meeting with Papini. It is here that his own idea of 'painting as representation' must be defined, starting from Cubism and moving through Denis, Rousseau and Gauguin. His writings from this period demonstrate a powerful desire to define an art in which the spectator's emotion is recreated through the apparent isolation of the objects represented, thus creating allegorical painting rich in unusual references and subtle cultural allusions. The mannequin appeared to take the place of the atelier model—a real character whose pose is as significant as its freedom from human psychological coercion. In Ferrara 1915 De Chirico and Carlo Carrà worked out a definition of metaphysical painting, whose philosophical bases were founded on the thought of Nietzsche, Schopenhauer and Weininger. The mannequins of *Trovatore* or *Ettore e Andromaca* make up a series that he would return to in later years—signs of a move towards the eternal present in classical mythology. Another key series in De Chirico's

production are the self-portraits, actual philosophical suggestions of the *pictor optimus*. Portrayed as a Turk, a bullfighter, Odysseus, by identifying himself with everyone he seems finally to be identified only with himself, in a deliberate reference to the mirror of the classical Narcissus (Fagiolo dell'Arco, 55).

BIBLIOGRAPHY
Giorgio De Chirico, catalogue, Munich Haus der Kunst 17 November 1982–30 January 1983, eds. William Rubin, Wieland Schmied and Jean Clair (Munich, 1982); Maurizio Fagiolo dell'Arco, *I bagni misteriosi–De Chirico anni Trenta: Parigi, Italia, New York* (Milan, 1991).
LS

Degas Edgar
Paris 1834–1917
Raised in a bourgeois environment, he enrolled in the Ecole des Beaux-Arts (1855) and frequented artists who were disciples of Ingres. During his travels in Italy (1856–60) he discovered the Florentine masters. At the Louvre he met Manet and exhibited at the first Impressionist show (1874) although he was not totally convinced by the movement. At the end of the 1870s he began to sculpt seriously, primarily bathing women, horses, and of course, ballerinas. One of his most famous bronzes is the *Petite danseuse de quatorze ans* (1880) executed in two versions, one nude and the other dressed in actual clothing (a tutu, ballet slippers, and a ribbon) with a wig of real hair. 'With the application of clothing and hair to bodies modeled in wax Degas created a realistic base on which to work. This procedure was adopted in sculpture when, wanting to reach a higher degree of realism, ready-made objects were applied to wax models or terracotta' (Louis Relin in *Degas scultore*, 58).

BIBLIOGRAPHY
Paul Lemoisne, *Degas et son œuvre*, 4 vols. (Paris, 1954); *Degas scultore*, catalogue, Florence Palazzo Strozzi 16 April–15 June 1986, eds. E. Camesasca and G. Cortenova (Milan, 1986); Henri Loyrette, *Degas: Passion and Intellect* (London, 1993).
MC

Dejneka Aleksandr Aleksandrovič
Kursk, 1899–Moscow, 1969

He studied at the Char'kov School of Art (1914–1918) and later at the Uchtemas art department from 1920 to 1925. He taught in the art departments at the School of Art (1934–46), the School of Decorative Arts (1945–53), and the Institute of Architecture (1953–57) in Moscow. He was one of the founders of the 'Society of Easel Painters' known as OST. He was indebted to the Russian popular tradition, and was influenced by French contemporary painting, but later turned to a synthetic realism. He traveled in the United States, France and Italy. His themes are the revolutionary epic, war, and modernist industry and sport.

BIBLIOGRAPHY
Russian and Soviet Painting 1900–1930, catalogue, Washington Hirshhorn Museum and Sculpture Garden Smithsonian Institution 12 July–25 September 1988 (Washington, 1988), 74; *Aleksandr Deineka. 1899–1969*, catalogue, Helsinki Konsthall 5–28 January 1990 (Helsinki, 1990); *The Great Utopia. The Russian and Soviet Avant-Garde, 1915–1932*, catalogue, Frankfurt Schirn Kunsthalle 1 March–10 May 1992 (New York, 1992), figs. 377–9, 381–5, 717.
RA

Delvaux Paul
Antheit-les-Huy, 1897
Delvaux's debut was post-Impressionist vein, but he soon changed over to an Expressionist vein. He later destroyed nearly all of his early work. His later painting was considered Surrealist—he himself declared that between 1932 and 1935 'Giorgio di Chirico and later Magritte showed me the path to follow' (Delvaux in *Paul Delvaux*, 7). Delvaux, however, never joined any group, and he maintained a isolation interrrupted only by his teaching at the Ecole des Beaux-Arts in Brussels. Working from a palette set in a minor key, his paintings are set in an atmosphere where pale, nude, nearly wax figures of women wander through columned architecture or half-deserted stations, under a leaden sky. 'Condemned to an eternal virginity, they wander like sleepwalkers from one room, one planet, one universe to another [...]. Their huge eyes have the gaze of frightened fawns and all sad animals, turned inwards towards their own interior,' (Langui in *Paul Delvaux*, 7–8).

BIBLIOGRAPHY

Paul Delvaux, catalogue, Amsterdam Museum Boymans-van Benningen, 13 April–17 June 1973; Marc Rombaut, *Paul Delvaux* (New York, 1989).
SDS

Demachy Robert
Saint-Germain-en-Laye, 1859–Hennequeille, Trouville, 1936
Born into a wealthy family of Paris bankers, he dedicated himself entirely to photography in 1880. He was part of the editorial board of the *Revue de photographie*, the publication of the Société Française de Photographie. He was elected a member in 1882 and became a spokesman and champion for the pictorial movement. After his first exhibition (1982) he began to experiment with duochrome rubber which allowed him to control every detail of his copies. His photographs were reproduced in *Camera Work* (1904) and a year later he was elected member of The Royal Academy of Art. 'His favorite models were women and children, dreaming girls languidly stretched on carpets, women of the world whose profile stands out against the hat string. Faces silhouetted against a united background, pervaded by a sweetness, with an impalpable nuance of sensuality that recalls something of Renoir' (Carole Naggar, in *Robert Demachy fotografo*, 5). He also published many articles on technique and theory.

BIBLIOGRAPHY
Bill Jay, *Robert Demachy: Photographs and Essays* (London, 1974); *Robert Demachy fotografo*, catalogue, Venice Palazzo Fortuny, January–February 1981 (Milan, 1981).
MC

Demenÿ Georges
1850–1917
French physiologist. Between 1891 and 1894 he collaborated with Etienne-Jules Marey, and assisted in the foundation of the Station Physiologique du Parc des Princes. Most of his work was devoted to physical education, and he was the professor of applied physiology at the Military School of Gymnastics at Joinville-le-Pont.

BIBLIOGRAPHY
Sur la cronophotographie, (1893); *Les bases scientifiques de l'éducation physique* (1902); *Mécanisme et éducation des mouvements* (1904).
PC

Denis Maurice
Granville, 1870–Saint-Germain-en-Laye, 1943
He studied at the Académie Julian where he met Ranson, Bonnard and Sérusier, and was active in the founding of the Nabis group, becoming its critical interpreter with the publication of his article *Définition du Néo-Traditionnisme* (1890). His painting became increasingly simplified, referring on the one hand to Japanese and Italian Primitivism, and on the other to religious themes with a particular focus on the Christian family. He experimented with Divisionism and Symbolism in illustration, large decorative panels, and murals for churches, public buildings and private homes. With Rouault and Desvallières he founded the *Ateliers d'Art Sacré* in 1919. He was also an important writer and prolific critic, and published his diary in three volumes between 1957 and 1959.

BIBLIOGRAPHY
Catalogo della XX Esposizione Biennale Internazionale d'Arte (Venice, 1936), 262; Robert Rosenblum, *I dipinti dell'Orsay* (Udine, 1991), 585; *Die Nabis. Propheten der Moderne*, catalogue, Zurich Kunsthaus, 28 May–15 August 1993, ed. Ursula Perucchi-Petri (Munich, 1993), 138–76.
RA

Depero Fortunato
Fondo, Trento, 1892–Rovereto, 1960
He trained at the Scuola Reale Elisabettiana in Rovereto. In 1913 he went to Rome, where he met and exhibited with the Futurist artists Balla, Cangiullo and Marinetti. With Balla he wrote the manifesto *Ricostruzione futurista dell'universo* in 1915. In 1916 he collaborated with Sergei Diagilev on thirty-five plastic-mobile costumes for Stravinsky's *Chant du rossignol*. The following year he met the Egyptologist and poet Gilbert Clavel. He drew a series of plates for his short story *Un istituto per suicidi*, and performed the *Balli Plastici* with him. Between 1917 and 1918 he painted many portraits of Clavel which explore the breakdown of form and new abstract dimensions of color and form. In 1919 he founded the *Casa d'Arte Depero* in Rovereto, an artisan center for applied arts. Along with Balla and Prampolini, he took part in the Paris Exposition Internationale des Arts Décoratifs et Industriels Modernes, where he exhibited fabrics, furniture designs, toys and advertising graphics (1925). In 1927 he published the bolted-book *Depero Futurista*, and a year later went to New York (1928–30, 1947–49) where he concentrated on advertising graphics. In 1950 he participated in *Futurismo e Pittura Metafisica* at the Zurich Kunsthaus; he also published the *Manifesto della pittura plastica nucleare*.

BIBLIOGRAPHY
Depero, catalogue, Trento Museo Provinciale d'Arte 12 November 1988–14 January 1989, ed. Maurizio Fagiolo Dell'Arco (Milan, 1988); *La Casa del Mago. Le arti applicate nell' opera di Fortunato Depero 1920–1942*, catalogue, Rovereto Archivio del '900 12 December 1992–30 May 1993 (Milan–Florence, 1992).
RA

Dix Otto
Untermahaus, 1891–Hemmenhofen, 1969
He first studied with a decorator in Gera (1905–09) and later at the Dresden School of Decorative Arts (1919–14). He was influenced by the Die Brücke Futurist group. He volunteered in 1914, first interpreting the war as a purifying event, but later becoming a harsh critic, as seen in his paintings and *acquaforti* on the war theme (1923–24). In 1919 he was among the founders of the Dresdner Sezession–Gruppe 19. He taught at the Dresden Academy of Fine Arts (1919–22, 1928–33) and later in Düsseldorf (1922–27). His art was accused of being degenerate, and he was publicly vilified and dismissed from his position. In 1920 he began to work in a realist vein, moving towards a 'realist objectivity' expressed in many portraits of friends, intellectuals and ordinary people. His theory of human types, with different occupations and interests, is portrayed with a wide-angle lens which deforms and contorts bodies and objects, heightening the drama and contrast of the images. His inspiration lies in the German tradition of the early sixteenth and the late nineteenth centuries, such as Dürer, Holbein, Lucas Cranach, Grünewald and Altdorfer. He began to exhibit again in 1946, when he started to work with many art institutions and schools.

BIBLIOGRAPHY
Otto Dix, catalogue, Genoa Villa Croce 3 July–14 September 1986, ed. Serge Sabarsky (Milan, 1986); *Dix*, catalogue, Stuttgart Galerie der Stadt 4 September–3 November 1991 (Stuttgart, 1991); *Otto Dix. 1891–1969*, catalogue, London Tate Gallery 11 March–17 May 1992 (London, 1992).
RA

Dubuffet Jean
Le Havre, 1901–Paris, 1985
A theorist and polemist as well as an artist, he began to paint in 1942. He rejected traditional art and revalued the freedom of expression characteristic of children and the alienated. He collected and exhibited what he called 'Art Brut', spontaneous forms of art. He explored the possibilities inherent in the expressive potential of matter and the language of ordinary man in *Prospectus* (1946) and *Asphysiante Culture* (1968). His thematic series, *Hautes Pâtes* (1945–46) and *Portraits* (1946–49), mixtures of different materials (asphalt, cement, sand, plaster) into painting, were a great success of the European Informal. In *Paysages grotesques* (1949–50) and *Corps de dames* (1950–51) he experimented with *graffito* and etching. The *Gymnosophie* (1950) depicts two obese women, a study inspired by *arte sauvage* and Art Brut, revealing his interest in material painting. Moving towards an obscure existential anguish, bodies expand, lose form, and take on metaphysical meanings linked to animal, vegetable, and mineral images. In the almost geological stratifications of *Sols e terrains* (1951–52) he explored the phenomenology of painting material; in his later *Assemblages d'empreintes, Tableaux d'assemblage, Texturologies* (1953–59), *Phénomènes* (1958–62), and *Matériologies* (1959–60) he created assemblages of different materials, ranging from newspaper to natural elements. In the Sixties, his anthropomorphic figures in *Haurloupe* achieved a breakthrough in painting, drawn from Dada and Expressionism, suggesting new approaches to different avant-garde currents (Pop Art, Op Art, Environment, and Performance).

BIBLIOGRAPHY
Jean Dubuffet: A Retrospective, catalogue, New York Solomon R. Guggenheim Museum (New York, 1973); *Jean Dubuffet & Art Brut*, catalogue, Venice Collezione Peggy Guggenheim Winter 1986–87, eds. Thomas M. Messer and Fred Licht (Milan, 1986); *Jean Dubuffet 1901–1985*, catalogue, Frankfurt Schirnkunstalle, 12 December 1990–3 March 1991 (Stuttgart, 1990).
RA

Duchamp Marcel
Blainville, 1887–Neuilly, 1968
He attended the Académie Julian in Paris, and his early portraits and landscapes (1908–12) reveal the influence of neo-Impressionism and later Cubism, to which he added a personal interest in motion. This is seen at its most striking in *Nu descendant un escalier n. 2* (1912) which moves towards Futurism. The great scandal and success created by this painting in Paris and New York caused him to abandon painting. He later developed a sort of aesthetic nihilism and introduced the concept of irony into three-dimensional objects which make up *Stoppages étalons* (1913–14). These works anticipate the ready-mades, decontextualized pre-fabricated objects 'defined, in general, as any common manufactured object, which is consecrated as a work of art only because of its selection by the artist without undergoing any alteration ...' (Schwarz). The first ready-mades were exhibited in New York during his years in America (1915–18), where he met Picabia and Man Ray with whom he created Dadaism. In the Twenties he studied and experimented in optics, filmed a Surrealistic short (*Anémic cinéma*, 1926) and worked extensively in experimental photography.

BIBLIOGRAPHY
Arturo Schwarz, *La Sposa messa a nudo in Marcel Duchamp, anche* (Turin, 1974); *Marcel Duchamp*, catalogue, New York Museum of Modern Art and Philadelphia Museum of Art 1973 eds., Anne d'Arnoncourt and Kynaston McShine (n.p., [1973]); *Marcel Duchamp*, catalogue, Venice Palazzo Grassi 1993, eds. Jacques Caumont and Jennifer Gough-Cooper (n.p., 1993).
MC

Ducos du Hauron Louis
Langon, 1837–Agen, 1920
A French inventor and photographer, in 1869 he wrote *La Couleur en photographie: solution du problème*, in which he developed the idea he patented in 1868. At the same time as Cros, he analyzed the colors of objects using three filters—green, purple and orange—and then synthesized them by projecting positive images on the screen or on paper. On the paper version, he used the

superimposition of positives printed in red, blue and yellow. Together with Bercegol's nephew he created a trichromatic screen procedure first marketed in 1909, the *Omnicolore*. He invented other procedures and instruments, including *trasformismo* (1888) which allowed him to achieve photographic anamorphosis, an aspect of 'recreative photography' or *analglyphs* (1894) which Gimpel would take up later.

BIBLIOGRAPHY
Nathalie Boulouch, ad vocem *Louis Ducos du Hauron*, in *Dictionnaire mondial de la Photographie, des origines à nos jours* (Paris, 1994), 197–8.
NB

Dumas Marlene
Capetown, 1953
She studied at the Academy of Fine Arts in Capetown (1972–75) and moved to Holland where she was admitted to the 'Ateliers 63' in Haarlem (1976–78) and attended the Psycologisches Institut in Amsterdam (1979–80). She initially worked in paper collage, utilizing photographs, newspaper, and occasionally texts. In the Eighties she began to paint expressive penetrating portraits and the human figure. Her major themes—eroticism, death, and fear—are usually viewed within a humorous context or possess a poetic aura.

BIBLIOGRAPHY
Miss interpreted: Marlene Dumas, catalogue, Eindhoven Van Abbemuseum n.d. (Eindhoven, 1992); *L' Orizzonte. Da Chagall a Picasso, da Pollock a Cragg*, catalogue, Castello di Rivoli Museo d'Arte Contemporanea 18 December 1994–23 April 1995 (Milano, 1994), 156.
RA

Dunning Jeanne
Granby, 1960
She attended Oberlin College in Oberlin, Ohio (1982) and the School of the Art Institute of Chicago (1985), where she had her first one-man show (*Feature*, 1987). She took part in the biennial show organized by the Whitney Mueum of American Art in New York, had a one-man show at the Hirshhorn Museum and Sculpture Garden, Washington D.C., and was exhibited at the group show *Micromega*, Centre Américain, Paris 1995. Her central interest has always been the study of the 'physicality' of things (*Detail 17*, 1993), and people, which she investigates analytically

through photography (*Sample 4*, 1990; *Crack 2*, 1991) so that '... to see her work is to become a subject of a structured experiment that clearly aims at the fundamentals of the perceptive psychology of us all ...' (Wittig, 142).

BIBLIOGRAPHY
Amy Gerstler, 'Jeanne Dunning–Roy Boyd', *Artforum*, vol. XXIX, 3 (November 1990), 174–5; Rob Wittig, 'Jeanne Dunning at Roy Boyd', *Art in America*, vol. 79, 1 (January 1991), 142–3; Judith Russi Kirshner, 'Jeanne Dunning–Feigen Incorporated', *Artforum*, vol. XXXI, 1 (September 1992); *Vivid–Intense Images by American Photographers*, catalogue, Berlin Raab Galerie 1993, ed. Victoria Espy Burns (Arese, Milan, 1993), 24.
VM

Eakins Thomas
Philadelphia, 1844–1916
After studying at the Pennsylvania Academy of Fine Arts (1861), where he would teach for the rest of his life, he traveled to Spain (1866; Ribera, Velasquez), and France, where he studied with Léon Bonat (1869) and Jean Léon Gérôme at the Ecole des Beaux–Arts. Considering realist painting as a form of scientific documentation, he developed his anatomical studies (*Thomas Eakins*, 77) by sculpting in bronze as well (*Thomas Eakins*, 78), which he made an integral part of his courses at the Academy (1879). Influenced by the experiments of Eadweard Muybridge and Etienne Jules Marey, he began work in photography (1880), especially stroboscopy, which he used not only as preparation for paintings, but considered an independent art form (*Thomas Eakins*, 81). In addition to his portraits and open–air scenes, his exploration in the real also includes an interest in the world of sports (wrestling, swimming, canoeing, boxing) which would be one of the most popular themes in the next generation of American painters (John Sloan, Rockwell Kent, and Edward Hopper).

BIBLIOGRAPHY
Thomas Eakins. Artist of Philadelphia, catalogue, Philadelphia Musem of Art 29 May–1 August 1982, ed. Darrel Sewell (Philadelphia, 1982), 77–8, 81; William Innes Homer, *Thomas Eakins. His Life and Art* (New York, 1992), 241 n. 230.
VM

Enrie Giuseppe *see* Shroud of Turin

Ensor James
Ostend, 1860–1949
From childhood onwards, Ensor was fascinated by the marvelous and the curious, which he derived from his family. He maintained a life-long attachment to the curiosity shop managed by his parents, just as he would never move from his birthplace, although well aware of its provincialism. These interests coincided with an artistic vision, freed from any allegiances to schools or trends (if we think of Bosch, Brueghel, van Ostade, Steen, Callot) in which the taste for the grotesque is accompanied by a corresponding taste for the visionary and the popular. Masks, such as the papier-mâché masks in Ostend at Carnival time, occupy a prominent role in his themes: '... I joyously withdrew to the realm ruled by the mask, made entirely of violence, light and brilliance. The mask is freshness of tones, sharp expression, sumptuous decoration, grand improvised gestures, spontaneous movement, exquisite turbulence ...' (Ensor, quoted in Edebau, 16). The strange gaiety of Ensor's works is, however, an exorcism of panic and death, that, not coincidentally, is often accompanied by skull masks (*Les masques et la mort*, 1897). '... once his masks are evoked and unconsciously revived, the painter maintains his distance: not the distance of imagination, too close to the Id, but an irritated moral judgement. Thus while he revives them, he also repudiates them, and damns the monstrous creatures; while he concedes them the salvation of a desperate gaiety, he ferociously attacks their connotations and opposes them with his own... intelligence and sensitivity ...' (Calvesi, 12). The Venice Biennale XXV dedicated a retrospective to him in 1950.

BIBLIOGRAPHY
Maurizio Calvesi, *Le maschere di Ensor*, in *Ensor. Dipinti disegni incisioni*, catalogue, Rome Campidoglio July–August 1981 (Milan, 1981), 11–4; Frank P. Edebau, *Ensor: l' uomo e il suo ambiente*, in *Ensor. Dipinti disegni incisioni*, catalogue, Rome Campidoglio July–August 1981 (Milan, 1981), 15–27; Xavier Tricot (ed.), *James Ensor. Catalogue raisonné of the paintings* (London, 1992), 2 vols.
LS

Epstein Jacob
New York, 1880–London, 1959
He attended the Art Students League in New York and the Académie Julian in Paris. He moved to London (1905) where he received an important public commission from the British Medical Association in 1907. He sculpted Oscar Wilde's funeral memorial (Paris, 1912–13) and was acquainted with Brancusi, Modigliani and Picasso. After his return to England, his work began to reveal Primitive influences. He joined the Vorticist movement, but refused to publish his work in its journal *Blast*. He was one of the founders of the 'London Group'. *Rock Drill* was inspired by his interest in the machine age (1913–15). He executed twelve preparatory drawings for the sculpture, which depicts a drill mounted on an easel operated by a plaster figure of a man. It symbolized the victorious power of machine–age man, recalling at the same time—the fetus in the rib cage—man's responsibility to future generations. In the second version, executed after the war, the man has changed into an armless bronze figure, victim of the destruction of World War II, where the power of machinery acquires a devastating potential. He later received other public commissions in London, and continued to exhibit, primarily in England. He returned to traditional sculpture, concentrating on Expressionist bust portraits.

BIBLIOGRAPHY
Evelyn Silber, *The Sculpture of Epstein* (Oxford, 1986).
RA

Ernst Max
Brühl, 1891–Paris, 1976
One of the leading figures in the history of the avant-garde, Ernst first became involved in Dada in 1919 during the deep Nihilist crisis he suffered as a consequence of the war. In Cologne, he was first more committed to the political aspects of the movement, but later dedicated himself entirely to art. He began work in collage at that time, which he defined as the 'lucky meeting between two different realities on an inappropriate plane', a technique that he would use throughout his entire career. 'Starting from a repertoire of pre-existing forms, he creates a montage of new images that reveal a completely Dada comic pleasure in his establishment of paradoxical relationships' (*Max Ernst. Retrospective*, 82). In 1920 he began to frequent various

groups in Paris, in which the Surrealists were making their first experiments. 'The adoption of a painting style that prefigures the iconography of Surrealism alienated Max Ernst from the restricted mentality that reigned in Cologne. Among the themes we find allusions to the reading of Freud's *Interpretation of Dreams* (1900) by Freud. His works evoke a situation which emanates strong a-logical evidence similar to what Freud called the manifest content of the dream' (*Max Ernst*, 96).

BIBLIOGRAPHY
Max Ernst. Retrospective, catalogue, Paris Centre Georges Pompidou 28 November 1991–27 January 1992 (Paris, Munich, 1991); Werner Spies, *Max Ernst. Collages. The Invention of the Surrealist Universe* (New York, 1991).
SDS

Fautrier Jean
Paris, 1898–Châtenay–Malabry, 1964
After his father's death he accompanied his mother to London (1908) where he attended the Royal Academy. He soon transferred to the less conventional Slade School, where he developed an interest in the late Turner. He returned to fight in France, and by 1922 he was back in Paris. He exhibited at Zborowsky (Paris 1926) at a dramatic crisis point in his artistic development, when he was painting landscapes marked by a strong realism. It was the moment of an unusual expressionism '... in which form tends to free itself from the limits of design ...' (Bucarelli, 149) which he would later renounce. He encountered André Malraux, who convinced him to illustrate Dante's *Inferno* (1928) and later the work of Eluard and Bataille. Meeting Paulhan, Ponge and Ungaretti, he began his work on matter. The famous series of *Otages* belong to the war years, painted in memory of the prisoners shot at Châtenay–Malabry, a massacre at which Fautrier was present. The *Otages* '... frame his new poetics of the "fragment" in the dramatic situation that the modern world finds itself in ...' (Bucarelli, 150). In 1952 the critic Michel Tapié made the *Informal* movement official with a study dedicated to Fautrier, Dubuffet and Wols. Indifferent to Cubism's spatial qualities and the geometric essentiality of constructivism, Fautrier created a painting in

which matter, design and color, the three canonical terms of traditional painting, are placed in relationship in completely new ways: '... matter is not only a means or a support, but a plastic fragment, the body of the image ...' (Bucarelli, 150). The invasion of Hungary inspired a second important series, the *Têtes de partisans* (1956). He won the Gran Premio of the Venice Biennale xxx (1960) and a year later, the Grand Prize at the Tokyo Biennale.

BIBLIOGRAPHY
Palma Bucarelli, *Jean Fautrier*, in *XXX Esposizione Internazionale d' Arte* (Venice, 1960) 149–55; *Linee della ricerca dall' informale alle nuove strutture*, in *XXXIV Esposizione Biennale Internazionale d' Arte Venezia* (Venice, 1968), n. 34; *Sei stazioni per artenatura–La natura dell' arte*, in *La Biennale di Venezia 1978–Dalla natura all' arte, dall' arte alla natura*, catalogue, Venice Giardini di Castello [Summer 1978] (Venice, 1978), n. 2 (*Torse nu d' ôtage*); Patrick Gilles Persin, 'Jean Fautrier', *L' Oeil*, 410 (September 1989), 64–9; *Jean Fautrier. Gemälde und Zeichnungen*, catalogue, Bremen Kunsthandel Wolfgang Werner 30 October 1992–6 March 1993 (Bremen, 1992).
LS

Filonov Pavel Nikolaevič
Moscow, 1883–Leningrad, 1941
On the advice of Isaak Brodsky (1884–1939), he attended courses at the Academy of Saint Petersburg between 1908 and 1910. Later (1910–1914) he came into contact with the avant-garde group 'Soyuz Nolodeži' (The union of youths) which included, among others, Natalia Goncărova, Kasimir Malevič and Kuz'ma Sergeevič Petrov–Vodkin (*Filonov*, 39). He was very active in various literary and Futuristic circles (1913) because of his acquaintance with Velimir Chlebnikov and Vladimir Mayakovsky (Groys, 157). Starting from a neo-Primitivism inspired by Goncărova's works, Filonov moved on to explore the latest European developments (such as Futurism and Expression) and began to incorporate Surrealist but still original references into his work (*Arte rivoluzionaria*, 39). He devised theoretical policies, summarized as 'analytic painting' (*Canon and law*, 1912, *Declaration of universal flowering*, 1923), and supported the October Revolution, becoming a member of the Idealogy Section in the Institute of Artistic Culture

(1923). In the changing political climate of the Thirties, he devoted himself to teaching, and continued to work, even if he was not allowed to exhibit. His work is now in the Russian Museum of State in Saint Petersburg.

BIBLIOGRAPHY
Arte rivoluzionaria dai musei sovietici 1910–1930, catalogue, Lugano Villa Favorita Fondazione Thyssen–Bornemisza 12 June–2 October 1988 (Milan, 1988), 39; *Filonov*, catalogue, Paris Centre Georges Pompidou 15 February–30 April 1990 (Paris, 1990); Boris Groys, 'Filonov's Organic Machines', *Art in America*, vol. 80, 11 (November 1992), 96–101, 157.
VM

Fischl Eric
New York, 1948
He lived in Phoenix, San Francisco, and later studied at the California Institute of the Arts in Valencia (1972). In Chicago, where he worked at the Museum of Contemporary Art, he developed an interest in early twentieth-century European art (Paikowsky 1983). He worked with his former professor, Allen Hacklin, teaching painting at the Nova Scotia College of Art and Design in Halifax, Canada (1974–78). He later moved to New York. He participated in the Venice Biennale (1984) in a group show at the United States Pavilion. After his early California abstract work, he began to work in a realistic vein, seen in his first one-man show at the Dalhousie Art Gallery (Halifax 1975), which is indebted to various painters such as Edgar Degas, Robert Henry, Rockwell Kent and Edward Hopper. He portrays subjects from everyday life covering the banal themes of middle-class American life, analyzed at various times of day, and almost always observed through the eyes of an adolescent: '... I would say that the focus of my work lies in the sensation of embarrassment and self-consciousness that everyone feels in the profoundly emotional events in all our lives ...' (Fischl, quoted in Paikowsky 1983).

BIBLIOGRAPHY
Eric Fischl–Paintings, catalogue, Montréal Québec Sir George Williams Art Galleries Concordia University 16 March–9 April 1993, ed. Sandra Paikowsky (n.p., 1983); *Eric Fischl–Paintings*, catalogue, Saskatoon Saskatchewan Canada Mendel Art Gallery 8 February–17 March 1985, ed. Bruce W. Ferguson (Saskatoon, 1985); Holland

Cotter, 'Postmodern Tourist', *Art in America*, vol. 79, 4, April 1991, 154–157; 183.
VM

Flanagan Barry
Pestatin, 1941
Very early, during his years at the St. Martin School of Art, Flanagan reacted to the inheritance of 'classical' sculptors like Moore and Caro, who was his teacher. He became interested in Pataphysics and contributed poetry to a journal he founded with some friends. He later became involved in the concerns of Arte Povera, and created assemblages and installations that use materials like canvas, sand and rope. In the Seventies he moved to Italy where he returned to more traditional materials like stone and bronze, still remaining, however, controversial in his subject matter. His hares, for example, immortalized in plastic poses, are parodies of figurative representation of the heroic statue, indicators of the impossibility, as he says, to take contemporary art sculpture seriously. His art rejects theories: 'moral positions are human remedies for human ailments, while Flanagan's art is fed by the amoral energy of nature. What he wants to bring to the public is energy, and not a theoretical or moral position' (Biggs in *Barry Flanagan*, 68).

BIBLIOGRAPHY
Barry Flanagan. A Visual Invitation, catalogue, Belgrade Museum of Contemporary ARt 1 October–5 November 1987 (Belgrade, 1987); *La Biennale di Venezia. Settore Arti Visive. Catalogo generale* (Venice, 1982), 116-9.
SDS

Fontana Lucio
Rosario di Santa Fe, 1899–Comabbio, Varese, 1968
The child of Italian parents, his earliest works were executed in his father's sculpture studio. He grew up largely in Milan (1905–22), and finally moved there permanently (1928) where he attended Adolfo Wildt's courses at the Brera Accademia. After graduation (1930) he had his first one-man show at the Milan gallery Il Milione, and came into contact with the Lombard abstract group. He joined the 'Abstraction–Création' movement (1934), and took part in the Prima mostra collettiva di Arte Astratta italiana (1935) in the Casorati–Paulucci studio of Turin. He

returned to Argentina during the war (1940–47) where he worked out his *Manifesto Blanco*. On his return to Milan he played a role in the birth of Spatialism. From 1951 onward, he confronted the problem of space with his *Concetti spaziali*, in which he penetrated and punctured the supporting surface with slashes and holes. He took part in many Biennales, including those of 1958, 1961 (his large paintings featuring Venice), 1966 and 1968.

BIBLIOGRAPHY
Lucio Fontana, *Concetti spaziali*, ed. Paolo Fossati (Turin, 1970); Enrico Crispolti (ed.), *Fontana. Catalogo generale* (Milan, 1986), 2 vol.; *Lucio Fontana*, catalogue, Vienna Hochschule für Angewandte Kunst 12 August–26 September 1992 (Vienna, 1992).
MC

Fotografia spiritica (Spiritualist Photography)
In the nineteenth century the popularity of para–normal phenomena began to merge with concepts based on Eastern religious mysticism. In the wake of these interests, Spiritualist photography began to spread as the interpretation of mediumistic and meta–psychic phenomena. A number of fairly controversial characters were involved in spiritualist photography, such as Edouard Isidore Buguet (born 1840), a medium–photographer sentenced for fraud in Paris (1875). In France there were also Thiébault and Saint–Edme, active around 1860, who devised advertising and spiritualist photo–montages whose images evoke phantasmagorical optics, while G. Simoni (1912) and Ada Emma Deane (1920–25) were spiritualist photographers. There was also a *Société d' études des phénomènes psychiques* which was active in Paris, and G. Delanne and C. Richet in Nancy studied the apparitions of the villa Carmen, home of a spiritualist. The United States echoed this interest (Littleton Views Company Publishers, *The Haunted Lovers*). The end of the nineteenth century saw a real repertoire of tricks and techniques, established for creating images of the 'invisible' spiritualist photography, which led to a theoretical interest between scientists and artists. In Italy, Enrico Morselli (1853–1929, a neuropsychiatrist associate of Lombroso's), worked in spiritualist photography and

took part in sittings with the medium Eusapia Paladino (1901–07), which served the basis for a later publication. The physician Dr. Enrico Imoda (d. 1911), along with the medium Linda Gazzeri, suggested '... capturing, with instantaneous magnesium flash photography, the ephemeral fleeting stereosis of faces and hands ...' (Imoda, 22). Recent research suggests that this type of photography influenced the birth of Futurism (Ragghianti, 214). In Imoda's photographs of spirits, Lista distinguished details which confirm the spiritualist nature of apparitions re-occuring in Futurist works (*Futurismo*, 112): '... Clearly in this case the collusion between painting and para–scientific research, by means of fraud and gullibility, led their own discourse to cross the borders of a mythical territory which is instead the specific task of art... In the name of usurped empiricist positivism, an artificial simulation of scientific method therefore acquired full authority as aesthetic research, initiating ... the break with the naturalist contents of the image'.

BIBLIOGRAPHY
William Crookes, *Researches in the Phenomena of Spiritualism* (London, 1874); Alexandre Aksakof, *Animisme et spiritisme. Essai d' un examen critique des phénomènes médiumniques spécialement en rapport avec les hypothèses de la force nerveuse, de l' allucination et de l' inconscient comme réponse à l' ouvrage du Dr. Ed. von Hartmann intitulé ' Le spiritisme'* (Paris, 1895); G. de Fontenay, *A propos d' Eusapia Paladino, les séances de Montfort l' Amaury, 25–28 juillet 1897* (Paris, 1898); Enrico Imoda, *Fotografie di fantasmi* (Turin, 1912); Giovanni Lista, *Futurismo e Fotografia* (Milan, 1979); Carlo Ludovico Ragghianti, 'Fotodinamica e fotospiritica', *Critica d' Arte*, 172–4 (July–December 1980), 213–5.
MBG

Fox Judy
Elizabeth, 1957
After attending Yale University (1978), she studied sculpture at the Ecole Superieure des Beaux-Arts (1979) and later at the Institute of Fine Arts at New York University (1983). She later taught at Middlebury College (New York 1989), at the School of Visual Arts in New York, and at the Artist Studio at Amherst College (1994). In 1985 she exhibited

in the group show *Young Masters of the East Village* (Limbo Gallery, New York 1985) and at *The East Village Art Collection* (The Palladium, New York 1985). After various one-man shows in the United States (New Haven 1977, New York 1987) she made her debut in Europe with *Jaguar Knight, Malanggan, Shiva Dancing, The Virgin Mary, Saint Theresa, Mohammed* (Christine König Galerie, Vienna 1994) and with *Judy Fox-Inez van Lamsweerde* (Kunstwerke, Berlin 1995). Although traditionally modeled (often in terra cotta or ceramic), her sculptures, generally of life-sized children (*Virgin Mary*, 1993; *Saint Theresa*, 1993), defy any hint of the academic and use symbols of mythological archetypes from different cultures: '... taken from the art history repertoire, according to their own ethnic identity. For example, *Saint Theresa* is a two-or three-year-old Latin-American baby portrayed like a Baroque saint ...' (Taplin 1994, 117).

BIBLIOGRAPHY
Margaret Moorman, 'The Age of Women', *Art News*, vol. 89, 2, February 1990, 161-163; Ken Johnson, 'Judy Fox at Carlo Lamagna', *Art in America*, vol. 78, 5, May 1990, 239-240; Rainer Metzger, 'Judy Fox, Christine Köning Galerie, Wien', *Kunstforum*, vol. 130, May 1995; Robert Taplin, 'Judy Fox at P.P.O.W.', *Art in America*, vol. 82, 5, pp. 117-8.
VM

Freud Lucian
Berlin, 1922
Moving to Great Britain in 1933, he studied in London at the Central School of Arts and Crafts (1938), and later at Goldsmith's College (1943). After the war he worked in Paris and Greece, and taught at the Slade School of Fine Arts in London (1954). From his earliest one-man show at the Lefévre Gallery (London, 1944), he has stood as one of the most important references in the world of English art. His first wife was the daughter of the sculptor Jacob Epstein, his friends have included artists such as the painters Graham Sutherland and Francis Bacon, and while his influences include contemporaries such as Picasso, Tanguy and Grosz, he also looks back to Dürer, Rembrandt and Ingres (*Lucian Freud*, 10–4). He represented Great Britain, with Ben Nicholson and Francis Bacon, at the Venice Biennale XXVII (1954). The creator of a precise form of realism in

which the artist distances himself '... emotionally from the subject so that it too can speak ...' his work attempts to achieve his objective of 'touching the senses by an intensification of reality ...' (Freud, quoted in *Lucian Freud. Dipinti*, 23).

BIBLIOGRAPHY
Lucian Freud. Dipinti e opere su carta 1940–1991, catalogue, Rome Palazzo Ruspoli 3 October–17 November 1991, ed. Bruno Mantura (Milan, 1991), 23; *Lucian Freud*, catalogue, Sidney Art Gallery of New South Wales 31 October 1992–10 January 1993, eds. Emanuel Capon, Henry Meyric Hughes and William Feaver (Sidney, 1992), 10–4.
VM

Gallina Pietro
Turin, 1937
The central theme of his work within the Pop art movement is the human figure, reduced to a two-dimensional silhouette etched into wood or stainless steel (*Ombra di ragazza seduta, Bambino, Sculture multiple*). The *Monovisore*, dating from 1968, is a machine conceived to focus the spectator's attention on slices of reality which are usually ignored. In 1970 he turned his interest to landscape work, with his *Nevigrafie*, prints made first in fresh snow and then into fiberglass. In later years he explored the links between nature and artifice. He currently lives in Turin, where he works in advertising.

BIBLIOGRAPHY
P. Thea, *La collezione d'arte contemporanea della Galleria Comunale di Cagliari. Gli artisti e le opere*, ed. A. Negri (Cagliari, 1983), 124–6; *Il Novecento. Catalogo delle opere esposte*, Galleria Civica d'Arte Moderna e Contemporanea di Torino, eds. R. Maggio Serra and R. Passoni (Turin, 1993).
VC

Garanger Marc
Normandy, 1935
He developed an interest in photography during his studies at the Ecole d'Instituteurs at Evreux (1951). He worked as a professional photographer at the Institut Pédagogique at Lyons (1958) where he met Roger Vailland. His most formative period was the time in Algeria doing his military service (1960–62) when he defined his *Femmes Algériennes* project (1960): '... their faces, beyond all

frontiers, [marked by] the same passions, the same laughter, but also the evidence of hard work, the violence of destiny, rebellion and the everyday ...' (1960). He later did reportage on his extensive travel throughout the world (Ivory Coast, the Tyrol, Turkey, and China). He has also created several compact disk videos, such as *Regard sur la planète*, 1988, *Louisiane*, 1989, and *Death Valley, Las Vegas e le Grand Canyon*, 1989.

BIBLIOGRAPHY
Marc Garanger, *Femmes Algériennes 1960* (Barcelona, 1982); Marc Garanger, *Femmes des Hauts Plateaux-Algérie 1960*, text by Leïla Sebbar (n.p., 1990).
VM

Garbari Tullio
Pergine Valsugana, Trento, 1892–Paris, 1931
After attending the Scuola Reale Superiore Elisabettiana in Trento (1906–08), he moved to Venice where he studied at the Accademia di Belle Arti, and became acquainted with the painters of Ca' Pesaro. His exhibitions (1910 and 1913) reveal affinities with the work of Felice Casorati, Gino Rossi and Martini, and display a gradual assimilation of the post-Impressionist influences of Trento–based painters, as well as the Sezessionists. He lived in Milan from 1915–1919, and became friends with Carrà, with whom he exhibited at the Galleria Chini in 1917. Among the works exhibited, his *Intellettuali al caffè* has much in common with *La musa e il poeta* by Rousseau (Basle, Kunstmuseum) in the emerging portrait of Baudelaire, and illustrates Garbari's personal ironic comments on the contemporary cultural elite. He abandoned painting almost entirely until 1927, to devote himself to poetry and literature, an interest since the 1910s. He worked for the Florentine review *La Voce*, was involved in the 'Questione Tridentina' and was associated with Giovanni Papini, Benedetto Croce, Carlo Belli and Gino Severini. He exhibited in Milan, Hamburg, Amsterdam, at the Aja with other artists from the 'Novecento' group, as well as at the Venice Biennale XVI (1928), the first Rome Quadriennale and the galleria Il Milione of Milan (1930). His last paintings move towards a refined Primitivism, in an insightful reintrepetation of the Catholic figurative tradition, expressed in extremely spiritual works. In 1931 he went to Paris where

he exhibited for the last time at the Galerie de la Renaissance with the '1940' group.

BIBLIOGRAPHY
Garbari. Trentino d'Europa, catalogue, Trento Palazzo delle Albere 14 April–10 June 1984 (Trento, 1984).
RA

Gatian de Clérambault Gaëtan
Bourges, 1872–Paris, 1934
Descended from a family whose ancestors include Descartes and Alfred de Vigny, he took a degree in medicine (1899) and became chief physician (1905) of the Special Hospital of the Paris Police, where he began to study psychic phenomena (mental automatism, passional psychosis) which he later described in his essays (*Gaëtan Gatian de Clérambault. Automatismo*, 21). Injured in World War I, he spent the years just before and after in Morocco, where he photographed the drapery of Arab costume (Tisseron). From 1923 to 1926 he taught a popular course on drapery at the Ecole des Beaux-Arts of Paris (*Gaëtan Gatian de Clérambault. Automatismo*, 11), based on material collected in Africa. Two years later (1928) he began to experience trouble with his vision, and committed suicide in 1934 after a failed cataract operation.

BIBLIOGRAPHY
Serge Tisseron (ed.) *Gaëtan Gatian de Clérambault-Psychiatre et photographe* (Paris, 1990); *Gaëtan Gatian de Clérambault. Automatismo mentale-Psicosi passionali*, ed. Paola Francesconi (Capodarco di Fermo, 1994), 11, 21.
VM

Gaudier-Brzeska Henri
Saint Jean-de-Braye, 1891–Neuville-Saint-Vaast, 1915
Henri Gaudier, known in art circles as Gaudier-Brzeska after his marriage to the Polish artist Sophie Brzeska (1911), completed his studies in Orléans, after work in Bristol and Munich, before taking up sculpture (1910). In London (1913) he met the American poet Ezra Pound and the painter Wyndham Lewis, with whom he worked in the Vorticist movement. He was actively involved in the French avant-garde, with a particular interest in Cubism. He was killed at the front at the beginning of World War I. His friendship with Ezra Pound, who was to become his first

authoritative critic (1916) was the inspiration for several works, such as the *Tête hiératique* (1914). As attested by the inscription carved on the back (1974), the copy exhibited here is the only known authorized version (*Henri Gaudier-Brzeska*, 115 n. 39). Soon after Pound's death, his companion Olga Rudge commissioned Isamu Noguchi, an American sculptor of Japanese origin, to create a circular base for its use as his funeral memorial in the Venetian cemetery of San Michele. As it proved unsuitable for the purpose, the piece was first temporarily, then permanently, left to the Fondazione Giorgio Cini in Venice.

BIBLIOGRAPHY
Ezra Pound, *Gaudier-Brzeska. A Memoir by Ezra Pound* (London, 1916), fig. XXI, 160 n. 9; *Henri Gaudier-Brzeska*, catalogue, Orléans Musée des Beaux-Arts, June–September 1993 (Orléans, 1993), 115 n. 39.
VM

Gauguin Paul
Paris, 1848–Atuana, 1903
Gauguin's sense of escapism and his love of exotic coloristic effects was instilled in him by a childhood spent in Lima and his family circumstances. Pisarro encouraged him to paint and pressed him to buy Impressionist works. His originality emerged in the scenic harmony displayed in the nineteen canvases he exhibited in the eighth Impressionist show. His visits to Pont-Aven (1885 and 1888), when he became friends with Van Gogh, and a trip to Martinique (1887) in which he discovered the symbolic value of colour, led him to the final definition of a style of his own, which successfully merges Cloisonnism and Symbolism. In 1891 he set sail for Tahiti, only to return ill and penniless two years later. He was back in Tahiti, however, in 1895. His last works, uniting the vivid coloristic treatment of the tropical landscape with the symbolism of Tahitian pagan rites, achieve a refined and eclectic exoticism whose origin seems to lie in expressive Primitivism and a taste for Japanese art, as well as the influence of Cézanne and Degas. The *Autoportrait* (1903) is the last work attributed to Gauguin. Here the artist appears for the first time wearing glasses and '... the simplicity of the pose, the austerity of the clothing and the hair, his gaze toned down by the glasses that make him

look like an old sage... evoke the self–portraits of an old Chardin or Bonnard ...' (Cachin, 30). He was the subject of a retrospective at the Venice Biennale XVI in 1929.

BIBLIOGRAPHY
Kuno Mittelstädt, *Die Selbst-bildnisse Paul Gauguins* (Vienna–Munich, 1968); Françoise Cachin, *Gauguin vu par lui–même et quelques autres*, in *Gauguin*, catalogue, Paris Grand Palais 10 January–24 April 1989, eds. Françoise Cachin, Isabelle Cahn, Charles F. Stuckley (Paris, 1989), 19–33.
LS

Genzel Johan Karl (Karl Brendel) *see* **Prinzhorn-Sammlung**

Gerstl Richard
Vienna, 1883–1908
Gerstl's work, which consists of around eighty paintings executed between 1904 and 1908, the year of his suicide, was never exhibited during his lifetime. The lack of informa-tion regarding his life, due to his ruthless elimination of any biographical traces prior to his suicide, makes it difficult to reconstruct the profile of an artist whose painting is a fusion of Expressionism and post–Impressionism. In 1898 Gerstl enrolled in the Academy of the Fine Arts under the direction of Christian Griepenk-erl. He studied with the Hungarian painter Simon Holosy, and he met the painter Heinrich Lefler, who, after having seen his Die Schwest-ern (*The sisters*) accepted him into his studio. However, Gerstl's philosophical, literary and linguistic studies (espe-cially Italian and Spanish) are much more revealing than his paintings. It was especially his interest in music that led to his friendship with Arnold Schönberg and Alexander Zemlinsky. The Schönberg family involved him in a complicated network of personal relationships. He and Schönberg were very close, so close that it seems that Gerstl actually guided Schönberg's first attempts in painting. His own painting moves from the Impressionism of Corinth and Liebermann to the work of Munch, Van Gogh, and Klimt, to forge a very personal style of his own. The self–portraits are a fundamental part of his production: '[he] engaged in a continual conversation with the large mirrors conspicuous-ly placed throughout his studio...[he] represented his nudity with such frankness his works were impossible to exhibit at the time... [he] scrutinized every detail of his face, making the progressive descent into despair and madness ...' (Kallir, 462).

BIBLIOGRAPHY
Jane Kallir, *Arnold Schönberg et Richard Gerstl*, in *Vienne 1880–1938-L' apocalypse joyeuse*, catalogue, Paris Centre Georges Pompidou 1986, ed. Jean Clair (Paris, 1986), 454–69; *Richard Gerstl 1883–1908*, catalogue, Vienna Kunstforum der Bank Austria 21 September–28 November 1993, ed. Klaus Albrecht Schröder (Vienna, 1993).
LS

von Geyer Otto
1843–1914
A German artist, he was a professor at the Königlichen Technischen Hochschule of Berlin. He attempted to establish a canon of propor-tions of the human body, by combining classical canons with anthropological data.

BIBLIOGRAPHY
Der mensch, hand und Lehrbuch der Masse, Knochen und Muskeln des men-schlichen Körpers für Künstler, Architekten, Kunst-Kunstge-werbe, Handwerker, schulen und zum Selbstunterricht (1902).
PC

Giacometti Alberto
Stampa, 1901–Coire, 1966
He grew up in Switzerland, traveled in Italy, from which he returned full of lofty enthusi-asm for Tintoretto, Giotto, and Cimabue, and arrived in Paris in 1922. In his early years in Paris he was attracted to African art and later worked in an increasingly Surrealist vein. In 1935 he defined his primary themes, which were soon accompanied by a special technique—*pastillage*—'which is almost a continual move-ment of particles of matter along the invisible currents that intertwine in empty space' (Bucarelli in *La Biennale di Venezia*, 1962, 108). At that time he began to produce classical elongated figures which were to become his trademark. In 1955 two important retrospectives (the Guggenheim in New York and the Arts Council in London) recognized his extraordinary contribution. He took part the next year in the Venice Biennale, with his famous series *Femme de Venise*, which he worked on throughout early 1956: 'they can be considered the compendium of all that he had learned about those particular forms' (Lord, 305–6). 'Photography, the cinema, x-rays, the discovery of Expressionist, African and oceanic art have led to the spreading of the conviction there is no longer anything left to be done for reality . People have surendered to abstraction' (Jean Clay in *Alberto Giacometti* 1995, 228).

BIBLIOGRAPHY
La Biennale di Venezia, (Venice, 1956); *La Biennale di Venezia*, (Venice, 1962); James Lord, *Giacometti. Una biografia* (Turin, 1988); *Alberto Gia-cometti. Sculture. Dipinti. Disegni*, catalogue, Milan Palazzo Reale 26 January–2 April 1995 (Florence, 1995).
SDS

Gie Robert *see* **Art Brut**

Gimpel Léon
Paris, 1878–1948
A French photographer, he worked as a reporter for the journal 'L'illustration' (1904). Along with the Lumière brothers, the inventors of the autochrome plate, he was the first to use this procedure for photographic reportage. He experimented with different possibilities of color cliché, without abandoning black and white which was better adapted to the photography of events. In 1908 he joined the Société française de photogra-phie and tried to improve autochrome in the field of instantaneous and reproduc-tion photography. In 1911 he carried out the first tests of anaglyph on autochrome. He produced autochromes revealing his artistic interest linked to contemporary painting and experimentation with neon light.

BIBLIOGRAPHY
Nathalie Boulouch, ad vocem *Léon Gimpel*, in *Dictionnaire mondial de la Photographie, des origines à nos jours* (Paris, 1994), 262.
NB

Givaudan G.
French photographer.

Godin Paul
1857
French doctor and anthropolo-gist who studied the change in the proportions of the body during growth. He wrote for the *Revue d'Anthropologie*.

BIBLIOGRAPHY
Recherches anthropométriques sur la croissance des diverses parties du corps (Paris, 1903); *Les proportions du corps pendant la croissance* (1910).
PC

Goldworthy Andy
Chesire, 1956
He attended Bradford Art College in Yorkshire in 1974–75, and the Preston Polytech-nic in Lancashire. In 1979 he won the North West Arts Prize, and moved to Bentham in Yorkshire. His work consists of atmospheric landscapes involving the use of found objects. He exhibited in 1981 at the Serpentine Gallery in London. In 1986 he took part in the St. Louis Arts Festival in the United States, and in 1988 he showed at the Takagi gallery in Nagoya, Japan and the Venice Biennale. In 1991 he exhibited his *Sand Leaves*, and in 1994 his show at the Setaga Museum of Fine Arts in Tokyo coincided with the publication of *Stone*, describ-ing his work executed between 1990 and 1993 in Great Britain, France, the United States, Australia and Japan.

BIBLIOGRAPHY
Stone (Harmondsworth, 1994).
VC

Goodwin Betty
Montréal, 1923
Self-taught, she began to draw when still only a child gifted with a natural talent. In the Fifties, with the arrival of the *New York School* in Canada, she decided to opt for figurative art and spent much time in museums painting still-lifes, landscapes and figure studies (*Centric 46*). She took part in her first group show in 1955 at the Musée des Beaux-Arts in Montréal (*Spring Exhibition*). She studied with Yves Gaucher at Concordia University of Montréal and, in the wake of Pop Art and Joseph Beuys, exhibited a series of etchings with objects from everyday life: *Gloves, Vest, Shirt* and *Hat* (1969–72). After an experimental phase she worked on the *Swimmers* series (1982), followed by *Red Sea* (1984), *Carbon* (1986), *Steel Notes* (1988) and *Figure/ Animal Series* (1990-91). The work *La mémoire du corps-XVII* (1991–92) is part of a cycle with which Goodwin, using the image of a psycho-logical treatment tub seen in a *reportage* on the life of Vincent van Gogh, reflects on the theme of the body, his experiences and 'his secret convulsions and traumas' (Louppe 1994).

BIBLIOGRAPHY
Betty Goodwin–Oeuvres de 1971 à 1987, catalogue, Montréal Musée des Beaux-Arts, 11 February–27 March 1988, ed. Yolande Racine (Montréal, 1987); *Centric 46: Betty Goodwin*, catalogue, Long Beach California State University 1992, ed. Diana D. du Pont (n. p., 1992); Laurence Loupe, 'Betty Goodwin', *Art Press*, n. 189, March 1994.
VM

Gromaire Marcel
Novelles-sur-Sambre, 1892–Paris, 1971
He abandoned his law studies to devote himself to painting, and he exhibited at the Salon de Indépendents (1911). During the war he met Villon, Léger, and Bonnard, and took up drawing. In 1919 he began to work as a film critic for the review *Le Crapouillot*. His *Art moderne* and *Notes sur l'art d'aujourd'hui* set forth his convictions on the permanence of art, easel painting as the most evolved form, the quest to render the era accessible to all, and the rejection of any form tainted with the academ-ic or avant-garde. In 1924 his reflections led to *La Guerre* (1925), the product of the trauma experienced during the war which culminated in his rediscovery of Catholicism. Here the painting assumes new meaning, and is no longer an assemblage of colors but an interior experience of the living universe. A representa-tive of French-Flemish Expressionism, his treatments of rural and working-class themes reveal the study of the French Romanesque art and the influence of Cézanne and Seurat.

BIBLIOGRAPHY
Catalogo della XXV Biennale di Venezia (Venice, 1950), 304 n. 101; *Marcel Gromaire 1892–1971*, catalogue, Paris Musée d'Art Moderne de la Ville de Paris 12 June–28 September 1980 (Paris, 1980).
RA

Grosso Giacomo
Cambiano, Turin, 1860–Turin, 1938
'He studied at the Accademia Albertina until 1884, and from 1889 he was professor of drawing. He exhibited eight paintings in Turin in 1884, one of which attracted particular attention and admiration, *La cella delle pazze*. He sent *L'inverno a Torino* to Venice in 1887. One of the most attractive paintings in the

Milan Mostra (1894) was his *Ritratto d' una Signora* in gray. [On exhibition were also] n. 129 *Il Supremo Convegno* sala D and n. 130 *La Femme sala C'* (*Prima esposizione*, 96). His *Testa di adolescente* is a study for the figure on the left of his *Supremo Convegno*, which won the Premio del Pubblico (550 votes) in the first Venice Biennale (1895), in spite of official protests by the Cardinal of Venice, Giuseppe Sarto (the future Pope Pius x) and Queen Marguerite of Savoy, who felt that the subject was indelicate. It was later destroyed in a fire in Chicago. Grosso, who became the director of Turin's Academia Albertina, saw his success confirmed both as a portraitist (*Ritratto di Cesare Lombroso*) and a landscape artist, and also worked extensively in photography. He was named a Senator of the Kingdom of Italy.

BIBLIOGRAPHY
Prima esposizione internazionale d' arte della città di Venezia–1895. Catalogo illustrato (Venice, 1895), 96; *Giacomo Grosso–Il pittore a Torino tra Ottocento e Novecento*, catalogue, Turin 1990, ed. G.L. Marini (with bibliography) (Turin, 1990).
VM

Gruber Francis
Nancy, 1912–Paris, 1948
The family moved to Paris in 1916, where he suffered from severe asthma and was unable to attend school. He took up painting with his father's support and the encouragement of Braque and Bissière. He studied at the Académie Scandinave (1929–32) with Dufresne, Friesz and Waroquier. He became a friend of Giacometti and Tailleux. His complex artistic training links the expressionist features of French Realism with surreal humour and a deep understanding of Flemish and German tradition. His early works were extremely visionary and figurative, and he would later work predominantly from the model in his studio, or observe cityscapes from his windows. He taught at the Académie Ranson (1942–43), and in 1947 he won the Prix National. Exhibited at the Salon d'Automne, the painting *Job* (1944) symbolized the misery of the oppressed who, like the artist, have experienced great suffering. It evokes the atmosphere of the Fourteenth arrondissement in Paris where Gruber lived.

BIBLIOGRAPHY
Ronald Alley, *Catalogue of the*

Tate Gallery's Collection of Modern Art (London, 1981), 343–4.

Guidi Virgilio
Rome, 1891–Venice, 1984
A student at the Accademia di Belle Arti in Rome, he studied Cézanne and Matisse, and was actively involved in the Caffè Aragno set, where he met Longhi, De Chirico, Bacchelli, Cardarelli and Ungaretti. He began to explore light and space, themes around which his æsthetics would later revolve. In 1920 he began to participate in the Venice Biennale, where *In tram*, exhibited in 1924, was a public and critical success. From 1927 to 1935, the year he moved to Bologna, he held the Chair in painting at the Accademia di Belle Arti in Venice. He returned to Venice in 1944, where he worked on the chromatic studies that anticipated the Corrente movement. Between 1947 and 1950 he conducted a reassessment of Mondrian in the *Marine astratte* made with pure planes of color. The Venice Biennales of 1954 and 1964 dedicated one-man shows to him.

BIBLIOGRAPHY
Virgilio Guidi, catalogue, Milan, ed. M. Rosci (Milan, 1991); T. Toniato, *Virgilio Guidi* (Venice, 1991); *XIV Esposizione Internazionale d' Arte della città di Venezia*, (Venice, 1924), 44.
LS

Guston Philip
Montreal, 1913–Woodstock, 1980
He moved with his family from Canada to Los Angeles where he met Jackson Pollock, with whom he attended the Manual Arts High School (1928). At the same time he began to study Italian painters of the Renaissance, especially Piero della Francesca (1930) and the *murales* of José Clemente Orozco (1932). He worked for the government *W.P.A.–Federal Art Project* (1935) where he was in contact with Willem de Kooning, Arshile Gorky, Stuart Davis and Jackson Pollock. In 1941 he taught at Iowa State University where he had his first one-man show (1944). He first attracted international notice in the early Fifties with the 'Action Painting' movement, but he always managed to find new inspiration, moving easily from the figurative to the abstract. In 1960 he took part in the Venice Biennale XXX. From 1973 to 1978 he was a professor at Boston

University.

BIBLIOGRAPHY
Philip Guston, catalogue, San Francisco Museum of Modern Art 16 May–29 June 1980, with an essay by Ross Feld (San Francisco, 1980); Paul Brach, 'An Act of Salvation', *Art in America*, 1 (January 1989), 130–5; Musa Mayer, *Night study: a memoir of Philip Guston* (London, 1991); *Philip Guston in the Collection of the Museum of Modern Art*, catalogue, New York Museum of Modern Art [Summer 1992], ed. Harriet Bee and Robert Storr (New York, 1992).
VM

Gutfreund Otto
Dvur Krácové, 1889–Prague, 1927
He studied at the School of Applied Arts in Prague (1906–09) with Josef Drahonovsky and with Bourdelle in Paris (1909–10). In 1911 he joined the Prague Cubist group of figurative artists (SVU). Between 1914 and 1920 he spent much time in France. Gutfreund is '... the first European sculptor, with the exception of Picasso, who transported the principle of analytical Cubism into three–dimensional forms ...' (Šmejkal, 487). The Expressionist deformations of some of his early sculptures transgress the classical canons of beauty, symmetry and harmony, becoming the expression of interior psychological states. In his comments on theory Gutfreund claims that '... the figure becomes the center that connects surrounding space with itself... the statue is no longer frozen, trasformed into space, but the expression of a flowing event, a continuous motion, with the same rhythm as the creative process, before the thought is fixed in an image ...' (Šmejkal, 488).

BIBLIOGRAPHY
Kupka, Gutfreund & C. nella Galleria Nazionale di Praga, catalogue, Venice Ca' Pesaro, Venice Biennale (Venice, 1980); František Šmejkal, *Otto Gutfreund*, in *Futurismo e futurismi*, catalogue, Venice Palazzo Grassi 3 May–12 October 1986, ed. Pontus Hulten (Milan, 1986), 487–8; *Otto Gutfreund 1889–1927: Plastiken und Zeichnungen*, catalogue, Berlin Otto–Nagel–Haus 21 January–16 April 1987, ed. Jiri Kotalik (Berlin, 1987).
LS

Guttmann Martin see Clegg & Guttmann

Guttuso Renato
Bagheria, 1912–Rome, 1987
He studied with Pippo Rizzo, a leading figure in the Futurist group from Palermo, and later moved to Rome in 1933 where he was associated with the Via Cavour artists, including Mafai, Cagli and Melli. Between 1935 and 1936 he lived in Milan where he became part of the 'Corrente' group (including Birolli, Fontana, Manzù, and Treccani). He moved to Rome permanently in 1937 and shared a studio with Colacicchi and Scialoja. His painting became a moral and civic statement, seen in his treatment of working-class and social themes. He traveled frequently in France where he met Picasso. He was one of the founders of the 'Fronte Nuovo delle Arti' (1947), with whom he exhibited at the Venice Biennale XXIV. This was followed by many other shows, evidence of his critical success. Based on a slightly different smaller-scale study, his painting *Caffè Greco* (1976) inspired Jörg Immendorf in his *Café Deutschland* series (1978). It evokes the atmosphere of the historic bar frequented by Rome's artists and intellectuals. The subjects portrayed are all contemporary —De Chirico in particular stands out, last of the century's great painters—except for Buffalo Bill, the only link with the past.

BIBLIOGRAPHY
Guttuso. Opere dal 1931 al 1981, catalogue, Venice Palazzo Grassi 4 April–20 June 1982 (Florence, 1982); *Renato Guttuso. Catalogo Ragionato Generale dei dipinti*, ed. Enrico Crispolti (Milan, 1985).
RA

Haas Michel
Paris, 1934
He initially studied philosophy, but soon dedicated himself exclusively to painting. His artistic training was particularly influenced by his long stays in Italy (Rome, Florence and Venice). In 1961 he became close friends with Bran van Velde, while van Velde was in Paris. His first exhibition was in Paris in 1975, which was soon followed by one in Geneva, where van Velde had moved. 'What interests me is the human being, his flesh, his life. And I like to take what I see. I like those visions that you have on the street, in the metro, in a café. And this is what I try to say, because this is what moves me' (Haas in *Opus International*, 32). It is the little daily encounters between people that interest him: meetings, separations,

reconciliations. Thus 'in his work Michel Haas does not tell a story. Only scenes, scattered moments, fragments of life of those human bodies whose only existence lies in their own physicality' (*Opus International*), 33).

BIBLIOGRAPHY
Michel Haas. Paintings and monotypes 1984-1989, catalogue, New York Jan Krugier Gallery–31 March 1990 (New York, 1990); Manuel Jover, 'Michel Haas', *Beaux Arts Magazine*, 101, May 1992, 88–90; Henri-François Debailleux, 'Michel Haas', *Opus International*, 97, Spring 1985, 32–33.
SDS

Hatoum Mona
Beirut, 1952
After receiving her degree from the Beirut University College (1972) she moved to London (1975) where she studied at the Byam Shaw School of Art (1979) and later at the Slade School of Art (1981). In the Eighties she taught at the Central Saint Martin College of Art and Design in London (1986–92) and the Jan van Eyck Akademie of Maastricht in Holland (1992–94). In her works (performance, video, video installations) she is concerned with the limitations of the human body ('... establishing paradoxical relationships between the private and the public, the personal and the social, the intimate and the political ...', van Assche in *Mona Hatoum*, 10). *Corps etranger* (1994) is a cylindrical audio-visual installation equipped with a sound track, which records and films the sounds emitted by the internal and external functioning of Hatoum's organs (van Assche, 13).

BIBLIOGRAPHY
Christine van Assche, *Vidéo et après–La collection vidéo du Musée National d' Art Moderne* (Paris, 1992), 150–2; Christine van Assche, *Introduction*, in *Mona Hatoum*, catalogue, Paris Centre Georges Pompidou 1994, with texts by Jacinto Lageira, Desa Philippi, Nadia Tazi and Christine van Assche (Paris, 1994), 10, 13.
VM

Hausmann Raoul
Vienna, 1886–Limoges, 1971
He studied painting and sculpture in Berlin (1900) where he showed inclinations towards Expressionism and Futurism. He worked for the reviews *Der Sturm* and *Die Aktion*, (1912) and with the

'Expressionistische Arbeitsge-meinschaft' in Dresden. During the war he explored the possibilities of photomontage with Hanna Höch. In 1919 he founded the review *Der Dada*, and became one of the leading figures in the Dada movement in Berlin. He became friends with Kurt Schwitters, and they experimented on sound poems and typography with Otto Freundlich, Hans Arp and Laszlo Moholy–Nagy. In 1922 he abandoned painting for photography and writing. He lived in Ibiza (1926–36) and worked on the novella *Hyle*, and later moved to Zurich, Prague, and Paris. After the war he continued to work as a painter, photographer, and writer, concentrating on the historical interpretation of the Dadaist movement in Berlin.

BIBLIOGRAPHY
Michael Erloff, *Raoul Hausmann: Dadasoph* (Hanover, 1982); *'Degenerate Art'. The Fate of the Avant–Garde in Nazi Germany*, catalogue, Los Angeles, Los Angeles County Museum of Art 17 February–8 September 1991 (Los Angeles, 1991), 248–9.
RA

Heine Maurice
Paris, 1884–Vernouillet, 1940
Heine was an active participant in the revolutionary developments taking place in the Surrealist group in the Paris of the late Twenties. Also politically active (he was one of the founders of 'Contre-attaque') he focused on the evolution of the Surrealist conception of love. He was responsible, from the Twenties to the Thirties, for the rediscovery of Sade, and wrote prefaces to his works as well as a distinguished study.

BIBLIOGRAPHY
I Surrealisti, catalogue, Milan Palazzo Reale 7 June–September 1989 (Milan, 1989).
SDS

Hélion Jean
Couterne, 1904–Paris, 1987
He attended the Institut Industriel du Nord in Lille (1920), and in 1921 he began to paint and work as an architectural designer. He was one of the founders of the journal 'L'acte' where he met Joaquín Torres-García. In 1928 he exhibited at the Salon des Indépendants. His painting began to lose its figurative qualities in 1929, when he met Arp, Pevsner and Mondrian. With Van Doesburg he founded the review *Art Concret* and the

group 'Abstraction-Création'. He traveled in Europe and the Soviet Union, and on his return to Paris met Ernst, Tristan Tzara and Duchamp. He exhibited in Paris (1932) and New York (1933) and was an associate of Miró, Lipchitz and Nicholson. He moved to the United States in 1936. In Paris he met Tanguy, Paul Eluard and Matta. In 1938 he returned to the figurative, and concentrated on the direct observation of reality, representing simple objects such as hats and umbrellas (*Charles*, 1939). In 1943 he recounted his war experiences in the book *They Should Not Have Me*. In 1946 he returned to Paris where he took up urban themes, exploring images taken from everyday life and his artistic experience (*A rebours*, 1947).

BIBLIOGRAPHY
Hélion. Peintures et dessins 1929–1979, catalogue, Saint-Etienne Musée d'Art et d'Industrie, September–October 1979 (Saint–Etienne, 1979); *Omaggio a Hélion. Opere recenti*, catalogue, Venice Collezione Peggy Guggenheim Spring 1986, ed. Fred Litch (Milan, 1986).
RA

Hill Carl Fredrik
Lund, 1849–1911
In January 1878 Hill left the world of reality behind forever as his illness, schizophrenia, took possession of his mind. Thus two distinct characters can be distinguished in Hill: first, the painter of in the French tradition of Courbet, Corot, and Pissarro, and later, the madman who was given 'a paintbrush and a box of chalk to keep him quiet in his dark room in Lund' (Kenneth Clark in *The Price of Genius*). Hill was in Paris during the time of the Impressionist *salons* (his work was accepted in 1873 and 1875), where he remained until the outbreak of his illness, when he had to return to his hometown. In his pre-illness production the most relevant element is his extremely conscious and controlled style. In the second half of his life, instead, 'he had no artistic problems—the concept had actually ceased to exist for him. He had reached the end of the road, and had no choice but to express the sentiment of total solitude, disillusion and despair that was annihilating him' (Nils Lindhagen in *Carl Fredrik Hill*, 147).

BIBLIOGRAPHY
The Price of Genius, catalogue, Pittsburg University Art Gallery

20 September–26 October 1974, ed. Carl Nordenfalk (Pittsburg, 1974); *Carl Fredrik Hill*, catalogue, Malmö Konsthall 10 April–7 June 1976 (Malmö, 1976).
SDS

Hill Gary
Santa Monica, 1951
In 1969 he was active in the Art Student's League in Woodstock in New York, a student of Bruce Dorfman. In 1973 he began to experiment in video tape, working for Woodstock Community Video (1974–76). In his early videos, *The Fall* and *Air Raid*, he used a sound image for ecological themes. With his installations *Hole in the Wall* (1974) he defied the Woodstock Artist Association, which did not consider the video a legitimate art form. He studied the potential of electronics at the Experimental Television Center in Binghampton, New York (1975–77). In the late Seventies the close relationship between image, sound, word and language began to emerge. He moved to Japan in 1984–85 where he produced *URA ARU (The Backside Exists)*. He included the mise-en-scene in the video *Why Do Things Get in a Muddle (Come on Petunia)*; in 1985 he edited a video program at the Cornish College of Art in Seattle; and in 1988 he was inspired by the writings of Maurice Blanchot (*Incidence of Catastrophe*). After an important exhibition at the Stedeljk Museum of Amsterdam (*Beacon*, 1990) he has dedicated himself almost exclusively to installations.

BIBLIOGRAPHY
Gary Hill, catalogue, Paris Musée National d'Art Moderne Centre Georges Pompidou 25 November 1992–24 January 1993 (Paris, 1992); *Gary Hill*, catalogue, Seattle Henry Art Gallery 1994.
RA

Hockney David
Bradford, 1937
After studying at the Bradford School of Art (1957), he transferred to the Royal College of Art in London, where he was a student with R. B. Kitaj, (1959), met Andy Warhol, and was active in the lively atmosphere of early Pop Art in London (1962). His first one-man show was the result of meeting the gallery owner John Kasmin (*David Hockney: Pictures with People in*, London 1963). In 1966 he moved to the United States, and has taught in several

American universities (UCLA, Berkeley). Deeply influenced by Picasso, as well as Francis Bacon, Larry Rivers and the sculptor William Turnbull, his paintings feature a profoundly stylized realism which brought him to international attention. At the same time he began to use photography and other techniques in his work (such as lithography and acqua-forte). In the Seventies he lived in London (1970) and Paris (1975), and had important one-man shows in major European and American cities. In 1975 he began to work in opera, starting with the *Rake's Progress* by Igor Stravinsky. He has designed sets and costumes for Mozart's *The Magic Flute* (1978), Erik Satie's *Parade* (1980), Wagner's *Tristan et Iseult* (1987) and Puccini's *Turandot* (1992).

BIBLIOGRAPHY
Marco Livingstone, *David Hockney* (Milan, 1988); *David Hockney. A Retrospective*, catalogue Los Angeles, Los Angeles County Museum of Art 4 February–24 April 1988, ed. Maurice Tuchman and Stephanie Barron, with comments by R.B. Kitaj and Henry Geldzahler (Los Angeles, 1988), 18; Antony Peattie, 'Hockney's Living Color', *Design Quarterly*, 156 (Summer 1992), 21–7.
VM

Hodler Ferdinand
Berne, 1853–Geneva, 1918
He was a student of Barthélemy Menn at the Ecole des Beaux-Arts in Geneva (1872–77), where his own personality began to emerge in his landscapes, portraits and large-scale compositions. He lived in Madrid from 1878 to 1879. The landscape was his most congenial subject, which he developed through 'parallelism', a new composition principle that uses repeated forms to give structural and decorative unity. He exhibited in Paris, Munich, Geneva, and the Venice Biennale (1899). He depicted Swiss heroes and history in his larger works. Two of his series were dedicated to death: his first in 1909 depicted Augustine Dupin, the mother of his son, and the second his companion Valentine Godé-Darel (1914–15). The scars inflicted by the deaths of his parents and brothers in early childhood are apparent in his depiction of the illness of Valentine Godé-Darel. In this expression of the tragic end of the vital forces of human nature, the clenched hands and the half-closed mouth testify to the suffering

of the beloved Valentine in her progressive and inexorable descent into death.

BIBLIOGRAPHY
Ein Maler vor Liebe und Tod. Ferdinand Hodler und Valentine Godé–Darel. Ein Werkziklus 1980–1915, catalogue, Zurich Kunsthaus 9 april–23 May 1976, ed. Jura Brüschweiler (Zurich, 1976); *Ferdinand Hodler*, catalogue, Locarno Casa Rusca 22 March–10 May 1892, ed. Bernhard von Waldkich (Locarno, 1992).
RA

Hoerle Heinrich
Cologne 1895–1936
In the years before the First World War, Hoerle was active in the cultural and artistic life of Cologne, and sported a fiercely satirical style which he usually brought to bear against Prussian military ambition. After his experience at the Front, his relationship with the war was dramatically intensified. Two lithographs appeared in 1920 (*Die Krüppelmappe*) dominated by images of soldiers who return maimed and disfigured from the front line, 'Crippled soldiers who had to to beg along the streets for survival, the emotional problems of young crippled veterans who had to re-adapt to everyday life and the psychological stress they suffered' (*The Dada Period in Cologne*, 28). The man who is physically transformed by the violence of society would become a metaphor also used to represent another of Hoerle's dominating themes, that of the *man-machine*, a human being which the technology of his workplace has transformed into a sort of robot who often has piston prostheses. Hoerle worked for many years in the quest for a true proletariat culture, merging his own socialist ideals with a figurative constructivism. His interest in Dada should be viewed from this point of view. In a show in 1919 Hoerle exhibited in the Dada Section, exploring its underlying idea, that the Sunday painter be brought into the pantheon of Art.

BIBLIOGRAPHY
Dirk Backes, *Heinrich Hoerle: Leben und Werk* (Cologne, 1981); *The Dada Period in Cologne*, catalogue, Toronto Art Gallery of Ontario, 10 September–6 November 1988 (Toronto, 1988).
SDS

Hopper Edward
Nyack, 1882–New York, 1967
He first worked as an illustrator in advertising. He later moved to New York (1906) where he attended the courses of Robert Henry, a painter who was a member of the well–known group 'The Eight'. Among his influences are John Sloan and especially Thomas Eakins whom he felt was '... greater than Manet ...' (O'Doherty, 70). After a trip to Europe (Paris and London) he moved to New York (1912) where he would live for the rest of his life. In 1913 he took part in the *Armory Show*, the exhibition which marked the first organic confrontation between American painting and the Old World avant–garde. His first one–man show at the Whitney Studio Club (New York, 1920) was followed by many others over the next several decades. He was invited to represent the United States at the Venice Biennale XXVI (1952). Known as a landscape painter, Hopper explored the theme of isolated figures, both male and female, throughout his entire artistic career, lost in their own thoughts '... as if they were a projection of his own intro-spective nature ...' (*Edward Hopper*, 42).

BIBLIOGRAPHY
Brian O'Doherty, 'Portrait: Edward Hopper', *Art in America*, 52 (December 1964), 70; *Edward Hopper–The Art and the Artist*, catalogue, New York Whitney Museum of American Arts 16 September 1980–25 January 1981, ed. Gail Levin (New York, 1980), 42; José Alvarez Lopera, *Modern Masters–Thyssen–Bornemisza Museum* (Madrid, 1992), 446, fig. p. 447.
VM

Houghton Miss *see* **Fotografia spiritica**

von Huene Stephan
Los Angeles, 1932
He attended the University of California in Los Angeles (1952–53), where he also studied painting and drawing at the Chouinard Art Institute (1955–59). In 1961 he took part in his first group show at the Pasadena Art Museum. He exhibited at the Venice Biennale XXXVII (1976) was professor at the Hochschule der Künste in Berlin (1979) and later also taught at the University of Hamburg (1986). After initial interest in *Abstract Expressionism* he took up sculpture, experimenting with various media to record the relationships between art and sound, influenced by Marcel Duchamp, Kurt Schwitters and the composition theories of John Cage. Never linked to a single genre, he draws freely from Meister Eckhart, Dürer, Goya, Blake and Daumier, but also uses Mozart (*Zauberflöte*, 1985) to reach his goal which 'is to unite word, sound, movement, to evoke a balance between the emotional and spiritual physical' (Metken, 1990).

BIBLIOGRAPHY
Stephan von Huene: Klang-skulpturen, catalogue, Baden Baden Staatliche Kunsthalle 10 July–4 September 1983, ed. Katharina Schmidt (n.p., 1983); *Stephan von Huene–Lexichaos*, catalogue, Hamburg Hamburger Kunsthalle, 8 June–8 July 1990 (Hamburg, 1990); Günter Metken, *On the production sounds through speech*, in *Stephan von Huene–Lyd Skulpturer, Sound Sculptures, Klang Skulpturen*, catalogue, Humlebaek Denmark Louisiana Museum of Modern Art 24 November 1990–13 January 1991 (Hamburg, 1990).
VM

Iba-Zizen M.T. *see* **Cabanis Emmanuel A.**

Immendorff Jörg
Bleckede, 1945
A German Neo–Expressionist, he had his first one–man show in 1961 at the New Orleans Club in Bonn. In 1964 he began to attend the courses given by Joseph Beuys at the Kunstakademie of Düsseldorf, which profoundly influenced his artistic training (Adams, 93). Between 1968 and 1970 he began to emerge in various works marked by heavy social and political content, loosely grouped together by the slogan LIDL (a '*nonsense*' word, referring to the world of infancy). His participation in the Venice Biennale XXXVII witnessed his confrontation with the realism of Renato Guttuso (Szeemann, 33) whose painting *Caffé Greco* (1976) inspired his own *Deutschland Café* (1978). In 1984 he opened the Café La Poloma in Hamburg, which soon became an important exhibition space for many artists. He lives and works in Düsseldorf.

BIBLIOGRAPHY
La Biennale di Venezia 1976–Ambiente, partecipazione, strutture culturali (Venice, 1976), vol. II, 332; Harald Szeemann, *The Long March or Incitements of the Times. A Compilation* in *Jörg Immendorf: Café Deutschland and Related Works*, catalogue, Oxford Museum of Modern Art 7 October–2 December 1984 (Oxford, 1984), 9–33; *Jörg Immendorf*, catalogue, Cologne Gallery Michael Werner 16 November–22 December 1990, ed. Rudolf Schmitz (Cologne, 1990); Brooks Adams, 'Anarchy and Innocence', *Art in America*, vol. 80, pt. II, 2 (February 1992), 92–7.
VM

Imoda Enrico *see* **Fotografia spiritica**

Ionin Nikolaj Aleksandrovič
Navolek, 1890–Saint Peters-burg 1948
He worked in Saint Petersburg as a graphic artist, painter and set-designer. He was a student of D.N.I. Kardovsky (1915–17), and studied at the Academy of the Fine Arts (1921–22), and the Institute of Painting, Sculpture and Architecture at the Russian Academy of Art with K. Petrov-Vodkia (1934–36).

Jacquin–Chatellier J.
French doctor who was a student of Claude Sigaud, one of the founders of typology in France. He studied morpholog-ical types and their influence on illness.

BIBLIOGRAPHY
Considérations morphologi-ques sur quelques faits sociaux (1923); *Morphologie des cancéreux* (1928); *L'homme, les hommes* (1932).
PC

von Jawlensky Alexei
Torsok, 1864–Wiesbaden, 1941
Jawlensky's artistic training was profoundly influenced by religious concerns which he absorbed from his family's strict observance of Christian-Orthodox tradition. He abandoned his military career for art (1896) and enrolled in Anton Azbé's school in Munich. Here he met Kandin-sky and was influenced by A. Zorn and L. Corinth. With Kandinsky and others he founded the *Neue Künstlerv-ereinigung* (1909). His interest in the human face intensifed in the years just before the war ('It had become necessary for me to find a form for the face since I understood that great art had to be painted only from religious emotion'. (Jawlensky, quoted in 1989, 86). It developed into a series of human definitions that sprang from the Coptic tradition of Fayyum and the icons of the Russian Orthodox church (*Head of Youth or Heracles*, 1912). He emigrated to Switzerland, where he studied Eastern philosophy and theology, and became acquainted with the theories of Blavatsky. In 1917 he began to paint a series that triggered that spiritualization of the face (*Mystic heads*, and *Faces of the Redeemer*) which would gradually evolve towards increasingly idealized forms. Forced by illness to reduce the face to a miniature, he began to execute small panels (*Meditations*) which resemble abstract icons (G. Leinz in *Jawlensky*, 1989).

BIBLIOGRAPHY
Alexei Jawlensky, catalogue, Locarno Pinacoteca Comunale, 3 Septmber–19 November 1989, ed. Rudy Chiappini (Milan, 1989); *Alexei Jawlen-sky. Catalogue raisonné of the Oil Paintings Volume One 1890-1914*, ed. M. Jawlensky, L. Pieroni-Jawlensky and A. Jawlensky (London, 1991); *Alexei Jawlensky, Il volto e il colore, aforismi, lettere, memorie*, ed. Maria Passaro (Milan, 1995); *Jawlensky*, catalogue, Milan Palazzo Reale 8 Aprile–4 June 1995, ed. Rudy Chiappini (Milan, 1995).
MBG

Job Enrico
Naples 1934
He studied at the Brera Accademia in Milan, and joined the Neo-Realist movement in the Fifties. He competed for the Premio Suzzara with his *La domestica a ore* (1950), and had his first one-man show at the La Colonna gallery in Milan in 1958. He began to move towards Informalism influ-enced by the Surreal. In 1960 he worked solely as a set- and stage- designer, and worked with Ronconi, Strehler and Zeffirelli. By 1968 he had moved to Rome, and returned to art, this time focusing on the happening. He had an exhibition in 1970 at the Naviglio gallery in Milan, which consisted of a heap of mannequins piled on a sun-baked patch of dry mud. He showed his *Autoritratto* (*Self-Portrait*) in 1971 in Modena (Galleria della Sala di Cultura) and Ferrara (palazzo dei Diamanti), which consisted of a wax cast melted by air projectors during the exhibi-tion. In 1972 he presented his *Metamorphosis* (Venice, Il Canale Gallery) in which men made of bread were offered to the birds and the public. In 1973 he took part in the International Kunstmesse in Basle. The next year he presented *Il mappacorpo* to the Diagramma in Milan, a photographic map of his body divided in numbered squares. In 1976 he went to New York with *Quando tutto sarà finito* (by Lucio Amelio) and *Until* (Fine Art Building). The same year he also participated in the Venice Biennale. Since 1983 he has worked exclusive-ly in stage design.

BIBLIOGRAPHY
Gillo Dorfles, *Enrico Job*, catalogue, Milan Galleria del Naviglio (Milan, 1970); Achille Bonito Oliva, *Autoritratto*, catalogue, Modena Galleria della Sala di Cultura and Ferrara Palazzo dei Diamanti (Modena, 1971); L. Vergine, *Il corpo come linguaggio* (Milan, 1974).
VC

Josephson Ernst
Stockholm, 1851–1906
Josephson settled in Paris at the end of the 1870s and experienced a series of bitter disappointments after numerous rejections of his work at the Impressionist *salons*. His work was too intensely focused on uniting the work of the great masters of the past with the modern manner, in an era which looked so intently to the future. His production of this period included bourgeois interiors in the style of Courbet or Renoir, painting *en plein air* of an Impressionist stamp, and portraits, for which he had a real gift. In 1888 he was struck by schizophrenia. The rest of his life was spent in a cycle between madness and mental hospitals. His painting, however, was not completely changed by his illness. There was simply an heightened emphasis on popular Nordic myth and folklore which had been present from the beginning. His interest in his Jewish heritage also intensified, with Old Testament echoes (and a focus on Creation, with particular reference to Michelangelo). 'The important fact is that his condition seemed to have offered him an extraordinarily prolific period, no longer blocked by the events that had absorbed him in the past. As Hartlaub wrote, his fall left intact [...] the "most intimate level of his being"' (Newton in *The Price of Genius*).

BIBLIOGRAPHY
The Price of Genius, catalogue, Pittsburg University Art Gallery 20 September–26 October

1974, ed. Carl Nordenfalk (Pittsburg, 1974).
SDS

Kandinskij Vassilij
Moscow, 1866–Neuilly–sur–Seine, 1944
He began to paint after his university studies in Moscow where he specialized in ethnology and sociology. He left Moscow for Munich (1896) where he attended Anton Azbé's school with Javlensky, and took courses taught by Von Stuck at the Academy. The years in Munich were years of exploration in which his studies in Van Gogh and Cézanne gradually culminated in the elimination of the object and the renunciation of naturalistic outline. Around 1912 he met Marc and Macke, wrote *The spiritual in art* (1912), founded *The blue knight* and painted his first abstract watercolour. On his return to Moscow, he was an active participant in the artistic developments connected with the October Revolution, although his plans for the Institute of Artistic Culture were rejected. Kandinsky returned to Germany where he taught at the Bauhaus school (1922). He published *Point, line, surface* in Dessau, 1926, which analyzes the formal components of the act of painting in an attempt to find instruments to investigate the hidden structure of painting. He moved to Paris permanently in 1933. It was this last period, when his interest in scientific theories re–emerged, which led him to insert abstract painterly motifs into his repertoire derived from the bimorphic and biological world (*Succession*, 1935).

BIBLIOGRAPHY
Vassilij Kandinskij, *Tutti gli scritti*, ed. Philippe Sers (Milan, 1980³); Hans K. Roethel and Jean K. Benjamin, *Kandinsky. Catalogue Raisonné of the Oil–Paintings*, 3 vols. (London, 1982–84); Vivian Endicott Barnett, *Kandinsky Watercolours*, 2 vols. (London, 1992); Jelena Hahal Koch, *Kandinsky* (New York, 1993).

Katharina *see* Art Brut

Kelley Mike
Wayne, 1954
An artist who is both transgressive yet moral and philosophical, Kelley was born as a *performer* on the West Coast in the Seventies. Kelly's work is situated within the world of conceptual art, but understood broadly (when, in the Seventies, this term included Acconci's body art, Laurie Anderson's music and William Wegman's narrative). Kelley himself draws on all kinds of influences (film, music, literature, psychology, politics). 'This wide spectrum of interest produces the effect of 'ruining' Conceptualism, taking it beyond its dry theories into open space' (Sussman 1993, 16). In this sense Kelley is strenuously opposed to Minimalism and its ascetic cleanliness: 'I like caricatures. I like destructive things' (*Art in America*, 165). The goals of his destructive art are certain established American myths, such as the sexism which he still sees prevailing in art (without falling into feminism), or religion. In 1987 corporeal abstractions began to appear in his art, such as rag-dolls, as well as excrement and parts of the body, in a kaleidoscope of the pathetic, amusing and sexual.

BIBLIOGRAPHY
Holland Cotter, 'Eight Artists Interviewed', *Art in America*, May 1987, 164–165, 197; *Mike Kelley*, catalogue, Basle Kunsthalle 5 Aprile–24 May 1992, ed. Thomas Kelein (Basle, 1992); *Mike Kelley. Catholic tastes*, catalogue, New York Whitney Museum of Modern Art 5 November 1993–20 February 1994, ed. Elizabeth Sussman (New York, 1993).
SDS

Kertész André
Budapest, 1894–New York
Kertész did not take up photography professionally until he was thirty, which makes his extraordinary dedication in portraying his Budapest—the city, the people, the street life and the surrounding landscape—all the more remarkable. Later, during the First World War he documented his fellow soldiers and life at the front. In 1925 he moved to Paris. Here, he became a model of modern reportage because of his work sold to many European newspapers and magazines (*Berliner Illustrierte Zeitung, Münchner Illustrierte Presse, Sunday Times*) and influenced younger generation of artists such as Brassaï, Henri Cartier-Bresson, and Robert Capa. Yet he also was deeply involved in the exciting experimental work that was taking place within the avant-garde in Paris of the Twenties and Thirties. Influenced by Surrealism, Kertész worked on a series of photographs entitled *Distor-*tions (1933), in which the image of the female body is dramatically disturbed using distorting mirrors. In 1936 he went to the United States with a year-long contract at a cinematographic studio. He was to remain there for the rest of his life, choosing not to return to the old world because of the political climate fostered by the pre-war situation in Europe. He worked for fashion magazines until 1962 when he dedicated himself exclusively to his own work. 'The composition of his photographs, revealing that fragments can be as revealing as the representation of an entire scene in portraying the mood and passions of the metropolis, display a clear break with the past' (*Photography*, 14).

BIBLIOGRAPHY
Photography: a Facet of Modernism. Photographs from the San Francisco Museum of Modern Art, catalogue, San Francisco Museum of Modern Art, eds. Van Deren Coke, Diana C. du Pont (New York, 1986); *André Kertész. La biographie d' une œuvre*, ed. Pierre Borhan, catalogue, *André Kertész. Le double d' une vie* Paris Pavillon des Arts 25 October 1994–29 January 1995 (Paris, 1994).
SDS

Kitaj R.B.
Cleveland, 1932
American by birth, Kitaj actually possesses a richly literary European artistic background. After years of travel in his youth (he first set off in a freighter, then joined the Marines) Kitaj made a name for himself in Great Britain. Friends with David Hockney since the early Sixties, he also associated with Francis Bacon, Auerbach, and Kossof, a group he named the London School, and had his first one-man show at the Marlborough Fine Arts Gallery. He is an artist who defies classification—he is a kind of eccentric conceptualist (his paintings are accompanied by long explanatory texts) who is, however, animated by a strong emotional component. On the other hand, while affirming the need for political commitment in the work of art, Kitaj has never been ideological. Kitaj 'is a sort of romantic traveler of the mind who, while he crosses the lands of the modern, struggles to maintain and record in a comprehensible fashion his personal experiences in this broken-down century' (Johnson, 79). But even more importantly, the unifying element in all his work is man: 'Kitaj's commitment to the portrait is an emphasis of the dignity and integrity of the individual' (Johnson, 85).

BIBLIOGRAPHY
Ken Johnson, 'R.B. Kitaj: Views of a Fractured Century', *Art in America*, March 1995, 78–85; *R.B. Kitaj*, catalogue, London Marlborough Fine Arts 8 June–20 August 1994 (London, 1994).
MLS

Klein Yves
Nice, 1928–Paris, 1962
Born into a family of painters, he was attracted by the Eastern world, which he studied in the Nice School for Eastern Languages. In 1949 he began experiments in the field of colour, culminating in his *Monochromes*. These were panels covered by a uniform layer of pure colour, which he exhibited at his first one–man show held at the Galerie des Solitaires (Paris, 1955). A refined, innovative artist, open to many different influences and trends, he was invited to chair two conferences held at the Sorbonne, on the *Evolution de l' art et de l' architecture vers l' immatériel* (1959). In the next year, he joined 'Nouveau Réalisme' and presented (9 March 1960) his *Atropométrie*, 'the ashes of my art' (J & J, *Yves Klein 1928–1962*, 56), impressions on paper of nude models smeared with colour. In 1962 he further evolved this technique in the *peintures feux-couleurs*, where the colours are worked by the heat of a flame.

BIBLIOGRAPHY
J & J, *Yves Klein 1928–1962. Selected Writings* (Wisbech, 1974); Pierre Restany, *Yves Klein* (Munich, 1982); *Yves Klein*, catalogue, Cologne Museum Ludwig and Düsseldorf Kunstsammlung Nordrhein–Westfalen, 8 November 1994–8 January 1995, ed. Sidra Stirch (Cologne, 1994).
VM

Klimt Gustav
Vienna, 1862–1918
He studied at the Kunstgewerbeschule (1876–83) and later worked with his brother Ernst and Franz Matsch in public building decoration. In 1890–91 the first traces of Art Nouveau begin to appear in some panels and portraits, which were to develop in his search for expressivity in the pathos and gestural quality of the body. In 1897 he was among the founders of the Viennese Sezession, and the review *Ver Sacrum*. He painted his controversial panels for the university, the *Beethoven Frieze*, which was presented at the XIV show of portraits and Sezession art. In 1905 he collaborated with the architect Hoffmann. He founded the Österreichisches Künstlerbund, and became its president in 1906. He met Schiele and traveled in Italy, London, Paris and Brussels. In 1910 he took part in the Venice Biennale. His work reveals influences of Slavic folk art color and Oriental decorative elements. The major features of his work are refined Symbolist taste, a mastery of color and detail, and the erotic *sfumato* of his drawing. The *Three ages of woman* (1905) plays on the stylistic contrast of the portrayal of the young woman with the child, and the naturalist drawing of the old woman. This play assumes symbolic qualities in the revelation of the infinite possibilities in the metamorphosis of youth, contrasted with the inexorable unambiguity of age which cannot escape reality. In the first phase—the dream—he uses decorative design, while in the second—the impossible dream—he returns to realistic drawing.

BIBLIOGRAPHY
IX Esposizione Internazionale d' Arte della Città di Venezia 1910. Catalogo (Venice, 1910), 58–60; *XXIX Esposizione Biennale Internazionale d' Arte* (Venice, 1958), 201–4; *Le Arti a Vienna. Dalla Secessione alla caduta dell' impero asburgico*, catalogue, Venice Palazzo Grassi 20 May–16 September 1984 (Venice–Milan, 1984), 101–4; Eva di Stefano, *Il complesso di Salomè. La donna, l' amore e la morte nella pittura di Klimt* (Palermo, 1985), 114.
RA

Kogler Peter
Innsbruck, 1959
He first exhibited at a group show at the Galerie Nächst St. Stephan (*Situationen*, 1979) and later had his first one-man show at the Galerie Krinzinger in Innsbruck (1983). In the Eighties he took part in the Venice Biennale XLII (*Aperto 1986*) and worked for the Edition Artelier in Graz, the publishing company founded by Petra and Ralph Schilcher specializing in silk-screen of young artists, experimenting with new print techniques using aluminium and polyester as well (Ripley 1991, 94). His most recent work has led him into installation video (*Ohne Titel*, 1994). In 1992 he

exhibited at Documenta IX and in 1993 at the Venice Biennale XLV (*La coesistenza dell' arte*). He lives and works in Vienna.

BIBLIOGRAPHY
Robert Fleck, 'Jeunes artists autrichiens du néo-actionnisme à la nouvelle abstraction', *Art Press*, 157, April 1991, 24–29; Deborah Ripley, 'Snob Appeal–Edition Artelier, Graz', in *Artscribe*, 86, March-April 1991, 94–95.
VM

Kokoschka Oskar
Pöchlarn, 1886–Villeneuve, 1980
He studied at the School for Applied Arts in Vienna (1905–09) and worked for the Cabaret Fledermaus and created new Art Nouveau decorative objects for the Wiener Werkstätte. Under the influence of the architect Adolf Loos he abandoned the decorative arts and executed a series of portraits which were outstanding in their use of color and powerful form. He contributed articles and drawings to the Berlin review *Der Sturm*. He returned to Vienna (1911–12) where he became an assistant in the School of Applied Arts. In 1913 he traveled to Italy with Alma Mahler, who was the subject of many portraits (*Mahler mit Puppe*, 1922). He enlisted at the outbreak of World War I and was seriously wounded. He drew and painted during his convalescence in the military hospital of Dresden. He met Käthe Richter, Fritz Neuberger, Walter Hasenclever and Ivan von Lücken whom he portrayed in the testimony to their close friendship *Die Freunde* (1917–18). In 1919 he taught at the Academy in Dresden; he took part in many exhibitions in Europe (such as the Venice Biennales 1922, 1932, and 1948). He began to travel throughout Europe and North Africa in 1924. The political climate in Germany forced him to move to Prague (1933) and he later emigrated to London. In 1937 the authorities confiscated 417 of his works exhibited in public museums, some of which were shown at the exhibition Degenerate Art. Kokoschka reacted with the painting *Bildnis eines Entarteten Künstlers* (1937). In 1943 he became president of the 'Free German League of Culture' and in 1947 he was granted English citizenship. Major retrospectives have been dedicated to him in Munich, Vienna, the United States and Venice (1948, sixty paintings). He founded the 'Schule des Sehens' (School of sight) in Salzburg (1953–62). In 1962 he moved to Villeneuve where he continued painting and exhibiting.

BIBLIOGRAPHY
Oskar Kokoschka 1886–1980, catalogue, Rome Palazzo Venezia, November 1981–February 1982 (Venice, 1982); *Oskar Kokoschka 1886–1980*, catalogue, New York Solomon R. Guggenheim Museum (New York, 1986).
RA

Kollmann Julius
1834–1918
German doctor and anthropologist who was a professor of anatomy at the University of Basle. He worked on the creation of an atlas of morphology.

BIBLIOGRAPHY
Beiträge zu einer Kraniologie der Europäischen Völker (Brauneohweig, 1881); *Plastiche Anatomie des Menschlichen Körpers für Künstler und Freunde der Kunst* (Leipzig, 1910).
PC

de Kooning Willem
Rotterdam, 1904
'Pioneer of what is now known as the movement of Abstract Expressionism' (Zilczer, 11), he emigrated illegally to New York (1926), where he would live for the rest of his life, after he attended the Rotterdam Academy from 1917–1921. He met the artists Stuart Davis, Arshille Gorky and David Smith (1934), and worked with them in the American Expressionism *W.P.A.– Federal Art Project*, in which he collaborated with Fernand Léger (1936). At the same time, he was active in the meetings of the 'American Abstract Artists'. In 1948 he was invited by Joseph Albers to teach at Black Mountain College. Since 1950, when he was associated with the 'Irascible Eighteen', he has been one of the leading figures in the contemporary art world. *Woman I* (1950–52), exhibited at the United States Pavilion at the Venice Biennale XXVII became the starting point of a reflection on women, developed over the years in different series of paintings with the same title, establishing an unusual innovative way of representing the human figure. As de Kooning himself declared: '[*Woman I*] does one thing for me: it eliminates composition, arrangements, relationships, light—all those stupid discourses on line,

colour and form ...' (*Museum*, 191).

BIBLIOGRAPHY
Andrew Carnduff Ritchie, *Willem de Kooning*, in *XXXVII Esposizione biennale internazionale d' arte* (Venice, 1954), 396 n. 69; *The Museum of Modern Art, New York. The History and the Collection*, catalogue, intro. Sam Hunter (New York, 1984), 191, fig. 275; Judith Zilczer, *De Kooning and Urban Expressionism*, in *Willem de Kooning from the Hirschhorn Museum Collection*, catalogue, Washington D.C. Smithsonian Istitution 23 October 1993–9 January 1994, ed. Judith Zilczer (Washington, 1993), 11.
VM

Kossof Léon
London, 1926
Although he has been exhibiting since 1957, Kossof only arrived at world recognition in the Eighties. Of Jewish background, born in London, the memory of his childhood, finanche the topography of London of those years, remains a primary source for his painting. David Bomberg, his teacher at the Borough Polytechnic, was a great influence: 'Bomberg was an indipendent man who took his risks: his teaching wasn't important in terms of technique, but rather in terms of the way to put myself in relation with the world as a painter' (Kossof, quoted in Fuller, 88). His Expressionism has in equal measure elements of objectivity and subjectivity. The world that emerges from his painting is permeated by a widespread sense of sadness, a sentiment however compensated for by the energy and positive qualities that emanate from the act of painting, vital, liberating, and therefore indirectly from his sign. 'Kossof–like Roualt, Soutine, and other Expressionists of the past–offers, with his painting, "another reality" inside that of the existing one. He suggests a sense of fusion with the world that is usually absent in the adult world. He creates a kind of "redemption through form", a hedonistic and aesthetic reparation. Perhaps this is the best that we can hope for'. (Fuller, 89).

BIBLIOGRAPHY
British Painting '74, catalogue, London Art Council of Great Britain 26 September–17 November 1974 (London, 1974); Peter Fuller, *The British Show*, Art Gallery of New South Wales (Sidney, 1985).
SDS

Kramlich David
see Burson Nancy

Kupka Františ ek
Opč no, 1871–Puteaux, 1957
As an adolescent he became interested in spiritualism and religious painting. He attended the Academy of Prague, where he was influenced by abstract Symbolism and folklore. During his studies at the Academy in Vienna (1892) he joined a theosophical society, and also studied Oriental religions and natural sciences. He made his living as a medium. In 1896 he moved to Paris where his paintings revealed the Symbolist thought he had absorbed in Vienna, in which the influence of Odilon Redon and Ensor blends with the philosophy of Nietzsche, Schopenhauer and the occult theories of Madame Blavatsky (*Isis Unveiled*, 1877). '... Man is a little world—a microcosm in the immensity of the universe. As a fetus, he is suspended by his three spirits in the matrix of the macrocosm ...' . Between 1910 and 1912 he began to invent a language aimed at the creation of forms without any link to the visible world, based on abstract geometry. His research developed from his knowledge of Futurism and Neo-Impressionism, the study of movement, and his interest in biological research, leading to his final rejection of figurative representation.

BIBLIOGRAPHY
Frantisek Kupka 1871–1957. A Retrospective, catalogue, New York The Solomon R. Guggenheim Museum, (New York, 1975); *Františ ek Kupka 1871–1957 ou l' invention d' une abstraction*, catalogue, Paris Musée d'Art Moderne de la Ville de Paris 22 November 1989–25 February 1990, (Paris, 1989), 77, n. 11.
MBG

Kustodiev Boris Michajlovič
Astrakan,1878–Saint Petersburg, 1927
He studied at Saint Petersburg with Ilya Ephimovič Repin (1844–1930) and abroad, in France, Spain, and later in Italy (1913). On his return to Russia he worked in stage design (Ostrovsky, Zamyatin) both in Saint Petersburg and Moscow (1920). Chagall's influence is felt in his works which examine the more human and popular elements in Russian life. In the Twenties he was an active member of cultural groups such as the ' The Painters' Union and 'Mir Iskusstva', whose members he

portrayed between 1916 and 1920 in the painting *The artists of Mir Iskusstva*: Igor Grabar, Nicolai Rerich, Eugenie Lanseré, Ivan Bilibin, Aleksandr Benois, Georgy Narbut, Nicolai Milioti, Kostantin Somov, Mstislav Dobužinsky, Kuz'ma Petrov–Vodkin, Anna Lebedeva and Boris Kustodiev himself (*Arte Russa* 227, n. 80).

BIBLIOGRAPHY
Mark Etkind, *Boris Kustodiev: Paintings, Graphic Works, Book Illustrations, Theatrical Designs* (Leningrad, 1983); *Arte Russa e Sovietica 1870–1930*, catalogue [Turin Lingotto 1989], ed. Giovanni Carandente (Milan, 1989), 223, 227 n. 80.
VM

Lachaise Gaston
Paris, 1882–New York, 1935
He studied sculpture at the Bernard Palissy school and the Académie National des Beaux-Arts in Paris (1985–1905). In 1906 he emigrated to the United States and settled in Boston. He associated with Lincoln Kirstein, Alfred Stieglitz and the artists who exhibited at *291* who were challenging the repressive spirit of Puritan America. In 1917 he married Isabel Dutand Nagle, the muse of his nude female drawings and sculptures. Profoundly influenced by Rodin, and indebted to the abstract arabesques of Brancusi and the expressive treatment of Matisse's nudes, Lachaise was also influenced by Eastern art which he used in an anti-classical manner. Convinced that to be truly sincere towards its subject, the portrait had to be nude, and avowedly incapable of portraying the male nude, he selected a model of the body of a mature woman, a source of creative energy, which he set against the ancient classical ideal. He fought the image of the boyish ageless woman found throughout fashion magazines and popular American culture. In the Thirties, obsessed by the generative power of women, Lachaise began work on his most radical pieces (*Abstract figure*, c. 1935) in which he reduced the female principle to the organs of life, celebrating at the same time the creative power of the artist (Rose 1991). In 1935, just before his death, the Museum of Modern Art in New York dedicated a retrospective to him, legitimizing his life work which had always been considered shocking.

BIBLIOGRAPHY
Gaston Lachaise: sculpture,

catalogue, New York Salander-O-Reilly Galleries 2 January–22 February 1992, ed. Barbara Rose (New York, 1991); Louise Bourgeois, 'Obsession', *Artforum*, April 1992, 85–87; Claude Fournet, *Au nom du corps, Connaissance des Arts* (May, 1992), 100–105.
MBG

Lamsweerde Inez van
Amsterdam, 1963
She studied at the Fashion Academy Vogue (1983–85) and at the Rietveld Academy of Arts, where she specialized in photography (1985–90). She held her first one-man show in 1990 in Amsterdam. In 1992 she took part in many group exhibitions in Holland, France, Italy and the United States; she has received commissions for public projects, makes documentaries for the Dutch Television Network, and received the *Photography Award of the Netherlands* and the *European Kodak Awards* in 1992.

BIBLIOGRAPHY
L' Hiver de l' Amour, catalogue, Paris, Musée d'Art Moderne de la Ville de Paris 1994 (Paris, 1994); *Judy Fox–Inez van Lamsweerde*, catalogue, Berlin Kunstwerke 1995 (Berlin, 1995).

Lang Gerhard
Jugenheim, 1963
Lang studied in several different areas of the arts in Germany in the Eighties, including visual communication, design and architecture. To commemorate the opening of Documenta VIII in Kassel, he took part in the project '7001° tree' together with Beuys and the people of Kassel. He is increasingly involved in photography. In the 'Deutsche Fotoage '93' in Frankfurt, he exhibited his work on *Paleoanthropische Physiognomie*. In 1994 he moved to London, where he continues to work in photography.

BIBLIOGRAPHY
Paleoanthropische Physiognomie, catalogue, Frankfurt Museum of Natural History 1993 (Frankfurt, 1993); *Das Zebra Streifen*, documentation of the performance Kassel 1993 (Kassel, 1993).
SDS

Lankton Greer
She attended the School of the Art Institute of Chicago (1975–78) and studied sculpture at the Pratt Institute

of Brooklyn (1978–81) where she had her first one-man show (*Art from the Ombilious*, 1981). She has exhibited her interpretations of the female condition in various group shows in the United States and in Europe since 1984 (Stockholm, Milan, Berlin, London).

BIBLIOGRAPHY
Nude, Naked, Stripped, catalogue, Cambridge (Massachusetts Hayden Gallery), 13 December 1985–2 February 1986 (Cambridge, 1985); Alfred Nemeczek, 'Frauenbilder von Künstlerinnen–made in New York', *Art: das Kunstmagazin*, 9 September 1986, 36–49.
RA

Lassnig Maria
Kappel am Krappfeld, 1919
Active on the post-war Austrian scene, Maria Lassnig has continued to make her presence felt in the European and American art world despite her isolated existence. Around 1950 she took part in Arnulf Rainer's 'Hundsgruppe'. In the Sixties her work signaled a return to the figurative, in her version of critical realism. One of the constants in her work is her interest in the human body. The self-portrait is her favorite theme: the body portrayed in her works is never simply itself, but often appears in a state of symbiosis with another foreign body, sometimes an animal (*Self-portrait with dog*, 1975). 'The human being [...] metaphorically extends to the animal its own experience of the body [...] It wants to escape its solitude in the hybrid animal' (Werner Hofman in *Maia Lassnig. Austria*).

BIBLIOGRAPHY
Maria Lassnig. Austria–Biennale di Venezia 1980, catalogue, Austrian Pavilion Biennale di Venezia 1980 (Vienna, 1980); *Maria Lassnig*, catalogue, Vienna Museum Moderner Kunst (Vienna, 1985); *Maria Lassnig. Mit dem Kopf durch die Wand–neue Bilder*, catalogue, Lucerne Kunstmuseum 28 April–11 June 1989 (Klagenfurt, 1989).
SDS

Laurent Emile
1861–1904
A French doctor and anthropologist, he worked as an intern at the central prison hospital in Paris and studied criminology. He attempted to verify Lombroso's 'criminal by birth' theory by researching social

and psychological factors.

BIBLIOGRAPHY
Les Habitués des prisons de Paris (Lyons, 1890).
PC

Lebel Jean-Jacques
Neuilly-sur-Seine, 1936
Son of the poet Robert Lebel, Jean-Jacques Lebel is one of the youngest representatives of Surrealism. He writes articles for and illustrates the reviews «Le surréalisme, même» and «Bief». In May 1968 he is one of the protagonists of the Prise de l'Odeon. Friend of the American writers of the Beat Generation a poet himself, he translates in French the poetry of Ginsberg, Burroughs and Corso. In 1955 he has his fiest individual exhibition at the Numero Gallery in Florence. He is also the author of several happenings and organizes artistic events.

bibliography
Pierre Restenay, *Une vie dans l'art*, Neuchâtel 1983; Françoise Janicot, *Poésie en action*, Paris 1984; Arnaud Labelle-Rojoux, *L'act pour l'art*, Paris 1988.
LS

Léger Fernand
Argental, 1881–Gif-sur-Yvette, Seine-et-Oise, 1955
He began his career as a architectural draughtsman in Caen and later in Paris where he studied at the Ecole des Arts Décoratifs and the Académie Julian (1903–5). In 1909 he met Archipenko, Soutine, Chagall and Robert Delaunay, and withdrew from post–Impressionism in an attempt to break the image down from a Cubist angle. His works exhibited at the Salon des Indépendants and the Salon d'Automne (1911) are divided into conical, cylindrical, and curved shapes in primary colors. After the war his works chronicle the speed and violence of urban industrial society. In 1920 he moved from the dynamism of the 'machine' age to the static quality of the human body, emphasizing the monumental aspect of massive form. The body is reconstructed in architectural terms. His paintings of the female form (*Femme au bouquet*, 1924) operate on a higher plane. With their enormous column–like arms and legs, hair grooved and sculpted like stone, and spherical faces sharply contrasted with the severe lines of the background, these women become

truly architectural monuments. Léger worked in a number of different genres: he collaborated on cinema and theater projects, executed important mural cycles, worked with Le Corbusier, sculpted, created mosaics and stained glass, and was an active lecturer on color and architecture.

BIBLIOGRAPHY
Gilles Néret, *Léger* (Paris, 1990); Lucio Cabutti, 'Fernand Léger', *Arte*, 259 (February 1995), 64–75.
RA

Leriche René
Roanne, 1879–Cassis, 1955
He specialized in surgery in Lyons. In 1910 he taught experimental surgery at the Medicine Faculty in Lyons, and by 1924 he became a professor in Strasburg. He received important honorary distinctions from the Académie di Chirurgie in France, and the Universities of Harvard, Glasgow and Cleveland. He discovered the predominating role of the nervous reflex system in the regulation of the organic functions, and specialized in bone and pain surgery. He was also a writer and philosopher who published his many discoveries.

BIBLIOGRAPHY
René Leriche, *La philosophie de la chirurgie* (n.p., 1951).
RA

Leroy Eugène
Tourcoing, 1910
Leroy has never left his native area of Lille, except for short trips in search of the work of artists who have influenced him (Rembrandt, Giotto, Toulouse-Lautrec). He began to exhibit in 1937 when his work was primarily figurative (flowers, still lifes, self-portraits). In time, layers of paint began to superimpose themselves on this figurative base, which never entirely disappears but remains a first step in the increasingly complex composition process, until its underlying original forms become almost unrecognizable. However Leroy continued to declare the centrality of resemblance, in his work: 'The image only achieves likeness when form escapes from the real [...] Its blues can be completely unreal, and yet so much more real when looked at in the end' (*Eugène Leroy*, 22). He came to international notice only in the mid-Eighties, when he had several important exhibitions and became a subject of interest for several

young German painters, especially Baselitz.

BIBLIOGRAPHY
Eugène Leroy, catalogue, Museo d'Arte Moderna (Villeneuve d'Ascq, 1987); 'Eugène Leroy. L'énergie de la peinture', *Art Press*, 162 (October 1991), 20–27.
SDS

Littleton Views Company Publishers *see* **Fotografia spiritica**

Liu Wei
Peking, 1965
He studied at the Central Academy of the Fine Arts in Peking (1989) and became one of the leading figures in the movement called 'Cynical Realism'. In his work, portraits of politicians, military leaders and bureaucrats, in which the trompe-l'oeil style is alternated with casual brushstrokes (*Chinese Exhibitions*, 63) critically examines the new path Chinese society is taking in the Nineties, lookings at the work of Western artist (Lucian Freud, Balthus) and trying to '... make the solemn ridiculous ...' (*China's New Art*, 76). He has taken part in many important international exhibitions, including *China's New Art: Post 1989* (Hong Kong 1993), *Mao Goes Pop* (Sydney and Melbourne 1993), *New Art from China: Post 1989* (London 1994) and the Venice Biennale XLV (1993).

BIBLIOGRAPHY
China's New Art, Post–1989–With a Retrospective from 1979–1989, catalogue, Hong Kong 31 January–25 February 1993, eds. Chang Tsong–Zung and Li Xian-Ting (Hong Kong, 1993), 76; *Chinese Exhibitions–I. The Remaking of Mass Culture–II. Wakefulness and the Weightless Present*, catalogue, São Paulo Brazil XXII Biennale Internazionale 12 October–11 December 1994, ed. Chang Tsong–Zung (Hong Kong, 1994), 63.
VM

Lombroso Cesare
Verona, 1835–Turin, 1909
A psychiatrist and anthropologist, Lombroso was a university professor first at Pavia and then in Turin. He taught legal medicine, public health, psychiatry, and criminal anthropology. With Ferri and Garofalo he founded the *Archivio* of psychiatry, penal sciences and criminal anthropology. Lombroso's theory starts from a severely

materialistic view of human nature; he based his new science of criminal anthropology on these assumptions, establishing a close link between physical and psychosomatic anomalies of individuals and the moral degeneration of the delinquent. He arrived at a rigid classification of anthropological criminal types. With the recognized prevalence of anthropological causes of crime, he saw the need to cure rather than punish the delinquent. Even if his work may be controversial today, Lombroso must be credited with having brought psychology and anthropology within the experimental disciplines.

BIBLIOGRAPHY
Cesare Lombroso, *L' uomo delinquente in rapporto all' antropologia, alla giurisprudenza ed alle discipline carcerarie* (Milan, 1876); Cesare Lombroso, *La perizia psichiatrico-legale coi metodi per eseguirla e la casistica penale classificata antropologicamente* (Turin, 1905); Giorgio Colombo, *La scienza infelice* (Turin, 1975).
SDS

Lopez García Antonio
Tomelloso-Ciudad Real, 1936
Raised in an artistic milieu, he moved to Madrid when still an adolescent and enrolled in the Escuela Superior de Bellas Artes de San Fernando (1950–55). Here in the post-war years he made contact with other artists and began to paint, sculpt and draw, in a strongly figurative and realist vein. This choice of reality, adopted in classical terms which initially idealized models, later became increasingly direct and austere, so that 'not wanting to omit any detail, making sure that the space, light and color are true, his paintings ended up becoming metaphysical' (*Antonio Lopez. Pintura*, 20). He is a great admirer of Greek sculpture which 'narrates aspects of the universe and human sentiment, in a unique richness and elevation' and considers sculpture, in its tangible permanence, the most complete art. He responds to the conviction that 'our era has discovered the beauty of horror as artistic material' (Lopez, quoted in Lafaye, 53), with work often defined as transcendant and atemporal. Little-known in France, rarely exhibited in Spain, he has been active in New York since 1965 (Staempfli Gallery 1965 and 1968, the Marlborough Gallery 1986, 1988, 1989). In

1992 he exhibited at the show *Otra realidad. Companeros en Madrid* at the Sala de Exposiciones Casa del Monte di Madrid.

BIBLIOGRAPHY
Antonio Lopez García. Paintings, Sculptures and Drawings: 1965–1986, catalogue, New York 3–26 April 1986 (New York, 1986); Jean Jacques Lafaye, 'L'artiste, le monde et le verbe', *Connaissance des Arts*, March 1991, 49–56; *Antonio Lopez. Pintura, escultura, dibujo*, catalogue, Madrid Museo nacional Centro de Arte Reina Sofía (Madrid, 1993).
MBG

Louÿs Pierre
1870–1925
A French sculptor, whose early acquaintance with the 'Parnassians' influenced him to become a poet. At 21 he founded the journal *La Conque*, where he published, in addition to his own poetry, works by Gide, Mallarmé, Verlaine and his friend Paul Valéry. Inspired by Greek erotic literature, his work has an extraordinary sensuality in which the licentious does not exclude the precision of erudition and the subtlety of psychological observation. He was also sensitive to the female consciousness. He recorded his observations with clinical precision, and worked extensively in erotic photography.

BIBLIOGRAPHY
Astarté (1893); *Chanson de Bilitis* (1894); *Aphrodite* (1896); *La Femme et le Pantin* (1898); *Les aventures du roi Pausole* (1901).
PC

Lumière brothers
Auguste (*Besançon, 1862–Lyons, 1954*) and Louis (*Besançon, 1864–Bandol, 1948*), were the children of a painter and photographer. After studying at the *Ecole professionelle et industrielle de la Martinière* in Lyons, they joined their father's studio where Louis revealed a particular aptitude for photography. At seventeen he invented a new system for manufacturing silver gelatine–bromide photographic plates which allowed the company to expand. In 1892 he founded the 'Societé Anonyme Antoine Lumière et Fils', directed by Auguste and Louis, which would become one of the most famous in Europe. Although photographic plate production remained the

company's major focus, the two brothers continued to do research on the image in motion. They were granted a patent for the *Cinématographe* in 1895, the device used in the first public projection of a film (Paris, Grand–Café du Boulevard des Capucines, 28 December). The *Cinématographe* was later adapted on an industrial scale by the Parisian engineer Jules Carpentier.

BIBLIOGRAPHY
Bernard Chardère, Guy and Marjorie Borgé, *Les Lumière* (Lausanne, 1985); *Verso il centenario: Lumière*, catalogue, Pesaro XXII Mostra Internazionale del Nuovo Cinema 14–22 June 1986, ed. Riccardo Redi (Rome, 1986).
MC

Lüpertz Markus
Liberec, 1941
Immediately after he left his native Rhine area for Berlin in 1963, Lüpertz began to work on a 'dithyrambic' art project, a term drawn from the world of ancient Dionysian cults. He founded, with Hödicke and Köberling, the Grogörschen 35 gallery in 1964, a cooperative of artists located in an old factory in Berlin. His Dithyrambic Manifesto (1966) declares that 'the grace of the twentieth century will be revealed in the dithyramb, which I have invented'. 'The dithyramb symbolizes fullness, which emerges from the restrictions and difficulties of everyday life, and the ecstasy that lies behind artistic banality' (Gohr in *Markus Lüpertz*). With Baselitz and Kieffer, Lüpertz became one of the major figures of new expressionist German painting in the Seventies. His characteristic style emerges from the violent gesture. 'To me motifs are only superficial inspiration. I have always considered myself an abstract artist. Which, to me, means an artist without responsibility. I have no responsibility towards subject matter. I am responsible for the genius of painting, for its rapidity, beauty and aggression. The motif is the opposite' (Dietrich, 9).

BIBLIOGRAPHY
Markus Lüpertz: 'Stil' Paintings 1977–79, catalogue, London Whitechapel Art Gallery (London, 1979); Dorothea Dietrich, 'A conversation with Markus Lüpertz', *The Print-Collector's Newsletter* (March–April 1983), 9–12; *Lüpertz–Retrospectiva 1963–1990*, Catalogue Madrid Centro de Arte Reina Sofia 1991 (Madrid, 1991).
SDS

Mac Auliffe Léon
1876–1936
French doctor and director of the pathological psychology laboratory of the Ecole Pratique des Hautes Études in Paris. He was one of the founders of typology in France, along with C. Sigaud and L. Vincent.

BIBLIOGRAPHY
Traité de morphologie médicale (Paris, 1912); *Les Tempéraments* (Paris, 1926); *La Personnalité et l' hérédité* (Paris, 1932).
PC

Magritte René
Lessines, 1898–Brussels, 1967
He studied at the Académie des Beaux-Arts (1916–18) where he explored various avant-garde currents, such as Futurism, Orphic Cubism, and New Objectivity. In 1923 he took part in a group show at the Cercle Royal Artistique in Antwerp with Lissitzky, Moholy-Nagy, Feinenger and Paul Joostens. He contributed to E.L.T. Mesen's review *Oesophage* (1924) and came into contact with De Chirico's painting. In 1927 he moved to Paris with his wife, and was associated with the Surrealist painters Paul Eluard, André Breton, Arp, Miró and Dali. He exhibited at the Exposition Surréaliste at the Goemans gallery (1928). On his return to Belgium (1930) many exhibitions followed in Europe and the United States (1938). His painting was inspired by the metaphysical spatiality of De Chirico and the use of paradoxically linked elements to create an effect of strangeness and mystery, approaching Surrealism. He reproduced utilitarian objects and familiar images, placing them together to twist their real significance. Painting becomes an instrument for knowing the world. The 'vache', a bizarre strain in this period (1948), was born in an exhibition at the Galerie du Faubourg in Paris. Magritte used a spontaneous language of caricature and cartoons in the vivid color bordering the outlines, but he was also inspired by James Ensor, the Belgian grotesque, Fauvism and Matisse and Manet (*Les voies et moyens*, 1948). In these paintings, (of which there are around thirty–five), he created a style which defied the dominant art of the time, which occasionally and accidentally coincides with Dubuffet's *Art Brut*.

BIBLIOGRAPHY
Magritte, catalogue, London The Hayward Gallery The South Bank Centre 21 May–2

August 1992, ed. Sarah Whitfield (London, 1992); *René Magritte. Peintures et gouaches*, catalogue, Antwerp Ronny Van de Velde 13 March–26 June 1994 (Antwerp, 1994).
RA

Maillol Aristide
Banyls-sur-Mer, 1861-1944
In 1885 he enrolled in the École des Beaux-Arts in Paris. In the 1890s he worked in tapestries, ceramics and decorative wooden panels, and was influenced by the Art and Craft movement. He was friends with many of the artists in the Nabis group. In 1900, partly because of eye problems, he abandoned tapestries and took up sculpture. In 1902 he held his first one-man show at the Galerie Vollard. His interest, first in Egyptian and Indian sculpture–which he encountered at the Esposizione Universale of Paris in 1900—and then in classical sculpture–born from his travels in Italy and Greece in 1908—merge in a taste for solid female nudes with massive volumes and comforting grandeur.

BIBLIOGRAPHY
Philippe Sollers, 'Les déesses de Maillol', *Art Press*, 103, November 1991, 55–56.
MLS

Malczewski Jacek
Radom, 1854–Krakow, 1929
Malczewski's artistic training was influenced by the quest for Polish independence, inspired by the writings of Adam Mickiewicz and Julius Slovacky. At the same time he was influenced by the teacher Adolf Dygasinski, one of the supporters of the 1863 insurrection, who instilled in him a love for the classical world, permeated by a pantheistic mysticism (1867–71). In the Eighties he defined his civil commitment with a series of realistic works, such as the first paintings on the theme of exile in Siberia (1882) and the controversial *Ellenai halála* (1883). In 1890 the artist made his first forays into Symbolism. His Romantically–inspired stand on the fight for independence, linked with his interest in folklore, make him one of the great precursors of the movement 'Young Poland'. His great allegorical syntheses from 1890–1897 (*Introduzione*, 1890; *Melankólia*, 1894; *Büvös Kör*, 1896) express his position on the three most important themes of his symbolic creation: the relationships

between art and nature, art and history, and art and life. *Thanatos I* (1898) is the first painting in a series on the theme of death that the artist would return to throughout the rest of his life. In the self-portraits he is represented surrounded by fantasy characters, dressed as a clown, a prisoner, in armor, disguised as Christ or Tobias, offering us '... a portrait of himself which is bitter, pathetic, suffering or ironic, which unmasks the disguises one by one, in an inexorable quest for a response to the questions of life and the role of creation ...' (Lawniczakowa, 33).

BIBLIOGRAPHY
Agniewska Lawniczakowa, *Jacek Malczewski*, in *Simbolo espressione metafora. Quattro pittori polacchi*, catalogue, Rome Palazzo Barberini 8 May–5 June 1981, ed. Giovanna De Feo (Rome, 1981), 33–44 (with extensive bibliography).
LS

Malevič Kazimir

Kiev, 1878–
Saint Petersburg, 1935
After a post-Impressionist Nabis phase, he worked in a Fauvist vein between 1906–11, portraying scenes from everyday life. Between 1911–13 he created machine-age works with cylindrical forms reminiscent of Léger. His painting drew on Cubist and Italian Futurist themes, and he moved towards the abstraction of Suprematism, based on the existence of an 'integrating additional element in the painting, which is the formula or sign by which not only structure and color can be synthesized, but also the degree of development of a given culture' (Carandente, 39). In *Two masculine figures*, the two characters are exactly the same, except for the slightly altered position of the left foot. 'In this composition the majestic figure stands side by side with the grotesque; the union of these apparently incompatible elements distinguished many of the paintings of the rural post-Suprematist genre' (Malevich, 178). The image of Renaissance man, independent in his individual microcosm, is explored in a series of portraits that mark a return to the figurative (Misler, 230). Malevich declared that 'the painter discovers the world and shows it to man': in his *Self-portrait* (1933) 'the likenesses of the master are pervaded by the awareness of his great mission... Malevič aspires to the Renaissance

idea of the exaltation of the hero, departing from the concept of waiting for the future of sacred painting itself' (Malevich, 186). In the *Portrait of Natalya A. Mancenko, the painter's wife* (1933), the hat and the dress show the influence of fifteenth-and sixteenth-century Renaissance medallion portraits. The gesture of the hand 'which recalls the oratorical gestures of ancient statues, also recalls the standing figures of the icons and frescoes of old Russia' (Malevich, 184).

BIBLIOGRAPHY
Malevich. Catalogue raisonné, ed. T. Andersen (Amsterdam, 1970); *Kazimir Malevič 1900-1935. Una retrospettiva*, catalogue, Milan Palazzo Reale 15 December 1993–30 January 1994 (Prato, 1993); Giovanni Carandente, *Kazimir Malevič e il Suprematismo*, in *Kazimir Malevič 1900-1935. Una retrospettiva*, catalogue, Milan Palazzo Reale 15 December 1993–30 January 1994 (Prato, 1993), 27–41; Nicoletta Misler, *L'ozio come autentica verità. Autoritratto d'autore*, in *Kazimir Malevič 1900-1935. Una retrospettiva*, catalogue, Milan Palazzo Reale 15 December 1993–30 January 1994 (Prato, 1993), 229–43.
LS

Man Ray

(Emmanuel Rudnitsky)
Philadelphia, 1890–Paris, 1976
After studying architecture and working briefly in advertising, Man Ray began to paint in 1911, basing his work on the juxtaposition of heterogenous objects. In 1915 he met Duchamp and Picabia, which proved to be a decisive moment in the history of the avant-garde. In the same year he also met Stieglitz and began to work in photography, which would be the medium of some of his most important works. His first 'rayograms' appeared in 1921–photos obtained by direct contact between the object and the photographic paper. His 'rayograms' and the objects (*Regalo*) (1921) represent the best and most original part of his oeuvre, but he also worked in many other areas, always approaching them from an unusual angle: 'I could paint with a spoon or with my hands, without anyone noticing the difference. It is the intention that gives sense to creation' (*Man Ray*, 7). And the same holds for the subjects of his works–Man Ray has always been a champion of ambiguity. In his *Belle Haleine–Eau de Violette* (1921) the linguistic game ('veletta'

instead of 'violetta', a veil concealing the metamorphosis) reveals Marcel Duchamp dressed as a woman. He lived in the Stated from 1940 to 1951, and then returned to Paris for good. 'I have always done things without effort. I have always looked for the biggest economy in achieving things, in painting objects. The slightest effort possible, for the greatest possible result. That's my rule'.

BIBLIOGRAPHY
Man Ray. L'immagine fotografica, catalogue, *Man Ray. Testimonianza attraverso la fotografia*, Venice San Giorgio 18 July–10 October 1976, ed. Janus (Venice, 1977); *Perpetual Motif. The Art of Man Ray*, catalogue, Washington D.C. National Museum of Art / Smithsonian Institute 2 December 1988–20 February 1989, ed. Merry Foresta.
SDS

Manzoni Piero

Soncino, Cremona, 1933–Milan, 1963
In the early Fifties he began to paint vaguely anthropomorphic images in tar and oil, projections of the collective unconscious, or detailed imprints of objects like keys and pliers. He took part in a group show organized by Fontana (Galleria Pater, Milan, 1957) and joined the 'Gruppo Nucleare'; he founded the review *Azimuth* with E. Castellani. In 1957 he began to treat the surface of the canvas with crude gesso and kaolin in his series of ontologically-influenced monochromes called *Achromes* (colorless). He used different types of materials, including canvas, fiberglass, ice, and bread. In the Sixties he executed the *Linee di lunghezza variabile*, drawn on paper placed in jars; the balloons of *Fiato d'artista*; fingerprinted hard-boiled eggs (*Consumazione dell'arte*, Galleria Azimuth, Milan 1960); and boxes containing *Merda d'artista*. His *Socle du Monde* dates back to 1961, and consists of an iron pedestal with reversed writing, representing the base of the globe, elected to a total work of art.

BIBLIOGRAPHY
Freddy Battino–Luca Palazzoli, *Piero Manzoni. Catalogue raisonné* (Milan, 1991).
RA

Marage René

La Flache, 1859
Marage studied the voice for

several years, focusing on practical applications for deaf-mutes as well as teachers of song and elocution. He photographed the voice, recording the vibrations produced by the vocal cords. After having studied the characteristics of the vibrations of vowels, he then tried to synthesize them by first reconstructing the vocal cords mechanically with tubes, then positioning them on artificial mouths made with casts, using amplifiers. This was the first example of the synthesis of the word.
MC

Marey Etienne–Jules

Beaune, 1830–Paris, 1904
A physiologist and professor of Natural Sciences at the Collège de France, he dedicated himself to scientific research and the problem of motion (blood circulation, pulmonary respiration, muscular contractions) inventing instruments to record vital movements. Around 1880, in the course of his research on the movement of birds, he developed an interest in photographic applications. He learned of Muybridge's experiments, and realized that his shots could not explain the question of the time element in movement. In 1882 he completed his first *fusil photographique*, an instrument which could achieve twelve successive images in the interval of a second, making it possible to recording the motion of a bird in flight. This instrument allowed Marey to obtain what Muybridge's photography could not: the unity of point of view and equidistance in time. Later, with the *chronophotographe*, a piece of equipment with fixed photographic plates on which instantaneous exposures remain printed one next to the other, he obtained sequences which he projected for scientists, artists and photographers.

BIBLIOGRAPHY
Italo Zannier, *L'occhio della fotografia* (Rome, 1988); Mario Verdone, 'Marey, la cronofotografia e la fotodinamica', *Terzocchio*, 63 (June 1992), 38–40.
MBG

Martini Arturo

Treviso, 1889–Milan, 1947
His artistic training was influenced by his relationship with G. Rossi and his association with the Scuola di Burano, and his attendance of A. von Hildebrand's school in

Munich, as well as his early ceramic apprenticeship, an experience that left him with an artisan's love for material. Another formative experience was his trip to Paris (1912) where he met Modigliani and Boccioni, and was active in the inititives of the Ca' Pesaro group. Martini always connected his female nudes to childlike emotion. In Treviso, his parents had rented a room to a prostitute: 'The prostitute often took me with her. One morning, she went out to the canal, lifted her petticoat and squatted over the water... There exploded a vision of her great buttocks, the trunks of her white thighs. This temple, this ecstasy. At two years of age, I was already twenty. I understood form. The *Saffo*, the *Pisana*, all my women are that revelation' (*Arturo Martini*, 86). For his *Pisana*, the heroine of Nievo's novel, Martini utilized not only erotic charge but Renaissance inspiration. 'Female sculpture, uterine, the sculpture of the Earth-Mother in living matter, regenerator, Catonian ... the work of Martini is an enterprise that dares, following the example of the stars, to raise its head, as one would rise up from an illness' (Clair).

BIBLIOGRAPHY
Arturo Martini, catalogue, Florence Palazzo Medici Ricciardi, 9 July–15 September 1991 (Milan, 1991); Jean Clair, *Il culo, la testa e le stelle*, in *Arturo Martini*, quoted, 25–34.
MLS

Mason Raymond

Birmingham, 1922
In 1946, when he arrived in Paris, Raymond Mason was an abstract sculptor attracted by pure form. But three years later he was already declaring that abstraction 'bored him to death'. Mason has worked over a long period of time on several works that are particularly significant in his development as a sculptor, each marking an important step in the evolution of his thoughts on art and life. A bronze group from the Sixties, *La Foule* (1963–68) portrays ninety-nine figures 'expanding like lava'. Distressed over the imminent closure of his beloved Les Halles, he then executed *Le Départ des fruits et légumes du cœur de Paris le 28 février 1969* (1969–71), displaying a detachment from any earlier sense of the metaphysical. 'Le Départ des fruits et légumes does not, like La Foule, lay bare the problem of being in the world: it is already the work which permits life to regain posses-

sion of its ambiguous situation, in which joy approaches despair' (Yves Bonnefoy in *Raymond Mason* 1985).

BIBLIOGRAPHY
Raymond Mason, catalogue, Paris Centre Georges Pompidou 11 September–11 November 1985 (Paris, 1985); *Raymond Mason*, catalogue, London Marlborough Fine Arts 25 October–23 November 1991 (London, 1991).

Matisse Henri
Chateau–Cambrésis, 1869–Nice, 1954
His models were Corot, Vermeer, Chardin and Fragonard, and later Gauguin and van Gogh. He was also, however, influenced by Oriental art, Persian ceramics, Moorish fabrics, Japanese woodcuts and African art. He took part in the Salon d'Automne with the Fauves (1905) a movement whose vivid colorism distinguishes it from the spatial concerns of Cubism. As Matisse commented on his conception of the portrait 'the nearly unconscious transcription of the significance of the model is the initial act of every work of art, especially of a portrait. Reason later dominates [...] and reconceives that first version which is then used like a trampoline ...' (Matisse, quoted in Monod-Fontaine, 49). The *Tête blanche et rose* (1914) which recalls the *Jeune femme au chapeau corbeille* (1914) portraying Matisse's daughter, contains some Cubist elements because of its '... arrangement of an orthogonal grid, as well as the parallel bands in the treatment of the face and bust ...' (Monod-Fontaine, 46). The *Autoportrait sans barbe* (1927) reveals to Matisse's interest in his changing appearance: using a realistic technique he notes '... the new proportions of his face, discovering, beneath its normal appearance, a stranger ...' (Baldassari, 206). The *Autoportrait* (1937) is part of a series of four carbon drawings. In them the format depends on an element of decisive differentiation: '... the composition is modified by a dimension provided by the surfaces to be covered. If I take a piece of paper of a given dimension I will draw something that has a proper relationship with its format. The drawing must possess a power of expansion which rejuventates the things surrounding it ...' (Matisse, quoted in Baldassari, 236). The *Autoportrait au chapeau de paille* (1945), homage to van Gogh's self-portraits of the same name, seems to reject explicitly the photographic portrait, whose '... anthropometric nature conceals, rather than reveals, what to Matisse constituted the identity of the model: a multiplicity of aspects, expressions, and points of view ...' (Baldassari, 289).

BIBLIOGRAPHY
Isabelle Monod-Fontaine, Anne Baldassari and Claude Langier, *Matisse*, (Paris, 1989); *Henri Matisse: A Retrospective*, catalogue, New York Museum of Modern Art 24 September 1992–12 January 1993, ed. John Elderfield, (New York, 1992).
LS

Matthias Eugen
1882
German artist who extolled a new aesthetic of the body, using the pure Aryan athlete as an ideal model.

BIBLIOGRAPHY
Der Männliche Körper (1931).
PC

Mattiacci Eliseo
Cagli, Pesaro, 1940
After receiving his diploma from the Istituto di Belle Arti in Pesaro and traveling in Europe, he took part in his first group show in 1961. At this time he was sculpting in metal, assembled from leftover pieces and parts forged by hand, showing a deep sensitivity to the location in which his works were placed. At his first one-man show in 1967 at the galleria La Tartaruga in Rome he exhibited a jointed yellow *Tubo* 150 meters long. He participated in many other shows, including the Venice Biennale XXIII. In 1975 he exhibited the *Recuperare un mito* at the L'attico gallery, a series of photographs dedicated to the pellirossa (Redskins or Native Americans). In 1976 he won the Bolaffi prize, and was the subject of a monograph. In 1978 he exhibited *Essere Respirare* at the La Salita gallery in Rome, and *Senza Titolo* at the Venice Biennale, which consisted of two pairs of spectacles hung from the wall facing each other. He held several one–man shows in the Eighties, at the Palazzo Mazzancolli of Terni in 1982, the Castelli di Miramare and San Giusto in Trieste in 1987, and the Galleria Civica in Modena from December 1988 to February 1989. In 1990 he took part in the show *Entretien. Quatres générations d'artistes italiens* at the Centre Albert Borchette in Brussels.

BIBLIOGRAPHY
Eliseo Mattiacci, catalogue, Modena Galleria Civica December 1988–February 1989, (n.p., 1988); B. Corà, *Eliseo Mattiacci* (Ravenna, 1991).
VC

Mayet Lucien
1874
A French doctor and anthropologist, he was a professor at the Lyons medical faculty, and a member of the Anthropological Societies of Paris, Lyons, Vienna and Berlin. He published many works on criminal anthropology, craniometry and alcoholism.

BIBLIOGRAPHY
Table pour servir au calcul rapide de l' indice céphalique (1901); *Les Stigmates anatomiques et physiologiques de la dégénérescence* (1902).
PC

Mazzoni Guido
Modena, 1450–1518
One of the major sculptors of the Italian Renaissance. He reached technical summits of extraordinary refinement and complexity, even resorting to live casting. He worked in bronze fusions, but is especially known as the master of a genre, the *Compianto sul Cristo morto*, eight figures in terracotta that spread throughout Northern Italy from the 1480s on. His first known work is the *Compianto sul Cristo morto* in the church of Santa Maria degli Angeli in Busseto, the only group of statues still found in its original niche. It was probably executed c. 1475–77. Later works include the *Compianto* once in San Giovanni della Buona Morte in Modena (1477–79), a *Madonna con bambino e donatori* known as the *Madonna della Pappa* (after 1480) now in the cathedral in Modena, and the *Compianto* once in Santa Maria della Rosa in Ferrara (1485), now in the church of the Gesù. He later worked in Venice in the church of Sant'Antonio in Castello, where he executed a *Compianto* (documented between 1485–89, now in the Museo Civico in Padua). In June 1492 he went to Naples (*Compianto* in Sant'Anna ai Lombardi in Monteoliveto) and from there he moved to France, in the retinue of Charles VIII. He was one of the first Italian artists to work in Paris. He executed the tomb of Charles VIII for the cathedral of Saint-Denis and assisted with work in the castles of Gaillon and Blois.

BIBLIOGRAPHY
A. Lugli, *Guido Mazzoni e la rinascita della terracotta nel Quattrocento* (Turin, 1990).
AL

McCarthy Paul
1946
He lives and works in Los Angeles. He is considered a subversive artist for his use of debased materials (which he calls 'the stream') and for his strong visual violence. He also makes performances, videos and, in later years, drawings, sculptures and photographs.
SDS

Meidner Ludwig
Breslau, 1884–Darmstad, 1966
He studied at the Academy of Breslau and then moved to Berlin (1905). He was in Paris from 1906–1907, where he met Modigliani. He returned to Berlin and frequented the Café des Westens, a historic avant–garde center (1908). He founded, with Richard Janthur and Jakob Steinhard 'Die Pathetiker', an artistic group with anti–Impressionist leanings (1912). At the same time, obsessed by the idea of catastrophe, he began to paint apocalyptic scenes. Meidner, who had renounced his Judaism and burned his Torah in his youth, had the first of his mystic religious experiences in December of the same year. In 1918 he had his first one–man show at the Gallery Cassirer. His violent and convulsive style recalls Bosch, Bruegel the Elder, Ensor and Van Gogh, but also reveals a debt to the Futurists and Delaunay. These were the years of increasing political commitment, pursued along with his artistic concerns and his writing. He supported the Bolshevist revolution, and rediscovered his Judaism, making a controversial public profession of faith (1929). The religious subjects which predominated in the Thirties gave way to self-portraits. The work selected for the *Entartete Kunst*, the 1937 Munich exhibition on Degenerate Art was *Selbstbildnis* (1912): the face with the protruding eyes marked by a convulsive grimace was held up as a symbol of the 'degeneration of a race'. In 1938 Meidner took refuge with his family in England where he would remain until 1952, the year of his return to Germany.

BIBLIOGRAPHY
Ludwig Meidner–An Expressionist Master, catalogue, Ann Arbor The University of Michigan Museum of Art 20 October–19 November 1978, ed. Victor H. Miesel (Ann Arbor, 1978); *Ludwig Meidner 1884–1966*, catalogue, Wolfsburg Kunstverein 2 June–14 July 1985, ed. Klaus Hoffman (Wolfsburg, 1985); '*Degenerate Art'. The Fate of the Avant–Garde in the Nazi Germany*, catalogue, Los Angeles, Los Angeles County Museum of Art 17 February–12 May 1991, ed. Stephanie Barron (Los Angeles, 1991).
LS

Melotti Fausto
Rovereto, Trento, 1901–Milan, 1986
After attending Luigi Comel's drawing courses in his hometown Scuola Reale Elisabettiana, he enrolled in 1918 at the University of Pisa, and completed his studies in Milan with a degree in electronic engineering. He took up sculpture in 1925, where he frequented the studio of Pietro Canonica in Turin and enrolled at the Brera Accademia in Milan, where he moved in 1928. Here he shared his studio with Fontana and in 1934 joined the Galleria del Milione group. The following year he held his first one-man show, after having taken part in the 'first group show of abstractart' in Casorati's studio in Turin. His work relies on geometric metaphysical abstraction, that leads him to the creation of slim , precariously balanced structures with magical effects. In 1935 he also joined the Abstration-Création movement. In the late Thirties his sculpture began to move towards more traditional forms (*I sette savi*, 1937, *L' architettura, La Pittura, La Scultura* and *La Ceramica*, 1940). Between 1941 and 1943 he lived in Rome where he concentrated on poetry and drawing. He became increasingly interested in ceramics in the Forties and Fifties. He produced metallic threadlike sculptures suspended in the air in the Sixties. Adelphi published his *Linee* in 1974, a collection of poetry and writings. The Venice Biennale dedicated a retrospective to him in 1986.

BIBLIOGRAPHY
Fausto Melotti. Sequenze d' amore, catalogue, Bollate Festival di Villa Arconati 1991, ed. G. Celant (Milan, 1991); Germano Celant, *Fausto Melotti*, catalogue raisonné (Milan, 1994).
VC

Michetti Francesco Paolo

Tocco Casauria, Chieti, 1851–Francavilla a Mare 1929
He attended the Accademia in Naples with Domenico Morelli, and was friends with the Catalan nobleman Mariano Fortuny and his circle until his death in 1927. He very quickly matured an independent style and achieved notice with his *Corpus Domini* (1877) shown at the Naples Esposizione. He had immediate and continuous success as a painter: he exhibited in Paris, Rome and Venice, where he showed his *La figlia di Iorio* at the first Biennale (1895). This painting would inspire Gabriele D'Annunzio to write his tragedy of the same name, and begin a long friendship between the two. Like many Italian artists in the late nineteenth century, he was also interested in photography as a preparation for drawing, as a process that furnishes material for artistic conception. In this field too he revealed his positivist mentality, and was alert to the phenomena of the real, of which '... he records individual exposures, treated like partial sketches together on a vast surface, where they are hung in superimposed strips ...' (*L'ultimo*, 12). He retired from his painting career, and at the turn of the century began to concentrate on aesthetically independent photographic research.

BIBLIOGRAPHY
Marina Miraglia, *Francesco Paolo Michetti fotografo* (Turin, 1975); *L'ultimo Michetti: Pittura e Fotografia*, catalogue n.p., ed. Renato Barilli (Florence, 1993).
MC

Miró Joan

Montroig, 1893–Palma de Mallorca, 1983
He studied contemporary art and went to business school in Barcelona. After working as an accountant (1910), he decided to devote himself entirely to painting. On his first visit to Paris (1919) he met Picasso. The next year after he began his custom of spending the winter in Paris and summer in Montroig where his family had a house in the country. Soon his painting, moving naturally towards the imaginative dream, encountered Surrealism. Miró was never conventional, however, and he was not interested either in the movement's theoretical debates nor automatism (the preparatory drawing is the norm in his work). In later years he used different techniques: from 1928–29 he worked in 'papiers collés', collage, and first worked in lithography; he also developed an interest in contemporary Dutch art. Back in Barcelona (1941) after the Civil War, he achieved world notice. In the Sixties he worked almost exclusively in sculpture. Although he is considered a spontaneous and childlike artist, 'his work, which seems to develop in the midst of total spontaneity, is regulated by constant debate '[...] Miró, who once claimed that he wanted to destroy art, and his own first of all [...] abandoned his conquests in order to resume his journey towards the unknown' (Chilo).

BIBLIOGRAPHY
Michel Chilo, *Miró, l'artiste et l'œuvre* (Paris, 1971); *Joan Miró. Retrospective de l'œuvre peint*, catalogue, Saint–Paul de Vence Fondation Maeght 4 July–7 October 1990 (Saint–Paul de Vence, 1990); Pere Gimferrer, *The Roots of Miró* (Barcelona, 1993).
SDS

Mondrian Piet

Pieter Cornelis Mondriaan, Jr. Amersfoort, 1872–New York, 1944
Until 1908 his work was naturalist and displayed the influence of academic landscape painting, Dutch Impressionism and Symbolism. In 1909 he exhibited his works at the Stedelijk Museum in Amsterdam. Between 1909 and 1910 he experimented in *pointillisme* and around 1910 he worked in a Cubist vein. He lived in Paris from 1912–14, and developed his own very personal abstract style. In 1917 he founded the De Stijl group with van Doesburg and Vantongerloo. The self-portrait, a figurative isolated example in a production completely based on abstraction, was the result of a promise he kept to his friend Slijper. The painting does not portray Mondrian as an initiate—he had been active since 1909 in the Società Teosofica—but as an artist, and a 1917 painting portrayed in the background, *Composizione n. 3 con Piani di Colore*, seems 'to symbolize the precariousness of his artistic status at the time' (*Mondrian. From Figuration*, 179).

BIBLIOGRAPHY
Mondrian. From Figuration to Abstraction, catalogue, Tokyo The Seibu Museum of Art 25 July–31 August 1987, ed. H. Henkels (Tokyo, 1987); *Mondrin e De Stijl. L'ideale moderno*, catalogue, Venice Fondazione Giorgio Cini 19 May–2 September 1990, eds. G. Celant and M. Govan (Milan, 1990); *Piet Mondrian 1872–1944*, catalogue, Haags Gemeentemuseum, 18 December 1994–30 April 1995 (Milan, 1994).
MLS

Mori A. *see* x–Rays or Röntgen

Morris Robert

Kansas City, 1931
An eclectic American artist, after his studies at Kansas City University (1948) and the California School of Fine Arts (1951), he served in Korea (1953) and taught in several secondary schools on his return. He held his first one-man show at the Dilexi Gallery (San Francisco 1957) and in the Sixties he was active in Minimalism—expressed in sculptures executed in different materials (1968). He organized a happening in Düsseldorf (1964) and was interested in Land Art (1971). He designed the Los Angeles Project II (1969) which was an attempt to interact with the climate of the city. After his participation in the Venice Biennale XXXIX (1980) and the cycles Holocaust and Firestorm in the Eighties, he worked on 'a profound meditation—or rather, a savagely bitter criticism—of the politics, sociology and morality of the Reagan era ...' (Johnson, 152) expressed in the aluminum encaustic-treated panels inspired by Goya (1989).

BIBLIOGRAPHY
Carter Ratcliff, 'Robert Morris, a Saint Jerome for Our Times', *Artforum*, vol. XXIII, 8, April 1985, 60–63; Ken Johnson, 'Robert Morris's Wake Up Call', *Art in America*, vol. 78, 12, December 1990, 150–156; *Inability to endure or deny the world: representation and text in the work of Robert Morris*, catalogue, Washington Corcoran Gallery of Art 8 December 1990–17 February 1991, eds. Christopher French, Terrie Sultan, Barbara Rose, Dena André.
VM

Morselli Enrico *see* Fotografia spiritica

Mottier N. *see* Cabanis Emmanuel A.

Munch Edvard

Löten, 1863–Ekely, 1944
The memories of a macabre childhood, marked by death and illness within the family, became the dominant themes of his painting. His pessimistic vision of existence was strengthened after he met August Strindberg (Berlin), and later Ibsen, for whom he did the stage sets for *Hedda Gabler* (1906). His controversial show at the Berlin Künstlerverein (1892) sparked the Expressionism of 'Die Brücke'. His painting can be summed up in his series *The frieze of life* (1893–1918), an open work in which he represents the interior growth of the individual and the male–female conflict. The last painting in the series is *Metabolism* based on the myth of the birth of Adonis. *The shout*, the symbol of the spiritual anguish of modern man, is probably his most famous work. His final years were devoted to a series of self-portraits which document his inexorable decline and loneliness.

BIBLIOGRAPHY
Gösta Svenæus, *Edvard Munch. Das Universum der Melancholie* (Lund, 1968); *Munch*, catalogue, Milan Palazzo Reale and Palazzo Bagatti Valsecchi 4 December 1985–16 March 1986, eds. Guido Ballo and Gianfranco Bruno (Milan, 1985); *Edvard Munch: The Frieze of Life*, catalogue, London National Gallery 12 November 1992–7 February 1993, ed. Mara–Helen Wood (London, 1992).
MC

Music Anton Zoran

Gorizia, 1909
He grew up in a family of teachers in Austro-Hungarian Gorizia, a cultural crossroads between the Slavic, Austrian and Italian worlds. During World War I he was a refugee in Stiria (1915) and then moved to Völkermarkt in Carinzia (1920). After attending the Zagreb Academy of Fine Arts (where he studied with Babic, a former pupil of von Stuck) he traveled to Madrid and throughout Dalmatia (1935). He took part in a group show in Lubyana (*I Pomladanska razstava*, 1935) and then had his first crucial encounter with Venice (1943). Arrested by the Gestapo for anti-German activities, he was deported to Dachau concentration camp whose life he portrayed in a series of drawings executed during work breaks (1944). He decided to move permanently to Venice (1945) where he painted some self-portraits, but was particularly interested in small horses and Dalmatian themes which he would bring to the attention of a large public. He exhibited at the Venice Biennale XXIV (1948), and lived in Switzerland and Paris where he opened a studio in Montparnasse (1953–59) which he used as an alternative to his studio in the Accademia. In later years he was in great demand with galleries and museums on an international level, and he exhibited different cycles such as *Non siamo gli ultimi* (1972), *Motivo vegetale* (1973), *Paesaggi rocciosi* (1976), *Interni di cattedrali* (1984), punctuated by views of the *Canale della Giudecca* series and *Punta della Dogana* (1981–82), which continue his never-ending investigation of Venice and its light.

BIBLIOGRAPHY
Zoran Music, catalogue, Rome Accademia di Francia Villa Medici 17 January–15 March 1992, ed. Jean Clair (Milan, 1992); *Zoran Music*, catalogue, Paris Galerie Nationales du Grand Palais 4 April–3 July 1995, ed. Gérard Régnier (Paris, 1995).
VM

Muybridge Eadweard

Kingston–on–Thames, 1830–1904
In 1852 he emigrated to the United States where he began his career as a landscape photographer in the service of the American government. His interest in the photographic study of movement began when the ex–governor of California, Leland Stanford, asked him to document the phases in the gait of a race horse (1872). Only in 1877 did Muybridge succeed in breaking down the movement of a horse in a series of exposures obtained by using 24 cameras, placed along the course, whose shutters were operated directly by the horse's motion and exposed the film at 2/1000 of a second. In 1881 is in Paris and his 'chronophotographs' of racehorses were projected in sequence with a praxinoscope at the house of the physiologist E.J. Marey, to an audience of photographers, scientists and artists. The publication of his findings aroused much interest and debate, and greatly influenced the painting and teaching of Thomas Eakins, among others. Between 1884 and 1887 he extended his research to other animals, including man, whose movements he photographed in both sports activities and

Bertesca gallery in Genoa. He then moved from analysis to the function of art in history, leading to works with explicit references to the Old Masters, such as *Giovane che guarda Lorenzo Lotto* (1967) and *L'invenzione di Ingres*, 1968. He also began to work in casts of classical statuary (*Mimesi*, 1975). In 1985 he exhibited at the Pinacoteca Comunale in Ravenna with *Tutto qui*, in 1988 at the Museo di Capodimonte in Naples, in 1989 at the Galleria Nazionale d'Arte Moderna in Rome, in 1990 at the villa delle Rose in Bologna, and in 1991 and 1993 at the castello di Rivoli in Turin.

BIBLIOGRAPHY
M. Fagiolo, A.C. Quintavalle, *Giulio Paolini* (Parma, 1976); G. Celant, *Giulio Paolini* (Turin, 1988).
VC

Parmiggiani Claudio

Luzzara, Reggio Emilia, 1943
He studied at the Istituto d'Arte in Modena, and became close friends with Morandi, whose understanding of art as an integral part of life influenced him profoundly. In 1965 he held his first one-man show of *oggetti parasurrealistici* at the Feltrinelli bookshop in Bologna. In the city he was associated with the poets from Luciano Anceschi's 'Gruppo 63' and the review *Il Verri*, including Nanni Balestrini, Corrado Costa, Adriano Spatola and Giuseppe Guglielmi. In 1967–68 he also made two equally important acquaintances, Emilio Villa and Vincenzo Agnetti, with whom he shared his studio in Milan when he created *Tavole temporali* (1968). This was the period in which he was primarily working on his 'misurazione' series (1967–70)—imprints of his own shoes on sheets of paper, and maps of the world crumpled up in glass jars. In 1970 he produced *Delocazioni*, which are imprints of canvases removed from the walls. In 1969 he began the *Barca* series, starting with *Zoogeometrico*, which culminated in the large *Barche* from the late Eighties. In 1989 he exhibited his *Iconostasi*, wrapped statues and canvases, at the Stein gallery in Milan. In 1989 he created *Terra*, a terracotta sphere with his handprints buried in the cloister of the Museo di Arte Contemporanea in Lyons. He has taken part in many Venice Biennale. In 1992 the Matildenhohe Institute of Darmstadt dedicated a large retrospective to him, and he was later a guest in Prague.

BIBLIOGRAPHY
C. Bernard, D. Ronte, *Parmiggiani* (Turin, 1987); *Claudio Parmiggiani. Iconostasi*, ed. K. Wolbert (Matildenhohe, Darmstadt, 1992).
VC

Payet D. *see* **Cabanis Emmanuel A.**

Pei-Ming Yan

Shanghai, 1960
He first came to attention in Dijon, France with the show *Duel des Hommes de Vertu* (1987, Atheneum) and took part in many other one-man and group shows (*Mouvements 2*, Centre Georges Pompidou, Paris 1991; *Primo vero*, Galerie des Anciens Establissements Sacrés, Lieges 1992) exhibiting portraits of famous people (*Mao*, 1993) or identified only by a generic title (*Tête*, 1992) or an abbreviation (*G.K.*, 1993), following his conviction that 'if man exists, so do his face and portrait' (Ming, quoted in 1994).

BIBLIOGRAPHY
Yan Pei-Ming, catalogue, Paris Palais de Congrès, 27 October–13 December, 1992, eds. Jean Daviot and Berhard Macardé (Paris, 1992); *Yan Pei-Ming. Visages-Portraits*, catalogue, Paris Nouveau Musée Institut d'Art Contemporain 17 January–13 February 1994, eds. Olivier Donat, Jean-Louis Maubant, and Pascal Pique (Paris, 1994).
VM

Penfield Wilder Graves

Spokane, 1891
After specializing in surgery, Penfield taught at the New York Neurological Institute from 1921 to 1928, when he moved to Canada. In 1934 he founded the Montreal Neurological Institute, a specialization center in neurology and neurosurgery. Penfield is known for his early studies on the consequences of mesencephalon damage, especially epilepsy. He studied the functions of the conscious mind, distinguishing the allocation of the areas controlling the movement of the different parts of the human body. Penfield outlined a theory of the cerebral functions linked to the mechanisms of perception, memory, behavior, the conscious and the higher functions. Among his most revolutionary contributions was the demonstration of the existence of a complete

receptor of experience in the brain, which can be made to function by electrical stimulation of the temporal lobe.

BIBLIOGRAPHY
H.H. Jasper, ad vocem *Penfield*, in *American Men of Science* (Lancaster, 1949), 504; *The Encyclopedia Americana. International Edition*, vol. 21 (New York, 1970), 1921.
SDS

Penone Giuseppe

Garessio, Cuneo, 1949
He made his début in 1968 with his nature studies, photographic documentation of growth in an attempt to visualize and alter its processes (*Alpi marittime*, 1968, *Continuerà a crescere tranne che in quel punto*, 1968). In 1969 he began his tree series, which consisted of wooden beams carved to reveal the tree inside the beam. A large number of these works were exhibited at the Stedelijk Museum in Amsterdam in *Ripetere il bosco* in 1981. He later concentrated attention on his own body with *Rovesciare i propri occhi* (1970) where he photographs himself wearing reflecting contact lenses, and *Svolgere la propria pelle* (1978), enlarged projections of the epidermis. The late Seventies were the years of *Patate* (1977) and *Zucche* (1978). He began his *Soffi* series in 1978, and in the Eighties he was producing the *Gesti vegetali*. He took part in the Venice Biennale in 1978 and 1980, and created the *Essere fiume* series in 1981. In 1984 the Arc Musée de la Ville de Paris dedicated a retrospective to him, and he took part in shows at the installation at the Chateau de Malle (Preignac) in 1985, the Musée de Peinture et Sculpture in Grenoble in 1986, the Galerie Buchman in Basle, and the Musée des Beaux-Arts in Charleroi. Some works from the series *Unghie* were exhibited at the 1988 Musée Rodin in Paris. In 1989 the villa delle Rose in Bologna gave him a retrospective, and in 1991 and 1993 he exhibited at the castello di Rivoli (Turin).

BIBLIOGRAPHY
G. Celant, *Giuseppe Penone* (Milan, 1989); *Giuseppe Penone*, catalogue, Turin Castello di Rivoli 1991 (Milan, 1991).
VC

Perrier Charles

1862
A French doctor and criminolo-

gist, he worked in the central prison in Nîmes, and studied criminal anthropometry and graphology.

BIBLIOGRAPHY
Du tatouage chez les criminels (Lyons, 1897); *Les Criminels, étude concernant 859 condamnés* (Lyons, 1900); *La Grande envergure et ses rapports avec la taille chez les criminels* (Lyons, 1908).
PC

Petrov-Vodkin Kuz'ma Sergeevič

Chvalynsk, 1878–Saint Petersburg, 1939
After his early work as an icon and landscape painter in Novgorod (1896), he attended the School of Applied Arts in Saint Petersburg. He studied first in Moscow, and later in Munich (1901) where he was the student of Anton Ažbe who started him off on Symbolist painting (*Arte rivoluzionaria*, 105). He completed his training with frequent journeys to Europe (Greece, Italy, France), where he became interested in Pierre Bonnard, Maurice Denis and the Nabis (1907). When he returned to Saint Petersburg he studied the Matisses in Sučukin's collection (1911). During the Revolution, he was a member of the Arts Council, worked in graphics, and began teaching (1918). At this point, realistic and historical themes begin to dominate his works, discussed in his publication *Euclid's space* (1932). He was invited to the Venice Biennale XIV (1924).

BIBLIOGRAPHY
Arte rivoluzionaria dai musei sovietici 1910–1930, catalogue, Lugano Villa Favorita Fondazione Thyssen–Bornemisza 12 June–2 October 1988 (Milan, 1988), 105; *Arte Russa e Sovietica 1870–1930*, catalogue, Turin Lingotto 1989, ed. Giovanni Carandente (Milan, 1989), 236; *Avanguardia Russa dalle collezioni private sovietiche. Origini e percorso 1904–1934*, catalogue, Milan Palazzo Reale 28 January–18 March 1989, ed. Enrico Crispolti (Bergamo, 1988), 164.
VM

Pfeiffer Ludwig

1843–1921
A German doctor and artist, he was an honorary professor at the Weimar Academy of Fine Arts. He studied human morphology in its applications to art, medicine and clothing design.

BIBLIOGRAPHY

Handbuch der Angewandten Anatomie, genaue Beschreibung der Gestalt und der Wuschfehler des Menschen nach den Mass und Zahlenvernhältnissen der Körperoberflächenteile (Leipzig, 1899).
PC

Picasso Pablo *see* **Topography of Pablo Picasso**

Pisani Vettor

Naples, 1934
Duchamp is the constant reference point throughout his work, who appears as early as his first one-man show in May 1970 in the La Salita gallery in Rome, *Studi su Marcel Duchamp 1965–70: maschile, femminile e androgino. Incesto e cannibalismo in Marcel Duchamp*. In 1970 he designed with Pistoletto the space for the show *Amore mio* in the palazzo Ricci in Montepulciano. In the same year he also exhibited for the Pascali prize *Uova mangiate, uova culturate* (1965) and *Agnus Dei* (1970) at the castello Svevo in Bari, on the theme of the sacred. He also took part in a group show at the L'attico gallery in Rome with *Fine dell'alchimia* and *Io non amo la natura*, and also exhibited in the collection *Vitalità del negativo nell'arte italiana 1960–1970* at the Palazzo delle Exposizioni with *Silenzio Marcel Duchamp*. In 1971 he exhibited at the São Paolo Biennale VII with *Marcel Duchamp. Les quatre doigts moulus de Meret Oppenheim*. In 1975 he put on *Il coniglio non ama Joseph Beuys*, at the Sperone gallery in Rome. He showed *RC Theatrum* at the Venice Biennale, the beginning of a theatre series he would work on throughout the Eighties. He participated in the Venice Biennale in 1978, 1984, 1986 and 1990, the Rome Quadriennale in 1986, the shows *Avanguardia/Transavanguardia* (Rome, 1982), *Arte italiana 1960–1982* (London, Hayward Gallery, 1982) and *Terrae Motus 2*, (Paris, Grand Palais, 1987).

BIBLIOGRAPHY
Arte e critica 1980, catalogue, Rome Galleria Nazionale d'Arte Moderna July–September 1980, ed. I. Panicelli (Rome, 1980); *Vettor Pisani. Il Teatro di Cristallo*, catalogue, Trento Galleria Civica di Arte Contemporanea December 1982–February 1983, ed. D. Eccher (Rome, 1993).
VC

Pollock Jackson

Cody, 1912–The Springs, 1956
He grew up in Arizona and studied at the Manual Arts High School in Los Angeles, where he met Philip Guston (Landau, 247). In 1930 he moved to New York and took courses with the regionalist Thomas Hart Benton, and was influenced by Albert Pinkham Ryder whose style is felt in his self–portrait (1930–1933) exhibited here (Landau, 32). The New Deal initiatives to fight the effects of the economic crisis gave him the opportunity to paint, along with his wife Lee Krasner, for the government in the *W.P.A.– Federal Art Project*, until 1943. In the same year Peggy Guggenheim organized his first one–man show in the Gallery Art of This Century (New York City). In 1946 he painted *Eyes in the Heat,* reflections on the nature of Long Island, anticipating the dripping technique which brought him international fame. The painting was selected for the Venice Biennale XXIV (1948, United States Pavilion) with other works from the Peggy Guggenheim collection.

BIBLIOGRAPHY
XXIV Biennale di Venezia, ed. Rodolfo Pallucchini (Venice, 1948), 347 n. 109; Francis Valentine O'Connor and Eugene W. Thaw (eds.), *Jackson Pollock: a Catalogue Raisonné of Paintings, Drawings and Other Works* (New Haven and London, 1978), 4 vols.; Angelica Zander Rudenstine, *Peggy Guggenheim Collection, Venice* (New York, 1985), 654 n. 150; Ellen G. Landau, *Jackson Pollock* (London, 1989), 32, 247.
VM

Prampolini Enrico

Modena, 1894–Rome, 1956
A student of Giacomo Balla (1871–1958), he was involved in Futurism very early on, as is revealed in a letter from Sironi to Boccioni 1913 citing his signing of various manifestoes. His artistic production takes into account several European movements and influences, such as Dada (1917), De Stijl, Bauhaus, and trends from the Section d'Or (1922) and the Cercle et Carré groups (1930, of which he was one of the founding members). This wide-ranging set of references put him into contact with the latest abstract developments. His constant quest to go beyond mere 'easel' painting led him to polymaterial works such as *Ritratto di F.T. Marinetti poeta parolibero* (*Prampolini 1913–1956*, 52 n. 8),

works which use different types of materials on the canvas. Their use was described and discussed in his *Dalla pittura murale alle composizioni polimateriche* (1934) and *L'arte polimaterica* (1944). From his first one–man show at the Galleria Sprovieri (Rome 1914) and his participation in the Venice Biennale XV (1926), he remained at the center of European cultural developments, and exhibited in many one–man and group shows. He was also involved in sculpture, theater, architecture and murals.

BIBLIOGRAPHY
Prampolini 1913–1956, catalogue, Modena Galleria Fonte d'Abisso, 7 December 1985–28 February 1986, ed. Achille Bonito Oliva (Modena, 1986), 52 n. 8; Giovanni Lista (ed.), *Enrico Prampolini– Carteggio futurista* (Rome, 1992); Rossella Siligato (ed.) *Prampolini–Carteggio 1916– 1956* (Rome, 1992); Jeffrey Schnapp, 'Heads of State', *Art Issues*, 24 (September– October 1992), 23–8.

Prinzhorn-Sammlung

This collection of over 5000 works preserved in the psychiatric clinic of the University of Heidelberg takes its name from the psychiatrist Hans Prinzhorn (Hemer, Westphalia, 1886–Munich, 1933), who from 1919 to 1921 catalogued and studied for the first time the artistic expressions of generally schizophrenic patients from various German and Swiss clinics, putting together material which had been collected from as early as 1890. Prinzhorn was primarily interested in the link between mental illness and expressive artistic phenomena, and he continued to gather much more material. In 1922 he published his findings in the essay '*Bildnerei der Geisteskranken*' ('Figuration of the mentally alienated') which was reprinted in 1923 because of the great public demand outside the scientific world. It was read by artists such as Jean Arp, Alfred Kubin, Paul Klee, Pablo Picasso and Max Ernst (Poley 1980, 58– 63). Until 1933 examples from the extraordinary collection were exhibited, works which are striking because of the spontaneity and immediacy of artistic expression, which reflect both the circumstances of hospital life as well as the symptoms of illness, including repetition of the same images. Although two works were exhibited by the Nazis in 1937 and denounced as *entartet* (degenerate) the collection

remained substantially intact. Except for an occasional show, a permanent exhibition of the Prinzhorn-Sammlung collection in the clinic in Heidelberg was only established in 1972.

BIBLIOGRAPHY
Hans Prinzhorn, *Bildnerei der Geisteskranken. Ein Beitrag zur Psychologie und Psychopatologie der Gestaltung* (Berlin, 1922); *Die Prinzhorn-Sammlung. Bilder, Skulpturen, Texte aus Psychiatrischen Anstalten (c. 1890–1920)*, catalogue, Heidelberg, Hamburg, Stuttgart, Basle, Berlin and Munich February– December 1980; Stefanie Poley, '... und nicht mehr lassen mich diese Dinge los.' Prinzhorns Buch '*Die Bildnerei der Geisteskranken*' und seine Wirkung in der modernen Kunst*, in *Die Prinzhorn-Sammlung*, catalogue, Heidelburg, Hamburg, Stuttgart, Basle, Berlin and Munich February–December 1980 (Königstein 1980), 55–69.
SR

Pullè Leopoldo F.

1850–1934
He held the Chair in Indo-European philology in Padua and Bologna. In his youth he had Socialist leanings, but later his affiliations were increasingly nationalist, and even Fascist. In addition to his interest in glottology and Eastern studies, he was also involved in ethno-anthropological research. He was a member of the SIAE (Società italiana di Antropologia ed Etnologia) and took part in their meetings (see discussion on the Aryans, Pullè 1897). He won the competition for the Società per tracciare la carta etnolinguistica d'Italia (Pullè, 1989). He was a follower of Cattaneo and Ascoli, and wrote the preface to the third volume of Cattaneo's *Scritti politici*, also published in the 'Archivio' under the title *Carlo Cattaneo come antropologo, come etnologo* (1902).

BIBLIOGRAPHY
Leopoldo F. Pullè, 'Sugli Ariani', *AAE*, XXVII, 1897, 441– 69; Leopoldo F. Pullè, 'Profilo antropologico dell'Italia', *AAE*, XXVIII, 1898, 19–168; Leopoldo F. Pullè, *L'Italia: genti e favelle* (Turin, 1927), 3 vols.
LS

Raetz Markus

Büren an der Aare, 1941
Raetz was influenced by Pop Art and Op Art very early on. He began to produce installations and drawings, expressing a constant interest in ex-

tremes, from enormous weight (his pink granite *Mimi* weighed six tons) to an extraordinary lightness (*Eva*). He lived in Poland, Holland, Morocco, and Spain and finally returned to Switzerland. His work was exhibited at the 4th, 5th, and 7th Documenta. His entire production is marked by states of passage: from the shapeless to the shape, from the invisible to the visible: 'Emptiness becomes full, more becomes less, visual reflections are submitted to a test of strength, reality is undermined, and the coherency of the world is veiled in doubt' (Bouyer, in *Dictionnaire de l'Art Moderne et Contemporaine*, Paris 1992, 519).

BIBLIOGRAPHY
Markus Raetz. Arbeiten 1962-1986, catalogue, Zurich Kunsthaus 1986 (Zurich, 1986).
SDS

x–Rays *or* Röntgen

Wilhelm Conrad Röntgen (*Lennep, 1845–Munich, 1923*), professor of physics at the University of Würzburg, discovered x–rays, or Röntgen rays, in 1895 (Ratti, 6). Working with a cathode tube in his research on the effects of an electrical discharge passing through rarefied gas, he became curious about a fluorescent halo effect. While experimenting with these radiations on his wife's hand, he realized the '... the soft parts were dissolving and becoming transparent, and the framework of bones stood out clearly ...' (Cardinale, 40). He understood that these radiations could see through opaque bodies, and this discovery soon led to many important practical applications and won him the Nobel prize (1901). This new field of studies had an immediate effect on the scientific community. Paul Oudin and T. Barethélémy's work in France led to the first radiograph (21 January 1896), followed by a photograph album by Remy and Contremoulins (Paris, 1897), and the experiments of Van Heurck in Antwerp (23 March 1896) and A. Mori in Italy. Unexpected possibilities opened up in the art world as well, which was profoundly influenced by early experiments in this technique, from Man Ray to Meret Oppenheim (*Rötgenaufnahme des Schädels Meret Oppenheim*, 1964) and Robert Rauschenberg (*Booster and Seven Studies*, 1967).

BIBLIOGRAPHY
Otto Glasser, *W.C. Röntgen und die Geschichte der*

Röntgenstrahlen (Berlin, 1959); Arduino Ratti, 'W.C. Röntgen e i fisici italiani del suo tempo', *Memorie dell' Istituto Lombardo–Accademia di Scienze e Lettere–Classe di Scienze Matematiche e Naturali*, vol. XXVII, Memoria 1 (Milan, 1977), 6, 8–9; Adelfio Elio Cardinale, 'Con il misterioso "raggio x" il corpo rimase nudo', *Il Corriere della Sera*, (8 April 1995), 40.
VM

Rainer Arnulf

Baden, 1929
Self-taught, he rejected traditional academic education, and was first influenced by Paul Nash, Francis Bacon, Stanley Spencer, Henry Moore, and Surrealist theory (1947). With Ernst Fuchs, Anton Lehmden, Arik Brauer and Joseph Mikl he founded the *Hundsgruppe* (1950) and began to work in photography (1951), initiating systematic research on relationships with other graphic techniques which still continues in his work today. The Surrealist period (*Zentralisationen, Blindmalerei*) was followed by his discovery of *Abstract Expressionism* (De Kooning, Pollock) and *tachisme* employed during his stay in Paris (1951). Rainer achieved international fame with his *übermalungen* painted where works of other artists (Emilio Vedova, Sam Francis, Victor Vasarely) were covered with superimposed layers of colour (1952–64). After the cycle of the *Kruzifikationen* (1956–57), he returned in the Sixties to the Surrealist theme of automatic writing assisted by the use of drugs (LSD, Psylocibin), and later worked on a re-evaluation of Leonardo, Rembrandt, Goya, Franz Xavier Messerschmidt (*Kunst auf Kunst*). At the same time as his *Fingermalerei* and *Handmalerei* (1973–80) he began to use the body as a painting instrument, spreading colour directly on the canvas first with the finger and then using the entire body. After *Piranesi-Zyklus* (1987) and *Shakespeare-Zyklus* (1988) he produced the series *Katastrophen und Desaster* (1991) and *Engel und Kosmos* (1994). He took part in the Venice Biennale XXXVIII (1978) when he had a one-man show at the Austrian Pavilion, and exhibited at the next Biennale as well (1980, *L' arte negli anni settanta*).

BIBLIOGRAPHY
Arnulf Rainer, catalogue, Recklinghausen (Germany) Kunsthalle, 18 September–6 November 1994, ed. Ferdinand Ullrich (Recklinghausen, 1994).
VM

Rauschenberg Robert
Port Arthur, 1933
After the war he enrolled at Black Mountain College, North Carolina, where he took courses with Joseph Albers (1948), and met the composer John Cage, as well as Merce Cunningham and David Tudor (1949). After his first one-man show at the Betty Parsons Gallery (New York 1951) he traveled extensively in Europe, especially in Italy with his friend the painter Cy Twombly. On his return to New York he began a long collaboration with Merce Cunningham's dance company (1953), and started his *Combine paintings*, canvases which use different materials assembled in a new way, linked by painting. His work occasionally resembled Pop Art, but was classified as New Dada, especially as revealed in the work of Marcel Duchamp and Kurt Schwitters. The prize he won at the Venice Biennale XXXII (1964) confirmed his importance at a European level and his paintings began to command very high prices on the market. A pioneer in technical and expressive innovation, he launched the R.O.C.I. in 1984 (Rauschenberg Overseas Culture Interchange), a 'planetary' scheme of traveling shows that involve his works (paintings, sculptures, videotapes), and the work of artists and artisans from all over the world.

BIBLIOGRAPHY
Robert Rauschenberg, catalogue, Düsseldorf Kunstsammlung Nordrhein–Westfalen 7 May– 10 July 1994, ed. Armin Zweite (Bonn, 1994), 196.
VM

Remy *see* x-Rays *or* Röntgen

Richer Paul
Chartres, 1849–Paris, 1933
Doctor, sculptor and art professor, in 1882 he was named the head of the laboratories of the Salpêtrière Clinic for mental illness in Paris. He began a systematic investigation of the physiono-my of the sick, using drawings and photographs in collabora-tion with Albert Londe, (*Nascita*, 39–40). In 1903 he was named professor of anatomy at the Ecole des Beaux–Arts. With Jean Martin Charcot (Paris, 1825–Nièure, 1893), the eminent neu-ropathologist at the same clinic, he published *Les démoniaques dans l' art* (1866), *Les Malades et les difformes dans l' art* (1889)

and an interesting interdisci-plinary study on the deformed face in the keystone on the door of the campanile of the church of Santa Maria Formosa in Venice. His drawings illustrate the characteristic symptoms of 'hysterical hemiplegia', a nervous disorder which causes a spasm in the lower half of the face and the tongue (Charcot, 87–91).

BIBLIOGRAPHY
Jean Martin Charcot and Paul Richer, 'Le mascaron grotesque de l'église Santa Maria Formosa à Venise et l'hémispasme glosso labié hystérique', *Nouvelle Iconogra-phie de la Salpêtrière*, I, 1888, 87–91; *Nascita della fotografia psichiatrica*, catalogue, Venice Ca' Corner della Regina 31 January–8 March 1981, ed. Franco Cagnetta and Jacque-line Sonolet (Venice, 1981), 39–40.
VM

Roberts William
London, 1895–1980
He worked as a poster artist in advertising, and then studied at the Slade School (1910–13) where he met Stanley Spencer and Paul Nash and, began to explore Cubism. He was active in Roger Fry's *Omega* project, and in 1914 he joined Wyndham Lewis' *Vorticist* movement, and signed the group manifesto in the review 'Blast'. He took part in the *Vorticist Exhibition* at the Doré Galleries (1915). Moving away from Lewis, he continued to work within the Cubist world until 1926–27, when he returned to traditional painting, rounding angular forms and animating his composition. He was interest-ed in the human figure, and portrayed people engaged in various activities, urban life, religious and classical subjects, and English country landscapes. *The Vorticist at the Restaurant de la Tour Eiffel* (1962) depicts one of the group's meetings at the Percy Street restaurant, celebrating the launch of the first issue of the journal 'Blast'. Ezra Pound, Wiliam Roberts, Wyndham Lewis, and the owner of the restaurant, Rudolph Stulik, are portrayed.

BIBLIOGRAPHY
William Roberts ARA. Retro-spective exhibition, catalogue, London Tate Gallery, 20 November–19 December 1965 (London, 1965); *Vorticism and its allies*, catalogue, Hayward Gallery 27 March–2 June 1974 (London, 1974), 32, 106–07, 110.
RA

Rodin Auguste
Paris, 1840–Meudon, 1917
Although he took drawing and sculpting courses from a very early age, he was not accepted by the Ecole des Beaux–Arts (1857). After working as a decorator, he moved to the studio of A.E. Carrier–Belleuse, with whom he worked on several monuments in Brussels. In 1875 he traveled to Italy where he was deeply impressed by the work of Michelangelo and Antonello whose influence would be felt in the bronze *Le Vaincu*, also known as *L' Age d' Airain* (1877), which caused a scandal at the Paris *Salon* because of its realism compared to the sculpture of the time. On his return to Paris he was excluded from competitions for several monuments, but he succeeded in establishing his reputation as a sculptor with his *St. Jean–Baptiste prêchant* (1878) in which he reconfirmed his tendency, on a larger scale, for anatomical realism and the depiction of movement. An important state commission for a door in bronze for the Musée des Arts Décoratifs inspired by Dante's *Inferno* from which it takes its name, *La porte de l' enfer*, occupied him till his death.

BIBLIOGRAPHY
Catherine Lampert, *Rodin: Sculptures & Drawings*, catalogue, London Hayward Gallery, 1 November 1986–25 January 1987 (n.p., 1987); Ruth Butler, *Rodin: The Shape of Genius* (New Haven–London, 1993); Mary L. Levkoff, *Rodin in His Time*, catalogue, Los Angeles, Los Angeles County Museum of Art 1994 (n.p., 1994).
MC

Rosso Medardo
Turin, 1858–Milan 1928
He studied at the Brera Accademia (1882–83) and was expelled for his rebellious conduct. His further training took place within the late Lombard *scapigliatura*, and he drew his formal solutions from the painting of Daniele Ranzoni and the sculpture of Giuseppe Grandi, creating a sculpture which breaks through the impenetrable surface of the plastic object, achieving an interrelationship between external and internal spaces (*Carne altrui*, 1883; *Impressione di un omnibus*, 1884). His conviction of the interference between subjec-tivity and objectivity was borrowed from the Impression-ists, merging it with his own positivist training and seeking movement in the dynamics of

light. In 1889 he moved to Paris where, praised by Degas and admired by Zola and Clemenceau, he became friends with Rodin and completed his education. Moved by the desire to 'forget matter', he finally abandoned full relief sculptures and statues. His figures become mobile, fleeting, and almost lose their plastic substance (*Conversazione in giardino*, 1896) and acquire a new expressivity (*Rieuse*, 1890; *Yvette Guilbert*, 1895). This progressive advance towards synthesis reaches its peak in *Madame X* (1896), 'in the circumscribing of the head alone, its almost total elimination of objects, and its unified modeling' (Caramel, 563). It is regarded as the work which achieves the highest degree of abstraction in the sculpture of the time (Scolari Barr, 49). In 1914 and 1950 the Venice Biennale dedicated one-man shows to Medardo Rosso.

BIBLIOGRAPHY
Catalogo XI Esposizione Internazionale d' Arte della Città di Venezia 1914 (Venice, 1914), 85–7; *Catalogo XXV Biennale di Venezia* (Venice, 1950), 65–70; Margaret Scolari Barr, *Medardo Rosso* (New York, 1963); *Medardo Rosso 1858–1928*, catalogue, Frankfurt Frankfurter Kunstv-erein, 20 January–11 March 1984, ed. Peter Weiermair [Frankfurt, 1984] with bibliog-raphy; Luciano Caramel ad vocem *Medardo Rosso* in *Futurismo e futurismi*, catalogue, Venice Palazzo Grassi 3 May–12 October 1986, ed. P. Hulten (Milan, 1986).
MBG

Russolo Luigi
Portogruaro, Venice, 1885–Cerro di Laveno, 1947
He abandoned the family tradition of music in 1901 to attend the Accademia in Brera. In Milan he was exposed to the theories of Romani and Previati, and he trained in Divisionist technique, while remaining alert to develop-ments in Symbolism as well. He met Boccioni whose thematic influence would be visible in his later engravings, featuring subjects linked to the industrial civilization. He signed the Futurist manifesto (1910), became one of the most animated participants in their evening gatherings, and he took part in many exhibi-tions in Italy and abroad. He joined in the Futurist quest (1910), focusing on the theme of movement, with works that recorded the moment of fusion between dynamic forces

(*Dinamismo di un' automobile*) or that adhere to the '... principle of simultaneity as mnemonic synthesis, in a key between Munch and Previati ...' (Calvesi, XLVI). He worked with the Bragaglia brothers and was interested in spiritualist photography. From 1913 he concentrated on his interest in music, published *L' arte dei rumori* (*The art of noise*, 1913) which explored enharmonic music and invented new instruments such as the *intona–rumori* ('noise-maker'). He returned to painting after the First World War and exhibited abroad. He directed three concerts at the Théâtre des Champ Elysées in Paris, before an audience that included Stravinsky, Ravel and Kahn. Russolo exhibited five works in the Futurist section presented by Marinetti at the Venice Biennale XVII (1930).

BIBLIOGRAPHY
Maurizio Calvesi, *Quattro maestri del primo futurismo italiano*, in *Venezia–Biennale 1968* (Venice, 1968), XLI–LII; *Russolo: l' arte dei rumori 1913–1931*, catalogue, Venice Ca' Corner della Regina 15 October–20 November 1977, ed. F. Maffina (Venice, 1977); Franco Maffina, ad vocem *Russolo*, in *Futurismo e futurismi*, catalogue, Venice Palazzo Grassi 3 May–12 October 1986, ed. P. Hulten (Milan, 1986); Carlo Pirovano (ed.), *La pittura in Italia–Il Novecento 1900–1945*, vol. I, II, (Milan, 1992), 1051–2; *Civico Museo d' Arte contemporanea* (Milan, 1994), 55.
MBG

Šadr Ivan Dmitrijevič
Shadrinsk, 1887–Moscow, 1941
He was educated in Saint Petersburg and at the Yekaterinberg School of Art and Industrial Design (Sverdlovsk), and studied sculpture in Paris with Auguste Rodin (1840–1917) and Emile–Antoine Bourdelle (1861–1929). Interested in large–scale monumental projects, he received many commissions from the Russian revolutionary government. These celebratory pieces were so successful that they were even reproduced on banknotes and stamps, and exercised a profound influence on Soviet art for many years. A skilled portrait sculptor as well, (*The artist's mother*, 1923; *Maxim Gorky*, 1939) he began the project and designs for the *Maxim Gorky* monument (Moscow 1952) which was completed by Vera Mukhina and collaborators after his death.

BIBLIOGRAPHY
Art in Soviet Union. Major Works by Soviet Artists from 1917 to the 1970is. Painting, Sculpture, Graphic Art (Leningrad, 1977).
VM

Saint-Edme see **Fotografia spiritica**

Saliger Ivo
Bilovec, 1894
He studied and worked in Vienna, and in 1930 left for Paris. After 1933 he became increasingly involved in German Fascism and developed an interest in ancient mythology, following the theories of the Nazi Alfred Rosenberg, who constructed a link between the ancient Greeks and twentieth century *Arier*. He painted the *Judgement of Paris* for the II Große Deutsche Kunstausstellung (Second Big Show of German Art) in 1939, one of the most popular themes in the Fascist world. Saliger transformed the famous three gods of myth into models of the feminine aesthetic ideals of the Nordic race. Paris's pose and scrutinizing gaze towards the three women submitted to his judgement, however, remove any sensual allusions to the myth.

BIBLIOGRAPHY
Kunst und Diktatur. Architektur, Bildhauerei und Malerei, in Österreich, Deutschland, Italien und der Sowjetunion 1922-1956, catalogue, Vienna 1994, ed. Jan Tabor (Baden, 1994); Berthold Hinz, *Die Malerei im deutschen Faschismus. Kunst und Konterrevolution* (Munich, 1974).
SR

Samochvalov Aleksandr Nikolaevič
Beshezk, 1894-1971
After finishing his studies in Saint Petersburg (1913) and at the Petrograd Academy (1914-18), he became a student of Kuz'ma Sergeevič Petrov-Vodkin (1878-1939), with whom he made an ethnological expedition in Turkestan in the summer of 1921 (*150 Jahre*, 177). He was an eclectic personality within the various art groups and movements in the Twenties ('Mir Iskusstva') and worked as a poster artist, porcelain decorator, book illustrator, graphic artist, sculptor and set designer (*Avanguardia russa*, 168).

BIBLIOGRAPHY

150 Jahre Russische Graphick-1813-1963, catalogue, Dresden Staatliche Kunstsammlungen Dresden Kupferstich-Kabinet 1964, ed. Werner Schmidt (n.p., n.d.), 176-7; *Avanguardia russa dalle collezioni private sovietiche-Origini e percorso 1904-1934*, catalogue, Milan Palazzo Reale, 28 January-18 March 1989, ed. Enrico Crispolti (Bergamo, 1988), 168.
VM

Savinio Alberto
Andrea De Chirico
Athens, 1891-Rome, 1952
The 'quintessential dilettante', Alberto Savinio was a writer, painter, and musician. With a 'light, soft, "mistaken", ironic', educational background (Scheiwiller in *Con Savinio*, 21) Savinio believed in the identification of 'supreme dilettantism' and 'supreme liberty'. In Paris in 1910 with his brother Giorgio De Chirico he was a frequent guest at Apollinaire's literary soirées; in 1917 the two De Chirico brothers were in Ferrara demanding the recognition of 'metaphysical painting'. In 1925 Savinio began to paint more seriously and in 1927 he returned to Paris. In comparison with his brother's work, his paintings explore psychological analogies between men and animals, which assume disturbing and monstruous shapes. In later years, Savinio regarded the growing excesses of the avant-garde with indifference, and remained fundamentally connected to 'human evidence': 'There is no rift between physical and metaphysical, and the metaphysical is the direct and natural continuation of the the physical. The metaphysical must be understood in this sense... a courageous, precise, complete attempt to find some "explanation for the world"' (Scheiwiller in *Con Savinio*, 21).

BIBLIOGRAPHY
Alberto Savinio, catalogue, Milan Palazzo Reale (Milan, 1976); *Con Savinio*, catalogue, Fiesole (Milan, 1981).
SDS

Schad Christian
Miesbach, 1894-Stuttgart, 1982
He had his first one-man show at the Salon Wolfsberg in Zurich, and invented the 'schadograph' in Geneva in 1918 (a kind of rayogram) where he met Tzara and the French Dadaists. In 1925 he settled in Vienna where in 1927 the first complete

exhibition of his works took place, leading back to the Neue Sachlichkeit. His fame as a realist of extraordinary expressive brutality is due to his portraits from the late Twenties, depicting close friends and personalities of contemporary Viennese society. In 1928 he moved to Berlin: Doctor Haustein of the anonymous portrait, who was to kill himself by swallowing cyanide when the Gestapo came to arrest him, kept a salon which was a favorite meeting point for the artistic, political and literary élite of the day. The chill gaze of Schad's portraits seem to create portrait-memorials very like 'mug shots'. 'Although... attached to the flesh almost as if it were his own true plastification [the shirt in Selbsporträt] he creates between himself and the flesh an implacable inalterable vacuum, which makes the true singularity, the true mark and the true stigmata (as well as the true space) of Schad's poetics' (Testori in *Christian Schad*, 1970).

BIBLIOGRAPHY
Christian Schad, catalogue, Milan-Munich Galleria del Levante, February 1970 (Milan, 1970); *Christian Schad*, catalogue, Berlin Staatliche Kunsthalle (Berlin, 1980).
LS

Schjerfbeck Helene
Helsinki, 1862-Stockholm, 1946
She arrived with a scholarship in Paris at the age of eighteen, and soon exhibited several naturalist works in the *salon* (*Fête juive*, 1883 and *Première verdure*, 1889). After studying the Old Masters on her grand tour of Europe, she returned to Finland in the 1890s. She taught for a period, but suffering from poor health, she decided to retreat into the Finnish countryside. Remaining outside both the local Romantic and Symbolist currents, she worked on her own personal expressive vision in solitude. The gallery owner Gösta Stenman, her agent, guaranteed her financial independence and organized her one-man shows in Sweden (1937). At the turn of the century she began to concentrate on the faces of the people of Hyvinkää and Tammisaari, the small towns of her retreat, which make up a gallery of portraits influenced by French Modernism (*Flicka med blått band*, 1903; *Flicka i svart*, 1906-07; *Maria*, 1912). Another constant factor in her work are the self-portraits that form an almost

uninterrupted series in the last two decades of her life. Schjerfbeck was working on them well into her eighties, and they are arresting in their increasingly economical brushstroke which reflects her search for an essential identity within Scandinavian Expressionism. The XXVIII Venice Biennale (1956) dedicated a retrospective to her with sixty paintings including her *Sjäwporträtt* (1912).

BIBLIOGRAPHY
XXVII Biennale di Venezia (Venice, 1956), 370-74; Lena Ahtola-Moorhouse, 'Helene Schjerfbeck', *Form Function Finland*, 1, 1992, 10-5; *Helene Schjerfbeck*, catalogue, Stockholm Galleri Axlund 3 April-8 May 1994, ed. Lena Holger (Stockholm, 1994).
LS

Schlemmer Oskar
Stockholm, 1888-Baden Baden, 1943
Invited to Bauhaus by Gropius in 1920, Schlemmer ran the stone sculpture and mural painting studios there, and until 1929 he also directed the theatre workshop, in which he created the *Triadic Ballet* (1924-26). In 1929 he left Dessau for the Breslau Academy, and in 1932 he went to Berlin to the Fine Arts Academy, where he was rejected by the Nazis. He moved from initial post-Impressionism, accompanied by his interest in scenic problems, to a Cubist phase, and later to a style approaching the abstract, which he employed on natural forms reduced to their fundamental structures. 'In all his wide-ranging production, Schlemmer was interested in clarity and balance, based on the exploitation of essential and geometric forms' (*The Bauhaus* 314).

BIBLIOGRAPHY
Oskar Schlemmer. Zeichnungen und Graphik (Stockholm, 1965); *The Bauhaus. Masters and Students by themselves*, ed. Frank Whitford (London, 1992).
SDS

Schneemann Carolee
Fox Chase, 1939
Since the Sixties she has been investigating the female universe from a profoundly radical point of view, through photography, installations and performance art (Klinger 1991, 39). She came to international notice with her performance Interior Scroll (New York 1975), which was followed by Up and

to including her limits (1976) and ABC-We Print Anything-In The Cards (1977). *Fresh Blood: Dream Morphology* examines the relationship between dreams and sexuality, a theme she also explored in the more recent *Cat Scan* (1990), where Egyptian mythology is used to achieve a more heightened awareness of the female condition. In *Cycladys Imprints* (1988-91) an installation with slides and sounds 'through the timeless symbols of the female body-the violin, the images of fertility, the vagina itself-Schneemann's work seem to assert that femininity is something which lies outside of time and changes, and is based on the body alone' (Joselit, 1991, 121).

BIBLIOGRAPHY
Bruce McPherson (ed.), *More than meat joy: Carolee Schneemann-complete performance works & selected writings* (New York, 1979); Linda S. Klinger, Where's the Artist? Feminist Practice and Poststructural Theories of Authorship', *Art Journal*, vol. 50, 2, Summer 1991, 39-47; David Joselit, 'Projected Identities', *Art in America*, vol. 79, 11, November 1991, 121.
VM

Schönberg Arnold
Vienna, 1874-Los Angeles, 1951
Arnold Schönberg explored an increasing dissolution of tonality within the world of music, constantly moving towards the atonal and dodecaphony. His crucial meeting with Mahler (1903) inspired him to begin composing. In 1904 his group of students included Alban Berg and Anton Webern, who later, with their teacher, would establish the School of Vienna, which was to exercise an enormous influence on the music of the post-war period. Schönberg pursued his musical composition along with his interest in the figurative arts, inspired by his friendship with Richard Gerstl (Vienna 1883-1908). In 1907 he met Kandinsky and the members of '*Der Blaue Reiter*'. In his painting the most frequent subject is his face, '... the borderline between the interior and the external world. The eye watches its own image watching itself ...' (*Arnold Schönberg*, 363). In a letter to Leopold Stokowsky, referring to *Selbsportrait* (1910), a self-portrait that does not resemble him at all, he writes: 'Today I am sending you... a *self-portrait*, as I call it-that I painted around 1911 [...] I was

defining my style at that time as "making music with colors and forms" ...' (*Arnold Schönberg*, 369). Kandinsky comments on his friend's work: '... Schönberg reproaches himself for his "faulty technique"... he is wrong, he is not unhappy in his painting technique but in his interior desire... I would wish this unhappiness for every artist, in every age. It is not difficult to make progress externally. It isn't easy to make progress internally ...' .

BIBLIOGRAPHY
I quadri di Schönberg, in *La musica la pittura l' epoca di Arnold Schönberg*, catalogue, Venice Museo Correr 10 April–14 May 1978 (Venice, 1978); *Arnold Schönberg–Das Bildernische Werk*, catalogue, Vienna Museum des 20. Jahrhunderts 1991, ed. Thomas Zaunschirm, (Klagenfurt, 1991).
LS

Schulze-Mittendorf Walter
1893-1976
German decorator and set designer. In 1927 Mittendorf created the famous futurist robot for Fritz Lang's *Metropolis*. Mittendorf recalled 'the last step in the process wasn't much fun for Brigitte Helm. We had to make a plaster cast of her entire body. Pieces of canvas cut in the form of armor were covered with two millimeters of substance, spread out with a rolling pin. We used these pieces to cover the gesso model of Brigitte, like a shoemaker stretches the leather over the model. Once the material hardened, the parts were polished and the exterior sculpted. Thus we created a suit of armour in which the actress could move. We then touched up the whole to create a technological aesthetic. And finally we sprayed the armor with 'cellon' paint mixed with silver to give her that metallic appearance that was so convincing in the film' (Mittendorf in Lotte Eisner, 82).

BIBLIOGRAPHY
Lotte Eisner, *Fritz Lang* (Milan, 1978), 82; *Fritz Lang. La messa in scena*, catalogue, Turin Circolo degli Artisti, 4–20 March 1993 (Turin, 1993), 117.
SDS

Schwarzkogler Rudolf
Vienna, 1940–1969
He attended the School of Graphic Arts in Vienna from 1957 to 1961. He was one of the leading figures in Viennese Actionism, along with Nitsch, Muehl, and Günter Brus. The provocative and aggressive movement defied the traditional aesthetics and moral values which dominated in the Sixties, and was based on the happening, with echoes of the Informal, Action Painting and Tachism. Between 1965 and 1966, Schwarzkogler performed six actions, one before a live audience, the rest filmed. He created still-lifes with objects and human bodies, metaphors of the vulnerability of man and existential denunciation. In 1966 he began to move towards a more deliberate exploration of pure sensuality. The group became even more aggressively addicted to the bodily functions, during the violent public exhibitions, serving a liberating function, celebrating ambiguity, sado-masochistic sensuality, and self-destruction.

BIBLIOGRAPHY
Eve Badura-Triska, Hubert Klocher, *Rudolf Schwarzkogler. Leben und Werk* (Klagenfurt, 1992).
RA

Segal George
New York, 1924
He studied literature, history and philosophy at Rutgers University (1942–46) and later at the Pratt Institute of Design and at New York University (1949). After working for some time at his parents' factory and taking up painting (in which he was influenced by Baziotes, de Kooning, and Hans Hofmann) he had his first one-man show at the Hansa Gallery (New York City 1956). He began to work in sculpture (1961), making plaster casts of human beings obtained by using a special surgical bandage, and placing them in everyday situations, in work similar to that being created by other Pop Art artists. He finally arrived as a professional artist in 1964 with the establishment of Pop Art on an international level which took place at the Venice Biennale XXXII. From that moment on he has been a leading figure in the art world, participating in numerous international art events. In his latest work he attempts a sculptural re-assessment of the paintings of the great contemporary masters (Cézanne, Picasso, Braque, Morandi) in a quest to rediscover the symbolic values of the sense of color (Orsi 1990, 67).

BIBLIOGRAPHY
Handbuch Museum Ludwig, catalogue, Museum Ludwig, ed. Karl Ruhrberg (Cologne, 1979), 723; Donatella Orsi, 'Perché Segal ha ucciso i suoi manichini', *Arte*, 208, June 1990, Year xx, 64–67; Berndt Finkeldey, George Segal: *Situationen, Kunst und Alltag* (Frankfurt on Meno, 1990).
VM

Segantini Giovanni
Arco, Trento, 1858–Engadina, 1899
He attended the Accademia in Brera (1874–77) and became great friends with the painters Mentessi and Longoni. He was therefore a product of Lombard naturalism, from which he drew his interest in luminous effects. The turning point in his life was his meeting with the art dealer Vittore Grubicy, who permitted him to fulfil his humanistic and pantheistic ideal by confronting art in the solitude of the fields and mountains. He moved to Brianza (1880–86) where his works demonstrate a gradual liberation from his academic training, and move deeper into naturalistic exploration. A last glimmer of 'Scapigliatura' is occasionally revealed in works such as *L' eroe morto* (1879), an ambitious and difficult project in which Segantini employed an iconography of death '... with the objective of extracting from the dark something never before achieved, in the hope of making some sense of it ...' (Grubicy). He moved to Grigioni (1886–94) where he began to explore his interest in allegory and Symbolism which was to feature in his later works.

BIBLIOGRAPHY
Luciano Budigna, *Giovanni Segantini* (Milan, 1962); Annie–Paule Quinsac, *Segantini. Catalogo generale*, 2 vols. (Milan, 1982); *Giovanni Segantini 1858–1899*, catalogue, Zurich Kunsthaus, 9 November 1990–3 February 1991, eds. Annie–Paule Quinsac, Günther Metken and Dora Lardelli (Zurich, 1990).
MC

Seglas Jules
1856
A French doctor who worked at the Salpêtrière clinic in Paris. Through the study of anthropometry he sought to establish a relationship between the morphology of the body and mental illness. He contributed to the journal *Nouvelle Iconographie de la Salpêtrière*.

BIBLIOGRAPHY
De l'examen morphologique chez les aliénés et les idiots (1889); *Leçons cliniques sur les maladies mentales et nerveuses* (Paris, 1895); *Séméiologie des affections mentales* (1903).
PC

Selke Willy
A sculptor and photographer, he developed new techniques in photosculpture, a procedure combining the industrial and the artisan which was originally conceived by François Willème. His works, presented to the new Société Générale de Photosculpture de France between 1863 and 1869, were a great public success. Twenty-four cameras were positioned in a radius around the subject in the middle, which they photographed in unison. The profiles thus obtained were projected onto a screen and modeled in clay blocks with a pantograph which was rotated by 15 degrees. The photosculpture was therefore the sum total of the profiles in clay, and the materials used varied from stucco to porcelain, to marble or bronze. Repeating the procedure in Reissig, Selke modified the technique. In the patent (valid from 2 July 1897) he described the procedure entitling it 'Technique for the plastic reproduction of bodies'. In 1899 he opened a studio in Berlin and several of his works were exhibited in Paris in 1901. In the course of his artistic career, Selke created reliefs of this markedly realistic taste, comparable in quality to those of Willème. Photosculpture, developed along with the cinematographic technique, gave Selke the opportunity to use a film camera, with the added infinite potential of luminous cuts achieving absolute mechanical identity.

BIBLIOGRAPHY
Wolfgang Drost, 'La photosculpture entre art industriel et artisanat. La réussite de François Willème (1830-1895)', *Gazette des Beaux-Arts*, October, 113–129; Wolfgang Drost, *Die herausforderung des Fortschritts an die Kunst. Von der 'technischen' zur 'kreativen', Photoskulptur (Willème, Pötschke, Reissig, Selke–Kammerichs, Ceroli)*, in *Sondertruck* (Heidelberg, 1986).
LS

Serrano Andres
New York, 1950
Of Hispanic background, Serrano studied painting and sculpture at the Brooklyn Museum Art School of New York from 1967 to 1969, and later began to experiment in photography. His work has affinities with Neo-Conceptual art and Surrealism, with special reference to Marcel Duchamp and Yves Klein. He regards photography as a false reality, a reality forged and directed by the artist. His works are constructed on opposites, such as the sacred and the profane, life and death, abstraction and representation. *The Morgue* (1992) is his last series of photographs, which are pictures of dead bodies and various details of body, each accompanied by a note indicating the cause of death. Serrano does not reveal the identity, political affiliation, religious beliefs, or social status of the deceased, and at times the fragmentation of the details make it impossible to distinguish sex, race or age. Serrano exhibited at the *Aperto 93* of the Venice Biennale XLV.

BIBLIOGRAPHY
Gianni Romano, 'La palette cachée d'Andres Serrano', *Art Press*, 159 (June 1991), 30–4; *Catalogo della XLV Esposizione Internazionale d' Arte* (Venice, 1993), 330–1; *Andres Serrano. The Morgue*, catalogue, Paris Galerie Yvonne Lambert 17 October–18 November 1993, ed. Daniel Arasse (Paris, 1993); *Andres Serrano*, catalogue, Lubyana Moderna Galerija 1 March–3 April 1994 (Lubyana, 1994).
RA

Severini Gino
Cortona, 1883–Paris, 1966
He met Boccioni and Corazzini in Rome in 1899. In 1906 he moved to Paris where he became friends with Modigliani, Utrillo, Braque, Picasso and Gris. In 1910 he was one of the signers of the *Manifesto della pittura futurista*, but he later claimed to be much closer to French Futurism, which started from the Divisionism of Seurat and Signac, unlike the Italian movement. He developed an interest in Cubism and between 1913 and 1914 he produced Cubo-futurist works inspired by the war. Together with motifs of the French and Italian avant-garde, his works combine the idea of a 'scientific' method of artistic representation derived from Formalist purity with the great Renaissance tradition. In 1922 he set forth his ideas in *Du Cubisme au Classicisme*, published the following year; his *Projections conjugées de la tête* drawings come from

the preparatory work. They are the emulation of the construction system of figures using joined orthogonal projections worked out by Dürer. He met Jacques Maritain and became interested in religious painting which reveals mystic inspiration. He decorated the churches of Semsale and la Roche, achieving that style that Maritain defined as 'classically-spirited transcendant realism' . *The Portrait de la famille Severini* (1936) concludes the series of family portraits executed in the mid-1930s. In this work 'the solemn arrangement of the figures and their sturdy volume are associated with a taste for the representation of detail (Gina's silk dress, the coral earrings) linked to a 'mythology of the everyday' of the Italian twentieth century.

BIBLIOGRAPHY
XIV Esposizione Internazionale d'Arte, catalogue (Venice, 1936), 41 (Portrait de la famille Severini); *Gino Severini prima e dopo*, works, catalogue, Cortona Palazzo Casali 12 November 1983–22 January 1984, ed. Maurizio Fagiolo dell'Arco (Florence, 1983); Daniela Fonti, *Gino Severini*, catalogue raisonné (Milan, 1988).
MLS

Sherman Cindy
Glen Ridge, 1954
After taking her degree at the University College of Buffalo (New York State) she exhibited her photography in the group show held at the Albright–Knox Gallery in Buffalo in 1976. The next year she began one of her *Film stills* series, photographs of the imaginary repertoire of a 'B' movie actress, which she used to explore the theme of the image in mass culture. In the Eighties the use of color is offset by the progressive elimination of back–drops in the *Back screen* series (1980), *The real Cindy* (1982), and *Costume Dramas* (1984), which were followed by *Freaks* (1986) and the *Tableaux vivants* (1989), all untitled and designated by number alone. In the *Tableaux vivant*s her interest in portraiture is heightened in this reappraisal of famous paintings (by Raphael, Caravaggio, etc.) in which Sherman impersonates the subject, as if to reappropriate their codes and begin a new phase (Meneguzzo, 16).

BIBLIOGRAPHY
Biennal Exhibition, catalogue, New York Whitney Museum of American Art 1985 (New York, 1985); Kees van der Ploeg, 'Cindy Sherman', *Flash Art International*, 143 (Summer 1990), 142; Marco Meneguzzo, *Make-up, make over*, in *Cindy Sherman*, catalogue, Milan Padiglione d'Arte Contemporanea 4 October–4 November 1990, ed. Marco Meneguzzo (Milan, 1990), 16 (extensive bibliography).
VM

Silverthorne Jeffrey
Honolulu, 1946
He studied at the Rhode Island School of Design in Providence (1969–77) where he specialized in photography. He worked as a freelance photographer and taught art history and photography at several universities, and has exhibited in many one-man and group shows. His primary themes involve death and the body, and focus on the subtle line separating *Eros* from *Thanatos*. In the first series dedicated to the morgue —*Morgue Work* (1972–74)—he created a one–way dialogue with death. In its chilling delicacy, *Beating Victim* (1972–74) recalls Géricault's studies for the heads of the *Radeau de la Méduse*, while other images from the *Morgue Work* series contain references to Beckmann, Goya and Manet. A perceptive observer of the human condition in the *Slaughterhouse, Female Impersonators* and *Prison* series, he moved on to collages of anatomical parts, and later returned to nude figures treated like the sculptures of Hans Bellmer. In *Letters from the Dead House* (1986–89) he returned to the theme of the morgue, this time using color and collage technique. He seeks to condense meanings and associations, linking popular culture and personal memories of death. He chronicled the daily struggle for survival on the Mexican border with the United States in *Texas/Mexico* (1986), portraying prostitutes, illegal immigrants, and the police. In *Detroit Negatives* (1991) he created collages on the theme of sex, using his own material and that of photographers from the Fifties to depict the sexual restlessness of the Nineties.

BIBLIOGRAPHY
Jeffrey Silverthorne. Photographs, catalogue, Stuttgart Galerie A, 24 September–10 November 1993 (Stuttgart, 1993).
RA

Shroud of Turin
The Holy Shroud of Turin (the sheet that Christ was wrapped in after his death, cf. Gospels, Matthew XXVII: 59, Mark XVI: 46; Luke XXVIII: 53) was a popular widespread cult in the Middle Ages when several different versions were worshipped. The most famous was that kept in the Turin Duomo since 1578, which originally came from Lirey in Champagne (1353–1418) and was later preserved in Chambéry by the Dukes of Savoy. The image of a body with Christ's traditional stigmata imprinted on a linen sheet (4.36 x 1.10 m.) was the subject of great controversy when Secondo Pia's photographic identification (1898) revealed that a positive image remained on the photographic plate, suggesting that it was not a product of painting but actual traces left by a human body. The similarity of the face with the traditional iconography of the dead Christ led to a second photographic identification (1931) by Giuseppe Enrie (Alba, Cuneo, 1886–Turin, 1911) with the assistance of Sorbonne experts Paul Vignon and Yves Delage. This revealed that the image is a self–impression of a body on a sheet left by vaporous emanations. A three–dimensional computer examination of the image was recently conducted by the Computer Sciences Department of the University of Turin, by a research group headed by the professors Giovanni Tamburelli and Nello Balossino.

BIBLIOGRAPHY
Giovanni Enrie, *La Santa Sindone rivelata dalla fotografia* (Turin, 1933); Thomas Humber, *La Santa Sindone* (Milan, 1978), 107; Giovanni Riggi, *Rapporto Sindone 1978–1982* (Turin, 1982).
VM

Sironi Mario
Sassari, 1885–Milan, 1961
He met Balla, Boccioni and Severini in Rome, and in 1905–06 he lived in Milan. From 1908–11 he traveled to Paris and throughout Germany. His production in the early 1910s reveals a futurism concentrated on the space-volume relationship drawn from Carrà's constructivism and Léger's cubism. In 1920 he signed, along with Dudreville, Funi and Russolo the manifesto *Contro tutti i ritorni in pittura*, and he established the new themes of the Periferie industriali o Paesaggi urbani. With Margherita Sarfatti and the gallery owner Lino Pesaro he founded the 'Sette pittori del Novecento' in 1922 in Milan. In his monumental *Nudo allo specchio* (1923) 'his composition is... delimited geometrically by three vertical rectangles and their diagonals', demonstrating that 'certain static constructivism' (Benzi in *Mario Sironi 1885-61*, 16) championed by Sironi. Here we see Sironi's achievement of the idea of monumental classicism so important to the twentieth century, as well the new classicism of language. Critics have always emphasized the abstract and hieratic value of his *Allieva*. This is the product of a 'moral classicism, etched on a melancholy which corresponds to the existential difficulties of construction, of the impossible achievement of perfection' (Benzi, 168). Raphael, Casorati, De Chirico and Masaccio, 'together with a faraway echo of the Neoclassical Picasso, are therefore the inspiring beacons of this painting, among the richest and most original in European painting of this century, because of the stately *dignitas*, and the dark color of the flesh (Benzi, 168).

BIBLIOGRAPHY
XIV Esposizione Internazionale d'Arte della città di Venezia, catalogue (Venice, 1924), 44; *Mario Sironi 1885-1961*, catalogue, Rome Galleria d'Arte Moderna 9 December 1993–27 February 1994 (Milan, 1993).
LS

Smith Kiki
Nuremburg, 1954
After completing high school in Newark (New Jersey) she became involved in theatre and art (she performed in Meredith Monk's Vessel, New York 1976). In 1976 she met the New York collective group Collaborative Projects (Colab: a group of forty artists including Jenny Holtzer, John Ahern, Carla Perlman, Robin Winters and others) with whom she worked and exhibited (Times Square Show, 1980). She had her first one-man show in 1982 (Life Wants to Live) at the Kitchen gallery in New York. At the same time she was active in the New York Experimental Glass Workshop, and was producing sculptures in bronze (Womb, 1985) and paper (Paper Body, 1987). During the Nineties she has been exhibiting at some of the major international art events, such as the Whitney Biennal (New York, 1991) and the Venice Biennale XLV (1993, Aperto 1993) in which her works explore her relationship with the body: '... it seems a theme very well-suited to me to speak through the body of the way we exist and live ...' (Kiki Smith, quoted, 1995, 31).

BIBLIOGRAPHY
Kiki Smith, catalogue, London Whitechapel Art Gallery 24 February–23 April 1995, ed. Catherine Lampert (London, 1995), 12; 31.
VM

Soffici Ardengo
Rignano sull'Arno, Florence, 1879–Poggio a Caiano, Florence 1964
He studied at the Accademia di Belle Arti and took courses from Giovanni Fattori at the Scuola Libera del nudo in Florence. He pursued his interest in literature and poetry along with his painting. In 1900 he set off for Paris and the Exposition Universelle and exhibited in the Salon des Independents (1901) and contributed to several reviews (*Plume, Revue Blanche*) and became close friends with Jean Moréas, Apollinaire, Braque, Rousseau and Medardo Rosso. His meeting with Picasso (1906) was a crucial turning point in his work, and marked the beginning of his mature style. He was present at the creation of the *Les Demoiselles d'Avignon* in Picasso's studio. He later showed the influence of those new trends that allowed reality to multiply itself by breaking down sides of rigid geometric forms of solid shapes (*Ardengo Soffici. Un percorso d'arte*). In 1911, he became a frequent contributor to Prezzolini's *Voce*, and he published his *Picasso e Braque* (24 August). In the same year he gave 'with his works (*I mendicanti, Donne che si lavano*) the confirmation of his opinions [...] In these exoticism and archaism are not cultural formulae, but are instead recognized as primary elements of cognitive perception and the synthesis of perceptible reality: not decorative but realistic language in the sense urged by Picasso' (Russoli, quoted in *Ardengo Soffici. Arte e storia*, 31).

BIBLIOGRAPHY
Guiseppe Raimondi, Luigi Cavallo, *Ardengo Soffici* (Florence, 1967); *Ardengo Soffici. Un percorso d'arte*, catalogue, Poggio a Caiano Villa Medicea 24 September–6 November 1994, ed. Luigi Cavallo (Milan, 1994); *Ardengo Soffici. Arte e storia*, catalogue, Rignano sull'Arno Villa di Petriolo 18 September–6 November 1994, eds. Ornella Casazza and Luigi Cavallo (Milan, 1994).
MBG

Sow Ousmane
Dakar, 1935
Although he participated in the *Festival des Arts Nègres* (Dakar, 1966), he decided to take up sculpture professionally when he was around fifty, inspired by the photography of German director Leni Riefenstahl (Berlin 1902) of the Nubians of southern Sudan (1978). His series *Les Noubas* (1984) was followed by *Les Guerriers Massäis* (1988), *Les Zoulous* (1991) and *Les Peuls* (1993), all studies of African tribes. He executed two other groups for the Bicentennial of the French Revolution, *Marianne et les Révolutionnaires* and *Toussaint L'ouverture et la vieille esclave* (1989). He was invited to the *Centre Culturel Français* (1991) and took part in Documenta IX.

BIBLIOGRAPHY
Leni Riefenstahl, *I Nuba* (Milan, 1978); Marie Lavandier, *L'œuvre d'Ousmane Sow* (Paris, n.d.); *Documenta IX*, catalogue, Kassel 13 June–20 September 1992, vol. I, (Stuttgart and New York, 1992), 223.
VM

Spagnulo Giuseppe
Grottaglie, Taranto, 1936
He attended the Istituto d'Arte per la Ceramica in Faenza. He moved to Milan in 1959, and enrolled in the Brera Accademia, but preferred working as assistant to Fontana and Pomodoro. After a brief stint as a ceramicist, he took up sculpture permanently, and had his first one-man show in the Salone Annunciata in Milan in 1965. His work uses different types of material—stone, clay, grès—and analyzes the relationship between figure and space, which is the theme of a series of terracotta and grès sculptures executed between 1962 and 1965, the year in which he replaced terracotta with wooden geometric configurations. In 1968 he began to work with iron, creating primary geometric forms whose interiors are deeply cut into. Next came the *Paesaggi* phase, clay beds arranged on a brick surface, on which he used the weight of his own body. Later works include *Archeologia* (1976) and *Lavoro elementare*, in which he returned to work in iron. In 1980 he was back with terracotta in works full of references to earth-linked myths: *Antigone e Mortanatura* (1980, *Turris* (1982), and *Autoritratto* (1983). He held one-man shows at the Galleria d'Arte Moderna in Turin (1977),

the Galerie Templon in Paris (1990) and the Kunstverein in Stuttgart (1991). He also took part in the *Arte italiana 1960–1982* show at the Hayward Gallery of London in 1982, and *Intersezioni. Arte internazionale 1970–1990* in the Budapest Museum in 1991.

BIBLIOGRAPHY
Giuseppe Spagnulo. Opere: 1964–1984, catalogue, Modena, ed. P.G. Castagnoli (1984); *Giuseppe Spagnulo*, catalogue, Duisberg Hamburg, ed. K.E. Vester (1985).
VC

Spencer Stanley
Cookham-on-Thames, Berkshire, 1891–1959
His work belongs to the realist British school that emerged between the wars. After attending the Slade School in London (1910–1912) the works of his early maturity demonstrate that he appropriated developments of modern art up to post-Impressionism, forging a personal style in which the 'figurative [form], expressive and imaginative, evokes the realistic image despite the different degrees of stylization and distortion'. His experiences in the war, in which he served as a volunteer (1914–18) turned him to works inspired by the horrors of the conflict and religious subjects, but especially mark the formation of his own conception of sexuality. 'During the war... I felt that the only way to get this horrible experience over with was abandon to all forms of excess, carnal, sexual, whatever you want to call it. It is there that the true joys of humanity reside' (Spencer, quoted in Wilson, 280). In 1925, the year of his first marriage, he showed an obsessive interest in sexuality that was also revealed in the nude portraits of his second wife, Patricia Preece (1935–36): 'central to these works' is the ability to explore the potential of the body and its gestures as the expression of an intense emotion or psychological state, the ability to permeate the body with tension, pleasure, or both' (*Stanley Spencer. The Apotheosi's*, 15–16).

BIBLIOGRAPHY
Simon Wilson, *Stanley Spencer et le Réalisme britannique dans les années 30*, in *Les Réalismes 1919–1939*, catalogue, Paris Centre Georges Pompidou 17 December 1980–20 April 1981, ed. Gérard Régnier (Paris, 1980); *Stanley Spencer. The Apotheosis of Love*, catalogue,

London Barbican Art Gallery 24 January– 1 April 1991, ed. Jane Alison (London, 1991).
MBG

Stratz Carl Heinrich
1858–1924
German doctor and anthropologist who studied the morphology of race, and published many popular works on the aesthetics of the body, especially the female.

BIBLIOGRAPHY
Die Frauen auf Java (Stuttgart, 1897); *Die Schönheit des weiblichen Körpers* (Stuttgart, 1898); *Der Körpers des Kindes und seine Pflege* (Stuttgart, 1903).
PC

Stubbing Tony
London, 1921–London, 1983
After fighting in World War II, he attended the Camberwell School of Art from 1947 to 1948. He trained in Edith Gordon's studio and later was a student of Sickert and Domingo Marqués. He exhibited for the first time in Cypress, where he served during the war, at the British Institute in Famagosta. In 1946 he returned to London and a year later he moved to Madrid, where he had a one-man show at the British Institute in 1947, and in 1954 at the Museo d'Arte Moderna. He was one of the founders of the 'Scuola di Altamira'. In 1959 he painted the sets for the ballet 'Saeta', produced by Ana Ricarda for the Marquis de Cuevas company, and for the 'Canzone dell'eterna tristezza' performed at the Théâtre Alhambra in Paris and the Edinburgh Festival in 1959. He was one of the founders of the International Centre for Esthetic Research founded in Turin with Marcel Tapié, and he exhibited at the show 'Arte Nuova' organized by Tapié, Angelo Dragone and Luciano Pistoi at the 'Circolo degli Artisti' in Turin in 1959. He produced many mural paintings between 1964–68. In 1968 he was forced to give up painting with his hands because of ill-health. He then dedicated himself to sculpture and set design, for the London Royal Ballet School.

BIBLIOGRAPHY
M. Tapié, *Morphologie Autre* (Turin, 1960); M. Tapiè, A. Dragone, L. Pistoi, *Arte Nuova*, catalogue, Circolo degli artisti (Turin, 1959).
VC

Stuß Otto *see* Prinzhorn-Sammlung

Tamburelli Giovanni *see* Shroud of Turin

Theimer Ivan
Olomuc, 1944
His first one-man show was at the Belgrade Theater in Coventry (1967). In 1968 he took part in the Danuvius Biennale in Bratislau, and in the same year he moved to Paris, where he studied at the Ecole des Beaux-Arts. Theimer uses a wide variety of material in his works, ranging from tempera to bronze and wax. He is interested in both the portrait and figurative art, but also paints Arcadian landscapes which challenge the modern industrial landscape, responding to a utopian vision of nature.

BIBLIOGRAPHY
Jean Clair, *Nouvelle subjectivité, notes et documents sur le retour de l'expression figuration et de la scène de genre dans la peinture de la fin du siècle* (Brussels, 1979).
LS

Thiébault *see* Fotografia spiritica

Tonks Henry
Solihull, 1862–London, 1937
In 1877 he began his studies in medicine and from 1880 he worked as a doctor at London Hospital. Ten years later he met the painter Frederick Brown, and attended his courses at the Westminster School of Art. He later became an instructor at the Slade School of London (1917), where he would teach for the rest of his life (Cattermole and Furber, 10). He left medicine permanently in 1894 to devote himself to painting, and was especially influenced by the Pre–Raphaelites and the French Impressionists. His long training in drawing, based on his anatomical research in the hospital, led to his *Studies of facial wounds* (1916) owned by the Royal College of Surgeons in London. He was to conduct '... the most vigorous defense of the traditional spirit in art in general, and of design in particular ...' (Charlton, 867) in the English art world from 1917–1930, in contrast to Futurism, abstraction and other avant–garde movements.

BIBLIOGRAPHY
George Charlton, *Tonks, Henry*

(1862–1937), in *The Dictionary of National Biography*, supplement 1931–1940 (Oxford, [1945] 1961³), 866–7; Lance Cattermole and Winifred Furber, 'Tonks the terrible!', *Artist*, vol. 100, pt. 3 (March 1985), 10–1, 25; Roy Caine, *The Surgeon as Artist*, in *Modern Painters*, vol. 3, pt. 2, (1990), 63.
VM

Topinard Paul
1830–1911
French doctor and anthropologist who worked in Paul Broca's anthropology laboratory. He studied anthropological biology and anthropometry, and established the first canon of the proportions of the 'adult European male', based on purely statistical data.

BIBLIOGRAPHY
L'Anthropologie (Paris, 1876); *Eléments d'anthropologie générale* (Paris, 1885); *L'Homme dans la nature* (1891).
PC

Topography of Pablo Picasso
It is unuseful to produce a biography of Pablo Picasso (Malaga, 1881–Mourgins, 1973), but given his presence throughout the show his works should be mentioned in chronological sequence. The following is a list with references to the numbers of the sections of the show (Sez.), Christian Zervos' classification (Z.), and those of the Musée Picasso in Paris (MP). When other indications are lacking, the works are to be considered as from the Collection of the Musée Picasso in Paris. Sez. III. 1: *Dessin pour 'Les Demoiselles d'Avignon'* (1906–1907, Basle Offentliche Kunstsammlung, Kupferstichkabinet; Z. vol. II n. 19); *Buste di Femme* (1907, Prague Národní Galerie inv. n. NG o 8022; Z. vol. II n. 16); *Étude pour 'Les Demoiselles d'Avignon'* (1907, MP 13, Z. VI n. 73); *Étude pour 'Les Demoiselles d'Avignon': nu debout* (1907, MP 535); *Étude pour 'Les Demoiselles d'Avignon': nu debout* (1907, MP 536); *Étude pour 'Les Demoiselles d'Avignon': nu debout* (1907, MP 5376); *Étude de nu au visage hiératique, les bras croisés au-dessus de la tête* (1908, MP 552); *Trois études: femme de dos au chignon, les bras levées* (1908, MP 553); *Tête di femme (Fernande)* (Autumn 1909, MP 243; Z. vol. II 573). Sez. III. 2: *Autorretrato con Peluca* (1896-1897, Barcelona Museo Picasso; Z. vol. XXI n. 48:

Portrait de l'artist en Gentil-homme du XVIII siècle); *Vieil homme assis* (1970–1971, MP 221, Z. vol. XXXIII n. 265); *Tête* (2 July 1972, private collection); Z. vol. XXXIII n. 436); Sez. IV. 3: *Nu dans un fauteuil* (3 October 1972, MP 1544; Z. XXXIII n. 513). Sez. V. 3: *Métamorphose I* (1928, MP 261); *Femme assise dans un fauteuil rouge* (1932, MP 139); *Une Anatomie: trois femmes II* (25 February 1933, MP 1090); *Une Anatomie: trois femmes VI* (27 February 1933, MP 1094); *Une Anatomie: trois femmes X* (1 March 1933, MP 1098). Sez VII. 2: *Nu couché sur fond jaune* (October 1967, private collection).

BIBLIOGRAPHY
Christian Zervos, *Pablo Picasso*, 33 vols. (Paris 1932–1978), voll. II, 16, 19; II, 573; VI, 73; XXI, 48; XXII, 265; XXIII, 436, 513; Marie Laure Besnard-Bernadac, Michèle Richet, Hélène Seckel (eds.), *Musée Picasso–catalogue sommaire des collections*, 2 vols., with an introduction by Dominique Bozo (Paris, 1985), vol. I, cat. nos. 107, 286, 302; vol. II, cat. nos. 135, 137, 138, 139, 211, 976, 980; Josep Palau i Fabre, *Picasso–I primi anni 1881–1907* (Barcelona, 1980), ed. cons. Milan 1982, 101, figs. 149, 522 n. 149.
VM

Trocme Philippe see
Cabanis Emmanuel A.

Tschackert Franz
Tschackert created the world's first transparent figure, the so-called man of glass (*Der gläserne Mensch*), working at the Hygiene-Museum of Dresden. In 1930 Tschackert presented the result of his experiments with glass resin (Cellen) and it was this synthetic material that allowed him to create his artificial 'flesh and blood' man. The immediate success of his work led to many shows all over the world. By 1945 workers from the Dresden Museum had probably created about another eight figures, some of them female as well. And it was during a show in Buffalo in 1937 (New York State), that the man of glass met the first woman of glass (Die gläserne Frau). In 1949 he returned to Dresden and began making his glass figures again, later moving on to glass animals as well.

BIBLIOGRAPHY
Ludwig Stephan, *Das Dresdner Hygiene–Museum in der Zeit des deutschen Faschismus*

(1933-1945) (Dresden, 1986); *Der Gläserne Mensch–Eine Sensation. Zur Kulturgeschichte eines Ausstellungsobjektes*, ed. Rosmarie Beier and Martin Roth (Stuttgart, 1990) (= Baustein 3 des Deutschen Historischen Museums, Berlin).
SR

Umgelter Louis see
Prinzhorn-Sammlung

Uncini Giuseppe
Fabriano, Ancona, 1929
In his early work he used *materiali poveri* (such as earth, coal, plywood, masonite) which he discarded in 1958–59 for reinforced concrete, as in the works exhibited in March 1959 at the La Salita gallery in Rome in a group show with Angeli and Festa. He also exhibited in Rome in 1960 in the group show organized by Pierre Restany *Cinque pittori Roma '60*. Together with Carrino, Biggi, Pace, Santoro and Frascà he founded the 'Gruppo Uno', which intended to go beyond the Informale, which inspired his *Cementi armati*. The *Ferrocementi* and the *Spaziostrutture*, with a hint of the late Sixties, sought the relationship between objects and their shadows, and were projected into their material form in iron and cement. The *Mura* (1969–1970) instead consisted of brick columns, arches, and buttresses. A large retrospective was dedicated to him in 1979 at the Palazzo dei Consoli of Gubbio. *La dimora delle cose*, exhibited at the Studio Marconi of Milan and the gallery Rondanini in Rome, is a series of mixed-technique work, including frescoes and bas-reliefs in reinforced concrete. He later produced the *Spazi di ferro* in iron and cement. In later years he has exhibited in many one-man and group shows, including the retrospective given him in 1989 by the Galleria dei Banchi Nuovi in Rome.

BIBLIOGRAPHY
Uncini, la logica fantastica, catalogue, Macerata Pinacoteca e Musei comunali, May–June 1983, ed. L. Marziano (Macerata, 1983); G.M. Accame, *Giuseppe Uncini. Le origini del fare* (Bergamo, 1989).

Vallorz Paolo
Caldes, Trento, 1931
He spent his childhood in Trento, and attended the Accademia in Venice for a year, where he studied under Guido

Cadorin. He exhibited for the first time in Trento in 1950, and then moved to Paris. There he studied at the Libre Académie de la Grande Chaumière and the Ecole du Louvre, and was associated with Klein, César, Giacometti, Restany and Burri. His first work was abstract, and he later moved into Informal geometric forms. In 1956 he abandoned painting, and in 1958 he designed and built a car with Tinguely, with whom he competed in the 24–hour event at Le Mans. He returned to painting, this time in an exploration of figurative subjects, and destroyed and repainted his earlier works. Of his old acquaintances he still sees only Giacometti. He exhibits in Paris, New York, London, Trento, and Milan.

BIBLIOGRAPHY
Paolo Vallorz, catalogue, Trento Galleria Civica di Arte Contemporanea April–June 1991 (Turin, 1991).
RA

Van Wieck Nigel
Bexley, 1947
He studied painting at the Hornsey College of Art (1968–72). His first group show was held at the Nottingham Arts Festival (1970) and his first one-man show at Marjorie Parr in London (1971). He later exhibited in New York (1971), Sheffield (1972), Edinburgh (1974), and Paris (1976). He moved to New York (1978) where he lives today. Although his work still lies within the tradition of Winslow Homer and Edward Hopper, his works reveal (*Two Manhattans*, 1989) 'people forgotten in their own solitude, [who] invite the observer to investigate through the psychological content, the vision of the solitude of the artist ...' (1993, 3).

BIBLIOGRAPHY
Recent Works by Nigel Van Wieck, London The Lefèvre Gallery, 7 October–6 November 1982 (London, 1982); *Stowe-on-the-world*, catalogue, Gloucestershire Fosse Gallery 1993, ed. Anne Horton (n.p., 1993).
VM

Vautier Ben
Naples, 1935
A leading art figure from the Sixties onwards, his work lies within the 'Fluxus' movement, which aims to exhaust the possibilities of art, moving beyond into the world of 'anti-art' or 'non-art' by means of event, gesture, audience participation and the use of

found objects. He uses writing to achieve this goal—by affixing his name to an object he deprives it of its own physicality and makes it rise to an abstract concept. Among his one-man shows are *Ben expose rien et tout* at the Laboratoire 32 in Nice (1960), *Essayez d'être naturel*, and exhibitions at the Centro di Informazione Alternativa in Rome in 1975, and the Museum of Contemporary Art in Montreal. He also took part in the opening of the Museo Sperimentale d'Arte Contemporanea in Turin in 1967, the Kassel Documenta 5, and the Contemporanea in Rome in 1973.

BIBLIOGRAPHY
L'esthétique de Ben (Nice, 1960); Ben Vautier, *Théorie* (Milan, 1975); *Tout Ben* (Paris, 1975).
VC

Warhol Andy
Pittsburgh, 1928–New York, 1987
After studying at the Carnegie Institute of Technology (1945–49) he worked in advertising graphics in New York. In 1960 his early work was inspired by comic-strip characters and he produced his Coca-Cola bottle series. He was a great admirer of Marcel Duchamp and his ready-mades, and he in turn focused his attention on the repetition of subjects, taken from the media and everyday life. He rapidly became one of the leading figures in Pop Art. In 1963 he founded the Factory which was to become the centre of the American underground culture of the time. Here he also made many experimental films and produced the rock band 'Velvet Underground'. Warhol found the portrait his most congenial subject: 'more than any other artist in the last thirty years Warhol revived the portrait as a grand genre. His portraits, both of himself and of others, have been a constant in his work from the very earliest days' (McShine, 19). Using a two-layer technique that granted his subjects a double identity, his series of portraits of American and European celebrities became very famous during the Seventies.

BIBLIOGRAPHY
Andy Warhol: A Retrospective, catalogue, New York The Museum of Modern Art, 6 February–2 May 1989, ed. Kynaston McShine (New York, 1989) (ed.it. Milan 1989); Henry Geldzahler, *Andy Warhol Portraits* (London, 1993).
MC

Wicki Chantal
Zurich, 1963
She studied at the Experimental School of Art (1983–84) and the Academy of Applied Arts (1985) where she was a student of Oswald Oberhuber. Her first one-man show was at the Galerie an der Klostermauer in St. Gallen in 1983. She works in both sculpture and painting. She creates bodies, in bronze or wax, united in a struggle of love or death. Her sculptures are inspired by Rodin's *Porte de l'enfer*; her figures cannot exist individually, but assume significance in the group, in union. Creation and destruction, and life-love-death, are her dominating themes, which she makes even more explicit in her paintings which portray well-known figures: 'whole figures, intensely expressed interweavings of bodies and faces'.

BIBLIOGRAPHY
Chantal Wicki. Neue Arbeiten, catalogue, Zurich Galerie Ursula Siegenthaler 21 February–23 March 1991, ed. Alice Villon-Lechner (Zurich).
RA

Wildt Adolfo
Milan 1868–1931
Giuseppe Grandi (1843–94) was his first instructor, and he later enrolled in the Scuola Superiore di Arte Applicata in Brera (1885–86). In 1894 a contract with the Prussian art patron Franz Rose, who bought the first version of each of Wildt's sculptures, guaranteed him financial independence (*Adolfo Wildt*, 155). He was part of the Sezession movement, and was especially influenced by Auguste Rodin (1840–1917) and Adolf von Hildebrandt (1847–1921). In 1912 he exhibited one of his most famous works at the Brera Triennale, *La trilogia*, later exhibited at the Munich Sezession (1913). He was friends with Vittore Grubicy de Dragon (1851–1920) and Gaetano Previati (1852–1920). His reputation was assured in the Twenties when he took part in several Venice Biennales (XIII, 1922; XIV, 1924; and XV, 1926) and exhibited his bust of *Benito Mussolini* in Sala 17 of the Italian Pavilion.

BIBLIOGRAPHY
XIV Esposizione Internazionale d'Arte della città di Venezia-Catalogo (Venice, 1924), 65 n. 33; *Adolfo Wildt 1868–1931*, catalogue, Venice Galleria d'Arte Moderna di Ca' Pesaro 8 December 1989–4 March 1990, ed. Paola Mola (Milan, 1989), 155.
VM

Wissel Adolf
Velber, Hanover, 1894–1973
After completing his studies in Hanover (set design) he enrolled in the Kassel Academy (1921). In 1924 he began to work as an independent artist, concentrating on rural scenes and portraits which contain echoes of the *Neue Sacklichkeit* movement (*The Romantic*, 493). He took part in the *Heroische Kunst* exhibition (Berlin 1935) and the annual shows *Grosse Deutsche Kunstausstellung* in Munich (1937–44). Adolf Hitler bought his painting *Kalenberger Bauernfamilie* (1939) (*The Romantic*, 493).

BIBLIOGRAPHY
The Romantic Spirit in German Art 1790–1990, catalogue, Munich Haus Der Kunst 2 February–1 May 1995, ed. Keith Hartley (Cambridge, 1994), 392, 394 cat. n. 197; 480 cat. n. 197; 493.
VM

Witkiewicz Stanislaw Ignacy
Warsaw, 1885–Jeziory na Polesiu, 1939
Son of an illustrious art critic, painter and writer who gave him an anti-conformist education, he began to produce Symbolist, Sezessionist and Expressionist works around 1908 (such as the so-called 'monster' cycle). In 1914, following the mental crisis caused by the suicide of his fiancée Jadwiga Janczewska, he joined Malinovski's scientific expedition to New Guinea. This inspired the world of his visions, which is like 'the nightmare of a terribly painful sensuality, the extraordinary dream of a tropical sun' (Degler, 38). In the years from 1919 to 1924 he became one of the leading spokesmen of the Formist group. In painting he limited himself to the portrait. In addition to using drugs to enhance his work, he established the Portrait Company 'S.I. Witkiewicz' and classified the portrait by genres: 'type A, the most finished, heightening a certain beauty, and type B, with a certain emphasis of characteristic features, down to type E, free psychological interpretation, according to the Company's intuition' (Krzyzanowska–Hajdukiewicz, 28).

BIBLIOGRAPHY
La ditta dei ritratti S.I. Witkiewicz, catalogue, Leghorn Casa della Cultura 8–25 February 1980 (Prato, 1980); Anna Krzyzanowska-Hajdukiewicz, *La ditta dei ritratti S.I. Witkiewicz*, in *La ditta dei ritratti S.I. Witkiewicz*, catalogue, Leghorn Casa della Cultura 8–25 February 1980 (Prato, 1980), 27–34; Janus Degler, *Cronaca della vita e delle opere di Stanislaw Ignacy Witkiewicz*, in *La ditta dei ritratti S.I. Witkiewicz*, catalogue, Leghorn Casa della Cultura 8–25 February 1980 (Prato, 1980), 35–42.
LS

Wols (Otto Wolfgang Schulze)
Berlin, 1913–Paris, 1951
He trained in Dresden as a photographer; in Berlin (1932) he came into contact with Bauhaus where he met Klee. He moved to Paris and worked in photography, moving in Surrealist circles that included figures like Tzara, Masson, Arp, Giacometti and Calder. He began drawing in India ink, and worked extensively in graphics during his reclusion between 1939 and 1940. He took refuge in Dieulefit (1942–45) and painted watercolors that evoke an microscopic organic world, or sketched faces and parts of the body, using fluid overflowing colors. When he returned to Paris he met Sartre and Paulhan; he began to paint in oil and created a kind of instinctive painting, breaking with pictorial tradition and moving towards the Informal. Wols created a photographic portrait of Paris, recording all the details of the life of the city. He devoted much of his work to the portrait, fragmenting images and using photomontage, and created Surrealist compositions, assembling fruit, vegetables, animals' entrails, fabrics and objects. His photographic work, always linked to his work as a painter, occasionally has erotic overtones or becomes an evocation of disgust or pain.

BIBLIOGRAPHY
Laszlo Glover, *Wols. Photographe*, catalogue, Paris Musée National d'Art Moderne Centre Georges Pompidou 1980 (Paris, 1980); *L' écriture griffé*, catalogue, Saint-Etienne Musée d'Art Moderne (Paris, 1993), 187–199, 214–215.
RA

Wulz Carlo *see* **Wulz, Photographic Studio**

Wulz, Photographic Studio
Giuseppe Wulz (*Tarvisio, 1843–Trieste, 1918*), student of the photographer Guglielmo Engle, made a name for himself in Trieste where he opened a photographic studio (1868) which was to be the oldest in Italy, and would be witness to more than a century of the life of the city (Zannier, 184). Using collodium and gelatine-bromide technique, he produced both large–scale cityscapes and portraits satisfying the taste of the times. His son Carlo (Trieste, 1874–1928) and his granddaughter Wanda (Trieste 1903–1984) were particularly successful in portraiture, and developed new expressive and artistic approaches to the genre. After her father's death, Wanda Wulz produced excellent work in this field, while she managed the studio on Corso Italia with her sister Marion until the early Eighties. After her death, the firm closed after more than one hundred years of production. The archive of the studio Wulz was bought and entirely re-organized by the Fototeca Alinari in Florence, where it can be consulted.

BIBLIOGRAPHY
Italo Zannier, *Wulz Giuseppe*, in *Fotografia italiana dell' Ottocento*, catalogue, Florence Palazzo Pitti October–December 1979, and Venice Ala Napleonica January–March 1980 (Venice, 1979), 184; Giovanni Lista, *Futurismo e fotografia* (Milan, 1979), 176 n. 172.
VM

Wulz Wanda *see* **Wulz, Photographic Studio**

Zhang Xiaogang
Kunming, Yunnan, 1953
He attended the Department of Oil Painting at the Academy of Fine Arts in Sichuan (1982) where he currently works today. In the Eighties he established himself as one of the most important emerging artists of his generation. From his earlist works onwards (*Panthom* series, 1984) he has tried to capture the expressive power of emotions, which, in his recent *Bloodline series* (1995), images of his relatives painted in the style of portraits from the Twenties, lead to 'a sense of resignation which permeates the canvas' (*Chinese Exhibition*, 43). To Zhang, the ability to paint becomes '... the vehicle through which I am able to explore the profound depths of the soul. In controlling it I can continue my quest for the significance of life and the value of liberty, and experience many things ...' (Zhang, quoted, in *China's New Art*, 107). His work has been exhibited in many important international group shows, including *China's New Art: Post 1989* (Hong Kong 1993), *Mao Goes Pop* (Sydney and Melbourne 1993), and *New Art from China: Post 1989* (London 1994).

BIBLIOGRAPHY
China's New Art, Post-1989– With a Retrospective from 1979–1989, catalogue, Hong Kong 31 January–25 February 1993, eds. Chang Tsong-Zung and Li Xianting (Hong Kong, 1993), 107; *Chinese Exhibitions–I. The Remaking of Mass Culture–II. Wakefulness and the Weightless Present*, catalogue, São Paulo, Brazil XXII Biennale Internazionale 12 October–11 December 1994, ed. Chang Tsong-Zung (Hong Kong, 1994), 43.
VM

Zorio Gilberto
Adorno Micca, Vercelli, 1944
He is part of the group of artists who created the Arte Povera movement. His early works display the working process, the interaction between primal forces and those produced by technology. His first one-man show was at the galleria Sperone in Turin (*Rosa-blu, Rosa, Tenda*) in 1967; in 1968 he took part in the group show *Rassegna di arti figurative: arte povera-azioni povere*, in Amalfi. In 1969 he had a one-man show at the Sonnabend gallery in Paris and he exhibited with other artists in the Kunsthalle of Berne and the Amtsterdam - Stedelik. In 1972 he participated in the Documenta in Kassel; and in 1973 the Quadriennale X of Rome. His investigation into the conventionality of verbal language, joined with the energy of the relationship between material and thought, is the theme of his works from the Seventies: *Odio, Fluidità radicale, Per purificare le parole* (containers full of alcohol provided with sports). He took part in the Venice Biennale in 1978 and 1980. In the Eighties he was constructing canoe-shaped forms, placed in a eurythmic balance, placed next to elements which enact chemical transformations of the material (*Canoe*, 1984). In 1982 he was part of a group show at the Guggenheim in New York. In 1985 he had a one–man show in the Kunstverein in Stockholm, and the Centre Georges Pompidou in Paris. He was again a guest at the 1986 Venice Biennale.

BIBLIOGRAPHY
Gilberto Zorio, catalogue, Lucerne Kunstmuseum (1976); *Gilberto Zorio*, catalogue, Prato Centro per l'Arte Contemporanea Luigi Pecci, ed. Germano Celant (Florence, Prato, 1992).
VC

Index of Artists

Aarau
Aargauer Kunsthaus Aarau

Aja
Haags Gemeentemuseum

Amsterdam
Stedelijk Museum

Antwerp
Ronny Van de Velde

Barcelona
Fondació Joan Miró
(bequest Maria Dolors Miró)
Museu Picasso

Basel
Kunstmuseum (lent Emanuel
Hoffmann-Stiftung)
Öffentliche Kunstsammlung,
Kunstmuseum
für Gegenwartskunst
Öffentliche Kunstsammlung,
Kunstmuseum
Öffentliche Kunstsammlung,
Kupferstichkabinett

Beaune
Musée Marey

Belfast
Ulster Museum

Berlin
Staatliche Museen zu Berlin,
Nationalgalerie

Bern
Kunstmuseum

Bologna
Collection Livio Collina

Bolognano, Pescara
Collection Lucrezia Durini
de Domizio

Bremen
Kunsthalle

Brescia
Civici Musei di Arte e Storia

Brussels
Andrée Levy Collection

Buffalo
Albright-Knox Art Gallery

Capetown
South African National Gallery

Châlon-sur-Saône
Musée Nicéphore Nièpce

Cologne
Galerie Christian Nagel
Galerie Michael Werner
Leon Gustantiner Collection

Columbus
Columbus Museum of Art,
Derby Found

Dakar
Ousmane Sow Collection

Darmstadt
Hessisches Landesmuseum
Darmstadt

Djion
Musée des Beaux-Arts

Dortmund
Museum am Ostwall

Dresda
Deutsches Hygiene-Museum

Düren
Leopold-Hoesch-Museum

Düsseldorf
Konrad Fischer
Kunstsammlung Nordrhein-
Westfalen

Edimburgh
Scottish National Portrait
Gallery

Emden
Kunsthalle, donation Henri
Nannen

Florence
Beatrice Monti Rezzori Collec-
tion
Biblioteca Nazionale Centrale
Museo di Storia della Fotografia
Fratelli Alinari

Frankfurt
Deutsche Bank AG
Städtische Galerie
im Städelsches Kunstinstitut

Gaggiano, Milano
Giuseppe Spagnulo Collection

Geneva
Galerie Analix - B&L Polla
Galerie Krugier-Ditescheim
Art Contemporain
Musée du Petit Palais

Gentilly
Philippe Comar Collection

Hamburg
Thomas Levy Collection

Heidelberg
Prinzhorn-Sammlung, Psychiatrische Universitätsklinik, Ruprecht-Karls-Universität Heidelberg

Helsinki
The Finnish National Gallery
Ateneum

Hong Kong
Wei Liu Collection
Xiaogang Zhang Collection

Humlebaek, Denmark
Louisiana Museum
of Modern Art

Innsbruck
Tiroler Landesmuseum
Ferdinandeum

Ithaca, New York
Herbert F. Johnson Museum
of Art Cornell University
(donation Samuel A. Berger)

Karlsruhe
Zentrum für Kunst
und Medientechnologie

Krakov
Muzeum Narodowe w Krakovie

Lausanne
Collection de l'Art Brut

Liege
Musée d'Art Moderne

Linz
Neue Galerie der Stadt

London
Andy Goldsworthy Collection
England & Co. Gallery
Eric and Salome Estorick
Foundation
Ivor Braka Limited
Jim Moyes and Joanna Price
Collection
Tate Gallery
The British Museum
The Royal College of Surgeons
of England
Saatchi Collection

Los Angeles
David Hockney Studio
Lannan Foundation
Rosamund Felsen Gallery
The Museum of Contemporary
Art, Collection Panza di Biumo
The Schönberg Estate

Lyon
Bibliothèque Municipale
de Lyon
Ecole Nationale Supérieure
de la Police
Musée des Beaux-Arts

Madrid
Antonio Lopez Collection
Fundación Colección
Thyssen-Bornemisza
Fundación Juan March
Penn Sicre Collection

Malibu, California
The J. Paul Getty Museum

Malmö
Konstmuseet

Marseille
Fonds Regional d'Art Contemporain Provence-Alpes-Côte
d'Azur
M.A.C. Galeries, Contemporaines
des Museées de Marseille,
donation César
Musée Cantini
Musées de Marseille

Milan
Alain Toubas Collection,
Compagnia del Disegno
Alessandro Grassi Collection
Angelo and Silvia Calmarini
Collection
Arturo Schwarz Collection
Civico Museo d'Arte Contempo-
ranea
Collezione di Paolo Curti
Fontana Collection
Fontana Foundation
Germana Agnetti Collection
Giorgio Marconi Collection
Mario Bellini Collection
Matteo Lorenzelli Collection,
Lorenzelli Arte
Pasquale Leccese Collection
Renato Cardazzo Collection

Modena
Claudio Parmiggiani Collection
Galleria Estense

Montreal
Musée d'Art Contemporain
Stephanie Dudek Collection

Moscow
Tret'jakovskaja Galereja
Muzej Revoljucii

Munich
Deutsches Museum von
Meisterwerken der Naturwissen-
schaft und Technik
Oberfinanzdirektion München
Städtisches Galerie im Lenbach-
haus

Münster
Westfalisches Landesmuseum
für Kunst und Kulturgeschichte

New Orleans
New Orleans Museum of Art

New York
Acquavella Contemporary Art
Hazel S. Kandall Collection
Joseph Helman Collection
Lois & Richard Plehn Collection
Louise Bourgeois Collection
Marlborough Gallery Inc.
Mary Carlson Collection
Pamela Jo Rosenau Collection
Philip Guston Estate
Richard Kahn Collection
Robert Rauschenberg Collection
Salander-O'Reilly Galleries
Solomon R. Guggenheim
Museum
Spencer Harper, III Collection
The Lachaise Foundation
The Metropolitan Museum
of Art
The Museum of Modern Art
The Pace Gallery

Nice
Ben Vautier Collection

Nurnberg
Germanisches Nationalmuseum

Oggebbio, Como
C. Raman Schlemmer Collection

Oslo
Astrup Fearnley Collection
Munch Museet
Nasjonalgalleriet

Osnabrück
Kulturgeschichtliches Museum

Paris
Alain Burger Collection
Alain Kahn-Sribert Collection
Angel-Sirot Collection
Avigdor Arikha Collection
Bernard Ruiz-Picasso Collection
Bibliothèque Charcot, Hôpital
de la Salpêtrière
Bibliothèque de l'Institute
de France
Bibliothèque du Musée
de l'Homme
Bibliothèque Nationale,
Cabinet des Estampes
Collection de la Cinémathèque
Française, Ateliers de Moulage
du Louvre
Ecole Nationale Supérieure
des Beaux-Arts, Département
de Morphologie
Emmanuel Cabanis Collection
Eugène Jean Leroy Collection
Fondation Dina Vierny, Musée
Maillol
Fonds National d'Art Contempo-
rain (F.N.A.C.)

Fonds Regional d'Art Contemporain de Basse-Normandie
François Petit Collection
Galerie André-François Petit
Galerie Daniel Templon
Galerie Di Meo
Galerie Pascal Lansberg
Galerie Yvon Lambert
Gérard Régnier Collection
Jacqueline Hélion Collection
Lewis Kaplan Collection
Librairie Alain Brieux
Lucien Treillard Collection
Marc Garanger Collection
Michel Haas Collection
Ministère de la Défense, Secrétariat d'Etat chargé des Anciens Combattants et Victimes de Guerre, Délégation à la Memoire et à l'Information Historique
Musée Carnavalet
Musée d'Art Moderne de la Ville de Paris
Musée d'Orsay
Musée de l'Assistance Publique, Hôpitaux de Paris
Musée des Collections Historiques de la Préfecture de Police
Musée du Service de Santé des Armées au Val-de-Grâce
Musée National d'Art Moderne, Centre Georges Pompidou
Musée National des Techniques du C.N.A.M.
Musée Picasso
Musée Rodin
Philippe and Denyse Durand-Ruel Collection
Raymond Mason Collection
Remo Guidieri Collection
Richer-Coutela Collection, Alain Sourdille
Société Française de Photographie (S.F.P.)
Vincent Corpet Collection
Yvon Lambert Collection

Pittsburgh
The Andy Warhol Museum, Founding Collection, Contribution The Andy Warhol Foundation for the Visual Arts

Poznan
Muzeum Narodowe w Poznaniu

Prague
Národni Galerie v Praze

Riverside
Wendy E. Ormond Collection

Rome
Centro Studi Anton Giulio Bragaglia, Raccolta Antonella Vigliani Bragaglia
Fabio Sargentini Collection
Galleria Nazionale d'Arte Moderna e Contemporanea
Gina Severini Franchina Collection
Nicola Maria De Angelis Collection
Vettor Pisani Collection

Rotterdam
Museum Boymans-van Beuningen

Saint-Moritz
Gilbert de Botton

São Paulo
Museu de Arte de São Paulo

Seattle
Gary Hill Collection

Southampton
Southampton City Art Gallery

St. Eraclio in Foligno
Primo De Donno Collection

St. Etienne
Musée d'Art Moderne

St. Gallen
Kunstmuseum

St. Paul-de-Vence
Fondation Maeght

St. Petesburg
Gosudarstvennyj Russkyj Musej

Stockholm
Nationalmuseum

Stuttgart
Galerie der Stadt
Staatsgalerie

Tammisaari
Tammisaaren Museo

Toronto
Alan and Alison Schwartz Collection

Turin
Centro Internazionale di Sindonologia
Francesco Casorati Collection
Galleria Christian Stein
Galleria Civica d'Arte Moderna e Contemporanea
Galleria Martano
Gilberto Zorio Collection
Giulio Paolini Collection
Istituto di Scienze Medico-forensi dell'Università di Torino
Massimo Sandretto Collection
Michelangelo Pistoletto Collection
Pietro Gallina Collection
Soprintendenza Archeologica del Piemonte
Teresa Giacometti Collection

Utrecht
Centraal Museum

Venice
Archivio della Fondazione San Servolo I.R.S.E.S.C. and Archivio dell'Ospedale Psichiatrico di San Clemente
Archivio Storico delle Arti Contemporanee de La Biennale di Venezia
Civici Musei, Palazzo Fortuny
Fondazione Giorgio Cini
Galleria Internazionale d'Arte Moderna Ca' Pesaro
Giancarlo Ligabue Collection
Giovanni Deana Collection
Italo Zannier Collection
Peggy Guggenheim Collection

Verona
Galleria dello Scudo

Vienna
Austria Center
Galerie Ulysses
Hubert Klocker Collection
Maria Lassnig Collection
Museum Moderner Kunst
Stiftung Ludwig

Österreichische Galerie
Peter Kogler Collection

Villeneuve-d'Asq
Musée d'Art Moderne de la Communauté urbaine de Lille (donation Geneviève and Jean Masurel)

Washington
Hirshhorn Museum and Sculpture Garden, Smithsonian Institution
National Gallery of Art (donation Lila Acheson Wallace)
The Phillips Collection

Wuppertal
Von der Heyt Museum

Zurich
Chantal Wicki Collection
Galerie Bruno Bischofberger
Kunsthaus
Kunsthaus, Graphische Sammlung

Amsterdam
Torch Gallery

Cologne
Galerie Rudolf Kicken
Galerie Tanya Grunert

Edinburgh
Scottish National Portrait
Gallery

Hong Kong
Hanart TZ Gallery

London
British Council
Michael Hue Williams
Whitechapel Art Gallery

Madrid
Galería Marlborough

Milan
Galleria Blu
Galleria GianFerrari

New York
Blum Helman Gallery
Galerie Saint-Etienne
Jason McCoy Inc.
Jayne H. Baum Gallery
McKee Gallery
Metro Pictures
& Cindy Sherman
Robert Miller Gallery
Salander-O'Reilly Galleries

588 Courtesy

Paris
Béatrice Soulé
Galerie de France
Galerie Liliane
& Michel Durand Dessert
Galerie Michèle Chomette
Galerie Pascal Lansberg
Galerie Samia Saouma
Librairie Alan Brieux

Philadelfia
Free Library of Philadelphia
Print & Picture Collection

Santa Monica, California
Smar Art Press Rosamund
Felsen Gallery

Stuttgart
Galerie A. Vera Amor

Venice, California
Louver Gallery

Verona
Galleria dello Scudo

Vienna
Christine König Galerie
Galerie Heike Kurtze

**Photography
Credits**

Aaltonen Hannu - Kuvataiteen
Keskusarkisto, *Helsinki*
Agent Foto, *Turin*
Amendola Amelio, *Pistoia*
Anders Jörg P., *Berlin*
Antony D'Offay Gallery, *London*

Basso Claudio, *Ormea, Cuneo*
Baudouin Eric
Berquet Gilles
Blot G., *Paris*
Bornard C., *Lausanne*
Bresson Yves, *St. Etienne*
Bühler Martin, *Basel*
Burke Christopher

Cameraphoto Arte, *Venice*
Celeste Lucio
Cergeva A., *Moscow*
Cesana Foto, *Venice*
Color Gruppen Humlebaek

Dell'Aquila Pino, *Turin*

Einstein Susan, *Los Angeles*
England & Co. Gallery, *London*

Faujour Jacques, *Paris*
Filè Peter, *Milan*
Foto Grosso, *St. Gallen*
Foto Studio 3, *Milan*
Fototechnik Dreieich, *Dreieich*
Franzini Claudio
Frese Peter, *Wuppertal*
Fritschi Adrian, *Zurich-Paris*

Galerie 1900-2000, *Paris*
Gariglio Luigi, *Bruino, Turin*
Gemini G.E.L., *Los Angeles*
Germain Claude,
St. Paul-de-Vence
Giraudon - Alinari, *Marseille*
Gonella Riccardo, *Turin*

Hatala Béatrice, *Paris*
Heald David, *Venice*
Hoffenreich L., *Vienna*
Hossaka Luiz, *São Paulo*
Hue-Williams Michael
Hyde J., *Paris*

Jarret Bruno / ADAGP, *Paris*

Keystone, *Paris*
Klinger I.L., *Heidelberg*
Kren Kurt, *Vienna*
Kubelka Peter
Kumpf W. - HLM, *Darmstadt*

Lannoy Marcel, *Paris*
Lejenx Corwal, *Beaune*
Licitra Salvatore, *Milano*
Linke Armin, *New York*
Lund Tord, *Stockholm*

Migeat Philippe, *Paris*
Morain André, *Paris*
Mussa Giorgio, *Turin*
Mussal Sartor Paolo, *Turin*

Oliver Steve, *Los Angeles*

Palan Oto, *Prague*
Paruum Photo, *Milan*
Pellion Paolo, *Turin*
Photogriffe, *Nice*
Phototheque des musees
de la Ville de Paris, *Paris*
Pollitzer Eric, *New York*
Popkova V., *Moscow*
Possel Milan, *Prague*
Prudence Cuming Associates
Ltd., *London*
Pulfer Wolfgang, *Munich*

Reinhold Ernst, *Munich*
Reunion des Musées
Nationaux, *Paris*
Ricci Enzo, *Turin*
Roberts, *London*
Rosenthal Lynn, *Philadelphia*
Royneland Tore, *Oslo*
Rzepka Adam / ADAGP, *Paris*

S.A.D.E. (Surrealism & Dada,
Even) Archives, *Milan*
Schiavinotto Giuseppe, *Rome*
Schlemmer C. Ramam, *Oggeb-
bio, Como*
Schmehling
Schmidt Richard, *Los Angeles*
Shunk-Kender, *Paris*
Silo, Cestmir
Spiler Jürgen, *Dortmund*
Squidds & Nunns, *Los Angeles*
Stalsworth Lee, *Washington*
Stoner Richard, *Pittsburgh*
Studio Luca Carrà, *Milan*
Studio Fotografico Scoffone,
Turin
Studio Otto, *Vienna*

Tesseraud J.L.
Tingaud Jean-Marc, *Paris*

Vandrasch Paolo, *Milan*
Villani Antico Studio Fotogra-
fico, *Bologna*
Vitali Guido, *Radda in Chianti,
Siena*

Walford Elke, *Hamburg*
Walker Valerie, *Los Angeles*
Wlmkuk, *Münster*

Zeidman Dorothy, *New York*

**Works of art documented
in the catalogue and not
in the exhibition for technical
reasons**

**Marcel Duchamp
e Man Ray**
«La Tonsure», 1924-25
Cat. Ref. II.21, ill. p. 115

Thomas Eakins
*A Man Walking Full-Face.
Marey-Wheel Photograph
by Eakins*, 1884
Cat. Ref. II.75, ill. p. 137

Robert Demachy
*Femme mimant une expression
sous hypnose (l' effroi)*,
c. 1900
Cat. Ref. II.139, ill. p. 168

Robert Demachy
*Femme mimant une expression
sous hypnose (la joie)*, c. 1900
Cat. Ref. II.140, ill. p. 168

Pablo Picasso
*Etude pour «Les Demoiselles
d' Avignon»*, 1907
Cat. Ref. III.13, ill. p. 200

Anonimo
*Masques en cire d' un blessé
de guerre*, 1917
Cat. Ref. IV.22, ill. p. 263

René Leriche
*Statuette d' un homme
atteint d' hémiplégie
post-commotionnelle*, 1918
Cat. Ref. IV.38, ill. p. 260

Jeffrey Silverthorne
*Morgue Work:
Old Man*, 1986
Cat. Ref. IV.63, ill. p. 270

G. Givaudan
*Profil d' Emile Givaudan
(«Méthode de la troncature
apparente par tranches
lumineuses»)*, c. 1920
Cat. Ref. IV.78, ill. p. 280

Pavel Nikolaevič Filonov
Živaja golova, 1926
Cat. Ref. V.3, ill. p. 315

Pavel Nikolaevič Filonov
Posle nalëta, c. 1930
Cat. Ref. V.4, ill. p. 316

Victor Brauner
*Project pour Anatomie
du désir*, 1935
Cat. Ref. V.47, ill. p. 342

Diane Arbus
*Exasperated boy with a Toy
Hand Grenade*, New York, 1963
Cat. Ref. VI.30, ill. p. 391

William de Kooning
Woman II, 1952
Cat. Ref. VI.55, ill. p. 398

Eugène Leroy
Autoportrait, 1962
Cat. Ref. VI.60, ill. p. 400

Chuck Close
Fanny (Fingerpainting), 1985
Cat. Ref. VII.16, ill. p. 414

Lucian Freud
Benefits Supervisor Resting,
1994
Cat. Ref. VII.21, ill. p. 416

Giorgia O'Keeffe
White Iris n. 7, 1957
Cat. Ref. VII.64, ill. p. 439

Michel Haas
Les Etreintes, 1994
Cat. Ref. VIII.69, ill. p. 483

Maria Lassnig
Der Verstopfte, 1991
Cat. Ref. VIII.94, ill. p. 490

Cindy Sherman
Untitled n. 223, 1989
Cat. Ref. VIII.127, ill. p. 500

**Works of art documented
in the catalogue and not
in the exhibition for scientific
reasons**

Giorgio De Chirico
Il Trovatore, 1917
Cat. Ref. IV.2, ill. p. 242

Printed
in June 1995
by Marsilio Editori®, s.p.a.
Venice